In a Post-Hegelian Spirit

In a Post-Hegelian Spirit

Philosophical Theology as Idealistic Discontent

Gary Dorrien

BAYLOR UNIVERSITY PRESS

Unless otherwise stated, Scripture quotations are from the New Revised Standard Version Bible, copyright 1989, Division of Christian Education of the National Council of the Churches of Christ in the United States of America. Used by permission. All rights reserved.

Cover Design by Savanah N. Landerholm
Cover image: Photo by Zbysiu Rodak on Unsplash

The Library of Congress has cataloged this book under ISBN 978-1-4813-1159-5.

Printed in the United States of America on acid-free paper with a minimum of thirty percent post-consumer-waste recycled content.

Books by Gary Dorrien

Logic and Consciousness

The Democratic Socialist Vision

Reconstructing the Common Good

The Neoconservative Mind: Politics, Culture, and the War of Ideology

Soul in Society: The Making and Renewal of Social Christianity

The Word as True Myth: Interpreting Modern Theology

The Remaking of Evangelical Theology

The Barthian Revolt in Modern Theology

The Making of American Liberal Theology: Imagining Progressive Religion

*The Making of American Liberal Theology:
Idealism, Realism, and Modernity*

Imperial Designs: Neoconservatism and the New Pax Americana

The Making of American Liberal Theology: Crisis, Irony, and Postmodernity

Social Ethics in the Making: Interpreting an American Tradition

Economy, Difference, Empire: Social Ethics for Social Justice

The Obama Question: A Progressive Perspective

*Kantian Reason and Hegelian Spirit: The
Idealistic Logic of Modern Theology*

The New Abolition: W. E. B. Du Bois and the Black Social Gospel

*Breaking White Supremacy: Martin Luther
King Jr. and the Black Social Gospel*

*Social Democracy in the Making: Political and
Religious Roots of European Socialism*

In a Post-Hegelian Spirit: Philosophical Theology as Idealistic Discontent

For Catherine,
Cherished friend and eminent theologian

Contents

Preface   ix

1 Introduction   1
   Modern Theology as Religious Philosophy

2 Kantian Foundations   29
   Creative Reason and Moral Freedom

3 Post-Kantian Feeling   73
   Romantic Idealism as Theology

4 Hegelian Intersubjectivity   113
   Dialectics of Spirit

5 Against Hegelian Spirit   165
   Marxism, Existentialism, and Wholly Otherness

6 Personal Idealism   205
   Why Subjectivity Matters

7   Whiteheadian Ordering   267
     God and Creativity

8   Neo-Hegelian Theonomy   309
     Religious Socialism as Theology

9   Struggling for Liberation   339
     Breaking White Supremacy and Sexism

10   Rethinking Relationality   387
     Theologies of Becoming

11   In a Post-Hegelian Spirit   443
     Divine Becoming and Discontent

Notes   505
Index   597

Preface

This book builds a post-Hegelian religious philosophy out of my interpretation of modern philosophical theology. It has an origin story dating to 2013 and 2014, when I lectured for a week to large ecumenical gatherings in St. Simon's Island, Georgia. In 2013 I lectured on social ethics and politics alongside biblical scholar Walter Brueggemann, who regaled the crowd in customary Brueggemann fashion with torrents of exegesis sprinkled with uproarious humor. The following year I lectured on theology and religious philosophy alongside the late biblical scholar Marcus Borg, in his last venue of this kind. Marcus was as sharp and engaging as ever, to the end. Every day, it seemed, there was a book signing before we commenced lecturing; perhaps the trauma magnified my sense of the frequency. The line on the left, for Walter and Marcus, was always very long. My line on the right was nearly always a modest affair, and some of my folks lined up just to talk. The second year one skittish soul, having heard me speak at least ten times, wanly observed that my books were awfully large and numerous. Did I have one that conveyed the gist of the others?

I began to say that *Economy, Difference, Empire*[1] distills much of my work in social ethics, but he cut me off: "I mean your *other* books, in theology and philosophy." One side of my work is theological and philosophical, and the other side explores the intersections of politics, economics, social theory, and social ethics. To my mind, these sides complement each other, but I recognize there is a difference in how I come through. My social ethical writings are driven by my convictions and are rife with them, taking positions on issues large, small, historical, and contemporary. My theological writings are analytical and reflective in the disciplinary modes of intellectual history, historical theology, and philosophy of religion; here I marshal various traditions of thought into a conversation and make arguments about them. At the podium, whatever the subject, I readily throw off scholarly restraints. Time is pressing, the audience is broader, and the speaker is compelled to cut to why-it-matters.

This book offers the gist argument that my friend in the book line requested. I teach at a seminary that is theological in its very name and at a university that excludes theological claims on principle. In both contexts we interrogate the truth claims of seminal religious thinkers in ways best described as religious philosophy and customarily described as philosophical theology. The subtitle of this book defers to the conventional category, but the book itself is geared to straddle the theology-versus-no-theology divide. Religious philosophy can be approached by all the methods employed in religious studies—comparative, phenomenological, analytical, historical, theoretical, and evaluative. It has a role to play in mediating the chasm that currently prevails between theological and religious studies approaches to religion. Kant, Hegel, Alfred North Whitehead, and Paul Tillich wrote broadly visionary works for ages that prized such thinking. Our postmodern age is dramatically otherwise, yet these thinkers shaped our fields of discourse to the point of shaping even the theories and movements that arose to throw off their influence. In particular, every post-something theory or critical approach traces in some way to Hegel. I will argue that Hegel was not a panlogical monist and did not fashion a closed system, but no matter which Hegel one holds in view, grappling with his thought binds thinkers on both sides of the chasm to each other.

My first glimmer that I had thoughts about such things occurred in my sports-dominated youth, perplexing over what it could mean that God is everywhere. I fixed in my youth on the crucifixes in Christian art, struck deeply by the image of a suffering God, and on the searing witness of Martin Luther King Jr., who became a martyred Christ figure when I was in high school. These two cross stories melded together in my thought and feeling. At Alma College I had four treasured teachers who helped me find my way into religious philosophy, although none meant to do so. Physicist Louis Toller persuaded me that nothing on earth is more wondrous than light theory. Sociologist Dave Lemmon taught me the canon of sociological theory and guided me to political economists, especially Karl Marx, Karl Polanyi, and Gunnar Myrdal. Philosopher Wesley Dykstra sent me to Aristotle and Kant, told me to waste no time on Hegel, and thus inspired my first plunge into Hegel's *Phenomenology of Spirit*—a wild, puzzling, obscure, rollicking monster of a book that hooked me like no other. Theologian Ronald Massanari, fresh out of graduate school and taking leave of Christianity, introduced me to Karl Barth and Paul Tillich, describing them as theological rivals who differently overthrew the liberal approach to theology.

Liberal theology, according to my religion professors and everyone I read, was long dead and refuted. Adolf von Harnack was the quintessential liberal theologian, and he was readily dismissed. The last significant liberal theologian was Walter Rauschenbusch, who died in 1918 and only mattered because of his social gospel activism, not his outdated theology. It would be hard to exaggerate the force of these conventions when I began reading theologians. The canon consisted of the so-called neo-orthodox titans who killed liberal theology—Barth, Tillich, Emil Brunner, Rudolf Bultmann, and Reinhold Niebuhr—but these figures had passed and it was hard to figure where theology was going. Massanari favored the new death-of-God theologies of Thomas J. J. Altizer and William Hamilton. Altizer and Hamilton made me skeptical about reading more theology. If that was where theology was going, I was inclined to stick with Marx, Polanyi, and Myrdal. I didn't belong to a church, so there was nothing holding me to theology except Jesus crucified and King. In this ambivalent mood I had two sophomore-year experiences that put me on a theological path.

One was reading Rauschenbusch's social gospel classic of 1907, *Christianity and the Social Crisis*. He described the teaching of Jesus as a message of radical social transformation. Christianity obscured the revolutionary spirit of the gospel, but it was not too late for the church to adopt the way and spirit of Jesus. The church is supposed to be a new kind of community that transforms the world by the power of Christ's kingdom-bringing Spirit. The idea of the indwelling and growing commonwealth of God is not merely part of Christianity; it's the central thing holding everything else together. Christianity is a kingdom movement that carries God into everything you do. In a concluding chapter titled, "What to Do," Rauschenbusch made a scintillating case for radical democratic socialism.[2]

His liberal theology and radical politics were equally compelling to me. I turned the pages exclaiming that this was what Christianity should sound like. For years I had felt that King laid hold of something in Christianity that the rest of the church somehow missed—something inspiring movement idealism and a real surge for social change. Rauschenbusch explained what was missing, and he expressed brilliantly the vision of a socially regenerative Christianity. The books that I read about the social gospel said it was an idealistic understanding of Christianity that briefly influenced liberal Protestantism before it was discredited by the neo-orthodox reaction, especially Barth and Niebuhr. Reading Rauschenbusch, I could see various problems. He loved idealistic rhetoric, said almost nothing about racism, and was proudly, stridently, vehemently anti-Catholic. But for grasping and expressing the prophetic core of the gospel, Rauschenbusch soared above everyone except King.

The same year I read James Cone's recently published manifestos for black liberation theology, *Black Theology and Black Power* (1969) and *A Black Theology of Liberation* (1970). These searing books sundered my recently acquired ideas about liberal arts education and theology. I told our college president, Robert Swanson, about Cone's books, vaguely aware that Swanson was a Presbyterian minister. To my surprise he said we should invite Cone to Alma.[3]

Cone rocked our campus with a fusion of his fiery first book, his powerful second book, a brief excursus on a song by the Rascals, and a stunning concluding section that was just for us. He talked about slave ships and auction blocks and lynching. He explained that black theology interprets Christianity and the American experience from the perspective of oppressed black Americans. He said very hard things about white liberals, white Christianity, white conceits, and King, describing nearly all white Americans as racists who couldn't imagine giving up their white privilege. He lightened the mood for a moment with a song that everyone knew: "All the world over, so easy to see! People everywhere, just wanna be free." Then he held up a copy of Alma's course catalog and ripped it to shreds from a standpoint that no one had ever heard at Alma College: We were being taught white theology, he said, and white philosophy, white sociology, white psychology, and white everything else as though nothing but white thinking counted as thought. And all of it was paraded in the name of universality and the liberal arts.

Rauschenbusch and Cone had no time or inclination to grapple with philosophers, so their names occur only occasionally in the present book.

This absence marks that philosophy is both indispensable to me and never quite what I most care about. Rauschenbusch and Cone have been in my head and heart since my college sophomore year, and both are featured in other books of mine.

In college I wrote a thesis on Karl Rahner's transcendental Thomism that drew on my studies of Kant, and a thesis on Marx's social theory that similarly featured Hegel, already accustomed to autodidactic philosophizing. My philosophical education resumed at Harvard University, where I absorbed Dieter Henrich's courses on Kant and Hegel, and at Harvard Divinity School, where George Rupp taught me to read Hegel as a source for comparative theology. I also heard John Rawls lecture on his theory of justice, but otherwise I lamented that Harvard philosophers were somehow content to reduce philosophy to language analysis and modal logic. A bit later, when I studied at Union Theological Seminary and Princeton Theological Seminary, I had similar experiences with the university philosophy departments at Columbia and Princeton.

This experience closely resembled my study of liberal theology. None of my teachers anywhere, except Rupp, taught about liberal theology per se. They took liberal methodologies for granted while assuming that liberal theology itself was passé. I was vaguely aware that this situation might be different at the University of Chicago Divinity School, Boston University School of Theology, and Vanderbilt Divinity School, strongholds of the old liberalism. I did not realize, during my graduate school years, that a liberal renaissance was quietly germinating among theologians who began their careers as epigones of the neo-orthodox giants and were reinventing themselves as latter-day liberals. Gregory Baum, Anne Carr, Edward Farley, Langdon Gilkey, Peter Hodgson, Elizabeth Johnson, Gordon Kaufman, Sallie McFague, W. Norman Pittenger, and David Tracy became prominent examples of this trend. But I was slow to see the trend that I featured, twenty years later, in volume three of *The Making of American Liberal Theology*.[4]

Much of my expertise in liberal theology is thus self-taught and was acquired after I preached liberal-liberationist sermons for seven years in Episcopal pulpits. I came through the door of solidarity activism and ministry, speaking for two Latin American solidarity organizations and a democratic socialist organization, and became an academic at the age of thirty-five. From my college days onward I embraced the liberationist starting point and liberationist criticism: theology must begin in solidarity with oppressed people and interrogate theological complicity in racism, sexism, class privilege, and colonialism. In seminary I learned to add heterosexual privilege to this list. But I did not construe liberationism as something that began with Cone or Gustavo Gutiérrez, since I was steeped in the Christian socialism of Rauschenbusch, King, Tillich, Leonhard Ragaz, and Rosemary Radford Ruether. Three of my first five books were about religious socialism. Moreover, beginning with liberationist questions and assuming liberationist criticism never precluded, to me, the necessity of grappling with liberal questions and liberal thinkers. The Schleiermacher agenda of addressing the challenges of critical disbelief cannot be wrong, even though it is only part of what theologians and religious philosophers must take up.[5]

Having written many books that run long on thick description, historical detail, winding arguments, and colorful stories, it is against my habit to boil down to the what-matters arguments featured in this book. Every chapter except the concluding chapter contains highly condensed versions of arguments and narratives I have developed elsewhere. The book moves toward its constructive post-Hegelian conclusion with swiftly summarized analyses and judgments. My desire to distill this half of my work owes much to the fact that *Economy, Difference, Empire* is singularly meaningful to me for representing the other half.

I have had only good experiences with publishers and editors, so my thanks to them could go on for several pages. I am especially grateful for the privilege of working in recent years with Rebecca Harkin at Wiley-Blackwell, Wendy Lochner at Columbia University Press, and Jennifer Banks at Yale University Press—stellar editors and friends. Above all the debts that I owe to publishers, I am grateful for the unfailing generosity, hospitality, and proficiency always extended to me by everyone associated with Westminster John Knox Press. My six books with WJK contain the majority of my theological writing, and the first versions of most of it. The late Stephanie Egnotovich edited all of them; eventually I won a few debates with my beloved friend over her aversion to short sentences. Daniel Braden (project editor), Catherine Carpenter (copyeditor), and Hermann Weinlick (copyeditor) worked on these books, superbly. I do not forget, and was reminded while writing the present book, what I owe to them and to everyone at WJK.

Chapter 1 mines my analyses of modern theology and philosophy in Gary Dorrien, *The Word as True Myth* (Louisville: Westminster John Knox, 1997); Dorrien, *The Barthian Revolt in Modern Theology* (Louisville: Westminster John Knox, 2000); Dorrien, *The Making of American*

Liberal Theology: Imagining Progressive Religion (Louisville: Westminster John Knox, 2001); Dorrien, *The Making of American Liberal Theology: Idealism, Realism, and Modernity* (Louisville: Westminster John Knox, 2003); and Dorrien, *Kantian Reason and Hegelian Spirit: The Idealistic Logic of Modern Theology* (Chichester, UK: Wiley-Blackwell, 2012.) Chapter 2 draws upon my discussions of Kant, Kantian idealism, and modern philosophy in Dorrien, *The Word as True Myth*; Dorrien, *The Barthian Revolt in Modern Theology*; Dorrien, *The Making of American Liberal Theology: Imagining Progressive Religion*; and especially Dorrien, *Kantian Reason and Hegelian Spirit*. Chapter 3 draws upon my discussions of Schleiermacher, Coleridge, and modern theology in Dorrien, *The Word as True Myth*; Dorrien, *The Barthian Revolt in Modern Theology*; Dorrien, *The Making of American Liberal Theology: Imagining Progressive Theology*; Dorrien, *The Making of American Liberal Theology: Idealism, Realism, and Modernity*; Dorrien, *Kantian Reason and Hegelian Spirit*; and Dorrien, *Social Democracy in the Making: Political and Religious Roots of European Socialism* (New Haven: Yale University Press, 2019). Chapter 4 draws upon my discussions of Hegel, Schelling, and post-Kantian idealism in Dorrien, *The Word as True Myth*; Dorrien, *The Barthian Revolt in Modern Theology*; Dorrien, *The Making of American Liberal Theology: Imagining Progressive Theology*; Dorrien, *The Making of American Liberal Theology: Idealism, Realism, and Modernity*; Dorrien, *The Making of American Liberal Theology: Crisis, Irony, and Postmodernity* (Louisville: Westminster John Knox, 2006); Dorrien, *Kantian Reason and Hegelian Spirit*; and Dorrien, *Social Democracy in the Making*.

Chapter 5 draws upon my discussions of Kierkegaard, Marx, and Barth in Gary Dorrien, *The Democratic Socialist Vision* (Totowa, N.J.: Rowman & Littlefield, 1986); Dorrien, *The Word as True Myth*; Dorrien, *The Remaking of Evangelical Theology* (Louisville: Westminster John Knox, 1998); Dorrien, *The Barthian Revolt in Modern Theology*; Dorrien, *Kantian Reason and Hegelian Spirit*; and Dorrien, *Social Democracy in the Making*. Chapter 6 draws upon my discussions of Bowne, Royce, Troeltsch, Knudson, Brightmann, Muelder, and personal idealism in Dorrien, *The Word as True Myth*; Dorrien, *The Barthian Revolt in Modern Theology*; Dorrien, *The Making of American Liberal Theology: Imagining Progressive Religion*; Dorrien, *The Making of American Liberal Theology: Idealism, Realism, and Modernity*; Dorrien, *The Making of American Liberal Theology: Crisis, Irony, and Postmodernity*; Dorrien, *Kantian Reason and Hegelian Spirit*; and Dorrien,

Social Ethics in the Making: Interpreting an American Tradition (Chichester: Wiley-Blackwell, 2008). Chapter 7 draws upon my discussions of James, Whitehead, Hartshorne, Meland, process thought, and the Chicago School in Dorrien, *The Making of American Liberal Theology: Idealism, Realism, and Modernity*; and Dorrien, *The Making of American Liberal Theology: Crisis, Irony, and Postmodernity*. Chapter 8 draws upon my discussions of Tillich and religious socialism in Dorrien, *Reconstructing the Common Good: Theology and the Social Order* (Maryknoll, N.Y.: Orbis Books, 1990); Dorrien, *The Word as True Myth*; Dorrien, *The Making of American Liberal Theology: Idealism, Realism, and Postmodernity*; Dorrien, *Kantian Reason and Hegelian Spirit*; and Dorrien, *Social Democracy in the Making*.

Chapter 9 draws upon my discussions of Du Bois, King, and Ruether in Dorrien, *The Making of American Liberal Theology: Crisis, Irony, and Postmodernity*; Dorrien, *Social Ethics in the Making*; Gary Dorrien, *The New Abolition: W. E. B. Du Bois and the Black Social Gospel* (New Haven: Yale University Press, 2015); and Dorrien, *Breaking White Supremacy: Martin Luther King Jr. and the Black Social Gospel* (New Haven: Yale University Press, 2018). Chapter 10 draws upon my discussions of Tracy, Hodgson, Farley, Keller, and postmodernity in Dorrien, *The Making of American Liberal Theology: Crisis, Irony, and Postmodernity*. Thanks to these publishers for permitting me to adapt material from these works.

I am grateful to many friends and expert readers for reading early or later versions of arguments made in this book. There are too many to name, but the short list includes Gregory Baum, Rufus Burrow Jr., Philip Clayton, John B. Cobb Jr., the late James Cone, Harvey Cox, Sheila G. Davaney, William Dean, Mary Doak, Frederick Ferré, Juan M. Floyd-Thomas, Nancy Frankenberry, the late Langdon Gilkey, David Ray Griffin, Roger Haight, William D. Hart, Stanley Hauerwas, Obery M. Hendricks Jr., Peter C. Hodgson, Michael Hogue, Jennifer Jesse, William Stacy Johnson, Catherine Keller, Christopher Latiolais, Vincent Lloyd, Kelly Maeshiro, Margaret R. Miles, Jürgen Moltmann, Christopher Morse, Robert C. Neville, Larry Rasmussen, Joerg Rieger, Donald Shriver, Jerome A. Stone, Marjorie H. Suchocki, Mark C. Taylor, Mark Lewis Taylor, Thandeka, John Thatamanil, Edgar Towne, Emilie M. Townes, David Tracy, Keith Ward, Sharon Welch, Cornel West, Demian Wheeler, Andrea White, Robert R. Williams, and Thurman Willison.

I am grateful to Carey Newman, the director of Baylor University Press, for taking on this book. I have long admired his work at Baylor and was mindful of it from early on because he came from WJK. I am equally grateful to managing editor Cade Jarrell, copyeditor Jon Haney, production manager Jenny Hunt, and editorial assistant Bethany Dickerson, all of whom worked superbly on the manuscript.

One style point and two terminological points are noteworthy. This book contains many quotations, some of which contain italicized emphases. I have a simple rule about italicized emphases: NEVER add or subtract one. Every cited italicized emphasis comes from the original quote. On occasion I will also refer to U.S. Americans instead of Americans; this usage registers the point that the USA is only one of the Americas. Lastly, most of the time I will employ "post-Kantian" in the customary sense of the term that includes Hegel, but my argument about Hegel's originality sometimes compels me to distinguish between the post-Kantian and Hegelian traditions.

1

Introduction

Modern Theology as Religious Philosophy

This book develops the post-Hegelian religious philosophy that I take from the post-Kantian tradition in modern theology, making an argument for a liberationist form of religious idealism. It mines Immanuel Kant, Friedrich Schleiermacher, and G. W. F. Hegel for my founding argument on intellectual intuition and the creative power of subjectivity. It sifts critiques of Hegel by Søren Kierkegaard, Karl Marx, Karl Barth, and Emmanuel Levinas, contending that all were penetrating but one-sided compared to Hegel. It features an extensive discussion of the personal idealist tradition, commending its empirical emphasis on human dignity and why personality matters. It appropriates the process tradition founded by Alfred North Whitehead and the thought of Paul Tillich, W. E. B. Du Bois, Martin Luther King Jr., Rosemary Radford Ruether, David Tracy, Peter Hodgson, Edward Farley, Catherine Keller, Sharon Welch, and Monica Coleman. It makes an argument about the religious character of Hegel's thought and a case for his theodicy of love divine. Like the Whitehead school, Hegel expounded a process theodicy of God salvaging what can be salvaged from history. But Hegel's tragic sense of the carnage of history cut deeper than Whitehead, lingering at Calvary.

To engage a thinker as notoriously complex and elusive as Hegel is to invite misunderstanding because many interpreters take for granted that Hegel fashioned a closed system. There is a basis for interpreting him as a panlogical right-Hegelian, an anti-Christian left-Hegelian, a

1

conceptual realist metaphysician in the mode of Aristotle or Spinoza, a social philosopher and phenomenologist who only pretended to care about metaphysics, the founder of postmodern nihilism, and a philosopher of love who developed a radically hospitable theology. I am in the last school, but I respect the others while contending that Hegel was both offensively wrong and brilliantly creative. Hegel broke open the deadliest assumptions of Western thought by conceiving being as becoming and consciousness as the social-subjective relation of spirit to itself. His concept of the cunning of reason (*Die List der Vernunft*) offered a dynamic, holistic, open, ambiguous, tragic, and reconciling idea of how revelation takes place, conceiving the divine as spiraling intersubjective Spirit.

Friedrich Nietzsche described the God of Western theism as the enemy of freedom and subjectivity. Martin Heidegger said that Western metaphysics wrongly took being for God. Emmanuel Levinas countered that Western metaphysics wrongly took God for being. I argue that Hegel undercut these critiques by creating a new category of thought subverting Western metaphysics—fluid, intersubjective Spirit, the dynamic whole of wholes that unifies thought and being in Spirit. Hegel's discovery of social subjectivity created a new kind of idealistic metaphysics, or something better named by dropping the categories of idealism and metaphysics. The closed system Hegel described by countless textbooks and the founders of postmodernism does not get him, notwithstanding that the bad parts of Hegel were terrible to the point of being repugnant.[1]

Liberal theology poses similar challenges as a subject, interlocutor, and discourse tradition. This book is disciplined by the tradition of Christian liberal theology while favoring the streams of it that engage multiple religious and philosophical perspectives. On my definition, theology is first-order reflection about matters of religious truth, liberal theology is a distinct species of it, and theology is open to mutual give-and-take with philosophy. But the liberal tradition contains a complex array of positions about religious philosophy ranging from robustly metaphysical to strategically philosophical to anti-metaphysical to anti-philosophical. Liberal theology is distinct for its approach to the authority question, not the philosophy question; one can be theologically liberal and take any conceivable position about metaphysics or philosophy. Theological liberals who minimize or oppose philosophy usually define theology as reflection on faith, not religious truth. Here the driving concern is to secure the autonomy of faith and theology. I am of a different mind, recognizing that theology and religious philosophy are different things, but disbelieving in the autonomy of faith or theology. On my terms, any time that we espouse convictions about religious truth, we are doing theology, whether or not it takes the form of a religious philosophy. Theology ventures into the perilous, cognitive, normative, existential work of adjudicating whatever it is that concerns us ultimately. It is about the things that individuals and religious communities care about sufficiently to stake their lives upon and invest their passion.

This definition of theology is geared to include theologies that rest on authority claims, those that rule out such claims, and those that negotiate between these approaches. Until the modern era, every Christian theology operated within a house of authority. The external authority of the Bible and Christian tradition established what had to be believed about very specific things. Liberal theology, first and foremost, was and is the enterprise that broke away from authority-based religious thinking. Liberal theologians variously rejected or relativized the external authority of Scripture and tradition, affirming their right to intellectual freedom. They invented the critical methods of theological scholarship, navigated between orthodox overbelief and atheistic disbelief, and reestablished the credibility of theology as an intellectual enterprise. But liberal theology took a mighty fall in the twentieth century for sanctifying bourgeois civilization.

In its glory years, liberal theology espoused a religion of cultural progress even in its socialist and anti-imperialist versions. This optimistic faith did not survive World War I in Europe or the Depression in the United States, to put it mildly. The heyday version of liberal theology came from the Ritschlian school theologians, who dominated theology in the late nineteenth and early twentieth centuries: Adolf von Harnack, Albrecht Ritschl, Wilhelm Herrmann, and Ernst Troeltsch. They swept the field by historicizing Christianity, idealizing bourgeois culture, producing major works of scholarship, and touting their own social relevance. Theologically the Ritschlian school was based on its commitment to historicism and the autonomy of faith. Then it splintered three ways over both claims, flanked on opposite poles by Herrmann and Troeltsch. Ritschlian liberals, it turned out, profoundly disagreed about historicism and philosophy. Their actual basis of unity was their Culture Protestant nationalism. German Ritschlian theology grew strong by reducing theology to bourgeois moral religion and baptizing Germany's conceits about itself. It thus set up liberal theology for a mighty fall, becoming an object of ridicule and overthrow. Later a similar toppling occurred in the United

States, with less drama. Liberal theology ever since has had this fateful history to overcome.

Historically and logically, the cornerstone of liberalism is the assertion of the supreme value of the individual, an idea rooted in Christian theology, the Magna Carta Libertatum of 1215, and Renaissance humanism. In all its historic forms, liberalism makes a defining appeal to the rights of freedom. As a political philosophy it originated in the seventeenth century as the threefold claim that individuals have natural rights to freedom, the state must prevent the tyranny of the mob, and religion must be separated from politics. As an economic theory it arose in the eighteenth century as a defense of free trade and self-regulating markets. As a cultural tradition it arose in the eighteenth century as a bourgeois humanistic ethic and a rationalist critique of authority-based belief. In liberal ideology the universal goal of human beings is to realize their freedom, all traditions are open to criticism, and state power is justified only to the extent that it enables and protects individual liberty.

These principles defined liberalism wherever capitalism spread, yielding liberal theologies that affirmed modern humanism, biblical criticism, and Enlightenment philosophy. England had the first trickle of theologies of a liberalizing sort and a nineteenth-century tradition of mildly liberal theology, but no movement of the full-fledged real thing until the end of the nineteenth century. Germany produced the great founding liberal theologies and the movements that propagated them. The United States sprouted a historic tradition of liberal theology in the mid-eighteenth century, but it yielded a Unitarian schism that thwarted the movement ambitions of early nineteenth-century liberals. By the time that England and the United States developed significant movements of liberal theology, liberalism itself had morphed into liberal democracy under pressure from democratic movements, variously contesting older traditions of liberal individualism and elitism.

Religion, from the beginning, was distinctly troublesome for liberal ideology. To the liberal traditions associated with Locke and Kant, the liberal state was naturally tolerant by virtue of deriving from a rational social contract, it existed to protect the natural rights of citizens, and religion had to be constrained by modern rationality. Thomas Jefferson and Benjamin Franklin espoused a liberalism of this sort in the United States, where it competed with a latter-day Puritan notion deriving from John Milton and the English Puritan revolution that prized faith and religious liberty. Here it was said that the state has a sacred duty to protect liberty—the theocratic seed of what became the American social gospel. In both cases, the liberal founders had an ambiguous relationship to their own rhetoric of freedom because liberalism arose as an ideological justification of capitalism *and* as tolerant relief from the religious wars of the seventeenth century. The champions of liberal ideology exalted human dignity while denigrating or denying the humanity of vast numbers of human beings. Theories of racial, sexual, and cultural inferiority disqualified most human beings from their rights, while liberals designed a supposedly natural political economy based on self-interested market exchanges that served the interests of the capitalist class.

The liberal state tolerated plural religious traditions, posing as a guarantor of the rights of individuals and communities to pursue diverse interests. Routinely it denied rights of citizenship and humanity to human beings who were not literate, white, male, and owners of property. Some liberals stoutly opposed the hypocrisy and injustice of privileged liberalism, demanding the rights of liberalism for all. Some vehemently opposed the assumption of white-dominated societies that social contract liberalism applied only to whites. The best neo-abolitionists and anti-imperialists in England and the United States campaigned for the extension of liberal rights to excluded communities: Britons John Hobson, Charles Marson, Stewart Headlam, and Scott Holland, and Americans Albion Tourgée, Ida B. Wells, W. D. P. Bliss, George Herron, Reverdy Ransom, and W. E. B. Du Bois. But they had to be called radical liberals or liberal socialists to distinguish them from what liberalism usually meant. Liberalism was better known for protecting capitalism and white supremacy than for defending the oppressed and vulnerable.[2]

Modern theology arose as an aspect of this story. It began when people began to search for the sacred. I mean that quite literally, because searching for the sacred is a modern phenomenon. For most of human history, the sacred was readily available. Every culture was organized around the sacred observances of a cult, which provided rituals and myths concerning birth, life, identity, community, sexuality, work, redemption, and death. The real world was the realm of the gods, whose history shaped human history. People did not talk about their lives as journeys in search of the sacred. They did not ask how their myths disclosed spiritual meaning. They understood history as myth and themselves as participants in sacred time and space.

In the modern age the sacred cosmos was demythologized by science, religion became a private option for individuals, and the sacred underpinnings of culture in cult were deconstructed to expose its configurations of desire and power. Culture had no attachment to a sacred realm but was real precisely as human work. Enlightenment thinkers contended that the inductive methods of science should be applied to all fields of knowledge and that religion is not exempt from the tests of critical rationality. If rationality is the only valid authority in science or philosophy, no respectable claim to religious truth can be secured by appealing to an authoritative scripture, church, or tradition.

The founders of modern theology took these verdicts very seriously. In the Bible, God created the world in six days, the fall occurred in a real space-time Eden, and God spoke audibly to living persons and intervened directly in history. In modern consciousness the world of the Bible was obliterated and the mythical aspects of biblical narrative became embarrassing to religious people. Early Enlightenment rationalists took the Bible as a flat text and corrected it from the standpoint of their own naturalistic worldview. They exposed discrepant accounts, or harmonized them; rejected miracle stories, or provided naturalistic explanations; stressed that the Bible contains myths, or deduced a rational system from the Bible. Generally, they conceived interpretation as taxonomy. A bit later, in the 1760s, the German founders of historical criticism—Johann Semler, Johann Eichhorn, Johann Jakob Griesbach, and Johann David Michaelis—made a course correction by deconstructing the history of the text itself. They proposed to study the Bible from a scientific standpoint stripped of dogmatic presuppositions. The founders of historical criticism revolutionized biblical scholarship by deciphering the historical development of the Bible. They had no nation, yet they had far more historical consciousness than scholars from the mighty nations of France and England. The German historical critics were the first to call themselves "liberal theologians," until Kant came along in the early 1780s, after which they called themselves Kantians.

Kant, Schleiermacher, and Hegel acquired their iconic standing in modern thought by surpassing early Enlightenment rationalism. All are important to me for theorizing Kant's insight that reason is an activity inseparable from will. I refuse to doubt that I think my thoughts and will my purposes, which does not mean that I believe in a substantive self that possesses thoughts and purposes. Persons think and feel; there is no thought without attention, an act of will; and thought is an act performed with a motive, which implies feeling. Kant revolutionized modern thought by showing that the mind is active in producing experience and freedom is the keystone to the vault of reason. But he made a mighty contribution to the liberal traditions of reducing theology to ethics and expunging metaphysical reason from religious thought. Schleiermacher vastly improved on Kant's reductionist approach to religion and showed how theology could get along without appealing to external authorities. But Schleiermacher's theology spun a novel form of fideism, unless one brushed aside what he said about the autonomy of theology, as many of his disciples did. Hegel provided a new basis for onto-theology by conceiving Spirit as a spiraling, dynamic I that is a We and a We that is an I—a triadic social structure unfolding in threefold mediation. But Hegel was nearly as arrogant as his reputation, making grandiose claims for philosophy and his system.

All three were chauvinistic about European civilization, parading Teutonic conceit as fully justified and virtuous. Kant saw only gradations of backwardness and inferiority whenever his lecture courses peered beyond Europe. He taught a course on race that he might as well have titled White Supremacy 101. According to Kant, Europeans were at the top, Africans were at the bottom, everyone else sorted out in between, and Europeans soared so high they verged on becoming a separate race. Schleiermacher said he singled out France and England for criticism in 1799 because he didn't really care about anyone else. What mattered was that Germany, not yet a nation, needed to catch up to France and England as a national power while preserving its spiritual and cultural superiority. Hegel cared very much about world history, contending that its axis was the Mediterranean Sea. He prattled to the end of his days that Africa proper held no historical interest, being stuck in "barbarism and savagery." North Africa was interesting only because the Phoenicians, Romans, Vandals, Byzantine Romans, Arabs, and Turks successively colonized it. Egypt owed its admittedly "great and independent culture" to its association with Mediterranean history. Asia was slightly interesting for giving birth to consciousness, but it got stuck in contradictions. Modern Europe was the land of spiritual unity, where the Spirit descended into itself, overcoming the so-called Middle Ages. Jerusalem mattered to Hegel because of Judaism and Christianity, and Mecca and Medina got comparable credit for Islam, but Greece was the light of history. Delphi, Athens, Rome, Carthage, Alexandria, and Constantinople loomed large in his imagination and feeling, but only for enabling Europe to unite the particular and the universal.[3]

America came out not much better on his telling. Hegel said that history deals with the past, philosophy deals with reason, America had no history, and he had his hands full dealing with Reason. So he gave short shrift to both American continents, despite claiming that the burden of world history would surely reveal itself in America, perhaps in a contest between the two continents. In North America, he noted, the native tribes were mostly destroyed and otherwise repressed. In South America and Mexico, the conquering violence was much worse, yet larger native populations survived. The Portuguese conquerors were more humane than the Dutch, Spanish, and English, but all were deadly violent and destructive, leaving North America to "the surplus population of Europe," while South America forged mixed-race republics based on military force. Hegel singled out the Creoles for evincing Hegelian self-awareness and autonomy, though of a low order. He thought the United States was better off than South America for being Protestant, industrious, and steeped in freedom consciousness, but he could not find an intellectual culture, and he believed its federalist government would not survive. It had survived into the 1830s only because the United States was perched between the Atlantic and Pacific Oceans. Sooner or later, Hegel said, the United States would discover that a large republic lacking a monarchy cannot defend itself from foreign invaders. The United States was doubly vulnerable for relying so exclusively on commercial trading. It was hard to say what the United States would become, once it developed its vast unsettled territory: "What has taken place there up to now is but an echo of the Old World, and the expression of an alien life."[4]

The Eurocentric hubris that Kant, Schleiermacher, and Hegel took for granted is an abyss separating me from the many things I admire about them and take from them. "Post-Hegelian" is decidedly both to me: leaving Hegel behind by passing through him. Right-Hegelian readings of Hegel miss what matters in his thought, while postmodern critics wrongly suggest that Levinas and Jacques Derrida discovered the problem of difference. Hegel blasted the monism of Parmenides, the Eleatics, and the ontological tradition, and he rooted reason and rationality in interhuman relation. Moreover, contrary to postmodern convention, I do not disparage the rhetoric of freedom that the Kantian and post-Kantian traditions bequeathed to modern thought. No philosophy has defended human freedom and dignity more powerfully than the post-Kantian tradition, and no philosophy has surpassed Hegel's grounding of social subjectivity in the struggle for freedom, recognition, and power.

My dance with Hegel is an elective affinity, making a case for his persisting relevance. My argument about modern theology says the same thing with stronger finality: we are never done with the questions that gave rise to it. How should theology deal with the challenges to belief that overthrew the external authority of Christian Scripture and tradition? What kind of religious belief is possible after science, the Enlightenment, and post-Enlightenment criticism disenchanted the world? How should Christian theology deal with the mythical aspects of Christianity and the results of biblical criticism? These questions were peculiar to the founders of modern theology and remain very much with us.

The Making of Liberal Theology

Every tradition of full-fledged liberal theology emphasized the individual's right to intellectual freedom, yielding six defining principles. My definition of liberal theology features these principles that liberals have espoused in various national contexts for three centuries. Liberal theology refuses to establish or compel religious beliefs on the basis of a bare authority claim, seeks a third way between orthodox overbelief and secular disbelief, accepts the historical-critical approach to the Bible, allows science to explain the physical world, looks beyond the church for answers, and seeks to make religious faith relevant to the modern world.

Modern theology began as a liberalizing impulse in contexts where Enlightenment movements delegitimized appeals to external authority to establish or compel religious beliefs. In Britain it began with the early Enlightenment deists and Anglican rationalists, spawned a vaguely liberal Broad Church tradition in the 1820s, and produced a full-fledged liberal movement in the late 1890s. In Germany, liberal theology began with the mid–eighteenth-century founders of historical criticism. In the United States, the founding liberals were mid–eighteenth-century rationalists influenced by British theology, with the exception that the American founders were Congregational descendants of the New England Puritans and chiefly concerned with alleviating Calvinism of its most objectionable features. Theology, to be modern, had to recognize contradictions, faulty history, and outright myths in the Bible. That required stripping Christian orthodoxies of unbelievable teachings and paying close attention to deist and atheist criticism—the mediating agenda signaled in the subtitle of the first fully modern work of theology, Schleiermacher's *Über die Religion: Reden an die Gebildeten unter ihren Verächtern* (*On Religion: Speeches to Its Cultured Despisers*, 1799).

Britons had long preceded Schleiermacher in producing Christian apologetic responses to rationalist criticism, and Schleiermacher had read similar fare from German scholars of his time. British critics ransacked the Bible for unbelievable things and skewered Christian doctrines, compelling Anglican rationalists Samuel Clarke and Joseph Butler to defend slightly alleviated forms of Anglican orthodoxy. In Germany, a deceased anonymous deist (Hermann Samuel Reimarus) caused a stir in the mid-1770s by portraying Jesus as a misguided political messiah lacking any idea of being divine. Schleiermacher, surrounded by cultured Romantic scoffers in Berlin, contended that true religion and the divinity of Jesus are credible on modern terms. He took for granted that theologians had to accept biblical criticism and modern science, engage modern culture and other religions, and make religious faith relevant to modern living, even though he had no models for doing so. His argument was constructive and new, never sealing an argument by citing Scripture or any ecclesiastical authority. Both things were crucial to the historic significance of *On Religion*. It offered a positive approach to theology without making any appeal to external authorities or traditions.

To say that liberal theology dispenses with external authority can be misleading. It does not mean that Scripture and tradition have no authority, or that liberal theology necessarily operates outside the sphere of the church. The first school of liberal theology, Kantian theology, did in fact dispense with scriptural authority and operated outside the Christian church and tradition. But it was possible on liberal terms to affirm a doctrine of scriptural authority, and to do so within the Christian church. Nearly every form of Anglican and Roman Catholic liberal theology has done so, and still does. Schleiermacher became the quintessential liberal theologian by grounding his theology in the Christian church, conceiving theology as interpretation of the church's experience of redemption. He did not call himself a liberal, because Kantians owned this category in his time. Neither did Schleiermacher speak of scriptural authority, because that sounded like a throwback to the original problem. But Schleiermacher inspired Mediating theologies in which liberals invoked the authority of Scripture on liberal terms: scriptural teaching is authoritative *within* Christian experience, not as an outside word that establishes or compels truth claims about particular matters of fact or doctrine.

In Germany, four schools of thought vied for influence, yielding Mediating fusions of two or more schools. Kantians grounded Christian truth entirely in the moral concerns of practical reason, conceiving theology as reflection on moral faith and freethinking criticism. The school of Schleiermacher located the essence of religion in religious feeling (*Gefühl*) and identified Christianity with the experience of redemption. Hegelian theologians construed Hegel's philosophical system as the highest explication of Christian doctrine. Ritschl founded the fourth major school by fusing Kant on moral religion, Schleiermacher on religious experience, and himself on social-ethical consciousness. Christianity is fundamentally a sociohistorical movement with a distinct social-ethical character founded on Christian faith alone.

All four of these schools and the Mediating variations of them positioned themselves between overbelieving church traditions and disbelieving critics. Unavoidably, they had to battle with conservatives for the right to liberalize Christian doctrine. But they worried more about the challenges to belief from outsiders. The agenda of modern theology was to develop a credible form of Christianity before the cultured despisers routed Christian faith from intellectual and cultural respectability.

During the Progressive Era there was a seventh plank that played a fatefully implosive role in German liberal theology, very little role in British liberal theology, and a permanently redefining role in American liberal theology: social Christianity. In Germany, liberal theology became wholly identified with Culture Protestantism, the bourgeois civil religion of an expanding German Empire, which set up liberal theology for a devastating crash. In England some Christian socialists were vaguely liberal in Maurice's fashion, but the full-fledged liberal theology movement spurned Christian socialism as a low-grade concern, or too Anglo-Catholic, or too left-wing. In the United States, liberal theology surged into the established churches through the social gospel, a cultural earthquake that should be called the Third Great Awakening.

The American social gospel had a deeper, wider, and more lasting impact on established churches than was true anywhere in Europe, owing to its abolitionist and evangelical Puritan roots plus America's lack of a state church. The ministers who founded it in the 1880s were stung by the accusation of socialists and trade unionists that churches did not care about the suffering of the poor and vulnerable. They knew it was true and resolved to do something about it. White social gospel leaders combated the ravages of industrialization and economic injustice, black social gospel leaders were neo-abolitionists who combated white terrorism and oppression, and the best social gospel founders on both sides of the color line combined these liberationist struggles. They proclaimed that churches had a mission to transform the *structures of society* in the direction of *social justice*, which they called *social salvation*. All three parts of this message employed language that did not exist before the 1880s. The novel idea that there is such a thing as social structure yielded the language of social salvation, social ethics, social justice, and the social gospel. Salvation, to be saving, could not be personal only. Evil is transmitted through inherited social structures, not only by personal sins.[5]

The American social gospel was politically activist and progressive, supporting cooperatives, the nationalization of monopolies, and the doctrine of social salvation. Here the movements for liberal theology and the social gospel fused together. It was possible to be one without the other, and there were notable examples on each side. Religious philosopher Borden Parker Bowne was a liberal who opposed the social gospel; theologian Augustus Strong was a conservative evangelical who supported the social gospel; and many black and white social gospel clerics resisted liberal theology. But the leaders of the social gospel—Washington Gladden, Richard Ely, W. D. P. Bliss, George Herron, Walter Rauschenbusch, Reverdy Ransom, Richard R. Wright Jr., Adam Clayton Powell Sr., Vida Scudder, and Harry Ward—said it made no sense to be one without the other. To them, the liberalizing impulse in theology and the social conscience of the social gospel were complementary aspects of the same struggle for freedom and progress. Liberal theology and the social gospel were deeply intertwined from the beginning of the social gospel upsurge.

In Britain and Germany, liberal theology had a stronger elitist character. British and German theological liberals took pride in belonging to a cultural elite, having been trained in highly prestigious universities. German theology was far more creative and profound than British theology, partly because Britain had no tradition of treating theology as a university discipline. For most of the nineteenth century, British liberals had to fight for the right to accept modern criticism. In both contexts, socialism was more serious and looming than in the United States and not a foreign idea, and liberalism retained its original character as the individualistic ideology of the middle class.

In 1860 a mildly liberal book, *Essays and Reviews*, caused a firestorm of condemnation that raged across England, Scotland, and Wales for months. It killed the possibility of liberal theology in Britain for the next generation, aside from temporizing Broad Church–Anglican versions and a handful of Presbyterians. British Anglicanism produced no explicitly liberal organization until 1898, when a group of low-church rationalists founded the Churchmen's Union for the Advancement of

Liberal Religious Thought. These founders naturally fixed on intellectual freedom, especially the right of Anglican clergy to be theologically liberal. Otherwise, they warned, the church would be discredited and theology was sure to be expelled from the academy.[6]

In Germany, liberal theology had a storied history reflecting the strengths of a German invention, the modern research university, and longtime dreams of a united nation and empire, which were not fulfilled until 1871. All four of the German schools of liberal theology had a Prussian nationalistic bent, plus leading scholars named after Kings Friedrich and Wilhelm. By 1889, the year of Ritschl's death, the Ritschlian school dominated modern theology. It built on the heritage of Luther, Kant, and Schleiermacher, stressing the irreducible autonomy of faith, now meshed with the new social consciousness. It was practical, anti-metaphysical, and comfortably ensconced in the churches, academy, and government. It provided theological ballast for Germany's expanding empire and was avowedly comfortable with Germany's mighty growing army. The Ritschlian school was so dominant that when it crashed after World War I, liberal theology as a whole nearly perished in Continental Europe.

I shall argue that the traditions of liberal theology deriving from Kant, Hegel, and Schleiermacher offer powerful wellsprings for religious philosophy. Yet the most dominating and defining liberal theology ever devised, Ritschlian theology, oscillated between minimizing its debt to philosophy and repudiating religious philosophy. This anomaly looms so large over my subject that it must be addressed before I proceed with my argument about the enduring relevance of liberal theology.

The Ritschlian Heyday: Liberal Theology without Metaphysics

Each of the liberal theologies deriving from Kant, Hegel, Schleiermacher, and the Mediating fusions of them claimed to give historical criticism its due, yet each was also a strategy to curtail its reach. Ritschl said this defensive posture was self-defeating. He cut his teeth on neo-Hegelian historicism, but concluded it was not really historicist. He absorbed the personal idealism and value theory of his Göttingen colleague and friend Rudolf Hermann Lotze, but denied it controlled his theology. Ritschl said theology needed to embrace historical consciousness, reclaim the kingdom-oriented religion of Jesus, accept Kant's division of knowledge, and defend the indispensable role of religion in society. The school he founded swept the field by doing all four things, albeit as Ritschlian theologians clashed with each other. The leading Ritschlians were theologian Wilhelm Herrmann, eminent church historian Adolf von Harnack, and history of religions theologian Ernst Troeltsch. Other German Ritschlians included Johannes Gottschick, Theodore Häring, Julius Kaftan, Ferdinand Kattenbusch, Friedrich Loofs, Martin Rade, Max Reischle, Friedrich Traub, and Georg Wobbermin.[7]

All grappled with Ritschl's historicism, judging that he got it approximately right (Harnack), or took it too far (Herrmann), or did not take it far enough (Troeltsch). All grappled similarly with Ritschl's attempt to expunge metaphysics from theology, judging that he got it right (Harnack), or didn't go far enough (Herrmann), or was wrong to try (Troeltsch). Liberal theology in the Ritschlian era projected a sunny, confident, outward-reaching progressivism that proposed to make peace with science and make Christianity socially useful, although Troeltsch warned that modern society and the Ritschlian school stood on tottering foundations.

Ritschl was born to the Prussian Union Church as the son of a conservative Lutheran bishop. He was schooled in Mediating theology under Immanuel Nitzsch at Bonn and Julius Müller and F. A. Tholuck at Halle, and subsequently studied under Ferdinand Christian Baur in 1845 at Tübingen. His relationship with Baur was stormy, competitive, and brief, but crucial to Ritschl's career. Baur began as a philosophical disciple of Friedrich Schelling, moved in mid-career to Hegel, and adopted Hegel's concept of the self-disclosure of Spirit in and through historical process. He taught Ritschl to interpret Christianity in Hegelian fashion as a total historical reality. Baur employed the conventional simplistic rendering of Hegel's dialectic, teaching that a thesis generates an antithesis yielding a synthesis. This idea helped Baur explicate his revolutionary claim that the key to early Christianity was the struggle between its "Judaizing" and "Hellenizing" factions. Peter and the other Jerusalem-based apostles espoused Jewish Christianity; Paul and the Gentile converts espoused Hellenistic Christianity; the New Testament book of Acts smoothed over the conflict; and Paul did not write the Pastoral Epistles.[8]

In his early career Ritschl accepted Baur's brand of historicism and his rendering of early Christian history, but in 1850 Ritschl turned against Baur's dictum that pure historicism is impossible. Ritschl claimed to interpret history without a philosophy, roiling Baur and his disciples. According to Ritschl, philosophy got in the way of understanding what happened in early Christian history. Accusations of bad faith ensued back and forth. Baur said the Johannine literature was a synthesis of the conflict between Judaizers and Hellenizers, which led to Catholicism. Ritschl said Catholicism was no synthesis, but rather a negation of Judaism by a triumphant Hellenistic faction that redefined Christianity in its own image. Catholicism stood for corruption and deracination, erasing the Jewish character of Christianity.[9]

Ritschl grieved that German theologians routinely denigrated the Jewish aspects of Christianity, often with anti-Jewish quotes from Martin Luther. He compensated by emphasizing Luther's anti-Catholicism and contending that Luther was not as bad on Judaism as his worst writings conveyed. Protestant theology, he taught, especially Lutheran theology, needed to reclaim its Jewish, ethical, historical, this-worldly, monotheistic heritage, discarding the pagan motifs it inherited from Catholicism. Paul de Lagarde, the founder of the history of religions school, was a vile anti-Semite who loathed Ritschl's pro-Judaism. Göttingen students who studied under Lagarde and Ritschl often steered a diplomatic path between them, yielding evasive theological and historical scholarship that erased this part of Ritschl's legacy.[10]

Ritschl sometimes exaggerated Baur's reliance on Hegel, but the break between Ritschl and Baur occurred over a real disagreement. Baur taught that every theology needs a philosophical basis, Hegel provided the best philosophy, and Christianity is the very life process of God explicating itself in thinking as spirit. Paul, Baur contended, shifted the focus of Christianity from the historical Jesus to the person of Christ. The unknown author of the Fourth Gospel provided a metaphysical foundation for Pauline universalism, replacing Paul's emphasis on justification with a love theology of new being in Christ. Good theology must be rigorously historicist, unlike the Gospel of John, and robustly metaphysical, like John. Ritschl countered that historicism is a golden key that makes metaphysical speculation unnecessary. From 1846 to 1864 he taught at Bonn; in 1857 he left church history to become a theologian; in 1864 he moved to Göttingen and changed the field of theology.[11]

He changed the field by contending that Christianity is inherently social, historical, and based on faith. Ritschl had two defining concerns: the challenge of Darwinian evolution and the bitter disputes between conservative confessionalists and Pietists in the Prussian Union Church. As a modern theologian, he was anxious to avoid religious conflicts with science; as a Prussian churchman, he was appalled at the erosion of the church's moral and social authority. His solution to the religion-and-science problem came straight from Kant: science describes the way things are or appear to be, while theology is about the way things should be. Religious knowledge is never disinterested, consisting entirely of value judgments about reality, especially judgments contributing to personal and social good. Ritschl explained in *The Christian Doctrine of Justification and Reconciliation* (1874): "Religious knowledge moves in independent value-judgments, which relate to man's attitude to the world, and call forth feelings of pleasure and pain, in which man either enjoys the dominion over the world vouchsafed him by God, or feels grievously the lack of God's help to that end."[12]

Ritschl took from Kant and Lotze—without putting it that way—that the goal of true religion is to attain the highest possible good. He said this idea and its content are in the Christian apostolic tradition and are discoverable by historical criticism. The point is not to uncover what Jesus really said. Quests of the historical Jesus kept getting this wrong, feeding the impression that Christianity should be based on whatever historical critics discovered about the Jesus of history. What matters, Ritschl contended, is to uncover the collective Christian experience of value inspired by Jesus: "It would be a mistaken purism were anyone, in this respect, to prefer the less developed statements of Jesus to the forms of apostolic thought."[13]

What makes a religion good is its concern with value. Historical research shows that the essence of Christianity is the kingdom of God as valued by the Christian community, which makes Christianity the best religion, since Christianity is concerned above all with the realization of social and ethical value. To be sure, the kingdom is valued as absolute only by those who follow Jesus. Outsiders don't care what Jesus taught about sin, redemption, or the kingdom. Ritschl stressed the logical upshot: Christian truth cannot be grasped outside the Christian community, for Christian faith is knowable only to faith. It is comprehensible only within the inner history of the church's life and practices. The value of the kingdom becomes a matter of knowledge within the inner history of the church's life. From this perspective, Jesus is the embodiment of humanity's highest ideal—the Redeemer of humankind who incarnates and inaugurates the realization of the kingdom.[14]

Personal redemption and social religion go together in the gospel. Ritschl's image for this double character became synonymous with the Ritschlian school: an ellipse determined by two foci, personal redemption and the kingdom of God. Christians know Jesus as their Redeemer and are commanded to follow him in building the kingdom of God. The mark of true Christianity is its mutually relational double character in which the religious and ethical dimensions perpetually interact and advance through history.[15]

The Ritschlian school offers the rare example of a school outshining its founder. Ritschl lacked personal magnetism, his writing style was clumsy and verbose, he kept revising his position, his German nationalism embarrassed his American followers, and he never quite decided how to defend his position. He absorbed Lotze's philosophy, but blasted theologians for espousing a religious philosophy, which provided fodder for the many Ritschlians who accentuated Ritschl's anti-philosophy trope. Herrmann surpassed him by doing so, and Harnack far surpassed him.

Like Ritschl, Harnack had a distinguished clerical father, but he grew up in Dorpat (today Tartu), a Russian majority town in Livonia where he belonged to a German-speaking Prussian nationalist elite. Harnack's proudly German identity cast a long shadow over his life and legacy. His early books on church history carried him swiftly from Giessen to Marburg in 1886, where he befriended Herrmann, and then to Berlin in 1888, where he became world famous. He wrote massive scholarly works that detailed the Hellenization of Christian doctrine and popular books that simplified Ritschl's theology. Britons and North Americans flocked to Berlin to hear him, marveling at his knack for cutting through tangled webs of doctrine and historical detail. Cordial, eloquent, and gifted with charm, Harnack was skilled at making his historical subjects come alive. He tempered his aristocratic bearing with a kindly disposition and a sincere evangelical piety, telling audiences that Jesus Christ is the central fact of human history. All that came before and after Jesus must be interpreted in light of his creative personality.[16]

Harnack's disciplined clarity was a central feature of his work and a key to his vast influence and productivity. His simple theology of the "Fatherhood of God and brotherhood of man" attracted people who were mystified by Schleiermacher and even Ritschl. Harnack said that religion is about the human problems of living, suffering, meaning, and death, not doctrines, and Christianity is the highest religion because it is precisely Jesus Christ and his gospel. Since Christianity is a life, not a doctrine, one must grasp its history to understand it. To understand a tree, one learns about its root and stem, bark and branches, and the way it blooms. Understanding Christianity is much the same, plus the only way to purify dogma. Harnack said the church's mission is to preach the gospel of personal faith, leaving the realms of politics and economics to experts in these fields. He supported Germany's welfare state and military expansion, contending that the greatness of Germany rested on two pillars: the German military and German scholarship.[17]

In 1903 Harnack assumed the presidency of the Evangelical Social Congress, helping the kaiser combat social democracy. Two years later he became director general of the Royal Library (renamed the Prussian State Library after World War I). Harnack held these two positions concurrently for six years, greatly expanding the library on Berlin's main avenue, Unter den Linden. In 1911 he gave up the Social Congress presidency because the kaiser had a new job for him: running the Kaiser Wilhelm Gesellschaft, which founded scientific research institutes.

Harnack never doubted that his prominence was good for liberal theology, although he lived to see it ridiculed by a postwar generation. He taught that historical theology breaks the power of traditions that fossilized Christianity into something alien to the gospel of Jesus. To a point he shared the deconstructive project of left-Hegelian critic David Friedrich Strauss, but judged that Strauss lacked a literary-historical understanding of his subject, being a prisoner of rationalistic narrowness. Thus he failed to comprehend the kind of literature he attacked. Strauss dismissed as mythical every Gospel account containing dubious history, but the Gospel writers made no pretense of presenting disinterested historical accounts. Harnack explained that the Gospels are testimonies of faith, not works of history. Their purpose is to inspire faith in the person and mission of Jesus.[18]

All four of the Gospels are products of Jewish didacticism under the short-lived conditions of first century Jewish Christianity, composed by a religious community in the last stage of its absorption by the Hellenistic church. To treat the Gospels as history or myth is to miss their unique character as the faith literature of a disappearing community of memory. With the triumph of Hellenistic Christianity, the peculiar gospel blend of faith and tradition became alien to the church. It was no longer a living possession. The Gospels became alien texts, though not lacking in historical material. Harnack judged that the gospel picture of the life and teaching of Jesus is basically reliable. Jesus taught that the kingdom of God is coming, the human soul is infinitely valuable under the rule and love of God, and believers hold the promise of righteousness and eternal life.[19]

Jesus pointed to the providential care of the Father, not to himself. His teaching centered on the coming kingdom—a cooperative social order in which human beings live under the rule of love and conquer their enemies by love. Ultimately, Harnack said, there is no difference between the God of Jesus and the kingdom proclaimed by Jesus, for both signify the same spiritual reality. The kingdom "is not a question of angels and devils, thrones and principalities, but of God and the soul, the soul and its God." The business of theology is to faithfully separate the unchanging "kernel," the gospel of Jesus, from the "husk" of its various cultural and doctrinal forms as expressed in the New Testament and church tradition.[20]

Harnack's scholarly renown lent immense authority to his theological judgments. He described the Gospel infancy stories as purely mythical and said that any story featuring angels, devils, absolute miracles, or apocalyptic prediction is mythical too. But the core of the gospel is not mythical, he insisted. None of the early church's mythical trappings impinge on its gospel core. A sentence such as "I am the Son of God" is not a gospel statement, but an addition to the gospel. Harnack did not blame the early church for adding to the gospel; it remembered Jesus in the light of its faith in him. But in modern Christianity, everything depends on keeping the crucial distinction clear. Christian faith must not be identified with the church's mythical or doctrinal expressions of its faith in Jesus. All forms of gospel husk inevitably become antiquated over time; every attempt to rationalize Christianity eventually becomes an obstacle to Christian faith. Even the favorite liberal construct, the "religion of Jesus," has this problem. Jesus believed in devils and he may have believed in an imminent apocalypse, both of which belong to the category of dispensable husk. Harnack said the gospel itself is timeless. It is never falsified or rendered obsolete, for its constitutive elements are eternal.

His voice was so commanding that he obscured for many that other kinds of liberal theology existed. Harnack taught liberal theologians to judge Christian history by its relationship to the gospel core and its results. With Baur, he insisted that the Hellenization of Christianity beginning with Paul is the central problem of Christian history. With Ritschl and against Baur, he contended that the heart of Christianity is not an idea but a spiritually and socially redemptive way of life.[21]

Harnack found little time for book writing after Germany marched into Belgium in 1914. World War I began for him on August 1, when the emperor asked him to compose a call to war. The enemy nations, when Harnack began, were France and Russia. Before he finished, he was told to add England, which stunned him; Harnack prized his British friends. He lost them swiftly. Some British scholars tried to distinguish between Prussian militarism (bad) and German scholarship (good, but cowardly about militarism). Harnack trembled with rage at reading such things. He would not accept moral criticism from acolytes of the British Empire. He believed that all Germans had an obligation to preserve the glorious legacy of German civilization, which rested on superior armed forces and a tradition of scholarly and artistic excellence. He believed that Germany's enemies caused the war by encircling Germany and that Western Christian civilization was at stake in Germany's fate. He signed numerous public declarations saying it defiantly.[22]

For all his iconic status, Harnack was never at the cutting edge of the Ritschlian school, and his eminence was misleading. One would not have guessed from his writings that the Ritschlian school seethed internally with controversy. At the very time that Harnack spoke with commanding assurance to a global audience, Ritschlian theologians sharply debated whether they had any ground of certainty or should want one. Herrmann and Troeltsch played the star roles in this drama, with Herrmann lurching to outright anti-historicism and Troeltsch taking the opposite tack as a ringleader of the *Religionsgeschichtliche Schule*.[23]

Johann Wilhelm Herrmann, born in Melkow, Prussia in 1846, had two role models of the tender piety for which he became known. The first was his father, a neo-Pietist Lutheran pastor who served humble congregations of poor and working-class people and was well versed in Schleiermacher. The second was his graduate mentor, neo-Pietist Lutheran theologian Friedrich August Tholuck, with whom Herrmann lived for over two years as his personal secretary at Halle, where Herrmann also studied under Julius Müller and Martin Kähler. Tholuck combined Schleiermacher and Hegel with apologetic arguments they eschewed. He befriended his students, taught them not to fear historical criticism, and radiated a childlike sincerity that made him a magnet for students eager to combine modern learning and personal faith.[24]

Herrmann was like his teacher in radiating joy and pious conviction. He taught at Halle for four years, becoming the first theologian to call himself a Ritschlian, and moved to Marburg in 1879, telling students that the living Christ can be known personally. Herrmann's early writings focused on the role of metaphysics in theology. *Die Metaphysik in der Theologie* (1876) and *Die Religion im Verhältnis zum Welterkennen und zur Sittlichkeit* (1879) argued that Catholicism, Protestant orthodoxy, and liberal theology shared the same fatal mistake of making theology depend on metaphysical arguments. Metaphysical reasoning is not a way into true religion, but a way of evading or losing the life of faith that constitutes true religion.[25]

Herrmann challenged Ritschl to say it this starkly, instead of allowing Kant to define what religion is about. True religion is an independent power through which God saves a lost human being. To incorporate religion into a general theory of knowledge is to treat being as a function of thinking. In biblical terms, it is to commit idolatry. Herrmann did not deny that morality plays an important role in the inner drama of salvation. People discover through morality that they are lost souls. Every saving encounter with Christ begins with an experience of inner moral conflict. But moral experience, he implored, is not saving. We are saved by faith, as Luther taught, not by moral achievement. Through faith we learn that God is unique, mysterious, and transcendent. The reality known to true faith is knowable only to faith, not to any other kind of cognition. Since philosophy and science have no access to divine reality, theology must not seek any support from these disciplines or any other discipline.[26]

Ritschl bristled at being pushed by Herrmann, and Herrmann battled with himself over how far he should go with fideism—faith as its own basis. For thirty years he equivocated on saying that religious knowing is fundamentally different from other kinds of knowledge and that all apologetic arguments are illegitimate. Herrmann's fideism drove his theology from the beginning, but he hedged because Ritschlian theology was deeply vested in arguments about the historical character of Christianity, and fideism cuts off theology from other disciplines. Why should the Ritschlian school retreat to an immunization strategy? Herrmann's bottom-line answer was that fideism is true: revelation cannot be established by something else. His battle with Troeltsch drove him to say it more and more categorically, dispensing with apologetic arguments. Troeltsch was fond of saying that as soon as one concedes an inch to historical criticism, it takes a mile. Sometimes he added that for conservatives, historical criticism was very much like the devil. Both remarks irked Herrmann, because historical criticism was a problem for liberals too, and Ritschlians were vulnerable to being devoured by it.[27]

In 1886 Herrmann's major work, *The Communion of the Christian with God*, ostensibly refashioned the Ritschlian school strategy. Many

anti-Ritschlians wrongly said that Ritschl based his theology on a picture of the historical Jesus constructed by historical criticism, and some
post-Ritschlians were beginning to say that Ritschl's interpretation of
Christian history wrongly rested on dogmatic presuppositions. Herrmann said both groups held a skewed idea of what it means to claim that
Christianity is historical. It does not mean that Christian faith is founded
on historical facts confirmed by historical criticism. Christianity is historical because it is grounded in an experience of communion with God
mediated by Christ that occurs in history. It is historical in the sense that
it bears the spiritual reality and power that makes history. As historical
reality, Christianity is comprehensible only to those who participate in its
effects, not to onlookers. What matters is the inner life of Jesus known to
faith, not the history-making life and teaching of Jesus.[28]

The book's first edition appealed to the inspiring personality of Jesus
as the basis of Christian faith, asserting that the gospel picture of Jesus
is historically reliable. The later editions cut back on the historical assur-
ances while continuing to describe Jesus as "the historical fact" through
which God's love is revealed to people of faith. In both cases, Herrmann
tried to strengthen Ritschlian theology by shifting from the life and
teaching of Jesus to the inner life of Jesus. Ritschl grasped from the beginning, however, that Herrmann was breaking ranks. He told Herrmann
he could scarcely find himself in the book. He had to read it several times
before he saw anything of value. Ritschl's core was the kingdom-bringing
effect of Christ's life and teaching, but Herrmann moved away from the
very notion of a critically established historical core.[29]

Herrmann judged that Ritschl's reliance on history took on the character of an apologetic device, diminishing the power of the gospel claim
to truth. Ritschl used historical science as a crutch, bringing readers to
Christianity by convincing them that his historical arguments about it
were correct. Herrmann countered that apologies for Christianity detract
from the gospel faith. Orthodoxies overload Christian teaching with
legalistic doctrines. Mystical theologies make Jesus peripheral to a quest
for unmediated communion with God. Metaphysical theologies distort
the gospel by turning it into an abstraction. History, to be sure, is slightly
different, because Christianity is historical, but history-as-apologetics is
no less problematic than dogmatism.[30]

No one has ever been saved by information. This claim acquired
mantra status for Herrmann. What saves is the person of Jesus as we
encounter and experience him. Put differently, we do not meet, in faith,

the historical Jesus sought by historians, but rather the living presence of the personality of Jesus. Christian faith is founded on the inner life of Jesus, which is known by faith. It has no basis outside itself. Pietism at its best, Herrmann said, got this right. Christianity is founded on a specific experience of sin and regeneration, and regeneration is the precondition of all theological knowledge. But Pietism degenerated into dogmatism and crude evangelism, a disaster for Protestantism. That is, it degenerated into a form of the apologetic mistake. Herrmann ripped it mercilessly for that reason. His alternative blended Schleiermacher and Tholuck in a revised Ritschlian framework. Like Tholuck he played up his Lutheranism, claimed Luther for his side, and professed no interest in a liberal Protestantism cut off from its Reformation roots. The key was Luther's doctrine of justification by faith.

Rightly understood, Herrmann argued, justification by faith opposes all attempts to make any other doctrine essential to Christianity or to establish support for Christianity on any basis outside the experience of faithful communion with God. By God's grace and through the mediation of Christ, Christians are brought into a saving communion of the soul with the living God. This is the gospel faith. Actual communion with God is the only nourishment on which faith can be fed. One does not become a Christian by accepting doctrines about God or Christ, for doctrines are expressions of a life of faith. They cannot be true for someone who is not in a faith-relation to God.[31]

Herrmann had only a slight acquaintance with Kierkegaard's thought, but he fastened on the same claim as Kierkegaard: Christianity is subjective except for the objective reality of divine revelation that we apprehend in faith. To put aside the knowledge that is obtainable only through faith is to be cut off from objective reality, that which makes reality possible. Herrmann's concept of revelation was cribbed from Schleiermacher and Hegel, though he felt no need to trace the genealogy, after two generations of Mediating theology. Revelation is that which brings human beings into actual communion with God. It is not propositional, but occurs as event. It is not to be identified with thoughts of faith, although faith produces true thoughts. Revelation occurs as events of grace that produce true thoughts of faith. It is revelatory experience of the divine, not lumps of propositional information.[32]

Jesus is the only objective anything that Christianity needs. We know in faith that God is real because we know the man Jesus whom God sent. Herrmann allowed that every reader inevitably asks to what extent the Gospels convey accurate historical information, and historical criticism rightly addresses this question. But the crucial religious question lies beyond the scope of historical reason. It is not what we make of the gospel story, but what the content of the story makes of us. Through faith and the fellowship of the Christian community we are led into Christ's presence and receive a picture of his inner life. The inner life of Jesus becomes part of our reality in the same way that any historical personality meaningfully enters our lives.[33]

This was still a type of Ritschlian theology, albeit without Ritschl's historical construction of the content of faith that Christians should believe. Herrmann judged that Ritschl's historical foundation made him the "last great representative of orthodox dogmatics." Ritschl never quite relinquished the concept of Scripture as a source of prescriptive ideas about the content of faith. The fact that Ritschl disliked *Communion* helped Herrmann throw off Ritschl. With each edition the book sounded more like Schleiermacher, and in 1906 Herrmann's *Christlich-protestantische Dogmatik* was emphatically in the Schleiermacher mode, while barely mentioning Ritschl.[34]

Herrmann completed his prolonged process of relinquishment in the years just before World War I, embracing what Troeltsch, not unfairly, called "the agnostic theory about the nature of religious knowledge." Troeltsch cautioned that Herrmann's anti-historicism was an instructive example of "subjective mysticism," the upshot of abandoning "firm and adequate knowledge." Less charitably he declared in 1911 that Herrmann's religious claims were "obscure and mystical," if not "violently" willful, and Herrmann's refusal to ground his claims in historical criticism was "almost incomprehensible to people who think historically and critically." Troeltsch said that Herrmann preserved the orthodox claim to a religious absolute, but failed the test of historical credibility.[35]

This clinging-to-orthodoxy image offended Herrmann, who replied that Troeltsch was the one clinging to a security blanket, a supposedly scientific historicism presuming its own certainty *and* its right to serve as the test of religious faith. By confusing religion and science, Troeltsch distorted the experiential character of religious truth. The history of religions approach reduced the truth of Christianity, the experience of Christ, to a mere idea. Herrmann made a clean break with all such confusions and his earlier concessions to them. Without giving up his belief that Christianity possesses a factual grounding in history, he denied that theology should establish a historical-critical ground for its religious claims. With no apologetic asides he insisted that all religious statements about God, creation, morality, and everything else are lifeless and groundless apart from their source in religion itself.[36]

Thus he urged theologians to see the Kantian revolution through by refusing Kant's frame. Kant liberated religion from its distorting connection to scientific reason, but failed to recognize that religion has its own truth. The early Schleiermacher corrected Kant's identification of religion with the ethical will, but his later system lost the Kantian recognition that religion belongs only to a particular kind of individual experience. Schleiermacher's dogmatic system deduced religious reality from the unity of human self-consciousness. Herrmann allowed that this strategy may have described the condition of the possibility of religion, but it obscured through its ostensible universality that which constitutes true religion itself. True religion, he said, exists historically only in the life of individuals, comprehensible only to those who live in it. What we need, we must be given. A person can become a truly live self (*das etwas für sich selbst sein will*) only by experiencing a reality that one cannot produce from within oneself. True religion is the simultaneously liberating and submissive response to revelation, which is the experience of a spiritual Power. To experience the working of this Power is to settle, or have settled for us, the question whether God is a reality. Only the Spirit gives life. Usually it works through the moral will, but it is never merely a product or function of morality. True religion is an awakening to the revelation of God's Spirit in all the life-giving movements of one's inner life.[37]

Herrmann and Harnack had the same status quo politics and the same reply to the *Religionsgeschichtliche Schule* claim that Jesus was a failed apocalypticist: the worldview of Jesus doesn't matter, because it is irrelevant to the question of faith and true religion, belonging to the same category as his belief in devils. The kingdom of God is the rule of God in the hearts of Christ-following individuals. It does not matter that Jesus and the early church believed many things that we do not believe, for what links us to Jesus is the revelatory experience of God as righteous, providential, and loving.[38]

Through such experiences we come to know the inner life of Jesus. Herrmann insisted that religion finds its true origin without remainder "in revelation understood as a unique personal experience" (*als ein eigenes Erlebnis erfasster Offenbaung*). In 1909, at the height of his debate with Troeltsch that drove him to say it more starkly than ever, Herrmann said his entire career was devoted to showing that the only true ground of religious teaching is "that experience which is its revelation." Faith is a spiritual gift of God's Spirit. Herrmann told his students that one would have to be secretly ashamed of the Spirit's gift to defend it with reasons.[39]

These ideas were immensely influential in twentieth-century theology, but not as liberal theology, and usually without citing Herrmann. A great deal of what came to be called neo-orthodoxy refashioned themes from Herrmann in orthodox dress: revelation is divine self-revealing, theology is the explication of a self-authenticating revelation, faith is not assent to doctrine or the outcome of an argument, history is not a basis or subject of faith, apologetics is not a legitimate theological enterprise, and Christian faith is not a worldview. Herrmann's liberal successors were left with the perplexing question of how the inner life of Jesus could be ascertained if the biblical testimony about it belongs to the period of second-generation Christian reflection. His Barthian and Bultmannian successors waved off the problem, replacing Herrmann's appeals to the inner life of Jesus with a doctrine of biblical authority. That kept Herrmann's legacy alive in theology, albeit in reworked form, through varieties of neo-orthodoxy that scorned Harnack and Troeltsch for stripping theology bare.

Troeltsch's thoroughgoing historicism carried him beyond the Ritschlian school, and his commitment to a personalist religious philosophy made him a leading theorist of the personal idealist school discussed in chapter 6. The Ritschlians found their actual unity by shilling for Germany's political and cultural establishment. They backed all five German chancellors from Otto von Bismarck to Theobald von Bethmann-Hollweg, defending Bismarck's welfare state, lionizing the German army and German state, and opposing the Social Democrats. Barth's contempt for *that* record seethed through everything he said about the Ritschlian school, long before Tillich disavowed his own German militarism. After the war, while routing the liberal establishment, Barth took for granted that Herrmann won the debate with Troeltsch. Pauline radicalism about faith was indeed the answer to the crisis and trauma of the postwar church, though not on Herrmann's liberal terms. Tillich, emerging from the war, agreed with Barth about Pauline faith and the Ritschlian school, but not about the liberal tradition. Two dominant ways of construing liberal theology flowed from what Barth and Tillich said about it. Both heaped ridicule on the Ritschlian school, Barth said the problem began with Kant and Schleiermacher, and Tillich said the liberal tradition was too great to be lumped with the Ritschlian school.

Liberal theology went down with the Ritschlian school, even as Ritschlians retained the major chairs in German universities. Barth said liberal theology betrayed Christ by construing faith as a human work and reducing God to an aspect of the world process. Barthian "crisis theology" was about the holy mystery and wrath of a Wholly Other God, beheld in faith and confessed in the language of paradox. Ritschl, Barth decided, was not worth refuting, having merely baptized the German bourgeois order. Harnack conferred scholarly prestige on Ritschlian theology. Troeltsch trivialized theology by reducing it to the ponderings of historicist onlookers. Schleiermacher was great, but also the beginning of the problem. Hegel was great, but Hegelian philosophy was a bad substitute for Christian revelation. According to Barth, Schleiermacher founded a bad approach to theology that led straight to the bankruptcy of Ritschl, Harnack, and Troeltsch. Halle theologian Martin Kähler and his protégé, Tillich, countered that liberal theology *was* the Ritschlian school and that Schleiermacher and Hegel should not be blamed for it. In both cases, liberal theology was defined as Christ-of-culture optimism and modernism.

Both versions of this polemical rendering were enormously influential to the end of the twentieth century. Often they were mashed together by theologians across the theological spectrum. Denigration and dismissal were so commonplace that even liberal theologians who rejected Progressive Era liberalism swallowed the regnant usage. American process theologian Daniel Day Williams, for example, wrote in 1949: "By 'liberal theology' I mean the movement in modern Protestantism which during the nineteenth century tried to bring Christian thought into organic unity with the evolutionary world view, the movements for social reconstruction, and the expectations of 'a better world' which dominated the general mind. It is that form of Christian faith in which a prophetic-progressive philosophy of history culminates in the expectation of the coming of the Kingdom of God on earth."[40]

Here, as usual, liberal theology was equated with the evolutionary ideology, cultural optimism, and social idealism of its social gospel heyday. A century of pre-Ritschlian liberal theology fell out of this definition, as did the American and British liberal theologies predating the social gospel. More important for twentieth-century theologians, liberal theology supposedly existed after World War I only among tiny bands of idealistic progressives who refused to get their clocks fixed. That did not describe Williams or any of the liberals that influenced him, notably

Whitehead, William Ernest Hocking, and Henry Nelson Wieman. Yet Williams recycled the very definition of his tradition that marginalized him and it.

The conventional usage was wrong at both ends. It ignored that the liberal tradition had its richest intellectual flowering before the Ritschlian school existed. And it denigrated an ongoing tradition that is still creatively refashioning itself a century after World War I.

2

Kantian Foundations

Creative Reason and Moral Freedom

The unavoidable thinker in modern philosophy and religious thought is Immanuel Kant. His thought was notoriously difficult and abstract, he wrote badly to heighten the difficulty, and many of his defining ideas did not originate with him. Though famous for rejecting authority religion and defining enlightenment as the courage to use your reason, he inherited both tropes from the early Enlightenment. Kant is the unavoidable modern thinker because he brilliantly expounded original ideas about what it means to have a thought and to experience moral freedom: reason and will are inseparable; reason is essentially an activity; free activity is reasonable; freedom itself is the unfathomable groundless ground of something that we fathom, the moral law within us; and we ought to do good.

He was indebted to René Descartes, John Locke, G. W. Leibniz, Jean-Jacques Rousseau, and David Hume. Descartes resolved to doubt nearly everything, conceiving epistemology as the philosophy of mind. Locke put epistemology at the center of philosophical debate, conceiving it as a map of the elements and associations of experience. Leibniz provided Kant's early model of German Enlightenment metaphysics. Rousseau contended that the Enlightenment diminished human happiness and betrayed the cause of freedom by corrupting modern Europeans; the only cure was to cultivate public morality and civil society. Rousseau's onetime friend and ally, Hume, though more skeptical than Kant realized, prodded Kant by arguing that there are no links between facts in the world of experience.

Kant distilled three terrible threats to enlightenment from these figures and his intellectual context: skepticism, determinism, and atheism. He aimed his three *Critiques* at this triplet of threats, building up to a defense of religion as moral activity. He fused rationalist and empiricist ideas into a theory of the creative power of subjectivity, the primacy of practical reason, and the grounding of reason and morality in something lacking a comprehensible ground, freedom. His first *Critique* opened the door to post-Kantian intellectual intuition, and his third *Critique* teetered on outright post-Kantianism—unless the first *Critique* was more "post-Kantian" than it seemed.

When Kant began his academic career in 1755, German universities and the German language were just beginning to acquire respect. There was no "Germany"; there was only a grab bag of principalities more or less held together by the so-called Holy Roman Empire. A century had passed since the Peace of Westphalia (1648), which ended the Thirty Years' War, fought mostly on German lands. Little intellectual life had arisen in the German principalities. England was the world's dominant power, exercising direct influence on German lands through its possession of Hanover. France was becoming the strongest nation on the Continent. The early Enlightenment was mostly English, Scottish, and French; the German version was very modest by comparison.

Usually Kant comes off as all thought and no life. Three theologian biographers established this convention shortly after he died, making him as machinelike as possible, after which German Romantics perpetuated the caricature. In 1804, the year of Kant's death, Ludwig Ernst Borowski, Reinhold Bernhard Jachmann, and Ehregott A. Christian Wasianski defended Kant from recent aspersions on his character. In their telling, Kant was a morally earnest academic habituated to a rigid regime of quiet and reflective dignity. Contrary to recent allegations, he was not petty, selfish, egotistical, subversive, or devoted to the French Revolution. Kant, they insisted, was a dutiful Prussian citizen, albeit with eccentricity issues. He was not harmful to public morals or the role of religion in modern society; in fact, he was the opposite. The biographers that knew Kant personally fixed on his later life and warded off any suggestion that he was a dangerous character.[1]

German Romantics, opposing German rationalism, seized on this picture, which reinforced the impression that Kant's biographers got him right. According to the Romantics, Königsberg was a provincial backwater from which Kant never roamed because he had no life and didn't want one. Heinrich Heine established the classic version of the Romantic account. In his telling, Kant was as regular and mechanical as the cathedral clock in Königsberg, so neighbors set their clocks by Kant's daily constitutional, consisting of eight trips up and down a quiet tree-lined alley. Everything had its precise time, and nothing was allowed to interfere with the production of thought.[2]

The Königsberg biographers depicted Kant as an obsessive thought machine to defend a local hero, who had to be thoroughly Prussian, non-republican, and no threat to religion. Subsequently the Romantics liked it because it lampooned the rationalist devotion to logical order and abstraction—never mind that Romantic philosophizing was based on Kant.[3]

Kant had a life, which was shaped by the tumultuous political, social, and intellectual events of his time. He ascended from a humble trade-guild family, took his genius to the local university, put a German stamp on the Enlightenment, sharply criticized traditional religion, fervently defended the French Revolution, dreamed of cosmopolitan global peace, and championed the conceits of his nation and intellectual class. Europeans, in his bigoted telling, were vastly superior in intelligence, character, and culture over all others; Africans were at the bottom of the human hierarchy; and Germans were the best of the Europeans. Thus he epitomized the best and worst of the Enlightenment.

He was born in 1724, the year after Prussian King Friedrich Wilhelm I expelled philosopher Christian Wolff from Prussia. Kant's father was a harness maker in Königsberg, and both of Kant's parents, especially his mother, were Lutheran Pietists devoted to a simple faith centered on street preaching, family devotions, personal morality, and knowing Jesus in one's heart. Kant was educated at Pietist schools affiliated with Königsberg's *Collegium Fridericianum*, very unhappily. He hated the emphasis on rote memorization and the punitive moralistic atmosphere. When Kant was thirteen his mother accidentally infected herself with smallpox by using the wrong spoon while caring for an afflicted friend, and died. Losing his beloved mother, and hating school, tormented Kant. He resented that his teachers forced him to write about the state of his soul and apparently believed they could punish children into being saved. In 1740, the same year that King Friedrich II allowed Wolff to return triumphantly to Halle, Kant entered the University of Königsberg, not quite grateful for the education that qualified him for admission.

German universities fought over rationalism versus Pietism. Leibniz, an objective idealist in the Platonic mold, was Germany's leading philosopher until his death in 1716. He opposed Descartes' skeptical idealism on rationalist grounds, depicting a perfectly rational and harmonious world ordained by God. Ultimately, he argued, the universe consists only of God and of non-composite immaterial "monads." Space, time, material things, and causality appear to exist only because God ordained a pre-established harmony among all that does exist. The idea of space is a concept or ideal, not a specific thing or intuition. We attain this idea by abstraction from particular distances that make the idea possible. After Leibniz was gone, his protégé Christian Wolff refashioned Leibniz's deterministic and optimistic system, which dominated German philosophy until Kant overthrew it in the 1780s.[4]

Wolff, besides popularizing Leibniz's ideas, ranged widely, prolifically, and eclectically, blending Leibniz with Descartes. He reasoned that immaterial souls (not Leibnizian monads) relate to bodies through a preestablished harmony. At Halle, a stronghold of Pietism, Wolff sparred uneasily with colleagues who distrusted his deductive rationalism. Pietism supplemented Protestant dogma with a strong emphasis on the necessity of inward spiritual experience and commitment. In 1721 Wolff put himself in danger by contending that one does not have to believe in God to arrive at sound principles of morality and politics. Morality requires respect for God, Wolff said, but it does not depend on divine commands. It depends on an antecedent comprehension of moral truth. Even ethical atheists respect God without realizing it.[5]

Wolff's colleagues, appealing to King Friedrich Wilhelm I, warned that Wolff's theory of rational harmony was fatalistic and thus offered an excuse to army deserters. The king was alarmed, having organized Prussia around the needs of the army. He banished Wolff, making him famous. Wolff was verbose and prolific, with a flair for drama. He fled to Marburg, became a popular lecturer and a symbol of intellectual freedom, and virtually invented German as a scholarly language while writing for other Europeans in Latin. In 1740 Friedrich II (Frederick the Great), a more reflective type than his father, ascended to the throne and called Wolff to come home.

Wolff returned to a hero's welcome in Halle just as Kant began his studies. Kant's hometown, though somewhat insular and outside the domains of the Holy Roman Empire, was no backwater. Königsberg was an important city in the northeastern corner of Prussia, near Poland

and the Russian border. Until 1701 it was the capital of Prussia, and it remained the capital of East Prussia during Kant's youth. The Prussian state was weak during Kant's youth, and most Prussians called themselves "Berliners," "Westphalians," and the like, not Prussians. Königsbergians called themselves Prussians, absorbing Poles, Russians, Lithuanians, Huguenots, Mennonites, Jews, and numerous Dutch and English merchants. The last group proved to be significant for modern philosophy, as the British Navy, needing Baltic timber for its masts, was deeply invested in Königsberg, which brought the Scottish Enlightenment to Kant's university and to him.[6]

Some of Kant's teachers, hearing of Wolff's return to Halle, hoped it augured a defeat for Pietism. But Friedrich II was more interested in expanding Prussia's territory than in changing its universities. Thus he left the universities more or less as he found them, and Kant cut his teeth intellectually on the battle between Pietistic empiricism and induction versus not-so-pious Wolffian rationalistic deduction. Most of Kant's teachers were Pietists, a few were Wolffians, and a few others were die-hard Aristotelians. Pietist philosophers J. F. Budde, J. Lange, A. F. Hoffmann, and Christian August Crusius conceived philosophy as the analysis of concepts given in experience, often charging that their rationalist opponents were infidels.[7]

Newtonian physics devastated metaphysical systems based on Aristotle, who taught that objects acquire impetus and that four causes explain the "why" of everything: the material cause is the material out of which something is made and the subject of change; the formal cause is the shape of what a thing becomes; the efficient cause is the primary source of changing and resting; and the final cause is the end for which something exists. Newton countered that the universe is a closed system with universal physical laws. Material bodies interact according to laws of motion concerning the uniformity of motion, change of motion, and mutuality of action, and absolute time, space, place, and motion are independent quantities constituting an absolute framework for measure.

The question for Kant's teachers was whether Newton devastated any possible metaphysics. Kant began his career as an Enlightenment rationalist in the mold of Leibniz and Wolff, holding out for a new form of metaphysical reason that established the authority of reason in all spheres of life. From 1744 to 1759 Kant sought to provide a new foundation for metaphysical claims about God, immortality, and the first causes of nature. In 1760 he took a skeptical turn that lasted six years, developing arguments about the sense-bound limitations of scientific knowledge that he later made famous in the *Critique of Pure Reason* (1781). In 1766 he suffered a six-year relapse, as he later viewed it, fashioning a modest ontology. In 1772 he turned against full-orbed metaphysics again, setting on a course that produced the *Critique of Pure Reason*.[8]

In each phase Kant grappled with the attempts of Leibniz and Wolff to provide a new mathematical foundation for metaphysics. Kant taught metaphysics, logic, mathematics, physics, and ethics in his early career, later adding geography to boost his income, as he made no salary. Until the Russians came, Kant relied entirely on his lecture income, spurning private instruction. From the beginning he was a popular lecturer. Professors and lecturers were required to base their lectures on a textbook, but Kant freely departed from the text, tossing off witticisms, advising students against taking too many notes, and flashing his dry humor, although he almost never laughed. He told students to think for themselves; Kant didn't want followers. Lecturing at a brisk pace, he made no effort to help slower students comprehend the material, yet his lecture hall was nearly always filled to capacity.

Kant's lectures featured Hume's first *Enquiry concerning Human Understanding* (1748) as soon as it was published in a German edition, in 1755. He respected Hume enormously, wrestling with Hume's skeptical treatment of causality, although he never read Hume's *Treatise on Human Nature* (1739), which was not translated into German until 1793. Wrongly, Kant believed that Hume was a transcendental realist (truth consists in the conformity of concepts to objects), and he restricted Hume's skepticism to the issue of causality. Had he read Hume's *Treatise*, he probably would have corrected both misconceptions. As it was, Kant studied only the *Enquiry*, Hume's summary version of the *Treatise*, which propelled Kant to transcendental idealism—the idea that truth consists in the conformity of objects to concepts.[9]

In the late 1750s Kant worked hard at providing a better foundation for Wolffian rationalism. Leibniz founded all knowledge on a few self-evident first principles. Wolff argued that all knowledge reduces to a single first principle. Kant reasoned that there are two: "Everything that is, is" (for true affirmative propositions) and "Everything that is not, is not" (for true negative propositions). Following Wolff, Kant derived the principle of sufficient reason from the principle of identity: nothing is true without a sufficient reason. Any subject, by virtue of being a subject, must have something in it that excludes the opposite predicate from being true of it. It followed for Kant that there must be a reason for everything that exists; reason justifies the principle underlying all knowledge of matters of fact, the principle of causality. This was the cornerstone of Kant's early rationalism. The principle of causality, to use Kant's later categories, is analytical, not synthetic a priori. But by the time that Kant developed these categories, he believed that causality is synthetic a priori.[10]

A bit to his surprise, Kant worked hard at securing a place in polite society, and succeeded. In 1758 Königsberg fell to Russia, without a fight, as a casualty of the Russian-Prussian Seven Year War. Kant soon judged that being occupied by a wealthier and more cosmopolitan nation had its advantages. Russian money, culture, and officers poured into the city, the Russians stayed for five years, and they brought a freer way of life, with a taste for beautiful things. Russian worldliness eroded Prussian customs; at the same time, Russian officers crowded into university classrooms, especially Kant's, who boosted his income by giving private instruction to officers. Local bankers, merchants, and nobles, noting Kant's suave intelligence, invited him to dinner parties, where Kant sparkled. Kant found himself becoming something of a dandy. He cultivated the social graces of his new friends and became a family favorite of Count and Countess Keyserlingk, especially the countess, whom he rated, for the rest of his bachelor life, far above other women.[11]

Kant enjoyed the ruminating banter that Hume and Rousseau published to popular acclaim, and he was inspired by his success at dinner parties. Thus in 1764 he published some banter of his own, *Observations on the Feeling of the Beautiful and Sublime*. In Kant's telling, women had a "strong inborn feeling for all that is beautiful, elegant, and decorated," while men came naturally to reason and achievement. Women had no use for geometry or the principle of sufficient reason. When men turned away from wickedness, they did so for moral reasons, although Kant said that very few men actually lived by rational and moral principles. Women, however, turned away from wickedness only because it is ugly: "They do something only because it pleases them." Kant didn't blame women for being that way, because they were not capable of principles. A woman that tried to understand intellectual things was a violation of nature; she might as well grow a beard. For a man, the worst insult was to be judged a fool; in morals, the worst thing was to be found a liar. For a woman the worst insult was to be called disgusting, and the worst moral failing was to be unchaste.[12]

These opinions were apparently well received by the women that Kant met at dinner parties; he had very little engagement with any others.

In his early career he took for granted that beauty is objective, existing in objects outside the mind, although he allowed that taste is subjective, varying among individuals. Beauty was not yet a point of dispute between rationalists and empiricists; both defined it as an objective, orderly, harmonious, and attractive unity of things, emphasizing unity. Kant added that beauty is also various, which inspired him to make judgments about places he had never visited and ethnic groups he knew mostly from books. In his rendering, the scale of pleasures ranged in quality from coarse sensual pleasures at the low end to "finer" feelings at the high end requiring cultivation and talent. At the extreme ends of the scale, he argued, it is unnecessary to distinguish between the sublime and the beautiful, but in the middle region this distinction is crucial.

The sublime evokes awe, while the beautiful evokes joy. There are three kinds of sublimity (terrifying, noble, and splendid) and two kinds of beauty (outward attractiveness and a combination of outward and inward attractiveness mixed with elements of the sublime). In all five cases, beauty and virtue go together to some degree. Kant's examples of the sublime included snow-capped mountains, nighttime, courage, honesty, unselfish zeal, and understanding, while the beautiful included flowerbeds, daytime, artfulness, pleasant flattery, refinement, and courtesy. By these standards he rated the Italians and French as epitomizing the feeling of beauty and the Germans, English, and Spanish as keepers of the sublime. The Dutch had no taste for either and the Russians he tactfully did not mention.[13]

Overall the English came off second best, next to the Germans, although Kant worried that Germans cared too much about what others thought of them. Kant wanted Germans to unleash their talents, fretting less about the opinions of others. He judged that Arabs were the noblest race in the "Orient" because they were hospitable and truthful; unfortunately, they were prone to "inflamed imagination," which turned even the propagation of Islam into a "great adventure." The Persians were "the French of Asia," excelling at poetry, courtesy, and pretty things. Since Persians loved pleasure, they devised a mild version of Islam. Kant respected that Japan was resolute like England, but Japanese resolution degenerated into a stubborn disdain of death. Otherwise he found the rest of the "Orient" devoid of finer feeling. Indian religion and culture were "grotesque" through and through, featuring idols, atonements, adventure, and the sacrifice of widows, and China was equally repugnant in its own way, producing the most grotesque painting and literature in the world.[14]

Kant realized that his aesthetic banter trafficked in stereotypes. All such generalizations were of limited validity, he allowed, and no people completely lacked finer feeling, except native Africans and their descendants. Kant pronounced, "The Negroes of Africa have by nature no feeling that rises above the trifling." Hume was Kant's authority on the humanity of black persons. Hume claimed that Africa never produced a significant thinker or person of accomplishment, and Kant agreed, contending that blacks were dramatically inferior to whites in mental ability. The religion of blacks was riddled with superstition and idolatry, Kant claimed, "a sort of idolatry that sinks as deeply into the trifling as appears to be possible to human nature."[15]

These bigotries were popular well beyond the dinner parties at which Kant moved up in society. He embraced the standard racism, sexism, and cultural chauvinism of his time and context with no acknowledgment that any of it contradicted his claim to enlightened cosmopolitanism, although the later Kant tellingly confined his worst racist asides to private notes. In his middle career he was best known for his book on aesthetics, which earned him a nickname: "the beautiful Magister." *Observations on the Beautiful and Sublime* was published when Kant turned forty. He believed that individuals reach maturity at forty, acquiring a character, the self-creation of an individual. Character doesn't just happen, and no one is born with it. The crucial issue for every individual is whether one will be governed by instinct or reason.

When Kant turned forty he resolved to strengthen his rational moral character by adopting certain maxims on which he acted all the time. A good maxim, such as "Take an evening constitutional," is a rule that one practices every day without exception. Kant was a worrier, frail in health, and plagued by nervous anxiety and constipation, all of which reinforced his homebody tendencies. In 1764 he became friends with Joseph Green, a maxim-following bachelor and English merchant who had moved to Königsberg in his youth. Green prided himself on his extreme punctuality and self-control. Gradually, Kant became Green's closest friend and adopted his way of life. Kant's regime of maxims helped him cope with his neuroses, even as they created some new ones, and sharply reduced his enthusiasm for social diversions. To Kant, living by maxims and fulfilling his intellectual potential became synonymous.[16]

Kant taught for fifteen years before he finally won a professorial position, in 1770. He kept trying to establish a new foundation for metaphysics, but in the 1760s he began to doubt it was possible. His doubts yielded early versions of arguments that later made him famous, especially his refutation of the ontological proof. In 1762, in *The One Possible Basis for a Demonstration of the Existence of God*, Kant opposed the Augustinian/Anselmian tradition of proving God's existence by definition, which Descartes and Leibniz amplified by deducing the existence of a perfect being from the concept of a perfect being.[17]

The classic form of the ontological argument, developed by Anselm, defines God as "that which nothing greater can be conceived." Anselm reasoned that that which exists in reality is greater than that which exists only in the mind. Since we have a concept of perfect being, it is undeniable that God exists in our minds as an object of the understanding. The question is whether God also exists as an extramental reality. If God existed in the mind alone, we could conceive of a being greater than that which nothing greater can be conceived. That is absurd, Anselm said; one cannot conceive of something greater than that which nothing greater can be conceived. God's nonexistence is not conceivable, for God is that which cannot be conceived not to exist. Since God cannot exist in the mind alone, God must exist also as an extramental reality.[18]

Descartes and Leibniz similarly espoused definitional proofs of God's existence, contending that God's existence is a necessary deduction from the concept of a perfect being. Descartes reasoned that just as geometry is not possible if one does not accept its axioms and postulates, metaphysics requires the concept of a being in which all perfections are united. If such a definition for God is accepted, the necessity of God's existence follows immediately as an implication of the logic of perfection. The nonexistence of God the perfect being is as inconceivable as a four-sided triangle. The reality of the unity of perfections bears the same degree of necessity and certainty as that of a triangle possessing three sides. Put differently, the concept of God necessarily involves God's existence. Leibniz took this argument a step beyond Descartes, arguing that God's perfect being is not only the source of all that exists but also of all possibility insofar as anything is real in possibility.[19]

Kant replied that all such ontological reasoning misuses the concept of existence. Rightly understood, existence is the absolute position of a thing, not a predicate or determination of something. A predicate is always posited with respect to some other thing, but "existence" and "being" are not concepts of things that can be added to the concept of a thing. Adding existence to a thing does not give it any additional properties; a real something contains no more than a merely possible something. In the *Critique of Pure Reason*, Kant explained that a hundred real thalers contained no more coin than a hundred possible thalers; to say that something exists does not add any value to it. *The One Possible Basis* lacked an equally homely example, but Kant told readers to consider that Julius Caesar and sea unicorns had all the same properties whether or not they existed. It did not matter that this argument seemed "strange and absurd," for Kant was applying logic, not common sense, to the ontological proof. In everyday discourse, he allowed, there is no harm in employing existence as a predicate, but Descartes and Leibniz harmed philosophy by doing so.[20]

In the late 1760s Kant decided that he had the wrong project. Rousseau was a crucial influence, contending that high culture and the academy subverted virtue. Kant resolved to do something on behalf of the good. Instead of establishing a rational foundation for religion and morality, which made both dependent on a speculative worldview, Kant reconceived metaphysics as the science of the *limits* of reason. The fundamental source of morality, he reasoned, is freedom, not a speculative worldview. Morality is founded on the power of the free will to prescribe laws. If metaphysics started there, with philosophical modesty and the power of freedom, it might do something enormously useful, establishing the universal rights of humanity. Scholastic and rationalist metaphysics both projected the source of morality into a world transcending human powers, which alienated human beings from their freedom. Both metaphysical traditions, like the rest of the academy skewered by Rousseau, ignored the true source of virtue, which is human freedom.[21]

For ten years Kant labored in silence, wrestling with Hume's contention that there are no links between facts in the world of experience. No one has ever seen causality; all we know are ideas and impressions. Kant, resolving to deal only with the pure thinking of reason, puzzled over the possibility of cognition, wrote lengthy scraps, and finally, in a four-month frenzy of writing and assembling, produced the *Critique of Pure Reason*, which pursued a single question: How does a mental representation relate to its object? Or in Kant's language, How does the mind intuit objects of sense data?[22]

Kant did not want to be an idealist. He rejected Leibniz's Platonic idealism, Descartes' skeptical idealism, and Berkeley's empirical idealism.

But thinking about thinking drove him to some kind of idealism. Kant reasoned that the hard problem has to do with the a priori concepts of the understanding. Empirical representations are effects corresponding to the objects given to a subject, and in mathematical concepts, the mind creates its objects in the act of knowing them. There is nothing in a mathematical object that is not in its concept. A priori concepts, however, are not the effects of objects given in experience, nor do they create their objects. So how do they correspond to objects? What can be known on an a priori basis apart from experience?

Kant focused his tremendous powers of intellection on these questions, disciplining himself to his maxims, ignoring his students, publishing nothing, and developing his theory. Very few students got a moment with him, and he lectured only to those who understood him, whoever they were. Kant wasn't sure they existed. He told a friend he had "almost no private acquaintance" with his listeners and didn't know if they understood him. When the first *Critique* was finally published in 1781, local readers were disappointed. The book had none of the juicy flair of his book on aesthetics. Kant's method was analytical; he focused relentlessly on the faculties of knowledge, which he disclosed by transcendental logic; the book was extremely long, sprawling, and at times structurally disjointed; and the age of bad writing in philosophy began with the first *Critique*, the greatest work of modern Western philosophy.[23]

Pure Reason and the Bounds of Sense

One of Kant's major achievements in the first *Critique* was to convince philosophers and the public that the history of philosophy led to him. Christian Neoplatonism Christianized Plato's doctrine of eternal forms: God the Father creates through the eternal Son of the Father, the mind of God or logos. Kant's theory of pure reason fused select aspects of the rationalist and empiricist traditions of philosophy, refashioning the Platonic forms and divine logos as the forms of intuition and categories of understanding, and the Platonic flux of matter as the sensible manifold of intuition. Rationalists taught that we know nothing about things-in-themselves except through pure reason and logic; thus they made substantive knowledge claims apart from experience. Empiricists taught that we know nothing about things-in-themselves except that which we glean from our experience of them; thus they contended that all knowledge derives from sensation and reflection.

Kant rejected and fused aspects of both traditions, describing the forms of intuition and categories of understanding as a priori, and thus universal. All knowledge has an a priori component that allows rational subjects to make synthetic a priori judgments about the world, and all knowledge is synthetic. But synthetic a priori claims are not about reality per se. Rational subjects possessing certain a priori principles make claims about a "reality" that they experience through these principles. Metaphysics is about the requisite conditions of experience, which Kant called transcendental. There are three forms of such conditions: sensibility, understanding, and reason.

The forms of sensibility are space and time, which are subjective conditions of knowledge. We view the world as spatial and temporal, not because space and time are out there as objects of perception, but because they are necessary conditions of all experience. Kant contended that human subjects, being finite, do not see things as they are in themselves. Intuition apprehends the data of experience through the pure forms of sensibility and organizes these objects of sense to conform to the pure concepts or forms that Kant, following Aristotle, called categories of understanding.[24]

Aristotle elaborated ten categories of understanding—substance, quantity, quality, relation, place, time, action, passion, position (the end result of action), and state (the end result of passion and position). Kant took over some of these categories, but Aristotle's scheme was empirically based, and it lacked a guiding principle aside from Aristotle's attempt to exhaust all contents of predication. Kant's system was transcendental, and, in his telling, rigorously systematic. To explain how such diverse entities as the particulars of the external world and the pure concepts of mind can be related, Kant pointed to the universal applicability of time, for both the particulars of the external world and the pure concepts of the mind exist in time. Time and space, he argued, besides not being realities that reason apprehends in the world, are not ideas innate in the mind either. They are essential preconditions of thought through which the mind receives representations of objects, "and which therefore must also always affect the concept of these objects." Human reason, through the transcendental imagination, makes sense of the world by applying its a priori categories of understanding to phenomena perceived by the senses. Then it unifies the objects of understanding through the three interrelated Ideas of reason: God, self, and world. Kant cautioned that these Ideas do not constitute knowledge, since they do not arise from sense experience and cannot be verified by it. The Ideas of reason have a regulative, not constitutive, function—helping us to make sense of the world without necessarily telling us anything about the world.[25]

Kant postulated twelve categories of understanding under four headings, insisting that exactly twelve such categories exist. The four headings were quantity, quality, relation, and modality. Unity (this one), plurality (more than one), and totality (all together) are categories of quantity. Reality (presence and more), negation (absence and more), and limitation (a compound of presence and absence, needing space and time) belong to quality. Subsistence (substance and accidents), causality (cause and effect), and social reciprocity (community) are relational. And possibility/impossibility, existence/nonexistence, and necessity/contingency are categories of modality. These categories, he argued, make knowledge of phenomena possible by unifying the manifold of intuition—the plurality of representations or sensations given by the object through intuition—into a thought for consciousness. There are three steps to knowing something. The manifold of pure intuition is given, it is synthesized by the imagination, and the concepts unify the synthesis. Our sensations are synthesized as intuitions through the categories of understanding and are unified by the imagination.[26]

Kant solved the riddle of causality by conceiving it as an a priori category of understanding, but that raised the possibility of employing causality, or another category, in scholastic fashion. Did his categories have a wider application than the concepts of space and time? If the categories enable knowledge claims about things not belonging to the world of spatiotemporal experience, how far can one take them? Scholastic theologians invoked the concept of causality in proving God's existence, yet they also claimed that God is beyond space and time. Is that legitimate? Kant agreed with Hume that invoking causality to prove God's existence is not legitimate. However, Kant rejected Hume's contention that the concept of causality, being derived from experience, is meaningful only within experience. Hume failed to grasp that the understanding might, through its concepts, create the very experience in which its concepts are found. Hume fell back on a weak resort to subjective necessity, confining causality to experience; he tried to explain too much by appealing to mere custom, a repeated association in experience.[27]

That failed to account for the scientific a priori knowledge that we possess in pure mathematics and the science of nature. Since the categories are a priori concepts, Kant reasoned, they are independent of experience. Since the categories are universal, the knowledge they yield is objective—Kant's refutation of skepticism. Causality is a necessary structure of the human mind, notwithstanding that its objectivity does not inform us what things are in themselves. To Kant, the tricky question was whether the categories, which make experiential knowledge possible through their independence from experience, also make other kinds of knowledge possible. In 1770 he made a case for saying yes. Now he made a torturous, messy case for the view that the categories, though necessary for experiential knowledge, do not provide substantive knowledge of objects independent of space and time.[28]

This analysis, the key to the first *Critique*, he called the Transcendental Deduction of the categories. Kant's first edition of the first *Critique* struggled for twenty-one pages with it, but failed to demonstrate the unity of pure apperception (the original consciousness that is the necessary condition of experience), objective consciousness, and judgment. Thus he rewrote this section in the second edition of 1787, pressing hard on the functional unity of the categories. In both editions Kant twisted and turned, piling up arguments that didn't always prove his points or stay on the subject. Kant scholar H. J. Paton, summarizing his painstaking efforts, remarked in 1936: "The crossing of the Great Arabian Desert can scarcely be a more exhausting task than is the attempt to master the windings and twistings of the Transcendental Deduction."[29]

But Kant's central contention in both versions of his Transcendental Deduction can be stated plainly: the categories are possible concepts to the extent that they make experience possible and *only* to that extent. They are empty when applied to anything beyond experience. The version of the Transcendental Deduction on which Kant rested in the second edition began with the manifold of pure intuition and a spontaneous act of combination performed by the understanding. This act of combination, which he called synthesis, is the source of all combination, and the category of unity presupposes combination.[30]

I have summarized as concisely as possible to get to this point, where Kant's epistemological forest can be glimpsed. The first *Critique*, though steeped in transcendental analysis, fiercely resisted applying it to subjects transcending the bounds of sense. Kant abstracted form from content with logical zeal, prizing the purity of pure concepts. He described some concepts as empirical, possessing a sensible content actualized in thought or reality, but the transcendental concepts that made knowledge possible were purely formal, lacking any content. Purely formal entities controlled the structure of all human knowledge of phenomena. So how do they apply to phenomena? How do pure forms impinge on sensuous particularity? If no category, such as causality, can be intuited through sense or observed, how does any category bridge to anything in the empirical world?

Kant answered that something mediates between the categories and appearances through the pure form of time—the transcendental schema. Since time is the pure form of inner sense, just as space is the pure form of outer sense, all representations and thoughts occur in time. The categories are actualized through time and applied to sensuous appearances, where the transcendental schema must be applied as a rule. The schema is a product of imagination, Kant reasoned, but it does not unify images. It unifies the determination of the sensibility. The schema is distinct from every image, and the schema—not images of objects—underlies all pure concepts. To apply a concept, the mind has to know the rule from which an image of the entity can be correlated with an image of the category, which is the schema, the category in time. For example, the schema of a triangle exists only in thought. No image of a right-angled or obtuse-angled triangle is as valid for all triangles as the schema underlying the pure concept of a triangle. The schema is a rule of synthesis of the imagination through which the categories and intuition come together to create the possibility of experience. To apply a concept, one must know how to make images.[31]

Philosophical idealism owes much of its notorious complexity to the puzzles of its emphasis on imagination and abstraction, and much to the fact that idealism is not just one thing. In normal conversation, when we use the terms "idealist" or "idealism," we use them in an ethical or political sense. An idealist is someone who has an idea of a moral or political ideal to which one might aspire. In metaphysics, however, the "ideal" can refer to spiritual or mental ideality as contrasted with the material or physical. Or it can refer to a normative ideal as contrasted with the substantive.

Idealism in the first sense, subjective idealism, is the idea that there is no reality without self-conscious subjectivity. The extreme form is Berkeley's doctrine that only the ideas of individual minds are real. Idealism in the second sense, objective idealism, is the idea that everything is a manifestation of the ideal, an unfolding of reason. Plato and Leibniz taught that all reality conforms to the archetypes of an intelligible structure; in Platonism, this is the theory of the forms. From an objective idealistic standpoint, one can readily affirm the equal and independent reality of the spiritual and material, but subjective forms of idealism are logically more expansive and exclusive. In subjective idealism, there is a strong logical tendency to make the concept of subjective mind do the work of the ideal or the rational, making it the world's entire reality. The logic of subjective idealism, if unchecked, drives toward the triumph of subjectivism.

The entire field of Kant studies is a battleground over the question whether Kant was a subjective idealist, an objective idealist, or something in between, and this debate colors every aspect of post-Kantian thought. Kant's transcendental idealism rested on the idea that truth consists in the conformity of objects to concepts. But how far did he go with conceptualism? Subjective and objective idealisms are both idealistic in claiming that reality depends upon the ideal or the rational. Subjective idealism, however, binds the forms of experience to the transcendental subject—the knowing subject that employs its categories of understanding to intuit objects of sense data. In subjective idealism, the transcendental subject is the precondition of the forms of experience, and the ideal or the rational is subjective or spiritual. Objective idealism, by contrast, detaches the forms of experience from the transcendental subject. Here the forms of experience apply to the realm of being as such, and the ideal or the rational is archetypal and structural.

This distinction correlates with the two main traditions of interpreting Kant. Many leading scholars, notably H. A. Prichard, P. F. Strawson, Jonathan Bennett, and Robert Paul Wolff contend that Kant was a subjective idealist. Advocates of this view emphasize Kant's affinities with Descartes, Hume, and Berkeley, arguing that Kant's transcendental idealism was the key to his system: we have no direct knowledge of reality. Immediate objects of perception are the ideas of a perceiving subject. All that we know are our own representations, the appearances of things. The reality of an independent world must be inferred from our representations.[32]

This school maintains that Kantianism is coherent only as a thoroughgoing form of subjective idealism in which we cannot know anything beyond experience. On this reading, which dates back to the earliest reviews of the *Critique of Pure Reason*, Kant's transcendental idealism was a rationalistic refashioning of Berkeley's idealism that lopped off Berkeley's empiricism and misguidedly appealed to the thing-in-itself.

The rival tradition of interpretation contends that Kant was insistently anti-subjective and that the key to his system was his determination to overcome the skepticism of Descartes, Hume, and Berkeley. Even if the thing-in-itself was a mistake, the objectivist aspects of Kant's thought must be taken seriously. Kant's "subjectivism" was actually a form of objective idealism in which the ideas of the knowing subject are *determined* by the intersubjective world of the concepts of the understanding.

In this reading, the ideas of the individual mind are not primary in Kant's system; rather, as Kant argued in the Transcendental Deduction, the a priori concepts of the understanding constitute an intersubjective order that is the necessary condition of any ideas that the individual mind may have. Contrary to the subjectivist interpretation, Kant's doctrine of the categories of understanding is epistemological, not psychological. The forms of understanding are conditions of the possibility of experience, not objects within experience. As the conditions by which something might be identified as subjective or objective, the forms of understanding are not subjective or objective. Leading exponents of this interpretation include the early twentieth-century Marburg school (Hermann Cohen, Ernst Cassirer) and, more recently, Karl Ameriks, Graham Bird, Henry Allison, and Arthur Collins. In this reading, Kant's transcendental idealism was much closer to Schelling and Hegel than to Berkeley and Hume.[33]

Both of these interpretive traditions have impressive proof texts from the first *Critique* and other works of Kant. Both are predisposed to make Kant's position logically consistent, even if that requires playing down or eliminating an important aspect of Kant's thought. A third tradition of interpretation, taking hold of these contradictions, maintains that Kant mixed the two doctrines. In some cases, scholars espouse "patchwork" theories, claiming that the first *Critique* incoherently patched together conflicting doctrines from different stages of Kant's development. Hans Vaihinger and Norman Kemp Smith wrote the classic works of patchwork theory.[34]

Another version of option three is that Kant tried to steer a middle path between subjective and objective idealism, leaving him with ambiguous doctrines about ideas and transcendental idealism. In this reading, Kant's critical idealism is best understood as a form of subjective idealism that struggled against subjectivist captivity. Ralph Walker, Frederick Beiser, and Sebastian Gardner espouse this interpretation, as I do, although I believe the patchwork theory gets certain things right about how Kant assembled his argument. Fundamentally, Kant's position was a form of subjective idealism, since Kant contended that the forms of experience derive from the transcendental subject. But Kant warded off extreme subjectivism by insisting that the matter of experience is given, and he provided the starting point of post-Kantian objective idealism by contending that the very possibility of self-consciousness depends on universal forms of experience. The categories of understanding bridge the so-called Kantian chasm between subject and object.[35]

Kant's discussions of transcendental idealism in the first *Critique* expounded his subjective idealist starting point, but he also made statements in the first and third *Critiques* about the universal forms of experience that qualified his subjectivism. The latter forms became, in a tangled process, the basis of post-Kantian objective idealism. Hegel was the first, in 1801, to spell out the differences between the types of subjective and objective idealism that Kant, Fichte, Schelling, and others were elaborating, and Hegel's rendering favored his own emerging position. By then, the term "absolute idealism" was in play as a name for the view that everything is ideal as an aspect or appearance of the absolute idea. Friedrich Hölderlin and Friedrich Schlegel, in the late 1790s, described their idealism as "absolute," a name that Schelling and Hegel took up. The new name signified that good idealism transcended subjectivity versus objectivity. Absolute idealism was about the "unconditioned" or the "in-itself," refashioning Spinoza's concept of substance.[36]

Kant revolutionized philosophy by asking two questions: How should one explain the possibility of knowledge? And how should one account for the reality of the external world? His dilemma, which has perplexed philosophers ever since, was that solving either of these problems undermines the answer that one needs to solve the other one. To solve the first question, one has to demonstrate some kind of identity between the knowing subject and its objects, for if the subject and object are completely distinct from each other, they cannot interact to produce knowledge. But to explain the reality of the external world, one has to establish some kind of dualism between subject and object; otherwise objects are not really independent of our subjectivity.[37]

The strongest case for reading Kant as a subjective idealist rests on everything he said about transcendental idealism. Kant began with Descartes in order to get somewhere else: I am conscious of my representations. Therefore, these representations and I exist. External objects, however, being mere appearances, are "nothing but a species of my representations." External objects are something only through somebody's representations. Transcendental realists supposed that objects of the senses, to be external, must exist by themselves. Kant countered that transcendental idealism, correctly understood, does not deny or doubt the existence of matter. He was an idealist only on the transcendental level; on the empirical level, Kant was a realist, on his terms. To him, everything depended on grasping that transcendental idealism is perfectly compatible with empirical realism, because matter is a species of representation. As long as one bears in mind that space is a representation within knowing subjects, there is no contradiction in describing matter as an external representation relating perceptions to things that appear in space.[38]

Kant defined transcendental idealism twice in the first *Critique*, and both times he described appearances as representations detached from objects in themselves. Appearances are distinct entities identified with representations, not aspects of an object-in-itself or a perspective on objects-in-themselves. He did not refer to appearances *of* things-in-themselves, a realist claim that would have rendered appearances as the way by which an independent reality manifests itself in human knowing. Appearances are representations, which depend entirely on the perceiving subject and do not detach from objects in themselves. Kant believed that his combination of transcendental idealism and empirical realism saved his position from subjectivism. Transcendental realism claimed too much about objects being what they appear to be, and empirical idealism led to skepticism about the existence of an external world. Kant said the objects of consciousness are real, whatever they happen to be in themselves. Our representations of objects in space are reliable, except when they are not.[39]

The first *Critique* wrestled with the problem of deceptive representations, and the second edition belabored the problem with a tortuous analysis of sensory illusions, false judgments, and delusions. Kant said that representations must be checked against empirical laws. He implored against the skeptical upshot of empirical idealism while tacitly conceding to skeptics that perception of external objects is not immediate. The validity of perceptions must be determined by empirical tests. He heightened the paradox by acknowledging that transcendental idealism has a special problem with spatial perception. Ideas, being representations belonging to inner sense, have no length, breadth, or depth, so how are things-in-themselves represented as spatial? Kant never solved this problem on his terms, but in the course of grappling with it he invoked a distinction about appearances that complicated his subjectivism.[40]

Essentially, he applied the distinction between the transcendental and empirical levels to the language of appearance. An appearance is a specific kind of thing in experience, an object of outer sense. But as a representation, an experience is transcendental, something set against the thing-in-itself that lies beyond all experience. In this transcendental sense of the term, an appearance involves a relation between perceiving subjects and independent objects. It is how a thing-in-itself appears to a perceiving subject.

To be sure, the idea of appearances as "aspects of things" (*rerum species*) is harder to dig out of the first *Critique* than Kant's subjectivist rendering of transcendental idealism. All of Kant's early reviewers missed it, and many interpreters still push it aside. But it is there. In his section on the Transcendental Aesthetic, Kant described the spatial appearances as being *of* things-in-themselves, having two sides. One side is the object viewed in and by itself; the other is through the form of the intuition of an object. The form appears in the subject to which the object appears, not in the object in itself. In his section on the Paralogisms of Pure Reason, Kant argued that the unknown substratum of matter produces in our senses the intuition of something extended. In his section on Phenomena and Noumena, Kant said the idea of an appearance implies that it is the appearance of some reality. This section famously distinguished between the appearances of things (phenomena) and the unknowable reality of things as they are in themselves (noumena). Kant strove for clarity by developing a doctrine of the transcendental object, but his second edition dropped the transcendental object for reasons that illustrate why Kant is so notoriously difficult to interpret.[41]

The concept of a noumenon, being unknowable, negative, and yet the true real, is inherently impossible to explain. Kant struggled with it in both editions, rewriting this section extensively in the second edition. In the first edition he developed a positive sense of the noumena, the transcendental object, which opened a Pandora's box of possibilities about special modes of intuition. In the second edition he slammed the box shut, eliminating the transcendental object from his sections on Phenomena and Noumena, the Transcendental Deduction, and the Paralogisms of Pure Reason. But he let it stand in the Antinomies of Pure Reason and the Second Analogy of Experience, apparently because tearing it out of the latter sections would have required more extensive rewriting than he could bear.[42]

In both editions Kant described the noumena as the idea of a thing-in-itself that is not an object of the senses and is not positive in any way. Essentially it signified the thought of something in general, in which one abstracts from everything belonging to sensible intuition. A noumenon is a thing so far as it is not an object of sensible intuition. But what kind of thing is that? How can it signify a true object by Kant's principles? In the first edition Kant admitted he could not prove that sensible intuition is the only possible kind of intuition, but he also could not prove that another kind is possible. In the second edition he tried to wrest more control over his most elusive concept by eliminating the transcendental object, at least in the most relevant sections. The noumenon had no positive content or sense, period. To apply the categories to objects that are not appearances would assume that some kind of intellectual intuition exists. But sensible intuition is the only type we know.[43]

The concept of intellectual intuition, to which Kant himself was driven, loomed large in every form of post-Kantian thought, sometimes invoking Kant's authority. Kant allowed that perhaps there are intelligible entities to which human sensible intuition has no relation. But since the concepts of understanding are forms corresponding to our sensible intuition, it is pointless to speculate on the subject; there is no knowledge. Kant realized that his critics would say the same thing about the thing-in-itself, but he needed the idea of the noumenon to account for the manifold of intuition and the incomprehensible ground of freedom. This idea was crucially important, wholly negative, and a thing of pure understanding. It cast a long, ironic shadow over modern philosophy and theology, as the whole idea of it was to impede metaphysical speculation. Instead Kant's dualism of known and unknown worlds sparked an explosion of high-flying metaphysical systems claiming that the world exists as the externalization of consciousness.

All of that was hard to see coming, however, when Kant published the first *Critique*. In the early going, it seemed that he labored in vain. The first *Critique*, in four years, got one review, which was so negative it scared off potential readers for years afterward. Philosopher Christian Garve, repaying a favor to an editor friend, Johann Feder, promised to review Kant's new book, which he assumed would be something like Kant's banter about aesthetics. Garve later confessed that reading the first *Critique* was an utter torment to him. In an anonymous review, he blasted Kant for spurning common sense in favor of a turgid, impossibly lengthy, scholastic mess of subjective idealism, and Feder ramped up the review's polemical tone, charging that Kant failed to acknowledge his obvious dependence on Berkeley.[44]

Kant despaired that nobody wanted to read such a difficult work. He wrote a new book, *Prolegomena to Any Future Metaphysic*, just to draw attention to the first *Critique* and to refute his one reviewer. Kant seethed at his only reviewer, at others who should have reviewed the book but didn't, and at colleagues who told him the book defeated them. He didn't mind being compared to Hume, because he admired Hume. But he and Hume disagreed about metaphysics, he deeply resented being compared to Berkeley, and he wearied of complaints that the *Critique of Pure Reason* was too hard to understand. Kant chided that many would-be readers tried "to skim through the book, and not to *think* through it." On the one hand, he sympathized, to some extent, because the book was undeniably "dry, obscure, opposed to all ordinary notions, and moreover voluminous." On the other hand, he was appalled: "I did not expect to hear from philosophers complaints of want of popularity, entertainment, and facility." Moving back to the first hand, Kant stooped to win an audience for his masterwork before it was too late by writing the *Prolegomena*. On the other hand, if any reader found the *Prolegomena* to be too difficult, "let him consider that every one is not bound to study Metaphysic."[45]

In the sense that mattered, Kant's *Prolegomena* was a success, helping to get a debate going about his position and the first *Critique*, though he misconstrued Berkeley and Hume. Berkeley's lack of synthetic a priori principles left him with no criteria of truth in describing experience, but Kant wrongly said that Berkeley's idealism committed him to this position. Berkeley was an empiricist idealist; it was his *empiricism* that drove him to claim that all experience is an illusion. Kant's rationalistic idealism was the answer to Berkeley's dilemma, but Kant didn't put it that way, wanting distance from Berkeley. As for Hume, Kant confessed that Hume shook him from his "dogmatic slumber" by interrogating the connection between cause and effect. Hume believed that the concept of causality is correct and indispensable, but reason does not establish the necessary conjunction between cause and effect that is inherent in the concept of causality. That is, reason does not establish how the existence of one object necessitates the existence of another object. Kant put the upshot colorfully: "Hence he inferred, that reason was altogether deluded by this concept, which it considered erroneously as one of its children, whereas in reality the concept was nothing but the bastard offspring of the imagination, impregnated by experience, and so bringing certain representations under the Law of Association."[46]

Kant went that far with Hume. What he rejected was Hume's con-clusion that because the causal relation is not rational, metaphysics is impossible—all we have are imagination and custom, which produce merely subjective necessities. Kant's prolonged dance with Hume got various things wrong. Kant wrongly described Hume as a transcen-dental realist, he restricted Hume's skepticism to the issue of causality, he overlooked that Hume exaggerated the implications of the causality problem, he failed to challenge Hume's mistaken assertion that the causal relation is the only way to establish the concept of a connection a priori, and he was probably wrong to claim that Hume did not deny the existence of necessary synthetic judgments. But Kant's self-defense in the *Prolegomena* got the biggest thing right, justifying the dense transcendental project of the first *Critique*, which drove readers to it. The a priori connections that Hume did not find, Kant deduced from the pure understanding.

The *Critique of Pure Reason* changed the course of modern philos-ophy by showing that the mind is active in producing experience out of its a priori categories. The seemingly unstoppable march of materialistic empiricism was stopped in its tracks. Enlightenment, on Kantian terms, dethroned the things of sense, offering a new way to color the world with-out bowing to antiquated dogmas. Powers of mind were shown to be fun-damental to human life and experience. On the one hand, metaphysics had a very limited role on Kant's terms, and so did religion. On the other hand, Kant rehabilitated metaphysical reason and thereby inadvertently sparked the explosion of post-Kantian metaphysics. To get as much out of reason as possible, Kant argued, and to give morality the exalted status it deserves, and to keep religion in its place as a servant of morality, we must distinguish between pure theoretical reason and pure practical reason.

Kant had only partly figured out what that meant when he wrote the first *Critique*. What really mattered to him—moral religion and the cre-ative power of freedom—he had yet to expound. The key to his system was the key to German idealism as a whole, bitter ironies notwithstanding.

Kantian Moral Religion

Kant had only a glimmer of the key to his system when he wrote the first *Critique*. He did not grasp why his critical idealism mattered; he had only his ethical misgivings about the Enlightenment. For most of his career Kant looked backward, trying to shore up metaphysics. The Enlightenment was courageous and ambitious, taking pride in espousing the authority of reason, naming itself the bearer of light. Kant prized it immensely, but worried about its impact on morality, religion, and the social order. This concern helped him to discover what his system was about. Kant did not recognize that his racism, sexism, and Prussian chauvinism violated Kantian ethics, even after the *Critique of Practical Reason* announced that freedom is the key to rationality, and thus the key to his system. Kantian idealism was about the emancipating and unifying reality of freedom, "the keystone of the whole architecture of the system of pure reason."[47]

The second *Critique* replicated the argument of the first *Critique* in much shorter compass, now on things that mattered more to Kant: value, purpose, God, immortality, and freedom. Kant argued again that reason is one and its deployment is triune as theory, practice, and aesthetic judgment. In moving from theory to practice, the categories of understanding become the moral law, and the sensible manifold of intuition consists of sensory intuitions and conflicting desires. The first *Critique* established the conditions of the possibility of knowledge, for the work of theoretical reason is to produce theoretical knowledge of what is. The second *Critique* established the necessary presuppositions of moral activity, for the work of practical reason is to produce practical knowledge of what ought to be. Kant argued in the first *Critique* that unaided theoretical reason does not establish the existence of transcendent realities such as God or immortality. Proofs of God's existence do not prove anything because reason is limited, conditioned, and sense-bound, restricted to the web of sense experience within the space-time continuum. Thus it cannot know of spiritual realities transcending space and time.[48]

The fundamental law of practical reason is the categorical imperative to act only according to that maxim which should be a universal law regardless of context. The place for religion, Kant said, is in practical reason, where the necessity of moral laws is unquestionable. He put it with typical laboriousness: "Now since there are practical laws which are absolutely necessary, that is, the moral laws, it must follow that if these necessarily presuppose the existence of any being as the condition of the possibility of their *obligatory* power, this existence must be *postulated*; and this for the sufficient reason that the conditioned, from which the inference is drawn to this determinate condition, is itself known a priori to be absolutely necessary."[49]

Kant's metaphysic revolved around two conceptual pivots, the idea of the ideality of space and time, and the idea of a cognizable and yet supersensible freedom. The latter belongs to practical reason and is the basis of morality, which is the basis of religion. To Kant it was terribly important to say that religion has a secure home and that it rests entirely in the moral concerns of practical reason. In *Foundations of the Metaphysics of Morals* (1785), *Critique of Practical Reason* (1788), and *Religion within the Boundaries of Mere Reason* (1793), he explained that human beings are moral agents as well as creatures of sense experience. Human experience includes a sense of moral obligation not subsumed under or explained by sense-bound theoretical reason. Freedom is a basic idea to which theoretical reason leads us, but we cannot prove its existence on theoretical grounds. Rather, our moral experience impels us to believe in the reality of freedom, which gives us the right to postulate the reality of God and immortality as the ground of moral faith.[50]

Kant did not believe that metaphysics is useless or that pure reason is not practical, contrary to standard misunderstandings of Kant. Otherwise his ethical theory of freedom and the moral law would have made no sense. Kant believed that two kinds of metaphysics were still imperative after he destroyed the old metaphysics: the metaphysics of nature expounded the a priori principles of what is, and the metaphysics of morals expounded the a priori principles of what ought to be. *Critique of Pure Reason* modeled a critical metaphysics of nature, grounding scientific rationality in a system of a priori knowledge from pure concepts. *Foundations of the Metaphysics of Morals* expounded Kant's ethic of the categorical imperative: autonomous rational beings provide their own moral laws by universalizing situations of norm conflict. *Critique of Practical Reason* expounded the a priori laws of conduct, conceiving the metaphysics of morals as the rational understanding of the moral law and its ramifications. *Religion within the Boundaries of Mere Reason* expounded the kind of religion that came from taking these arguments seriously.

Emphatically Kant based religion on morality, not the other way around, because religion is essentially moral and has no warranted claim to knowledge except by its connection to morals, where the mode of knowing is strictly practical. In the preface to the second edition of the *Critique of Pure Reason* he put it boldly, declaring that he had found it "necessary to deny *knowledge*, in order to make room for *faith*." However, the closing section of Kant's first *Critique* and his subsequent writings on practical reason made moral arguments for God's existence that seemed, to many interpreters, to erase Kant's distinction between knowledge and faith. Did he not make a knowledge claim for religion through its connection to morality? Did his moral arguments for God's existence not amount to a substitute natural theology?[51]

Here Kant's interpreters have quarreled for centuries. Some hold fast to the dichotomy between faith and knowledge, others claim that Kant (wisely or not) crafted his own form of natural theology after destroying the traditional types, some contend that he failed to sustain a consistent position, and others contend for a mixture of these views: for example, that he ultimately rejected his own misguided argument. Critics who see little difference between Kant's moral arguments for God's existence and the traditional speculative proofs usually contend that he undermined or contradicted his own argument.[52]

My view rests on two interpretive judgments. One, Kant generally held to his distinction between knowledge and faith, which corresponded to his distinction between theoretical reason and practical reason. But two, these distinctions broke down at the point of intersection between the two *Critiques*—Kant's grounding of freedom in moral experience, which yielded his arguments for God and immortality.

Kant regarded his moral arguments defending God's existence as justifications of faith or belief, not as claims to knowledge. To him, as in German, faith and belief were the same thing, *Glaube*. Kant held that faith and knowledge are valid, justified, and "sufficient" (*zureichendes*) ways of holding judgments. Both are forms of conviction (*Überzeugung*) as distinguished from a mere opinion (*Meinung*)—a judgment lacking sufficiency. But faith and knowledge are sufficient in different ways. There are three degrees of sufficiency in holding a judgment: opinion has no sufficiency, faith has subjective sufficiency alone, and knowledge (*Wissen*) has subjective and objective sufficiency. One does not hold opinions about mathematical problems, because here we either have knowledge or no business holding a judgment. But belief is a slippery area, because terribly important issues are at stake, yet knowledge is lacking. Kant defined belief as the "theoretically insufficient holding of a thing to be true" from the standpoint of practical reason. Believing refers either to a skill, which is concerned with contingent ends, or to morality, where the ends are absolutely necessary and religion is grounded.[53]

Theoretical knowledge, Kant reasoned, is universal, being valid for everyone. But moral faith is no less universal, however lacking in objective sufficiency. There is such a thing as a justified, even necessary, conviction that is subjective in character. Faith, being essentially different from knowledge, cannot be built up or strengthened by appeals to proofs, theoretical claims, or evidence. Faith is personal and subjective, holding to crucially important convictions without claiming that objective sufficiency applies to them. In the realm of faith, which Kant called "moral faith" when describing the ideal, something has to happen: the believer is compelled to conform to the moral law. Kant moved straight to the upshot: "The end is here irrefragably established, and according to such insight as I can have, there is only one possible condition under which this end can connect with all other ends, and thereby have practical validity, namely, that there be a God and a future world."[54]

Without a divine Moral Guarantor there can be no moral unity of ends. We cannot pursue the good if we do not believe it is real and attainable. God is not a moral being, since God's duty and desire are never in conflict. God is the Moral Governor who brings nature and morality into harmony—the kingdom of God. To act as moral beings, Kant insisted, we must postulate the idea of God as a condition for the possibility of the highest good, believing as we must in order to live as we ought. Kant put it personally, referring to his belief in God and a future world: "I am certain that nothing can shake this belief, since my moral principles would thereby be themselves overthrown, and I cannot disclaim them without becoming abhorrent in my own eyes." He could not imagine living with himself if he did not live in a moral universe. The alternative was moral nihilism and despair. Life had no meaning on these terms, and his passionate intellectual and moral endeavors would have been pointless.[55]

On the one hand, Kant cautioned that no one *knows* if there is a God and a future life; on the other hand, he called his conviction of God's existence a "moral certainty," because he never really doubted the existence of moral truth. Every day he pursued the truth and struggled to obey the moral law; he would not pretend to believe that life might really be meaningless. To Kant there was a crucial difference between saying, "It is morally certain that there is a God," and saying, "I am certain that there is a God." The former statement smacked too much of an unwarranted theoretical claim; it went too far. Moral certainty is personal and practical, taking the form of the second statement, which Kant did say. Since he knew that he stood in no danger of losing his moral convictions, and since believing in God and a future world were deeply interwoven with these convictions, there was no chance that he would lose faith in God. Thus, it was no exaggeration to say, "I am certain that there is a God."[56]

Does that mean that everyone who wants to be good has to believe in God? Kant believed that dogmatic atheism is definitely out of bounds; one cannot be faithful to the moral law and negate its ground simultaneously. At a minimum, one must say that God might exist. Kant called this minimum a "negative belief." He doubted that negative believing gives rise to moral sentiments, yet at least it serves as a check on nihilistic evil sentiments. Outright atheism is intolerable; religious skepticism, although tolerable, is far from the ideal; at the other end of the scale, all forms of religious authoritarianism were repugnant to him, plus all varieties of religious ceremony, ecclesiastical organization, and mysticism. Kant was contemptuous of ceremonial worship, which struck him as self-degrading. He loathed petitionary prayer, which struck him as pathetic wheedling. He refused to attend religious ceremonies, even when his responsibilities as university rector required him to participate. *Religion within the Boundaries* abounded with put-downs of "priestcraft," religious dogma, superstition, "religious acts of cult," and everything else that detracted from the one true religion of enlightened moral faith.[57]

Everything that human beings do to please God, except for conducting themselves morally, is a stupid waste of time and energy. *Religion within the Boundaries* said it repeatedly. Kant was incredulous that anyone believed that salvation has anything to do with going to church, accepting biblical myths as historical, or holding a particular theory of justification. Morality, too, as he explained in *Foundations of the Metaphysics of Morals*, is not really moral if it is handed down or compelled by authority. To Kant, autonomy was the supreme principle of morality. A moral belief accepted on the basis of authority is no more legitimate than any other kind of belief accepted on the basis of authority. In situations of moral perplexity, one should ask, "What should everyone do in this situation?" Kant put it formally: "Act only according to that maxim by which you can at the same time will that it should become a universal law." True morality, Kant taught, is action in accordance with self-given maxims that deserve to be universal laws for all rational beings, and true religion, subjectively considered, is the acceptance of one's self-given moral duties as divine commands and nothing else.[58]

Kant had a version of the doctrine of original sin and even the rudiments of a Christology, but to him, sadly, historic Christianity was about the wrong things. Instead of expounding its sacred narrative exclusively in the interests of morality, Christianity compelled people to believe propositions about matters of history and dogma. Instead of focusing on what human beings must do to become worthy of salvation, Christianity, especially Lutheranism, focused on dogmas about things God supposedly did to win our salvation. *Religion within the Boundaries* distinguished between the parts of Christianity that reflected its basis in "pure rational faith" and the parts that degenerated, however inevitably, into sectarian dogmas distracting from pure moral faith. Kant argued that no appeal to revelation is needed to see that human beings have a disposition (*Gesinnung*) to evil. From a purely rational perspective it is terribly obvious that "radical evil" afflicts every human heart. True religion battles against evil and spurns everything else as a distraction.[59]

Kant said no one understands where this radical evil came from. It is inscrutable, yet certain things about it can be read off from the universal human condition. It cannot be known in itself, nobody is free of it, and persons freely adopt it. He identified three grades of this natural propensity to evil. Everywhere, human beings show the frailty of human nature by failing to comply with moral norms against lying, cheating, murder, and the like. Second, human beings everywhere adulterate moral incentives with immoral ones. Third, human beings everywhere show the depravity of human nature by adopting outright evil maxims. On frailty, even the morally earnest Apostle Paul was an example, lamenting his inability to follow the moral law that he preached. On impurity, Kant noted that persons rarely if ever act out of a pure motive of moral duty, even when they act according to the moral law. On depravity, every page of history displays the corruption and perversion of the human heart, which uses the power of free moral choice to do evil, reversing the ethical order of things.[60]

This is what religion should be about and against, Kant implored. The propensity to evil in human beings is evil itself, even if it did not originate in a free act in time; Kant read the Adam and Eve story as an illustration of the problem, not an explanation. As for how this propensity could be morally evil if it did not originate in a free act in time, Kant said it originated in a free act that was not in time. Every propensity is either physical or moral, but there cannot be a physical propensity to moral evil, because moral evil is necessarily a by-product of freedom. Nothing is morally evil that is not the consequence of a freely chosen deed, and every moral propensity includes a subjective determining ground of the power of free will that precedes every deed.

This idea of a subjective determining power, an echo of Kant's defense of the noumenal realm in the first *Critique*, was the noumenal ground of moral freedom and the basis of Kant's distinction between two kinds of deeds pertaining to moral evil. The determining noumenal ground of freedom yields acts of free will that transcend time, while the second kind of deed is empirical, applying to acts in time. Original sin (*peccatum originarium*) is grounded in noumenal reality, which is inscrutable and not phenomenal. Derivative sins (*peccatum derivativum*) are empirical transgressions of the moral law in time. Original sin remains in the human heart even if one resists committing derivative sins: "The former is an intelligible deed, cognizable through reason alone apart from any temporal condition; the latter is sensible, empirical, given in time (*factum phenomenon*)."[61]

Kantian religion, like the ethic of which it was part, was centered on the moral aspiration of being worthy of happiness. In religious form it asked, "How can I be well-pleasing to God?" Kant stressed that this question is not about escaping divine punishment, an egocentric and amoral question that misses the point of religion. The object of moral aspiration is a pure heart, not a utilitarian outcome such as avoiding hellfire or attaining the greatest good for the greatest number, degraded schemes for which the moral good is merely instrumental. Kant argued that morality is an intrinsic good and that only the truly good will is good without qualification. All morally reflective people know they are not as good as they ought to be. The moral ideal is to be so pure in one's willing that one would be pleased with oneself even if one knew one's heart as fully as God knows it. Toward this end Kant had a place for the Christ figure, which he called the "personified idea of the good principle."[62]

All human beings have a duty to strive for moral perfection, Kant reasoned, but as sinful beings we lack the moral power to attain a perfectly good will by our powers alone. Thus it is helpful to have a God-like human prototype of moral perfection that came down from heaven to take up our humanity. Human beings, being "evil by nature," do not renounce evil on their own, or raise themselves to the ideal of holiness. Christianity is the plausible and saving idea that a God-like human prototype lifts human beings to holiness by descending into their life and providing a moral example. To Kant the figure of Christ was the exemplary idea of a human being fulfilling his moral duties, spreading goodness as far as possible through teaching and example, and taking on suffering for the good of the world and even his enemies. Here Kant followed the lead of G. E. Lessing's "The Education of the Human Race," which attributed a large, but strictly moral, importance to Jesus and the Bible. A great deal of liberal Protestantism took exactly that tack.[63]

Religion within the Boundaries circled back to the evils of church religion, speaking to the moment. Kant railed against priests, public prayers, petitions to an all-knowing God, and other superstitious delusions. He warned sternly that such "fetish-making" is not harmless to society. Wherever it took hold, it took over, corrupting true religion. Clerical religion, instead of inculcating moral faith, personal integrity, and the loyalty of subjects, inculcated hypocrisy and sham. Kant fumed against Prussia's religious corruption, which began, in his view, when Friedrich Wilhelm II became king in 1786. The golden age of Frederick the Great gave way to Frederick's self-indulgent, adulterous, mystical, Rosicrucian brother, who appointed a slick Rosicrucian and Freemason, Johann Wöllner, as minister of ecclesiastical affairs. Kant despised Friedrich Wilhelm II and his semiofficial prime minister, Wöllner. He thundered that Prussia's leaders should care about being good, not about ritual and preserving their privileges. Prussia's supposed elect, he said, imagining themselves the favorites of heaven, did not compare to humble, ordinary, dutiful Prussians, "which proves that the right way to advance is not from grace to virtue but rather from virtue to grace."[64]

This frontal challenge defied the king to respond, which occurred ten months after Kant's book was published in January 1794. Kant risked a bad ending to his career after achieving distinction in late life. But having waited until the near-end of his career to write a book on religion, he had reason to believe that his renown, however recently acquired, would save him.

Debating Kantianism

Kant believed he established a secure basis for believing in reason and moral religion. His critics made him famous by condemning both beliefs as ridiculous. Two rival groups led the way in opposing the Kantian revolution. One was the *Popularphilosophie* movement, a German counterpart to French *philosophe* led by Christian Garve, Johann G. H. Feder, J. A. Eberhard, and J. Engel. It blended Leibniz and Wolff, incorporating strands of Lockean empiricism, Scottish commonsense realism, and French *philosophe*. The popular philosophers were Prussian liberal advocates of intellectual freedom, religious tolerance, and mild reform, and opponents of democracy and radicalism. They took for granted the need for elite rule, including a strong state, and their own privileges, funded by royal patronage. They were committed to enlightening the public and defeating Pietist opposition to the Enlightenment. On both counts they lauded Frederick the Great for defending intellectual freedom. Before Kant published the first *Critique*, the popular philosophers generally admired him. Afterward, following Garve and Feder, they adamantly opposed him, forging an unlikely alliance with Pietist critics.[65]

Friedrich Heinrich Jacobi and Johann G. Hamann led the Pietist critics, though each had a complicated relationship with Pietism. Kant's attack on common sense was terrible, they said, and his elevation of reason over faith—including faith in common sense—was even worse. Jacobi and Hamann held out for the primacy of Christian faith, which they tied to common sense, indebting them to the same Scottish commonsense realism as their *Popularphilosophie* rivals. Both groups of Kant's critics admired Scottish philosopher Thomas Reid (1710–1796), who taught that sensation automatically causes belief in external objects. To oppose common sense is a kind of madness or perversity.[66]

Reid taught that sensations are mental acts that give rise to knowledge, but they are not the direct objects of knowledge. The objects are the things of the external world towards which the acts of sense are directed. We do not acquire our beliefs about external objects by comparing ideas; rather, such beliefs are caused by the occurrence of a sensation and are included in the very nature of a sensation. Believing anything else defies the facts of experience. The Jacobi Pietists and popular philosophers agreed that Kant's blend of skepticism and dogmatism defied experience. He skewered common sense and religion, yet revived dogmatic metaphysics with a pre-Lockean belief in a priori ideas. His idealism contradicted common sense; his technical vocabulary and dogmatic method smacked of a new scholasticism; and he harmed Christian faith, or natural religion, or both. Both groups charged that Kant distorted reason in the name of defending it, which confused the public about the real thing. Both attacked his idealism of space and time, countering that space and time are a posteriori concepts abstracted from particular distances and intervals, not a priori intuitions. The popular philosophers were so ardent about refuting Kant that they launched two anti-Kantian journals, Feder's *Philosophische Bibliothek* and Eberhard's *Philosophisches Magazin*. Both made a creed of Feder's thesis that Kantianism was Berkeley's solipsism wrapped in obscurantist scholasticism.[67]

Kant hated having to defend himself, so he pressed his friends to do it. Johann Schultz published a helpful exposition of the first *Critique* in 1784, and Jena philosopher Karl Leonhard Reinhold specialized in warmhearted renderings of Kant's idealism. But it was Kant's critics who lifted him to prominence. The popular philosophers made him famous by attacking him constantly. Others piled on, notably Kant's former student Johann Gottfried Herder, a Lutheran pastor and church official. Herder said the Enlightenment was a disastrous conceit and Kant's abstract separation of thought from language culminated the disaster. Herder's friend Hamann similarly protested that Kant's mistaken purism of reason stripped philosophy of its vital basis in sensation and ordinary language. Jacobi became prominent by poking holes in Kant's faith in abstract reason and charging that Kant did not believe in real objects. Jacobi said Kant perpetuated the Enlightenment prejudice against sensation by turning real objects into subjective determinations of the soul devoid of real objectivity, reducing empirical objects to mere appearances.[68]

Hamann was a minor civil servant in Frederick the Great's despised tax office who got his job with Kant's help. His lowly station helped him see the despotic side of Frederick's purportedly enlightened regime; Hamann had to defer to tax experts that Frederick imported from France. Embittered, but also liberated by his humiliation, Hamann developed an enigmatic writing style specializing in parody. Theologically he was a Lutheran believer in the self-emptying of God and the divine power of powerlessness. He loved the kenotic hymn of Philippians 2, in which Christ willingly gave up equality with God to take the form of a slave. Hamann applied the spirit of kenosis theology to Enlightenment presumptions about the objectivity of reason, charging that Kant's belief in the abstract purity of philosophy was ludicrous. For two years Hamann labored on a metacritique of Kant's first *Critique* that Herder nagged him to finish; it totaled only ten pages when Hamann completed it in 1784. But Hamann's work anticipated the post-Kantian protest against Kant's dualism and the postmodern critique of hypostatized reason.[69]

Hamann said Kant's project labored under a mistaken abstraction, a vain attempt to liberate reason from history, experience, and language that yielded arbitrary dualisms and concepts breeding concepts: "Receptivity of language and spontaneity of concepts! From this double source of ambiguity, pure reason draws all the elements of its doctrinairism, doubt, and connoisseurship." Hamann was sarcastic, but also penetrating. He derided Kant's pride in abstracting a purely formal transcendental subject=X, which Hamann called "a windy sough, a magic shadow play, at most." Kant's object, Hamann said, a special faculty called reason, does not exist. What exists are rational ways of thinking and acting in specific languages and cultural contexts. Kant's idealism, like Plato's, got in the way of dealing with anything real. Hamann was sensitive about offending Kant in public, he died in 1788, and his book was not published until 1800. But he had a subterranean influence through Jacobi and Herder.[70]

In 1784 the *Berlinische Monatsschrift* sponsored a series on the question, "What is Enlightenment?" Kant's answer was aggressive, triumphal, self-congratulatory, a bit preachy, and more than a bit snobbish: "*Enlightenment is mankind's exit from its self-incurred immaturity.*" Immaturity, the inability to reason independently, is self-incurred if caused by a lack of courage and resolve, not a lack of intelligence. The Enlightenment was rightly named because its motto was "Have the courage to use your *own* understanding!" According to Kant, enlightenment needed nothing but freedom; moreover, the kind on which it depended was "the most harmless" of all freedoms, "the freedom to make a *public use* of one's reason in all matters."[71]

Kant cautioned that the enemies of such freedom were many and pervasive. Military officers commanded good Germans to march and not argue; tax collectors commanded them to pay and not argue; clerics commanded them to believe and not argue. Kant said only one ruler in the world allowed people to argue as much as they wanted, although he required obedience. Frederick the Great, being enlightened, did not fear shadows; plus, the king had "a large, well-disciplined army as a guarantee of public peace."[72]

It was too soon to speak of an enlightened age, because darkness prevailed over much of modern life, especially in religion, where "immaturity is the most harmful as well as the most dishonorable." Nonetheless, Kant said, the present age was indeed "the age of enlightenment," or what was the same thing, "the century of *Frederick*," because the king of Prussia allowed his subjects to argue freely, making public use of their reason, even on matters of government. Kant lauded Frederick as the "shining example" of enlightened rule who restrained civic freedom to allow the flourishing of spiritual freedom. It was a very good thing that Prussia had a large army and a firm hand at the top. The seed of German freedom blossomed under the "hard shell" of an enlightened ruler, improving the character of the people, who thereby became "more and more and more capable of *acting freely*," which created the preconditions for a more liberalized government.[73]

Hamann and Herder took a dimmer view of their age, stressing that German freedom did not extend much beyond the privileges of intellectuals like Kant. Hamann protested that every line of Kant's apologia reeked of snobbery and sneering. What kind of "conscience" accused humble religious people of immaturity and cowardice "when their blind guardian has a large, well-disciplined army to guarantee his infallibility and orthodoxy?" How did Kant dare to mock the supposed laziness of ordinary people struggling under the yoke of monarchy? Hamann said Kant's pride and joy, the public use of reason and freedom, was "nothing but a dessert, a sumptuous dessert." What mattered was the "daily bread" of a life of dignity, on which Kant gave the king a pass. Hamann gagged that his friend denigrated ordinary Germans and all women with the same conceit: "The *self-incurred immaturity* is just such a sneer as he makes at the whole fair sex."[74]

That barely scratched the surface of Kant's conceit, as he showed whenever he spoke about racial inferiority. Eighteenth- and nineteenth-century naturalists generally followed the father of modern taxonomy, Swedish zoologist Carl Linnaeus (1707–1778), in dividing Homo sapiens into four categories: American (which Linnaeus described as copper colored, choleric, and regulated by custom); Asiatic (sooty, melancholic, and governed by opinions); African (black, languid, and governed by caprice); and European (fair, sanguine, and governed by laws). They disagreed about monogenesis versus polygenesis. Kant was a defender of monogenic human unity, but he left room for soft-polygenic beliefs by reasoning that monogenesis produced four distinct races: "(1) The white race; (2) the Negro race; (3) the Hun race (Mongol or Kalmuck); and (4) the Hindu or Hindustani race."[75]

All other racial groups derived from these four races, Kant taught. The Hun and Hindu races were mediating types; thus he gave them short shrift. In Kant's view, whites and blacks were "the base races" standing at opposite ends of the racial continuum, a "self-evident" truism needing no proof. Kant figured that nature equipped the human species to exist and adapt in much the same way it equipped all organic life. Both were endowed with natural adaptive capacities he called "seeds" (*Keime*)— predispositions hardwired into the organism as a whole. Once a race formed, it resisted further transformation. Kant believed that all four races were prefigured *in potentia* in the first human beings, the stem genus. This prototype, although lost, must have closely resembled the white race, because whites were obviously superior to all others. Kant said this "without any prejudice." Human beings were best fitted for the temperate climate in which the white race flourished, whites had the best skin color, and no race remotely compared to whites in cultural accomplishment.[76]

But even that did not quite express the extent of white superiority for Kant, because it separated whites from other races only by degree. Whites, to be sure, were a race, Kant allowed; however, they progressed so far beyond other races they were no longer a race in the ordinary sense of the term. The white race, by advancing in the direction of enlightened cosmopolitan perfection, was moving beyond race. It was expanding globally to bring the world to perfection, recreating the world in its image. Kant told his students that no race on earth stood a chance of thwarting the global dominion of race-transcending white people. The Hindu people were educable in the arts, but not in the sciences. They never changed, were too calm to change the world, and had no capacity for abstract concepts. Native Americans were even worse off, lacking drive, passion, and romance. They were lazy and apathetic, had few children, and didn't even cuddle. The "Negro race," in Kant's telling, had some virtues, but none that helped it advance. Negroes were educable to a degree, Kant allowed; they were sensitive, had some drive, and a sense of honor. But they were so talkative and vain, filled with affect and passion, that they were fit only to be servants.[77]

Kant did not say, in public, that the nonwhite races would have to be weeded out for the world to reach its enlightened destiny. But in a note to himself, he did say it: "All of the races will be stamped out; they will undergo an inner rotting or decay leading to their utter eradication." Native Americans and people of African descent were incapable of ruling themselves; moreover, he lamented the spectacle of "interbreeding" (*sich vermischen*) in Mexico, where Spanish colonizers created a new race. That would never work, and it detracted from the benefits of Spanish colonization.[78]

Kant believed that race itself would end when the white race prevailed. The triumph of enlightened civilization went hand in hand with the triumph of whiteness. More precisely, the triumph of enlightened civilization was inseparable from the triumph of whiteness, being identical with it, although Kant was guarded about how he said it in public. The business of "stamping out" the other races (*Alle racen werden ausgerottet werden*), after all, had a brutal side to it; Kant was glad that Prussia did not have to get into the colonization business to make history and nature come out right. The lower races lacked sufficient capacity to develop; thus, their "inner rotting" would lead to their dissolution. In the meantime, England and France, "the two most civilized nations on earth," were keen to bring capitalism (England) and cultured refinement (France) to backward parts of the world.[79]

Kant would have preferred to see the French take the lead in this area, on account of their refinement. The "trust-inspiring civility" of French society contrasted sharply with the "haughty rudeness" of the British, who spoke the language of interest and commerce, preferred to dine alone, and, although benevolent with their own kind, treated foreigners like dirt. Kant surmised that Britons got their appetite for imperialism through geographical circumstance, not natural character. They had no natural character, as the "old stock of Britons" dissolved from centuries of German and French immigration. Protected by geography from foreign invasions, the British islanders became a nation of aggressors, "a mighty nation of maritime commerce." The "mercantile spirit" pervaded British society and fueled its appetite for conquest. Thus, the British projected a rude and materialistic idea of civilization, which taught the world a vital lesson—one must make a character for one's self. Britons did not expect anybody to love them, which Kant admired. They merely demanded respect, building a more or less liberal order through which they allowed people to live according to their own will.[80]

Kant rolled his contempt for Jews into the same bigoted rhetoric of inferiority, with the difference that Jews were resident aliens, "Palestinians living among us." He wrote little about European Jews because he took for granted they were degenerate—the opposite of pure reason, embodying the grubby impurity of matter. He called them "a nation of deceivers" and "a whole nation of merchants," which meant the same thing: nearly all Jews were consumed with the spirit of usury. Kant respected philosopher Moses Mendelssohn and a few others, strictly as exceptions. According to him, Jews ignored the moral norms and legal regulations of decent society pertaining to material gain. Honor meant nothing to them, for they turned deception into a way of life, cheating the very people "among whom they find protection."[81]

According to Kant, the only moral principle to which Jews subscribed in dealing with their European protectors was "buyer beware." He resented their dishonesty and lack of gratitude, but claimed to put aside moralizing about both, a "futile project." Jews were not going to be shamed out of being usurious cheaters. Instead of assimilating into decent society, they clung to their religion, "an old superstition that is recognized by the government under which they live." Instead of building up the European nations that gave them refuge, they compensated their losses and struggles by cheating their protectors.[82]

Kant absurdly understated the Jewish underpinnings of Christianity. On the conceptual level, he said, there was "absolutely no connection" between Judaism and Christianity. Jewish religion, at its founding, was a collection of statutory laws supporting a political state, lacking any spiritual or moral character. It had the Ten Commandments, but they were purely external. Later it added moral appendages, but they were foreign to Judaism. Kant explained, "Strictly speaking Judaism is not a religion at all but simply the union of a number of individuals who, since they belonged to a particular stock, established themselves into a community under purely political laws, hence not into a church." All genuine religions teach a doctrine of eternal life, Kant insisted. Thus, Judaism flunked an elementary test of being a religion. Kant said Christianity rested on "an entirely new principle . . . a total revolution in doctrines of faith."[83]

On this theme he had a large legacy, legitimizing a de-Judaized Christianity that Schleiermacher, the early Hegel, Harnack, and Herrmann recycled, to mention only major liberal religious thinkers.[84]

Cosmopolitan Peace and Kantian Freedom

By now the bitter paradoxes and fateful hypocrisies are fully in view. The Kantian revolution proffered enlightened justifications of bigotry while championing liberating doctrines of universal freedom and human dignity. It featured this contradiction at its birth and inspired generations of successors that heightened the contradictions. Kant taught that if one universalizes the moral question and obeys the answer, one will never denigrate the humanity of another person. Human beings are to be treated as ends in themselves, not as means to an end. Every person's humanity—the matrix of capacities that enable rational self-conscious activity—must be recognized as an end in itself, except that Kant did not do so, and the Enlightenment yielded new rationalizations of bigotry.

Kant transformed modern thought by establishing that experience is never merely given. The meaning of experience is always a creative construction. The process by which we achieve self-consciousness about our relation to the world is fundamental to every claim that we make about knowing anything in any field of inquiry. Before Kant, it was possible to conceive nature per se as the source of meaning. Even Berkeley assumed that sense experience is produced outside the human mind. Kant made idealism critical by showing that human experience and creativity are never mere epiphenomena of the things of sense.

Kant and post-Kantian idealism unleashed a new self-consciousness about the irreducible role of creative imagination in all knowing and the contestability of all norms. Moreover, Kant realized that Hamann was at least half right about the limits of German enlightenment. Until the French Revolution, Kant harbored deeper republican convictions than his writings showed. Keeping his privileges required a certain amount of brownnosing of local potentates, or so he told himself. But when the French Revolution broke out in July 1789, Kant was ecstatic. He told his students and friends that the revolution represented the first real-world triumph of philosophy, in which a government would be constructed on the basis of rational principles. This was a cause on which old-style rationalists, new-style rationalists like him, and the young generation headed toward Romanticism could agree.

Upon learning that France had formed a republic, Kant exclaimed, "Now let your servant go in peace to his grave, for I have seen the glory of the world." Staunchly he defended the storming of the Bastille, the National Assembly's abolition of feudal privileges, and the building of a new order. After the Terror began and "Jacobin" became a fearsome epithet in Prussia, Kant still defended the revolution. In print he played a careful hand, defending a constructionist version of social contract theory while denying that citizens had a right to rebellion. Kant reasoned that the French Revolution was not a rebellion because Louis XVI abdicated, in effect, when he called the National Assembly. In class, with friends, and at dinner parties Kant opined enthusiastically about the revolution, even before nobles. His friends blushed at his republicanism; some brushed it off as a personal quirk not to be counted against his towering stature. Kant played the game adroitly, perceiving where the line of danger was, until Wöllner informed him in October 1794 that tolerating *Religion within the Boundaries* was out of the question for Friedrich Wilhelm II.[85]

Wöllner charged that Kant distorted and maligned Christianity and failed to uphold his duty as a teacher of youth. His "continued obstinancy" would not be tolerated. Kant, stewing over the parallel with Wolff, fixed on a key difference: that he was seventy years old. Though wealthy by this point, he was very concerned not to be fired, forced into retirement without a pension, or, especially, banished. So he capitulated, while denying he had done anything wrong. Kant insisted he had never disparaged religion, neglected his duty as a teacher, or denigrated Christianity. He had modeled tolerance to his lecture audiences and readers. But to show his sincerity as the king's loyal subject, he vowed to stop writing about religion, which was enough for the king, who prevailed without causing a furor. Kant kept silent about religion until the king died three years later, whereupon Kant returned to writing about religion. He reasoned that Friedrich Wilhelm II made the issue personal; thus the promise ended with the end of him.[86]

In between the promise and the king's death, Kant wrote a classic of idealistic ordering, "Perpetual Peace: A Philosophical Sketch," which replaced the law of nations (*Völkerrecht*) with cosmopolitan law (*Weltbürgerrecht*) stating the rights of human beings as citizens of the world. Kant blasted the existence of standing armies, protesting that standing armies make it too easy for nations to fall into war; plus, paying people to kill turns them into machinelike tools of the state. He argued that every state should have a republican constitution founded on the principles of freedom for all members of a society, the dependence of all members on a single common legislative structure, and legal equality for all citizens. Moreover, the rights of nations should be secured through a federation of free states, a type of world federalism. First and foremost, Kant considered himself a cosmopolitan citizen of the world, not a Prussian. The hope of the world, politically, lay in founding a federative global union taking a maximal view of human rights and moral legitimacy. Religiously, the hope of the world was to build a cosmopolitan civil religion that took the same view of human rights and moral rightness.[87]

Kant's liberalism was an expression of the emancipating project of modernity, which he called the giving of the law to one's self. Hegel called the same idea the concept's giving itself actuality. In both cases, Kantian idealism was about the realization of truth in free self-determination. Kant contended in the second *Critique* that freedom is the only idea of speculative reason whose possibility we know a priori. We do not understand this idea, yet we know it as the condition of the moral law, something we do know. If we had no freedom, we would not be able to grasp the existence of the moral law within us. To Kant, the concept of mind as a subject of knowledge was impossible lacking the idea of a world governed by laws. No concept of mind as a subject of knowledge is possible lacking the idea of a world governed by laws. In any concept of mind, some concept of the world is implied; otherwise there would be no self-understanding of the mind.[88]

Each time that Kant described what his system was about, he used a different metaphor of reason to describe the actual multidimensionality of an apparently dualistic system. In the first *Critique* he described reason as an organic totality that coordinates the dualistic structural distinctions between sensibility and understanding, reason and understanding, and reason and judgment. Each cognitive faculty exists for the sake of the others and for its own sake. Reason, more broadly than the specific faculty of reason that is distinct from experience and understanding, embraces all cognitive faculties, aiming at a totality that makes experience complete. Kant said that pure speculative reason is peculiar in two ways. It measures its own capacity by the different ways it chooses the objects of its thinking, and it takes account of the many ways by which problems are put before it. Regarding the first peculiarity, nothing in a priori cognition can be ascribed to the objects of thought except that which the thinking subject takes out of itself. Regarding the second, pure speculative reason, considered as a unity of principles of cognition, is a unity that subsists for itself. Every part exists for the sake of all the others and its own sake, "and no principle can safely be taken in *any one* relation, unless it has been investigated in the *entirety* of its relations to the whole employment of pure reason."[89]

For example, Kant's distinction between reason and understanding yielded his distinction between the intellectual world and the sensible world. But reason cannot be a unifying principle if it does not aim for a totality of combination that completes experience. Thus, even Kant used an organic metaphor for reason, even in the first *Critique*. Dieter Henrich explains that Kant needed a "feedback loop" between his ontological system and his theory of how the various faculties of mind combined with each other. Though Platonic dualism ran deep in Kant's thought, even Kant needed a basis for defining what his philosophy was about. Fichte, Schelling, and Hegel, perceiving the problem on Kant's terms, devised systems that were strong on this point.[90]

Kant's epistemology was a philosophy of mind, not a science of formal objects. He began with the self and its mental activities, not a formal theory of rules about logical or objective realities. Henrich observes that a reader of the first *Critique* might expect Kant to incorporate his cognitive framework into an ontological framework. But that never happens. Kant derived his idea of the two worlds from his theory of an active self, a self that requires something given. The idea of something given yielded the distinction between noumena and phenomena, two worlds constituting Kant's operative ontological framework. However, once Kant put into play the theory of two worlds, he could not return to the self, because it could not be construed as a member of one world or the other, and Kant could not conceive the self as a relation between two worlds as long as he conceived it as merely a subject that combines what is given to it.[91]

Kant took three passes at describing what his system was about. In the first *Critique* he explained that he tried to solve the problem of metaphysics. In the *Critique of Judgment*, in a discussion prized by post-Kantians and especially Hegel, Kant contended that his philosophy demonstrated the continuous transition from acts of understanding to reason to practical reason, including the apprehension of beauty. This was a larger boast than claiming to solve the problem of metaphysics; Kantian philosophy was a theory of the achievements of mind. Then he made a larger claim in his essay "What Real Progress Has Metaphysics Made in Germany since the Time of Leibniz and Wolff?" Kant argued that reason has a destination; his philosophy was structured to justify it. Rightly conceived, philosophy swings on two hinges, like a door. One is the ideality of space and time; the other is the reality of the idea of freedom.[92]

The destination of reason is the idea of freedom. In his last attempt to explain what his system was about, Kant took hold of his breakthrough theme in the second *Critique* that reason is a vault whose keystone is freedom. All other ideas, he reasoned, gain stability and objective reality only by attaching themselves to the idea of freedom. Even the necessary ideas of God and immortality become real only through "the fact that there really is freedom, for this idea is revealed by the moral law." If we do not insert the keystone to the vault of reason, the vault will not work. When we insert the keystone of freedom, the vault becomes self-supporting. Freedom is autonomy, the self-originating of law, as in the categorical imperative—an absolute law that is precisely the law of freedom without remainder.[93]

Freedom belongs to reason, not to understanding, because freedom makes absolute commands that one act in a certain way and requires the totality of a subject's volitions. In addition, Kant argued, freedom is practical, extending beyond theoretical reason. Freedom is a type of causality; it determines laws for the intelligible world, and it causes actions with knowable effects in the sensible world. It belongs to the intellectual world, yet it has effects on the sensible world. Kantian idealism was a theory about the connection between the principles of the intellectual world and the sensible world through practical reason and the subordination of everything to freedom. This idea that freedom is the link between the intellectual and sensible world and the unity of the self was Kant's feedback loop from his ontological framework to the principles of his system, even though he never quite put it that way. As Henrich says, "We need understanding in order to get to totality; we need totality in order to get to freedom; and we need freedom in order to get to the significance of the total system."[94]

If we do not believe in our freedom, we cannot trust anything our reason tells us, and freedom engenders ethical idealism, Kantian betrayals notwithstanding. Thus Kant's legacy includes, most notably, generations of abolitionists, radical liberals, freethinkers, religious socialists, feminists, peacemakers, generic progressives and liberals, world federalists, and human rights activists for whom freedom and ethical idealism *had* to go together.

3

Post-Kantian Feeling

Romantic Idealism as Theology

For all the complexity of Kant's system, it was beautifully simple at its core. Kant was certain of only one thing: we ought to do right. If we ought to do right, there is one speculative idea that we know on an a priori basis: the idea of freedom. We do not understand this idea, yet we know it as the condition of the moral law, something that we know. Kant's insistence on the actuality of the moral law made room for the actuality of freedom that is necessary to grasp the moral law within us, which is simple, absolute, sublime, and not that hard to figure out. To find it, all we have to do is universalize the moral question. To do the right thing, however, we have to fight the radical evil within us, using all the good religion we can get.

Liberal theology started there, with Kant's critical idealism and moral religion. To many liberal Protestant thinkers, Kant provided a secure home for religion that withstood the harshest disbelieving criticism and assigned an important role to religion. But Kant disowned his protégé, J. G. Fichte, for sounding too atheistic, and before Kant finished his third *Critique* there were already post-Kantians in Jena, Berlin, Frankfurt, and Homburg who rejected his dualism, the thing-in-itself, and Kantian religion. Friedrich Schlegel inaugurated post-Kantian Romanticism, F. W. J. Schelling conceived three kinds of absolute idealism before he turned thirty, G. W. F. Hegel lagged behind his friend Schelling until he surpassed him, and Friedrich Schleiermacher lagged behind his friend

Schlegel before blooming as a theologian. Samuel Taylor Coleridge, paying close attention to the post-Kantian upsurge, brought it singlehandedly to England. Schleiermacher and Coleridge had three crucial things in common, besides genius. They deeply absorbed Kant's philosophy. They were too religious to accept Kant's moralistic rendering of religion, construing Kantian idealism as a doorway to spiritual meaning. And they grounded post-Kantian religion squarely in Christian churches.

Friedrich Daniel Ernst Schleiermacher was born in 1768 in Breslau (today's Wroclaw in southern Poland) and named after Friedrich II, in whose army his father Gottlieb Schleiermacher served as a Reformed chaplain. Gottlieb struggled with Calvinist theology, drifted through a rationalist phase, and periodically catechized his three children on his occasional stopovers at home. Schleiermacher credited his mother with raising him to love God. In 1778 Gottlieb experienced a Pietistic conversion upon meeting the Moravian community at Gnadenfrei in Upper Silesia, in Prussia. The Moravian Brethren practiced a communal, devotional, warmhearted religion centered on Christ's expiatory sacrifice on the cross. Gottlieb could not join them without losing his commission, so he settled for bringing his family into the Moravian fold. Non-Moravian schools, he told his children, abounded in moral depravity. Schleiermacher was fourteen when he and his brother Carl were placed in the Moravian boarding school at Niesky, while sister Charlotte enrolled in the school at Gnadenfrei. He never saw his parents again. His mother died shortly afterward, and his father traveled two thousand miles per year with the army. But Schleiermacher exchanged letters with his father until Gottlieb's death in 1794, and he craved intimate personal relationships for the rest of his life.[1]

The Moravians were fervently devoted to Jesus, teaching that religion can only be awakened, not really taught—two predispositions that stuck with Schleiermacher after he threw off Moravian theology. The Niesky school had a monastic ethos, protecting students from the evils of the world, and a lax curriculum centered on Pietistic instruction. It stressed the depravity of human nature and the supernatural means of grace, prizing communion with Jesus, which depended on a breakthrough of grace by the Holy Spirit. To be saved was to gratefully accept Christ's atoning sacrifice for sin. Schleiermacher appreciated that Moravians spurned the penitential severities of other Pietist groups, wanting students to experience the joy of salvation: "Here it was that that mystic tendency developed itself, which has been of so much importance to me, and has supported and carried me through all the storms of skepticism."[2]

Upon moving to the Moravian seminary at Barby, however, Schleiermacher rebelled against monastic seclusion, censorship, and orthodox theology. Barby students were forbidden to read modern writers, notably Johann W. Goethe, so Schleiermacher read Goethe intently. The teachers railed against J. S. Semler and biblical criticism, so Schleiermacher yearned to study at Halle. School administrators cracked down on Schleiermacher's group of rebels, prohibiting independent studies and expelling an English student. Schleiermacher told his father in a letter that things were going badly for him, mainly because he didn't believe in substitutionary atonement.

How could a loving God subject human beings to everlasting punishment for their sins? But if that was unbelievable, Christ's expiatory sacrifice was unnecessary, plus making no sense. Schleiermacher explained: "I cannot believe that He, who called Himself the Son of Man, was the true, eternal God; I cannot believe that His death was a vicarious atonement, because He never expressly said so Himself; and I cannot believe it to have been necessary, because God, who evidently did not create men for perfection, but for the pursuit of it, cannot possibly intend to punish them eternally, because they have not attained it." Asking for permission to enroll at Halle, Schleiermacher signed off, "Your distressed and most dutiful Son."[3]

Gottlieb's reply was anguished and furious: "Oh, thou insensate son! Who has deluded thee, that thou no longer obeyest the truth, thou, before whose eyes Christ was pictured, and who now crucifiest him? You were so well started, who has held you back from obeying the truth?" Had Friedrich become so degenerate in merely a few months? Or were his previous letters filled with hypocrisy and deception? Had he never tasted "one little drop of balsam" from the wounds of Jesus? It seemed to Gottlieb that his son had chosen a different god; thus he disowned him: "With heartrending grief I discard thee, for discard thee I must, as thou no longer worshippest the God of thy fathers, as thou no longer kneelest at the same altar with him—yet, once more, my son, before we part—oh! tell me, what has the poor, meek, and humble-hearted Jesus done to thee, that thou renouncest his strength and his divine peace? Did you find no consolation when you laid before Him your need, the anguish of your heart? And now, in return for the divine long-suffering and patience with which He listened to you, you deny Him?" As for Halle, where Schleiermacher's (maternal) uncle Samuel Stubenrauch taught theology, Gottlieb was willing to pay for three semesters, as a farewell gift. Since his son longed for the world's approval, he might as well find out if his soul could feed on the world's husks.[4]

Schleiermacher's reply was sensitive but unyielding. His feeling of "wretchedness" was unbearable, especially at grieving his father. He had never been a hypocrite—"I did really feel it"—but could not continue to feel devoted to doctrines he no longer believed. He implored his father to stop overreacting; their views were not so different: "You say that the glorification of God is the end of our being, and I say the glorification of the creature; is not this in the end the same thing? Is not the Creator more and more glorified the happier and the more perfect his creatures are?" Schleiermacher said he felt "the most sincere love and filial grati-tude towards the all-good God, who, even in the midst of the painful circumstances that are now besetting me, lets me experience such far preponderating good." Did that count for nothing? Why did Gottlieb insist that mere doubts about atonement theory and Christology made his son an enemy of God? Didn't they pray to the same God? Since he was still a Christian, Schleiermacher asked his father to reconsider casting him aside.[5]

Gottlieb half relented, withdrawing the expulsion, though he grieved that "pride, egotism, and intolerance have taken possession of you." Thus it repulsed him that Schleiermacher claimed he was inspired by the love of Christ. Schleiermacher transferred to Halle, Prussia's leading univer-sity, though its golden age had ended. He studied Kant under Johann August Eberhard, lived with Stubenrauch, a moderate supernaturalist with rationalist leanings, and absorbed Eberhard's respect for Kant, although Eberhard found Kant too skeptical. Otherwise Schleiermacher got little from his two years of academic training, being hard to impress and prone to melancholy. Stubenrauch retired to a country pastorate in Drossen, taking Schleiermacher, who floundered in lonely doubt that he believed in anything besides Kantian ethics.[6]

Schleiermacher was depressed and physically ill in Drossen. He tried to study for the Reformed Church's theology exam, but brooded that theology was pointlessly complex and scholastic, fixed on conceptual sub-tleties proving nothing. He mused that Christianity probably should be tossed aside and replaced with Kantian ethics, except that Kant's moral argument for God was not believable either. To regain his ministerial vocation, Schleiermacher had to feel religious, which could not happen in lonely Drossen, although he passed his theology exam in 1790. He took a private tutorial position with the family of a nobleman, Count Wilhelm

Dohna, at Schlobitten in East Prussia, and perked up. Count Dohna and his wife, a born countess, were conservative monarchists, friendly, refined, and great talkers, with twelve children. Schleiermacher adored one of the teenaged countesses, awakened emotionally, and stayed with the Dohna family for three years, preaching philosophical sermons at a local church. Later he recalled that he first awakened to "the beauty of human fellowship" in the Dohna home: "I saw that it requires freedom to ennoble and give right expression to the delicate intimacies of human nature."[7]

Still short on intellectual ambition, Schleiermacher did not pass his second theology exam until 1794, winning an appointment two years later as a Reformed chaplain at Berlin's main hospital, Charité Hospital. Berlin, the vanguard of Romanticism, offered salons and café banter that enthralled Schleiermacher. He befriended wannabe aesthetes who pondered Goethe's *Wilhelm Meister's Apprenticeship* (1795), a coming-of-age novel about a young man's emotional, intellectual, and artistic development. They vowed to find unity in their lives by devoting themselves fullheartedly to something worthy of devotion. One important friend was Marcus Herz, a prominent physician and former student of Kant's, who hosted gatherings of intellectuals in his home. Another was the rising poet and writer Friedrich Schlegel, who moved to Berlin in 1797. Schleiermacher's closest friends were women, especially Herz's multilingual, cultured, comely wife Henriette Herz, who was less than half the age of her husband.[8]

Schleiermacher and Henriette Herz had an intimate Platonic relationship for many years. They met nearly every day, usually spending entire afternoons together, and traveled abroad together, writing to each other whenever they were separated. To Schleiermacher the essential prerequisite for friendship was a highly developed capacity to describe one's feelings. He and Herz constantly poured out their feelings to each other. Both stressed that they connected emotionally, not sexually, and made a comical pair in appearance, as he was small and slight, and she was very tall and full-figured. He observed, "Her colossal, queenlike figure is so very much the opposite of mine." She observed, "He had an irresistible inward craving to commune with friends, to open before them every fold and crevice in his heart and mind, and an equal craving for signs of life and love from his friends."[9]

Schleiermacher's life turned a corner upon befriending Henriette and her husband, who introduced him to Schlegel. Schlegel was brilliant, mercurial, and ambitious, aspiring to write "progressive, universal poetry" that strove infinitely for an unattainable ideal, "free of all real and ideal self-interest." He coined the term "Romanticism" and urged that the essence of poetry is in its romantic element—the feelings of the human spirit. In Berlin he fell in love with a married woman, Dorothea Mendelssohn Veit, the daughter of philosopher Moses Mendelssohn, which led to a scandalous affair leading to her divorce. Schlegel's barely disguised fictional account of his passionate relationship with Dorothea, *Lucinde* (1799), made him famous, though also reviled, prompting them to move to Jena.[10]

Schleiermacher loved and admired Schlegel, defended him, and put off his exhortations to start writing books. He said he lacked the ambition to be an author; it didn't help that he felt vastly inferior to Schlegel intellectually. To his sister Charlotte, Schleiermacher rejoiced at finding an intellectual companion and inspiration: "I always felt the want of a companion to whom I could freely impart my philosophical ideas, and who would enter with me into the deepest abstractions. This great void he has filled up most gloriously. To him I can not only pour out what is already in me, but by means of the exhaustless stream of new views and new ideas which is ever flowing into him, much that has been lying dormant in me, is likewise set in motion."[11]

The key Romantic tropes were already there in Schleiermacher's friendship with Schlegel—the prizing of inward feeling, vision, idealism, expression, and the growth of individuality. Schleiermacher had an early inkling, however, of what might go wrong. He told Charlotte that Schlegel, though "infinitely superior to me," lacked "tenderness of feeling" and any appreciation of the "pleasing trifles of life." Schlegel was fiery and strong, spurning the gentle, the beautiful, and the pacific: "He will always be my superior; but I shall know and understand him more thoroughly than he will ever know and understand me." Schleiermacher prized tender feeling and intimate friendship above everything else. He knew that he needed both in large amounts. He told Henriette he was so dependent on intimacy and affection that he sometimes doubted if he was an individual: "I am the least independent and least self-sufficing of mortals. . . . I stretch out all my roots and leaves in search of affection; it is necessary for me to feel myself in immediate contact with it, and when I am unable to drink in full draughts of it, I at once dry up and wither. Such is my nature; there is no remedy for it; and, if there were, I should not wish to employ it."[12]

Very unhappily, Schleiermacher fell in love with Eleonore Grunow, the wife of a Berlin pastor, with whom he pleaded to dissolve her unhappy marriage in order to marry him. In the meantime he brooded over the book that Schlegel and Henriette Herz urged him to write. Schleiermacher winced at the hostility of his friends to religion, telling Herz, "My religion is so through and through heart-religion, that I have not room for any other." Some of his friends were old-style rationalist debunkers; some adopted Kantian ethics with God left out; some treated religion as a backward form of something precious, romantic striving. Schleiermacher partly sympathized with these views, but judged that none grasped the unique content and importance of religion. Moreover, Schlegel's faith was nature-religion, a variant of option three. Schleiermacher employed a version of Kant's analytical method, distinguishing the essential spirit or "idea" of pure religion from its historical forms. Though he complained of being a slow reader, slow to grasp ideas, and slower yet in writing, he wrote an epochal work of ruminating genius in a few months, *On Religion: Speeches to Its Cultured Despisers* (1799), passing the chapters to Schlegel and Herz as he wrote them.[13]

His opening sentence highlighted his novel apologetic task: "The subject I propose to discuss has been massively denigrated by the very people from whom I especially claim a hearing." Schleiermacher allowed that this was not a very promising project. His friends were taken with "suavity and sociability" and "art and learning," giving no thought to religion. His subject belonged to a past age that his friends supposedly saw through: "I am quite aware of all this." Yet he felt compelled to say that they understood very little about religion: "To me, what seems a divine impulse makes it impossible to withdraw my overture inviting precisely you, the cultured detractors of religion, to hear me out."[14]

His friends wrongly identified religion with forms and dogmas, missing what matters in religion: spiritual feeling. To Schleiermacher, piety was "the maternal womb in whose sacred obscurity my young life was nourished and prepared for a world still closed to it." Long before he became an adult, his spirit "found its vital breath in piety." Piety—spiritual feeling—had sustained him through years of loneliness, religious doubt, and intellectual confusion, making him capable of friendship and love: "As I began to sift out the faith of my fathers and to clear the rubbish of former ages from my thoughts and feelings, piety supported me. As the childhood images of God and immortality vanished before my doubting eyes, piety remained."[15]

Viewed from the outside, Schleiermacher allowed, religion appeared to turn on two things, providence and immortality. He did not blame the cultured despisers for believing that religion is about fearing or revering the providential rule of an eternal being and expecting an afterlife. But these were mere external dogmas, like other institutionalized opinions and practices. Religion is about the *source* of the external factors, which can only be known from the inside. Schleiermacher shared the contempt of his friends for most forms of organized religion: "These doctrines and systems very often move forward without having anything at all in common with religion. Personally, I cannot even speak of this without feeling revulsion." Most religious systems are loaded with superstitions, sacrifices, and coarse moral schemes. Even rationalistic forms of modern religion fixed on externals, replacing crude doctrines with "ill-assembled fragments of metaphysics and morals." Schleiermacher shuddered that "rationalistic Christianity" was very short on actual religion, though in a later edition he changed the reference to "purified Christianity," because his younger readers had no memory of dry deism.[16]

If you pay attention only to religious externals, he said, "you do not yet know religion itself at all, and religion is not what you are objecting to." Schleiermacher chided his friends for being so superficial: "How easygoing your mode of inquiry has suddenly turned out to be! I am astonished at this voluntary ignorance of yours! Why don't you look at the religious life itself?" He implored them to look especially at experiences of sublime mystical feeling, "moments in which one's feeling is wholly absorbed in an immediate sense of the infinite and eternal and of its fellowship with the soul." To understand religion is to grasp the inspirations of pious soul, "that effusion of insight and ardor which issues from a spirit truly surrendered to the universe. Without this you will experience nothing of religion."[17]

"Surrendered to the universe" smacked of pantheism to many readers, which Schleiermacher denied in the supplementary notes of the book's subsequent editions. *On Religion* was studiously vague in its references to God or the Divine, using *Gottheit* (Deity) most often and *Universum* next most often, along with a slew of supplementary terms: *Ganz* (whole), *geistige Welt* (spiritual World), *Sein* (being), and *Urwesen* (original being), plus longer phrases meaning the same thing, such as "the object of piety," "the supreme being in this world," "the Spirit of the Whole," "the source of spiritual life," "the supreme Spirit of the world," "the unity of the whole," "being in its totality," "the eternal fountainhead," and "the World

Spirit," among others. Schleiermacher used "God" only in specifically Christian contexts or when describing how his acquaintances normally referred to the divine. He reasoned that he could not change the preconceptions of his readers about divine reality if he relied on the word "God," because it immediately conjured up the very connotations he was trying to dispel. Schleiermacher worried less, to his subsequent regret, about the pantheistic connotations of his favored monikers, an impression he compounded by singling out Spinoza, "that saintly outcast," as his role model: "The supreme Spirit of the world permeated his being, the infinite was his beginning and end; the universe was his sole and everlasting love. In sacred innocence and deep humility he saw himself mirrored in the world of the eternal and perceived how he himself was its most worthy image. He was full of religion, of the Holy Spirit." To Schleiermacher, Spinoza's sublime spiritual witness, if not his identification of God with Nature, was the gold standard of piety.[18]

This passage was cited against Schleiermacher for the rest of his life as proof of his pantheism, notwithstanding his repeated denials. Thirty years later he was still defending the Spinoza passage and denying the motive usually attributed to it—he tried to replace the Christian God with a pantheistic God of nature that was functionally equivalent to atheism. According to Schleiermacher, the point of the Spinoza passage was that piety, being everywhere, existed even where the cultured despisers of piety "sought it least." Spinoza, at the end of the eighteenth century, was wrongly idolized by disbelievers and wrongly condemned by guardians of orthodoxy: "Yet almost no one had noticed his genuinely human, inwardly gentle, and most attractive personality and his deep devotion to the supreme being. If I had been a more cautious person, who always anticipated the worst from his readers, then I would have left a little space to mention that my words provide very little occasion for considering me a Spinozist. But given what I am, that thought did not even occur to me."[19]

Instead Schleiermacher pressed a Kantian argument that moved significantly beyond Kant's moralism. Kant uncoupled religion from science while treating consciousness of the moral law as a fact of pure reason; the basis of his moral religion was the sheer givenness of the moral law as a demand. Schleiermacher took for granted Kant's dichotomy between religion and science, but added that religion has no special expertise in morality either. Religious feeling, not the moral law, is the crucial given that cannot be derived from something else: "At the very outset, religion waives all claims to anything belonging to the two domains of science and morality. It would now return all that has been either loaned or pressed upon it from those sources." Religion is not about explaining or ordering the world, because spiritual feeling is a deeper aspect of human experience than theoretical reason, practical reason, or even sensation.[20]

In formal terms, Schleiermacher fashioned a third way between Continental rationalism and Kant's critical idealism. Leibniz and the rationalist tradition described feeling as a confused and primitive form of knowledge. Feeling is self-transcending and intentional, so it counts as a form of knowledge, albeit a poor one. Kant denied that feeling is self-transcending or intentional, and thus denied that feeling is a form of knowledge. Feeling is an autonomous faculty consisting of an emotive, noncognitive mode of consciousness that "knows" no truth beyond psychological experience.[21]

Schleiermacher disputed both of these put-downs of feeling. The rationalists were wrong to count feeling as low-grade knowledge, and Kant's faculty psychology wrongly obscured the fundamental unity of the self as a whole agent. With the rationalists, Schleiermacher conceived feeling as a direct, self-transcending apprehension of reality, something not reducible to a mere psychological state. Feeling is the general organ of the subject's receptivity and the preconceptual organ that makes possible all thought and experience. It is the immediate presence of undivided being that unites the self to her world, bringing the self into apprehension of the world as a whole. Contrary to rationalism, however, feeling is not a lowly form of cognition, because it is not a mode of knowing or doing at all, and contrary to Kant, feeling is not a third faculty alongside the theoretical and practical faculties. Knowing and doing are determinate, mediated modes of consciousness.[22]

Schleiermacher conceived feeling as self-consciousness as such, the autonomous, unifying dimension of the self that pre-reflectively apprehends the world as a whole. "Feeling" (*Gefühl*) was his term for the prerational apprehension of reality affected by the self in its immediate self-consciousness. Schleiermacher anticipated the phenomenology of Edmund Husserl and the panexperientialism of Alfred North Whitehead. His emphasis on the intentionality and concreteness of consciousness preceded Husserl's phenomenology of the lifeworld as the constantly presupposed subsoil of thought, and his contention that experience comes into being by feeling the feelings of one's world preceded Whitehead's organic panpsychism. To Schleiermacher, true religion was essentially contemplative, "the immediate consciousness of the universal being of all finite things in and through the infinite, of all temporal things in and through the eternal." It was rooted in an awareness of "the infinite nature of the whole, in the one and all, in God."[23]

Since religion is about relating to everything, Schleiermacher believed his strategy did not commit the Kantian mistake of confining religion to a box. Religion had to be liberated from science and morality, but not divorced from them: "For what else is science than the existence of things within you, within your reason? What else is art and culture than your existence in things on which you bestow measure, form, and order? And how can either science or art and culture spring to life for you except insofar as the eternal unity of reason and nature, the universal being of all finite things in the infinite, thrives within you?"[24]

Religion is the unifying ground of science and culture. It flows out of spiritual experience and inspires all intellectual, cultural, and moral activity. Schleiermacher put it epigrammatically: "True science is perspective fully achieved; true praxis is art and culture created of oneself; true religion is sense and taste for the infinite." The irreducible ground of religion is the self's pre-reflective awareness of its absolute dependence on the eternal ground of being: "To seek and to find this infinite and eternal factor in all that lives and moves, in all growth and change, in all action and passion, and to have and to know life itself only in immediate feeling—that is religion."[25]

He stressed that true religion does not consist of believing or knowing something about the nature of reality. As soon as one identifies particular factors with the divine, one moves out of the religious sphere. *On Religion* implored against the mythical impulse of hypostatizing God as a being outside the world of human experience and natural causality. In a later edition Schleiermacher expanded on the problem of myth, "a purely ideal object explicated in the form of history." Myth reduces God to an object of thought by separating God from the world. Any concept of God as an outside being that interferes in history or natural events reduces religion to "vain mythology." Schleiermacher shared the Enlightenment rationalist critique of mythical consciousness without adopting the rationalist strategy of expunging Christianity of myth. As long as one recognizes that Christian myth is mythical, he reasoned, and as long as one bears in mind that the Spirit of the Whole is not a being outside the world, it does no harm to retain mythical language in theology and the life of faith.[26]

True religion finds the eternal factor at work in all that lives and has being. We feel our dependence on the unity that underlies "the coinherence of the world," including our relationship to every part of the world. Schleiermacher cautioned that no feeling should be regarded as a "genuine stirring of piety" on the basis of anything particular in the world. Feeling is genuinely religious only as revelatory experience of the Spirit of the Whole. It is God, the sole and highest unity, being felt. One cannot conceive the world as a universal whole apart from a divine ground, and the only way to experience God is through the stirrings of genuine religious feeling that the world in its unity brings forth. The aim of spiritual living is to become one with the universe, Schleiermacher's idea of immortality. Since religious feeling is always related to the Divine, never attaching to any mere particular, the content of religious feeling is eternal, like the Divine. Instead of longing to live forever as a separate being, which Schleiermacher considered the very opposite of true religion, religious feeling longs for union with the Divine Spirit of the Whole.[27]

On Religion did not rest with Romantic religious individualism. Schleiermacher cautioned that religion is either social or nonexistent, because "it is man's nature to be social." One cannot be vitally religious alone. The more that one is vitally stirred by something, "the more strongly his drive toward sociality comes into play." Thus Schleiermacher risked alienating the friends that might have gone for Romantic individualism. To be religious, he insisted, one has to deal with other people, including religious organizations like the Christian church. The true church, to be sure, is a spiritual fellowship having "nothing directly to do with the profane world." Schleiermacher called it the social form of true religion. But social religion does not spring into existence straight out of religious feeling. It has to develop out of institutions that cope with the profane world and variously address "the illnesses of humanity." The true church emerges only out of compromised, backward, and easily denigrated churches in the real world—institutions that provide enough of the "atmosphere" of true religion to inspire new forms of social religion.[28]

On Religion had perfect pitch for the post-Kantian Romantic generation that wanted to be, in the idiom of a later time, spiritual but not religious. Many readers shared Goethe's reaction that Schleiermacher's rendering of the essence of religion was wonderful and his rearguard attempt to support church Christianity was disappointing. Others celebrated that he mixed the best of Enlightenment rationalism, Pietism, Kantian critical idealism, and Romanticism without giving up on church

Christianity. Many chewed over Schleiermacher's cheeky remarks about his intended audience, reading themselves in or out of it.

Schleiermacher stressed that he wrote only for liberal, educated, aesthetically sensitive types, namely "the cultured sons and daughters of Germany." It was sad that he had to aim at such a small group, but what else could he do? "It is not blind partiality for my native soil or for my fellow citizens or for those who use the same language that makes me speak as I do. It is the deep conviction that you alone are prepared—and in this respect deserving—of having the sense for sacred and divine things awakened in you."[29]

Only the privileged children of Germany seemed capable of attaining true religion. Britons were too greedy and power seeking to be religious, he opined. They cared only about things that enhanced their wealth and position, their zeal for science was merely "a sham maneuver," and their vaunted prudence was "a bauble." Too many Germans unduly admired the pushy British Islanders. Britons prattled a lot about freedom, but usually to justify their insatiable greed: "These people are never in earnest about anything that goes beyond ostensible utility." For example, they stripped the life out of science, "using it only as deadwood to fashion masts and helms for sailing in pursuit of gain." They did the same thing with religion, only worse, since British religion had nothing to do with true religion. England's corrupt state religion was religiously antiquated and morally bankrupt, yet somehow the English prized it: "They know nothing of religion, except that everyone preaches attachment to antiquated practices and defends its precepts."[30]

By his lights the French were even worse, unspeakably worse: "One who honors religion can scarcely bear to look their way. In their every action, their every word almost, they trample its holiest ordinances under foot." Only ten years removed from the fall of the Bastille, Schleiermacher felt no need to indulge anybody's lingering sympathy for the French Revolution; Napoleon took power eight months after Schleiermacher completed *On Religion*. Schleiermacher said the French were unspeakably rude and lacked any capacity for true religious feeling: "What does religion abhor more than that unbridled arrogance by which the leaders of the French people defy the eternal laws of our world? What does religion more keenly instill than that humble, considerate moderation for which they do not seem to have even the faintest feeling?" The "dazzling beguilement of revolution" turned normal French rudeness and impiety to sheer madness. An entire nation turned against God, no pious voice had any chance of being heard, and France paid a terrible price for it, albeit without realizing it.[31]

Twenty-two years later, in the book's third edition, Schleiermacher allowed that he might have exaggerated slightly about England, though not beyond the boundaries of normal rhetorical "stress." Germans admired British civilization far more than it deserved at the turn of the century, and Britons had not yet developed their enthusiasm for mission work and Bible distribution. Still, a great deal of this mission work was bound up with England's undiminished zeal for territorial expansion and enrichment. When the English bothered to promote Christianity, they did so as a secondary business that propped up what they really cared about. Nothing had changed concerning English greed, English science, and English religion; Schleiermacher had no second thoughts about the French; and he noted that he spoke only of England and France because Germans at the turn of the century were not interested in anybody else: "It seemed superfluous to direct similar attention elsewhere."[32]

On Religion gave Schleiermacher a splash of renown, though less than Schlegel's. Meanwhile he struggled with his aversion to Schlegel's stormy sensuality and impetuousness, confiding his true feelings to friends while defending Schlegel publicly. He told Eleanore Grunow that Schlegel was a font of repugnant pronouncements who stood above most intellectuals as a moral being. For example, though Schleiermacher admired Goethe and Schelling as thinkers, he could never love them, because they were just thinkers. Schlegel, by contrast, bore "the whole world in his heart with love." He was offensive by the letter of the law, but also highly moral and loving.[33]

Schleiermacher applied a similar distinction to himself, as he spent six years trying to persuade Grunow to divorce her husband and marry him. The couple met in 1799; soon he was urging her that every woman had a right to her own individuality; and in 1802 Schleiermacher left Berlin for a poorly endowed position as a court chaplain at Stolpe in Pomerania to give Grunow sufficient freedom to choose him. His friends were mystified that she captivated Schleiermacher, since she lacked the qualities he usually esteemed: sentimentality, sensitivity, beauty, broad culture, and intellectual playfulness. Schleiermacher said he admired the strength and richness of her feeling and her ability to express it. At Stolpe he ministered for two years to several tiny Reformed congregations, worked on a translation project of Plato's works that he shared with Schlegel, wrote a book on ethical theory, and pleaded for a positive verdict from Grunow. Schleiermacher surprised himself by adopting the disciplined habits of a scholar, though his book on ethical theory was not very good, as he wrote it in the process of learning the material.[34]

In 1804 he accepted a teaching position in ethics and pastoral theology at the University of Würzburg. This was a breakthrough, but the Prussian throne intervened, countering with a marginal position at its flagship, Halle. Schleiermacher's Prussian loyalty prevailed, taking the lesser position and its lower pay. For a year he taught as an adjunct Reformed professor at all-Lutheran Halle, after which he was admitted to the full faculty in the fall of 1805, just as Grunow renounced him, which devastated Schleiermacher. He told his friends Ehrenfried and Henriette von Willich that he was crushed with sorrow and pain "that will never leave me . . . but whatever can be made of the ruins, I will make of them." Heartbroken, he began his academic career, making Halle the first integrated theological faculty in Prussia.[35]

He got a cool reception at Halle, still a stronghold of mildly rationalist Lutheran Pietism, but flourished. Schleiermacher's former teacher, Eberhard, spurned him, sniffing that Halle legitimized an outright atheist as a theologian and preacher. Many of Schleiermacher's colleagues regarded his supposed pantheism as a disingenuous form of atheism. Halle had rationalists, Pietists, and conservatives, plus mixtures of these types. They were open to historical criticism and demythologizing, but not to Schleiermacher's rejection of a hypostatized God of being who intervenes in history. At the same time, classical philologist Friedrich August Wolf, a Goethe disciple and leading myth critic, disparaged Schleiermacher for clinging to theology. It took Schleiermacher's scholarly work on Plato to change Wolf's mind about his worth as an academic and colleague. Schleiermacher lectured on philosophy, systematic theology, ethics, New Testament, and a field he invented: hermeneutics, the study of interpretation. He taught that no text can be understood without comprehending how understanding occurs, and to interpret any text, one must enter the frame of mind of the author. Schleiermacher lectured on hermeneutics for the rest of his career, without publishing his theory that the interplay of whole and part is essential to all understanding. To comprehend a text, one must understand the cultural and linguistic whole in which it is embedded and its individual parts.[36]

In August 1806 the Prussian throne, learning that Napoleon offered Hanover to England, issued an ultimatum to Napoleon, who responded by smashing the Prussian forces at Auerstadt, Jena, and

Halle. Schleiermacher witnessed the fall of Halle to the French invaders and bewailed the incompetence of the Prussian army. His house was plundered and occupied by French troops, students were expelled from the city, the university was dissolved, and Schleiermacher's university church was turned into a grain store. His patriotism soared in response. Unlike Goethe and Hegel, who admired the French conqueror, Schleiermacher seethed with rage at the crushing of old Prussia. He vowed to remain in Halle as long as he had potatoes and salt, aspiring to build a new, reformed, militant Prussian state that expelled the French imperialists and unified the German principalities. In November 1806 he told Henriette Herz, "We are living here in a most feverish state. . . . The rod of wrath must fall upon every German land; only on this condition can a strong and happy future bloom forth. Happy they who live to see it; but those who die, let them die in faith."[37]

In that mood he fixed on the hope of a united German nation that leaped beyond its feudal mosaic of city-states, princedoms, and ministates. Prussia was a glorious cultural entity yet to be realized politically; relinquishing it was not an option. Schleiermacher's Romantic aestheticism faded, including his fixation with the individuality of the self; now he stressed that individuality is pointless if it does not serve the common good of the nation. To live under foreign domination was no life at all; history itself is a life of struggle, resistance, sacrifice, and waiting upon the will of God. Schleiermacher vowed to join the struggle for the fulfillment of God's purpose, which surely entailed expelling the French conquerors.

But the French dismembered Prussia and abolished its western universities, granting Halle to Westphalia, which forced Schleiermacher to rethink his pledge to Halle. To help Prussia recover, he had to return to Berlin. In 1807 he moved to Berlin, plunged into social activism, and grieved over the death of his friend Ehrenfried von Willich, an army chaplain who died in a typhoid epidemic during the siege of Stralsund. Von Willich's widow, Henriette von Kathen Willich, was nineteen years old and a mother of two children. Schleiermacher already had a tender fatherly relationship with her. She called him "beloved father," and he called her "my dearly beloved daughter" and "my dear child." In May 1809 Schleiermacher married her, in the same month that he became minister of Trinity Church in Berlin. Each became devoted to the other, though she rarely attended his sermons, finding his preaching incomprehensible and short on Pietistic orthodoxy.[38]

For the rest of his life Schleiermacher was an every-week preacher at Trinity Church and a professor at the University of Berlin, of which he was a major cofounder. He served on the organizing commission of the new university, headed by Wilhelm von Humbolt, which took seriously the reported vow of King Frederick Wilhelm III that Prussia needed to make up for physical loss through intellectual gain. To Schleiermacher, the founding of the University of Berlin in 1810 was foundational for the renewal of Prussian life. He served as university rector in 1815 and as dean of the theological faculty four times, teaching all fields of theology except Hebrew Scripture (dogmatics, encyclopedia, exegesis, church history, practical theology, and New Testament), and also taught philosophy (aesthetics, dialectics, ethics, hermeneutics, pedagogy, and psychology). His pulpit at Trinity Church became the focal point of his academic, political, and ecclesiastical efforts to renew Prussian life and culture, where Schleiermacher tested what could be said against Prussian conservatives and the French conquerors. In 1813 Napoleon's forces retreated from Russia in defeat; Schleiermacher exhorted students to rout the vanquished invaders in Breslau. The following year he called for a constitutional monarchy and parliament.[39]

Founding the University of Berlin raised the question of theological encyclopedia: How should theology be taught in a modern university? Fichte, joining the faculty at Berlin, strongly suggested that debates over theological encyclopedia had no place in a modern university because theology didn't deserve its own department. Schleiermacher, speaking as a theologian, university cofounder, and administrator, contended that theology is an integral discipline fully meriting department status. He divided theology into three distinct but related fields called philosophical theology, historical theology, and practical theology, describing theology as a positive science because it flows from the given of God-consciousness. The three parts form a whole through their common relation to a particular mode of faith, "a particular way of being conscious of God." The given of God-consciousness is positive because it takes historical forms. Philosophical theology utilizes the framework and methods of philosophy of religion. Historical theology includes exegetical theology, church history, and dogmatic theology. Practical theology is the crown of theological study, covering principles of church service and church government.[40]

His claim that the theological disciplines possess an organic unity was novel. Confessional theologies featured biblical or creedal loci lacking internal connections. Rationalist theologies rested on philosophical first principles. Kantians prized moral religion and their own scientific rationality; to them, the idea that theology obtains its organic unity as a discipline of the church was plainly anti-liberal. Schleiermacher's approach rested on the unifying religious self-consciousness shared by Christians in the church. Theology is critical reflection on the corporate experience of the Christian community. This argument redefined how religion should be taught in the modern academy. It helped that Schleiermacher's model was friendly to Pietist appropriation. It also helped that he was church centered *and* often read as a Romantic individualist; readers favored the Schleiermacher closest to their own sensibility. He shared this double legacy with his contemporary, Samuel Taylor Coleridge, who brought post-Kantian idealism to empirical, Lockean, anti-Germanic, anti-Kantian England, offering the Church of England an up-to-date recovery of logos reason.

Recovering Transcendental Reason: Samuel Taylor Coleridge

Coleridge barely survived decades of opium addiction, near-death experiences, and wasted genius to become a post-Kantian philosopher and spiritual oracle. He was nine years old in 1781 when his father, an Anglican parish priest, suffered a fatal heart attack and Coleridge was shipped to a wretched charity school in Greyfriars, London. Introverted, bookish, intensely lonely, brilliant, and inclined to reverie, he was scarred by spending the rest of his childhood in a Dickensian orphanage. Coleridge got his first dose of opium after catching rheumatic fever. His assiduous reading got him into Jesus College, Cambridge, in 1791, where he embraced the Unitarianism and Jacobin radicalism of his favorite tutor, William Frend, who got expelled.

Coleridge morphed to a communist-nature Romanticism he called "Pantisocracy," combined with hard partying. He dropped out of Cambridge, joined the large Dissenting community in Bristol, and teamed with radical poet Robert Southey to promote Pantisocracy. He and Southey married the sisters Sarah Fricker and Edith Fricker in 1795, the same year that Coleridge met William Wordsworth, the turning point of his life. Coleridge founded a radical journal, the *Watchman*, and wrote sonnets. Some were long and formal in John Milton's style; most were direct, personal, and spontaneous, introducing a new kind of English poetry. In 1796 he shut down the journal, deeply in debt and miserable in his marriage, contemplating two options: study Kant and Romanticism in Germany, or settle down as a Unitarian pastor in Bristol.[41]

He preached one Unitarian sermon, found a benefactor, and plotted a trip to Germany with Wordsworth. The Napoleonic Wars cooled Coleridge's ardor for radical politics and pushed British politics to the right. For the rest of his life he denied, wrongly, that he had ever been a Jacobin radical and emphasized, rightly, that he had always been religious, yearning for the infinite spiritual source and power of all things. Coleridge and Wordsworth invented English Romanticism while scratching for a living and planning their trip to Germany. They bonded over shared genius and their desire to write about things considered inappropriate for poetry: everyday occurrences, rural life, seascapes, fantasy, madness. They believed that poetry should be naturalistic and imaginative. Wordsworth was longer on naturalism, and Coleridge emphasized imagination, but each had both. In 1798 they put English Romanticism on the map with a stunning collection of poems titled *Lyrical Ballads*. There were twenty-three poems, only one was a ballad, and only four were by Coleridge, as Wordsworth wrote faster and considered himself the stronger figure. But Coleridge's poems were breathtaking: "The Rime of the Ancient Mariner," a sublime medieval ballad; "Kubla Khan," a symbolic poem about the Asian emperor Kublai Khan; part one of the narrative poem "Christabel," an abduction story of protean ambiguity, with Gothic motifs, later favored by vampire novelists; and "The Nightingale," a conversation poem celebrating the instinctive joy of nightingale songs, which refuted Milton's notion of the nightingale as a melancholy bird. These were the greatest poems that Coleridge ever wrote, along with the second part of "Christabel," which he completed in 1800, and "Dejection: An Ode," published in 1802 after his health collapsed.[42]

Lyrical Ballads got Coleridge and Wordsworth to Germany, where they soon parted, as Coleridge wanted to study Kantian philosophy and Wordsworth wanted seclusion with his sister muse, Dorothy Wordsworth, to write poems. Coleridge spent ten months in Germany, notably four months at Göttingen, where he heard Eichhorn lecture, plotted a book on Herder, bought a trunk of books on Kantian philosophy, and spurned pleas from his wife to come home. His infant son Berkeley died of smallpox and Coleridge refused to come home, destroying his marriage. In 1800 he moved to Keswick to be near Wordsworth. Coleridge was already on the downward path, at age twenty-seven. He suffered from depression, anxiety, overwork, rheumatism, marital misery, financial insecurity, and his devastating dependence on laudanum. It crushed him to realize that Wordsworth looked down on him. Coleridge sustained their friendship by telling himself that Wordsworth was right: even his best poems were overwrought, comparing poorly to Wordsworth. Coleridge fell in love with Dorothy Wordsworth's best friend, Sara Hutchinson, plus her entire family, which was uplifting for a while, but also maddening, as he could not marry his true love and she didn't want him anyway.

His health collapsed in January 1801 and he struggled with opium addiction for the rest of his life. Coleridge poured out literary criticism, journalism, and poetry, pondered his religious philosophy, and filled notebooks with his reflections on Kant, Fichte, Schelling, Herder, subjectivity, polarity, and the Trinity. He loved the idea of a transcendental ground of freedom and spirituality, telling a friend he was finished with atheists. He returned to Anglicanism and the Trinity, conceiving the Trinity as a triunity of unity and distinction held together by Will, not being. He took a three-year cruise in the Mediterranean by himself, half expecting to die, drifting from Malta to Sicily to Rome. He wrote a pastoral letter to Sara Coleridge's wayward younger brother George Fricker, recalling that he had been a Socinian for many years and sometimes almost a naturalist, but his terrible health problems and sorrows forced him to look into himself, which drove him back to the New Testament Christ. Rationalistic religion lost Jesus and his redemption, Coleridge said. It lost the tri-union of God as Will, the idea of Jesus as logos, and the focus of Christian salvation on the redemption of corrupted will. Even the Anglican rationalism of Locke and Joseph Butler conceded too much to the mechanistic culture of atheism, producing more infidels. Coleridge, knowing he desperately needed saving, gently advised Fricker that modern people needed to look "into their own souls, instead of always looking out."[43]

That was in October 1806, near the end of Coleridge's first brush with death. He rallied upon returning to Keswick and made a splash as a bravura public lecturer in London. Coleridge was one of the great talkers, and best when he riffed without notes. He founded a newspaper, the *Friend*, and tried to persuade readers that post-Kantian philosophy was superior to British empiricism. He lived with Wordsworth, who wearied of Coleridge's chaotic, sullen, slovenly, opium-fueled, demanding, half-crazed behavior in his home, leading to a break with Wordsworth that devastated Coleridge. He crashed spectacularly, nearly dying of overdosed benders. From 1811 to 1814, just as Coleridge disintegrated, the narrative verse-romance that he and Wordsworth pioneered soared as a popular genre. Coleridge despaired at missing his cultural moment. He realized he had to face his demons or die; writing and lecturing no longer kept them at bay. He enlisted medical treatment and confessed to friends, but not family, that he risked lethal overdose every day.[44]

For years Coleridge had crammed his notebooks with material for a major work on the divine unity of the world, titled *Logosophia*. It would draw deeply on Kant, Fichte, and Schelling, but in Coleridge's Anglican fashion, ending with a commentary on the Gospel of John. Hegel was not in his canon because Coleridge absorbed Kant, Fichte, and Schelling before Hegel came along, and he remained closer to Schelling afterward. Coleridge struggled and failed to write his masterwork, until it occurred to him that he should start with a literary autobiography. That would get him rolling toward the metaphysical section, plus make it comprehensible. This plan got him started on a rambling rendering of his literary career, but Coleridge decided the metaphysical part couldn't wait, because it was foundational to everything he believed. He rewrote the book extensively, now titled *Biographia Literaria*. It started with memoir, moved to metaphysics, and ended with literary criticism, but scraps of each section spilled into the others. The memoir section was not a confession; Coleridge said almost nothing about his addiction or marriage. He modeled the memoir on Wordsworth's *Prelude*, except as prose, stressing the distinction between fancy and imagination that Wordsworth borrowed from Coleridge.[45]

Coleridge said there are two kinds of imagination. The primary imagination is the living power of all perception, "a repetition in the finite mind of the eternal act of creation in the infinite I AM." The secondary imagination is an echo of the primary imagination that differs from it only in the degree and mode of its operation: "It dissolves, diffuses, dissipates, in order to re-create; or where this process is rendered impossible, yet still at all events it struggles to idealize and to unify." In both cases, imagination is essentially vital and transformative, inspiring all creativity. Fancy, on the other hand, is merely passive and mechanical. It imitates and distorts, but does not create. Coleridge praised Wordsworth as the poetic genius of the age, but Wordsworth never studied Kant, so he did not grasp the meaning of the poetic revolution that he and Coleridge inaugurated. Then Wordsworth canonized an unimaginative account of it that marginalized Coleridge, wrongly on both counts. Coleridge told friends that for many years he wrongly exalted Wordsworth over himself to the detriment of his reputation; *Biographia Literaria* settled that score.[46]

But Coleridge had greater things at stake. His subject was the unifying transcendent meaning of human experience from rational perception (which he called Understanding) to artistic vision (which he called Imagination) to transcendent intuition (which he called Reason). Kant and Fichte, he said, saved him from the Locke and Hume tradition he imbibed at Cambridge. Locke was too confident of his ability to deduce concepts of the understanding from experience without appealing to a priori concepts. Hume realized that a pure concept such as "pure mathematics" had to have an a priori origin, but he could not explain the unification of synthetic judgments in the understanding. Coleridge lauded Kant for showing that the understanding itself, through its transcendental concepts, authors the experience in which its concepts are found. Kant revolutionized philosophy by doing so, but there were problems with Kant, as Schelling showed. Coleridge walked readers through Schelling's critique of Kantian dualism, which corrected Kant without lapsing into Fichte's subjective idealism.[47]

Here Coleridge had a tricky problem, which he handled badly. He was deeply dependent on Schelling, who had no English audience until Coleridge created one for him in *Biographia Literaria*. He worried, as he confessed, what critics would say about his dependence on Schelling—justifiably, because Coleridge pasted entire paragraphs of Schelling's work straight into his book with no acknowledgment, presenting Schelling's words as his own. Coleridge's metaphysical position was identical to Schelling's, which made him look like a mere epigone, with or without the plagiarism. But Coleridge had always been motivated by religious concerns, unlike Schelling. He could have said so, noting that Schelling took a religious turn in 1809, which would have highlighted that Coleridge worked out his religious thought independently of Schelling and before Schelling had such concerns. Instead he claimed that he never read much of Schelling, what he read was piecemeal and late, and he didn't mind if the overlaps were credited to Schelling. Coleridge was sufficiently traumatized by what he borrowed from Schelling that he failed to explain how his position differed. He was drawn, for religious reasons, to thinkers that conceived reality as a dynamic relationship of opposite poles. He loved Giordano Bruno, Nicholas of Cusa, and Jacob Boehme for this reason. All described the life process as a constant generation of polar opposites that are not mere contrasts. Bruno had a theory of dynamic polarity. Nicholas had a similar theory of the coincidence of opposites, which he fashioned into a logos theology. Boehme had a mystical, dipolar logos theology marred by alchemical speculations. Kant's dialectic of sensibility and understanding made him the greatest thinker of dynamic polarity. Kant led Coleridge to Schelling, who improved on Kant.[48]

Schelling came late to a Christian understanding of divine reality as panentheistic distinction-in-unity, and never with Coleridge's emphasis on the Trinity. Philosophically, however, Schelling and Coleridge had the same absolute idealism. Nature is the sum of all objective things, and intelligence (or, the self) is the sum of all that is subjective. Nature is exclusively represented and lacking in consciousness, while intelligence is exclusively representative and conscious. The objective and subjective mutually exclude each other, yet all positive knowledge requires a reciprocal concurrence of these two factors. To Coleridge it was better to say, with Schelling, that mind derives from nature and nature derives from mind, than to say with Fichte (and arguably Kant) that everything derives from an act of free self-positing. *Biographia Literaria* rambled, but also sparkled, to a concluding vision of divine creative power communicated through imagination. Coleridge spiritualized post-Kantian thought distinctly, declaring that reason is in accord with faith, and faith is but the continuation of reason into the twilight, stealing into darkness.[49]

The reviews were horrible. Nearly every reviewer blasted Coleridge for publishing a sprawling disorganized mess of a book. Reviewers exhausted the connotations of obscure, inscrutable, and unhinged to dismiss Coleridge's metaphysical sections, sometimes pointing knowingly to his personal afflictions. Whatever German idealism was about, English readers didn't need to know. The reviews were so savage that Coleridge got a backlash reaction that made his later career possible. England's Romantic movement was still reviled, except by radicals and a handful of academics. Percy Bysshe Shelley had less than a hundred readers when he died in 1822, but Shelley, Mary Wollstonecraft Shelley, and John Keats lifted up Coleridge as the genius of Romanticism. Coleridge rose with the Romantic ascension that canonized Shelley and Keats; he enjoyed the irony that he owed his renaissance to radical feminists.[50]

In his last years he worked on a strange, prolix book originally titled *The Beauties of Archbishop Leighton*. Coleridge loved Robert Leighton, a seventeenth-century Anglican divine whose scriptural commentaries helped Coleridge survive his overdose meltdown of 1813. Coleridge reprinted Leighton's best passages and responded to them—a commentary on a commentary titled *Aids to Reflection*. The book morphed into a collection of aphorisms, playing up Coleridge's opposition to rationalist apologetics. One was immortalized by citation: "He, who begins by loving Christianity better than Truth, will proceed by loving his own Sect or Church better than Christianity, and end in loving himself better than all." To Coleridge, this aphorism was about the necessity of doubt and intellectual openness. God is not a Christian, and if God is the author of Truth, there is no reason to fear any truth.[51]

For twenty years he had pondered a revision of Kant's distinction between sensibility (*Sinnlichkeit*, the power to receive representations) and understanding (*Verstand*, the power of reasoning by means of representations). In 1806 Coleridge adopted the post-Kantian convention of calling it the distinction between Reason and Understanding. Reason correlates with noumena and Understanding with phenomena. In essence, Coleridge spiritualized Kant's transcendentalism by conceiving Reason as constitutive, the revelation of an immortal soul, not merely regulative. The Understanding apprehends contingent things of experience, while Reason works in the realm of necessity and universality, containing within itself the revelatory law of its conceptions. In *Biographia Literaria* Coleridge invoked the distinction between Reason and Understanding as a parallel to that of imagination and fancy, describing Reason as transcendent intuition. *Aids to Reflection* pressed hard on the upshot.[52]

Coleridge was a Kantian concerning the ground of morality, and thus of religion: it must be intuitive if the notion of moral truth is to be secured. Just as Kant distinguished between the sense-bound knowledge of pure reason and the intuitive, constitutively human knowledge of practical reason, Coleridge described the Understanding as sense bound and Reason as sense transcendent. The Understanding processes knowledge derived wholly from experience, while Reason gives birth to thought and life-enhancing action. The Understanding is discursive, but Reason is fixed. The Understanding is a reflective faculty that abstracts, names, and compares, bringing no immediate truths. Reason is essentially spiritual, the realm of conscience, contemplation, and insight—the transcendent power of intuition. The wellspring of religion is the revelatory power of being, Reason, not the sense-bound knowledge of the Understanding. The Understanding produces theologies, but has no knowledge of religious experience, since religion is about powers of will and being, not understanding. This claim yielded Coleridge's most famous epigram:

"Christianity is not a theory, or a speculation, but a life. Not a philosophy of life, but a life and a living process." So how can the truth of Christianity be proved? He had a two-word answer: "Try it." And what kind of life is it? He said it was the life of being redeemed.[53]

Coleridge was slow to get the followers he wanted in the Church of England, though he lived to see it happen, at Cambridge. In 1825 precious few Britons were willing to struggle with post-Kantian metaphysics. His first group of Anglican followers came along at Trinity College, Cambridge, enthused by *Aids to Reflection*. They read Coleridge as the prophet of a Broad Church third way between High Church and Low Church Anglicanism, although Coleridge's greatest theological disciple, Frederick Denison Maurice, decried party-line thinking itself. Coleridge, to Maurice, was the apostle of modern Anglican unity, not the founder of a third party. For many nineteenth-century Anglicans, Coleridge's emphasis on the corruption of the will helped to mitigate his sharp rejection of juridical atonement. Salvation is precisely redemption of the will. American evangelical Calvinist James Marsh, introducing the American edition of 1829, caught the book's evangelical note, and something equally important: Coleridge offered deliverance from Locke. Evangelicals should not be empiricists, Marsh said, but they had no alternative until Coleridge showed that knowing and being are inseparably linked. Young Unitarian minister Ralph Waldo Emerson, reading the American edition, skipped past Coleridge's insistence that the will is essentially corrupt. What mattered to Emerson was the book's intoxicating transcendentalism, especially the distinction between Reason and Understanding. It enthralled him to find an alternative to Hume's naturalistic skepticism in Coleridge's claim that the self possesses an active power of self-determination.[54]

Emerson copied into his journal Coleridge's maxim *Quantum scimus sumus* ("We are what we know"). Coleridge's next sentence was equally important to him: "That which we find within ourselves, which is more than ourselves, and yet the ground of whatever is good and permanent therein, is the substance and life of all other knowledge." These maxims set Emerson free to preach Emersonian sermons. In 1830 he declared, "Every man makes his own religion, his own God, his own charity." The root of religion is firsthand, he said. For the truly religious person, religion is not derived "from the Bible or his neighbor." The idea of God is "the most elevated conception of character that can be formed in the mind. It is the individual's own soul carried out to perfection."[55]

From there it was a short step to conceiving "salvation" as friendship, a notion Emerson developed in a series of sermons, and to write in his journal, "God in us worships God." He told Second Church in Boston that God would never bring a report to Reason that contradicted God: "To reflect is to receive truth immediately from God without any medium. That is living faith." On the other hand, to base one's faith on claims of the Understanding is to kill it. Faith is not about trusting in the veracity of particular bits of knowledge: "A trust in yourself is the height not of pride but of piety, an unwillingness to learn of any but God himself. It is by yourself without ambassador that God speaks to you."[56]

Emerson developed his signature ego-theism while he was still a pastor. "God in us worships God" led to his famous Neoplatonist assertion in "The Over-Soul" that the "simplest person, who in his integrity worships God, becomes God." Though Emerson still delivered sermons draped with rational evidence, he chafed at the demand for two-handed preaching. Sense knowledge has no bearing on genuine religion, so the customary Unitarian appeals to evidence were pointless, except as a concession to insecurity. Good religion projects a good God out of the self and does so without apology. Emerson resigned from Second Church in October 1832, a year after his beloved wife Ellen died of tuberculosis. Her death devastated him, eliminating his attachment to the church, turning him inward looking.[57]

He journeyed to England and met with Coleridge, Wordsworth, and Thomas Carlyle, judging that all fell woefully short of him: "They have no idea of that species of moral truth which I call the first philosophy." All were dense compared to him, failing to grasp "the extent or the harmony or the depth of their moral nature."[58]

Many American transcendentalists shared Emerson's excitement at making a new religious beginning. His friend Frederick Henry Hedge, a Unitarian minister and son of a Harvard logic professor, declared in 1833 that the true Kantians in America were young liberals steeped in Coleridge. Harvard professors, steeped in Locke, were too simplistic to understand transcendental thinking. Hedge said that Americans had to stop deriding the obscurity of Coleridge and German transcendentalism. Kantian idealism was comprehensible apart from Kant's abstract complexity, and it was possible to take Kant's subjective idealism too far, as Fichte did. Hedge said that Schelling and Coleridge got the right balance. Emerson loved that Hedge talked down to Harvard professors, lauding him as "an unfolding man" whose "living leaping Logos" of an article showed the way.[59]

That got a movement going. In 1836 Hedge, Emerson, and Unitarian minister George Ripley founded a discussion club, eventually called the Transcendental Club. It met whenever Hedge visited Boston from his congregation in Bangor, Maine—thirty times in four years. The core group counted twenty-five members led by Amos Bronson Alcott, William Henry Channing, James Freeman Clarke, Convers Francis, Margaret Fuller, William Henry Furness, Theodore Parker, Elizabeth Palmer Peabody, Sophia Ripley, and Henry David Thoreau. The transcendentalists looked past Coleridge's Anglican encumbrances, lauding him as the prophet of liberated self-authenticating Spirit. Fuller, a feminist literary critic who edited the *Dial* after Emerson founded it in 1839, declared of Coleridge: "To the unprepared he is nothing, to the prepared, everything." Coleridge had said the same thing about Wordsworth's "Intimations Ode." Preparedness had a double meaning in Fuller's usage, because only Hedge and Parker knew the German tradition. Hedge studied for four years in Germany, and Parker was a prodigy autodidact. Most American transcendentalists got their German idealism through Coleridge or French transcendentalist Victor Cousin. Hedge refused to write for the *Dial* because the Emersonians took license with their intuitions and dropped Unitarian Christianity. He spent his later career pleading that Unitarianism worked better within Christianity than as a supposedly pure, nonhistorical, universal religious humanism. Post-Christian Unitarianism, Hedge warned, was a minor religious movement with historical and cultural blinders of its own. It would never scale up, and it rejected Christianity too proudly, not fathoming why Coleridge and Schleiermacher stayed in Christian churches. Coleridge became the icon of Broad Church Anglicanism by claiming his spiritual home. Schleiermacher became the quintessential liberal theologian by constructing a church-based liberal theology.[60]

Christian Theology of Religious Feeling

Throughout his career there were disputes about the weight of Schleiermacher's Romanticism, idealism, and purported pantheism over his theology. He parried with and deflected these arguments constantly, pleading to be understood as he understood himself. But that rarely happened. Routinely Schleiermacher was described, even by allies, as having brought theology into line with a dominant pantheism, idealism, liberalism, or Gnosticism. This outcome had something to do with Schleiermacher's prolonged wavering over his philosophy, which cast an ample shadow over his work. More important, his lengthy prolegomena to his system, *The Christian Faith* (1821, 1830), gave a strong impression of doing theology philosophically. Schleiermacher's introduction ranged over the nature of theological knowledge and the nature, history, and types of religion before taking up doctrinal topics that were themselves prolegomena to Christian revelation. There were over 250 pages of it before he got to his starting point—the God-consciousness of Jesus and Christianity.[61]

In his early career Schleiermacher sought to mediate between Jacobi's fideism and Schelling's transcendental idealism, proposing to conjoin religious feeling and speculative reason as two sides of the human spirit that correspond to each other. Schleiermacher's dialogue, *Christmas Eve* (1806), contained idealist speeches taking this line; more directly, in his lectures of 1811 on dialectic, Schleiermacher argued that the immediate consciousness of God in human beings is expressed through both sides of the human spirit. If feeling and reason do not belong together, the consciousness of God must be split—which would not *be* consciousness of God. Theology and philosophy must go together. Schleiermacher reached for the maximally idealist way of saying it. Since knowing is the totality of all personal existence and never merely a personal consciousness, "knowing is the pure coinciding of reason with being." The congruence of reason and being is unequivocally necessary, since "nothing can proceed from being as such than what also has its subjective grounding in reason as such." If it were conceivable that there might be something different in reason than in being, the very reality belonging to reason would be lost along with the necessity of being: "What we find instead is a reciprocal action in which both endure."[62]

This was the customary post-Kantian construal of the absolute in transcendental terms as the condition of the possibility of experience, replete with the usual post-Kantian equivocations about "identity" not meaning pure coinciding or mere congruence. To Schleiermacher, identity referred to two distinguishable but mutually presupposing categories or two interlocking domains that are distinguishable but inconceivable apart from each other. Unlike Kant, who posited a Moral Guarantor solely as a postulate of practical reason, Schleiermacher posited that God is a necessary postulate of theoretical reason as well. Against Schelling and other absolute idealists, he contended that the divine cannot be known as such but must be *presupposed* as the identity of thought and being. We cannot know God as we know objects of thought, nor can we understand the identity between knowing and the known. We can only presuppose God *as* this identity: "Except to assert that the deity as transcendent being is the principle of all being and as transcendent idea is the formal principle of all knowing, nothing more is to be said of it in the domain of knowing. All else is simply bombast or an admixing of the religious, which is out of bounds here and can actually have only a corruptive effect if placed within the bounds."[63]

Schleiermacher had all of that against him after he claimed to exclude philosophy from his dogmatic system. He continued to say there is no conflict between theology and philosophy, because both are in accord with immediate self-consciousness. But he strenuously denied importing any philosophy into his dogmatics, because philosophy cannot provide the basis for faith. Schleiermacher insisted that theology needs no basis or content other than that which is given to it by the religious self-consciousness of the Christian community. This was all that he claimed to do in *The Christian Faith*, once he got past the cumbersome necessity of locating Christian piety descriptively within the context of world religious history. Constantly he was accused of doing no such thing, which galled him. Instead of achieving real disagreements, he had to protest that he really believed what he said he did, which was ignored or dismissed.

Ten years of hostile reviews and replies came to a head in Schleiermacher's preface to the second edition of *The Christian Faith*, where he denied "most emphatically" that he was the "head of a new theological school" or had founded anything: "I have invented nothing, so far as I remember, except my order of topics and here or there a descriptive phrase." He did not invent a modern theology, his own theology, or anything at all. He merely disclosed the religious truth of Christianity that is common to all Christians and all genuinely religious people. Christianity does not rest on certain ideas derived from reason or revelation, and neither should theology. If theology rests on ideas, intellectuals are sure to own it. Schleiermacher merely explicated Christian religious self-consciousness, distinguishing two elements. There is a consciousness of God derived from a feeling of absolute dependence that is constitutive of human nature. And there is a modification of this God-consciousness caused by every person's inability to give complete reign to God-consciousness in one's heart. The remedy to this problem is the saving influence of Jesus Christ.[64]

He titled his dogmatics *Glaubenslehre*, doctrine of faith, but gave central place to piety (*Frömmigkeit*), not faith, defying a century of rationalist condemnation of Pietism. Schleiermacher began with a theory about the fundamental openness of the self to an other in self-consciousness. In any moment of consciousness, we are aware of our unchanging identity *and* its changing, variable character. This twofold experience discloses the essential constitutive elements of self-consciousness, a self-caused element (*ein Sichselbstsetzen*) and a non-self-caused element (*ein Sichselbstnichtsoge-setzthaben*), which he called the Ego and the Other. The Ego expresses the subject for itself, while the Other expresses the coexistence of the ego with an other. The double constitution of self-consciousness makes it possible for the self, which is constituted only in *relation* to an other, to feel its absolute dependence.[65]

We exist as affective, active, self-conscious creatures only in coexistence with an other. Every self experiences a feeling of dependence, which is common to all determinations of self-consciousness expressing an affective condition of receptivity, and a feeling of freedom, which is common to all determinations expressing movement and change. These feelings are one, Schleiermacher argued, for the subject and the corresponding Other are the same for both.[66]

The totality of all moments of the feelings of dependence and freedom comprises a single reality corresponding in reciprocal relation to an other that makes self-consciousness possible. Since every moment is determined by what is given, which includes objects towards which we experience feelings of freedom, the feeling of absolute dependence cannot be captured or realized in any single moment. But self-consciousness is always awareness of absolute dependence, "for it is the consciousness that the whole of our spontaneous activity comes from a source outside of us in just the same sense in which anything towards which we should have a feeling of absolute freedom must have proceeded entirely from ourselves."[67]

Pre-modern theologies appealed to a notion of God's actuality derived from Scripture, tradition, or rationalistic proof. Schleiermacher's dialectic of freedom and dependence pointed to God's possibility and the limits of the human-spiritual relation. Theology, he argued, rightly approached, is human reflection inspired by the feeling of utter dependence on God and the experience of Christ as Redeemer. Theology begins with and reads off piety, presupposing the affective condition of persons in their innermost self-consciousness. Just as religion is immediate self-consciousness, the dependency and actualization of a self grounded in feeling and involved in thinking and willing, Christian theology is a positive and self-conscious use of language by a subject of religious feeling. There are two levels of self-consciousness—sensible and immediate. At the level of sensible self-consciousness, the self deals with perceptions, ideas, and other objects of awareness. Immediate self-consciousness grounds and unifies all acts of thinking and willing. Feeling is related to immediate self-consciousness, the irreducible essence of the self and presence of undivided existence. Religion, a product of feeling, stands for a person's position as the being on which God and world converge. God is not a being, but rather that which holds all being together, giving integrity to all things.

The essence of any faith is the affective element distinctive to it constant within its various expressions. Schleiermacher allowed that the essence of Christianity is hard to discern among Christianity's profusion of traditions and misguided doctrines, yet it does shine through: the redeeming influence of Christ. Every form of Christianity is rooted in some experience and understanding of Christ's redemptive influence. Every form of Christianity speaks in some way of Christ aiding or making possible the passage from sin or captivity to righteousness.[68]

He acknowledged that most theologies are dreadful in this area. Schleiermacher shuddered at juridical atonement theories in which Christ suffered on the cross to satisfy God's wrath or honor: "The forgiveness of sins is made to depend upon the punishment which Christ suffered, and the blessedness of men itself is presented as a reward which God offers to Christ for the suffering of that punishment." He stressed that atonement theories of this type, besides being morally repugnant, utilize magical thinking. It is ridiculous to imagine "something so inward as blessedness" as being brought about "externally, without any inner basis." Schleiermacher countered that sin is anything that arrests or impedes God-consciousness. Evil is a state of God-forgetfulness, not a state of disobedience to God. To be saved is to be transformed from a state of arrested God-consciousness to a state of potent God-consciousness through the redeeming example of Jesus.[69]

This was the key to the distinctiveness of Christianity. Schleiermacher reasoned that religions are like animal life and grades of consciousness in holding developmental histories. Some are more developed than others, and Christianity is more developed than all. The appropriate rule in this area is that only the true can be the basis for grasping the higher truth of Christianity. Some religions are too similar to Christianity to be entirely false. Moreover, if "primitive" religions contained nothing but error, how was it possible for human communities to move from these religions to

Christianity? All religions are true insofar as they are rooted in piety, which is the consciousness of absolute dependence.[70]

But Schleiermacher argued that other religions construe redemption as a derivative aspect of a controlling doctrine or institution. In Christianity the redeeming influence of Jesus is the key to everything else. His pivotal section on the essence of Christianity put it in the form of a definition: "Christianity is a monotheistic faith, belonging to the teleological type of religion, and is essentially distinguished from other such faiths by the fact that in it everything is related to the redemption accomplished by Jesus of Nazareth." As the unique embodiment of constantly potent God-consciousness, Jesus creates and embodies the possibility of salvation. The redeeming influence of Jesus is the "primary element" in Christianity, which exists only on the basis of this faith and its proclamation. Christianity exalts the redeeming work of Christ and the corresponding experience of redemption in piety. This two-sided concept was the heart of Schleiermacher's theology: "Within Christianity these two tendencies always rise and fall together, the tendency to give pre-eminence to the redeeming work of Christ, and the tendency to ascribe great value to the distinctive and peculiar element in Christian piety."[71]

Despite having friends, a soul mate, and a Redeemer who were Jews, Schleiermacher insisted that Christianity has no special relationship on the level of religious feeling to Judaism. The early Christians who converted from heathenism to Christianity did not have to make a greater leap than those who converted from Judaism to Christianity. To be sure, Jews had a monotheistic tradition on their side, but the Greek and Roman worlds were prepared for monotheism. The greater chasm was between the Jewish religion of law and the Christian religion of grace. Heathens had nothing like that to cross, so more of them came into Christianity. On this basis, Schleiermacher said the "most definitely Jewish" aspects of the Bible had the least value.[72]

Christianity was never a renewal movement within Judaism; it was about all things being made new through a godly example, Jesus Christ. Schleiermacher put it bluntly, with an echo of Kant. The first desire of every uncorrupted heart is to become good, "but to become good, we need an example we can always rely on." Only a perfect example of the good adequately guides our feeling and inspires our reason in the direction of the good: "And it is Christ who gives us this sublime example. . . . He spent the best years of his life going around among the fallen, though for the most part they were ungrateful, to preach the truth to them and to practice virtue among them. Never discouraged by mockery, disdain, persecution, or misinterpretation of his purest motives, his virtue remained ever constant. Everywhere he sought out misery to alleviate it with his gentle healing hand, as he alone always could."[73]

Christ the Redeemer was for Schleiermacher the image of perfected humanity, "the image of a soul constantly at one with God." Christ gave himself for and to human beings so that all people might become one with him, making his righteousness their own. The love that Christ bears for humankind is divine, and through his perfectly God-conscious influence Christ ignites love divine in human hearts. Thus Christ is rightly exalted above all others.[74]

Schleiermacher was emphatic that everyone needs Christ, not merely God-consciousness, because all human beings need fellowship with God, which God-consciousness does not assure. It is possible to be truly religious through the experience of dependence alone, but to have true fellowship with God, one must experience the Redeemer: "The distinctive feature of Christian piety lies in the fact that whatever alienation from God there is in the phases of our experience, we are conscious of it as an action originating in ourselves, which we call Sin; but whatever fellowship with God there is, we are conscious of it as resting upon a communication from the Redeemer, which we call Grace."[75]

Sin-consciousness came into existence only through God-consciousness; Schleiermacher shared Calvin's principle that grace precedes sin-consciousness. Human beings become aware of their sin only after their God-consciousness is awakened. But in Christian experience there is no relation to God (and thus no awareness of sin) that is not bound up with Christ's redeeming influence: "In the actual life of the Christian, therefore, the two are always found in combination: there is no general God-consciousness which has not bound up with it a relation to Christ, and no relationship with the Redeemer which has no bearing on the general God-consciousness." Human subjects owe to Christ the salvation from sin that his redeeming influence brings to their awareness. Because Christians experience Christ as love, they know that God is love. Because they experience Christ as Redeemer, they know they are sinners under God's judgment and grace.[76]

The churchy and traditional feel of *The Christian Faith* surprised many readers of *On Religion*; meanwhile many theologians protested that Schleiermacher stripped Christianity of its cognitive content. By the 1820s Schleiermacher and Hegel were colleagues at Berlin, Schleiermacher was less exalted than Hegel, and Schleiermacher's theology was intensely controversial. Breslau philosopher Christlieb J. Braniss advised Schleiermacher to choose between claiming that God does not intervene in history and Jesus was without sin. Bonn theologian Johann F. F. Delbrück said Schleiermacher's system was incompatible with apostolic Christianity. Leipzig theologian Heinrich Gottlieb Tzschirner said Schleiermacher made Christian faith depend on fantasy. Erlangen theologian Isaaco Rust said Schleiermacher paganized Christianity with his corrupting appeal to feeling. Gotha General Superintendent Karl Gottlieb Bretschneider said Schleiermacher's system was much like Vatican theology and far from Reformation theology. The crowning insult belonged to Hegel, who said Schleiermacher's emphasis on the feeling of absolute dependence reduced religion to something immature and lacking autonomy. Hegel deadpanned that if Schleiermacher was right, "a dog would be the best Christian, since a dog is most strongly characterized by this feeling and lives primarily in this feeling."[77]

Schleiermacher tried to wave off his critics. He had no system of his own, so how could he have opponents? If critics proved that he cut Christianity to fit an idealist or pantheist worldview, or ignored the historical Jesus, or contradicted himself, or paganized Christianity, or Romanized theology, or worst of all, negated Christian freedom, he would renounce *The Christian Faith* and not bother with a second edition. As it was, proof was lacking, so he replied, "I am not what they take me to be."[78]

That did not stem the tide of accusation. Tübingen historicist Ferdinand Christian Baur claimed that Schleiermacher's idealistic Christology was Gnostic. Heidelberg theologian Heinrich J. T. Schmid took the opposite tack, likening Schleiermacher's philosophy to the Alexandrian school. Baur, Bretschneider, and Tzschirner contended that Schleiermacher's doctrines of God and Christ smacked of Schelling-style idealism. Rust said Schleiermacher was a fideist like Jacobi, forsaking the intellectual defense of Christianity. Schleiermacher advised his critics to get together, because they embarrassed themselves with contradictory accusations. He especially disliked the Tübingen school's constant polemic that he was a Gnostic; Schleiermacher paid attention to critical scholarship about Jesus, even from Tübingen, and based everything on the life of Christ in Christians, so he found the Gnostic charge ridiculous. Similarly, the idea that absolute dependence is incompatible with freedom struck him as laughably simplistic, especially coming from the originator of Hegelian dialectic.[79]

Some critiques he took more seriously. Bretschneider denied that feeling and self-consciousness are identical, because some feelings are unconscious or semiconscious, while self-consciousness requires the awareness of one's "I." Feeling can refer only to what is already an object of thought; what matters is the object that produces the feeling, which gives Christianity its specific content. One must have an idea of God before any knowledge of God's determination of one's being is possible. Schleiermacher replied that he had a right to conceive feeling more narrowly, and the upshot about prior knowing was exactly what he disputed. His Romantic starting point was axiomatic for him, not something he could prove. No prior conception of God comes from piety, because it is not read off from the mode of determination of one's being. Schleiermacher knew plenty of intellectuals with sophisticated ideas about God who lacked any feeling for these ideas. If it was possible to have an idea of God without any feeling for it, it followed that no particular idea of God, considered in and of itself, is necessarily constitutive in piety.[80]

As for pantheism, he wearied of having to deny it. His only consolation was that he was tagged an idealist (*Ichheitler*) as often as a pantheist (*All-Einheitler*). Schleiermacher took back nothing from *On Religion*: "Even the sophisticated tone that predominated in it should not be eliminated because it has successfully countered the false sophistication of frivolous negativism." *The Christian Faith* was not pantheist either, because Schleiermacher did not traffic in worldview isms. He explicated the God-consciousness developed in Christianity and nothing else: "Whoever thereby thinks of some philosophy must inevitably become confused, and I have detected such confusion in nearly all of the more extensive reviews of my work."[81]

Even his staunchest allies stoked confusions on this matter, to his distress. Bonn theologian Karl Immanuel Nitzsch, a leading figure in Mediation theology and editor of its journal *Theologische Studien und Kritiken*, was a key example. Nitzsch defended Schleiermacher as a theologian of faith and a critic of dogmatic and speculative doctrines, but he argued that *The Christian Faith* incorporated its distinctively Christian content into a concept of universal religious knowledge. Nitzsch made a Schleiermacher-like argument against his version of Schleiermacher, criticizing *The Christian Faith* for crossing the line into religious philosophy. Schleiermacher repeated his stock reply: Christianity and speculative reason are harmonious *and* they do not belong together. Any notion that Christianity and speculative reason determine each other is toxic for both: "I have been most careful not to deviate even a hair's breadth from this rule." More importantly, "I have never needed a rational theology for my piety, either to nourish it or to understand it. And I have had just as little need of the sensuous theocracy of the Old Testament."[82]

Since virtually every reviewer of *The Christian Faith* misconstrued it, always attributing a religious philosophy to his rendering of the church's faith, Schleiermacher allowed that he must have done something wrong. He was tempted to reverse the two parts of the book's next edition, beginning with Christian consciousness and ending with the parts about religion and method. But that would make for a long anticlimax. You have to set the table before you eat. So Schleiermacher tried harder to make readers understand that he kept his philosophy and theology separate and that his theology merely explicated the faith of the church—its experience of redemption. He did not believe in Christianizing a pre-Christian god or a god of the philosophers, because he believed that in Christ everything is made new.[83]

Schleiermacher found it sad that so many children of the Enlightenment scorned the pinnacle of their heritage and culture, the spirit of Jesus. He implored them not to mock something they did not understand. The cultured despisers of Christianity, in their "proud delusions," ignored that even their weaker lights were borrowed from Christ: "The truths which they attribute to reason's own speculations have been spread abroad only through Christianity." If liberal culture wanted to move forward, it needed to hold onto its spiritual center.[84]

These were the keynotes of the first full-orbed liberal theology, which surpassed in influence all other modern theologies. It worked better as a defense of religion than as an argument for choosing Christianity, and thus had a longer legacy on the former ground. Schleiermacher's strongest argument was about the integrity of religious experience, not his case for Christianity. He tried to have it both ways, defending a theory of religion and a claim about the superiority of Christianity, which made him self-deceiving about the role of idealistic metaphysics in his theology. He took idealism so much for granted that he could deny doing so; idealism was the air that Schleiermacher breathed and the language he spoke.

Very carefully, he avoided conflicts with the old rationalist criticism and the historical criticism of his friend and Berlin colleague Wilhelm Martin L. de Wette. If piety is the essence of religion, religion is safe from historical refutation. If Christianity rests on the experience of redemption through Christ, the heart of gospel faith is not in jeopardy.

Schleiermacher believed that Jesus died on the cross, but he also believed it doesn't matter what happened in the resurrection. What matters is to know Christ as Redeemer, not to believe something about Easter appearances. Christianity needs no foundation besides the experience of Christ's redeeming example and influence *in the church*. Schleiermacher insisted that the personal aspect of Christian existence is necessarily bound up with communal and social aspects. To follow Christ includes being in communion with others on the same path; the church is the Christ-following community in which God-consciousness is the determining power. Many who never read his books heard the gospel through Schleiermacher's eloquent, convictional preaching of it.[85]

His immense prestige as a preacher, Prussian patriot, and thinker built a huge following for Schleiermacher's understanding of Christianity and legitimized it. At home he sustained a loving marriage with a younger spouse who became enamored of occult visions and prophecies. In the church he watched many of his protégés become prominent clerical leaders. In the academy his approach to theology became something of a new orthodoxy, just as he predicted. To many Prussians who knew little or nothing of his theology he was a national hero. The so-called "Restoration" of 1815 launched a new political order, state absolutism, under the guise of the old order of the eighteenth-century princes. Schleiermacher, to many, exemplified the right blend of realism and idealism in dealing with the new order, advocating liberal reforms, working within the system, and standing up for Germany. At his funeral in 1834, thirty thousand Berliners poured into the streets in a display of public mourning unparalleled for a German academic. The funeral procession took several hours. Schleiermacher's friend Heinrich Steffens later recalled: "It was not something arranged but a completely unconscious, natural outpouring of mourning love, an inner boundless feeling which gripped the entire city and gathered about his grave; these were hours of inward unity such as have never been seen in a metropolis of modern times."[86]

Though Schleiermacher claimed he founded no school, he was keenly mindful of the one that formed around him led by Nitzsch, J. K. L. Gieseler, Gottfried Christian Friedrich Lücke, Carl Ullmann, August Twesten, and F. W. C. Umbreit. This industrious group was highly effective in winning academic positions and a place in the church. It pressed for reconciliation between Christianity and science and a union between the Lutheran and Reformed churches. In Schleiermacher's last years he was usually ranked alongside Hegelian theologians Karl Daub and Philipp Marheineke. He had written only one large book; except for disciples, it was hard to foresee how his influence would grow. One reader in Schleiermacher's time, Joachim Christian Gass, got it right, telling Schleiermacher that his system heralded "a new era, not only in this one discipline, but in the whole study of theology in general." A decade later, on the day of Schleiermacher's death, church historian August Neander went further, also accurately: "From him a new period in the history of the Church will one day take its origin." Schleiermacher's school played a large role in creating his legacy. By 1850 he clearly stood above all modern theologians. By 1875 he had nothing like a rival, even as Ritschl sought to improve on him. By 1900 his stature was higher still, to the point that he appeared as the founder of an era, not merely a school or movement.[87]

Thus he caught up to Hegel, at least in theology, decades after both were gone. Hegel endured years of frustrated humiliation as a high school principal, while Schleiermacher rose to eminence in Berlin, but that changed after Hegel wrote his *Science of Logic* and *Encyclopedia*, won a chair at Berlin, and dominated German philosophy. Hegel grieved that Schleiermacher trivialized the truth of Christianity. When Hegel learned that Schleiermacher was writing a dogmatic system, he feared a disaster for Christianity and German civilization, so he taught an emergency course on religion. Schleiermacher ignored the Trinity, yet presumed to speak for the church. To Hegel, that was pathetic. The doctrine of the Trinity brilliantly expresses the dialectical movement of Spirit—God coming into self-knowledge. Hegel admonished that if Schleiermacher could not deal with the Christian doctrine of God, he needed to find a different line of work. Meanwhile Hegel found the great fixation of his later career, the course on religion, which he taught four times and revised constantly.

The first time he blistered Schleiermacher personally. The second time he carried on mercilessly against Schleiermacher, buttressed by the publication of *The Christian Faith*. The third time, Hegel took more interest in his own philosophy of religion, and the fourth time he plunged deeply into world religions, but in every lecture cycle he blasted Schleiermacher. At least Kant talked about something important, moral duty, but Schleiermacher talked about feelings. Hegel chided that feelings are subjective, ephemeral, indiscriminate, and very low on cognition. Hopes and wishes are feelings, and people hope for bad things all the time. Merely feeling something doesn't make anything good or true. One can feel that one is courageous, noble, compassionate, or truthful, but what matters is to be actually courageous, noble, and so on. It doesn't matter that feelings contain good things, because bad things are there too. Conversely, neither does the existence of the content depend on feeling, for all sorts of nonexistent imaginary things exist there. Hegel protested that if feeling is the justifying element of religion, the distinction between good and evil is nullified, for evil is every bit as present in feeling as the good.[88]

Once he warmed to this theme, Hegel had trouble letting it go, notwithstanding his proximity to Schleiermacher's office. Feeling has a place, Hegel allowed, but at the bottom. Dependency has a place too, but at the bottom of any progressive scale of values. Feelings and dependency go together, for in feeling we are at our most dependent. Hegel stressed that people of virtue and accomplishment do not spend a lot of time talking about their feelings. Moreover, people appeal to their feelings when they cannot defend what they are saying, which breaks the commonality between people. Hegel sympathized when people said that God must be felt in one's heart. He assured them he knew what they meant. But what mattered was to hold fast to goodness and truth, not to have nice feelings. Hegel did not have to invoke the Christianity of his dog; his students knew the punch line already.

Schleiermacher, nobly, did not respond in kind. Privately, he told friends that at least he didn't incorporate Satan into God, like Hegel. Hegel was terribly unfair to Schleiermacher. There are subtle differences between the German words for "sensibility" and "feeling" (*Empfindung* and *Gefühl*). To Schleiermacher, sensibility was a product of sensations, which are received in a mode of immediacy as they are found. Feeling, on the other hand, is the activity of a self, an act of consciousness integrating sensations in a reflected totality. Feeling reflects a deeper, higher, and more active form of self-consciousness than sensibility.[89]

In other contexts, Hegel said the same thing. But to Hegel there were bigger things at stake than fine distinctions or his reputation for being fair; thus he blasted Schleiermacher repeatedly. Hegel believed it would be disastrous if Christian theology retreated to subjectivity or the faith of the church. If Christian theologians were unwilling to defend Christian doctrines, somebody had to do it. So Hegel became an unlikely founder of a theological school. Hegel versus Schleiermacher, ever since, has framed a perennial debate in theology.

4

Hegelian Intersubjectivity

Dialectics of Spirit

The greatest philosopher of the modern experience, G. W. F. Hegel, was deeply rooted in Plato, Aristotle, Spinoza, and Kant, and made a creative advance on all of them. He inspired nearly every great philosophical idea and movement of the past two centuries and put dynamic panentheism into play in modern theology. Yet no thinker is as routinely disputed, debated, and misconstrued as Hegel, because his greatest book defies categorization and is notoriously hard to understand, his logical system resembled a gigantic mill, he developed multidimensional concepts that interpreters stripped down and translators couldn't translate, he seemed to celebrate Prussian absolutism, he seemed to sweep differences into the interiorizing logic of his system, and his thought was too Christian for most philosophy departments, so philosophers cast aside his Christian tropes or said they weren't really Christian.

There are many different interpretations of Hegel. The long-dominant one is that he expounded a closed panlogical system, an interpretation variously put forth by countless textbooks, Kierkegaard and the later Friedrich Schelling, every right-Hegelian from Philipp Marheineke to Stanley Rosen, the analytic tradition headed by Bertrand Russell and G. E. Moore, and the doyens of postmodern criticism, Derrida, Levinas, and Gilles Deleuze. On this view, Hegel developed an absolute idealistic metaphysic based on Kant's transcendental ego, Aristotle's final causation, and Hegel's logical mill, identifying thought with sense and being. His system was his logic, a teleology into which he folded all of history. Even if Hegel discovered social subjectivity—which is rarely recognized on this reading—his thought was too panlogical to make room for real subjectivity. Hegel's monist teleological ontology was a totalizing shell lacking any room for real difference or contingency; thus, Hegelian "difference" is really sameness.[1]

The second historic school of interpretation began with left-Hegelians in the 1830s and was refashioned by left-Hegelians in the 1930s. David Friedrich Strauss founded the left-Hegelian tradition in 1835 by contending that Hegel devised a radical theological basis for a new Christianity, albeit with pious encumbrances that Strauss eliminated. In the early 1840s Bruno Bauer, Ludwig Feuerbach, and Arnold Ruge said that Strauss did not go far enough, for Hegelianism makes sense only as post-Christian radical humanism, not a reconstruction of Christianity. Young Karl Marx cut his intellectual teeth on this contention, briefly self-identifying as a left-Hegelian. In the 1930s Russian-born French philosopher Alexander Kojève renewed the atheist left-Hegelian reading by contending that Hegel construed Christianity as an enemy of freedom. Hegel's dialectic of master and slave is the key to Hegelianism, he sought to complete the French Revolution, he conceived Christianity as a form of slavery, and the key to Marxism is Hegel's dialectic, applied to actual history. Georges Bataille, Jean Hyppolite, Jacques Lacan, and Maurice Merleau-Ponty absorbed this argument directly from Kojève in his famous lectures at the Ecole pratique des hautes; later they were joined by Max Horkheimer, Herbert Marcuse, and Jean-Paul Sartre in expounding Hegelian neo-Marxism.[2]

A latter-day offshoot of the left-Hegelian tradition similarly reduces Hegel to phenomenology, social philosophy, and sometimes logic, while dropping Marxian assumptions and apologetics. Here the Hegel that matters is the social philosopher who discovered social subjectivity and theorized about discourse and the struggle for recognition. Some interpreters in this camp contend that Hegel was essentially a post-Kantian or more Kantian than he seemed; some allow that he unfortunately espoused a teleological spirit monism; and some claim that Hegel was a closet humanist who used religious language strategically. However these differences sort out, Hegel remains philosophically relevant for his phenomenology and social philosophy; thus he can still be taught in philosophy departments, shorn of his baleful metaphysics, ontology, and philosophy of nature. Leading proponents of this approach include Frederick

Beiser, Robert Brandom, Judith Butler, Jürgen Habermas, Axel Honneth, Rolf-Peter Horstmann, John McDowell, Terry Pinkard, Robert Pippin, and Robert C. Solomon. Catholic versions of this argument variously advanced by William Desmond, Charles Taylor, and Merold Westphal contend that Hegel's onto-theology was bad ontology and bad theology compared to Catholic philosophical theology, since nobody believes that the universe is spirit positing itself out of rational necessity.[3]

A fourth category of interpreters draws upon the left-Hegelian emphasis on phenomenology and social subjectivity without lopping off or explaining away Hegel's religious basis. Many interpreters in this line are religiously musical, sometimes emphasizing that Hegel began and remained a philosopher of love who fused phenomenology and ontology. To grasp why religion mattered to Hegel, one has to take seriously what he said about it, without recycling right-Hegelian theology. Strauss and Ferdinand C. Baur were pioneers of this approach in the nineteenth century; later interpreters in this category include John W. Burbidge, Martin J. De Nys, Emil Fackenheim, Hille Haker, Dieter Henrich, Peter C. Hodgson, Eberhard Jüngel, Richard Kroner, Quentin Lauer, Thomas A. Lewis, George Rupp, Dale M. Schlitt, Andrew Shanks, Paul Tillich, Robert R. Williams, Rowan Williams, and me.[4]

Another interpretive school resumes the metaphysical reading of Hegel without returning to the right-Hegelian system or any particular interest in religion. Here it is argued that Hegel was a conceptual realist with a robust metaphysic in the line of Aristotle or Spinoza. Leading advocates of this view include Stephen Houlgate, James Kreines, Robert Stern, Kenneth Westphal, and Christopher Yeomans.[5]

The sixth line of interpreters derives from the deconstructionist tradition of Heidegger and Derrida, but disputes the panlogical reading of Hegel espoused by Derrida, Levinas, and Deleuze. Here it is argued that Hegel's emphasis on negation, groundless freedom, and difference paved the way to postmodern deconstruction. Leading Hegel interpreters in this line include Bruno Bosteels, Clayton Crockett, Catherine Malabou, Jean-Luc Nancy, Mark C. Taylor, and Slavoj Žižek.[6]

All these interpretive traditions have a basis in Hegel's thought. I shall argue that Hegel's system is a creative interpretation of Christian ideas and that Hegel made a breakthrough advance on his closest philosophical company, J. G. Fichte and Friedrich Schelling, by theorizing an intersubjective concept of Spirit as the *Gestalt* of the world, not a *Gestalt* of consciousness. The "I" exists concretely as self-recognition in others, not as the "I am I" of Kantian idealism. But I acknowledge that there is a basis in Hegel's work to interpret him as an inflated right-Hegelian or a contradictory puzzle, because Hegel was impossibly complex and elusive.

In the mid-1790s Kant was elderly and fading, Fichte was prominent for amplifying Kant's subjective idealism, and a group of youthful post-Kantian idealists in Berlin, Jena, and Frankfurt began to talk about the absolute. Fichte struggled with the ethical problem of the other, which Kant ignored, but the first edition of Fichte's *Wissenschaftslehre* (*The Science of Knowledge*), published in 1794, was an extreme version of subjective idealism, taking Kant's methodological idealism all the way to a totalizing ego philosophy. Fichte never overcame the cul-de-sac impression of his original edition, even though he revised the book constantly afterwards. He went down in the history of philosophy as the apostle of taking Kant to an absurdly solipsistic conclusion, even though Fichte flipped to ontological idealism in his edition of 1804, asserting the priority of being over the ego. One notable post-Kantian, Hegel, kept up with Fichte's shifting position and was influenced by him, while rejecting Fichte's core assumption that sociality is a threat to freedom and rationality. Others such as Samuel Taylor Coleridge didn't bother to keep up, typing Fichte's position as egomania. In the early going, however, Hegel seemed far less brilliant than the company he kept. Schelling, Schleiermacher, Friedrich Schlegel, Friedrich von Hardenberg (Novalis), Friedrich Hölderlin, and August Ludwig Hülsen were promising post-Kantians smacking of genius. Coleridge was an English outsider known for his poetry. Hegel, showing no sign of genius, was an insider to this discussion only because he was a friend of Schelling and Hölderlin.[7]

The absolute was a variation on Spinoza's doctrine of substance. To Spinoza, the key to substance was its independent or self-sufficient essence, something that does not depend on anything else. Substance had to be infinite, because anything less than the whole of all things would depend on something outside itself. Schelling called it "the unconditioned," the "in-itself," or, interchangeably, the absolute, a usage that Hegel and the absolute idealists adopted.[8]

The absolute idealists said that Kant failed to explain the reality of the external world, he turned nature into a mere instrument or medium of moral action, and Fichte made both problems worse. Nature, to Kant and Fichte, was subordinate to the striving of a moral subject, deriving its value from ethical ends imposed upon it. To the absolute idealists, nature was an end in itself worthy of spiritual appreciation. Schelling, a boy genius and Romantic, was the highest achieving post-Kantian until 1810, when he flamed out from heartbreak. Hölderlin, equally brilliant and Romantic, wrote shimmering lyric poetry until 1802, when he descended into schizophrenia. Hegel, a slow starter, got his fundamental concept, love, from Hölderlin, notwithstanding that Hegel was only briefly a Romantic. Then Hegel fashioned love into his richest concept, Spirit, surpassing Schelling by discovering the idea of a self-transforming social subject of experience and action.

Georg Wilhelm Friedrich Hegel was born in Stuttgart, in the southern German duchy of Württemberg, in 1770, near the end of the premodern reign of kings. His Lutheran family had been in Swabia for nearly a century and a half, inhabiting a Protestant enclave surrounded by Catholic territories. His father was a lawyer, a financial official in the duchy court, which made him a member of the non-noble notable class, the *Ehrbarkeit*. Hegel grew up highly self-conscious of his in-between status while attending Latin school and the Stuttgarter *Gymnasium Illustre*. From the beginning he read voraciously to acquire ideas and outperform his classmates. His mother died when he was eleven, and Hegel never warmed to his father. In 1788 he enrolled at Tübingen, where virtually all Württemberg notables had studied since the fifteenth century. Officially, Hegel enrolled as a theology student. He had G. E. Lessing in his head, imagining a literary career as an Enlightenment religious intellectual. As it was, he would not have received state funding had he not aimed for the ministry.[9]

Tübingen had declined drastically from its storied past as an outpost of semifeudal scholasticism. Nepotism was rampant; professors still came from a small number of privileged intermarried families; and not much was left of the university besides the Protestant seminary, the *Stift*. Hegel derided the school as a pathetic throwback. He cut classes, sneered at theologically conservative faculty, and befriended Schelling and Hölderlin, his seminary classmates. The three friends studied Jacobi and Kant, bonding with a young Kantian on the faculty, Carl Immanuel Diez. Schelling and Hölderlin absorbed Kant's critiques and became intellectual partners to each other, while Hegel failed to keep up. The difference played out for twenty years.

Schelling and Hölderlin had brilliant early careers and Hegel did not. Schelling poured out books blending Spinoza, Kant, and Fichte, winning Fichte's attention. Hölderlin tutored for the family of a Frankfurt banker, wrote poems and a novel that naturalized the forms of classical Greek verse, fell in love with the banker's wife Susette Gontard, looked out for Hegel, and was crushed when he had to forsake Gontard. Hegel wrote a breezy Kantian essay that wasn't very good, casting Jesus as a Kantian, and wrote a better essay about love divine, groping for his theme. In 1798 Fichte was fired from Jena, being too contentious not to get fired from every job he ever held. Schelling won the position as a rising star who said that Fichte should not have conceived nature as an organic product of consciousness. Good idealism, Schelling argued, derives nature from mind and mind from nature. The human ego is the highest potency of the powers of nature. Nature is the source of creative intelligence, and reason is able to abstract from the subjectivity of the ego to reach the point of pure subject-object identity.[10]

In 1800 Hegel wrote a painfully awkward letter to Schelling that saved his career. He was floundering, as he half admitted. Hölderlin had begun to unravel, causing him to leave Frankfurt, which stranded Hegel. Hegel asked to be rescued without quite saying it. Schelling came through, inviting Hegel to live with him in Jena, the hub of German Romanticism. Jena boasted Friedrich and Dorothea Schlegel, August and Caroline Schlegel, two renowned Romantic journals, J. C. Friedrich Schiller, Novalis, and Schelling's journal. Schelling gave Hegel a job as his coeditor, and Hegel repaid the double favor by writing a book defending Schelling, *The Difference between Fichte's and Schelling's System of Philosophy* (1801). Schelling had written so many books that no one except Hegel managed to keep up. Hegel explained that Schelling was better than Fichte because Fichte conceived the absolute as subjective in the form of cognition, while Schelling conceived it as objective in the form of being.[11]

Schelling and Hegel, working together in the early 1800s, argued that Kant wrongly dichotomized between form and content, which yielded a strangely abstract philosophy that knew only appearances, not reality. Kant described a real problem, but fixed on an elementary mode of self-consciousness in which form and content are separate, yielding a dualistic theory of knowledge predicated on the dichotomy between a knowing subject and its objects of consciousness. Schelling and Hegel acknowledged that Kant's first and third *Critiques* had passages smacking of objective idealism that cut against Kant's dualistic impasse—the key to improving upon Kant. Objective idealism, or better, absolute idealism, reconstructed Kant's principle of subject-object identity. It was not about the self-knowledge of a finite subject. It was about the self-knowledge of the absolute within a finite subject. Instead of trapping subject-object identity inside the circle of its own representations, the answer was to lift subject-object identity outside this circle by equating the self-knowledge of a knowing subject with the self-knowledge of the absolute.[12]

Post-Kantian idealism, as conceived by Schelling and Hegel, reworked Spinoza, Kant, Fichte, and the Platonic doctrine that all knowledge participates in divine self-knowledge. My knowledge is not merely something that I know from my own consciousness. It is knowledge of the absolute through the object itself. Schelling put it vividly: "Not I know, but the all knows in me, if the knowledge that I call mine is an actual and true knowledge."[13]

We do not know the absolute. The absolute knows itself, through us. Human subjects lack any power to know the absolute, which is not something that exists outside human subjects. Schelling and Hegel got that far together. Then Schelling got in trouble for marrying Caroline Schlegel, whose husband August took it generously, but Jena was outraged, causing Schelling to flee to Würzburg in 1803. Now Hegel was stranded again with no real job, a marginal lecture post at the University of Jena, and no major book. For three years he wrote scraps of books and kept starting over. In 1806 he finally got rolling on what became *The Phenomenology of Spirit*. Schelling, at the time, was in a Parmenidian phase, envisioning the absolute as pure self-identity, an ultimate identity of thought and being in which only forms are different, and even forms are only quantitatively different, not qualitatively. That was a dead end, occurring shortly before Schelling's beloved Caroline died of dysentery in 1809 and Schelling lost his book-writing ebullience. Hegel reasoned that absolute idealism, to justify its claim to knowledge, needed an account of the coming-to-be of knowledge itself. Nobody *begins* with absolute knowledge, as if it could be shot from a gun. To Hegel, the crucial question was whether the absolute could be grasped and expressed as subject, not only as substance.

This was the burden of *The Phenomenology of Spirit*—to show that finite knowledge is bound up with knowledge of the infinite. Plus, Hegel was desperate to win an academic position, amid Napoleonic smashing that dissolved twenty-two German universities. The fact that he half admired Napoleon helped him cope with Napoleon's dramatically negative impact on his job prospects. Schelling, Hegel believed, had the right project, describing the dialectical development of consciousness in which the universal and the particular come together. But Schelling confined himself to what is revealed in nature and history, which led to

Parmenidian nowhere. Hegel pressed on to the logical Idea, pure thought itself, which is not the idea of something.

Hegel completed his sprawling, rollicking, brilliant *Phenomenology* in 1806 shortly after Napoleon routed Jena. The book was a panoramic extravaganza that Hegel failed to reorganize after he found his argument. There were chapters on philosophical method (the preface), Hegel's method (the introduction), Consciousness, Self-Consciousness, Reason, Spirit, Religion, and Absolute Knowing, but Hegel structured it on the triad of consciousness, self-consciousness, and reason, so most of the book fell under the third category. Reason became the culmination of a triad ("C") and the heading ("AA") for all that followed on Spirit, Religion, and Absolute Knowing, all in the severely formal style that Kant bequeathed to philosophy. Hegel declared that prefaces are pointless in philosophy, which expounds universal truth. Then he took off on a forty-five-page preface, by far the book's best chapter, followed by ten pages of introduction, the book's original introduction. *Phenomenology* raced through methodological debates, epistemology, religious beliefs, stories, smart-aleck asides, ethical theory, Greek tragedy, medieval court culture, modern science, pseudoscience, Romanticism, and much more. It turned on Kant's distinction between understanding (*Verstand*) and reason (*Vernunft*), with a post-Kantian twist that Hegel carried over from his *Difference Between* book. Understanding is finite, sticks to fixed determinations, is based on the principle of noncontradiction, works on things given to it, and conceives the finite and infinite as mutually exclusive. Reason is infinite, apprehends the dialectical interplay of differences, works on materials that it gives itself, and apprehends the reciprocal interrelation of the finite and infinite. Every Hegel book and lecture series afterward turned on this distinction.[14]

In *Kantian Reason and Hegelian Spirit* (2012), I analyzed a forest of theories and debates about *Phenomenology*. Here I will cut straight to what I think. Those who claim it is two or more books, or no book at all, have ample evidence to cite from its bewildering swirl of subjects and strange structure, for Hegel ended up with a different book than he started. He began by replying to Kant about how consciousness relates to objects, the relation of a self to an object. Then he found himself writing about the social relation of spirit to itself. Hegel's subject became a self-relation in relation to an object—a social, temporal, historical, self-transforming subject of experience and action. His second preface was vastly better than the first one because the book was a voyage of discovery, as he told his students. Many believe he should have wrangled a real book from the messy first draft that he published. I believe he shifted course in the Reason chapter without failing to deliver a coherent argument.[15]

Kant described his transcendental inquiry into the a priori presuppositions of physics as a "phenomenology" of the transformation of appearances into experience. Hegel took Kant's phenomenology of the movement in nature as his model, proposing to track the movement of spirit in history. *Phenomenology* is an analysis of the development and shapes of Spirit, with a systematic part leading to a historical part that blends both kinds of interpretation of the movement of Spirit's thinking itself. Hegel was indebted to Plato, who constructed the world out of pure abstract universals, and to Aristotle, who taught that the knower and the known have a transparent relationship; in a crucial sense, the thinker and the thinker's thoughts are one. But *Phenomenology* was stunningly original in theorizing the emergence of social subjectivity. Hegel rejected empirical, naturalistic, and transcendental understandings of subjectivity. He named the book perfectly, as it tracked the emergence of social subjectivity in structures of life.[16]

Phenomenology dispensed with the chapters on logic that Hegel had planned, making room for his elaborate rendering of the collective self-determination of Spirit toward Absolute Knowing—a creepy-sounding destination that misleads all interpreters who read *Phenomenology* as closed-system metaphysics. "Absolute Knowing," to Hegel, was the *eros* of philosophy, not the static imputation of divine omniscience into human wisdom. On the other hand, the no-unity theories about *Phenomenology* are exaggerated, as the book was always a phenomenology of spirit. Persistently, through all of Hegel's prolix theorizing, storytelling, and seeming digressions, he sought to penetrate behind the views and stories on display to the human reality they reflected. *Phenomenology* was a theory of knowledge *and* a philosophy of history *and* an introduction to Hegel's system, but none of these things conventionally. It asked what kind of spirit was behind and within the subjects that Hegel analyzed. It tracked the yearning of the "unhappy consciousness," trapped in a world of despair and death, for which the real is always somewhere else, in eternity. The many scholars who see no feeling in Hegel miss that he described the unhappy consciousness as a feeling—the lived experience of an agonizing (*schmerzliche*) struggle with despair and death. *Phenomenology* was a *phenomenology* of Spirit because Hegel's method was descriptive, allowing the immanent development of the subject matter to disclose itself. In the unhappy consciousness, the pure subjectivity of substance is experienced immediately, unlike the experience of substance as object.

Hegel took for granted that philosophy is about the absolute: "The True is the whole." But the whole, the absolute, realizes itself only through its development; its very nature is to be a *result*, "the spontaneous becoming of itself." The absolute is the self-reflection and self-determining activity of the "I," a transforming *process*, not a special kind of substance. Hegel countered the supposition that the absolute cannot be a result, noting that "absolute" and "divine" do not express their content any more than "zoology" expresses all animals. All such terms and their use in propositions contain a "becoming-other" that is either mediated or must be taken back. His famous definition of mediation was a gloss on the absolute as self-determining activity: "Mediation is nothing beyond self-moving selfsameness, or is reflection into self, the moment of the 'I' which is for itself pure negativity or, when reduced to its pure abstraction, *simple becoming*." There is no truth without reflection, which is a moment of the absolute.[17]

The process of becoming is a return to simplicity. Hegel analogized that an embryo is a human being in itself, but not for itself. It becomes a human being for itself only through the cultivation of reason, which makes itself what it is in itself. Just as Aristotle defined nature as purposive activity, Hegel defined reason as purposive activity, "the unmoved which is also *self-moving*, and as such is Subject." Viewed abstractly, the power of reason to move is "*being-for-self* or pure negativity," which ends at the same place as the beginning because the beginning *is* the purpose. Hegel did not shrink from teleology, although he allowed that externalist forms of it brought teleological reasoning into disfavor. The actual, he argued, is the same as its idea in only one sense: "The immediate, as purpose, contains the self or pure actuality within itself." Existent actualities are unfolded movements of realized purpose; the self *is* the restless unfolded becoming that relates to itself and returns to itself.[18]

Hegel loved one idea above all others: the absolute as *Spirit* (*Geist*). This concept was not merely his refashioning of Kant's transcendental ego or transcendental unity of apperception, although plenty of Hegel interpreters read him that way, draining the idea of its intersubjective drive for recognition. Hegel reasoned that if truth is actual only as system, and if substance is essentially subject, "the spiritual alone is the *actual*." Spirit is that which has being in itself, that which relates itself to itself, that which has "other-being" and being-for-self, and that which, in its self-externality, abides within itself. In other words, Spirit is that which is in and for itself. It is an object to itself and reflects into itself. At first, Hegel cautioned, the being of Spirit in and for itself is only for human subjects, as spiritual substance. But insofar as Spirit is its own self for itself, this self-generation is the "objective element" of its existence. Only in the modern age did the supremely sublime idea of the absolute as unfolding interpersonal Spirit emerge. Hegel said this was what modern religion and science should be about, for science is precisely Spirit developed to the point of knowing itself as Spirit.[19]

Here I am compelled to say a word about the forest of interpretations, because much of the Hegel literature expounds Geist only as a Kantian logical concept. J. N. Findlay's right-Hegelian classic, *Hegel: A Re-Examination* (1958), is a venerable example, as is R. C. Solomon's much-quoted "Hegel's Concept of *Geist*" (1972). Findlay rightly traced Hegel's concept of Spirit to Kant's doctrine of transcendental self-consciousness and to Fichte's doctrine of the self-positing Ego—a being incapable of existing except through the act of self-consciousness in which it asserts its own being. To Fichte, the endlessly striving activity of the Ego was practical, seeking to know the world and to ethically change it. Hegel, Findlay said, adopted Fichte's schematic opposition between ego and non-ego without accepting Fichte's verdict that philosophy rests on a pure "ought," a matter of faith. To Hegel, Spirit is the truth of everything, the principle of unity and universality that fully understands the world by conceiving the world as the material of its own activity. Hegel taught that the truth of the world "lay in self-conscious Spirit," and no other way of viewing the world catches the truth.[20]

Solomon followed Findlay's interpretive line, described Hegelian Geist as "some sort of general consciousness," employed "spirit" and "mind" as interchangeable terms for it, denied that Hegel was any kind of mystic, and defended Hegel against the charge that he abused Kant's doctrine of the transcendental ego. In a subsequent book, *In the Spirit of Hegel* (1983), Solomon wonderfully humanized Hegel in his context, describing him as a "very humanist" conceptual anthropologist and an "anti-religious and anti-metaphysical proponent of the varieties of human experience." But if Solomon was going to defend Hegelian Geist, it had to be stripped of mystical and interpersonal content even as he acknowledged that Hegel's actual usage of Geist was "fundamentally a religious concept" geared to overcome the disharmonies in Christianity. To understand Hegel, Solomon argued, we must put aside Hegel's own instructions. Hegelian Geist makes sense only as Hegel's admirable resolution of the perplexities left by Kant's ego. Descartes and Kant drove philosophy into the ditch of methodological solipsism in which a philosophical proposition can be justified only from a first-person standpoint. Knowledge of any X implies an I that apprehends the X. Hegel, Solomon said, delivered philosophy from the solipsistic I by rendering the subject of philosophy as subject, not an individuated person. Hegelian Geist, the transcendental ego, is literally general—the unifying principle of consciousness and the underlying rational will behind all the activity of practical reason. It is Kant's transcendental ego shorn of the unwarranted assumption that there is "one ego per person." Solomon allowed that Hegel sometimes personified Geist in the singular as the divine subject. But these parts of Hegel have to be scuttled to save what Hegel really meant and achieved.[21]

Some interpreters acknowledge that Hegel conceived Geist as a Kantian logical principle *and* as intersubjective striving. H. F. Fulda identifies the logical sense of Hegelian Geist in terms of Fichte's ego that divides itself, opposes itself to itself, and overcomes this disunity by restoring its identity. The other, on this account, is an outcome of the logical operation of negation, lacking any independent status. But Fulda says that Hegel also conceived Geist as the process of self-abandonment and finding selfhood in the other. Instead of rendering the ego as absolute, like Fichte, Hegel construed self-knowledge as a process of self-externalization that requires an intersubjective other. Determinate negation, on this account, is an element in self-recognition in and of the other; the other mediates self-knowledge. Fulda does not relate these two conceptions of Hegelian Geist, though he does say that the second sense, not the logical ego, is primary for Hegel.[22]

Robert Pippin says that Hegel failed to integrate the chief threads of his concept of Geist until he succeeded only partially in his later work. Pippin robustly explicates Hegel's doctrine of social subjectivity without believing that it solves the problem of the Kantian ego or justifies Hegel's entire project. Hegel did not demonstrate that conceptual determinations of any and all kinds develop internal to any subject's *self*-understanding. Rather, he elaborated a "radical and complex" theory of a collective, socially self-realizing subject that he justified only in parts. Pippin lacks Hegel's religious impulse, but acknowledges that Hegel did not fall back on a Neoplatonist theory of conceptual emanation. The socially self-realizing Spirit of *Phenomenology* is supposedly the same subjectivity described in the *Logic*. Pippin, doubtful that it is the same subjectivity, argues that Hegel synthesized his logical and social-subjective concepts only when he wrote the *Encyclopedia* and shifted gears, developing the idea of objective Spirit.[23]

That may be correct. On the other hand, Pippin has the usual problem of interpreters who seek to salvage something from Hegel without sharing his religious motivation. The significance of recognition in Hegelian Geist was overlooked in Hegel scholarship until the 1980s partly because it reflects the core religious character of Hegel's thought. Spirit emerges, in *Phenomenology*, as a consequence of reciprocal recognition—the I that is a We, and a We that is an I. The transcendental ego is an abstraction from Spirit, which first emerges as intersubjective recognition. Hegel boldly claimed to improve on Neoplatonist Christianity by conceiving reason as a dialectical unity of opposites; reason is determined as self-recognition in others, not as a self-contained Logos or transcendental ego. The I exists concretely as self-recognition in the other, the doubling of consciousness and mutual self-recognition. Knowledge in its first phase, immediate Spirit, is mere sense-consciousness, the early stage of awareness at which Kant got stuck. Hegel argued that single individuals are incomplete Spirits. Even a robustly autonomous rational will is no substitute for social subjectivity. Genuine knowledge is earned only at higher stages of the coming-to-be of Spirit, which are social and spiritual. Sadly, modern idealists succumbed to new formalisms. Kant had no answer to the problem of how pure concepts relate to anything real; he had only a lifeless schema endowing forms with some determination of the schema as a predicate. Predicates such as objectivity, magnetism, or contraction could be multiplied to infinity, each could be used as a form for another—and almost nothing was learned![24]

The thing-in-itself doctrine was similarly anemic. Hegel allowed that the inner world is empty for consciousness before consciousness finds itself in it. Kant was right that we have no knowledge of this inner world in its immediacy. But this is not because reason is so limited, Hegel argued. In the void *nothing* is known, or, considered from the other side, the inner world is the *beyond* of consciousness. A blind person placed amid the wealth of the supersensible world and a seeing person placed in pure darkness or pure light see the same nothing. If nothing further happens to our inner world in our connection to the world of appearances, we can only stop at the world of appearances, perceiving something as true even as we know it is not true. In that case, Hegel said, we are better off with fanciful imagination than with Kant's emptiness, for even reveries are better than emptiness.[25]

The inner world comes into being from the world of appearances that mediates its coming to self-consciousness. Hegel reasoned that appearance is the essence and content of the inner world, for inward being is essentially the *truth* of appearance. Kant's supersensible realm, cut off from anything known, is in fact appearance qua appearance. Hegel did not mean the supersensible world *is* the sensuous world, or even the world as it exists for immediate sense-certainty. The world of appearance is the world of sense-knowledge and perception *posited* as an *inner* world, not as something that positively *is*. The inner world comes into being in-itself, as a universal lacking content, for the understanding. The inner essential is the truth of appearance, which stands in a negative—but not merely negative—relation to appearances. Self-consciousness arises from the "play of forces" that are immediate for the understanding. Force and its expression are dialectical, involving solicited force (a passive medium) and soliciting force (an active, negative unity). In itself, the play of forces is nothing; Hegel said it exists positively only as a mediating agency. The inner world becomes connected to the understanding through the mediating play of forces, which is the movement of the understanding through which the inner world fills itself out for the understanding. In other words, the understanding is driven to the principle in all things. The play of forces is immediate for the understanding, but "the True" is the simple inner world.[26]

Consciousness already involves self-consciousness, and self-consciousness is thoroughly mediated and dependent upon structures of reduplicated relation. Self-consciousness is essentially a return from otherness. In conscious self-certainty, Hegel explained, what is true for consciousness is something other than itself, which vanishes in its experience. In self-consciousness, we enter "the native realm of truth." The breakthrough to self-consciousness is a reflective movement in which self-consciousness distinguishes from itself "only itself as itself." Here, otherness appears in the form of a being, as a distinct moment, and in the unity of self-consciousness with itself, which is essential to self-consciousness.[27]

Self-consciousness, in its lowest form, *is* desire. The sensuous object of desire is only a means; what self-consciousness ultimately desires is unity of the I with itself. Self-consciousness, without yet realizing it fully, desires its own desire. Consciousness becomes aware of itself as self-consciousness by realizing that the other that it contemplates is an internal self-distinction repulsed from its I. Consciousness of the other, in its first stage, is simply a consciousness of the otherness of self-consciousness.

It is consciousness of distinction, the moment of self-consciousness. For self-consciousness to realize itself completely, it must realize its universality. This is what Hegel called Reason, grasping the world as a moment of self-consciousness driven by desire. Until self-consciousness becomes Reason, only observers know it. Self-consciousness in its early development does not understand its own appearance as the realization of Reason, and it is not merely the Cartesian ego. Hegel was an Aristotelian who conceived subjectivity as embodied in the world. Life, or more precisely, the lifeworld, is the context in which self-consciousness emerges as a social infinite. The Cartesian pre-reality ego, on this account, is an abstraction from the restless infinity of life.[28]

Kant taught that in making judgments, we follow the rules spontaneously prescribed for us by the Understanding, which are produced by the requirements of every self-conscious subject's reasoning. Hegel questioned on what authority the Understanding issues its purported rules for a universal self-consciousness. What if our desires are like sensory impressions? What if they acquire normative significance only because we confer significance on them? Hegel judged that Kant's ethic of issuing laws to oneself lacked a credible warrant. In its place he socialized the problem, analyzing the relationship of slave and master as an example of independence and dependence in self-consciousness.

The Struggle for Freedom and the World as Spirit

Self-consciousness exists only in being acknowledged; it exists only for another. Hegel explained that when self-consciousness encounters another self-consciousness, it comes out of itself, finding itself in an *other* being; moreover, it supersedes the other in doing so. Sociality is as essential to the being of self-consciousness as pure self-consciousness. The I of immediate self-consciousness exists for itself; its dissolution leads to a consciousness that exists for another; in the beginning these two shapes of consciousness coexist in an unequal union of opposition and dependency. One is the master (*Herr*), whose essential nature is to be for itself. The other is the slave or vassal (*Knecht*), whose essential nature is to live for another. Each is the "negative" of the other, each demands recognition from the other, and each has a need for the other to affirm that the law one enacts is right.[29]

Hegel told an idealized story about the struggle between them. A fight to the death ensues between a master and slave. The master prevails because he does not fear death as much as the slave; the slave consents to bondage out of this fear. There are no laws; each experiences the other as making brute demands in a predatory struggle for survival. When the master attains dominance, he becomes the author of the law.

This seems to be a resolution of some kind, however terrible for the slave. But the master's dominance does not work even for the master, because the slave, as a slave, cannot provide a warrant for the master's authority, and the master's self-consciousness depends on the things he consumes, which he owes to the slave's labor. The master's autonomy depends on the mediation of the slave; he is not a master if the slave does not recognize his authority. But the master has no reason to believe that the slave has any authority to confer authority on him. In Hegel's telling, the master simply imposes his lawless will on the slave. The slave, on the other hand, by obeying the master's rule, internalizes the idea of a moral right. Through his labor he becomes a reflective agent, learning there is such a thing as subjecting oneself to an external law. Previously he simply feared for his life; now he masters himself, relying on his self-chosen obedience to the law, and he begins to notice that the world is created by his labor. Seeing himself reflected in the products he makes, and thus no longer alienated from his labor, the slave achieves self-consciousness, rising above the trivial, possession-oriented consciousness of the master.[30]

This is the most famous section of the *Phenomenology*. It has a rich legacy in Marxist and socialist conceptions of the class struggle, owing partly to Marx's acknowledgment that Hegel grasped the social determination of the self and the importance of alienated labor in history. The master-slave trope influenced Nietzsche's critique of master-slave morality, Martin Buber's analysis of relationality and the struggle for recognition, Simone de Beauvoir's account of the dynamics of gender relations, and Frantz Fanon's critique of colonial racism. It is a key to Hegel's influence in psychoanalytic, political, structuralist, poststructuralist, postcolonial, critical race, and feminist theory, where Hegel's grounding of right in intersubjective purpose and his insights into psychological and sociological conflict are foundational. It got its longest self-standing run in twentieth-century neo-Marxism, building on Kojève's contention that the entire *Phenomenology* is a proto-Marxist critique of oppression—a philosophical anthropology demonstrating that human beings are self-made and historical without remainder. The latter interpretation was taken over by Marcuse, Sartre, Hyppolite's canonical commentary on the *Phenomenology*, and two generations of neo-Hegelian Marxists seeking a thicker account of human sociality than Marx's.[31]

Kojève read the *Phenomenology* as a tale about the Slave alone being able to create a new world of his making where freedom reigns. He explicitly discarded whatever metaphysical meaning Hegel had in mind, fixing on the parts of Hegel's analysis that were congenial to Marxism. In neo-Marxist readings, the Slave's first ideological resort was Stoicism, through which he tried to persuade himself that he was actually free by virtue of possessing an abstract idea of freedom. But that didn't work, and the Slave opted for Christianity after it arose, becoming a Christian Slave. The Slave became the equal of the Master before God, now enslaved to a divine Master. Hegel, on this account, taught that the Christian God reduces the Slave to the most absolute slavery imaginable in exchange for being told that he deserves to be treated as a child of God no less than the old masters. The motive for accepting abasement is the same as before, except this is worse. The storied Slave accepted slavery out of fear of losing his biological life. The Christian Slave accepts slavery as the price of his eternal life.[32]

Hegelianism, thus construed, is about something antithetical to Christianity—the triumph of freedom. The Hegelian struggle for freedom runs through Christianity in order to abolish it. Everything that Hegel said about the cunning of Reason in history drives toward this verdict. His thought was cloaked in Christian concepts because he conceived the evolution of Christianity as progress toward the atheistic freedom to come. Bruno Bauer, moving from right-Hegelian theology to left-Hegelian atheism in the early 1840s, instructed Marx on the "secret of Hegel," briefly a bond between Bauer and Marx. This claim fueled decades of debate between atheist left-Hegelians and Christian right-Hegelians, it was renewed in the 1920s by the rediscovery of the "young Marx," and it won canonical status in Kojève's legendary lectures. To save a Hegel worth saving, Hegel had to be dedicated to abolishing Christianity.[33]

Recent varieties of similar strategies, usually dropping the Marxian apologetics, reduce Hegel to social philosophy and phenomenology, or interpret Hegel as a transcendental Kantian, or treat the left-Hegelian reading as a precursor to postmodern deconstruction. Whatever gets salvaged from Hegel is usually whatever the interpreter prizes as real philosophy. Klaus Hartman launched a school of thought contending that Hegel was not metaphysical. Many took this option, discarding Hegel's Spinozist metaphysics, dialectical logic, *Naturphilosophie*, and religious philosophy. Sometimes the rational core to be salvaged consists of Hegel's system of categories, phenomenology, and/or Kantian transcendentalism, although some defend Hegel's metaphysics as a form of conceptual realism. Many others rest the case for Hegel primarily on his social philosophy, following the lead of Jürgen Habermas and Terry Pinkard. Pippin says that Hegel accepted Kant's destruction of precritical metaphysics only to devise a systematic metaphysics of his own "as if he had never heard of Kant's critical epistemology," conceiving the true infinite on idealistic terms as the pure self-relation of thought. Charles Taylor renders a similar verdict on what is living and dead in Hegel's thought, contending that the idea of a true infinite emerging from a self-contradiction inherent in finitude is intelligible only on the basis of a pre-Kantian ontological claim that the universe "is posited by a Spirit"—which no modern philosopher believes. Hegel's social philosophy is living and his ontology is dead, for his ontology rests on pre-Kantian metaphysics.[34]

Hegel, however, without Spinoza, dialectic, the philosophy of nature, and Christianity, is not Hegel. The only reason to salvage him for philosophy departments on these terms is to acknowledge that he greatly influenced modern philosophy, albeit on terms not conforming to analytic tests of true philosophy. Hegel criticized classical metaphysics on Kantian terms *and* he reconstructed metaphysics on post-Kantian terms. The either-or that Pippin and Taylor differently impose on Hegel brushes past Hegel's third possibility, which he expounded in *Phenomenology* and developed in the *Science of Logic*. Western metaphysics dating back to Parmenides was based on the ontology of being; Kant shredded the ontology of being, reducing philosophy to epistemology and method; Hegel transformed Western metaphysics by conceiving being *as* becoming. To put it this way acknowledges that Hegel had a defining ontological commitment, which many philosophers construe as pre-Kantian dogmatism. But if *any conceivable* ontology is ruled out as dogmatic, all manner of skeptics and neo-Kantians must be censured as dogmatists. Hegel made the greatest attempt to save modern philosophy from this fate by fashioning a metaphysic of becoming out of the Kantian framework. The left-Hegelian tradition that launched the nonmetaphysical reading of Hegel had the considerable twofold problem, from its beginning, that Hegel unfailingly called himself a Christian philosopher whose entire scheme explicated the truth of Christianity. Then the Kojève school read radical liberationist meanings into Hegel that he never came close to saying. One can get from Hegel a theory about the necessity of reciprocal relationships for the establishment of healthy self-consciousness and socially decent law, and a remarkably proto-Marxist insight into the dynamics of alienated labor. Beyond that, one has to spin hard to make Hegel sound like Marx, a fact that Marx noted sharply.[35]

Hegel conceived the logic of Spirit as the desire of the I for unity with itself. Natural religion, art-religion, and revealed religion play crucial mediating roles in the self-realization of Spirit. The "unhappy consciousness" of self-consciousness shows the pain of the Spirit wrestling in a world of sorrows to know itself, but the unity of the individual self-consciousness and its changeless essence remain "a beyond" for self-consciousness. Reason, struggling with the pain, still lacks religion, exhausting itself in the immediate struggle; thus it misses the absolute. The ethical conscience, Spirit coming into its truth, finally yields religion, in which Spirit becomes self-conscious. The Spirit of religion—the totality of Spirit—moves away from its immediacy toward the realization of what it is in itself. Thus it assumes specific *shapes* constituting the different moments of this movement. Each religion, selecting from the shapes that belong to each of its moments, picks out the one that fits its actual Spirit.[36]

Hegel took a brisk tour of the "natural religions" of Persia, India, and Egypt, which led to the religion of art, in which the Greeks specialized. As usual, he dwelt lovingly on the Greek story, where Spirit no longer mixed thought and the natural incongruously. In the religion of art, Spirit put itself into shapes of ethical self-conscious Spirit, advancing from knowing itself as substance to knowing itself as a Subject that creates its own outer shape. Moving up to revealed religion, the two standpoints held together with equal strength: substance alienated itself from itself to become self-consciousness and self-consciousness alienated itself from itself to give itself the nature of a thing. Hegel stressed that it didn't just happen. The incarnation of the Spirit as a self-conscious Being had to happen in a favorable moment of history, and it had to be *believed*. Believers had to see, feel, and hear the divinity in God's incarnation for the self-consciousness of the Spirit to be actual in them.[37]

Hegel ruled out tame versions of seeker religion. Revelatory unveiling does not begin with an inner thought or feeling. It begins with the recognition of God's existence as an individual self-consciousness. The self of existent Spirit takes the form of complete immediacy. It is not something produced, as in natural religion or art-religion, nor is it thought or imagined. It is the sensuously beheld incarnation of the divine being. Spirit is the knowledge of oneself in self-abandonment. Absolute religion is about God knowing God in humanity.

Philosophy employs concepts and religion employs picture thinking, so Hegel preferred philosophy, but what matters, he said, is that philosophy and revealed religion seek the same knowledge. Everywhere, through the ages, human beings search for the knowledge that the highest forms of religion and philosophy attain. The yearning of the unhappy consciousness for eternity, while trapped in a world of despair and death, is eternal. Speculative reason knows God as thought, it knows this thought as being and existence, and it knows existence as the negativity of itself. It knows the negativity of existence, the self, as simultaneously individual and universal. All of world history presses toward this revelation of beholding absolute being and finding itself in it.[38]

Christianity reveals, in partial form, the Spirit that seeks to be universalized in the understanding, not merely in religion. Hegel interpreted the life, death, resurrection, and ascension of Christ, and the sending of the Holy Spirit, as movements in this dialectical process. Christ was the individual man that absolute being revealed itself to be. In Christ, absolute Being accomplished in itself the movement of sensuous being, rose up for consciousness as a sensuous existence, and rose up in the Spirit. The consciousness that saw and heard Christ was merely immediate; it knew this objective individual as Spirit, but not itself. When Christ vanished, the immediacy was broken. At Pentecost, Spirit remained the "immediate Self of actuality," but now as "the *universal self-consciousness* of the community." The original Christian community reposed in its own substance, a universal Subject, which was not merely Christ, but also the consciousness of the community and what Christ was for this community, "the complete whole of the individual as Spirit."[39]

Spirit is a process of three moments beginning in pure thought (logic), moving into otherness and pictorial presentation (nature), and moving from nature into realized self-consciousness (Spirit knowing Spirit). Put differently, the first distinct moment of Spirit is Essence, God the Father. The second moment is Being-for-self for which the Essence is, God the Word. The third moment is Being-for-self in which the Spirit knows itself in the other, God as Spirit. The existence of the Word, Hegel argued, is nothing more, nor less, than the Spirit's hearing of its own self.[40]

Christianity construes the death and resurrection of Christ as bringing about the redemption of the world and inauguration of a universal life of Spirit. But this affirmation, Hegel said, negates the picture thinking in which it is made. The death of the Mediator, a particular being-for-self, gives rise to a universal self-consciousness. The universal becomes self-consciousness *and* the pure Spirit of thought becomes actual. The death of Christ marks not only the death of a particular being-for-self, but that of a pictured deity. The picture God dies in the death of Christ so that God as self-knowing Spirit may live. God suffering and dying on a cross is the abolition of the impassible picture God that does not suffer and is an exception to tragic anguish. There is no reconciliation without opposition and anguish, and no divine love that is exempt from divine anguish. The death of God, to Hegel, was the negation of the difference between theism and atheism. Christianity is a picture story about the movement of self-certain Spirit abandoning its unity nature and unchangeableness to embrace the suffering of the world and return to itself. Christianity apprehends in pictorial form the universal process by which Spirit redeems the world by desiring, sundering, suffering, reconciling, and coming to know itself.[41]

Years later, lecturing on religion, Hegel stressed that his thinking was Christian and that theology needed reconstructing just like philosophy. *Phenomenology* similarly vested unsurpassed importance in Christian ideas, even on a Marxist reading, without the apologetics. Every aspect of Hegel's system reworked the doctrines of the incarnation, cross, and Trinity, showing that every reconciling action has built-in conflict, sacrifice, tragedy, and anguish. In absolute knowing, self-consciousness surmounts the consciousness of revealed religion as such and becomes aware of itself in all the forms of its blood-soaked history. The intuition of the divine achieved in religion at its highest, which Hegel called the "beautiful soul," gives way to the divine intuiting itself. Spirit appears to itself in time only for as long as it does not grasp its pure notion. When Spirit realizes itself, overcoming the externality of objective substance, time is annulled. Everything that is outward must be transmuted into Spirit realizing itself. Spirit empties itself into the world of sensuous particularity in its creation of the world as an experience of itself. Reality is precisely and nothing less than the collective, spiraling, intersubjective self-thinking of Spirit.[42]

Hegelian Theo-Logic

The coming of Hegel, though late to begin, was perfectly timed and momentous. After Hegel published *Phenomenology of Spirit* in 1807, he taught high school for seven years, waiting for an academic opening that he fretted would never come. He was forty-six years old before he won a professorial post, at Heidelberg. His rise to prominence, when it finally came, rested chiefly on his *Science of Logic* and his ability to attract theological followers. On both counts, Hegelianism had a more problematic legacy than Hegel at his best deserved.

In 1812 and 1813 Hegel published the first two volumes of his logic, on being and essence. In 1816 he published volume three, on concepts, and won the Heidelberg chair. Napoleon had crashed and German monarchs were seeking to restore their authority. Hegel, well known for his liberal republican politics, resolved to play a careful hand upon winning a perch in the academy.

He divided his logic into three books because he divided everything into triads, except when his hurried writing of *Phenomenology* didn't turn out that way. Teaching *Gymnasium* students taught Hegel how to summarize his thoughts in capsule form, which paid off as he composed a summary of his system, *Encyclopedia of the Philosophical Sciences* (1817). Thinking has three operations or moments, he taught: understanding, which is abstract; dialectic, which is negative; and speculation, which is positive. Abstract thought—understanding—fixes the meaning of concepts so they can be used correctly. Dialectic is the movement of thought in which the formulae of the understanding supersede themselves, passing into their opposites. Speculative reason synthesizes the two contraries in a way that both preserves and dissolves them into a new reality. Hegel told students that dialectic, when done intelligently, is more than a seesaw of pro and con. Plato and Socrates were masters of dialectic, and Kant revived it in modern times, countering the one-sidedness of understanding.[43]

This was clearer than anything that Hegel said about dialectic in *Phenomenology*, where he used the term only a few times and did not describe it as a thesis generating an antithesis that leads to a synthesis. *Phenomenology* was not even stringent about using triads. It was based on the triad of consciousness, self-consciousness, and reason, and it subdivided consciousness into sensuous certainty, perception, and understanding. But the book had only two headings under self-consciousness, and Hegel's sprawling account of reason, which consumed almost three-fourths of the whole, had a complex fourfold division. *Phenomenology* was free flowing in applying its more or less triadic scheme to a surging waterfall of concepts, figures, events, rhetorical forms, and philosophical moves. It paired skepticism against Stoicism, which led to the unhappy consciousness, but Hegel did not claim to deduce one from the other in dialectical fashion, as skepticism is not the logical antithesis of Stoicism.

Science of Logic, however, was a philosophy of formal logic, an argument about the types and limitations of judgment and inference. Here the dialectic was named repeatedly, featured, and stringently applied with deductive zeal, demonstrating the point of Hegel's logic: the concept is a *movement* that determines itself to be. There is a logical movement from subjectivity to objectivity to idea that overcomes the impasse of Kantian dualism, rehabilitating metaphysical reasoning on post-Kantian terms. If the concepts of mind are universals, Hegel argued, they bridge the Kantian divide between knowing subjects and objects of consciousness. There is no rational basis for dichotomizing between subject and object, or form and content. The idea unfolding is precisely the co-inhering of everything.

Hegel divided logic into being, essence, and concept (or notion), each of which had normative structures that depended on the kinds of judgmental relations at issue. Dramatically, in his opening paragraph, he declared that the Kantian revolution transformed philosophy, except in logic. Philosophers no longer taught or wrote about ontology, cosmology, rational psychology, or natural theology—all had "vanished" from the field, obliterated by Kant. But the "higher standpoint" of modern philosophy, which tracked the movement of spirit's awareness of itself, had not encroached on the structure of logic—until now. Hegel believed that logic is not immune to movement, the life process of self-determination into being. The unity that precedes all acts of judgment is pure knowing. Thus he began his logic with the category of pure being, a "thought" lacking any determination.[44]

The simple act of trying to conceive pure being—the primordial unity of thought and being—immediately generates paradoxes. Hegel argued that these ruptures are implicit in the very nature of the unity and are brought out by the act of judgment. Logic must think about thinking, and it must not rest content with rules about the forms of logical judgment and inference. Rather, logic must deal with the process of reasoning that generates the forms. Hegel put it bluntly: "What logic is cannot be stated beforehand." Instead of beginning as formal logic always did, with symbols and rules of thought, logic must begin "with the subject matter itself."[45]

So his logic began with pure being—pure indeterminateness and emptiness, the most elementary feature of thought. Pure being, as a thought, does not restrict the context in which it is used, and despite being completely indeterminate, it is something that can be thought.

But Hegel stressed that this thought immediately generates a paradox, that being and nothing are identical. When we focus on pure being, we realize that we are thinking nothing; when we think nothing, we are led straight back to being. In both cases, lacking any determination, there is nothing to think. But there is something we think about in both cases, the two thoughts seem to be identical, and yet they are radically different. We cannot predicate being as a category of existence without predicating nothing as a category of existence. Thinking about being takes us straight to nothing and vice versa. The antithesis, nothing, is not merely the logical contradiction of pure being, for it is related to being as a contrary. Hegel allowed that nothing (*Nichts*) might be called "not-being" (*Nichtsein*), as long as one keeps in mind that it stands for the absence of all determination, not the denial of being. In the dialectic of being and nothing we confront a fundamental contradiction between identity and opposition: being is a pure positive (reality without unreality) and nothing is a pure negative (unreality without reality).[46]

This contradiction yields the third category, becoming—the passage of being into nothing, or of nothing into being. Hegel observed that when we try to think about being or nothing, our thought passes from one to another, erasing the thought with which we began. Becoming is this movement in which being and nothing are distinguished by a difference which immediately resolves itself. It is not a unity that abstracts from being and nothing; rather, becoming is the "unseparatedness" of being and nothing. As the unity of being and nothing "it is this *determinate* unity in which there *is* both being and nothing." Being and nothing are both in the unity, but only as vanishing moments. They do not self-subsist, for both sink to the status of distinct but "sublated" moments of simultaneous preservation and dissolution. Hegel distinguished between two moments of becoming, which he called "ceasing-to-be" and "coming-to-be." Ceasing to be is being passing into nothing, where nothing is equally the opposite of itself, coming to be. Coming to be is nothing passing into being, where being transitions into nothing, ceasing to be. Hegel reasoned that these moments do not reciprocally cancel each other externally, for "each sublates itself in itself and is in its own self the opposite of itself." *Everything* is an intermediate state between being and nothing.[47]

The next round of the dialectic begins with the synthesis of the first and second kinds of becoming as one thought—being becoming out of nothing which came out of being. This is not pure being; Hegel called it *Dasein,* "a being," usually translated as "determinate being." Determinate being is the first moment of a dialectic which becomes something by being "qualified," which involves a change of determination going beyond a limit, which sets off the dialectic of finitude and infinitude, and so on. Hegel famously declared, "We call dialectic the higher movement of reason in which such seemingly utterly separate terms pass over into each other spontaneously, through that which they are, a movement in which the presupposition sublates itself."[48]

"Sublate," not really an English term, has to work hard in English versions of Hegel, whose German term *aufgehoben* was equally distinctive. There is no dialectic without it, and *Science of Logic* was a huge waterfall of dialectics. The doctrine of being began with being, nothing, and becoming, which led to determinate being, finitude, and infinity, which led to being for self as such, the one and the many, and repulsion and attraction. All had dialectics of their own, creating simultaneous cases of reduplicated relation. For example, the dialectic of determinate being, under determinate being as such, contained the dialectics of determinate being in general, quality, and something; under finitude, it contained the dialectics of something and other, determination-constitution-limit, and finitude; under infinity, it contained the dialectics of the infinite in general, alternating determination of the finite and infinite, and affirmative affinity. Hegel's logic of essence had similar dialectics, which began with essence as reflection within itself, moved to appearance, and culminated in actuality, all with three logical moments divided into triads of their own. His system culminated in his "subjective logic," the doctrine of the notion, which moved from subjectivity (the notion, the judgment, the syllogism) to objectivity (mechanism, "chemism," teleology) to the Idea (life, the idea of cognition, the Absolute Idea).

The conventional account, a staple of philosophy textbooks for centuries, is that Hegel used a three-step method of thesis-antithesis-synthesis. This formula is not wrong, but it is not right either. As a shorthand formula it describes the general structure of Hegel's method in *Science of Logic* and his subsequent major writings. But Hegel *never* employed this formula, it misses his multidimensional complexity, and in many renderings it simply ignores the pragmatic commitments that motivated all of Hegel's work, not excluding *Science of Logic.*[49]

In *Science of Logic, Encyclopedia of the Philosophical Sciences,* and Hegel's last published book, *Philosophy of Right* (1821), dialectic expounded the fundamental categories of understanding, including concepts, forms of judgment, and forms of syllogism. He began by describing a category, A. Then he showed that A contains a contrary category, B. Then he showed that category B contains category A; thus, both categories are self-contradictory. This mutually contradictory outcome, though negative, yields a positive outcome, category C, which Hegel called the "negation of the negation" or the "determinate negation." Category C contains A and B, uniting them, but in a way that both preserves and abolishes them—Hegelian *aufgehoben*. Sublation is the process in which A and B are rendered no longer contradictory and not a source of contradiction in C. By rendering A and B to be no longer self-contradictory, category C is able to preserve and abolish A and B as a new, reciprocal reality. Hegel explained, "It is a fundamental determination which repeatedly occurs throughout the whole of philosophy, the meaning of which is to be clearly grasped and especially distinguished from *nothing*. What is sublated is not thereby reduced to nothing. Nothing is *immediate*; what is sublated, on the other hand, is the result of *mediation*; it is a nonbeing but as a *result* which had its origin in a being. It still has, therefore, *in itself* the *determinateness from which it originates*." At this point, the next round of the dialectic begins anew, with C playing the "thesis" role that was previously played by A.[50]

Kant revolutionized modern philosophy by insisting there are exactly twelve concepts of pure thought. Hegel demonstrated that there are at least eighty-one. Patiently, with tremendous concentration on how thinking actually works in logical reasoning, he made a case for taking seriously the Heraclitan world of becoming, the unity of thought and being, and the logical connection between these notions as a movement from subjectivity to objectivity to idea. His triads were not uniform, as Findlay noted. Sometimes the second member of the triad was an obvious contrary of the first, as in the relation of essence and appearance. Sometimes the contrast was much weaker, as in the relation of whole and parts to force and its manifestations. The same thing was true of the third members. Some, like measure synthesizing quality and quantity, worked very well. Sometimes Hegel's third member was merely one thing in which two concepts could be united (as in the mediation of identity and difference by the Ground). In other cases, as in the reconciliation of the mechanical and the chemical by teleology, Hegel stretched.[51]

His vast scheme of logical categorizing and dialecticism overwhelmed the pragmatic aspect of his thought, but it was there. Hegel sought to demonstrate that it is in the very nature of thought, and thus of life, to generate complexity from simplicity. The other, by turning upon itself, transforms the opposite into its immediate. Otherness becomes immediacy, otherness reduplicated. Hegel had the same normative concern in every dialectic that he unfolded: to show that the world is always coming to be and ceasing to be. What we are really doing when we distinguish being from nothing is to work out the kinds of inferences that are credible within a world that is always coming and ceasing to be. *Science of Logic*, despite its 844 pages of logic-chopping rigor, espoused the sociohistoricized Reason of *Phenomenology* and its worldview: the world is in flux, heading toward the realization of Spirit. To say that we know something is not to make an objective comparison. It is to make a normative ascription about the entitlement of the person making the claim. Pinkard explains, "Our ascriptions of knowledge are not comparisons of any kind of subjective state with something nonsubjective but instead are *moves within* a social space structured by responsibilities, entitlements, attributions, and the undertakings of commitments."[52]

Science of Logic put an end to the question whether Hegel had a position independent of Schelling's. *Phenomenology* was too puzzling to settle the question, but Hegel clearly stood on his own by the time he taught, for two years, at Heidelberg, and published the *Encyclopedia*. At Heidelberg he acquired a following, though nothing like his subsequent cult following at Berlin. Two of his best friends on the Heidelberg faculty were theologians, Karl Daub and Friedrich H. C. Schwarz, an augur of his Berlin career; Hegel also befriended Georg Friedrich Creuzer, founder of the scientific study of mythology. Upon moving to Heidelberg, Hegel exorcised a nine-year psychic torment by rescuing his illegitimate son Ludwig from an orphanage, overruling his wife Marie Hegel, with whom he had two children. *Encyclopedia*, though essentially a summary manual of Hegel's system, coined the term "objective spirit" for his concept of the social and political embodiments of spirit. Part one was a short version of Hegel's logic; part two dealt with philosophy of nature; part three covered the philosophy of mind. Part two made some bad choices on scientific subjects, not for the first time. In *Phenomenology*, Hegel rattled on for twenty-five pages about phrenology. In *Encyclopedia*, he opposed Lamarckian evolution, defended the fixity of natural kinds, and opposed Newtonian light theory, which rendered this part of Hegel's system to early obsolescence. He had scientific colleagues at Heidelberg who tried to warn him. But mostly he grew accustomed to being called the German Aristotle, a title he took to Berlin in 1818.[53]

Hegel had scorned Prussia for decades. Even the king of Prussia couldn't speak decent German. The language and fashions of the Prussian court were French, the literature was French, and France owned the world. Germany had a serious identity crisis—and not just to Hegel—until the University of Berlin became a powerhouse. Then Hegel virtually dictated the terms of his appointment. In 1818 the burning debate in German philosophy was Hegel versus Fries, although Schelling, silenced by heartbreak and trauma, still had the most adherents. Fries, recently appointed at Jena, combined neo-Kantianism, psychology, conspiratorial anti-Semitism, and liberal activism. He and Hegel despised each other, which earned Fries a disparaging and fateful reference in Hegel's last book, *Philosophy of Right*.

Hegel began to write *Philosophy of Right* as soon as he moved to Berlin. His aim was to justify the Prussian reform movement to which he and Schleiermacher belonged, establishing what counted as a "right" in general and what was necessary for the realization of freedom. Hegel argued that the goal of free mind is "to make freedom its object, i.e., to make freedom objective as much in the sense that freedom shall be the rational system of mind, as in the sense that this system shall be the world of immediate actuality." The course of history can be deduced from absolutely free will, a logical concept. *Philosophy of Right* was not quite a self-contained system, as Hegel derived historically messy ideas about property, the family, and civil society from his master concept. But the book had a strong logical cast, featuring a dialectic of being, essence, and notion, which led to a dialectic of natural will, arbitrary will, and universal free will, which led to a dialectic of abstract right, morality, and ethical life.[54]

Hegel made arguments for a two-house parliamentary government, a constitutional monarchy, freedom of the press, freedom of public opinion, trial by jury, individual rights based on property, and universal standards by which a person could claim to own property. In an argument that caught the astute attention of young Karl Marx, Hegel supported representing the estates of civil society in legislative bodies, which presented legislative content to a constitutional monarch, who added the royal "I will" to legitimize legislation as an expression of the general will. Hegel's idealism was central to his political philosophy. The general will must be *willed*, he argued; it cannot be merely the outcome of a mechanical clash of interests. Even in this area, the most pilloried aspect of Hegel's thought, the mechanical-system Hegel of the textbooks is not right, though Marx detected Hegel's cult of the state and his favoritism toward the bourgeoisie. Hegel, to his credit, tried to stoke a public argument about the right kind of social contract theory. But the early reviews ignored the body of his argument, aiming solely at his snarky, pithy, aggressive preface, which engulfed him in unwelcome controversy for years and permanently damaged his reputation.

The backstory was a tale of misgivings and suspicions. Hegel was sincere about defending the reform movement, but he loathed demagoguery and the anti-Semitism that usually went with it in the student fraternities, and he pegged Fries and Kantian theologian Wilhelm Martin L. de Wette as unbearable demagogues. In addition, Hegel and Schleiermacher were wary of each other, as Hegel had low regard for religious feeling and Schleiermacher had low regard for speculative philosophy. In 1811 Schleiermacher told the Academy of Sciences in Berlin that speculative philosophy was not really a discipline and it didn't belong in the university. Largely on Schleiermacher's influence, Hegel was never admitted to the Academy of Sciences. Moreover, during the crucial years of post-Napoleonic reordering in Prussia, Hegel avoided conflicts with the conservative government, so reform activists viewed him with suspicion. His defense of constitutional monarchy was beyond the pale for some, he seemed too comfortable with his privileges, and he defended the king's firing of de Wette from his professorship at Berlin. Even conservatives on the faculty senate protested de Wette's summary dismissal, but to Hegel, de Wette had become a badly mannered embarrassment to the university.[55]

In that mode, Hegel wrote a nasty put-down of Fries (by name) and de Wette (unnamed) in the preface to *Philosophy of Right*. Fries, Hegel pronounced, was the "ringleader of these hosts of superficiality"— indulging the student fraternities, flattering their leaders, appealing to "heart, emotion, and inspiration," and embarrassing serious academics. Fries prattled about the hopeful, communal rise of the people, united by "the holy chain of friendship," which would change society by pursuing "every single project of popular education and popular service." Hegel snorted, "This is the quintessence of shallow thinking, to base philosophic science not on the development of thought and the concept but on immediate sense-perception and the play of fancy."[56]

Philosophy of Right, by contrast, was long on moral duty, law, rational rigor, and rational order. It replaced Hegel's previous enthusiasm for the people with sober descriptions of civil society and the state, which he summarized in a fateful phrase fashioned from one of his favorite sayings. Usually Hegel said, "What is actual is what is efficacious." This time, intending to say the same thing, he declared, "What is rational is actual and what is actual is rational." Many readers and nearly every reviewer, including conservatives, took that as an endorsement of the status quo—Prussian royalist autocracy. The rest of the book, whatever it said, didn't matter. The reviews focused exclusively on Hegel's attack on Fries and ostensible defense of the existing order.[57]

Adding to the drama, Fries had been fired recently from Jena on trumped-up accusations. Hegel, it turned out, was a bully who kicked a rival after he was down. Fries supplied a quotable explanation for what happened: "Hegel's metaphysical mushroom has grown not in the gardens of science but on the dunghill of servility." Hegel fought back by insulting his critics. In his telling, all were stupid and insipid, carried away by a few sentences they didn't understand, judging a book they hadn't read, which would have been over their heads anyway. That made it worse. Hegel's penchant for scathing sarcasm magnified a flaw in his moral character. Somehow the defender of republican freedom believed his first order of business, after the old powers were restored, was to put down persecuted liberals.[58]

Hegel never came up with a good explanation of "somehow." His early years at Berlin went poorly on that account, as colleagues and onlookers shunned his arrogance. He told an inquirer that his book "greatly offended the demagogical populace" because most people wallowed in "superficial self-conceit." But Hegel weathered the storm by giving free reign to the gregarious side of his personality. He served the university energetically in a variety of capacities and won a large and devoted student following. He damaged his health by overworking, although not on books. Becoming a great figure placed demands on his time that precluded new books. Hegel's growing fame brought a stream of visitors to Berlin, a responsibility he took seriously, just as he had always been a dutiful teacher. The visiting traffic, and his swelling student following, crowded into his lectures on logic and metaphysics, philosophical encyclopedia, history of philosophy, natural law and political science, and the philosophies of art, nature, and world history. In 1821 Hegel threw together an emergency course on philosophy of religion after learning that Schleiermacher would soon publish a dogmatics.[59]

Philosophy of religion was beginning to emerge as a discipline in the wake of the downfall of rational theology, a branch of metaphysics.

Hegel wanted to make a contribution to it, and the Schleiermacher news hastened his resolve. He told Karl Daub, "I hear Schleiermacher is also in process of having a work printed on dogmatics. The epigram occurs to me, 'One can go on paying for a long time with chips, but in the end one has to pull out one's purse all the same.' We'll have to wait and see whether this purse too will yield nothing more than chips." After volume one of Schleiermacher's system appeared, Hegel wrote to his protégé H. W. F. Hinrichs: "From Daub I look for an open declaration whether this really is the dogmatics of the United Evangelical Church that one has had the brazen effrontery to offer as such—admittedly only in a preliminary first part." Hegel, too, belonged to the Evangelical Church of the Prussian Union, and was quite certain that Schleiermacher did not speak for him. How did Schleiermacher summon the audacity to speak for the church as a whole?[60]

In that frame of mind Hegel lectured on religion for the first time, for four hours per week for seventeen weeks, drawing 49 official auditors. In 1824 he returned to religion, drawing 63 auditors. In 1827 the official tally rose to 119 students, one of the largest crowds of his career. In 1831 he lectured on religion for the last time, though no enrollment data exists. Always he attracted guests and lecture-grazers. His lectures began with a long discussion of the concept of religion, followed with a longer section on determinate religion, and ended with the consummate religion, Christianity. He was a dreadful speaker, drawling and slow, often pausing to clear his throat, gasp, stare into space, or fumble with his manuscript. He began most sentences with the word "thus," and sometimes stuttered. These deficiencies were converted to endearing local lore as his fame ascended; listeners prized his mannerisms as part of the Hegel experience. Hegel was sufficiently ponderous and deliberate that creating a verbatim transcript was never difficult for his students, who made money by selling the transcripts. He made use of these transcripts when he repeated a lecture cycle.[61]

His lectures in 1821 were rough and improvised, exuding unusual directness for Hegel. His lectures in 1824 were the best of the series—lively, fluid, and engaging—which reflected his hard work on a fresh subject, plus his determination to discredit Schleiermacher's system. By the time that Hegel returned to religion in 1827 and 1831, he had a systematic command of his subject and was back to writing more formally, with slightly fewer polemics against Schleiermacher. Having launched the series to refute Schleiermacher, Hegel heightened his polemic after

Schleiermacher gave him additional fodder; later he featured his command of something new, Hegelian philosophy of religion; at the end he was most interested in the history of religions.

Hegel shuddered to think that modern theology might content itself with Schleiermacher's subjectivism. The antidote was a philosophy of religion that unified the Western understandings of religion and God under a single, modern, rational rubric. Hegel began, "Gentlemen! The object of these lectures is the philosophy of religion, which in general has the same purpose as the earlier type of metaphysical science, which was called *theologia naturalis.*" Hegel's prototype was Leibniz-Wolff rational theology, a division of metaphysics usually following rational psychology and cosmology. He did not dwell on the differences between his project and Wolff's, except to observe that the Kantian revolution occurred between them, changing everything. Hegel explained, "The doctrine that we can know nothing of God, that we cannot cognitively apprehend him, has become in our time a universally acknowledged truth, a settled thing, a kind of prejudice." Before Kant, all science was a science of God. After Kant, educated people took pride in knowing nothing of God. Hegel put it sharply: "It is the distinction of our age, by contrast, to know each and every thing, indeed to know an infinite mass of objects, but only of God we know nothing." In former times people desired, above all things, to know God: "Our age has renounced this need and the efforts to satisfy it; we are done with it."[62]

Hegel was scathing about the upshot of this turn, which turned God into "an infinite phantom, far removed from our consciousness" and reduced human cognition to "a vain phantom of finitude, to schemas [that are] the fulfillment of appearance." He featured this theme in every series, protesting that on Kantian terms it is impossible to make any sense of Christ's command to "be ye perfect as your Father in heaven is perfect." If one knows nothing of God and God's perfection, the command means nothing. Modern people, thinking themselves wise, reached "the last step in the degradation of humanity," where the profoundly simple words of Jesus became incomprehensible. Hegel set himself against this pathetic outcome, and on the side of Christianity, "according to which we should *know* God *cognitively,* God's nature and essence, and should esteem this cognition above all else."[63]

All human beings have some knowledge of God, Hegel insisted; otherwise they wouldn't be human beings: "No one is so utterly depraved, so lost, so bad, and so wretched as to have no religion at all or to have [no] knowledge or awareness of it." Even people who loathe or deny the spirit within them still have it: "Since we are human beings and not animals, [religion] is not an alien sensation or intuition for us. But what matters is the relationship of *religion* in human beings to *everything else* in their world view, consciousness, cognition, purposes, and interests; this is the relationship that philosophical cognition is concerned with and upon which it essentially works."[64]

The Spirit, he insisted, is the subject and object of religion. There are not two kinds of spirit, any more than there are two kinds of reason. The Spirit of God and the spirit of humanity—divine reason—have the same essence: "Human reason, human spiritual consciousness or consciousness of its own essence, *is* reason generally, is the divine within humanity." Spirit divine is not something hypostatized before or beyond the world, "for God is present, is omnipresent, and strictly *as spirit* is God present in spirit." Hegel declared that religion is "a begetting of the divine spirit, not an invention of human beings but an effect of the divine at work, of the divine productive process within humanity." It is a product of Spirit divine, spirit realizing itself in consciousness. Religion emerges first as faith; it is faith precisely in the mind of God being revealed in nature and history; and it saves the world: "So we must have faith that what has emerged in the world is precisely reason, and that the generation of reason is a begetting of the spirit and a product of the divine spirit itself."[65]

Modern theology fell short of knowing much of anything about what matters in religion. The fact that modern theologians played down the Trinity was terribly instructive; Hegel shook his head that Schleiermacher relegated this doctrine to an appendix. He countered that this doctrine expresses how Spirit is explicated; it is precisely God grasping at what God is for God's self within God's self. God the Father makes God's self an object for God's self (the Son), remaining the undivided essence within this differentiation of God's self within God's self; in this differentiation, God loves God's self while remaining identical with God's self—the Holy Spirit.[66]

Hegel perceived that historicism was gaining in modern theology. De Wette and Heinrich Paulus, respectively, espoused Kantian Romantic and Kantian rationalist forms of historicism, and Ferdinand C. Baur headed a school of post-Kantian historicists at Tübingen. Hegel cautioned that historicism is a very limited tool, enabling useful work with ancient texts, but not with religious truth. Historical knowledge, he explained, is pitifully low order: "This cognition is no concern of ours, for if the cognition of religion were merely historical, we would have to compare such theologians with countinghouse clerks, who keep the ledgers and accounts of other people's wealth, a wealth that passes through their hands without their retaining any of it, clerks who act only for others without acquiring assets of their own." To be sure, clerks earn a salary, "but their merit lies only in keeping records of the assets of other people. In philosophy and religion, however, the essential thing is that one's own spirit itself should recognize a possession and content, deem itself worthy of cognition, and not keep itself humbly outside."[67]

Historical theology is secondhand, a mere ledger entry lacking any spiritual content of its own. Hegel took the theology of feeling more seriously, if only because Jacobi and Schleiermacher turned it into "an established preconception." Hegel blasted Schleiermacher in every lecture cycle, sometimes noting that Jacobi paved the way for the academy to take Schleiermacher's mere feelings with such seriousness. Always, Hegel countered that feelings are subjective, ephemeral, indiscriminate, and very low on cognition. In 1822, writing the preface to Hinrichs' book on philosophy of religion, Hegel defended the compatibility of reason and religion, neglected to discuss his protégé's turgid book, and allowed that religious faith has a place for spiritual feeling. However, if Hegel was going to say something nice about religious feeling, he couldn't resist a swipe at Schleiermacher. This was the occasion on which Hegel, reprising Schleiermacher on absolute dependence, observed that on Schleiermacher's terms, a dog makes the best Christian.[68]

Thought, Hegel argued, is the ground upon which God *is*: "The universal is in thought, *only* in thought, and for thought." Thinking is spirit in its freedom. It supplies the content of truth, "the concrete deity," and it delivers this content to sensibility, creating religion. Empirical understanding, to be sure, is mere observing, the external vantage point of the onlooker. When one views consciousness from a higher, spiritual standpoint, one moves far beyond mere observing. Hegel explained, "I forget myself in plunging into the object. I immerse myself in it as I seek to cognize and to conceive God. I surrender my particularity in it, and if I do this I am no longer in the relationship which, as an empirical consciousness, I wanted to maintain." Now one perceives the relationship of consciousness; in the higher understanding, one takes upon oneself a relationship to whatever one perceives. God becomes "no longer a beyond for me," and one becomes interwoven with the object, spirit thinking itself. Hegel loved Meister Eckhart on this theme, helpfully informing students that Eckhart was a fourteenth-century Dominican monk. Eckhart sermonized, "The eye with which God sees me is the eye with which I see him; my eye and his eye are one and the same. In righteousness I am weighed in God and he in me." To Hegel, that was deeper and truer than the theologies of Kantians, Schleiermacher, and historicists.[69]

Kant and Fichte didn't understand religion, because religion is about making oneself such that the spirit dwells in one's being; it is practice of the presence of Spirit divine. Kant and Fichte reduced religion to a "merely moral standpoint," contending that the good must be brought out and realized within oneself as a religious duty. They wrongly assumed that the good is not already there in and for itself. In the Kantian picture, Hegel explained, the world stands waiting for rational moral agents to introduce the good from without. In the Hegelian picture, God is good and prevalent in the world; thus, the rational moral agent's role is to "rid myself of my subjectivity, do my share and play my part in this good, in this work, which is accomplished eternally and divinely." Hegel said the highest good is no mere ethical prescription; it is willing what God wills, "on which account it is the business of the singular subject to realize itself through the negation of its singularity."[70]

That raised the question of pantheism, which Hegel wearied of answering, but did so anyway. He was not a pantheist. But more importantly, nobody was a pantheist; Hegel had never met one: "It has never occurred to anyone to say that everything, all individual things collectively, in their individuality and contingency, are God—for example, that paper or this table is God. No one has ever held that." Spinoza and "Oriental pantheism" made "all is one" statements that smacked of pantheism, but neither taught that God is everything. They taught that the divine in all things is the universal aspect of their content, "the *essence* of things." Hegel observed that when Krishna or Vishnu said, "I am the luster or brilliance in metals," they superseded the idea of *everything* being God. Krishna is the luster in metals, not all metal and everything else. As for Spinoza, he was not a pantheist, and certainly not an atheist. Spinoza's accusers said he was a pantheist, so he was really an atheist. But that was only because they could not liberate themselves from the finite. To those who screamed "atheist," God stood on the other side of the finite realm. Hegel believed that Spinoza espoused acosmism, the view that finite things are absorbed into the infinite. To Spinoza, there was no aggregate of finitudes, otherwise called the world; thus, the ostensible pantheist formula, "all is one," did not apply to him, as the "all" vanished without a trace.[71]

As for the charge that "pantheists" like Spinoza and him, taking all to be one, made good to be one with evil, and thus abolished religion, Hegel countered that this accusation blended two kinds of misunderstanding. If God were actually everything, God *would* be sublated. But nobody said that. In the Hegel/Spinoza view, it was the finite that is sublated, and the distinction between good and evil was sublated implicitly—in God as the true actuality. Hegel said there is no evil in God, quashing rumors about his theodicy. But the distinction between good and evil is valid only if God is evil. Hegel did not believe that evil has any ontological status, much less that such an affirmative element exists in God. He affirmed, "God is good and good alone." The distinction between good and evil does not exist in the divine One, for it arises only with distinction in general. There is no distinction between good and evil until God is distinct from the world, especially human beings. The distinction between good and evil does not apply to God as such. Evil becomes an issue only with the rise of distinction, and the goal of human life is to be one with God, eliminating distinction. Hegel declared, "This is the most sublime morality, that evil is what is null, and human beings ought not to let this distinction, this nullity, be valid within themselves nor make it valid at all. We can will to persist in this distinction, can push it to the point of opposition to God, the universal in and for itself. In so doing we are evil. But we can also deem our distinction to be null and void, and can posit our essential being solely in God and in our orientation toward God. In so doing we are good."[72]

In every lecture cycle his longest section was the middle one, which he called *Die bestimmte Religion*, best translated as "determinate religion." Hegel offered an extraordinary feast of interpretation, unmatched by any thinker of his time, although much of what he said was wrong. Systematic Western research on Buddhism and Hinduism was just beginning in Hegel's time, his sources on Chinese religion and so-called "primitive" religion were equally thin, and Hegel's low view of Islam deterred him from reading much about it. On Buddhism he relied on travel literature and focused on the doctrine of nirvana. On Hinduism he made extensive use of reports by officials of the East India Company, though he also cited translations of the Code of Manu, the Mahabharata, and the Bhagavad Gita. For Persian religion (Zoroastrianism) Hegel relied on a German translation of a French translation of the Zend-Avesta. For Egyptian religion he leaned on Herodotus and Plutarch, though he also cited current secondary scholarship. On Roman religion he featured his schoolboy favorite, Gibbon's *Decline and Fall of the Roman Empire*, plus Karl Philipp Moritz; on Judaism he relied on his reading of Hebrew Scripture, emphasizing the Pentateuch, Job, and the Psalms. As usual, Hegel showed that he knew the Greeks best of all, although he changed his mind about the standing of Greek religion. His chief contemporary source was Creuzer's four-volume myth criticism, although Hegel did not let friendship prevent him from disagreeing occasionally with Creuzer.[73]

Very few scholars of Hegel's time knew as much as he did about world religions, and no philosopher came close to him. As in *Phenomenology*, his treatment of determinate religion was a phenomenology of the forms of consciousness assumed by Spirit as it advanced through the history of religion. Though Hegel conveyed a vast amount of historical information, his account was phenomenological (describing concrete states of consciousness) and speculative (privileging the absolute idea as an interpretive construct). On the model of his logical triad of being, essence, and concept, he conceived religions in the mode of determinateness and finitude, interpreting "Oriental nature religions" as religions of pre-reflective immediacy or undifferentiated substance, Jewish religion as differentiation in the form of particularity, Greek religion as differentiation in the form of necessity, Roman religion as differentiation in the form of external purposiveness, and Christianity as the true, infinite, consummate religion. Roman religion had a special role in Hegel's account because it showed the limitations of determinate religion. It was universal, transcending ethnic or national religions, yet it was too prosaic to have much depth or transcendence.[74]

Hegel worked hard on his account of determinate religions. He reached his definitive conception of Christianity as the consummate religion in 1824 and pretty much recycled it afterwards. He reached his definitive conception of the concept of religion in 1827. He never reached a definitive conception on determinate religion, still revising and amplifying substantially in 1831. His most significant change of mind centered on Jewish religion. In 1821 he repeated the standard tropes of his long time Grecophile anti-Jewish prejudice. In 1824 he revised this view significantly, and in 1827 he reversed his old position, lifting Jewish religion above the Greeks, all the while claiming that Schleiermacher got this issue disastrously wrong.[75]

When he began lecturing on religion, Hegel routinely dismissed Judaism as a servile, legalistic, ingrown religion that should have expired. This was a prejudice straight from his earliest writings; *Phenomenology* had barely granted Judaism a mention in its panoramic rendering of humanity's developing self-consciousness. By 1824, however, Hegel had spent three years intently studying religion, and his friend Eduard Gans convinced him it was wrong to write off Judaism. Hegel did not give up believing that Judaism reeked of servile consciousness and the master-slave relationship, and he did not distinguish between temple and rab-binic Judaism or historicize the relation of "Judaism" to Hebrew faith. Like Islam, he argued, only with less fanaticism, Judaism has no con-cept of a dialectically self-mediated deity. Judaism, like Islam, has only the severe, forbidding One, who is not relational and does not sanction human freedom. Parenthetically Hegel added that Schleiermacher's con-cept of religious dependence was in this mode; Schleiermacher's mode of piety was Jewish, not Christian. Hegel emphatically disliked the Hebrew conviction that Jews alone are God's people and that God alone is their God.[76]

But this time he also saw the sublimity, wisdom, and true spirituality in Jewish faith. The sublime, Hegel asserted, manifests itself in ways that transcend appearance and reality, so the reality "is simultaneously posited as negated." The idea associated with the sublime is exalted above that in which it appears, making its appearance "an inappropriate expression." Hegel admired the sublimity of the prophets and Psalms, and the Gene-sis creation myth, especially "Let there be light." Sublimity in religion is nature represented as wholly negated, subordinate, and transitory; by that standard, Hebrew religion is strong on sublimity. Moreover, the Jewish God is more spiritual than previous deities. Jewish religion conceives the finite spirit as essentially consciousness and God as the object of con-sciousness as God's own essence. In consciousness, Hegel explained, the Jewish God *is* God's own purpose; God is to be recognized and venerated by all people (Ps 117:1-2). Hegel commended the universality of God's purpose in the opening chapters of Genesis, though he judged that Juda-ism fell woefully short of it. The universal wisdom of Jewish faith "did not become truth for the people of Israel," stuck, as they were, in provin-cialism and determinacy. Nonetheless, it was wisdom of a high order.[77]

Hegel explained that Jewish religion, unlike Persian religion, had a problem with evil, and a compelling answer as to how evil came into the world. Persian religion, being dualistic, conceived evil as existing in the same way that good exists. Good and evil issue forth from the wholly indeterminate. In Jewish religion, however, God is power, the One is subject, and God is the Creator of all that is. The reality of evil is perplexing, for the God that created all things is absolutely good. Hegel pointed to the myth of Adam and Eve eating from the forbidden tree, the tree of the knowledge of good and evil. The difficult point for Hegel, as for Adam, was that God forbade humanity to acquire knowledge from this tree: "For this knowledge is precisely what constitutes the character of spirit. Spirit is spirit only through consciousness, and the highest consciousness lies precisely in such knowledge. How then can this have been forbidden?"[78]

Hegel, answering his own question through the myth, reasoned that knowledge is a two-sided gift, rife with danger. Human freedom is free to embrace good and evil, including the capacity to do evil. Hegel noted that Judaism never did much with the myth of the fall. Only in Christianity is this myth seized upon as an explanation of the reality and universality of evil. Christianity grasps the truth in the myth—evil derives from human nature, it exists as the counterpart of human freedom, and the knowledge of good and evil constitutes likeness to God. But this is fundamentally Jewish wisdom.[79]

Previously Hegel claimed that the Jewish emphasis on "fear of the Lord" valorized servility, making Jewish religion the antithesis of freedom. Now he claimed that Israel inaugurated the first religion of freedom because it commanded fear of the Lord, which delegitimized earthly rulers, abolished idols and dependency, negated human negativity, and yielded absolute trust in the Creator of all things. Jewish religion was grounded in something affirmative, the divine-human relationship, even though the people of Israel did not grasp the radical implications of their covenant with God or actualize their universality. In both cases Hegel set his view against Schleiermacher's purported one. In 1821 he claimed that Schleiermacher was wrong for preaching fear of the Lord, a religion of passive dependence and servitude. In 1824 Hegel said that fear of the Lord is actually something affirmative and creative—except when Schleiermacher said it, for Schleiermacher preached a religion of passivity and dependence. Hegel declared, "So absolute fear is not a feeling of dependence, but casting off all dependence and purely abandoning oneself in the absolute self, vis-à-vis which and in which one's own self evaporates and dissolves."[80]

But that was virtually identical with Schleiermacher's concept of absolute (*schlechthinig*) dependence. To Schleiermacher, being absolutely dependent was about being freed from dependence on all finite things, exactly in the sense of Hegel's "casting off all dependence and abandoning oneself in the absolute self." Schleiermacher and Hegel had the same panentheist concept of how the world process operates and how God saves the world. Both were influenced by Spinoza and compelled to live it down. In content, though not in style, there was no difference between Hegel and Schleiermacher in this area. Hegel misconstrued Schleiermacher's concept of absolute dependence. Had Hegel read the second edition of Schleiermacher's *Glaubenslehre*, which stressed that religious feeling is redemptive by liberating the self from worldly dependence, it might have helped, but not likely. Hegel hated that Schleiermacher elevated piety over reason, always the source of his animus. Plus, Schleiermacher blocked him from the Academy of Sciences. Meanwhile Schleiermacher puzzled over Hegel's fixation with putting him down.[81]

For his highest category, Hegel alternated between *Die vollendete Religion* ("The Consummate Religion") and *Die offenbare Religion* ("The Revealed Religion"). The former predominated, expressing Hegel's conviction that Christianity is religion in its quintessential expression, or as he put it, "the religion in which religion has become objective to itself." Spirit is revelatory, he argued, the essence of God as spirit is "to be for an other," and true religion is revelatory as spirit for spirit: "God is this process of positing the other and then sublating it in his eternal movement. Thus the essence of spirit is to appear to itself, to manifest itself."[82]

The very idea of absolute spirit is to be the unity of divine and human nature. The reality of God is implicit in the definition of God as absolute Spirit. If God is defined as absolute Spirit, God necessarily exists. Hegel admired Anselm's ontological proof of God's existence, but he had his own version based on his logic. Rightly, Anselm rested his proof on the presupposition underlying all philosophy, the reality of perfection. God is that which is most perfect—that than which nothing greater can be conceived. If God is merely a concept, God is not what is most perfect, for the perfect is that which has being, not merely something that is represented. Being is necessarily contained in the concept of what is most perfect, assuming that that which is merely imagined is less perfect than that which is real. Hegel put it concisely, restating Descartes' restatement of Anselm's proof: "God contains all reality; being is a reality; therefore he also contains this reality, being."[83]

But Kant demolished the presupposition that we can pluck being from the concept of God. Hegel accepted Kant's verdict that a fact cannot be derived from a concept. "Existence" and "being" are not concepts of things that can be added to the concept of a thing, for existence and being are not predicates. The content of a quart of milk is the same whether I imagine one or hold one in my hand. If being is not a predicate, it is not a reality, and thus it is not a determination of content or something contained in the concept of God. To the extent that Hegel accepted Kant's terms, he was chastened by Kant's disproof. Anselm's proof was circular; its conclusion was already contained in the presupposition of metaphysical perfection—the unity of thought and reality. Hegel accepted that modern philosophy, after Kant, had to start with the difference between concept and being, thought and reality, ideal and real, from the standpoint of the knowing subject.[84]

But to Hegel, the modern presupposition that sense experience contains reality was no more credible than the classical presupposition it replaced. Post-Kantian philosophy, beginning with the difference between concept and being, had to show that concept and being are unified by the negation of their antithesis. This was the point of Hegel's logic—to *demonstrate*, not merely presuppose, that being is contained in the concept. The concept, as Hegel put it in the *Encyclopedia*, is a movement that determines itself *to be*; it realizes itself in the process of determining itself into being, objectifying itself for itself: "The Idea is truth in itself and for itself—the absolute unity of the notion and objectivity. Its 'ideal' content is nothing but the notion in its detailed terms: its 'real' content is only the exhibition which the notion gives itself in the form of external existence, while yet, by enclosing this shape in its ideality, it keeps it in its power, and so keeps itself in it." This definition, Hegel argued, that the Idea *is* the absolute, is itself absolute. Everything comes back to it: "The Idea is the Truth: for Truth is the correspondence of objectivity with the notion."[85]

The concept progresses from subjectivity to objectivity to idea. On this basis Hegel refashioned the ontological proof, stressing that Anselm, Descartes, Spinoza, and Leibniz had presuppositions, and so did Kant, and so did Hegel. Kant made some shrewd arguments, but the others had better presuppositions. Anselm presupposed perfection; Descartes, Spinoza, and Leibniz presupposed that God is the first reality; Kant countered that a concept is merely a concept, not something that corresponds to the concrete. The old metaphysical view was based on absolute thought, the unity of concept and reality, while Kant's view was based on the concrete. Hegel contended that the metaphysical view is superior in taking thoughts to be the concrete, not empirical human beings and actuality. The Kantian view is contradictory because it accepts the one-sided subjective concept *and* the concrete as equally valid. Hegel cautioned that to treat empirical reality as real is to bypass the subjective concept. The part that Kant got right was in holding up the subjective concept as the starting point; this was an advance on the metaphysical tradition of beginning with an abstract concept of perfection. Hegel summarized, "The older view is at a great advantage in that it is founded on the idea; in one respect the modern view is more advanced, in that it posits the concrete as unity of the concept and reality." But modern thought had a tendency to lapse into mere empiricism, owing to Kant's contradictions and dualism. The way forward, Hegel said, is to track the movement of the Idea in its realization of itself.[86]

The divine Idea explicates itself in three forms: eternal being, the form of universality; being for others, the form of appearance and particularization; and absolute presence-to-self, the form of return from appearance into itself. Whenever Hegel explained why Christianity is the consummate religion, he began with the Trinity and featured the Trinity. The three modes of divine being correspond to three modes of subjective consciousness. God in God's eternal essence is in pure thought, present to God's self yet manifest. God as being for others is represented, shaping consciousness in its relation to the other. God as absolute presence-to-self is subjectivity as such, partly as immediate subjectivity (disposition, thought, representation, sensation) but also as concept (reason, the thinking of free spirit). Hegel stressed that the Trinity is the fundamental truth in Christianity and his philosophy. Essentially it is the idea of God differentiating God's self while remaining identical with God's self in the process.[87]

He played down the usual talk about the Trinity being mysterious. Christians and non-Christians routinely said the Trinity is mystical and speculative, and thus mysterious. They assumed that only sense experience yields certainty, something lacking in the case of the Trinity. Hegel was defiantly of another mind: "What is for reason is not a secret. In the Christian religion one *knows*, and this is a secret only for the finite understanding, and for the thought that is based on sense experience." In the mode of sense experience the distinctions in God's being are immediate, and natural things are treated as reality. But this is the mode of externality, Hegel said: "As soon as God is defined as spirit, externality is sublated, and for sense this *is* a mystery; for sense everything is external to everything else—objects change, and the senses are aware of them in different ways."[88]

The change perceived by sense is itself a sensible process occurring in time and space. The sun comes into being, making life possible, but some day it will pass out of existence. Hegel urged his students to think beyond the everyday actuality of temporal existence: "The being of a thing is *now*, and its nonbeing is separated from now; for time is what keeps the determinations apart from another, external to one another." Even the understanding, like sense experience, separates being from nonbeing, holding fast to abstractions that are apprehended or conceived as existing on their own account. Hegel noted that people routinely scoffed at the Trinity at this level of comprehension, deriding a literalistic understanding of three equals one. Reason, making sense of the Trinity, employs the relationships of the understanding, "but only insofar as it destroys the *forms* of the understanding." Everything concrete contains contradictions, which are resolved only in the idea, "and the resolution is spiritual unity." Hegel's favorite example was the statement, "God is love." This expression makes God present to sensation, construes God as a loving person, and conceives God as inherently relational. God is conscious of God's self only in the other, and there is no consciousness of God apart from consciousness of the other.[89]

Obviously, Hegel acknowledged, the Trinitarian form of Father, Son, and Spirit is childlike, and it conveys a merely figurative relationship. "Love" would be a more suitable term than "Spirit" in this triad, for the Spirit does not enter into this relationship. The Father and the Son are Spirit no less than the third mode, and the Spirit of love is what is truthful. But at the level of spiritual expression, Hegel said, the childlike form of Trinitarian theology is indispensable. In Christ, God appears in sensible presence: "He has no other figure or shape (*Gestalt*) than that of the sensible mode of the spirit that is spirit in itself—the shape of the *singular human being*." God must generate the Son to distinguish God's self from God's self in a way that what is distinguished remains wholly God in God's self, "and their union is love and the Spirit." The witness of love/Spirit is the "infinite anguish" of being conjoined as conflicting elements of infinite and finite, objective and subjective.[90]

Hegel had begun as a philosopher of love, writing post-Kantian essays that tried to keep up with Fichte and Schelling. Hölderlin persuaded him that love—not Kant's transcendental unity of apperception or Fichte's absolute ego—is the golden principle of unification and synthesis. Henrich observes, "Once Hegel adopted the concept of love as the basic principle of his thinking, the system came forth without interruption. The theme 'love' was replaced by the richer structure of life—for apparent reasons—and later by the still richer concept of spirit (*Geist*)."

Hölderlin, however, a tortured genius, conceived love as deriving from original Being. His holism was a type of love mysticism, unifying all in the One. Hegel's holism of love was a coalescence of modes of relation, as Henrich explains: "The event of coalescence itself, and not a ground out of which coalescence derives, is for Hegel the true absolute, the 'all in all.'" This was why Hegel insisted that the absolute must be conceived as Spirit, not as Being. The concept of love, for Hegel, was an ontological principle *and* a principle of social subjectivity. Human consciousness moves from the exclusive particularity of I to the inclusive universality of We through reciprocal recognition. The inner relation of the self to itself is mediated by the love of another that unites the lover and the beloved. Robert R. Williams aptly remarks that Hegel interpreted the kingdom of God normatively as "a community founded on the beautiful rule of love." He was dead serious in construing human intersubjectity as patterned on the relation of love manifest in incarnation.[91]

By the time, however, that Hegel's religion lectures wound their way to the life of Jesus, he was in a hurry to get to Good Friday. Hegel's long discussions of the Trinity set up the next thing that really mattered to him: the death of God on the cross. He reasoned that he didn't need to separate his treatment of Christ incarnate from his explication of the Trinity; plus, Hegel had little at stake in the Gospel stories about the teaching, miracles, and travels of Jesus. Turning to Good Friday, he cited Johannes Rist's Lutheran passion hymn of 1641, "O Traurigkeit, O Herzeleid":

> O great woe!
> God himself lies dead.
> On the cross he has died.
> And thus he has gained for us
> By love the kingdom of heaven.[92]

The suffering and death of Christ on the cross disclose the very nature of God as loving, self-sacrificial, and affirmative. They also posit God's negation—"in death the moment of negation is envisaged." Hegel admonished against making Calvary merely about the sacrificial death of Jesus, an individual: "Heretics have interpreted it like that, but what it means is rather that *God* has died, that *God himself is dead*. God has died: this is negation, which is accordingly a moment of the divine nature, of God himself." God could not be satisfied by anything else than the negation of God's own immediacy: "Only then does God come to be at peace with himself, only then is he spiritually posited." As Father, God is closed up within God's self; as Son, God becomes the other and negates the other for the sake of love. This negation reconciles all who are separated from God to union with God.[93]

Humanity is posited in God's death as a moment of God's being. Hegel put it with stunning, proto-Lutheran, radical insight, counting on German memories of Luther's similarly searing theology of the cross: "Death is love itself; in it absolute love is envisaged. The identity of the divine and the human means that God is at home with himself in humanity, in the finite, and in [its] death this finitude is itself a determination of God." God, to Hegel, was not an exception to tragedy or exempt from it. There is no reconciliation that does not presuppose and include opposition, conflict, and anguish. The death of God is the ultimate disruption of life—the gift of love divine that reflects the anguish *in* love divine. The death of Christ is a death in God reflecting the inseparability of divine anguish from divine love. On Calvary, Hegel taught, the abstract divine being of the unhappy consciousness died, turning the cross into a symbol of hope. God is self-communicating spirit and self-sacrificing love, not a jealous monarch or being. God suffered and died on Calvary because God is love and loving unto death, accepting nothing less than reconciliation. Through God's self-sacrifice in Christ, God reconciles the world to God's self and reconciles God's self eternally with God's self.[94]

Hegel said the crucial point of the story is the next part. God raises Christ from the dead to the right hand of God. The nature of God is accomplished: Spirit pouring itself out for the other and returning to itself. A spiritual community takes up the story that this is God's story, revealing who God is. Hegel stressed that the Christian community recognized Christ as a determination of the nature of God raised to the right hand of God. The revelation is not what Jesus said, what he looked like, his miracles, or anything else on the level of sense experience. What mattered is the nature of God as spirit, the witness of Spirit to spirit, the negation of Calvary as an essential moment in the life of God, and the consummated self-realization of Spirit. The spiritual community adopts this story and sustains it; there is no life of faith without the community.[95]

But only philosophy can justify the content of the consummate religion, not bishops or history. Hegel put it aggressively: "The story may be full of the passionate disputes of bishops at church councils and so on—this is of no account." The content in and for itself is what matters, not the transmission of church doctrine. Only philosophy, which deals with concepts, can adequately handle the content of true religion, not religion, which deals with pictures. Mixing two concepts of history, Hegel unleashed one of his most famous statements: "Only by philosophy can this simply present content be justified, not by history (*Geschichte*). What spirit does is no history (*Historie*). Spirit is concerned only with what is in and for itself, not something past, but simply what is present. This is the origin of the community."[96]

Hegelian theologians fiercely debated what that meant, especially after Hegel was gone. Had Hegel used the term *Historie* in both sentences, he might have been construed as saying that history as bare literal fact justifies nothing and is not the point. Many of his more orthodox disciples took him that way. As it was, Hegel used the term *Geschichte*—interpreted history, or the meaning of history—in the first reference, which raised unsettling questions about the extent to which he regarded *any* historical basis as being intrinsic to Christian truth.

Hegel did not teach that philosophy should replace religion or that the historical core of Christianity is entirely dispensable. He taught his students that philosophy is originally dependent upon and must continue to be fed by religious experience. But he was careful not to say how much of the gospel narrative must be historically credible if Christianity is to be accepted as the true religion. The logic of his argument pressed in the direction of minimizing historicity. He could be sloppy with his terms, as in the example from his 1824 lectures noted here. In his subsequent lectures Hegel used the terms "divine history" and "eternal history" more frequently, emphasizing that God *is* the eternal history. The process by which God self-distinguishes and self-reintegrates is historical (*geschichtlich*). But Hegel left open, for Hegelian theologians, the question of how much one needs to believe about past historical (*historisch*) events or the historical (*geschichtlich*) process in which Spirit comes to self-realization.[97]

His emphasis on the Trinity raised a similar question differently. Repeatedly he was accused of puffing up the Trinity to cover up his pantheism. Most critics of this sort came from the theological right, which Hegel ignored. But there were liberals and Pietists in Schleiermacher's orbit who said the same thing, and in 1826 young Pietist theologian Friedrich August Gottreu Tholuck, recently transferred from Berlin to Halle, offered a novel version of the anti-Hegel argument that Hegel did not ignore. Tholuck was fervently pious, learned, not yet prominent, and worried that people with dubious Christian credentials were treated as leading Christian thinkers. Hegel was example A. Hegel's robust

Trinitarianism did not impress Tholuck, as Tholuck regarded the Trinity as an unfortunate Nicene pickup from Aristotelian and Neoplatonist philosophy. Pietists of Tholuck's type were comfortable with rationalist criticism on this topic and with Schleiermacher's consignment of the Trinity to an appendix. Tholuck suggested that Hegel covered his lack of pious feeling with a doctrine of dubious Christian merit. Hegel replied that he would never "put off such a basic doctrine" on the basis of a merely historical argument, as Tholuck did. Hegel declared, "I am a Lutheran, and through philosophy have been at once completely confirmed in Lutheranism. I detest seeing such things explained in the same manner as perhaps the descent and dissemination of silk culture, cherries, small-pox, and the like."[98]

Hegel shook his head at the thought of a nonmetaphysical Christianity. He believed that theologians who spurned metaphysical ideas trivialized the great Christian truths. To friends he groused that pious sincerity provides no immunity from degrading Christianity. To Tholuck he put it plaintively: "Does not the sublime Christian knowledge of God as Triune merit respect of a wholly different order than comes from ascribing it merely to such an extremely historical course?" Hegel could see a new anti-intellectualism coming that dressed up its backwardness with supportive quotes from Schleiermacher; Tholuck epitomized the type. However, Hegel struggled to keep his sarcasm in check when he warmed to this theme. Pietism had a vast following in Hegel's denomination. Hegel sustained a respectful tone with Tholuck; even writing to him was a sign of respect.[99]

With Roman Catholic critics, however, Hegel was less circumspect. Routinely he blasted the Catholic Church for opposing intellectual freedom. In class he mocked the doctrine of transubstantiation, worrying about what it meant if a mouse ate a host. A Catholic priest, responding to complaints from Catholic students, filed a protest to the Ministry of Religious and Educational Affairs. Hegel's reply was scathing. He found it astonishing that a Lutheran professor of philosophy at a Royal Prussian university might be told not to criticize Catholic dogmatism. He warned officials not to offend him, as he would take it as "a personal offense, indeed as an offense perpetrated by the High Government." As for the accusations that he was anti-Catholic, he said that some were based on "misunderstandings," others were "errors and misunderstandings born of feeblemindedness," some were obvious "falsehoods," and others displayed "malicious disparagement." Summing up, Hegel circled back to, "Don't offend me." If Catholic students couldn't bear to hear a Lutheran philosopher criticize their church, they shouldn't take his class. Meanwhile officials needed to do their jobs—protect academic freedom and refrain from offending Hegel.[100]

In his last years Hegel defended his Christian basis, attended to his followers, took notice that nearly all were theologians or religious philosophers, and cautioned that his philosophy was not a closed rational system. He did not claim to understand the content of an unknowable thing-in-itself; even to claim to know it exists would be too much. The absolute, he said, if it is absolute, is not something beyond our knowledge of it. The absolute holds such knowledge within itself—its very self-knowledge. Hegel taught that religion, art, and philosophy are the three basic practices by which people become aware of humanity's highest purposes, and religion is distinctly important because in it one joins a community dedicated to experiencing unity with the divine. One cannot be religious by one's self, because religion is about transcending one's individuality to achieve union with the divine through ritual practices and symbolic representation. In his 1827 lectures on religion, Hegel told students that whenever they philosophized about religion, they engaged in religious thinking, which leads beyond mere thinking: "Religion is for everyone. It is not philosophy, which is not for everyone. Religion is the manner or mode by which all human beings become conscious of truth for themselves."[101]

Thus he wanted theological followers, and got them. The breakthrough for Hegel occurred in the early 1820s, when two distinguished speculative theologians, Karl Daub and Philipp Marheineke, converted to Hegelianism. Daub, a struggling type of deep moral integrity, completed a massive two-volume work on the nature of evil in 1818. Marheineke, a serene, self-confident type and Hegel's colleague at Berlin, finished a dogmatic system in 1819. Both were followers of Schelling, espousing Schelling's concept of the absolute as an undifferentiated ground of being revealed through intuition. But both were uneasy with Schelling's emphasis on revelatory intuition. Hegel convinced them that his system retained the best parts of Schelling's idealism without Schelling's subjectivism. Daub and Marheineke, upon becoming Hegelians, drew their students to Hegel's circle, which expanded rapidly. By 1830 there were many Hegelians, most of them theologians or religious philosophers, notably Agathon Benary, Friedrich W. Carové, Kasimir Conradi, Johann F. G. Eiselen, Friedrich C. Förster, Georg Andreas Gabler, Eduard Gans, Karl

Friedrich Göschel, Leopold Henning, Hermann Hinrichs, Heinrich G. Hotho, Christian Kapp, Heinrich Leo, Karl Ludwig Michelet, Johann Karl Friedrich Rosenkranz, Heinrich T. Rötscher, Isaak Rust, and Karl Friedrich Werder. [102]

From the beginning there were debates about the Hegelian line on religion and politics. These debates famously intensified after Hegel died in 1831 and the Hegelian movement split into factions. Most of the literature on Hegelianism contents itself with a facile distinction between establishment "right-Hegelians" and the younger, politically radical, mostly atheist left-Hegelians. The so-called "right-Hegelians," in this telling, were politically accommodating, theologically conservative, and led by Marheineke, Förster, Hinrichs, and Göschel. The left-Hegelian ringleaders were David Friedrich Strauss, Ludwig Feuerbach, Bruno Bauer, and Friedrich Theodor Vischer. Strauss announced the left-right divide in his demolition of Christian myth, *The Life of Jesus Critically Examined* (1835); Feuerbach contended in *The Essence of Christianity* (1841) that Hegelianism made sense as a glorification of the human species, not God, since God is a projection of human desire; and Karl Marx cut his left-Hegelian teeth by reading Feuerbach and the early Bauer.[103]

But this simple right-left scheme does not work even with these leading examples, as Strauss was a monarchist and only Göschel in the "right" group was theologically conservative. Most Hegelians were not conservative in either theology or politics, despite going down in history as "right-Hegelians," and some of the leading Hegelian opponents of the youthful left insurgency—Rosenkranz, Julius Schaller, and Johann Eduard Erdmann—were equally youthful. The simplest possible rendering of the Hegelian movement has to distinguish among its right, centrist, and left factions, sort out various combinations of theology and politics, and leave room for individual cases. The fissures that erupted in the 1830s had roots in the Hegelian school over which Hegel personally presided.

In 1827 the Hegelians founded a flagship journal, *Jahrbücher für wissenschaftliche Kritik* (*Yearbooks for Scientific Criticism*), directed by Gans. Hegel spent his last years monitoring in-house back-and-forth, complaining that most of it was not worth his time, and doing it anyway; his school mattered to him. Religiously and politically, most Hegelians were in the middle with Hegel, although he drifted rightward politically in his later years. From the beginning there were Hegelian theologians who did not espouse Hegel's panentheism, notably Göschel, Conradi, and Rust. Hegel was gentle with them. He liked having traditional theists on his side, as long as they didn't mislead the public about Hegel's concept of God. On politics the main issue in Hegel's time was accommodation versus liberal reform. Hegelians had to be careful in this area, as government censorship made it perilous not to be an accommodationist. It was much easier to debate religion, as young Marx soon discovered. In Hegel's time most prominent Hegelians were accommodationists, led by Marheineke and also Conradi, Förster, Gabler, Göshel, Henning, and Hinrichs. There was a liberal reform faction led by Gans and Carové that, by 1835, had grown into the dominant Hegelian party, attracting Agathon Benary, Ferdinand Benary, Hotho, Michelet, Arnold Ruge, Wilhelm Vatke, and Werder. Both groups claimed Hegel for their side. Liberals pointed to Hegel's republican principles and his longtime defense of the French Revolution. Accommodationists pointed to his defense of constitutional monarchy and his later-years grumpy conservatism.[104]

Politically, Göschel bonded with establishment Hegelians over accommodation, though he had a populist streak; religiously he was a special case because he reached a large audience. Göschel's *Aphorisms on Ignorance and Absolute Knowing* (1829) defended Hegel's absolute knowing against the theology of ignorant feeling espoused by Schleiermacher, Jacobi, Fries, de Wette, and Tholuck. According to Göschel, Hegel's speculative philosophy preserved faith by raising it to the level of knowledge. Reason, the divine logos, is not a mere human faculty, unlike the understanding. Reason is revelatory, as demonstrated by Hegel. To think out of reason, one must be enlightened by "his day of Pentecost."[105]

Hegel cheered this popular rendering of his thought, with one caution: he did not begin by assuming the truth of Christianity. If his philosophy was Christian, as he believed it to be, it was only such by virtue of being led there by the self-determination of reason. His system moved toward the Christian principle, and ultimately affirmed Christianity as the consummate religion, but it did not begin with the principle of any religious tradition. Elsewhere Hegel gently advised Göschel that believing in a God hypostatized apart from the world is not Hegelian; he should let go of the separate supernatural realm, if he could.[106]

Being a celebrity wore on Hegel, but he worked hard at building up his following and legacy. In 1831 he died suddenly, probably of a gastrointestinal disease. His death was an enormous shock in Berlin, and deflating; even Hegel's enemies acknowledged he was a historic figure. His funeral featured a massive procession through the streets of Berlin, not quite on Schleiermacher's scale, but huge for an academic; Hegel was buried next to Fichte at Dorothea Cemetery.

Förster and Marheineke gave the funeral orations; Marheineke's status as the university's new rector added weight to his pronouncement. Förster, at Hegel's graveside, declared, "Let the dead bury the dead; to us belongs the living; he who, having thrown off his earthly chains, celebrates his transfiguration." In case anybody missed the analogy, Marheineke said it explicitly at the Great Hall of the university: "In a fashion similar to our savior, whose name he always honored in his thought and activity, and in whose divine teaching he recognized the most profound essence of the human spirit, and who as the son of God gave himself over to suffering and death in order to return to his community eternally as spirit, he also has now returned to his true home and through death has penetrated through to resurrection and glory."[107]

That was a portent; Hegelianism was no longer merely an academic theory. It was a modern religious movement led by an academic spiritual community. To comprehend the infinite through Hegel's dialectic was to attain infinity. Marheineke said it pointedly, telling mourners that Hegel's comprehension of the Spirit's self-realization in nature and history enabled him and others to be elevated to a state of spiritual being. Immediately the Hegelians formed a society to publish a complete edition of Hegel's works, beginning with his lectures on the philosophy of religion. The ringleaders were Marheineke, Förster, Michelet, Gans, Hotho, Henning, Ludwig Boumann, and Johannes Schulze. They were prolific and industrious, armed with movement zeal, intellectual self-confidence, and religious fervor. The fact that most Hegelians were religious had consequences for theological and philosophical faculties for decades. Factions developed quickly. So-called "right-Hegelians" defended the doctrine of immortality, treated gospel history as constitutive to Christian truth, and sometimes balked at Hegel's panentheism. Centrist Hegelians stuck closer to Hegel's formulations on religion and built up a dominant liberal Hegelian party on matters political and cultural. Left-Hegelians adopted political radicalism and turned against religion. Each group took what it wanted from the multiple meanings of Hegel's concepts.

Perhaps he rehabilitated the classic Christian worldview on modern terms by refashioning the Platonic idea that reason rules the world. Perhaps the religious sheen was a cunning way to propagate atheism. Or perhaps Hegel was right that his fluid, spiraling, relational, tragic panentheism of divine love and suffering changed how the supposed choice between theism and atheism should be conceived. On the latter reading, my own, it is not a coincidence that Hegel was the first to grasp what it means to say that Christ represented humanity. Orthodoxies teach that Christ represents the God-given dignity of the human species as such; Christ is the Second Adam successor of the First Adam, on the same level as the (purely mythical) First Adam. This Christ has long buttressed ecclesiastical and theological imperialism and exclusivism, presuming to represent the interest of humanity as a whole, as feminist theologian Dorothee Sölle recounted in *Christ the Representative* (1967) and Andrew Shanks recounts in *A Neo-Hegelian Theology* (2016).[108]

Hegel was the first to counter that Christ represents the God-given dignity *of human individuality* as such, not the human race. A church that claims to represent the entire human species can justify almost anything, as church history shows. Or it can set up its own overthrow, as happened in Feuerbach's criticism. Feuerbach simply overturned Christian orthodoxy, deifying the human race while getting rid of God, mistakenly believing that he refuted Hegel. Hegel stressed that human individuality is specific and ethical, like Jesus. Christianity, he argued, rightly understood, has to oppose slavery, because the infinite worth of God in human beings that Christ manifests inheres in individuals, not in a species as such. In Christianity, "human beings are considered according to what they are inherently, and they are inherently posited as something absolutely valuable, are taken up into the divine nature." It followed for Hegel that human individuals "count not as Greeks, Romans, Brahmans, or Jews, as high or low class; instead they have infinite worth as human beings and, in and for themselves, they are destined for freedom."[109]

Hegelianism, to many, was exactly what Hegel said about Christianity: it repressed its own genius, the principle of subjectivity that fuels the struggle for freedom. But there are better ways to read Hegel, and however that plays out, the basis of a liberating holistic theology is definitely there.

Against Hegelian Spirit

Marxism, Existentialism, and Wholly Otherness

No one compares to Hegel as a font of ideas that shaped modern philosophy. Maurice Merleau-Ponty put the point aggressively for his generation: "Hegel is the foundation for all of the great advances that have taken place in philosophy in the last 100 years, e.g., Marxism, Nietzsche, phenomenology, German existentialism, and psychoanalysis." Merleau-Ponty had in mind Marx, Feuerbach, Kierkegaard, Nietzsche, Heidegger, Edmund Husserl, Sigmund Freud, Theodor Adorno, Simone de Beauvoir, Henri Bergson, Bernard Bosanquet, F. H. Bradley, Frantz Fanon, Max Horkheimer, Karl Jaspers, Alexandre Kojève, Georg Lukács, Jacques Lacan, Rudolf Hermann Lotze, Herbert Marcuse, Otto Pfleiderer, Josiah Royce, Jean-Paul Sartre, Max Scheler, Ernst Troeltsch, all flat-out Hegelians, and himself. A subsequent list might include Judith Butler, Gilles Deleuze, Jacques Derrida, Jürgen Habermas, Axel Honneth, Emmanuel Levinas, Jean-Luc Nancy, Charles Taylor, Mark C. Taylor, and Slavoj Žižek. A similar list in theology would include nearly every significant German theologian of the nineteenth and twentieth centuries, every British religious Hegelian, and others.[1]

Marx, Kierkegaard, and Levinas stand out among the philosophical critics, and Karl Barth among the theologians. All scored against Hegelian totality and systematic closure. All construed Hegel as a right-Hegelian who systematized the totalizing transcendental ego of post-Kantian idealism. Marx and Kierkegaard, from opposite standpoints, corrected Hegel by contending that knowledge is peculiar to the situation of the knower. Barth and Levinas refashioned Kierkegaard's critique of Hegelian immanence and Kierkegaard's concepts of infinite qualitative difference and transcendence. All four were deeply indebted to Hegel and made important critiques of his thought, yet all were one-sided compared even to the stereotyped Hegel they described. Marx reduced Hegelian holism to one of its dimensions; Kierkegaard raged for subjective one-sidedness; Barth and Levinas resorted to irrational constructs of Wholly Other otherness to get away from Hegelian problems.

Marx's critique of Hegel was distinct from the other three and contributed mightily to the Hegelian legacy described by Merleau-Ponty. It yielded Marx's incomparably important critique of capitalism, including the many things that Marx got wrong. Marx took incisive aim at the Hegelian cult of the state and Hegel's willingness to defend it with archaic arguments. But Hegel had a richer account than Marx of human sociality, Hegel's thought had profound religious dimensions that Marx wrongly denigrated, and Hegel's ethic of recognition held up far better than Marx's impossible anarcho-communist utopia.

Marxian Criticism and Political Economics

Marx grew up comfortably in the German Rhineland family of a Jewish lawyer, Heinrich Marx, an Enlightenment deist who converted to Protestantism the year before Marx was born in 1818. The Marx family had two maids and a vineyard; Heinrich Marx was devoted to Voltaire, Rousseau, and Lessing; and he switched religions to keep the way of life that Rhineland Jews had gained under Napoleon. Marx studied law for a year at Bonn, partying riotously. In 1836 he transferred to the University of Berlin, where he fell hard for Hegel's system and switched to philosophy. He befriended a radical atheist theologian, Bruno Bauer, who told Marx that theory was becoming more practical than any practical career. Marx and Bauer assured each other that religion is backward and suffocating. Hegel's ostensibly Christian philosophy, they judged, was actually a cunning form of atheistic humanism. Marx took pride in possessing the secret of Hegel, wrote a doctoral dissertation on ancient Greek philosophies of nature, and returned to Bonn in 1841 to begin an academic career that never got started.[2]

Marx, Bauer, and a fellow anti-Christian left-Hegelian, Ludwig Feuerbach, wrote articles for a Young Hegelian journal, *Deutsche Jahrbücher*, mostly about religion and philosophy. Politics was a dangerous topic in autocratic Prussia, and Marx was unsure of his politics anyway. Writing about religion from Feuerbach's humanistic standpoint was a cunning way of writing about politics. In December 1841 Prussian king Frederick William II issued a paternalistic censorship instruction forbidding attacks on Christianity. Marx seethed and radicalized, abandoning any hope of an academic career. He protested that modern Prussia would have silenced Kant and Fichte on religion and morality. He wrote slashing articles for a liberal paper, *Rheinische Zeitung*, honing his scathing arsenal of contrasts, polemical caricatures, slogans, insults, sneers, italicized declamations, and chiasms. In November 1842 Marx met Friedrich Engels, the son of a wealthy cotton textile manufacturer. Engels fell in with Marx's crowd of radical Hegelians at Hippel's bar in Berlin, but by then, Marx was shedding his bourgeois graduate school conceits about being free and knowing Hegel's secret. Thus he was slow to warm to Engels, then on his way to a business career in Manchester, England.[3]

Marx fled to Paris in 1843 after losing his battle with government censors, married his cultured childhood sweetheart, Jenny von Westphalen, who came from an aristocratic Prussian family, and befriended Engels after landing a job editing the Franco-Prussian Yearbook (*Deutsch-Französische Jahrbücher*). Engels said the working class suffered all the problems of capitalism without receiving its benefits. Socialism had to be achieved by a revolution of the working class against the bourgeoisie; there was no parliamentary road to it. Marx bonded with Engels over this conviction while rethinking what he believed about Hegel. Left Hegelians struggled with Hegel's embarrassing defense of Prussia's constitutional monarchy; Marx judged that Hegel's political theory had a worse defect than its accommodating outcome—Hegel's endorsement of the liberal idea of an autonomous political sphere. States and the legal regimes of states, Marx reasoned, are rooted in the material conditions of life. Hegel wrongly split off the state from civil society, which underwrote his disastrous attempt to preserve the medieval system of estates in a modern legal framework. Hegel began with the state, rendering the human subject as a subject state. Real democracy, Marx said, is the opposite, beginning with particular human subjects. Hegel's pretentious theorizing about civil (*bügerlich*) society abstracted from its class character as *bourgeois* society, masking what mattered. Marx put it epigrammatically: "Just as it is not religion which creates man, but man who creates religion, so it is not the constitution which creates the people, but the people which creates the constitution."[4]

This critique cut deeper than the warhorse accusation that Hegel deified the Prussian state. Marx pioneered the claim that the real problem with Hegel was his veneration of civil society. Hegelian civil society veiled the terrible divisions of bourgeois society, which the Hegelian state more or less unified. Marx pointed to an archaic foible in Hegel's *Philosophy of Right* and his unabashed defense of government bureaucracy. The foible was Hegel's strained defense of limited primogeniture rooted in landed property and family tradition. Hegel said that modern government bureaucracy retained and refashioned the social value in ancient primogeniture. A decent society needs a class of officials that devotes itself to public service and is free from the pressures and corrupting temptations of politics. Marx countered that ancient primogeniture was based on private property, both were indefensible, and the modern state rests on both. This critique became a pillar of neo-Marxist theory after Marx was gone, but Marx never published it—the germ of his subsequent verdict that true democracy has no state at all.

Marx moved on to Feuerbach, who said that Hegel's idealism was the last refuge of theology, a rationalistic mystification of the absolute. Philosophy, to get real, had to begin with finite realities perceived by the senses. Marx lauded Feuerbach for proving "that philosophy is nothing but religion conceptualized and rationally developed; and thus that it is equally to be condemned as another form and mode of existence of human alienation." In that spirit Marx dramatically told his friend Arnold Ruge: "I am speaking of a *ruthless criticism of everything existing*, ruthless in two senses: The criticism must not be afraid of its own conclusions, nor of conflict with the powers that be." He did not grope for a new dogma, he told Ruge. Marx proposed to interrogate all dogmatisms, such as (German) Wilhelm Weitling's Communism, a "dogmatic abstraction," and (French) Pierre-Joseph Proudhon's anarchism, a "one-sided realization of the socialist principle." Marx scoffed that imagining utopias does not change the world. To do that, philosophy must ruthlessly criticize everything, beginning with religion and politics, which are terribly important because they stir human passions, interpret the world, and get people in trouble. Weitling and Proudhon commanded the world to bow down to their truth. Marx proposed to unveil "new principles to the world out of its own principles." Like Feuerbach, he sought to awaken the world from "its dream about itself," changing human consciousness. The real sins of individuals and societies were not what people confessed in church.[5]

In April 1844 the Prussian government accused Marx of high treason for his offensive articles, the following January he was banished from Paris, and Marx fled to Brussels, where he remained until Europe erupted in revolutions. In 1845 he decided that Feuerbach's invaluable critique of philosophy applied to Feuerbach. It was one thing to demythologize the self-alienated consciousness of all religious projection, showing how religion creates an imaginary world as an escape from the real world. Feuerbach deserved unstinting praise for that. However, Feuerbach over-looked "that after completing this work, the chief thing still remains to be done." Feuerbach's secular humanism was not very deep and it never left his head. Marx reasoned that religious consciousness is a *social* product, religious individuals belong to specific societies, and all social life is essentially practical. The antidote to religion is to transform society at the level of social practices, not to explain an abstract individual's religious consciousness: "The philosophers have only *interpreted* the world, in various ways; the point, however, is to *change* it."[6]

To care about the human ravages of religion is to struggle for a society purged of religion. Marx and Engels agreed that "Critical Criticism" had to begin there. Their first two collaborations sought to get German idealism out of their heads by developing a materialist theory of history. *The Holy Family* (1845) blasted Marx's former friend Bauer and his brother Edgar Bauer for turning politically conservative, sticking with Hegelian idealism, and skewering Proudhon. The Bauer brothers said the Spirit of freedom moves history forward. Marx and Engels countered that the movement of the masses, not some idealized "Spirit," moves history forward.[7]

The Holy Family was discursive, winding, and tedious, a running commentary on obscure articles. Marx worked harder on *The German Ideology* (1845), contending with Engels that Hegelian enlightenment was still religious—the last rationalistic resort of a spiritual project, "the rule of thoughts." Hegel glorified the German middle class and obscured "the wretchedness of the real conditions in Germany," Marx and Engels said. They began, by contrast, with the premise of human history: concrete individuals distinguished themselves from animals as soon as they produced their means of subsistence and thus indirectly produced their material life. The mode of production, whatever it is, is always crucial, expressing the specific mode of life of a people: "As individuals express their life, so they are. What they are, therefore, coincides with their production, both with *what* they produce and with *how* they produce."[8]

Every division of labor through human history marks a specific form of ownership. Tribal ownership came first, a form of extended family structure tied to hunting, fishing, and farming production. Ancient communal and state ownership models came next, where citizens held power over slaves only in their community, and town and country antagonism appeared. In more developed forms, states were pro-town or anti-town, and towns fought internally over industry versus maritime commerce. The third form of ownership, feudalism, replaced the town focus of antiquity with the vaster expanse of the country. The Roman conquests made feudalism possible, which was still a form of communal ownership, with peasant serfs replacing the slaves. Feudalism gave rise to corporate property—the feudal organization of trades—and it had very little division of labor, since every country contained within itself the town and country polarity.

Marx and Engels insisted that the production of ideas is always interwoven with the material activities of human agents. Human beings produce their ideas within and through particular forms of production and material life. They put it epigrammatically: "Life is not determined by consciousness, but consciousness by life." They turned political, taking aim at typical bourgeois debates about democracy, voting, aristocracy, and the like. These debates were a distraction from what mattered. To rattle on about democracy and voting was to ignore the real struggle of the laboring masses not to starve or freeze. For a moment, Marx and Engels turned lyrical, writing a fanciful passage that stood out in Marx's entire subsequent corpus. In all societies preceding the coming communist society, one was a hunter, a fisher, a shepherd, or even a cultural critic—pointedly they left out slaves, serfs, and factory workers. But to not starve, one had to stick with hunting, fishing, shepherding, or criticizing. Losing your livelihood was life threatening in all previous forms of life. In a communist society, they said, no one would be consigned to one thing or forced to stick with it: "Each can become accomplished in any branch he wishes, society regulates the general production and thus makes it possible for me to do one thing today and another tomorrow, to hunt in the morning, fish in the afternoon, rear cattle in the evening, criticize after dinner, just as I have a mind, without ever becoming hunter, fisherman, cowherd, or critic."[9]

Revolutionary deliverance would somehow create brilliant multipurpose human beings that abolished the division of labor. Communism was precisely the abolition of, and liberation from, the rule of human products that gains power over human communities, grows out of control, constrains human expectations, and blights the lives of the many. Marx joined the League of Communists in December 1847, believing that the impending revolution would far exceed what happened in France in 1789. He and Engels wrote *The Communist Manifesto* flush with that conviction. It resounded with motivational language, came at the outset of Marx's ultra-left phase, and conveyed only one side of his complex thought. But it was by far his most famous work, and it defined true Marxism for many. The opening sentence declared that Europe was haunted by the "specter of communism." Marx and Engels knew that was absurd. Europe in 1848 was at war over bourgeois freedoms, not communism. Europe had very few communists, and Marx was just beginning to meet them. In section two, he and Engels announced the funeral of the bourgeoisie, but in the final section they urged proletarians to make alliances with it. The bourgeoisie was corrupt, inevitably hostile to workers, and dying, yet proletarians should help bring it to power, working with Chartists in England, petty-bourgeois radicals in France, agrarian reformers in the United States, and the bourgeoisie itself in Germany.[10]

Once the bourgeois revolution took place, the proletarian revolution would replace it. Marx and Engels said the bourgeois revolution in Germany would be the "prelude" to an immediate proletarian revolution. That sounded like an immediate transition to a communist revolution, skipping an intervening period of bourgeois government. Marx called for alliances with radical liberals, flirted with conspiratorial insurrection, and in April 1849 stopped calling for alliances, urging workers to form their own parties. He also used the fateful phrase, "dictatorship of the proletariat." In April 1850 Marx and Engels signed the declaration of the World Society of Revolutionary Communists: "The aim of the association is the overthrow of all privileged classes, their subjugation by the dictatorship of the proletariat which will maintain the revolution in permanence until communism, the last organizational form of the human family, will be constructed."[11]

Marx fled to England after the revolution failed, holing up in the British Museum. In 1859 he published his first critique of capitalism, *A Contribution to the Critique of Political Economy*, attaching a simplistic preface that seemed to espouse mechanistic determinism, later called vulgar Marxism. Marx played a stormy role in the First International, battling with anarchists over the role of the state in facilitating a transition to communism. In 1867 he published his masterwork, the first volume of *Capital*, and seethed that almost no one read it. In his second edition of 1873, Marx said that German intellectuals tried to kill the book by ignoring it, just as "they had managed to do with my earlier writings." Marx owed his few reviews to his socialist following, a point of pride and frustration to him. Economics, he lamented, was a "foreign science" in Germany, where capitalism had a delayed beginning and the professors "remained schoolboys." Thus *Capital* got shallow reviews complaining that the book was dry, long, cumbersome, and boring. Most reviewers failed even to recognize that he adopted the deductive method of the Smith/Ricardo English school.[12]

One reviewer, catching Marx's favorable reference to Hegel, admonished that the Hegel vogue was long past and Marx needed to get his clock fixed. Marx set the record straight. Yes, he was a protégé of Hegel, "that mighty thinker," because Hegelian dialecticism was powerfully important to him. Hegel recovered and refashioned an indispensable form of ancient Greek thought, he rightly put conflict and negation at the heart of all things, and Marx employed distinctly Hegelian tropes in his theory of value. But Marx contended that his dialectic was the opposite of Hegel's. To Hegel, ideas were ultimate reality, and real things were exemplifications of ideas. Marx said Hegel's idealism turned everything upside down. Hegel fashioned the life process of the human brain—the process of thinking—into an independent subject, which Marx called "the demiurgos of the real world." To Marx, "the ideal is nothing else than the material world reflected by the human mind, and translated into forms of thought."[13]

That was an echo of the early Marx's protest that Hegel taught German academics how to glorify their culture and society. Thirty years later, intellectual fashions had changed, and Marx told "peevish, arrogant, mediocre" intellectuals they had no reason to look down on Hegel, a colossal thinker who got crucial things right. Hegelian dialecticism was vastly superior to the simplistic worldview that German academics took from English economists. Hegel grasped that everything is in motion, everything has a transient nature and a momentary existence, and thus, the ever-fluid process of life "is in its essence critical and revolutionary." On the other hand, Marx contended, it was terribly important to repudiate what came from Hegelians who ignored Hegelian negation and/or couldn't get religious idealism out of their heads. Marx boasted that he managed it fresh out of graduate school. Hegel stood the dialectic on its head; Marx turned it on its feet and thereby discovered "the rational kernel within the mystical shell." Both claimed to be "scientific" in the sense of German *Wissenschaft*—a systematic body of knowledge in which objectively necessary relationships are established—but Marx believed that he better earned the name, having deconstructed Hegel's bourgeois ideology about civil society.[14]

Capital came late in Marx's career, and it needed many years afterward to grow into its career as the basis of Marxism—a fundamental critique of capitalist political economy. It expounded a labor theory of value and capital that amplified Ricardo's labor theory of price, with a radically different upshot, and a theory of capital, surplus value, and exploitation that expounded what was at stake in the proletarian struggle. The book's first three chapters summarized the theory of value and money that Marx developed in *A Contribution to the Critique of Political Economy*, which settled his previous uncertainty about whether alienation is primarily a by-product of commodity production per se or the appropriation of the product by capitalists. The early Marx seesawed on this question, but in *Contribution* he argued that capitalist appropriation is the crux of the matter.

His thought reversed the logic and history of classical economics. Marx began, like Smith and Ricardo, with the concepts of supply and demand, competition, and the market. But unlike classical theory, Marx did not move into quantitative formulas about market relations and the flow of exchange value. He applied Hegelian dialectics to economics, seeking to reveal the essential-whatever behind the phenomenal appearances of market relations. Marx's pursuit of this post-Kantian project led him to examine production and relations of production, first generally, and then specifically under capitalism. *Contribution* was the overture to *Capital*. Marx scrapped his first introduction to *Contribution*, explained that it was pointless "to anticipate results which still have to be substantiated," and substituted, fatefully, the only summary of his philosophy he ever published: human beings enter relations of production in the social production of their experience that correspond with a given stage of economic development and are independent of their will. The totality of these relations of production is the "real foundation" of society, "on which arises a legal and political superstructure with corresponding forms of social consciousness. The mode of production of material life conditions the general process of social, political, and intellectual life." Social existence determines consciousness; philosophies and ideologies rationalize economic interests; and no social order perishes until the productive forces for which it is sufficient are developed.[15]

The tight summaries of the preface provided proof texts for vulgar Marxists for decades to come. Had Marx stuck with his ambivalence about preface summarizing, he might have inspired much less vulgar Marxism. *Contribution* plunged immediately into its gritty, detailed, demystifying business, analyzing capital in general. It began with commodities and commodity production, distinguished between use value and exchange value, and developed an analysis of money as a universal measure of value and medium of exchange. It favored Ricardo over Smith, because Ricardo emphasized the problem of production. Marx argued in *Contribution* that exchange relations—the appearances of the market—express the *social* relations of labor activity and the division of labor that fundamentally constitute society itself. Under feudalism, capital consisted mostly of tools and secondarily of money capital, retaining an agrarian character. Under capitalism, the reverse took place. Agriculture became largely a branch of industry, dominated by capital. The same thing happened to rent.

Put differently, in pre-capitalist societies the relation of laborers to their work was natural and human. Human relations were undisguised throughout the process of production, exchange, and consumption. Under capitalism, Marx said, the same relations are veiled through institutions shrewdly dubbed the "free market" and "private property." Relations between people are replaced by what appear to be relations between things. Marx's unwieldy name for this process, *Verdinglichung*, had no English equivalent; translators usually opt for "reification." The problem of alienation is distinctive to capitalist society, he contended. To be sure, "natural relations" still exist in capitalist societies wherever landed property remains the decisive factor. But wherever capital predominates, it changes everything: "Capital is the economic power that dominates everything in bourgeois society. It must form both the point of departure and the conclusion and it has to be expounded before landed property. After analyzing capital and landed property separately, their interconnection must be examined."[16]

Marx got that far in *Contribution*, which summarized parts of his sprawling unpublished notebooks of 1857–1858, *Grundrisse der Kritik der Politischen Oekonomie*. He had worked out his method and the gist of his argument, but needed a deeper base of evidence for his challenge to classical theory. That required nearly another decade of work. Textbook economics treated the behavior of money as the essence of economic activity. Commodities are objects of human want and need, all societies turn commodities into money and back again in a circular flow of exchange value, and economics tracks the flow of money in satisfying human needs and wants. *Contribution* explored Marx's seemingly simple question of where the value of a commodity comes from in order to show, as Marx argued powerfully in *Capital*, that the capitalist system of production and exchange renders human labor literally inhuman by turning commodities into fetishes. Marx spurned conventional presumptions that money originated in circulation, capitalists bought commodities below their value, and sold them above their value. Convention was superficial, and wrong. Capitalists bought and sold commodities at their value, but somewhere they withdrew more value from circulation than they put into it. The answer to the riddle lay in the process of production itself, which made it structural and objective, not a function of something subjective like a desire.

He distinguished between the use value of a commodity (a property intrinsic to the commodity) and its exchange value (the value relative to other commodities in an exchange situation), asking how it could be that commodities with different use values were measured in the same units. Marx cautioned against the appearance that commodities are readily understood. Use values, he allowed, such as making a table out of wood, are not mysterious, and neither are the determining factors of value, which are functions of human organisms. The exchange process, however, turns a commodity into "a very queer thing, abounding in metaphysical subtleties and theological niceties." Marx's theory of commodity fetishism built on this insight. Commodities are mysterious because they stamp the social character of human labor upon the product of labor *as an objective character*, and they present the relation of the producers to the sum total of their labor as a social relationship *between the products of their labor*, not between the producers. Capitalism renders the social relations between who makes what, who works for whom, and the production time required to make a commodity as economic relations between objects—the value of a given commodity when compared to another commodity. The market exchange of commodities thus obscures the actual human relations of production, "social things whose qualities are at the same time perceptible and imperceptible by the senses." Perception, Marx reasoned, requires a physical relationship between physical things. An actual passage of light occurs between an external object and the optic nerve of an eye. But there is absolutely "no connection" between the physical things that become commodities and their labor-produced value, on the one hand, and the physical nature of the commodity and material relations arising out of the exchange process, on the other.[17]

Marx called commodity fetishism "the fantastic form of a relation between things." To find an analogy, one had to take flight into the misty world of religion, where productions of the human brain appeared as really existing individuals that interacted with human beings. Commodity fetishism was very much like religion: "This I call the Fetishism which attaches itself to the products of labor, so soon as they are produced as commodities, and which is therefore inseparable from the production of commodities." Capital is more expansive than commodities, Marx argued, because all manner of societies at various stages of economic development created commodities. The barter system began with a social division of labor that separated use value from exchange value. Capitalism, however, rests on historical conditions that were not given with the mere circulation of money and commodities. Capitalism sprang into life only when an owner of the means of production and subsistence engaged a laborer in the market selling his or her labor-power: "And this one historical condition comprises a world's history. Capital therefore announces from its first appearance a new epoch in the process of social production."[18]

Marx blasted Ricardo and his school for blithely assuming surplus value. Economists, he protested, screened out most of their subject, capitalism—a social system of intense accumulation of commodities. Though Ricardo rightly identified labor productivity as the originating cause of surplus value—Marx's favored term for profit—Marx said the entire Ricardo school was conveniently incurious about how profits are generated. Surplus value consists in the difference between the labor value of products and the payment for the labor *power* expended in production by workers. All pre-capitalist systems conceived money as a means of exchanging some commodities for others: commodity-money-commodity. Capitalism, Marx argued, turns money into something else: capital to be sought for its own sake. Capitalism is about money being used to obtain more money: money-commodity-money.[19]

Ricardo and Adam Smith, discussing the value of labor, reversed and obliterated what was actually at issue. Marx chided that to invoke the value of labor as an abstract concept is no more meaningful than to invoke the value of the earth. The real value of labor arises from relations of production, which are categories for the "phenomenal forms of essential relations." Every science except economics recognized that things in their appearances often represent themselves in inverted forms. Classical economists, by contrast, carried on the old physiocrat doctrine of a necessary price, rephrased by Smith as the "natural price" of labor, a commodity value expressed in money. Marx countered that what economists called the value of labor is in fact the value of the labor power of a human personality—a value as different from its laboring function as a machine is different from the work it performs.[20]

Capitalism changed the world by turning the scattered, individually owned means of production into powerful levers of production. This process moved from simple cooperation to manufacturing to modern industry, transforming individual instruments of labor into mighty productive forces that turned the means of production into *social* means of production. Marx stressed that products became *social* products, joint productions of laborers operating machinery workable only by collectivities. Capitalism socialized the producers, the means of production, and the products, yet bourgeois society treated all three as though nothing had changed; the means of production and products still belonged to individuals.

Capitalism abolished the conditions upon which individual owners owned their own products and brought them to market, but it allowed owners of the means of production to appropriate the products of labor to themselves, notwithstanding that others did the producing and created the value. This contradiction, to Marx, was the key to the crisis of capitalist civilization. The more that the capitalist class attained mastery over the many fields of production through the new mode of production, the more it reduced individual production to marginal status. Capitalists socialized production without socializing appropriation. They got away with it by firing troublemakers, thwarting unions, holding down wages, rewarding compliant lawmakers, and maintaining an industrial reserve army of unemployed workers. The latter concept inspired one of Marx's most colorful passages in *Capital*: "This antagonism vents its rage in the creation of that monstrosity, an industrial reserve army, kept in misery in order to be always at the disposal of capital; in the incessant human sacrifices from among the working class, in the most reckless squandering of labor-power, and in the devastation caused by a social anarchy which turns every economical progress into a social calamity." Repeatedly Marx said the accumulation of capital at one pole corresponds with an accumulation of misery and brutality at the other pole. He said it so emphatically that orthodox Marxists were stuck with it, although Engels played it down after witnessing the capitalist boom of the 1880s and early 1890s.[21]

Marx owed to Hegel the language and method of dialectical conflict, negation, and social transformation on which he based the Marxian advance on Ricardo. The capitalist mode of appropriation, he argued, is a consequence of the capitalist mode of production, which produces capitalist private property. The production of capitalist private property is the "first negation" of individual private property, after which capitalist production begets its own negation: "It is the negation of negation." Capitalism does not reestablish private property in a modernized form for the producer. It *gives* individual property to the capitalist from the social bounty of modern expropriation and accumulation. Marx seethed that capitalist apologists had the "effrontery" to describe wage slavery and the "despotism of capital" as economic freedom. He stressed that the transformation of individual private property into capitalist private property was far more wrenching, violent, and protracted than the current struggle to transform capitalistic private property into socialized property. Capitalism, after all, expropriated the mass of the people "by a few usurpers." The proletarian revolution expropriated a few usurpers for the sake of the many.[22]

W. E. B. Du Bois allowed that Marx might have erred about the labor theory of value, surplus value, and the inevitability of socialist revolution. He could have added that Marx certainly did err about the falling rate of profit, ever-worsening misery, economic determinism, inevitable catastrophe, proletarian dictatorship, and the inevitable dissolution of the state. Still, writing in 1933, Du Bois rightly said it was hard to avoid the verdict that labor, not gambling, is the foundation of value, that "business acumen" is a euphemism for exploitation, and that something is terribly wrong with a system that generates fantastic inequalities. Marx was "a colossal genius of infinite sacrifice and monumental industry, and with a mind of extraordinary logical keenness and grasp." This was the highest accolade that Du Bois ever gave to anyone, and the highest possible on his scale of values, since Du Bois prized work, love, and sacrifice above all things, "and the greatest of these is sacrifice."[23]

Marxism is best construed as a critique of capitalism, not as a constructive theory of anything else. It is the most powerful and illuminating critique of the capitalist system ever conceived, no matter how many things Marx got wrong, and Marx knew very well what he owed to Hegel. Like Kierkegaard, Marx brilliantly corrected Hegel by expounding the distinct situation of particular knowing subjects, and like Kierkegaard, nearly everything that he wrote bore the marks of contending with Hegel.

Kierkegaard and the Hegelian Whole

There are many Kierkegaards, because Kierkegaard tried out multiple authorial personas through his pseudonyms, and he was the greatest religious thinker of the mid-nineteenth century. He skewered the modernist project of replacing biblical truths with a myth of modern progress even as his emphasis on individual subjectivity made him as idealistic as any post-Kantian. In Kierkegaard's case the personal drama looms over and within everything. He was steeped in family tragedy, wracked with emotional torment, bitterly competitive with his only surviving sibling, had one friend as an adult, and chose romantic heartbreak over his one chance at normal happiness. Aptly he noted of himself, while recalling one of his statements about Socrates, "His whole life was a personal preoccupation with himself, and then guidance comes along and adds something world-historical to it."[24]

The first part was obvious. Guidance, in his meaning, was divine; Kierkegaard believed that his life had a religious purpose. The last part, about world-historical significance, was an astounding conviction, considering his circumstances; Kierkegaard believed, rightly, that he was too brilliant not to be discovered as a major thinker.

He spent his entire life in and around Copenhagen, except for four trips to Berlin and a pilgrimage to his father's roots in Jutland. Kierkegaard was unknown outside Denmark when he died in 1855, and he remained unknown for decades afterward. In the early twentieth century he entered the canon as the first existentialist and an influence on the dialectical theology generation. In the late twentieth century he survived the canon busting of deconstructionists, who hailed him as a forerunner of postmodernism, not that he would have cared about postmodernism. Kierkegaard's postmodern credentials are real; he subverted authorial authority, specialized in indirect communication, ridiculed the pretensions of theoretical systems, and said that truth is subjectivity. Thus he acquired postmodern interpreters who denied that he made any arguments or held any convictions. But he cared passionately about the radical possibility of becoming a Christian, roaring with convictions about it.[25]

Kierkegaard never doubted his intellectual power to do anything he willed, except to be delivered from melancholia, over which he had no power. He said he was tormented every day of his life, and could have gone either way with it, either hating human beings and cursing God, or loving human beings and praising God. In later life he stressed that he never rejected Christianity, even in his early twenties when he blew his father's fortune on angry, rebellious, frivolous self-indulgences. But despair took hold of him; Kierkegaard needed to be rebellious and alienated just to find his own thoughts. For our purposes we cut to his battle with Hegel.[26]

Kierkegaard chafed at Hegel's apparent low regard for individual subjectivity. In 1835 Kierkegaard wrote in his journal, "What I really need is to be clear about *what I am to do*, not what I must know, except in the way knowledge must precede all action. It is a question of understanding my destiny, of seeing what the Deity really wants *me* to do; the thing is to find a truth which is truth *for me*, to find *the idea for which I will live and die.* And what use here would it be if I were to discover a so-called objective truth, or if I worked my way through the philosophers' systems and were able to call them all to account on request, point out inconsistencies in every single circle . . . if it had no deeper meaning for myself and for *my life?*"[27]

He shucked off his father's Protestant orthodoxy, he said, shortly after entering college. Then he chafed at Hegelianism, a substitute colossus, though his doctoral dissertation, *The Concept of Irony*, employed Hegel's dialectic of possibility, actuality, and necessity, interpreting Socrates as an ironist of absolute negativity. Kierkegaard said the irony of Plato's Socrates was world-historical, something much higher than romantic irony. Then he struggled to get Hegel out of his head, appalled that it was so difficult.[28]

His early books stewed and thrashed over his agonizing decision not to marry Regine Olsen. *Either/Or* (1843), two volumes "edited" by Victor Eremita, contained the writings of a young man reflecting the aesthetic view of life and an older friend's defense of the ethical way of life. *Repetition* (1843), by Constantin Constantius, told the story of a young poet who had to break his engagement for ethical reasons and despaired of mere repetition in the ethical sphere. *Fear and Trembling* (1843), by Johannes de Silentio, explored the idea of faith transcending the ethical, centering on Abraham's willingness to sacrifice his son Isaac at God's command. *Prefaces* (1844), by Nicolaus Notabene, consisted entirely of comical prefaces. *The Concept of Dread* (1844), by Vigilius Haufniensis, offered a psychological reflection on original sin and a critique of philosophical systems. *Stages on Life's Way* (1845), a sequel to *Either/Or*, assembled documents discovered by Hilarious Bookbinder.[29]

Kierkegaard wrote in pseudonyms to get him out of the picture, reasoning that the ideas mattered, not him. More important, by using pseudonyms he could be different people, and say whatever he wanted to say, without having to defend himself. *Philosophical Fragments* (1844), by Johannes Climacus, contrasted the paradox of the "God in time" to philosophical idealism, epitomized in Socratic recollection. Kierkegaard wrote it in his own name and switched to Climacus the day before it was published. Then he wrote *Concluding Unscientific Postscript* (1846), again as Climacus, screaming irony in the title, and anti-Hegelianism.[30]

Johannes Climacus claimed he was not a Christian or a philosopher, and he lacked even an opinion. He was "an idler from love of ease" and an opponent of systems who came only to dance "in the service of Thought." He hoped to honor God and find some pleasure in dancing, but he would not risk anyone else's life in playing the game, unlike system builders. His dance partner was the thought of death; the dance itself was with death, in opposition to opinion. Others could bring their philosophy baggage to the dance, but he would not dance with them.[31]

Philosophical Fragments had five acts, in the manner of classical drama, and two main characters, Socrates and Christ, whom Climacus called "the God in time." An interlude between the last two acts, questioning whether the past is more necessary than the future, suggested the passage of time; otherwise the context was timeless, featuring dialogue carried by the two main characters, which was interrupted at the end of each chapter by the reader's remarks, to which Climacus replied. The book featured G. E. Lessing's haunting question about whether it is possible to base one's eternal happiness on historical knowledge, something merely probable and contingent. Its dramatic narrative featured Climacus' question: How does Christian paradox differ from Socratic recollection? Another question, never posed by Climacus, loomed over *Philosophical Fragments* and virtually shouted in *Concluding Unscientific Postscript*: Was despair the motivating force of Kierkegaard's dialectic? Did he merely replace Hegel's abstract negation with the despair of subjective spirit?

Socrates, pondering that a knower cannot seek what one already knows or does not know, taught that all learning and inquiry is a kind of remembering. The learner dispels one's ignorance by coming to oneself in the consciousness of what one already knows. The truth comes from within an individual, not without; the teacher is merely a prod to recollection. Climacus prized Socrates for awakening minds in the streets and marketplace. In Socratic idealism, each individual is one's own center. Climacus preferred the magnanimity and brilliance of Socrates to organized Christianity, which gave titles and rank to mediocre pastors, professors, and church officials mediated "in a common madness."[32]

He took for granted the Socratic model of recollection, especially the primacy of the moment of recognition, laying a heavy burden on it: "The Moment in time must have a decisive significance, so that I will never be able to forget it either in time or eternity; because the Eternal, which hitherto did not exist, came into existence in this moment." This was the crucial presupposition of the dance. Climacus reasoned that if the moment is to have decisive import, the seeker must be "destitute of the Truth" up to the moment of recognizing it. If the seeker possesses the truth as ignorance, the moment is not decisive; it is merely occasional. Moreover, even to call someone a seeker is problematic, for one cannot seek the answer unless one recalls it. There is no moment until one recognizes that one is in error in relation to truth, not wanting the truth. But how does it help to be reminded of something that one has not known and does not recall?[33]

Climacus allowed that the Socratic teacher helps learners to recognize they are in error. But that merely drives the learner further from the truth; ignorance is bliss compared to learning that one is devoid of the truth. So the teacher, being merely accidental, drives the learner away; there is no moment between teacher and learner. The Socratic teacher is merely an occasion, "even if he is a God." No one can be taught to see one's error or one's responsibility for it, even if everyone else sees it: "For my own Error is something I can discover only by myself, since it is only when I have discovered it that it is discovered." This being in error by reason of one's own guilt, Climacus explained, is called *sin*. There is an apparent freedom in learning that one is in error and is morally responsible for it, for to be free is to be what one is by one's act. But there is no real freedom in being free from the Truth. To be exiled by one's own self is to be in bondage, a slave to sin.[34]

Socrates was no help with that, for the Socratic view has no moment. Hegelian idealism was no help either, because Hegel said *every* moment is necessary and the fullness of time. The moment that makes a real difference, Climacus conjectured, has a distinct character. It is brief, temporal, and transient, like all moments, and also past, like every moment in the next moment. But it is also decisive and filled with the eternal, something deserving the name, "the Fullness of Time."[35]

Climacus got that far without appealing explicitly to Christianity; *Philosophical Fragments* was a thought project about thought self-produced. He confessed that he plagiarized Christian ideas, not needing to be Christian to grasp the Christian truism that love needs nothing to satisfy its own desire. Love is the cause of all suffering, because God is love and God desires in love to share the condition of the lowest and most vulnerable. God is like the seed of an oak planted in earthen vessels, bursting them apart, which is what happens when God implants God's self in human weakness. The movement that satisfies itself completely is love—the condition of its own need, the only need that is not a privation. Love creates and satisfies its own need because love and its movement are the same thing.[36]

Philosophical Fragments, abounding in paradox, cautioned against slighting paradoxes, "for the paradox is the source of the thinker's passion, and the thinker without a paradox is like a lover without feeling: a paltry mediocrity." Every passion, at highest pitch, wills its downfall, and reason is not satisfied until it collides with something resulting in its undoing. The "supreme paradox" of thought is that reason tries to discover something that thought cannot think. Proofs of God's existence fall into that category; Climacus waved them off, rehearsing Kant's argument that existence is not a predicate, without mentioning Kant. Reason, like paradox, when played out, ends in frustration, for reason and paradox are linked by passion, and both will their downfall by passion. To Climacus, everything depended on the Moment, the discovery of something that makes a difference.[37]

The incarnation of God, he said, is not secondary to the God's teaching; the incarnation *is* the teaching that makes a difference: "If the God had not come himself, all the relations would have remained on the Socratic level; we would not have had the Moment, and we would have lost the Paradox." The God's appearance as a servant is actual, not a disguise. Climacus said the object of faith is a contradiction, the paradoxical Moment. Faith is not seeing, for God incarnate is not immediately knowable. Neither is faith an act of will, for human volition operates within the condition of sin and error. Faith is a miracle, the recognition of something absurd, the eternal given in time, a gift of grace.[38]

Climacus refused all entreaties to make faith less paradoxical, offensive, or risky. He did not believe the past ever becomes necessary, because necessity is wholly a matter of essence; Climacus was more essentialist than Hegel on this point. Nothing is necessary when it comes into existence; the essence of the necessary is to exclude coming into existence. Anything that becomes actual retains the possibility with which it emerged. Climacus insisted that faith cannot be distilled from even the most detailed account. The "historical fact" of the incarnation is what matters, not any details about it. He wanted to leave it there, but realized he could not call the incarnation a historical fact without saying something about its historicity. So he obliged: "If the contemporary generation had left nothing behind them but these words: 'We have believed in such and such a year the God appeared among us in the humble figure of a servant, that he lived and taught in our community, and finally died,' it would be more than enough." All that is needed is to say that the God shared our life and died.[39]

This was the answer to Lessing's question, to the extent that Climacus had an answer; he could not help those lacking a high threshold for paradox. There *can* be a historical departure for an eternal consciousness, and it *can* be of more than merely historical interest *if* it is the unique historical fact of the eternal incarnated in the Moment. But basing one's eternal happiness on historical knowledge is out of play, for the Moment is recognized only in faith. Gospel salvation features "a new organ, Faith; a new presupposition, the consciousness of Sin; a new decision, the Moment; and a new Teacher, the God in Time."[40]

The irony of Climacus was that he waxed urgently and insistently on the Moment without giving himself to it. He was more Christian than those who turned Christ into a theory or a historical conclusion, yet he was still an outsider. He had one question—how he might become a Christian. It didn't matter that he was born in Copenhagen and raised in an ostensibly Christian culture. Of Kierkegaard's early pseudonyms, Climacus was the one closest to him. Climacus lived on the great questions, read books about Christianity and philosophy, was skilled at dialectic, and described the leap into faith, yet wavered over taking it.

Climacus was also the most strenuous of Kierkegaard's pseudonyms in insisting that a point of view should speak for itself without calling attention to an author and without solving problems that readers need to solve for themselves. In *Concluding Unscientific Postscript*, the sequel to *Fragments*, Climacus lauded *Fragments* for not rationally solving the problem it posed. He praised *Either/Or* for letting readers decide whether they favored the aesthetic or ethical ways of life. He commended *Repetition* for refraining from dogma, as the modern age already had "too much knowledge" and not enough inwardness. He lauded the authors of *Repetition* and *Fear and Trembling* for refusing to write for "paragraph-eaters," information-hungry types lacking any clue of inwardness. He praised *Stages on Life's Way* for refusing to reach a conclusion, which denied to readers a feeling of safety, throwing them on their own. He understood that nineteenth-century sophisticates, being immersed in world-historical problems, looked down on his "egotistical vanity" in laying so much stress on his "own petty self." But Climacus was unbowed: "It is not I who have become so presumptuous of my own accord, but it is Christianity itself which compels me to ask the question in this manner. It puts quite an extraordinary emphasis upon my own petty self, and upon every other self however petty, in that it proposes to endow each self with an eternal happiness, provided a proper relationship is established."[41]

Luther got this right; in the end everybody does their own dying. So Climacus would not apologize for spurning the Hegelian spirit of the age. He was slightly daunted that *Fragments* was ignored, noting gamely: "It has created no sensation, absolutely none." *Philosophical Fragments* sold 229 copies in three years, its only reviews were brief and dismissive, and Kierkegaard had trouble finding anyone who had read it, although a few acquaintances, offering polite conversation, asked about a sequel. Having burdened the tiny Danish public with fifteen books in two years, Kierkegaard knew better than to let Climacus complain about the public's reading habits. Pressing on, Kierkegaard decided to write one more book, fully intending it to be his last; Climacus cheekily said of it, "The one thing I am afraid of is a sensation, particularly if it registers approval."[42]

Concluding Unscientific Postscript assured readers that Climacus respected the vast fortress of knowledge erected by scholars, and he even respected their pious belief that they were getting more objective. He only disputed that their knowledge had any bearing on faith. Anyone who believes in biblical inspiration must regard historical criticism of the Bible as a violation of its spirit, and anyone who pursues historical criticism without believing in biblical inspiration cannot expect to have inspiration emerge as a result of pursuing critical study. No claim about the reasonableness of faith makes faith more possible. The condition of faith is passion, "infinite personal interestedness," which objectivity eliminates. Objectivity is about acquiring certainty, but certainty and passion do not go together. Decisiveness is rooted in subjectivity; Climacus put it quotably: "Christianity is spirit, spirit is inwardness, inwardness is subjectivity, subjectivity is essentially passion, and in its maximum an infinite, personal, passionate interest in one's eternal happiness." Arguments settle nothing, because Christianity is about an individual's relationship with God, and nothing else.[43]

Only an individual, in an act of private interiority, can make the leap of faith, which concerns something that cannot be thought, and which must be accepted *by virtue* of its absurdity. Still, it was possible to put it philosophically. Climacus had two theses: (1) a logical system is possible, and (2) an existential system is impossible. A logical system cannot include anything that exists or has existed. Climacus got his bearings from logician Adolf Trendelenburg, who taught that movement is an inexplicable presupposition of thinking and being, a common factor between them, and a factor in the continued reciprocity between them. Formal logic necessarily defines a realm of pure being in which any relation to actuality is hypothetical. Climacus thus dismissed Hegel's claim to introduce movement into logic, which was ridiculous for being unthinkable. Logic is indifferent to existence in the sense of actuality; to Climacus, Kant's dichotomy between the analytic and the synthetic held firm.[44]

Hegel taught that logic coincides with metaphysics as the science of grasping the essence of things in *thought*. The whole knows itself by virtue of the process of reflection, and negation—the only principle of thought—negates the prior, hence itself. The beginning *is* and *is not* because it is the beginning—the negation of the negation. Climacus said this is to make no beginning at all. Hegel talked nonsense about his starting point; he didn't begin the way he claimed, which is impossible, which he turned to his advantage by playing a sleight-of-hand game. Denying that philosophy must settle for a hypothetical starting point, Hegel claimed to begin with pure being—an absolute, abstract starting point lacking any presupposition, pure immediacy. Climacus was incredulous. How does one begin with the immediate? Did Hegel begin with immediacy immediately, something not mediated? That was absurd, because everything Hegel said about immediacy was a product of reflection.

Climacus overlooked that Hegel wrote *Phenomenology*, a tour de force of mediated reflection, precisely to make this point. Hegel did not claim that his logic began with no reflection behind it. However, he appeared to claim, very problematically, that the reflection of *Phenomenology* led to the realm of pure thought. Climacus did not pick up on the difference. Climacus said a beginning is possible only when reflection comes to a halt, which occurs only by an act of will, a leap.[45]

When Climacus denied that a system of existence is possible, he did not mean it does not exist. Reality is surely a system for God, he allowed; however, reality cannot be a system for any existing spirit, for systems are final, and "existence is precisely the opposite of finality." Existence holds things apart, while the system brings things together with finality.

Idealism has the real world against it, where the chasm between thought and being is terribly real. Climacus did not mean that existence is thoughtless, but he pressed the distinctions between thought and being, subject and object, and God and creation. Thought is abstract, static, and expressing necessity, while being is temporal, having resulted from becoming. Abstract categories are not involved in becoming; therefore Climacus rejected objectivity, founding the individual on the dialectical opposition of thought and being and its existential expression.[46]

Climacus insisted that Christianity is perfectly in line with this analysis, caring only about subjectivity. The highest task of every human being is to become subjective, which awakens an ethical impulse. When Hegelians tried to wring an ethic out of Hegel, they said the more ethically aware that one becomes, the more one sees the ethical in the world process. Climacus said that was flat wrong. The more that one develops in ethical subjectivity, the less one cares about the world-historical process. When individuals devote themselves to becoming subjective, "everything is beautifully arranged." World history is for God, kings, and eternity to worry about. The vocation of an individual is to become subjective.[47]

When Hegelians went on about universal history, Climacus had to stifle rude questions. Hegel wrote about many German thinkers and one Chinese thinker. Was there, perhaps, an imbalance here? Closer to home, Climacus wondered: What does it mean to die? If Hegel had any wisdom about *that*, he was interested. Does the ideality of thought overcome death by thinking it? But Hegelian idealism, fixing on a bigger picture, offered no help where one really needs it, the meaning of one's death.[48]

Climacus never quite addressed his relationship to the post-Kantian idealism that spawned Hegel. Everything depends, he said, on never forgetting that the subject is an existing individual and that existence is a process of becoming. Human existence (*eksistens*) is a special type of becoming, not merely the existence actualized in rocks and plants. To forget this point, at any point, is to be plunged into the fantastic "chimera of abstraction" of modern philosophy. From the standpoint of the existential individual, the identity of thought and being is an *expectation* of the creature. It cannot be a truth as long as the creature lives in time. This is where modern philosophy went wrong, wherever it was; Climacus did not go back to Descartes, Berkeley, or Kant to make a case. It was enough to point to the post-Kantian outcome, "the fantastic realism of the I-am-I," where philosophers bantered about a fantasy world rooted in their own selves while forgetting themselves.[49]

If an existing individual could actually transcend one's self, the truth for that person would be final, and it might even look like idealism. But nobody transcends one's existence. Climacus said the I-am-I is a mathematical point, not something that exists. Everybody could occupy it at once; one does not get in the way of another. He did not deny that individuals experience the unity of finite and infinite that transcends existence, but this realization occurs only momentarily, in the moment of passion. All of Climacus' dialectical reasoning about subjectivity, passion, existing, the moment, and truth as subjectivity drove to this point. Speculative philosophy holds passion in contempt, yet passion is the culmination of existence: "In passion the existing subject is rendered infinite in the eternity of the imaginative representation, and yet he is at the same time most definitely himself."[50]

Academics were sure to call this a variant of subjective idealism. Climacus didn't care what they called it, as long as he didn't come off as a post-Kantian. Modern philosophers tried in every conceivable way to enable the individual to transcend oneself objectively, with utter futility. Climacus countered that existence is persistent and unyielding. If philosophers were so intent on escaping it, they should advocate suicide. The I-am-I is a "fantastic rendezvous in the clouds," not an identity of the finite and the infinite, since neither is real. But Climacus featured the same point that Hegel took from Aristotle—there is a real link between the knower and the known. Realizing where that led, Climacus distinguished between essential knowledge and accidental knowledge, contending that only the former inwardly relates itself to existence, having an essential relationship to existence. That smuggled the union of thought and being into his thought by another name, which he denied, on the ground that he did not derive one abstraction from another. The knower is "essentially an existing individual," Climacus reasoned, and only "ethical and ethico-religious knowledge" qualifies as essential knowledge, bearing an essential relationship to the knower's existence.[51]

Mediation, to Climacus, was a mirage, the enemy of truth-as-subjectivity. From an abstract standpoint, nothing comes into being; everything simply is. There is no mediation without movement; thus mediation has no place in abstract thought. In essential knowing, subjectivity is the truth. He offered a definition: "An objective uncertainty held fast in an appropriation-process of the most passionate inwardness is the truth, the highest truth attainable for an existing individual." We cannot say, objectively, at what point the fork in the road arrives for us, "where the way swings off," because wherever it happens, it is subjective. We do not know what God is doing, where history is going, or what anything means, but these objective uncertainties intensify the infinite passion of our inwardness, where truth is known. Truth is the willingness to accept objective uncertainty "with the passion of the infinite." Climacus put it plainly—truth and faith are equivalent. If God could be known objectively, there would be no need for the risk of faith. Because God cannot be known objectively, we must believe: "If I wish to preserve myself in faith I must constantly be intent upon holding fast the objective uncertainty, so as to remain out upon the deep, over seventy thousand fathoms of water, still preserving my faith."[52]

If subjectivity is the truth, the truth is, objectively, paradoxical. Contrary to Hegelian talk about everything working itself out in the truth as a whole, Climacus said that Hegelians didn't even know about tomorrow, or the intentions of another person, much less what God is doing. No existing individual can understand God, which is why "God became flesh" is the absolute paradox. The incarnation is the ultimate absurdity—the eternal truth coming into being in time as an existing individual. It is also religiously offensive, the rankest idolatry from a Jewish perspective. The absurd cannot be rationalized or defended; it can only be believed in fear and trembling: "It behooves us to get rid of introductory guarantees of security, proofs from consequences, and the whole mob of public pawnbrokers and guarantors, so as to permit the absurd to stand out in all its clarity."[53]

Climacus realized that Hegel's rationalism turned on itself, qualifying everything that Climacus said about it. *Aufheben*, besides abolishing and preserving, means neither of these things because it means both at once. Climacus remarked, "Speculative philosophy removes every difficulty, and then leaves me the difficulty of trying to determine what it really accomplishes by this so-called removal (*aufheben*)." He knew the Hegelian reply that negation is primary in sublation. But in that case, Hegelianism eliminated paradox and decision, reducing both to something relative. Hegelian theology had the paradox and a strategy to abrogate it. Thus it lifted itself above Christianity. Hegelian theologians did not say that Christianity is the truth; they said their understanding of Christianity constitutes the truth of Christianity. Climacus shuddered at the presumption.[54]

Christianity is like love, he said. It is either a life-giving passion or it is nothing. The "most stupid thing ever said" about Christianity is that it is true "to a certain degree." Climacus found this idiotic sentiment to be prevalent in modern Christianity. He spent many years dawdling aimlessly, watching others get ahead while he frittered away his life, until he realized that modern people forgot what it means to exist. Finding his calling, it occurred to him that he should communicate indirectly, "for if inwardness is the truth, results are only rubbish with which we should not trouble each other." God communicates indirectly. God is in creation, but is not there directly. Paganism is about relating to God directly. In Christianity, God is hidden, holy, invisible, mysterious, and transcendently other: "God has absolutely nothing obvious about him." The sheer elusiveness of God triggers an "irruption of inwardness," an infinite desire for the divine that cannot be grasped.[55]

Despite believing that Kant ruined modern philosophy, Climacus had his own version of subjective idealism and the thing-in-itself: "The ethical reality of the individual is the only reality." He made a rare illusion to Kant, explaining that individual existence is the thing-in-itself that cannot be thought. Hegel, taking the Kantian problem too seriously, fantastically vanquished idealistic skepticism by means of pure thought, without breaking from Kantian skepticism. Climacus would have saved the entire post-Kantian tradition the problem of rethinking Kant's dualism. Jacobi got it right; the best response is to reject Kant's skeptical account of what cannot be known. Instead of trying to climb a ladder of being, or thought, or their identity, to heaven, it is better to have faith in the transcendent God who created a real world and human minds. Human beings think and exist as creatures in the divine image, and existence separates thought and being, but God does not think or exist. God creates and is eternal. One becomes a spirit in the transparent grounding of the divine creative power that posits the self. What matters is to become a Christian, not to understand Christianity.[56]

By the end of the *Postscript*, Climacus had answered the question he never asked—yes, despair was the motivating force of his dialectic. Climacus replaced Hegel's abstract negation with the despair of subjective spirit, sin-consciousness. Religiousness A, differently perfected by Catholicism and modern Protestantism, retained the idealistic assumption that truth is something to be recollected. God is immanent, eternal truth is rationally accessible, and one seeks to transform one's pathetic, guilty, resigned existence through religion. Paganism and every world religion practiced Religiousness A, a remedy for guilt and meaningless, but not despair. Despair is totalizing and infinite, relating to the eternal.

Climacus said that only Religiousness B deals with despair. Here, God is wholly transcendent, paradox and offense are central, despair is a howling reality, and one gives up the illusion of awakening to the eternal within. Finding salvation is completely about relating to a transcendent God.[57]

Kierkegaard had to wait for a generation that did not believe in the progress of modern culture and which shared at least some of his radical rejection of history. To him, history had no answers and did not clarify ideas. History muddled ideas and corrupted them, distorting whatever it touched. Kierkegaard had one historical norm, "New Testament Christianity," which he used as a club to ridicule local clerics. But he never bothered to defend this idea historically, realizing where that would take him. He tried to write a book on religious authority after a local pastor received visions and preached passionate sermons about them, but had to put it aside. What could he say? To be discovered, as he knew he would be, Kierkegaard had to be read in German by youthful thinkers who were disillusioned with history, notably Barth and Tillich.[58]

Kierkegaard stood out from his time by not belonging to it. Liberal theology, believing in reason, historical criticism, and modern cultural progress, was about the wrong things. It let go of any real connection to New Testament Christianity and sought to replace muddled state church orthodoxies that were hopelessly compromised. Kierkegaard spurned Schleiermacher-style liberalism as a boring and enervated waste of time. He repudiated post-Kantian idealism aside from the parts he borrowed and renamed. Had he lived to see the social gospel, he would have blasted that too. All got in the way of the one important thing he shared with the modernizing age he rejected: its idealistic impulse, which he absolutized.

Historicism undermined his pure contemporaneousness with Jesus. Rational objectivity and metaphysics opposed truth as subjectivity. Dogmatism distorted Jesus and Christian subjectivity. Liberalism was about perfecting modern culture, not following Jesus. Kierkegaard was keenly aware that he offered a dubious advertisement for the pure ideality he promoted. His early pseudonyms deflected the objection by pointing to the ideal, using their imaginations, while pondering the leap. The pseudonym closest to him, Climacus, unfolded a sprawling argument for leaping without quite doing so. Kierkegaard's later books put his name to reflections reflecting post-leap Christian consciousness, yet he was still the same melancholic genius absorbed with himself who savaged clerics, frittered away his father's fortune, and ridiculed women, democracy, and liberalism. He created one last pseudonym, Anti-Climacus, to manage the problem. Anti-Climacus knew what the ideal was, because he actually lived it. But who was that, and how did he know?[59]

Kierkegaard's rage for subjectivity radiates in every direction as critique and witness. It yielded existentialisms, anti-historicisms, postmodernisms, and other isms he would have cared nothing about, and speaks evermore to uncountable individuals, as he expected. He got his first splash of translated attention just before Tillich's generation headed off to World War I. By the time that Tillich came out of World War I, he needed Kierkegaard and Nietzsche desperately, and for the same reason. Both roared for life and personality in the face of the abyss. Tillich knew from his own experience why existential writers resonated so powerfully after the war. The only kind of theology worth writing struggled with the traumas of suffering, meaninglessness, despair, and being damned. Barth agreed with Tillich about that, which was the basis of their crisis theology alliance—Pauline radicalism about faith, mediated by Kierkegaard.

Barth, Kierkegaard, Hegel, and Levinas

Karl Barth, in 1918, was a Reformed pastor in Safenwil, Switzerland, a bitter critic of World War I, and a work in progress as a theologian. He was appalled that his teachers, Adolf von Harnack and Wilhelm Herrmann, cheered for Germany's war against France, Britain, and Russia. He gave angry sermons against the war and tried to rethink what Harnack and Herrmann had taught him. Barth knew what he was against—capitulating to nationalism. But to what extent did the war compel him to disown the liberal theology in which he was trained? He couldn't go back to the conservative orthodoxy of his upbringing, so what gospel should he preach? This question drove Barth to Paul's Epistle to the Romans, yielding his first book, *Epistle to the Romans*, in 1918. Barth expounded a post-Kantian idea of the "world of God" as the hidden motor of history, still operating in a liberal framework. Then he read clueless reviews of his book, read Kierkegaard's slashing attack on Hegel and modern Christianity, and rewrote the *Romans* book. The second edition was seething, slashing, and otherworldly, draped in Kierkegaard's concepts. Kierkegaard exploded into modern theology in Barth's second-edition *Romans* (1921)—mostly for blasting theologians, modern Christianity, and Hegel.[60]

Between the two editions, Barth gave a spectacular address at Tambach declaring that all human history stands under the sign of sin, death, and judgment. History is not a life process brought to fulfillment by a divine indwelling. History is the life of the old world that exists under the judgment of death. The "object" of theology is not an object at all, or a process within or among other objects. Writing theology, Barth said, is like trying to draw a bird in flight. Apart from the movement, theology has no standpoint or ground. Apart from the movement of the Spirit that transcends and penetrates human history, theology is "absolutely meaningless, incomprehensible, and impossible."[61]

Second-edition *Romans* carried on in that vein, describing the crisis of the postwar moment as a permanent universal condition that negates all human strategies of salvation. Human history, Barth said, stands under the crisis of judgment—the presupposition of Paul's message. God is unknown, "and precisely because He is unknown, He bestows life and breath and all things." God's power is completely different from the powers of observable forces: "It is the KRISIS of all power, that by which power is measured, and by which it is pronounced to be something and—nothing, nothing and—something." God is neither a power alongside other powers nor a supernatural power standing above other powers. Barth reasoned that God's power is "that which sets all these powers in motion and fashions their eternal rest. It is the Primal Origin by which they all are dissolved, the consummation by which they all are established." God's power is "pure and preeminent" and beyond all other powers.[62]

Luther taught that faith directs itself toward invisible realities; only that which is hidden can provide an opportunity for faith. Barth stressed that this is a Pauline theme: "The Gospel of salvation can only be believed in; it is a matter for faith only. It demands choice. This is its seriousness." The gospel is a scandal to those who cannot accept its inner contradiction, but to those who cannot escape the necessity of the contradiction, the gospel becomes a matter of faith: "Faith is awe in the presence of the divine incognito; it is the love of God that is aware of the qualitative distinction between God and man and God and the world; and therefore it is the affirmation of the divine 'No' in Christ, of the shattering halt in the presence of God." The righteousness of God is manifested wherever God's faithfulness encounters human faithfulness.[63]

Nearly all of Kierkegaard's concepts were there: the infinite qualitative distinction between time and eternity, the divine incognito of the incarnation, the scandal of faith, the sickness unto death, the dialectic of revelatory unveiling, the leap, the paradoxical gospel, and the Moment. The only Kierkegaard trope that Barth left behind was his preoccupation with how one becomes a Christian, which was too self-absorbed for Barth's purpose. Like Kierkegaard, Barth insisted that faith is "always a leap into the darkness of the unknown, a flight into empty air." Faith cannot be communicated to oneself or to one from another; it must be revealed. Because the revelation in Christ is that of God's righteousness, it is necessarily "the most compete veiling of His incomprehensibility." Through Christ, God is revealed "as the Unknown, speaking in eternal silence." Just as Kierkegaard argued that true Christianity is destroyed when it becomes a form of direct communication, losing its capacity to shock, Barth asserted that in Jesus "the communication of God begins with a rebuff, with the exposure of a vast chasm, with the clear revelation of a great stumbling block." To have faith in Jesus is to call upon God in God's utter incomprehensibility and hiddenness, embracing "the absolute scandal of His death upon the cross."[64]

Salvation is about the invasion of the eternal into time in the Moment, which is not a "moment" *in* time, but the eschatological Moment in which redeemed sinners are clothed with the righteousness of God: "We remove from the 'Moment' when the last trump sounds all likeness to the past and the future, and thereby proclaim the likeness of all times, of all past and future." The fact that Paul lived long ago, Barth said, is irrelevant to the truth of his message. If Paul was right, we lack any ground except eschatological hope: "We are deprived of the possibility of projecting a temporal thing into infinity or of confining eternity within the sphere of time."[65]

The dialectic of time and eternity made paradox the essential language of faith. Barth's text abounded with metaphors of disruption and cleavage. For him, as for Kierkegaard, God was an impossibility whose possibility cannot be avoided. "God is pure negation," Barth declared. "He is both 'here' and 'there.' He is the negation of the negation in which the other world contradicts this world and this world the other world. He is the death of our death and the non-existence of our non-existence." Barth likened God's grace to an explosion that blasts everything away without leaving a trace. Grace is not a religious possibility standing alongside sin; it is a "shattering disturbance, an assault which brings everything into question." Then how does the new world of the Spirit make contact with the existing world of Adam? In a striking image, often quoted, Barth said it touches the old world "as a tangent touches a circle, that is, without touching it." Because the new creation does not touch the old world, "it touches it as its frontier—as the new world." Christianity is true only as eschatology.[66]

That eliminated the possibility of systematic theology, among other things. Barth was fine with that, until he became a theology professor: "If I have a system, it is limited to a recognition of what Kierkegaard called the 'infinite qualitative distinction' between time and eternity, and to my regarding this as possessing negative as well as positive significance: 'God is in heaven, and thou on earth.'" Within time, the receiver of grace experiences eternity in the absolute moment of revelation and anticipates the complete overcoming of time by eternity.[67]

Did that mean that God is part of the dialectic of finite and infinite existence? Did the prohibition on projecting temporal things into infinity apply to the dialectic itself? Many religious thinkers said yes. The necessary precondition for faith was to become unconditionally turned inward, as Kierkegaard said. Crisis theology had no basis apart from Kierkegaard's dialectic of existence and its theory of truth as existential encounter. Both had a long run in theology after Barth resolved to eliminate Kierkegaard's tropes from his theology, opting for Reformed dogmatics. There were neo-orthodox, liberal, and Tillichian versions of existential theology in Protestantism alone, in addition to Martin Buber's *I and Thou* version and the Catholic existentialism of Gabriel Marcel. Then came the postmodern discovery of Kierkegaard, who had never fallen out of the canon. Kierkegaard thrilled postmodernists, who saw him as a forerunner to themselves, usually with the caveat that Kierkegaard was a Christian theologian, something beyond the pale. Levinas said that Kierkegaard had a theologian's obsession with salvation, an "egoist's cry," whereas his own perspective was "absolutely nontheological."[68]

Tillich, though influenced by Kierkegaard, recognized that existential tropes were too reactive and personal to carry theology by themselves. The focus on anxiety, despair, courage, and personal encounter was too individualistic and privatizing. A larger vision was needed in which the existential fixation with personal meaning played a role. Barth let go of Kierkegaard for a more prosaic reason—he became a professor of dogmatic theology, and thus an exponent of Reformed confessions that Barth had never learned during his academic training. In the mid-1920s Barth resolved to purge the existential tropes from his theology, which he attempted in his first volume of dogmatics, *Christliche Dogmatik* (1927). Then he repeated his experience of rewriting the same book after judging that *Christliche Dogmatik* did not go far enough. Barth got his bearings by rooting his dogmatic theology in the confessional life and language of the Reformed tradition, a shift signaled by changing the title of his work to *Church Dogmatics*. He did not oppose making use of philosophy per se, though he was often accused of being anti-philosophy. Barth said it was fine to appropriate philosophy on an ad hoc basis. What mattered was not to subordinate theology to any specific philosophical system, no matter whether the philosophy came from Plato, Aristotle, Thomas Aquinas, Kant, Hegel, Kierkegaard, or Heidegger.[69]

Church Dogmatics, unfolding in twelve massive volumes, became a monument to the independence of theology—in this case, neo-Calvinist theology—from philosophy and all other forms of intellectual and cultural endeavor. Yet for all of Barth's resistance to philosophy, especially of the speculative colonizing type, he was a quasi-Hegelian, admiring Hegel above all philosophers. His theology had key affinities with Hegel's, especially in its revelatory Trinitarian objectivism and its capacious ambition. Like Hegel, Barth traced the objective unfolding of divine Spirit in three-fold form, arguing that God is who God is in God's *action*. But Hegel epitomized the philosophical colonization of theology, just as Troeltsch epitomized historicism run amuck. Hegel's God was the *event* of reason writ large, the whole of wholes; for Barth, the Christian God was either wholly Other or not really God. Hegel's God self-revealed out of logical necessity; to Barth, that was terribly wrong, since the revealed God of Christian grace is the threefold sovereign *One* who *loves* in *freedom*. Barth took for granted the closed-system interpretation of Hegel, treating Hegelian negation and tragedy as subordinate elements of a system. Yet he appreciated the difficulty of refuting Hegel. With keen admiration of a kind, Barth cautioned his students to think three times before they disagreed with Hegel, "because we might find that everything we are tempted to say in contradiction of it has already been said within it, and provided with the best possible answer."[70]

To Barth, the Hegelian system was a stupendous perfection of the "philosophy of self-confidence," the realization of Western idealism. If one believed in idealizing reason, one could not do better than Hegel. In fact, if the Enlightenment had the right project, using only one's understanding, it was pointless to stick with Kant, who left the mind in a hopeless conflict with objects of mind and the contingencies of history. Hegel got somewhere by folding objects, history, and human destiny into his theory of mind. Barth said Hegel was the "great perfecter and surpasser of the Enlightenment," resolving the conflicts between reason and revelation, subject and object, the God in us and the God in Christ, and thought and being. Moreover, he did it "to a highly satisfactory conclusion." Hegel left out nothing and thought everything through. Barth explained, "It is nothing less than everything which is in question, and everything must continually be in question, the ultimate included, for the ultimate, too, in the self-movement of truth, must ever and again become the first." Knowing exists only in the event, like God—the idea or mind of all events.[71]

Barth admired Hegel's audacity in making philosophers and theologians deal with Christian concepts, especially the Trinity. He stressed that Hegel's peers "had absolutely no desire for a renewal of the doctrine of the Trinity. In propounding it Hegel was theologizing in his own way, alone and acknowledging no master, against the philosophers and the theologians." Hegel, to his immense credit, did not shrink from claiming certain knowledge of truth. He was not content, like Schleiermacher, to secure a home for Christianity in personal feeling; Hegel reached for the Creator of heaven and earth, the Lord over life and death. Barth explained, "Knowledge of God could be the knowledge of irreconcilable contradictions and their eternal vanquishing in the mind. Knowledge of God could mean the passage through the contradictions of reason to the peace that is higher than all reason, and the emergence into these contradictions in comforted despair." This was Hegel's audacity, to make the modern age see itself through the looking glass of Christian truth. Barth described Hegelian philosophy as a "theological invasion" that challenged intellectuals to found their precious modernizing consciousness on a theology, just as Hegel allowed his philosophy to be transformed into a theology.[72]

On Barth's account, Hegel failed because modern culture let him down. The greatest modern philosopher was a great success, but not on the scale he sought. Modern consciousness did not seek to understand itself in its own depth, and it did not want to be reconciled with Christianity. Non-Hegelian liberal theologians, imitating their secular colleagues, judged that Hegel was too demanding. His conditions were too theological, and he claimed too much in claiming to know about God. Barth begged to differ. The problem was that Hegel did not bring enough Christianity into his system and thus failed to demand enough of modern consciousness.[73]

Barth acknowledged that Hegel had a robustly positive and historical understanding of revelation, not mentioning that it was the linchpin of Barth's theology. Moreover, Hegel "emphatically affirmed" the uniqueness and divinity of Christ; Barth did not question that Hegel was "really" a Christian. Those who doubted it were usually secular types who refused to believe that Hegel meant what he said, since that made Hegel unlike them. But Hegel conceived God and Christ as elements of a system, construing Christ as the gift of necessity, not of free grace: "With Hegel, God and man can never confront one another in a relationship which is actual and indissoluble; a word, a new word revelatory in the strict sense, cannot pass between them; it cannot be uttered and cannot be heeded." Barth said Hegel had no concept of objective revelation apart from the objectivity of everything that exists for consciousness. Hegelian revelation, like all knowledge of other kinds, must pass through objectivity, since knowledge is bound up with the moment of perception. This objectivity includes the objectivity of revelation. Hegel granted that objective revelation is revelatory at the level of religious imagination, but he charged philosophy with the job of raising religious imagery to forms of thought suited to mind.[74]

Barth pressed hard on the upshot for Christianity. Even if Hegelians allowed ministers to speak in picture language, Hegelianism is about reducing that which is revealed to its logical content. Reason, in Hegelian theology, is as revelatory as the imagination; plus reason has a higher calling. Barth offered a striking picture to describe it: "When God manifests himself the philosopher of religion has already understood him in the preliminaries of this act, and he already has the lever in his hand which he has only to depress to advance from God's act of revealing to the higher level of God being manifest, in which every given thing, all duality, is annulled, all speaking and listening has lost its object and been transformed again into pure knowing, the knowing of the human subject, as it originally proceeded from him." Barth allowed that Hegel had a stronger concept of God's aliveness than most theologians of his time; however, it was the aliveness of thought being thought by living selves. Hegel's God lives as the life of human thinkers, a "merely thinking and merely thought God" before whom actual human selves either stand as idols or dissolve to nothing.[75]

Barth realized that Hegel could be read differently on divine and human personality, and he did not rest there. Even if he was wrong about equating Hegel's God with human acts of life, he knew that Hegel abolished God's sovereignty. Hegel's God, Barth said, is "his own prisoner." Hegel had a concept of divine omniscience as God's comprehension of all things, but Hegel's God has no freedom not to self-reveal. In Hegelian dialectic, a mind that does not manifest itself is not a mind, and

Hegel described God as being utterly manifest. Barth explained, "Hegel, in making the dialectical method of logic the essential nature of God, made impossible the knowledge of the actual dialectic of grace, which has its foundation in the freedom of God." Hegel's God cannot be free for human beings because Hegel's God is not free from human beings. Barth countered that God is free in God's relationships to all that is not God. Precisely because God is sovereign, God is free to transcend all that is other than God's self and to be immanent within all things. God is free to be the God of radical Christian grace poured out on all humanity for the salvation of the world.[76]

Levinas shared much of Barth's position without sharing any of his theology. Born in Lithuania in 1906, Levinas became a French citizen in 1930 and taught at the Ecole Normale Orientale of the Alliance Israelite Universelle in Paris. His major work, *Totality and Infinity* (1961), argued that every belief about relating to the Wholly Other, or entering deeply into Otherness, violates the ethical. This was the root of his signature ideas of the face of the other and the absoluteness of separation: "The perception of individual things is the fact that they are not entirely absorbed in their form; they then stand out in themselves, breaking through, rending their forms, are not resolved into the relations that link them to the totality." Levinas described the uncovered face as a symbol of this standing out and rending: "The nakedness of the face is not what is presented to me because I disclose it, what would therefore be presented to me, to my powers, to my eyes, to my perceptions, in a light exterior to it. The face has turned to me—and this is its very nudity. It *is* by itself and not by reference to a system." Any real relationship to the absolute would ruin its absoluteness, making it relative. The absolute "absolves" itself from the relationship in which it presents itself, preserving its absolute transcendence: "The same and the other at the same time maintain themselves in relationship and *absolve* themselves from this relation, remain absolutely separated. The idea of infinity requires this separation."[77]

This was the opposite of Hegel's idea of the absolute moving into real relation with the other, becoming absolute in communion. Levinas described Hegel as the modern champion of the "ancient privilege of unity" linking him to Parmenides and Spinoza. To the unifiers, Levinas said, separation and interiority were irrational, metaphysics suppressed separation, and the metaphysical being absorbed the being of the metaphysician. Separation was conceived as a fall from grace, or a privation, or a provisional rupture of the totality. But no philosopher of unity ever explained "whence came this accidental illusion and fall, inconceivable in the Infinite, the Absolute, and the Perfect." Levinas commended Descartes for conceiving the infinite as positive, upholding the language of exteriority against the unifiers. Leibniz, toward the same end, espoused atomism; Kant, on the other hand, claimed that the infinite presupposes the finite, which amplified the finite infinitely—"the most anti-Cartesian point of Kantian philosophy."[78]

Levinas allowed that Hegel rightly returned to the Cartesian doctrine that the infinite is positive, but Hegel excluded all multiplicity from it: "He posits the infinite as the exclusion of every 'other' that might maintain a relation with the infinite and thereby limit it." Hegel's infinite encompasses all relations and can only do so. It refers, like Aristotle's God, only to itself, albeit at the end of a history. Levinas wanted nothing to do with Hegelian infinity, likening Hegel's relation of a particular to infinity to the entry of an individual into the sovereignty of a state: "It becomes infinite in negating is own finitude." That supposedly described the Hegelian state, a tyranny willed by the reason of individuals that smothers their personality. Levinas stood up for "the finitude of man before the elements, the finitude of man invaded by the *there is*, at each instant traversed by faceless gods against whom labor is pursued in order to realize the security in which the 'other' of the elements would be revealed as the same." The other absolutely other, he said—the wholly other Other—does not suffocate individual freedom. It founds the freedom of individuals and calls them to ethical responsibility: "The relation with the other as face heals allergy. It is desire; teaching received."[79]

If one has to have a God who is wholly other and all-powerful, or the wholly other of being, it would be hard to improve on the critiques of Barth and Levinas. Both rightly criticized Hegel for claiming to know too much about God; Barth rightly censured Hegel for his hegemonic conceits about the superiority of philosophy; and Levinas commendably objected out of ethical passion, developing a purportedly phenomenological description of face-to-face encounters. Barth and Levinas opposed Hegel on fundamental things, and sometimes they were right. But both scored too easily by assuming the rationalist-totalizing Hegel, and Levinas' polemic was really against Western philosophy itself—supposedly an ego-logy that reduces the other to the same. The face, as rendered by Levinas, is not phenomenological, being neither an appearance nor an ontological theme. There is no phenomenon and no ontological theme, for the self and its other are not parts of a totality. The face expresses the ethical transcendence of the other, presenting an ethical demand not to kill. To Levinas, the ethical demand of the face is prior to ontology and theory. Thus it is expressed only in paradoxes, such as "that which is approachable by a thought that . . . thinks more than it thinks." Steven G. Smith and Robert R. Williams observe that Levinas' argument is not even rational, for it hangs on an infinite transcending any conceivable totality. One cannot have a phenomenological account of something that is not evident, or an ontological account of something that is wholly beyond being. In that case, Williams asks, what justifies calling the thought of Levinas philosophy?[80]

Levinas said he set himself against the entire Western tradition, based on Platonic ontology, in which love is perfected when two people become one: "I am trying to work against this identification of the divine with unification or totality. Man's relationship with the other is better as difference than as unity: sociality is better than fusion. The very value of love is the impossibility of reducing the other to myself, of coinciding into sameness." But Hegel never said that fused sameness is the ideal. Hegel's blend of phenomenology and ontology is about sociality, not sameness—with the advantage of being rationally phenomenological and ontological.[81]

Williams presses the irony that much of Hegel's thought has influenced recent philosophy through Levinas. Both expounded philosophies of love upholding the difference and dignity of the other. Both were vehement critics of the Eleatic monism of the ontological tradition, although Levinas interpreted Hegel as a monist. Both rejected the priority of union in the metaphysical tradition, specifically Parmenides and the Eleatics. Hegel put it sharply: "Being, the One of the Eleatic school, is only this abstraction, a sinking into the abyss of the [abstract] identity of the understanding (*Verstandesidentität*)." Derrida, noting the affinities, aptly observed that Levinas ironically affirmed Hegel whenever he attacked him: "Levinas is very close to Hegel, much closer than he admits." Hegel criticized the same things in classic monist ontology as Levinas *without* writing off ontology as a hopelessly mistaken enterprise. For all of Levinas' broadsides against ontology, he did not avoid it. *Totality and Infinity* is an anti-ontology abounding with the language of ontology. Smith explains, "He answers the question of being by displacing it. Thus far, however, he produces only paradox and apparent logical bad faith."[82]

One link between Hegel and Levinas is that Hegel always had Jacobi in mind. Levinas came closest to formulating a positive position in *Otherwise than Being*, which resounded with Jacobi/Kierkegaard fideism.

Levinas insisted that self and other cannot be expressed as a totality, the mistake of Western philosophy. But Levinas described a conjuncture of self and other in which each absolves itself from the other within their relation, remaining absolute within the relation. Williams observes that Hegel similarly conceived the other as being free and going free in the final phase of reciprocal recognition; only then does the self return to itself in satisfaction, enriched by the other. Hegel said it emphatically when he discussed love and forgiveness as conditions of reciprocity; he did not reduce the other to the same. The difference is that Hegel never said, like Levinas, that the self and other remain absolute within relation. If the relation is real, there must be an effect on each other. Hegel and Levinas similarly rooted reason in the interhuman relation, contending that reason has a social dimension and structure. Levinas, however, denied that this affirmation should be expressed theoretically. His skepticism purportedly protected the priority of the ethical over theory; the ethical holds priority over any truth claim. But this claim of ethical priority is presumably about the priority of justice. If it is not a claim about the truth of justice, what is it? Williams registers the Hegelian point: philosophizing on the basis of skepticism is self-refuting. One rejects the very thing that one needs to make a case.[83]

Levinas held that in common with Derrida, who at least saw the problem of anti-Hegelian dependence on Hegel, and with Deleuze, who culminated the tradition of postmodern anti-Hegelianism by exaggerating the exaggerations of Levinas and Derrida. Deleuze claimed that Hegel had no concept of difference, because getting rid of difference is the sole, defining, consuming problem of Hegelianism. Nothing is contingent or exterior in Hegel's ontology; everything is the same; Hegelianism is the culmination of Western hyperrationalism: "Contradiction resolves itself and, in resolving itself, resolves difference by relating it to a ground. Difference is the only problem." The postmodern doyens thus wanted no help from Hegel except as a contrast-foil. To them, Hegelian difference was just pretend, a showy distraction concealing a totalitarian outcome.[84]

But the postmodern founders were wrong about Hegelian difference, and the threat of totalitarianism is not what imperils the world under neoliberalism and postmodern fragmentation. Hegel insisted that external difference is real and always implies self-difference. External difference is grounded in every thing's immanent self-opposition. Every finite being is different from all other finite beings and things because every finite being is already not identical with itself. Moreover, the threat of totalitarianism that alarmed Levinas and Derrida pales before the racist nationalism and xenophobia, nihilism, political dysfunction, and eco-apocalypse that afflict us today. Hegel's rendering of social subjectivity and his fixation with tragic reconciliation have much to offer to societies in which social-anything—aside from trivial social media chatter and capitalist sociality—is very hard to achieve.

6

Personal Idealism

Why Subjectivity Matters

The schools of theology deriving from Kant, Schleiermacher, and Ritschl were arguments for keeping philosophy in a very restricted place. The Hegelian exception was so high-flying it often reinforced the Protestant predisposition to steer clear of philosophy or keep it on a short leash. The most creative attempt to mediate this situation in theology came from personal idealists in Germany, England, and the United States. In Germany the leading personal idealists were Rudolf Hermann Lotze, Rudolf Eucken, Otto Pfleiderer, and Ernst Troeltsch. In England they were Andrew Seth Pringle-Pattison, Hastings Rashdall, James Ward, and William Temple. In the United States they were Borden Parker Bowne, Albert C. Knudson, and Edgar S. Brightman. Personal idealism was never just one thing in any of these contexts. It could be theistic or non-theistic; it could be empiricist or rationalist; and it could be neo-Kantian, post-Kantian, or Hegelian. But all personal idealists said the existence of personality should make a crucial difference in how one interprets reality. And all personal idealists who were religious said that minimizing philosophy is no way to renew theology.

Lotze (1815–1881) was the major theorist of theistic personal idealism until his protégé Bowne surpassed him. Lotze fused Leibniz on activism, Berkeley on immaterialism, and Kant on epistemology and the ethical conception of personality, building a new argument for theism from the personalistic aspects of their thought. His legacy radiated into

England, where Anglicans dominated theistic personal idealism and sometimes cited Lotze, and into the United States, where Methodists were the leading theistic personal idealists and often cited Lotze. Later there was a French tradition of theistic personal idealism dominated by Roman Catholics. The American tradition was the most significant of all by virtue of having the longest run, drawing deeply on Lotze and Troeltsch, and attracting Martin Luther King Jr. in its fourth generation.

Bowne got his personal idealism straight from Lotze, at Göttingen. Essentially it was the view that personal spirit is transcendently real and the basis of the organic unity of nature. The soul is known immediately as the experience of consciousness, as Descartes said, and is essentially active, as Leibniz said. Self-consciousness is the necessary presupposition of all thinking and the world of objects, as Berkeley said, and the mind produces experience out of its transcendental categories, as Kant said. Personality is the single reality that cannot be explained by anything else. Bowne believed that Lotze got important things wrong. Lotze was a determinist and a monist, but Bowne was a good Methodist who believed in free will, the metaphysical reality of finite persons, Wesleyan piety, and the empirical experience of the world as real and plural. Later Bowne befriended William James and emphasized that he was a pragmatist too. Still later, Bowne's American disciples added crucial planks to so-called "Boston personalism": the social gospel, Schleiermacher-style liberal theology, social consciousness, and Hegelian holism. But all personalists followed Bowne in contending that science does not explain the reality or unity of consciousness because science is necessarily mechanistic. It is possible to move from mind to matter, but matter cannot be the ultimate or sufficient cause of mind. Bowne took experience as a whole as his datum, questioning how reality should be conceived on the basis of particular experiences as interpreted by thought. On this basis, personal idealists implored theologians not to abandon metaphysical reasoning. Religion isn't much of anything if it is not thought, feeling, willing, and moral caring about reality.[1]

American personalism was epistemologically dualistic, ethically Kantian, metaphysically pluralist, theologically liberal, experiential, and, from the second generation onward, devoted to the social gospel. Knudson earned his doctorate under Bowne in 1900; Brightman was Bowne's last doctoral student, completing his doctorate in 1912; the third generation, led by Walter Muelder, took over in the 1940s. Every personalist said it was important to see the sacred light in every human being. But Boston personalism had a patchy record of doing so until Muelder became its institutional and intellectual leader.[2]

Bowne and Personal Idealism

Bowne ranged widely over psychology, physics, evolutionary theory, epistemology, ethics, and theology, caring most about the religious aspects of philosophy. Born in 1847 in Leonardville, New Jersey, he grew up in a pious Methodist family that traced its ancestry to the first generation of English Puritans who lived in Salem, Massachusetts. Bowne's mother, Margaret Bowne, devoured Wesleyan holiness literature. His father Joseph Bowne was a farmer, local preacher, and court judge, and was devoted to personal sanctification, though without his wife's mysticism. Joseph Bowne opposed slavery, alcohol, emotional displays, and sloth, passing these dispositions and his learning to his brilliant, polymath, mostly autodidactic son. Bowne had no formal schooling until he enrolled at New York University in 1867. There he wrote a book on Herbert Spencer and graduated as class valedictorian in 1871. Bowne's first book argued that Darwinism is credible as scientific explanation and worthless as a philosophical theory of meaning or causation. He blasted Spencer's mechanical rendering of mind as the product of whirling atoms—a simplistic reductionism lacking any concept of the primal cause of things. Bowne took this conviction to Halle and Göttingen, studying for two years under philosopher of religion Hermann Ulrici (Halle), Oxford logician John Cook Wilson (Göttingen), and Lotze.[3]

Lotze taught that science rightly explains nature mechanistically and philosophy transcends science. Mechanism, though absolutely universal in extent, is completely subordinate in significance to consciousness. Good philosophy tracks the movement of spirit in Hegel's fashion without Hegel's vagueness about personality. Lotze rejected Berkeley's theory of knowledge, which required Kantian correction, and embraced Berkeley's subjective idealism: logically speaking, only persons exist. Personality is the ultimate reality, because God is personal. God's existence and teleological agency are known principally through feeling. Bowne absorbed Lotze's teaching and challenged him. On one occasion Bowne observed that a thunderstorm was approaching. Lotze replied, "That is nothing [compared] to the storm of questionings you have raised in my mind concerning my own philosophical system." He wanted Bowne to complete a doctorate with him, but Bowne didn't care about degrees. In 1876 Bowne landed at Boston University, a seven-year-old Methodist institution desperate for intellectual prestige. Bowne lifted the university nearly by himself, pouring out seventeen books and two hundred articles, serving as dean of the Graduate School of Arts and Sciences from 1888 to 1910, opening the Graduate School to women, and spurning job offers from rival schools. "Ephraim is wedded to his idols," he told suitors. "Let him alone." Making Boston University respectable was a Methodist spiritual mission to Bowne.[4]

For most of his career Bowne puzzled over what he should call himself. For a while he tried to settle on "transcendental empiricist," but that did not name what mattered most to him. Sometimes he said that he fused objective idealism with a Kantian form of Berkeley's idealism, but that was laborious; plus Bowne was averse to citing others. He rarely cited or credited any thinker. In some contexts he called himself a theistic idealist or a realistic idealist, but these tags were insufficiently specific. "Personal idealist" captured his system better than anything else, but University of California-Berkeley philosopher George Holmes Howison claimed it, so Bowne had to call himself something else. Mostly he called himself an objective idealist, with caveats, until 1909, the year before his death. Bowne settled on "personalist," which made him the first personalist "in any thoroughgoing sense." He said he agreed largely with Lotze, but transcended him; held half of Kant's system, but rejected the rest; and had a "strong smack" of Berkeley, while rejecting his theory of knowledge.[5]

Bowne's career coincided with the Hegel vogue in England that overtook British philosophy. He welcomed the powerful influence of Oxford neo-Hegelian T. H. Green in British philosophy, which launched a gusher of Hegelian philosophies. Green did not clearly affirm or deny that he identified the human spirit with the absolute, and his successors were profusely variegated on this issue. A prominent school of British absolute idealists played down or denied the individual personality of selves, or the personality of the absolute, or both. F. H. Bradley, Bernard Bosanquet, and Richard B. Haldane were leading British absolute idealists, teaching that all relations are internal and everything is logically connected to everything else. "Individual personality" has meaning, at best, only in relation to its total context. The whole is individual and universal, a *concrete* universal containing all things. Divine Spirit and human spirit are unified, although Bradley and Bosanquet cautioned that even to put it this way risks confusion, reinforcing the old dualism. J. M. E. McTaggart, another prominent British absolute idealist, dispelled this confusion by eliminating God. McTaggart said that true Hegelianism conceptualizes ultimate reality as a system of eternal selves forming an unconscious unity. Another stream of British absolute idealists, religious

thinkers headed by the brothers John Caird and Edward Caird, emphasized the personality of the absolute and thus conceived Hegelianism as
the best Christian philosophy, suitable for appropriation by Anglican
theologians.[6]

Bowne was the foremost American post-Kantian personal theist,
defending the reality of personal selves and a personal God, and pushing
back against absolute idealism. He shared this cause with British personal
idealists Andrew Seth Pringle-Pattison, James Ward, C. C. J. Webb, and
later, William Temple. In the United States his allies included Howison
and Harvard neo-Hegelian Josiah Royce, with significant differences.
Howison described God as noncreative personality and human beings as
noncreated, coeternal partners with God. Royce conceived the absolute
as the ground and originator of community—a personal, temporal being
who preserves the past, sustains the present through interpretation, and
anticipates the future. Bowne said the true relation of God and humanity
is interpersonal communion, not identity or absorption. Human persons
are distinct from the divine person while sharing God's purposes. The
crucial thing is to get purpose right, which Kant and the absolute idealists
failed to do.[7]

Bowne accepted Kant's basic account of knowledge as an a priori
synthetic activity of mind, as well as Kant's epistemic distinction of subject and object. But Kant's restriction of pure reason to knowledge of
phenomena was disastrous, as every post-Kantian said. Kant missed that
experience yields certain clues about reality that deserve to be regarded as
genuine knowledge. Bowne said it with commanding authority throughout his career, not bothering with scholarship that would have troubled
his simplistic interpretation of Kant as a subjective idealist. He didn't
need to complicate the questions of what Kant argued or what his system
was about, since he knew that Kant got purpose wrong. The problem
was that Kant found a role for purpose/will only in practical reason and
aesthetic judgment, not as a category of knowledge.

Bowne put it forcefully in *Theory of Thought and Knowledge*. No experience is intelligible apart from the Kantian categories of understanding.
Through these rules of mind, reason reaches the world of things that
appear, through sense perception, of being ready-made. But the Kantian categories alone leave perceivers adrift among isolated things and
events. Space and time are separating, and mechanical causality is not
unifying either. Reason needs a higher category to unify its objects. It
has such a category in purpose—the elevation of causality to intelligent

and volitional causality. There is no knowing without self-conscious intelligence, and intelligence is nothing without purpose. Bowne's critique of Kant had an echo of Arthur Schopenhauer's post-Kantian theory of metaphysical will, but Schopenhauer was an atheist who described willing as blind and insatiable. Idealists routinely wrote off Schopenhauer as a pessimist, or ignored him. Bowne said that good idealism accentuates the personalizing factor. The enemy is every kind of impersonal worldview. No mechanical conception is unifying or personalizing, no matter how intensely atoms whirl: "The unity and system demanded must be internal, and this true inwardness can be found only in self-determining, self-conscious causality, guiding itself according to plan and purpose."[8]

Bowne did not claim that purpose belongs on the same plane as Kant's categories of understanding or the pure forms of sensibility. Every event has a cause, and all objects are in space and time, but few events require a purpose. When we view things in isolation, as science usually does, purpose seems negligible. Bowne allowed that it plays little role in elementary experience. But purpose is crucial to higher forms of thought, being indispensable to reflection and constitutive of it. The necessity of purpose is hidden to intuition but revealed to reflection. Bowne drove home the post-Kantian upshot: mere mechanical causality is meaningless, catching thought in a self-destructive regress. Without meaning, reflective thought has no basis of maintaining itself or attaining systematic wholeness: "It is only when thought becomes systematic and aims at completeness that the rational significance of purpose is seen."[9]

The vocation of reason is to make sense of all dimensions of human experience. Bowne shook his head that Kant restricted theoretical reason to knowledge of phenomena, a low-grade enterprise, which excluded the deepest and most certain knowledge that reason possesses: the reflective self's knowledge of itself. Outward things may be viewed as phenomena, but not the self that views these phenomena. There are no phenomenal objects of knowledge without a perceiving subject. Lacking a more or less unified self, there is no secure knowledge of anything. Bowne would have spared Kant his strenuous grappling with the thing-in-itself, a futile substitute for the extra-phenomenal ground that knowledge requires.

Every post-Kantian got the latter point right, but many balked at recognizing why personality matters. In book after book, Bowne defended the integral self and its importance for faith: experience itself is the primary fact of knowledge; the personal self is the subject of experience; anything that reason affirms beyond this fact must be for its explanation.

Only a living, personal intelligence delivers reason from suicidal skepticism. Mechanical causation cannot be the last word about existence because mechanical causation is self-refuting as a last word. The truth of this word cannot be trusted, being a mere outcome of mental events. Bowne took Spencer far more seriously than he took Schopenhauer or Nietzsche, so he did not keep up with atheistic trends. It seemed obvious to him that Spencer's form of disbelief would capture minds long after flashy irrational versions were forgotten. Bowne's focus on Spencer was a species of respect—interrogating the strongest type of disbelief, which was stronger for not being atheist, combining deism and positivism. Bowne told students not to cower before the culture of disbelief: "A purely logical and contemplative intellect that merely gazed upon the relations of ideas, without choice and initiative and active self-direction, would be absolutely useless in explaining the order of life."[10]

Personal idealism, on Bowne's terms, was Christian theism refracted through modern philosophy—a theory of the fecundity and invisible personal ground of life. The reflective self is the ground of all knowing and being, yet this ground is invisible, for no one has ever seen a self. Bowne was fond of saying that the human body is an instrument for expressing and manifesting its inner life. To him, post-Kantian idealism mattered because it saved what matters in Christian theism while dispensing with centuries of Christian dogmatism. Every self knows itself in immediate experience and knows other selves only through their effects. Thus every self is as formless and invisible as God. All the meanings by which we live, and the motives that move us, are invisible. The drama of life has its seat in the invisible world of meanings, passions, and relations of personal wills. Bowne stressed that most of what matters in life is not only out of sight, but cannot be pictured. The seat of this drama is in consciousness, not in space, for the mind is neither in space nor time.[11]

This was an argument about the seat of the world's reality, not the unreality of the world of things. Bowne repeated as often as necessary that the world of objects is really out there. What matters is to conceive the world in terms of itself, in the incommensurable terms of life and feeling, not in phenomenal terms. Kant put philosophy on the right track, but never reconciled the contradictory impulses of his attempt to unite reason and experience. Bowne said the world of things is the expression of a thought world that is behind or immanent within being. The mind of God is as necessary for philosophy as for theology, and for the same reasons.

Bowne did not claim to prove that personal theism is true. It was enough to say that personal theism explains the world better than materialism, atheism, and other hypotheses. He grieved at latter-day Christian scholastics and apologists who took the bait from skeptics, proffering indefensible proofs. Bowne stressed that every field of thought contains an element of faith and will, and pragmatic usefulness is an important test of believing anything. The world exists through a mind analogous to the human mind, which makes the world of things and the world of thought commensurable, which makes life intelligible. The God postulate, he allowed, might seem a mystery-X solution to an unsolvable problem: What was God doing before creation? Bowne acknowledged that if time is infinite and the cosmic process in time might be finite, Christianity has a serious problem with God's procreative activity. God must have done something before the creation of the universe, yet God must have needed to wait, owing to the potency of number, for this procreative eternity to pass before being able to do anything. That was absurd, so Bowne stuck with Neoplatonist Christianity: God is timeless. The world was not created in a particular moment of the eternal flow of God's time, for God has no eternal flow of temporality. Creation is the beginning of all things, including time. No such eternity as that presumed in the what-was-God-doing question exists. Temporal terms mean something only with reference to the cosmic process, which is relative. God, however, is absolute—the self-existent, timeless I AM whose being lacks temporal ebb and flow.[12]

Bowne put pluralistic idealism on the map of American philosophy, with able support from Howison at Berkeley, G. T. Ladd at Yale, and George Herbert Palmer at Harvard. He had treasured friendships with Royce, Royce's Harvard protégé W. E. Hocking, and especially James, despite disagreeing with them. James mocked Bowne's integral self, quipping that Bowne crawled into a hole and pulled the hole in after him. Yet James counted Bowne as a pragmatic, empirical, and ethical ally in the fight against mechanistic and rationalistic dogmatism, and he taught Bowne's books at Harvard.[13]

Bowne was committed to being a good Methodist and was annoyed at having to defend himself to church leaders. He had a penchant for cutting sarcasm that wounded church audiences, but he showed up at church conferences and kept offending. His favorite kind of humor, besides sarcasm, was ironic. Often he began a conversation by saying, "Now let us have a word about pure being." Bowne said most of the

Bible is tiresome and obsolete, contributing little to healthy, regenerative, progressive religion. What matters in the Bible is the doctrine of creation—the concept of the world as personally created and personally related. As long as Christians hold fast to the biblical view of the divine-human relation, it doesn't matter how much myth biblical scholars find in the Bible. Bowne welcomed the comparative study of religion, but said it had a bleak future, because modernity crushes religions.[14]

Religions are tested every day for goodness, beauty, and credibility, he explained. No religion that retains superstitious dogmas has any chance of surviving the onslaught of modern science, technology, and criticism. Thus most religions had no future at all. Bowne said that only Christianity had a chance of withstanding the global rush of Western science and culture, and this chance was fading. He grieved that many churches still taught the doctrine of biblical inerrancy, an idol of "ignorant ark-savers" lacking any comprehension of the Bible as literature. Bowne stressed that churches opposed every form of progress before some made belated adjustments: "Texts have been arrayed against astronomy, geology, political economy, philosophy, geography, religious toleration, anti-slavery, mercy to decrepit old women called witches, anatomy, medicine, vaccination, anesthetics, fanning-mills, lightning-rods, life-insurance, women speaking in church and going to the General Conference. All of these, particularly the last, have been declared, solemnly and with much emotion, to make the Word of God of none effect."[15]

That had to stop, Bowne pleaded. Otherwise the culture of disbelief would surely win. Atonement theology, long handled gingerly by the best Methodist theologians, was a major candidate for theological revision. Bowne stumped for a purely moral interpretation that discarded even the word "atonement" as irreparable. In its time, he said, the New Testament's dramatic language of sacrifice and ransom brought sinners to God, but that was in the shadow of the altar and temple. Dragging this language into the modern age was disastrous for Christianity. Bowne judged that two contradictory notions in the New Testament undergird classical teaching on this subject. The first is substitution, based on the sacrificial system of Hebrew religion. The second is the imputation of Christ's merit and righteousness to sinners. Objective atonement theories try to make these notions comprehensible and compatible. The satisfaction theories make forgiveness unnecessary and unreal, negating God's forgiveness and even love. Love is ascribed to Christ, but God is pictured as a wrathful incarnation of primitive justice, needing to be appeased by sacrifice. Objective atonement is about justice, Bowne said, not the grace and love of God, and the justice is repugnant, impugning God's virtue. Moreover, atonement justice exists only in theory, making no change where salvation is needed. The real problem is terribly concrete. No word of forgiveness cancels the destructive consequences of sin. To be sure, there is such a thing as the cancellation of personal guilt, but there is no such thing as forensic cancellation of the concrete consequences of sin. Not even God can remove the results of sin with a word, yet orthodox theology settled for salvation that is not saving.[16]

Liberals were constantly accused of sentimentalism, making salvation purely subjective. Bowne countered that a sentimentalist is a person who fails to grasp that consequences cannot be forgiven. Orthodoxy fixed on the forensic penalty for sin, which changes nothing. Liberal humanism was weak *and* sentimental, treating sin as mere ignorance. Liberal theology, with or without the social gospel, said that salvation is saving only if it delivers people from their bondage to selfishness and changes the conditions that perpetuate selfishness and abuse. Bowne put it sharply, contending that liberal Christians wanted what God wants, a righteous world: "If we wish the thing, we must fulfill the conditions. It is God's purpose to have and to bless only a world wherein dwelleth righteousness. However inconvenient we may find it, and however strong our desire for sport may be, the unrighteous must come to grief; and God will never depart from his moral laws to make it otherwise."[17]

He put it sharper, knowing that being a Methodist gave him advantages over liberals speaking to Calvinist or Lutheran audiences. To wish to be saved from the penalty of sin, but not from sin, is the essence of degradation. Anyone who says such a thing, Bowne declared, no matter how orthodox, lacks the slightest idea or experience of redemption: "There can be no salvation for him. He knows neither the Scriptures nor the moral reason." Real salvation is from sin, not from penalty. It delivers the sinner to a life of active righteousness, reconciled to the holy will of God. Bowne said it with Wesleyan sanctification flourishes: knowing Christ is supposed to make a person righteous. But this was a characteristically liberal theme, with or without the Wesleyan flourishes. John Wesley felt obligated to incorporate his teaching about justification and sanctification into classic Christian orthodoxy, but modern theologians needed to privilege the truth, not Bible verses and traditions. The only objective aspects of salvation are the terribly concrete consequences of sin. Orthodox theologies were perversely subjective in picturing a monster

God *and* in lacking objectivity in the one area where something objective was at stake.[18]

Every late nineteenth-century American liberal theologian defined true religion in Victorian categories, and most liberal preachers did so before "Victorian" was a name. Unitarian icon William Ellery Channing and Congregational theologian Horace Bushnell said the fundamental problem of life is the conflict between the higher and lower impulses of human beings. Bowne said the same thing after Darwinism traumatized the church. Even the radical feminist Elizabeth Cady Stanton sounded like a Victorian preacher when she held forth on the struggle of enlightened spirit against nature. Cady Stanton told audiences that true religion is about the triumph of a rational-spiritual self over its carnal impulses. After Darwin, liberal theologians routinely preached that progress takes place through the gradual emergence of the spiritual in humankind and its growing victory over animal nature. Bowne put it with customary vigor: "The method of procedure is growth and development. There are animal beginnings with moral endings. Love and law are omnipresent throughout the whole of the work; and judgment is possible only at the end."[19]

This way of conceiving the problem of sin had a fateful trajectory. If progress takes place through the gradual emergence of the spiritual in humanity and its growing victory over animal nature, it follows that the human sense of sin is the consciousness that accompanies humanity's process of growth. The sense of sin is a necessary stage in the evolution of humanity. Explicitly, liberal theologians taught that animal beginnings gradually give way to moral endings. Implicitly, the upshot was that sin is a stage that can be outgrown. Nineteenth-century liberal theologians took their animal beginnings very seriously, but the next generation of theologians believed that progress was advancing at a very rapid rate. The world was getting better; the power of disease was broken; American power and democracy were expanding; education was expelling the evils of ignorance; religious orthodoxy was dethroned; the kingdom of God was within reach. The rationale for straining out sin language was built into liberal rhetoric about it from the beginning. By the time that Knudson reiterated Bowne's position in 1933, minus the Victorian encumbrances, the backlash against liberal theology was devastating, shredding weak versions of it.[20]

The personalists who built a school after Bowne was gone had no inkling that "liberal" and "progressive" would become sneer terms, and were incredulous when it happened. Meanwhile they had to make a major adjustment when they built the school, because Bowne lacked a social gospel conscience. Bowne rejected the defining social gospel principle that Christianity has a social mission to transform social structures in the direction of social justice. There is no such thing as society, he would say, so all the new language about social structures and social justice was misguided. Bowne feared that the social gospel emphasis on democracy was leveling, a barrier to enlightened progress. For all his criticism of Spencer, he spurned social gospel ideas about where to draw the line between good and bad Darwinism. To him, good Darwinism had a debatable amount of room for social Darwinist politics, because government often impeded social progress, being the rule of bureaucratic mediocrities. Bowne's battle was against ignorance and atheism, not social injustice, although he made an exception for women, who deserved the benefits of liberal rights, and he recognized that social gospel progressives were more right than wrong about social Darwinism. He considered himself a true progressive, but in the individualistic liberal sense that preceded the social gospel. Bowne took pride in keeping his balance on these topics, somehow writing voluminously about American social progress without mentioning that black Americans were lynched, despised, and disenfranchised amidst all of it.

He felt the lure of social Darwinism, observing that from the standpoint of abstract moral principles, or a utilitarian concern for human progress, it was hard to oppose the application of Darwinian principles to politics and society. Darwinian weeding out, he claimed, yielded stronger communities. Moreover, he grasped why condemnations of Christian "slave morality" were fashionable, although Bowne kept Nietzsche's name out of it: "Christianity has been denounced as more injurious than any crime in its practical sympathy for the weak and defective." Bowne warned that whenever these perspectives framed the issue, Christians lost the argument. Any appeal to abstract moral principles or the utilitarian greater good favored social Darwinism. The Christian argument operated on a different basis—the moral revolution that Christianity wrought in the world. Bowne identified true Christianity with the belief that all human beings are loved by God and bear God's Spirit. This teaching, he argued, surpasses all moralities based on tribal and ethnic traditions, common sense, and abstract reasoning. Christianity makes every person the bearer of sacredness and heir of eternal life: "By making the moral law the expression of a Holy Will, it brought that law out of its impersonal abstraction and assured its ultimate triumph. Moral principles may be what they were before, but moral practice is forever different."[21]

His disciples pointed to this argument when they claimed that personal idealism was the best philosophy for the social gospel, never mind that Bowne spurned the social gospel. They recalled that Bowne campaigned for progressive religion, albeit with caustic remarks about shallow thinking, stupid bishops, and ecclesiastical backwardness that Bowne's disciples were too politic to repeat.

In 1904 Bowne was formally accused of heresy on the Trinity, miracles, biblical inspiration, atonement, and redemption. He put up with a heresy trial in the New York East Annual Conference of the Methodist church, indignantly defending himself against overmatched accusers. This episode wounded Bowne's moral pride, notwithstanding that most of the assembly admired him. Bowne seethed against church reactionaries for the rest of his life. In 1905 his Boston University colleague Hinkley Mitchell was fired for teaching biblical criticism; Bowne declared that Mitchell was a paragon of scholarly virtue and the bishops were dopes. Human beings, he said, are prone to conservatism, institutions are more so, and excellence is always imperiled by the rule of mediocrities. Progress depends on the courage, imagination, and faith of educated visionaries. Repeatedly he said that Protestant churches didn't deserve to survive if they censured their best thinkers: "When the inferior men are brought to the front, then lower interests become prominent. The financial aspects of religion are brought forward and emphasized. The value of place likewise becomes significant, and we tend to have men in prominence who have very little interest in the truth as such, but rather in maintaining the present order, in securing position and the perquisites of religious place."[22]

Bowne implored church leaders not to censure scholars and scholarship they didn't understand: "Questions of scholarship can only be settled by scholarship." Progress in religion, he contended, is no different from progress in other fields; it requires the flourishing of discussion and criticism. The very notion of deciding a question of fact by authority or ignorant votes is absurd. Authority makes itself ridiculous when it presumes to dictate, and majorities are equally absurd when they do not respect evidence. Bowne stressed that if the Catholic Church had gotten its way, "modern civilization would never have developed, and humanity would have been ruined." Modern theologians needed to defend hard-won intellectual freedoms that churches had opposed in the first place. Thus he cast off the first commandment of church etiquette: be nice. The church's best thinkers had to stop being nice about a shameful situation. Liberal theology had barely begun in American Congregationalism, and it still did not exist in Bowne's beloved Methodism.[23]

But liberal theology and the social gospel took over the elite divinity schools and seminaries during this period. Bowne was by far the leading American religious intellectual of his time and thus forgiven for being old school about liberal individualism. He had notable philosophical disciples at DePauw University (L. R. Eckardt), University of Southern California (Ralph T. Flewelling), Vanderbilt (H. C. Sanborn), and Syracuse (G. A. Wilson), and he buoyed a flock of religious thinkers, especially George Albert Coe at Union Theological Seminary and Henry Churchill King at Oberlin College. Many clerics who knew nothing of Kant derived confidence from believing that Bowne handled Kant and Spencer. Bowne was comparable to Troeltsch for sheer intellectual firepower and did not compare to Troeltsch as a scholar. Bowne did not know the Kant-Schleiermacher-Hegel tradition as deeply as Troeltsch knew it, and he over-relied on his ability to argue, never developing the discipline or skill set of a scholar. His disciples thus leaned on Troeltsch when they built the personalist school—while saying they owed it all to Bowne.[24]

Ernst Troeltsch and the Theology of Religion

Ernst Troeltsch was a restless battler who renewed and amplified F. C. Baur's ambitious attempt to combine historicism and metaphysics. He grew up in Haunstetten, near Augsburg, idolizing his workaholic, studious, Lutheran, politically conservative father, a medical doctor. Lacking his metaphysical itch, Troeltsch would have become a scientist. As it was, he studied theology at Erlangen, transferred in 1886 to Göttingen to study under Ritschl, Lotze, and Paul Lagarde, and decided that Lagarde was right about Ritschlian historicism. Real historicism does not begin with Christian questions or favor any religion. Troeltsch befriended his classmates Wilhelm Bousset, Hermann Gunkel, and William Wrede, especially Bousset. All were cagey about Lagarde's anti-Semitism while helping him establish the *Religionsgeschichtliche Schule*. To Troeltsch and his classmates, the methodological issue was consuming. They believed the history of religions approach marked an advance on Ritschl just as Ritschl marked an advance on Baur's Tübingen school. Troeltsch taught successively at Göttingen, Bonn, Heidelberg, and Berlin. He made his early mark while teaching at Bonn in the early 1890s, loathed mediocre Heidelberg after moving there in 1894, became the major theologian of the history of religions school, and was thrilled when he got to Berlin in 1915.[25]

He was prone to dramatic announcements. In 1897, while complaining that he had no intelligent colleagues at Heidelberg, Troeltsch announced that "a grand new discipline, the history of religion" dismantled the claims of Christianity to superiority and universality. Instead of beginning with Christianity, this approach began with religion. Against the Ritschlian idea that Christianity is an independent entity grounded in faith, this approach took seriously "this maelstrom of historical diversity," shredding the idea of an independent sphere. Everything historical is relative, Troeltsch argued, which does not mean that historical relativism is a final truth. Historical relativism must be qualified by three fundamental truths supported by historical consciousness: mind has an independent potency not derived from nature, all religions are identical at their core, and some forms of religious consciousness are more advanced than others in advancing beyond nature and historical provincialism.[26]

Troeltsch said it is pointless just to explore, as though exploring were an end in itself. A theologian must have a compass—a religious philosophy that grounds whatever transcultural claims the theologian makes. In his early career, Troeltsch leaned on Hegel and Lotze for it. The basic reality of religion is the same everywhere because the human spirit is the same everywhere. Humanity has a common dynamism of spirit that advances in different ways through the mysterious movement of divine Spirit in and through the human spirit. The more that religions advance toward their ultimate goal, the more they strive for the fullness of truth, moving beyond the spell of nature and local mythology. Nearly every religion, Troeltsch argued, is a nature religion still bound to its mythology. Buddhism is a partial exception, but Buddhism is too pessimistic, otherworldly, and monastic to be a universal religion of redemption, and Neoplatonism is too mystical. Only Christianity breaks with nature religion, getting to universal redemption. In Christianity, God is experienced in the individual heart and the outward social world, and all people are included in God's plan.[27]

Troeltsch loved grand generalizations. In 1902 he declared at the outset of *The Absoluteness of Christianity and the History of Religions* that the modern world created "a unique type of culture" by taking an "unreservedly historical view" of all things human. In antiquity, he said, history was the history of single states. In Catholic culture it became the history of humankind, but everything was interpreted through church dogma. Modern culture took the next step by affirming the universal ambitions of the Catholic idea while dissolving its dogmas in the flow of events.

To modern historical consciousness, all things are in play as subjects of interpretation.[28]

Troeltsch shared Baur's fascination with the early Christian attempt to define its relationship to other religions, breaking from nature religion. Paul devised the first strategy, construing Christianity as a new, independent, universal religious power. But Paul relied on Judaism and his unrepeatable inner experiences in theorizing what Christianity is about. Later generations had no recourse to Paul's vision of Christ, his inner struggle with the limits and demands of Jewish law, or his ecstatic experiences of the Spirit. To make Christianity intelligible to Christians and outsiders, the church formulated the doctrines of revelation and the incarnation, which led to the Logos theory: all moments of truth contained in the world's various religions and philosophies are expressions of the mind of God at work in the world, and Christ is the perfect revelation of the divine mind, the incarnation of divine Reason.

Troeltsch said these two approaches served the church remarkably well, until the modern era. The Pauline tradition relied on the miracle of an inner renewal transcending all natural powers and a structure of dogma about it, while the Logos tradition treated non-Christian religions as blinkered anticipations or reflections of the absolute truth revealed in Christianity—the essence of religion. In the modern context, Troeltsch argued, Logos theology works better than Pauline theology, which is too subjective. In Logos theology, especially its Hegelian versions, history is subordinated to the concept of a uniform, self-actuating power or universal principle, and this concept is raised to the status of a universal norm or ideal constituting that which is of value in all events.[29]

But Troeltsch was too historicist to keep saying that Logos theology apprehends the essence of religion. Historical consciousness does not know an all-inclusive principle that regulates the emergence of everything individual, constitutes the essence of all value, and is the norm of all things. It knows only concrete, individual things conditioned by their context. He allowed that historical consciousness may grasp ideas that are said to be universally valid, but it knows no values that coincide with actual universals. Rather, it knows ideas that appear in individual form and make their claim for universal validity by resisting other ideas. Idealistic theories of graded progression miss what actually happens. History offers no evidence of gradual progression to higher orientations, and Harnack's kernel-and-husk strategy was no better, wrongly supposing that the absolute and the relative are separable.

Absolutizing the kernel, instead of preserving a credible absolute, also absolutizes the husk; meanwhile the relativity of the husk relativizes the kernel. Troeltsch decided that searching for a transhistorical absolute within history is counterproductive, for the crucial religious ideas are always bound up with the leading ideas of a given age. The truest parts of Christianity are not things that can be lifted above history. Christianity is a historical movement, so even the retrograde aspects of Christian tradition have a place in it.

True historicism focuses on the particularities of historical periods and the interrelationships of cultural structures. No historical period is a mere rung on a ladder; each has its own ethos and meanings. Baur's historicism was a breakthrough in its time, but it operated in scale-oriented theories about early Christianity and Catholicism. Real history does not unfold in schemes about logically related members of ascending series. So Troeltsch gave up the Hegelian idea of an absolute working itself out through the permutations of history—taking for granted the right-Hegelian view that Hegel was a monist with a closed system. In its place, Troeltsch adopted the neo-Kantian value theory of Wilhelm Windelband and Heinrich Rickert, reasoning that critical consciousness does not exclude norms. The task of critical history is to discern the value orientations that occur in history and construe them as a unified whole. These norms, and whatever ways they are unified, are always individual, particular, socially conditioned forms of striving toward a goal. History consists of relative, situated tendencies toward an absolute goal that is never completely realized in history. Religion is about cultivating and realizing value orientations, and some religions do it better than others. What matters is to achieve the highest values.[30]

Historicism has room for comparative judgments; in fact, making critical comparisons is fundamental to historical reason. Troeltsch still had a compass, still railed against aimless exploring, and still called for a history of religions theology, denying there was any contradiction in this idea. Theology needed to theologize a fully historicist account of world religions. He said it would be absurd—a capitulation to nihilism—if theologians refused to discern value orientations in history and make value judgments about them. The best judgments emerge from the critical comparison of value orientations. Historical criticism begins with descriptions of historical phenomena, which lead to a position about value orientations, which requires philosophical reflection. The very fact that religions are comparable shows that they are related "to something common and universally valid within them." Historical reason identifies orienting goals and ideals, not universal principles.[31]

The early Troeltsch believed that politics was beneath him, until his friend Max Weber persuaded him otherwise, which yielded Troeltsch's famous writings on social ethics. His social ethic was basically conservative, integrating four principles: conservatism, democracy, nationalism, and liberalism. Troeltsch took pride that his generation did not venerate the old Kantian and Hegelian cultural goals of the state. To his generation, schooled in the ascendancy of Germany under Bismarck, politics was obviously about power, power was the essence of the state, and a strong army was the backbone of the state. He argued that patriotic feeling and liberal liberties are very important, though secondary to aristocratic privilege and popular sovereignty, because only conservatism and democracy ascribe an intrinsic ethical value to the state. The ethical value of a state rests on the spirit of its political institutions, the richness and depth of its culture, and the ethical ideas permeating its society, plus nationalistic feeling. A good state upholds ethical principles that penetrate the inner structures of its institutions and define the social good. Troeltsch worried that modern society tottered on unstable foundations. He implored that democracy had to be rescued from the Social Democrats and feminists, telling Germans they were right to love their growing army.[32]

The early Troeltsch related a distinct concept of traditional doctrine to a critical understanding of the modern intellectual and religious situation, very much in the fashion of Ritschl and Harnack. But soon he decided that Ritschl got both things wrong. Ritschl assimilated a dubious rendering of the Christian story to an equally questionable interpretation of the modern situation, covering up the actual contrasts between them. This judgment yielded Troeltsch's unexpected fixation with the history of Protestantism and the emergence of the modern world. He told himself he was laying the historical groundwork for his systematic theology and philosophy of religion. But the more he studied modern problems, the more he found himself pulled into social ethics, which set him on the path of his landmark book, *The Social Teaching of the Christian Churches* (1912).[33]

Troeltsch offered detailed descriptions of social teaching in the early Christian movement, early Catholicism, medieval Catholicism, and varieties of European Protestantism. Adopting Weber's concept of ideal types, he argued that the Christian community developed three types of Christianity rooted in three distinct models of social organization. The gospel of Jesus was a religion of free piety, strong on spiritual intimacy and lacking any concern with creating a religious community, which yielded three kinds of Christianity: an institutional church model dispensing objective means of grace and redemption, a sectarian model of true believers living apart from the world, and a mystical faith stressing inward spiritual experience. Troeltsch respected the sectarian type for standing for something, and he liked the mystical type, but neither had a viable social philosophy for the modern world. Only the church type, he said, had the capacity to be creative and expansive. In nineteen centuries, Western Christianity produced only two major social philosophies: medieval Catholicism and Calvinism. The first was built on the spiritual unity of a feudal, patriarchal civilization featuring a supreme church. The second created a covenantal Protestant Christendom by combining asceticism, pietism, Free Church ecclesiology, state church governance, democracy, liberalism, and vocational diligence. By the nineteenth century, both were spent forces. The Catholic doctrine of the Catholic State was as laughable as the Catholic opposition to evolution and historical criticism, and Calvinism fared little better under modern criticism. There was no serious Christian social philosophy in modern times. There was only the glimmer of one in Christian socialism.[34]

Troeltsch was admiring and dismissive of Christian socialism, for two reasons on both counts. At least the Christian socialists tried to apply Christian norms to modern society, and they did so by rejecting centuries of authoritarianism and conformism in Christian ethics. So he gave them two cheers for breaking through, while judging them doubly naïve. Somehow Christian socialists believed they could transform the conditions of the world, just like the naïve sectarians of the past. And somehow they believed they recovered the original gospel faith, despite having been educated in modern universities. Theologically they were innocents, invoking Jesus as though his words blazed through the centuries. Politically they were innocent and dangerous, fantasizing about an international proletariat that refused all calls to war except perhaps class war. Troeltsch said that even if Christian socialism became the church's third great social philosophy, the church needed something else: a truly modern, critical, effective, and inspiring way of engaging the world through Christianity. He confessed that he didn't know what it was: "If the present social situation is to be controlled by Christian principles, thoughts will be necessary which have not yet been thought."[35]

All he could say was that Christianity provides a strong basis for personality and individuality, and only Christianity does so. This was the crucial thing that Christianity contributes to a better world—the belief in personality as a universal principle and value. Only Christianity embraces and unites all human souls, through its concept of Divine Love. Ethically, only Christianity solves the problem of inequality, by viewing all people as children of God loved by God. Troeltsch said Christianity is the consummate religion of love and personality, promoting charity as the fruit of the Christian Spirit. Beyond that he was chastened about the relevance of modern Christianity. Once the church lost its doctrinal certainties and social power, there was no answer; there was only the search for a new one. Meanwhile Troeltsch gave flaming, racist, militaristic speeches during World War I that fired up crowds with patriotic gore and might have destroyed his legacy had he not lived long enough to become a postwar European internationalist.[36]

In the aftermath of war and defeat, he lost his personalist compass and dropped his conceits about German superiority. As late as 1922, in his book *Der Historismus und seine Probleme*, Troeltsch had a version of his idea that Christianity is true as the consummate religion of personality. He even had a metaphysical substructure for it—a monadology derived from Leibniz in which every particular, conditioned, individual finite spirit "participates intuitively" in the divine Spirit. Troeltsch theorized that history consists fundamentally of individual totalities—*wholes* such as families, social classes, states, and schools of thought that synthesize psychical processes and natural conditions. Historical wholes, he reasoned, are original, partly unconscious, integral unities of meaning and value. A universal history should focus on them. But Troeltsch's attempt to write a universal history ended in failure, driving him to the reluctant conclusion that a universal history is not possible, or is possible only in a qualified way—he could be quoted either way, being conflicted.[37]

Sometimes he argued for a universal history leading to a modern cultural synthesis resting on four pillars: the ancient Hebraic tradition, classical Greece, the Hellenistic-Roman period, and the Occidental Middle Ages. Non-Western history had little to contribute to universal history, and Troeltsch barely glanced at non-Occidental philosophies of history. But elsewhere in *Der Historismus und seine Probleme*, and emphatically in his unfinished last book, *Der Historismus und seine Überwindung* (1924), published after his death, he argued that the dream of a universal history must be relinquished. On occasion, in the former mode, Troeltsch still argued that historical wholes possess a common spirit or mind that is properly the object of historical reason, theology, and especially the philosophy of history. In his last book he argued, with seeming finality, that we know nothing of "humanity" or a Common Spirit. All we know are particular groups, families, races, classes, schools, and sects from six thousand years, a tiny fraction of the human experience.[38]

In the end he replaced his nationalism and his Christian universalism with Eurocentrism. Troeltsch said the idea of personality is too Christian to be universal, and he regretted having said otherwise. In place of his vision of historical development as the shaping of community life in accordance with a universal norm epitomized in Christianity, he settled for "Europeanism." In place of claiming that Christianity is the best religion, he said it was the best religion for Europe. Troeltsch still made a strained appeal to universality: "For us there is only the universal history of European culture" (*Universalgeschichte der europäischen Kultur*), or, stressing Europeanism as an idea, "For us there is only a universal history of Europeanism" (*Weltgeschichte des Europäertums*). In both cases he accepted that any idea claiming universality is as thoroughly particular and historical as any other idea. No historically conscious European has an idea of universality or a concept of values that is not decidedly European.[39]

To Troeltsch, this became an argument for granting "ism" status to Europeanism, alongside capitalism, liberalism, and Expressionism, if not above them. Europeanism, he contended, has a vital, scientific, and liberating historical individuality. It valorizes individuality and critical rationality more than any other culture, and its carryover into the United States is a major point in its favor. Troeltsch took pride that Americans looked to Europe for high culture and intellectual leadership, filling their museums with European art. His American personalist admirers appreciated that he lightened up on nationalism and regretted very much that he relinquished the personalist principle. Certainly, Troeltsch was right that personal individuality is a Christian idea; it didn't come from anywhere else. But how could that be a proof that personality is not universal?[40]

Albert C. Knudson, Edgar S. Brightman, and the Personalist School

The Bowne disciples who built the personalist school held fast to the personalist principle. Albert Knudson, a product of Methodist piety and a graduate school conversion, was born in 1873 in Grandmeadow, Minnesota, to immigrant parents from Norway. Like Schleiermacher, Knudson had a clerical father who was impeccably orthodox. Like Schleiermacher, he remained deeply pious after he turned theologically liberal. Unlike Schleiermacher, Knudson suffered no parental trauma for turning liberal, later recalling that his father had "an instinctive reverence for the honest convictions of others." Thus he felt free to explore religious alternatives as an undergraduate at the University of Minnesota. Knudson's favorite teacher, Williston S. Hough, was a Hegelian, steering him to Royce and Edward Caird. For a while, Knudson felt edified. He liked that Hegelianism flew above the plane of sense, but Caird's concept of a unity implied in subject and object that transcends subject and object left Knudson in a fog. Did Hegel describe the Christian God? Was he Christian, or merely vaguely religious? By the end of his college studies, Knudson felt more confused than edified. Naturalistic materialism was never an option for him, commonsense realism merely scratched the surface, and Hegelian idealism was strangely elusive. That left him with a single certainty, his religious experience, which got him to Boston University School of Theology, where he studied Hebrew Bible under Mitchell, church history under Henry C. Sheldon, and theology under Olin A. Curtis.[41]

Curtis was an old-style conservative, Sheldon was a cautious moderate, and Mitchell converted Knudson to biblical criticism. Theologically, Knudson drifted to a moderate liberalism; philosophically, he was still perplexed by the end of his seminary program. If he had no philosophical foundation, how could he know his theology was credible? He noticed that his teachers looked up to Bowne, even those who disagreed with him. Knudson had to figure out what he believed about epistemology and metaphysics, so he studied philosophy under Bowne in the academic year 1896–1897. He later called it the year of *Aufklärung*, an illumination. Bowne's riveting lectures were enthralling to Knudson: "Here at last I found a thinker and a system of thought that matched my own mind. It would be difficult to express the degree of satisfaction that the year brought me. Not only was there the stimulus that came from the keenest, profoundest, and most masterful mind I ever knew, but the content of the teaching met my need as nothing else had done." Knudson found his philosophical foundation: "On the most fundamental questions he expressed himself with a freedom, precision and grace that the present writer has never heard equaled."[42]

His highest compliment for Bowne was, "He had a system. . . . He worked out a comprehensive theory of reality and of the intellectual, moral and religious life." Knudson's rationalism was stronger than

Bowne's, which colored his interpretation of Bowne's thought, but he got the essential Bowne exactly right: "First, personality is the key to reality, and second, life is the test of truth." Bowne taught Knudson to conceive the history of thought as a variety of epistemological and metaphysical perspectives. His teaching was clarifying and dazzling, but also, to Knudson, vital, inspiring, and real: "It brought me a mental relief and an intellectual illumination that may be described as akin to a redemptive experience. . . . He saw distinctly the true aim of all sound philosophy, and knew with the unerring vision of a seer how best to realize it. To listen to him or to follow him in his books was to see the mists arise from the valleys, and the clouds and the shadows fall away." It seemed to Knudson that personal theism was a consuming spiritual passion to Bowne: "It was his whole soul, not merely his intellect, that was a source of light." He and Bowne took long walks through the Fenway, discussing philosophy. Knudson told friends that upon returning from these conversations he often recalled the lines that Wordsworth wrote near Tintern Abbey: "I have felt a presence that disturbs me with the joy of elevated thoughts."[43]

Knudson was the blessed child, for Bowne did not converse with students. Even Brightman got only a one-word answer, a terse one-sentence answer to a question, and a terse one-sentence compliment in two years of studying under Bowne. Then Brightman told audiences for the rest of his life that Bowne's dignified bearing and intellectual power "made him seem almost a superman." Knudson studied for a year in Berlin under Harnack, Bernhard Weiss, and Julius Kaftan, underwhelmed by the German titans. None compared remotely to Bowne. He taught at Iliff School of Theology for two years, married Mathilde Johnson, and got a pleasant surprise from Boston University in 1900: a doctorate in philosophy based on his studies with Bowne. He moved to Baker University, where he taught philosophy, Bible, church history, sociology, and economics for two years, then did the same thing at Allegheny College for three years, still lacking a field of specialization. In 1905 the Board of Bishops fired Mitchell, and a painfully conflicted Knudson accepted the university's offer to come home. Knudson grieved for his beloved teacher, but somebody had to teach Hebrew Scripture at his alma mater. He emphasized religious themes, took a light pass at historical criticism, and became a popular teacher and author, albeit while realizing that he did not teach or write cutting-edge scholarship.[44]

In April 1910, just after Knudson departed for a sabbatical leave at Berlin, Bowne suffered a stroke in class and died. Knudson cabled a grieving tribute declaring that Bowne's incomparably brilliant light was "destined to be that which shineth more and more." That was a clue to his future, though Knudson resisted it, declining to take Bowne's position. He felt he was too old to return to philosophy and had to redeem his years of effort to become a competent biblical scholar. At the same time, he agreed to succeed Sheldon in theology when he retired, which would allow several years of preparation. But Sheldon held on until 1921. Knudson was forty-eight years old when he launched his career as a theologian, regretting that it took so long. On a popular level, personalist theology was burgeoning through the works of Francis McConnell, George Albert Coe, Henry Churchill King, Boston Congregational pastor George A. Gordon, and Pacific School of Religion religious philosopher John Wright Buckham (a protégé of Gordon). All acknowledged their debts to Bowne *and* supported the social gospel. The founding of the Federal Council of Churches in 1908 was a boon for the social gospel, and McConnell's election to the episcopacy in 1912 was a boon for personalism and the social gospel. Knudson wished he had written personalist books from the beginning; now he was eager to make up for the lost years. He had a partner in this work, as Brightman joined the faculty in 1919, with Knudson's help.[45]

Edgar Brightman was as religious as Bowne, equally gifted intellectually, and a far better mentor to students. He was born in 1884 in Holbrook, Massachusetts, where his warmhearted, theologically conservative father was a Methodist pastor and his deep-thinking mother tutored him in French, botany, and literature. Brightman was intellectually voracious throughout his life. As a youth he devoured Bible commentaries and ancient history, taking long walks on the seashore. At Brown University he shucked off his parents' theological conservatism, mastered Greek, Latin, German, and French, studied Plato, Kant, and Schopenhauer, and absorbed his teacher Alexander Meiklehohn's devotion to logic. Brightman successively fell under the sway of Kant, Schopenhauer, Royce, Hegel, and James, dropping James upon realizing that a proposition could be perfectly useful and wrong, just before Brightman enrolled at Boston University School of Theology. There, Bowne converted him. It seemed to Brightman that Bowne combined the best parts of Royce and James without committing their errors. After Bowne died, Brightman studied at Berlin under Harnack, whom he greatly admired, and at Marburg under Herrmann and neo-Kantian philosopher Paul Natorp. He formed a close friendship with the kindly Herrmann, who inquired about Bowne and helped Brightman work out the argument of his doctoral dissertation on Ritschl's theory of knowledge. Brightman argued that Bowne's emphasis on the unity of the subject corrected Ritschl's empiricism.[46]

In his early career he taught at Nebraska Wesleyan University and Wesleyan University, until Boston University called, at Knudson's urging. For many years Brightman was the only professor whose primary affiliation at the university was in the Graduate School, though he also taught at the College of Liberal Arts and the School of Theology. In 1925 he became the first Bowne Professor, feeling the weight of the title. Brightman devoted his early years at Boston to the school ambition he shared with Knudson, telling audiences that Bowne was the greatest American Christian thinker of his generation, conveying "an air of victory, a triumphant and infectious faith."[47]

Bowne vanquished his opponents, Brightman said; ironically, doing so made him forgettable. Americans no longer remembered how dominant Spencer's mechanistic system, John Stuart Mill's empiricism, and absolute idealism had been, because Bowne shredded these philosophies. Bowne deserved more credit than he received, and there were more personal idealists than it seemed. Brightman cited many of Bowne's disciples and counted Hocking as a personalist. He did not believe that World War I played much of a role in deflating the reputation of personal idealism. Brightman was too intellectual to pause over grubby historical factors. The chief problem, he said, was that Ritschlian pragmatism swept the field of theology, persuading theologians to eschew metaphysics. The social gospel called for a better social order, not a better philosophy. To Brightman, this was a showcase example of a half-truth becoming the enemy of truth: "For much as we need a new social order, we need God more; if not, let us cease at once all talk of religion."[48]

Modern Christianity needed the social gospel, but it also needed to make God intelligible, a job for the best religious philosophy. Varieties of materialism, positivism, and realism abounded, all trumpeting the triumph of worldly power and the mundane. Absolute idealists rightly defended the objectivity of value but wrongly let go of personality. The Chicago school made room for an idealizing divinity that was personal or not, depending on the theologian, but always on the basis of empirical science, a dead end. Brightman implored personal idealists to speak up for the best philosophy and refute the bad ones, just as Bowne had done. Personal idealism faded only because Bowne's disciples underperformed and pastors stopped reading philosophy. The former point was an exhortation to himself; the latter point, Brightman put bluntly: "The clergy should read more philosophy, and, if the suggestion be not too bold, come to think more philosophically."[49]

Brightman and Knudson built the personalist school on that basis. Though Brightman had less partisan spirit than Knudson, he stressed that schools are the vehicles of progress in philosophy. The history of philosophy consists of free thinkers working together to form schools of thought; it is not a record of unique individuals thinking unique thoughts. A field lacking schools would not be much of a field. Brightman said the fledgling personalist school needed to be wary of the problems of schools, but it had perfect right "to be loyal to its own insights, to acknowledge, with pride and gratitude, its debt to Bowne, in short, to be a school."[50]

The point was not to lift up Bowne as the Thomas Aquinas of Methodism. Brightman said personalists had to maintain an "open-minded temper," rethinking problems in logic, epistemology, psychology, value theory, and society. The usual struggle with absolute idealists had to be waged in new ways, and Brightman worried about a new version of the theory of internal relations, the organic naturalism of Samuel Alexander, C. Lloyd Morgan, and Alfred North Whitehead. It was holistic, relational, and temporal, like absolute idealism, but based on relativity physics and evolutionary theory, not a theory of mind. It was synthetic, scientific, and comprehensive like the old Spencer school, but based on updated science. Brightman felt its intellectual power and dreaded it as a new form of impersonal explanation, countering with four books. *Introduction to Philosophy* (1925) became a widely used textbook. *Immortality in Post-Kantian Idealism* (1925) surveyed beliefs about the immortality of the soul. *Religious Values* (1925) argued that values are conscious experiences of persons and have no meaning apart from consciousness. *A Philosophy of Ideals* (1928) conceived experience and nature as ideal systems that derive their existence and meaning from their embodiment of ideals. Ideals are not merely useful inventions; they reveal the structure of the real world that indwells and transcends humanity.[51]

Brightman attracted able students and took pride in mentoring female students, notably Georgia Harkness. In 1922 he told Harkness that his classes were packed and he was maxed out on work. He took up the Bowne role by writing his early books, but the role that lacked a precedent was Knudson's—theologizing personal idealism in an academic, American, ecumenical fashion. Knudson published his first theological book, *Present Tendencies in Religious Thought*, in 1924, and followed it with a movement manifesto, *The Philosophy of Personalism* (1927).[52]

Personal idealism, to Knudson, was the best philosophy for Christian theology and the vehicle through which he belatedly liberalized Methodist theology. Methodism had never produced a notable liberal theologian, so Bowne told Methodists they needed to learn from others, especially Schleiermacher, Ritschl, and Troeltsch. Like Schleiermacher, Knudson described theology as a scientific explication of Christian experience. Like Ritschl he conceived the Christian experience of revelation as both the ground and norm of Christian truth. Like Troeltsch he emphasized the idea of the religious a priori that he and Troeltsch dug out of Kant and Schleiermacher. Knudson insisted that Schleiermacher's theology and the Wesleyan tradition rested on the same thing, Methodist fundamentalism notwithstanding. In liberal theology and in Methodism, experience serves an apologetic function and a normative one. It is the wellspring of religious claims and the basis on which Christians defend their claims. This is what it means to say that personality is the key to reality and life is the test of truth. Personality is interpreted experience, and life is experience itself.[53]

Knudson's rendering of personal idealism renewed the idea behind Bowne's first name for it, transcendental empiricism. Personal idealism was empirical in its focus on experience, but transcendental in its contention that that which explains everything (personality) cannot be explained. The transcendental categories of thought are revealed in the experience of a self; they do not create or determine the self's experience. There are no innate ideas; there are only immanent rules of mind that condition experience and determine its form. The content of experience is derived from the sensibility, which would lack any form lacking the creative activity of thought. The categories alone make experience possible and are structural in human reason, exactly like our moral nature, which has its own a priori—the categorical imperative. Without the immanent principle in our moral nature, moral experience would be impossible.[54]

Knudson took over Troeltsch's claim that the same argument applies to the religious nature of human beings. Schleiermacher paved the way to it by applying Kant's argument to the religious sphere, rendering religion as a special mode of feeling, not a mode of knowing or doing. But Schleiermacher held back from saying that the same Kantian arguments about a priori knowing and morality apply to the religious nature. Religion—sense for the infinite, our need of God—is too special to be merely another a priori element of human nature. So Schleiermacher did not speak of a religious a priori. He described religion as a unique experience distinguished from the rational nature of human beings,

not identified with it. Ritschl and Herrmann took this argument further than Schleiermacher, with Herrmann lurching to an almost complete antithesis between religion and theoretical knowledge. Troeltsch
brought religion back into the circle of reason by invoking the rational
a priori of religion, and Knudson wholly endorsed what Troeltsch said
about it: the religious a priori is purely formal, in the Kantian sense, and
entirely unique, extending Schleiermacher. As a formal principle it has
no existence apart from experience and history, so it cannot prove God's
existence, establish a rational religion, or the like. It simply establishes
that there is a rational principle immanent in the religious experience
of human beings. Knudson loved Troeltsch's saying that being religious
"belongs to the a priori of reason." At the same time, the religious a priori
manifests itself only in religious experience, so it is independent of theoretical, moral, and aesthetic knowing.[55]

   To Knudson, relativism was by far the greatest enemy of religion.
Dogmatic relativists, by the 1920s, were more destructive than old-style
atheists, who at least believed that some truths are fixed. It pained Knudson that Troeltsch capitulated to relativism at the end, but that confirmed
why personalists had to be vigilant. Knudson said it strenuously, writing
a punchy chapter titled "Militant Personalism." He detailed Bowne's relationships to other versions of idealism, admitting that Bowne ignored fellow theorists and scholarship, so somebody had to historicize personalism
to move it forward. Modern theology, he said, was in a bad way. Compared to the Ritschlian heyday, contemporary theology was dreadfully
depressing, everywhere reducing theology to "a crude realism, dualism,
pragmatism, or positivism." The Chicago school took pride in its shallow
pragmatism and naturalistic empiricism. Union Theological Seminary
threw in completely for social gospel activism and pragmatism. The most
prominent American theologian of the 1920s, Yale theologian Douglas
Clyde Macintosh, was a product of the Chicago school. In Continental Europe the situation was even worse, because Barthian irrationalism
swept the field. Knudson grieved that postwar European theologians
willingly erased two hundred years of progress in theology, enticed by
neo-orthodox dogmatism. Theology, he said, needed desperately to regain
the courage to struggle with metaphysical problems.[56]

   Knudson carefully delineated various philosophies of personality
before explaining Bowne's version. He ran through McTaggart's atheistic
personalism, German neo-Hegelian William Stern's pantheistic personalism, French idealist Charles Renouvier's relativistic personalism, and the

flock of absolute idealists headed by Royce and the Caird brothers who ascribed personality to the absolute. He noted that Hocking described the absolute as personal, despite playing down personality; explained that Howison was entitled to the personalist name, despite denying God's creativity; and cheered that Mary W. Calkins, another protégé of Royce, personalized the absolute. Thus he stressed that Bowne's version of idealism was not the only one that qualified as personalist, notwithstanding that Bowne defined the term exclusively as a description of his combination of positions. Personalism, to Knudson, was shorthand for personal idealism. One could be a personalist without believing in a personal God or any god, because personal idealism is defined by a single postulate, the reality of the self or soul or "I." Personalists believe in the reality of finite persons. A personalist can deny God's existence, but not the reality of a personal self.[57]

Knudson's friend and faculty colleague George Croft Cell had long warned him not to trust Bowne's historical scholarship. On Kant, Croft detailed Bowne's misrepresentations under the categories (1) doubtful, (2) inaccurate, (3) misleading, and (4) wrong, judging that (3) and (4) predominated. Knudson realized that he had to clean up Bowne's faulty scholarship before he made a case for Bowne's position. Moreover, another generation of idealist theorizing had occurred since Bowne's death. He responded with seventy pages of meticulous table-setting, playing up a movement point he shared with Brightman: there were many personal idealists of Bowne's type, many other kinds of personal idealists, and many other kinds of idealists. Once he set the table, however, Knudson argued aggressively that it makes little sense to say that reality is personal if one does not affirm the reality of a personal God.[58]

Only personality is ontologically real. Knudson cited Bowne and Pringle-Pattison interchangeably on this point. The personal agency of human beings is inexplicable, the surest datum we possess, and the only clue we hold to the mystery of our existence. The key to the problem of human knowledge is human experience (the empirical plank), which all subjects know directly, but the explanation cannot be explained (the transcendental plank). Knudson judged that Bowne's late-life description of his position was nearly right. Bowne should have acknowledged Leibniz's influence on him, but otherwise he rightly pointed to Lotze, Kant, and Berkeley. Bowne distinguished between thought and reality because he was sufficiently realistic to acknowledge that reality is more than thought. But he took an idealistic view of nature, rejecting metaphysical realism.

The natural world has no independent reality of itself; nature is a phenomenal order constantly reproduced by a power or powers outside itself.
Knudson pressed hard on the freedom of the will, viewing the will as
a stronger force than reason. He did not claim that reason bridges the
chasm between thought and reality. Faith alone, he said, crosses the Cartesian divide; in the final analysis, all knowledge rests on faith.[59]

As for the ontological reality of the soul, Knudson stressed what
he and Bowne did not mean. They did not mean the soul is a material
substance, as in popular piety, or an immaterial substance, as in Plato,
or a thinking substance, as in Descartes' identification of the soul with
consciousness. They did not believe the soul is any kind of substance. Pre-
modern philosophies assumed that substance is a more fundamental idea
than that of cause, but modern consciousness regards activity as essential to being, denying reality to forms of existence lacking the power of
action. Thus Leibniz conceived the soul as the spiritual cause of material
phenomena. Berkeley conceived it as the perceiving activity that creates
ideas and the world of things. Kant said the mind creatively builds up its
world for itself, though he made no claim about the nature of the nominal
self that lies beyond the bounds of sense.

To Knudson and Bowne, Kant was the hero of this story, and the
goat. They exalted Kant for dethroning the things of sense and for contending that persons are moral ends in themselves. And they grieved over
the bad Kant who marred his own magnificent achievement by ruling out
knowledge of transcendental things in themselves, including knowledge
of human souls. Kant's agnosticism, they argued, was devastating for
the Protestants who absorbed it. To renew liberal theology, theologians
had to begin by asserting the reality of the soul as a knowable first principle. The soul that is known to consciousness is the conscious soul. The
nature of the only soul known to us is revealed in conscious experience.
Descartes took the right path by identifying the soul with consciousness,
construing the existence of the soul as immediate and certain, while
matter is an uncertain inference. But Cartesian dualism was impossible,
conceiving the body as an automaton. Knudson espoused the Lotze/
Bowne option of conceiving the knowing agent and the agent's activity
as one. The soul bears the force of reality by its consciousness of its unity
and self-identity. The reality of the soul is revealed in and through self-
consciousness and self-direction.[60]

That made personalism less dualistic than classical theism and Descartes, but still epistemologically dualistic in affirming the distinction of

subject and object. It was a type of objective idealism, but Knudson's version was less rationalistic than absolute idealism, affirming the primacy of practical reason. The other duality that Knudson carefully calibrated was between knowledge and faith, which held the key to negotiating the perennial dualities of transcendence and immanence, freedom and divine sovereignty, epistemological realism and absolute idealism, agnostic dualism and epistemological monism, pragmatic relativism and intellectual absolutism, and metaphysical monism and pluralism. Here again, Kant's legacy had to be corrected, because the line separating knowledge and faith was not as sharp as he said. Bowne showed that knowledge is not limited to the phenomenal world, theoretical reason employs faith assumptions of its own, theoretical reason cannot dispense with metaphysical categories, science is not value-free, purpose is constitutive in thought, and ideas of the good are constitutive in purpose. Thus he showed that faith and reason must work together. Knudson and Bowne treasured Leibniz for puzzling that anyone might question the existence of the soul and yet claim to know anything.[61]

Knudson had far more partisan spirit than Brightman, who criticized Bowne for writing too pedagogically and never joining the American Philosophical Association. Knudson remembered what he owed to Bowne, refusing to criticize him personally. He also appreciated that Bowne wrote his books while running the Graduate School. Brightman said he would be a Ralph Barton Perry analytic realist if he could not be a personalist. Knudson could not imagine being anything but a personalist. Brightman chafed when students asked for the party line on a philosophical issue. Knudson did not chafe, holding ample zeal for what he called "the polemic aspects of the subject."[62]

It showed whenever he wrote about Barthian theology or the Chicago school. Knudson struggled to imagine how the Barthians could be serious; his most generous description of the Barthian movement was "sophisticated irrationalism." He blasted the "amazing superficiality" of the Chicago school, amazed that Chicago theologians found humanistic naturalism to be profound. Macintosh, he said, though better than his Chicago teachers, was still crudely realistic, a product of "the picturing type of mind." Knudson warned that neither faith nor reason can rest in the realist position. The idea of spatial substance is contradictory, as is the idea of impersonal substance, so reason is forced to transcend them. Faith has the same problem in a realist epistemology because from the standpoint of faith the impersonal can have no intrinsic worth: "Its value is purely instrumental, and since it is such, no impersonal thing can be self-existent, for self-existence carries with it the idea of existence for itself, and this implies intrinsic value." Materialism, he admonished, is a conquering aggressor. Theologians who make bargains with it help to kill God and the soul. The only way to prevent the conquering tyranny of things of sense is to deny them true ontological reality.[63]

Knudson took little interest in Hegel except for his saying that the real is the rational and the rational is the real, for which Knudson granted immortal credit to Hegel. Whatever is irrational, Knudson said, is unreal and impossible: "Only as being is shaped by the categories of thought can it be given an intelligible content." This was his word of judgment against Barthians who wrapped themselves in paradoxes, and against realist and naturalist theologians who sold out the primacy of spiritual things, and against social gospel theologians who disdained metaphysical claims. None of these strategies would persuade modern people to take religion seriously.[64]

To those who objected that personalist theory is too systematic, rationalized, and sharply defined, Knudson said that serious thinking is systematic, rationalized, and sharply defined. There is no tenable middle ground between a mechanical and a personalist worldview. James and Perry described personalism as a confection of compromises between rival systems holding no strong center of its own. Knudson said the synthesizing and reconciling spirit of personalism was a virtue. Many cited Hume or James to the effect that no metaphysical glue binds together the so-called self in its states of consciousness. Knudson replied that the eye does not see itself, either; yet without the eye, nothing can be seen. The self is like the human eye. To say it is real is not to claim that it manifests itself to consciousness as a distinct object. It is to say that the self is a special kind of object, different from the things of sense, which is given immediately in experience. We cannot escape this experience; we assume its existence even when we try to analyze it away. When critics cautioned Bowne that consciousness cannot be any definite thing, he replied, "Of course I cannot be unconsciously conscious or consciously unconscious. I cannot conceive of being both dead and alive at the same time." Knudson reached for Augustine's similar clincher: it would be impossible to deny the existence of a self if a self did not exist to make the denial.[65]

The School of Theology lost its dean, James A. Beebe, just before Knudson wrote *The Philosophy of Personalism*. University president Daniel L. Marsh offered the position to Knudson, who balked. His theological

scholarship and movement activism had just begun. Marsh assured
Knudson he would get plenty of administrative assistance, allowing him
to keep writing. Faculty colleague Earl B. Marlatt worried that being a
dean might dissipate Knudson's otherworldly charm, "the air of elsewhere
that hovers over you like a halo. I should miss that." But Knudson thrived
in his new position, using it to make the seminary a bastion of personal
idealism. He and Brightman sustained a close friendship and intellectual
partnership, renowned for their enormous energy and disciplined productivity. Knudson maintained a grueling schedule of administrative tasks,
teaching, and prolific scholarship. Brightman assumed leadership roles in
professional associations and expanded his range of intellectual interests.
Knudson was the more approachable personality. Friends and students
called him "Knoody." Brightman was courtly, dauntingly brilliant, and
usually serious, though he had a sense of humor and wrote a stream of letters to readers and former students, constantly updating his index cards.
Both were logical drillmasters in the classroom. Knudson made friends
more readily, but both were greatly respected by colleagues and students.
Knudson guided the school, and lifted it, for nearly thirteen years.[66]

Personalism and God in Process

Knudson inherited his essential principles from Bowne and defended
them. Aside from the religious a priori, his chief contributions to personalism were in cartography and theological application. Brightman was a
different kind of thinker. He prized his intellectual independence and
wrote strictly as a philosopher of religion, not a theologian. In his early
career he was down the line with Bowne, aside from occasional friendly
references to Hegel. In mid-career he broke with Bowne on divine omnipotence, shortly afterward he rejected Bowne's doctrine of divine nontem-
porality, and then he decided that Bowne's theory of personality was
short on psychological facts. Brightman reduced the party-line feeling
of Boston personalism by instigating debates on God's finitude, whether
time has an effect on God, whether personalists should be temporalists,
and what it means to make conscious experience the point of departure.
He changed what personalism was, or could mean, on these topics, training nearly all its third-generation theologians and religious philosophers.
For many years, troubled that Bowne's integral self smacked of metaphysical glue, Brightman worked on his own theory of personality; his last
name for it was the "shining present."

In his early career, Brightman's belief that ideals disclose the structure of the real caused him to pass lightly over the problem of evil. In *Religious Values* he said this problem is filled with "seemingly irreducible mysteries," but the same thing is true of freedom, error, the experience of value, and the relation between mind and body. He leaned on Leibniz to explain how natural evils can exist in a good world, affirming that the "deepest reality is good." *An Introduction to Philosophy* lingered a bit longer over this subject, explaining that natural evils are aspects of the best possible world, apparently playing some role in God's work of creating a co-creative community of moral agents. The early Brightman betrayed no feeling that the terrible moral and natural evils of the world are not really analogous to the mind-body problem. What mattered was to defend religious idealism; thus he relegated the tragic realities of life to a folder marked "unsolved problems."[67]

But Brightman felt the tragic realities more deeply than his books conveyed. As a child he was struck in the eye with a stick by a playmate and permanently lost his vision in this eye. As a youth he knew a man who fell into insanity and did terrible things. Another acquaintance destroyed his nervous system in a swimming accident. Two years into his first marriage, Brightman lost his beloved wife to cancer. During World War I he taught military psychology as an ROTC captain at Wesleyan University, tracked German newspapers for the federal government, grieved at losing his affection for Germany, and subsequently grieved that he aided the American war effort. Brightman's early books repressed these experiences, exuding his determination to live in his head. To change his mind about anything, he had to find his way through books and arguments. The tragedies in his own experience, however, gnawed at him, and he puzzled over moral evil, natural evil, and God. In the late 1920s he read books on evolutionary science that moved him to rethink his concept of God.[68]

Is the existence of an omnipotent and omnibenevolent God the best hypothesis that one can make in the light of empirical evidence? This was Brightman's version of the theodicy question. Being steeped in Bowne and Royce had turned him away from natural science and its low-grade knowledge. Returning to evolutionary science forced him to confront what he called "surd" evils in creation and history—evils serving no good purpose that pervade the natural world. Brightman refused to doubt that God is good. The question became: How can God be all-good *and* all-powerful if the world overflows with meaningless evil? Brightman decided that God's omnibenevolence is defensible only if one relinquishes the doctrine of divine omnipotence. He said it plainly in his breakout book, *The Problem of God* (1930).[69]

James famously ended *The Varieties of Religious Experience* by speculating that God might be finite and plural. If one pays attention to religious experience and properly doubts every version of absolute unity, one has to be open to polytheism, "the real religion of common people." In 1917, British science-fiction writer H. G. Wells recycled "my friend and master, that very great American, William James" on the finitude of God, contending that God is not a unifying Creator. The real God is finite, and credible belief in God wells up from individual feeling alone. To American readers, these were the precedents for claiming that God is finite. More importantly to Brightman, in 1809 Schelling contended that God is limited by something within God's nature. Schelling postulated that the original unity of reality—the Eternal One—longed to give birth to itself. This original One was a striving will, and the oneness was best represented as the principle of chaos, or darkness. God, the principle of light, emerged out of chaos and ordered it, uniting the principles of order and disorder within God's being. Human beings are the consequence of this divine ordering, uniting chaotic darkness and ordering light, like God. Brightman had Schelling, James, and Wells in mind when he became the first American Christian thinker to transgress the usual caveats on this subject. He had a roadmap to what counted as transgression, in two recent books by McConnell.[70]

McConnell argued that God is limited by virtue of being morally good, creating a material universe, and allowing human freedom. In *Is God Limited?* (1924) he said that every theology limits God in some way, and the best Christian theologies emphasize limitations in God that are self-willed or that inhere in the divine nature. McConnell respected Wells for stressing that suffering is out of proportion with sin, but Wells crossed a fateful line by setting a finite God against the material universe. McConnell said any concept of a limitation on God from without must be ruled out, because it makes God a finite entity dependent on something else. He had no answer beyond his stew of Leibniz, Bowne, and postwar humility, but he implored readers not to solve the problem badly: "No solution of this mystery has ever been offered except those that add to our sense of woe. . . . There is no explanation in terms of our present knowledge. We hate desperately to say that the Divine Creator is back of all this pain because he must be, but does it make it any easier to say that this pain exists because he prefers it?" In *The Christlike God* (1927) McConnell took a provocative next step by arguing that the God of Christianity suffers pain along with and for the sake of suffering existence. It is more important to say that God is like Christ than to say that Christ is like God.[71]

Brightman had a complex reaction to these books. He treasured McConnell as a friend and personalist leader, welcomed that McConnell stretched classical theism as far as possible, embraced McConnell's controversial Patripassianism without employing his language about "Christly" experience, and flatly rejected McConnell's counsel. The time had come to see the matter through by concluding that God is actually finite. Brightman argued that God is creative, supreme, and personal, yet genuinely limited within God's nature by "given" experiences eternally present. God's will controls this "given," but does not create it.

He pressed four arguments toward the verdict that God is a conflicted finite being. Evolution is stunningly wasteful and violent. God's nature as a conscious being and God's granting of free will to human beings set limits to God's will. God's nature is not merely goodness but also dialectical struggle, characterized by the same dynamic of assertion and negation that pervades all reality. And God is perfect in will, but not in achievement. These arguments melded into a single thesis: given the facts that we possess about the suffering-causing evils of the world that far exceed moral guilt or moral use, we must revise the classical view of either God's goodness or God's power. *The Problem of God* espoused the latter option. Since God is loving and good, God would eliminate the evils that persons are not responsible for if God were able to do so, but evidently God is not able to do so. A nonrational "given" in God's consciousness apparently thwarts God's capacity to achieve the divine purpose. God attains goodness only after a struggle with given limiting factors that inhere in the divine being. The kind of God "required by the facts," Brightman argued, is fully worthy of being worshipped, for this God is infinitely good and loving, always working for a good and loving end. But Christians needed to face the facts about evils that a good God would not create or will.[72]

This proposal accepted McConnell's sanction against outside limitations on God, but pressed the idea of inner limitation to the point of positing a disabling conflict within God's being: God's power is limited by coeternal nonrational elements within the divine being that oppose God's rational divine will. Brightman urged readers not to fear the idea that God is finite, although he later preferred the formulation that God is a finite-infinite Being, since God is infinite in time, goodness, and love.

The Problem of God won plaudits, condemnation, and profuse commentary for many years. Some reviewers chided that Brightman's God seemed to be cowered by the given. Flewelling blasted the given in the *Personalist*, protesting that Brightman made the problem worse with a conjuring trick that solved nothing. If God bears moral responsibility for control of the given, as Brightman claimed in defending his Christian standpoint, are these restrictions within God's nature according to God's will? Are they determining? Flewelling argued that if God is self-limited, God must be held morally responsible for the defeat and obstruction of God's will. If God is not self-limited, the given is a power beyond God's control that controls God. In the former case, the given is a most undesirable servant. In the latter case, it is God's Frankenstein. Flewelling admonished, "We cannot get around this dilemma by any subterfuge of language."[73]

That spoke for many personalists, including Knudson. Brightman argued that the given within God's experience consists of various laws of reason, such as logic and mathematical relations, as well as various impulses and desires, the experiences of pain and suffering, the forms of space and time, and "whatever in God is the source of 'surd' evil." His influential textbook on the philosophy of religion defended his finite-God thesis, arguing that God is absolute as the ultimate source of creation, plus infinite in the sense that God has no beginning or end and is not limited by anything external to Godself, but limited by the given. The theory of God's given-finitude might not be *the* truth, but it is surely "an advance toward the truth."[74]

Though controversial in church circles, Brightman was increasingly viewed as a religious leader, not merely a philosopher of religion. He wrote books on spiritual experience and treasured his work with seminarians. He and Knudson agreed to disagree about God's inner conflicts, read each other's manuscripts, praised each other extravagantly, and usually offered only small points of criticism or correction. Brightman taught his students that logical coherence is the sole criterion of truth, religious experience furnishes data for truth about religion, and all truth is hypothetical. Good theology is rigorously logical, though logic is no substitute for experience. Brightman hated Bowne's slogan that life is more than logic, which Bowne borrowed from Lotze and James repeated. Obviously life is more than logic, but nothing about experience validates beliefs that are not logically consistent!

Brightman and Knudson said it constantly to seminarians, grieving that Nietzsche, Kierkegaard, and Barth unleashed a flood of irrationalism in theology. Brightman said his aggressive rationalism posed no conflict with his deep spirituality, because he was an idealist. Always he added that he was an idealist on the basis of its truth claims alone, but he honored religious experience wherever he found it. Brightman studied Hindu, Buddhist, and Islamic texts, and was a close friend of Swami Akhilananda, whose spiritual practices he followed. His books stuck to his fields of expertise, but he urged Christian audiences to learn about experiences of the divine in other religions: "Any consciousness of the presence of God is religious experience. It makes no difference whether it is conventional or unconventional; a stereotyped 'conversion' experience or a blissful vision on the mountain top. If we are aware in any way of the presence of the Divine, we are having a religious experience."[75]

Brightman felt spiritually linked to all who devote themselves to a superhuman order of reality and value. His spiritual ecumenism did not extend to people who took a purely humanistic or naturalistic approach to religion. He shared Knudson's feelings about the shallow futility of the Chicago school, and shook his head at idealists who turned out to be atheists. It offended Brightman when atheists won teaching positions at divinity schools, because they harmed religion while living off it. He said that religion would survive even if personal idealism did not, but the concept of personality had to be clarified, because personal idealism is true, it supports religion like no other philosophy, and it needed a better formulation than Bowne provided.

Brightman wearied of reading that personalism identifies the real with the human. It was tempting to say that this mistake derived from not understanding objective idealism, but even that was too generous, because the ego of Fichte's idealism was not Fichte. Personalism, to Brightman, was a theory about the objective structure of things, conceiving the real as a complex of selves or an episode in the experience of a cosmic self. Brightman allowed that personalists defined personality in a general way as a self-conscious unity of experience; a person is a conscious unity. But this did not mean that personality equals reflective self-consciousness. All experiences are self-experiences. Personality is any consciousness of any kind experienced as belonging to a unitary whole. On the other hand, to say that the self is a conscious unity excludes any union with anything that is not the self's consciousness. The self has a body, but is not a body. It is not a part or process of the body. Brightman wanted no part of his body to be identified with him, even though he swam and walked. Whatever one remembers to be part of the unity of one's consciousness is part of oneself, and whatever does not fall within the unity of one's consciousness is not part of oneself.[76]

Idealist theory was prone to overanalytical distinctions, notoriously in Fichte's case. Brightman, sensitive to the problem, waved off the "I and me" dialectics of the Fichte and Schelling tradition, including Bowne's distinction between the agent-self and the agent's acts that are products of the self. To Brightman, it was enough to say that the self is the present unity of consciousness as now experienced. He knew he was a person because in his immediate experience he found he was such a being: "I find myself; I do not invent myself. I am experience." To be sure, credible claims to knowledge also require understanding, relation, and interpretation. Experience contains immediacy (the presence of feelings, relations within the given) and references beyond immediacy (memories, things, relations beyond the given). Immediate experience as such is not knowledge, but no person has any knowledge that is not immediate experience at some point. All knowing is mediated by immediate experience; it becomes knowledge by virtue of its coherence and adequacy. The claim that one experiences a self in immediate experience is an inference that, to be credible, must be based on coherent and adequate knowledge. Immediate experience is potentially rational, but self-knowledge requires reason. Through memory and anticipation, he argued, the self experienced in immediacy links itself to a past self and a future self, while reason judges the claims of both memory and anticipation. As a subjective fact, the self is self-known as a rationally remembered and anticipated unity of consciousness.[77]

But the self is more than a subjective fact. Brightman was not as Cartesian as he seemed, because he believed that the self is not merely a unity of reflective self-experience. It is always interacting with something that is not itself; it can be known from within and without. Introspection is a teacher, but so is empirical observation. Both are necessary to the making of a self. Brightman affirmed that philosophy shares ample ground with psychology in this area, *and* takes guidance from scientific disciplines, *and* has its own tasks and trajectory, which are metaphysical. Philosophy provides a view of the whole of experience by criticizing, unifying, and supplementing science. It presses certain questions distinctively, such as the criterion and nature of value, and it theorizes certain facts distinctively, such as the unity of personality.

Psychology does not ask whether personality is the key to reality; personalist philosophy asks the question and answers that personality is cosmomorphic, not anthropomorphic. Brightman observed that space is found in human experience, yet everyone agrees that space is cosmomorphic. Similarly, everyone attributes cosmomorphic status to time and mathematics; Plato taught that God geometrizes. Brightman pressed the personalist question: If space, time, and mathematics are cosmic principles despite being found in human beings, what about the principle of personality? Critics said that Lotze and Bowne interpreted the universe in personal terms, rendering God in humanity's image. Brightman said that if God made human beings in God's image, human personality is cosmomorphic. Moreover, if personality *is* a clue to objective reality, it is more fundamental than space, time, or mathematics, all of which presuppose and require personality in order to be or be experienced. Personal idealism is not the claim that the universe is a copy of the psychology textbook self. It is the claim that the real is a complex of selves. Space, time, and mathematics without personality would be meaningless, and the great cosmomorphic truths would disintegrate into shards of vanishing experience. Personality does not require space, but space, time, and number are attributes of personality.[78]

Knudson said that personality combines conscious unity (individuality), identity (consciousness), and free activity (will). Later he added a fourth feature, self-control. Brightman made a similar argument with different language and a stronger objective idealist emphasis that the real is a complex of selves. He distinguished among the form of personality (the laws of reason), the content of personality (the brute facts of experience), and the activity of personality (its power of will to make choices and direct consciousness). Brightman and Knudson both excluded the body because it is not present in consciousness and because they were dead serious about purging anthropomorphic elements from personality. For all his revisions of Bowne, Brightman was as thoroughly idealistic as Bowne and Knudson, affirming that spirit and matter are aspects of a single unitary process, the process of divine will. Personal idealism is not about the superiority of mind over matter, a form of dualism. It is the belief that nothing truly impersonal exists. A stone has no personality of its own, but even a stone is part of the conscious activity of the divine person. Matter is the energizing of the will of God, not mere stuff. Brightman and Knudson indulged protégés who took idealism halfway; Harkness became a notable example in 1937, resorting to a halfway dualism. But they said it is better to go all the way. The relation of mind and matter is actually a relation of spirit and spirit. Nature is a divine language symbolizing what Brightman called "the purpose and the reason of the divine mind."[79]

The seed of an idealism that prized the natural world was there, especially in Brightman's increasingly temporal, tragic, holistic version of idealism. But none of the second-generation personalists developed it. Brightman's emphasis on the structural complexity of the self similarly distinguished his idealism from Knudson's reductive claim that "person" is a narrower idea than "self." Knudson contended that a self is not a person if the self lacks a requisite degree of intellectual and moral development. Brightman wanted nothing to do with the racist legacy of reductively simple ideas of the person. The unified and unifying nature of the self was, to him, the key to the importance of a self/person. A personality is a complex whole in which form, content, and activity are united inseparably. Brightman restlessly kept rethinking what that meant, which marked another difference from Knudson, who took little interest in rethinking idealistic epistemology or his prejudices while writing his belated books.

Knudson's books—*The Doctrine of God* (1930), *The Doctrine of Redemption* (1933), and *The Validity of Religious Experience* (1937)—fulfilled his academic ambition. Deftly he diagnosed the crisis in theology, explaining that theology won little respect in modern thought because it was anti-authoritarian and anti-metaphysical. These were very different kinds of problems, he said. Theologians inherited the cultural hangover from Christianity's long authoritarian past. It took enormous energy to show academics in other fields that theologians no longer bowed to an external authority. Modern theology was far more modern than it got credit for being. Knudson implored theologians to keep trying to break through, but not with a thin gruel of positivism or pragmatism. He understood why theologians fled from metaphysics, because the academy turned against it. Philosophers reduced philosophy to logic and analysis, shunning the great questions, trying to be relevant to shallow cultural trends. Knudson fought on both fronts, showing that good theology was anti-authoritarian and robustly willing to engage the great metaphysical questions.[80]

His method was rationalistic and empirical in the manner of Schleiermacher, Troeltsch, and the normative sciences, examining the relevant data of Christian experience and history, shunning all appeals to external authority, and resting on the claims of reason and critically interpreted experience. Knudson amplified the religious a priori by adding Rudolf Otto's analysis of religious awe, realizing that his previous formulation was too rationalistic. Otto's classic *The Idea of the Holy* (1917) helped Knudson affirm that the rational and irrational aspects of religion both spring from hidden depths of the spirit. Moreover Otto showed that the numinous feeling of religious awe and the religious concept of divine goodness are bound together in an inward union that has its own a priori character. The religious a priori includes a sense of ought that we cannot escape. The value of a merely subjective law of right is merely practical and aesthetic. The moral law is the ground of an objective belief only if it is absolute—a Kantian theme that Knudson pressed in every book.[81]

Methodist theology, to become modern, had to start over. Knudson quoted Wesley on the centrality of religious experience, but selectively. He said his theological predecessors—English Methodists Richard Watson and William Burt Pope, and American Methodists Miner Raymond and John Miley—did "creditable work," but operated within the authoritarian evangelical framework. He embraced Wesley's emphasis on spiritual experience, free will, and the personal and moral character of God, plus another Wesleyan notion that Knudson did not identify as specifically Wesleyan, the belief that theological affirmations should be based on four distinct sources of witness and affirmation. Methodist theologian Albert C. Outler, writing in the early 1960s, aptly named it "the Wesleyan Quadrilateral." Wesley, in this rendering, added a fourth important source, Christian experience, to the traditional Anglican troika of Scripture, tradition, and reason, and was never a Biblicist. Outler said Wesley's theological disciples were evangelical Biblicists who did not catch the significance of Wesley's emphasis on the testimony of the Holy Spirit as an impression on the soul, so the distinctly Wesleyan approach to theology was lost for over a century. Knudson played a key role in establishing this understanding of Wesleyan theology, but he did not describe it as distinctly Wesleyan, and as a liberal he did not speak of Scripture or tradition as authorities for theology. Knudson described the Bible as the church's normative source of information about the founding of Christianity. He described church tradition similarly as an important source of information, expanding this category to include psychology of religion, the history of religions, and philosophy of religion. On reason and experience in theology he lauded Wesley chiefly as a forerunner to Schleiermacher and Ritschl, citing Wesley's dictum that experience is "the strongest of all arguments . . . and the most infallible of all proofs."[82]

Much of Knudson's success in liberalizing Methodist theology owed to his vigorous defense of the divine personality of Jesus and God.

Methodologically his theology was deeply liberal, but his personalism was a bulwark against liberal-Jesus historicism. Christianity was founded, he insisted, on the *impression of divinity* made by the *personality of Jesus* on his disciples. There is no Christianity apart from this double impression, and no other Jesus known to anyone. The liberal historicist dichotomy between the religion *of* Jesus and the religion *about* Jesus is misleading, because Christianity was not founded on the person or religion of a non-divine historical Jesus, a construction imagined by historicists. Knudson said the disciples beheld in Jesus the sanctity of an exemplary man and God's gracious outreach to them. They heard in the message and life of Jesus the voice of a man and the voice of the divine. The New Testament radiates this double impression on every page. To reduce it to something simpler is to sunder the irreducible basis of Christianity. The notion that theology must press to an imagined Jesus behind the gospel text is a naturalistic prejudice, not a rational necessity.[83]

The same thing was true of the liberal retreat from a personal God. The Chicago school treated nature as metaphysically real and God as real, at most, only in a secondary sense as an aspect or product of nature. By defining God as a law or process, the Chicago theologians attributed reality to God only in the sense that a law or social process is real. That is not the Christian God, Knudson protested. Personal idealism, being modern, stressed the personality *of* God, not the personality *in* God that classical theism described. It made a difference to be informed by the modern understanding of a person and the demand of science for a unitary world ground. But giving up God's personal metaphysical reality was not in play. To say that God is personal is to ascribe intelligence and freedom to God. Lacking intelligence and freedom, God cannot be good, and if God is not personal, there is no possibility of personal communion with God. Everything is at stake in this question, Knudson argued. He was intrigued by Brightman's idea of a moral struggle in God, but rejected Brightman's idea of a dualism in the divine consciousness, because religion needs two things: a supreme good and an ultimate unity. Giving up God's omnipotence lost both things. Knudson said it is not enough to say that God has good intentions, or even that God is the most powerful being in the universe. There is no perfect goodness or unity without an all-powerful unifying ground.[84]

The personalists tended to share Schleiermacher's low regard of Trinitarian doctrine. Knudson saw three viable options on this topic. The first affirmed the Trinity as a symbol of God's inexhaustible complexity without claiming to know the inner structure of God's being. Classical theology, going too far, said that God has one essence, two processions, three persons, four relations, and five notions. Knudson regretted that metaphysical theology had this legacy to overcome. The second option featured the Sabellian emphasis on manifestation without disclaiming a direct relation with God's essential nature. God's triune manifestation as Father, Son, and Spirit surely relates to God's inner Trinity of essence, which the Sabellians obscured by playing the Trinity of manifestation against the immanent Trinity: all that we know is that God has been manifested to us in three modes. But even a modified Sabellianism disclaimed any knowledge of how the Father, Son, and Spirit are distinct or related in God's inner being. Option three, which Knudson took, was McConnell's "Christlikeness" argument. It made a place for Christ in God's life and carried the Christ-spirit into the divine, construing the Trinity as the Christian belief that God loves the world with sacrificial love because Christians have seen God in Christ. This belief defined Christianity long before anyone conceived the fellowship of Father and Son as a fellowship in the divine Spirit. McConnell said the late-coming Holy Spirit could have been an ideal interest; it did not have to be a person. Knudson seized on this point, arguing that there is nothing in the idea of love or self-consciousness that demands an ascription of personality to the Holy Spirit. Trinitarian doctrine would have made more sense had the church not felt compelled to equalize the Father, Son, and Spirit as persons.[85]

On sin and redemption, Knudson expounded Bowne's positions, emphasizing that there is no sin apart from free-willed moral choice. His Christology was straight from Schleiermacher, and he usually avoided Methodist references, except on Christian experience. Olin Curtis taught that Wesley's teaching on the close relation or simultaneity of justification and sanctification holds nearly the same epochal significance for the doctrine of holiness as Luther's doctrine of justification by faith and Athanasius' doctrine of the incarnation. Knudson corrected his teacher and most of the Wesleyan heritage, chiding that Wesley did not compare to Luther and Athanasius: "It was a theological provincialism, and has been gradually losing its importance." The idea of sanctification, Knudson argued, is still needed in Christianity, but not in the mystical perfectionist form that Wesleyans fossilized. The social gospel changed what sanctification means in Protestantism, teaching that individuals and society must be saved from sin, regenerated, and made new: "The conversion of individuals here and there will not suffice. Society itself must be converted, inwardly and outwardly transformed, so that it may be a fit home for the children of God. Nothing short of this will satisfy either the secular or the religious mood of our day."[86]

Knudson would not have said so lacking the social gospel tidal wave. He had a streak of cultural racism mixed with the liberal superiority complex he shared with Bowne, which caused him to scoff at white progressives who seemed too ardent about racism, anti-colonialism, and equality. By Knudson's reckoning he was as liberal as an enlightened person should be on these topics, but lacking pressure from the social gospel, he would have been less so. The social gospel dragged him along, enabling Boston University to become a bastion of progressive activism on his watch. Muelder, DeWolf, and S. Paul Schilling helped to pull Brightman to the left politically, which enhanced his influence after they became important theologians. They came of age intellectually while Brightman tilted toward Hegel, stopped repressing his tragic sense of life, and changed his mind about Bowne's eternalism. They heard Brightman move toward the view that personalists should be temporalists because freedom, activity, and purpose all require time, and everything real changes.

In 1933 Brightman began a dialogue with philosopher Charles Hartshorne, who had joined the University of Chicago faculty in 1928. Hartshorne studied under Quaker philosopher Rufus Jones at Haverford College, finished his undergraduate degree at Harvard in 1921, and completed his doctorate at Harvard in 1923, studying under Hocking, Perry, and logician C. I. Lewis. He already believed, when he got to Harvard, in the essentially emotional and social character of experience. At Harvard, Hartshorne embraced Hocking's panpsychic view of matter and his belief that God is not immutable. His dissertation, "The Unity of Being," argued for the unity of all things in God's developing being. At the time his chief influences were Hocking and Royce, plus Lewis for his logical rigor. Hartshorne knew little about Whitehead and did not mention him in his dissertation. In search of intellectual guidance, he studied under Edmund Husserl at Freiburg and Martin Heidegger at Marburg, with disappointment in both cases; phenomenology seemed shallow to him. He returned to Harvard as a research fellow in 1925, a year after Whitehead joined the Harvard faculty, and thrilled at meeting a genius, Whitehead, plus reading another genius, Charles Sanders Peirce. Hartshorne embraced Whitehead's temporal, panexperiential concept of reality as active independent droplets of experience, though he rejected

Whitehead's idea that God is an actual entity. Upon landing at Chicago he encountered another philosophy department that was averse to metaphysics, so Hartshorne reached out to Brightman.[87]

Swiftly they cut to philosophical differences. Hartshorne objected to Brightman's belief that a self merely infers the existence of other selves, declaring, "Literal participation in each other's being is about my strongest belief. Are we not parts of each other, members of one another?" Hartshorne believed that selves literally overlap, something has to bind them together, and what binds them must overlap. Brightman replied that whenever he tried to imagine intersubjectivity, he felt swamped in chaos, plus unfaithful to experience. He and Hartshorne held similar ideas of God, but that did not overturn Brightman's belief that each person is defined by an immediate experience that characterizes that person alone. We experience only ourselves directly; everything else is inferred.[88]

Hartshorne countered that other persons can be inferred from one's existence by the impression that they are necessary to one's existence; Brightman said this argument surrenders empirical and psychological evidence too completely to a logical claim. A flower is nourished by its soil, but the flower is not the same as the soil. Hartshorne protested that Brightman bifurcated experience and its object. Brightman replied that protecting the integrity of the only direct experience given to any knower is as essential as not identifying a cause with its effect. I am directly aware only of my own experience. Hartshorne reasoned that if a self is directly aware of the sun, the sun becomes a part of the self. Brightman said this supposedly direct awareness is really a direct awareness of myself referring to the sun. No part of me is part of the sun or of God. In his book *Man's Vision of God* (1941) Hartshorne argued that all individuals are part of God, and God's being thus includes all the beliefs that individuals hold. Brightman replied that God must believe many absurd and contradictory things. He tried to dissuade Hartshorne from panpsychism, advising that Hartshorne didn't need it to affirm the temporal panentheism they shared. Hartshorne persisted that embracing false beliefs within one's being and believing falsely are not the same thing. To have a belief as part of oneself is not necessarily to believe the belief.[89]

Back and forth they debated the logic of parts and wholes. Hartshorne reasoned that just as a small line can be part of a large surface without causing any contradiction between the line's smallness and the surface's largeness, a large mind might contain a small mind without accepting the smaller mind's false beliefs. That was picture thinking, Brightman replied; a theory of mind cannot be based on the model of space relations. Each thinker contended that his philosophy best protected the precious "en" of panentheism. Brightman lamented that Hartshorne ended up with an impersonal God as a consequence of breaking apart the unity of immediate experience. Whiteheadian theory was fragmenting, despite its language of wholeness, interrelation, and organic process. It broke down the distinction between self and world that secures the self's unity and the distinction between God and the world. And it yielded the creepy verdict that God's knowledge of Brightman was ontologically identical with Brightman's actual being for himself. Hartshorne came back with a personal truism. He was not, to be sure, any part of Jane Austen, but Jane Austen was definitely part of him. Moreover, he and Austen were both parts of God as God presently exists, but not as God once was. Brightman shuddered at the notion that consciousness includes Jane Austen, the sun, one's nervous system, someone else's nervous system, and other objects of consciousness. The essence of a person, he argued, is one's shining present—a notion he vowed to develop while jousting for ten years with Hartshorne.[90]

Brightman respected Hartshorne and cheered his impact at Chicago. Hartshorne and Henry Nelson Wieman briefly pulled the Chicago School of Theology in a Whiteheadian direction, contending that the school's lack of a metaphysical basis was a weakness. But Wieman decided in the early 1930s that Whitehead's system was too metaphysical, which delayed the Whiteheadian turn at Chicago until 1945, when Hartshorne's protégé Bernard Loomer became dean of the Divinity School. Not even Brightman believed in the 1930s and 1940s that Whiteheadians had a plausible alternative to personalism, and most personalists paid little attention to Whiteheadians or Wieman. The magisterial works of Brightman and Knudson, heaped on top of Bowne's corpus, persuaded many that personalist theory was already fully realized.

This impression daunted Muelder and DeWolf in their early careers. Brightman, however, was a restless type who did not believe, as Knudson claimed, that Bowne solved the perennial problems of philosophy. Brightman taught himself Spanish in order to communicate with Latin American philosophers. He wrote articles about trends in Latin American philosophy, self-teasing, "It takes a good deal to jar a man out of provincialism." In *The Future of Christianity* (1937) he looked forward to a Christian church that recognized Buddhism, Hinduism, Confucianism, and Islam as fully valid ways to God. Brightman argued that metaphysical religious philosophy is indispensable to overcoming the dogmatism in all religions. Religious authority should be vested in God alone, "a God who not merely tolerates differences of opinion, but also uses those differences as a means of bringing his followers nearer to him, and nearer to one another." All God concepts and religions are fallible forms and symbols of a single transcendental reality. Brightman idealized the grandest conceivable ecumenism while cheering small steps toward it. Every gain is a victory for "a more generous view of divine purpose." Sometimes he pressed on sensitive points. Despite disbelieving that Jesus is the only way to salvation, liberals rarely said so. Brightman said this was a serious mistake: "Modernists have often failed to be convincing because they have failed to face the most difficult points in the old view; and anyone who supposes that the battle is won for modernism either in Christendom at large or in the United States must base his supposition on his preferences rather than on the actual facts."[91]

In three books on ethics and value theory—*Moral Laws* (1933), *Nature and Values* (1945), and *Persons and Values* (1952)—Brightman delineated three types of moral laws, argued that a serious moral theory must be universalistic, and contended that ethical principles and laws must be open to criticism and revision from multiple standpoints. Always he moved from the abstract to the concrete in a progressive fashion that made each law dependent upon and inclusive of the laws that preceded it. Brightman regretted that this facet of his thought won little notice, but Muelder and DeWolf kept it in play after he was gone, teaching it to their students. Meanwhile Brightman worked on his metaphysical system, completing thirteen chapters before he died in 1953. *Person and Reality* established that the best kind of personalism is temporal, holistic, panentheistic, and spurns metaphysical glue.[92]

With Schopenhauer, Brightman believed that metaphysics is one of humankind's deepest needs. With Hegel, he believed that truth is the whole and metaphysics is the holy of holies of any civilization. In class he blasted Hegel's political conservatism and Prussian chauvinism, but patiently schooled students in the complexities of Hegel's thought. Brightman's system conformed to logical norms while standing before the court of appearance. The key test of any hypothesis is whether it makes systematic coherence out of experience. He turned away from Bowne's divine eternalism on the ground that nothing real is static, and he never liked Bowne's soul-language.

Change and activity, Brightman taught, are "the essence of the real." God is never less than a person ontologically, but believing so underscores the importance of disbelieving that God is supertemporally eternal, contrary to Bowne and Knudson. "The real endures; the real changes; the real grows. God is the real or at least the most significant part of the real." To be sure, Brightman said, reason establishes that the changes in experience conform to law, and it finds evidence of eternal form "which the changes never violate." But God is not an abstraction. God is a concrete, living reality, "an ever enduring creator" manifest as energy, creative process, concentration, integration, and will. God's existence is "an eternally changing present," a concept better construed on temporal idealist terms than on Whitehead's organic monism, and distinct from the atemporal abstractions undergirding Bowne's atemporal God and bordering-on-substantial self.[93]

Brightman never believed that the "that" which experiences is identical with its experiences. In *A Philosophy of Religion*, he coined the term "situation-experienced" to designate the complex personal unity within which sensing, willing, feeling, desiring, remembering, and reasoning takes place. Sometimes he called it the "datum-self." In his last years he called it a "shining present." The name was a figurative abstraction, for the shining present does not shine literally, nor does "present" hold a single literal meaning. Brightman stressed the Hegelian point that every now is a was that can never be again. Shining presents are what Whitehead called "perishing occasions," innumerably various and lacking any continuous substance. Yet every shining present contains "messages from the past as well as traces of unremembered events and interactions with contemporary reality." Shining presents are interactions registered partly as sensations and partly as other feelings of the impact of events on us, like Whitehead's prehensions of causal efficacy. They look to the future with yearnings and plans, marked by inner experiences of confusion and clarity, disorder and order, aimlessness and purpose, and hate and love, regardless of whatever outer relations may obtain. A shining present is whatever a person is at the present moment. Brightman put it more precisely: "Wherever there is any awareness or feeling of any kind, there is a shining present." It is a conscious awareness, a "situation-experienced" always to be distinguished from any situation-believed-in.[94]

Brightman moved as far as he could from the language or suggestion of a substantial soul without giving up Bowne's view that conscious experience is the starting point of philosophy and the key to reality. He referred unsolvable transcendental questions about the ground of the unstable self to a category marked "illuminating absent." The shining present, he allowed, undoubtedly depends for its existence on something beside itself, but to call this ground its soul is not to explain anything. The unity and continuity of experience need to be explained, but "the soul" is not an explanation. A soul conceived as a transcendent, unchanging, unity-continuity substance cannot account for the uncountable succession of temporal shining presents. Every shining present is crammed with clues, signs, messages, and effects it did not create. It can understand these pieces of evidence only if it perceives its mind as "a receiving station for messages from beyond." It can interpret these messages in whatever way it prefers, but it cannot know anything about its own past or future, or about other minds, nature, or God, "except on the basis of interpretation of the evidence now at hand." The shining present is all that we have. Thus the only source of evidence that we have for God is immediate experience.[95]

For all his rationalism, and for all the clashing in philosophy over rationalism versus empiricism, Brightman never doubted that all philosophers are in fact empiricists, taking their stand in the stream of their own experience—a fog of blind groping, attempts to privilege a particular kind of experience, and attempts by metaphysical types to be as comprehensive as possible, rendering nothing human as foreign. Metaphysics, he said, is about trying, fallibly, to show how different aspects of experience fit together. The evidence that God is temporal begins with the fact that all immediate experience is temporal. Immediate experience is the source of whatever evidence there may be for God. Every reason for believing in God is an interpretation of a shining present datum. Building on a point stressed by Hegel, Bergson, Heidegger, and Whitehead, Brightman argued that experience is always a duration featuring a real before and after. One cannot intelligibly speak of an experience occurring at no time and containing no temporal sequence. Heidegger said that Kant construed pure reason as essentially temporal, recognizing no difference between time and "I think." Brightman, not sure if Heidegger exaggerated, believed for sure that Kant held that time is essential to our inner life and space is not. Time is the universal content and form of every experience. If God is a real being, God must stand "in real relations to our temporal experience." The temporal character of every shining present points to the temporal character of God, manifest to experience as the ground of time and events in time.[96]

Moreover, all spatial processes are temporal, and universals are recurrent patterns. Brightman noted that space does not provide a world apart from temporal processes. As soon as one moves from the shining present to the world it implies, one encounters everywhere the reality that the world evolves in time. Time is the presupposition of all events, change, and evolution. To describe the development of life, mind, and the stellar universes by referring to a time transcending divinity "is fantastic." Brightman acknowledged that Neoplatonism and classical theism endured precisely on the idea of a timeless order or divinity. But universals do not exist apart from particulars. Every attempt to exalt a timeless superior—something utterly beyond all temporal process, change, and particulars—commits the fallacy of reification. Every timeless entity imaginable is a recurring pattern in the temporal process of thought and being. Absolute idealists tried to overcome time by absorbing it in the absolute. Bradley said the timeless Absolute abolishes the special character of time by possessing it as an isolated aspect. Brightman countered that this "horrible" concept proved his point, exactly what Hegel lampooned when he described Schelling's idealism as the night in which all cows are black. At least Plato saw the problem when he allowed the Eleatic Stranger to ask how it could be that motion, life, soul, and mind are not present to absolute being. Brightman said this was the right question: "We must either carry time into the timeless ideas of the Absolute or else have an Absolute without intelligible relations to experience."[97]

Grafting Neoplatonism onto Christianity had always been problematic, because Christianity is essentially temporal and historical. To say that time is not real for God is to nullify the Christian idea that the divine is immanent in history. Brightman put it bluntly: all struggle is temporal, moral struggle is fundamental to Christianity, and every realized ideal is in time. He appreciated the metaphysical assumption that the concept of eternity is a natural a priori for abstract thought. Plato loved the timeless truths of geometry, spurning time as a corruption of eternity and becoming as a corruption of being. Maimonides taught that no relation exists between God and time. Thomas Aquinas attributed eternity to God without referring to experience. To Thomas it was enough to restate the abstract conception of eternity, with Aristotle's endorsement. Brightman said the scholastics specialized in squeezing real experience out of ideas. Modern religious thinkers enamored of physics, notably F. S. C. Northrop, liked that no squeezing was required, because physics excludes personality, value, and the epistemological problem. Brightman countered that physics is a very limited tool for thinking about God: "If there is to be any theology or any theism, it needs a broader base than that."[98]

Last and foremost was the Kant factor. Too many idealists took license from Kant's doctrine of the ideality of time, reasoning that time, being purely subjective, does not apply to things in themselves or to metaphysical reality. Bradley relegated time to Kantian appearance, and McTaggart described it as a distorted reflection "of something in the real nature of the timeless reality." Brightman judged that Bowne got "lost and embrangled" in the same puzzles about time that confused Berkeley. In *Theism* Bowne said God is timeless in God's absolute, self-related existence and that absolute intelligence and will lay behind all temporal limits and conditions as their source. In *Metaphysics* he said the creative activity that produces the temporal order "has no temporality in itself." In *Philosophy of Theism* he said the cosmic process, though not being in time, produces the form of time by its incessant change. Brightman puzzled at the concept of timeless change, noting that Bowne made other statements in the same books that bordered on recognizing the metaphysical importance of time. In *Theism* Bowne said there is no a priori reason to deny that the cosmic process might be coeternal with God. In *Metaphysics* he said change is "a fact of reality itself," never merely phenomenal. In *Philosophy of Theism* he said God is the founder of the world process, which is changing and thus essentially in time, and "hence the divine activity therein is essentially temporal."[99]

Bowne's inconsistency was not what mattered. What mattered was that he missed the very thing he cared passionately about. Despite defending the reality of personal life, Bowne failed to see that making time depend on personality makes time metaphysically real. Persons act and endure, Brightman explained, experiencing changeless truths within the changing processes of consciousness. Each pole of the temporal/eternal axis is necessary to the other: "The temporal is just as necessary to the eternal as the eternal is to the temporal." Lacking either pole, we are left with mere abstractions, not an explanation of experience as a whole. Kant's ideality of time was an abstraction because he developed it solely in relation to objects of sense.[100]

It took three generations to unfold the radicalism in Boston personal idealism, notwithstanding that every personalist touted Kant's teaching about human dignity. Bowne, Brightman, and Knudson built an impressive school, but Bowne had superiority issues, Brightman was a pure intellectual, and Knudson never threw off his racial conceits, holding back what Boston personalism needed to be.

Exhausted from overwork, Knudson gave up the dean's office in 1938 at the age of 65, but continued to teach on a full-time basis until 1943. He prized his standing in the middle mainstream of American Protestantism on social issues, and sealed it by opining on anti-colonial struggles in the postwar aftermath. Knudson acknowledged that the West's regnant powers were often oppressive and expansionist—dominating foreign peoples, exploiting resources, and controlling markets. He respected Muelder's anti-imperialism, but insisted there was such a thing as good imperialism, a "benevolent and progressive type of colonial or imperial rule that has been developing during the past half century or more." Good imperialism is linked with democracy and freedom, Knudson said. It is "energetic and expansive, but not despotic," emphasizing consent and cooperation while eschewing domination. He boasted that Anglo-Saxons were usually less racist than their Teutonic cousins, though he allowed that the Josiah Strong wing of the social gospel flamed with "national self-glorification" and racial chauvinism. Knudson said he sympathized with the "rising tide of resentment" among colonized peoples. But strong anti-imperialism was too simple: "Many of the subject peoples are not ready for self-government. They still need a long period of tutelage." The major Western powers, in his telling, still had a "civilizing mission to perform" in vast parts of the world such as the African continent.[101]

That was a throwback to the baleful tradition that denuded Kantian personalism of its universalism. Colonial apologists claimed for centuries that slaves and children lacked the requisite intellectual and moral development to qualify for the rights of persons. Knudson said this was a personalist position. Slaves and children were selves, but not persons, because they lacked the intellectual freedom and moral responsibility that defined personality. Knudson did not say that Christianity and Kantian personalism compelled anti-racist universalism, since he didn't believe it. His faculty successors felt keenly what was wrong in this picture. Even Boston personalism had a history of sabotaging what it supposedly believed. Muelder and DeWolf rectified this situation at Boston University, building on Brightman's principle that racism is "a repudiation of the ideal of personality."[102]

Walter Muelder and Third-Generation Personalism

Muelder was the leading theorist of third-generation personalism and the exemplar of its social gospel spirit. He grew up in Methodist social gospel personalism, earned his doctorate under Brightman in 1933, taught at Berea College and the University of Southern California, and returned to Boston University in 1945 to serve as dean of the School of Theology. The glory of the personalist tradition is that King is in it, but Muelder symbolizes what Boston personalism became as a school of thought.

Muelder's father, Epke Hermann Muelder, was a German-speaking immigrant and Methodist pastor who hauled his wife and three young children to Boston University in 1908 to clarify his religious beliefs; Walter was a toddler at the time. Epke Muelder studied under Bowne and Knudson, knew Brightman as a classmate, converted to social gospel personalism, witnessed Bowne's fatal stroke in 1910, and completed his doctorate in 1913. Walter Muelder imbibed his father's faith and followed him to Boston University. Under Brightman's guidance, Muelder studied for a year at Frankfurt with Paul Tillich, Karl Mannheim, and Max Horkheimer, writing a dissertation on Troeltsch's philosophy of history. The third generation was thus determinately schooled in Brightman's personal idealism and linked to his contacts in German idealism just before the Nazis obliterated the latter.[103]

Muelder adopted Brightman's signature positions, appreciating that Brightman complicated Bowne's self by adding psychological and social structural aspects. But the personalist self was still too individualistic and ahistorical, lacking Troeltsch's idea that history consists of "individual totalities"—*wholes* that synthesize psychical processes and natural conditions. Muelder took over Troeltsch's idea that historical wholes such as families, social classes, states, cultural epochs, revolutions, and schools of thought are original, partly unconscious, integral unities of meaning and value that possess a common spirit or mind. Historical wholes reverberate with creative personality; thus, individual persons are empirically given totalities. Personality is the bearer of common spirit—the relation of individual and society—and the key to meaning and value, even as personalities interact with impersonal forces in physical environments.[104]

This idea became the linchpin of Muelder's revision of personalist theory. Personality is a principle of individuality, human community, and ultimate reality, applying univocally to divine reality and the individual person. Theology and ethics read off from that which is given, the social bond between finite persons and divine reality, as well as the problems of ideal ends and their realization. Christian ethics is directed toward ideal ends that are aspects of ideal personality. The essential problems of Christian ethics are those of the self's relation to oneself, other finite persons, and ultimate personality. Development is temporal, practical, inherently teleological, and suffused with meaning and value. All experience is mediated and historical. Theory and practice are necessarily related, as Marx and James contended, and experience and reason are historically conditioned, as Troeltsch contended. Muelder grieved that Troeltsch gave up his best idea at the end of his life. Why relinquish the principle of personality just because some cultures do not appeal to it and Buddhism seeks redemption by escaping from it? He stuck with Troeltsch's mid-career vision of historical development as the shaping of community life in accord with ideal norms, basing his social personalism on it. Muelder reasoned that it must be possible to make room for relativity without falling prey to relativism. Brightman helped by conceiving personality in organic, structural, temporal, pluralistic terms, but Brightman gave short shrift to historical consciousness.

The challenge was to historicize personalist theory by socializing the personalist self, overcoming Bowne's exaltation of the human mind as the repository of personality. The ideal of individual fulfillment, Muelder reflected, transcends every historical epoch, but personality is not a static phenomenon. Human experience, being temporal, is always implicated in the historical process, and since it is always social and historical, there must be such a thing as social subjectivity. Muelder could have dug it out of Hegel, but that would have required battling over interpretations of Hegel, and he accepted Troeltsch's reading that Hegel was a monist. So Muelder borrowed from sociologist John E. Boodin the concept of a social mind—the idea of an objective spirit existing on the same level as personal minds. The social mind is not distinct from personal minds, but exists within them. Its total content transcends the limitations of individual minds, which participate in the social mind and achieve awareness of each other through the social mind.[105]

Muelder called it "the communitarian dimension of personality." He developed it in the 1930s and refined it throughout his career. For years he puzzled over Boodin's claim that intersubjective continuity is substantive. Does the social mind contain a real compounding of will and consciousness? If it contains a real fusion of wills, what happens to the integrity of the individual person? How should we understand or secure the consciousness of personal privacy? These quandaries were not as forbidding to Muelder as they were to Brightman in his dialogue with Hartshorne. Muelder settled on the view that the social mind consists of energy fields interacting with each other and within which persons interact. Social interaction takes place on both levels, below consciousness and on the level of shared meanings. Experience is social, however one construes intersubjectivity. The consciousness of objective spirit exists in individual minds, which participate in spirit and achieve awareness of each other through it. The self is not, as Bowne claimed, an individual center of experience that is merely influenced by its social environment. It *is* its social experience and unique individual experience. The self is conscious, the individual person is self-conscious, and both are historical and therefore temporal.[106]

Muelder was trained by Brightman and Knudson to guard the difference between personal idealism and even the best kinds of absolute idealism, as espoused by Royce and Hocking. Absolute idealism blurred the integrity of personal selves and/or God, even when it personalized the absolute and/or selves. Royce's first book, *The Religious Aspect of Philosophy* (1885), argued that when a finite mind entertains an erroneous idea, it must contain an (erroneous) idea and its (false) object, while simultaneously intending the true object of the idea. The mind would not be able to intend the true object if the object was not somehow available to it. Moreover, the highest good is attainable only collectively, because it involves harmony. Royce said the first need of all human beings is to cultivate "the sense of community, the power to work together, with clear insight into our reasons for so working." The early Royce held out for comprehensive cooperation, "the Universal Community." By 1913, in *The Problem of Christianity*, he believed that a certain kind of community must be the vehicle for it, which he called "the Beloved Community." It was another name for the kingdom of God, "the Realm of Grace" that Royce described as one of the three defining ideas of Christianity, along with sin and atonement.[107]

Muelder's teachers taught Royce on this subject while conveying that he shortchanged Christian theology. Muelder felt keenly that Royce, Troeltsch, and Rauschenbusch were better than his teachers on the essential sociality of salvation. He did not claim that the self is merely a collection of social relations. Muelder said the self is a real subject, "a *socius* with a private center." A self develops and becomes known by sharing its experiences and meanings with others. With Bowne and Brightman, Muelder affirmed that each person acts from a creative center, personality means freedom, and the highest virtue of personality is love. Beyond them he contended that because personality is always a social whole with an individual center, it must be conceived as a historical-communitarian category. Because personality is the most concrete category of existence and value, it is in personality that existing wholes and the highest existing value are both apprehended.[108]

Muelder's early writings crackled with prophetic passion and youthful idealism. For six years he taught amid Appalachian poverty at Berea College and played a leadership role in the local Socialist Party. For five years he taught at the University of Southern California, chaired the Los Angeles Church Federation's Commission on Race Relations, and protested America's wartime internment of Japanese Americans. Muelder's writings lost the crackle after he became a middle-aged seminary dean and ecumenical leader, but he stuck to his pacifist, socialist, feminist, anti-imperialist, and racial justice commitments, changing the image of the School of Theology.

In December 1944 he wrote a plea for revolutionary pacifism that raised the hackles of Methodist conservatives. The West, Muelder said, was not ready for the coming crash of empires and the revolutionary challenges of a postcolonial world. Even American Christian radicals didn't realize what was coming: "Unless the revolutionary energies unleashed around the world in the last half decade are permitted to find creative and constructive expression in terms of rapidly expanding freedoms, self-government, and human equality, the remainder of the present century is bound to resemble a downward spiral, a maelstrom sucking into its vortex of violence more and more of the institutions of civilization."[109]

He acknowledged that anti-war activists and anti-imperialists were beaten down. Americans broadly supported their nation's war, pacifists felt defensive, and the civil rights of conscientious objectors were often violated. Many pacifists felt defensive because the government provided alternative service for conscientious objectors, raising tortuous questions about the ethics of supporting the war in alternative ways. Moreover, the pacifist movement lacked a unifying philosophy. It was a grab bag of Gandhian sentiments, sayings of Jesus, and fragments of radical philosophies and traditions often conflicting with each other. Anarchist and collectivist pacifism had almost nothing in common, and both contradicted most forms of Christian pacifism. American pacifism was therefore weak, demoralized, defensive, and morally confused.

Muelder said there were practical advantages to being so diffuse. People commit themselves to nonviolence in different ways and for various reasons.

But Christian pacifism had to improve its present condition, making a contribution to nonviolent theory and practice. Christianity *and* the anti-war movement needed a religious philosophy of love divine, the human person, and the good society. Did that smack of hopelessly abstract, divisive, and distracting theology and metaphysics? Muelder countered that movements for peace and justice need unifying principles. Communism and Fascism were based on morally repugnant cosmologies, yielding terrible evils: "First principles function as long-time purposes, and the conceptions inevitably canalize the resources of energy and power."[110]

Muelder wanted Christian pacifists to proclaim that religious truths are real and transforming. Christianity is the living of Christ's way, a way of life that says "yes" to the light. He also believed that anti-war movements are transforming, at least potentially. It meant something, he said, that anti-war activists usually cared more than others about racial justice and poverty. The leading activists in these fields were pacifists; now was the moment to expand and scale up. If religious pacifists pushed into "wider and wider vistas," they might yet save the world, penetrating "deeper and deeper" into the hearts of people and the chaos of the world: "The movement must be fearlessly mystical, fearlessly practical, and fearlessly intellectual."[111]

Conservative Methodists were appalled that this guy was the incoming dean at the School of Theology. They protested bitterly against his appointment. Later they erupted again when *Reader's Digest* published an exposé on "Methodism's Pink Fringe." Stanley High, a member of the Federal Council of Churches' Commission on International Relations and a former liberal, told *Digest* readers in 1950 that Muelder led "a powerful and growing" left-wing movement in American Christianity, "a serious liability for Protestantism as a whole." High warned of sinister motives: "That such a left-wing minority is officially tolerated is, in itself, an indication of the success of their tactics in concealing their real aims behind a humanitarian facade." Muelder stewed over the controversies he evoked, not wanting to hurt the school. At a personal low point he submitted his resignation to Daniel L. Marsh, who refused to accept it. Afterward Muelder kept a copy of the letter in his pocket as a reminder that no position was worth compromising his integrity. Often he advised students to make sure that if they got fired, make it for good reasons.[112]

He pulled the school in his direction, pointedly on racial justice. The early Muelder conceived racism as moral bias, like most white liberals; subsumed racism under class oppression, like most socialists; and emphasized—better than most liberals—that racism is a culturally generated evil. To abolish racism Americans had to integrate American society and ensure equal opportunity to social goods. Then Muelder read *An American Dilemma* (1944) by Swedish sociologist Gunnar Myrdal, witnessed the early civil rights movement, and changed his mind, arguing that racism has structural dimensions that defeat one-factor solutions. Ideas about racial superiority and inferiority are individual totalities welded into multiple layers of culture, economy, and society. Like Myrdal and political sociologist Robert M. MacIver, Muelder contended that racism is a distinct problem with multiple and cumulative causes, and nothing less than aggressive racial integration would break it.[113]

Myrdal showed that white fears and black grievances about race were inverted. White Americans feared racial intermarriage above everything else, followed by fear of personal and social equality, fear of joint use of schools and other public places, fear of equal voting, fear of equal standing in law courts, and fear of equal economic opportunity. To black Americans, the list of racial grievances was exactly reversed. Blacks cared most about economic opportunity, next about legal justice, next about voting, and so on. The right to intermarry was a distant last. Myrdal said there was some ground for optimism in the fact that blacks did not want what whites most feared. To Myrdal the American dilemma was that white Americans had an admirable creed they dared not practice out of fear and loathing of black Americans. Muelder stressed that racial integration should ensure the rights and opportunities of all citizens to participate as equals in society, accepting cultural differences. Any concept of racial integration as cultural conformity is self-defeating. Segregationists equated community with identity, repressing black Americans to preserve white American culture and domination. Following MacIver, Muelder countered that difference and separateness are not the same thing. Accepting difference leads to true community, not to separatism. Moreover, American Christians had a moral responsibility to show that integration worked. In this area especially, Muelder said, actions were more important than words. It started with integrating Christian congregations.[114]

Muelder was disciplined, idealistic, rigorous, and charitable, combining a prophetic spirit and institutional realism. He espoused social gospel ideals with an institutionalist's wary eye for selfishness, collective egotism, structural evil, and inertia. To Muelder, America's racial pathology was the supreme example of evil reproduced in social structures with multiple and cumulative causes. Myrdal taught him how to talk about it sociologically, but to Muelder, taking structural evil seriously was a major reason to renew the social gospel socialism of Rauschenbusch.

Rauschenbusch's Christian socialism exemplified how to hold together gospel ideals and structural realities. Muelder stressed that Rauschenbusch recognized the limits of bourgeois moralism and the harsh realities of the class struggle: "He had neither a merely optimistic view of human nature, nor a belief in inevitable progress, nor a lack of understanding of what Marx so realistically stated." Rauschenbusch was a pioneer, holding fast to truths that others neglected, including the terrible reality of collective evil. Muelder liked him on cooperation, responsibility, democratic socialism, and his insistence that competition creates a reign of fear that thwarts the values of the kingdom. Rauschenbusch was a salvation preacher, proclaiming the power of the gospel to redeem individuals and the social order. Thus he reaped a slew of insults: moralist, idealist, sentimentalist, and utopian. Muelder replied that Rauschenbusch made gospel claims and was neither sentimental nor utopian. Neo-orthodoxy may have scored a few points against him, but it did wrong in disparaging him, and it certainly did not improve on him. To Muelder, "Rauschenbusch was undoubtedly working along the correct line." Christianity needed to return to Rauschenbusch-style socialism, with better social scientific tools.[115]

Two generations after Rauschenbusch wrote sizzling prose and called for radical economic democracy, Muelder wrote workmanlike prose and commended "the responsible society." Both sought to persuade and inspire, but in very different times. The World Council of Churches (WCC), at its inaugural assembly in Amsterdam in 1948, condemned the denial of freedom under communism and the denial of social justice under laissez-faire capitalism, calling for an ethic of "the responsible society." Muelder adopted the spirit and language of this call. In 1952 he joined the WCC Faith and Order Commission and served it for twenty-three years, writing in 1953, "The conception of a responsible society commands respect when seen in contrast to ideologically extreme positions."[116]

Muelder implored the WCC to stand for freedom and democracy without exceptions, speaking "boldly in Christ's name both to those in power and to the people, to oppose terror, cruelty and race discrimination, to stand by the outcast, the prisoner and the refugee." A responsible society, he said, respects persons as intrinsically valuable, recognizes personality as the ground of all values, cherishes freedom as the development of personality, and makes freedom responsible for social justice. Muelder was slightly nostalgic for the ecumenical movement that preceded the Cold War and demanded economic justice. From 1925 to 1939 it commended economic democracy and called for cooperation between labor and capital. Then World War II led to the Cold War, which engulfed the entire planet and extinguished the ecumenical dream of economic democracy. Muelder regretted this retrogression, but was very much an advocate of WCC ecumenism, and a steward of it—condemning Soviet Communism as a totalitarian tyranny, rejecting Cold War militarism, and holding out for coexistence between the Soviet Union and the capitalist West.[117]

Identifying so closely with WCC ecumenism blunted Muelder's prophetic edge, except on the rights of women, on which his WCC work pushed him ahead of his time. In the mid-1950s Muelder cochaired the WCC Commission on the Co-operation of Men and Women in Church and Society. The work appalled him. Muelder wanted desperately to believe that the church is not inherently anti-feminist and conservative, but he said the "pattern of male domination" was overwhelming in American churches and American society. He charged that churches did not apply the norms of social justice to women, were not open to discussion on this subject, and dismissed important secular critiques. One culprit was the regnant neo-orthodoxy in theology; Barth treated Ephesians 5 as the last word on the subject, as did neo-orthodox biblical scholar Floyd V. Filson. Even liberal scholars tried to wring a bit of equality from the biblical motif of mutual submission. Muelder was incredulous. How could theologians ignore social scientific analysis of gender and gender relations?[118]

He implored that significant changes in one aspect of culture have effects in all other aspects of culture: "No one aspect of culture is always the cause of changes elsewhere. Causation in a complex cultural whole is pluralistic and tends to be cumulative." Since cultural change is always caused by dependent variables of differing intensities and power, no particular factor relating to biblical teaching, economic interest, social convention, or anything else is fully definitive or determinative. To make intelligent judgments about gender relationships and the rights of women, theologians must address "the whole range of cultural expression." It was ridiculous to settle disputes over women's rights by quoting Christian

Scripture and tradition, because both are culturally conditioned. Moreover, Muelder wrote, Christian claims are supposed to address the total culture, not merely the Christian community.[119]

Christianity needed to sweep away centuries of Hebrew tribalism, patriarchy, Hellenistic dualism, and asceticism that lay behind obsolete Christian thinking about sexuality and gender roles. Muelder judged that very little in Christian tradition is helpful. Besides needing new answers to old problems, Christianity had to ask new questions about how to nurture, valorize, and sustain relationships of genuine equality and mutuality. For example, what should the church say about the fact that female professionals often internalized masculine values? Muelder said Christianity had almost no wisdom in this area because the church sanctified male domination and lacked any history of asking relevant questions. Women exerted little pressure to reform the church's teaching and practices, and the proportion of women enrolled in graduate professional schools was no greater in 1958 than in 1918. Muelder blamed the culture of early marriage and the cultural conservatism of churches: "It is imperative that we draw upon the redemptive resources of our faith in order to achieve the full benefit of the mutual responsibility and fellowship within the Church and at the same time contribute to better interpersonal relationships in the family, the work situation, and society in general."[120]

That was a decade before the feminist eruption of the late 1960s. Brightman was the greatest of the personalist thinkers and an exemplar of personalist thought, but Muelder made personalism more relevant, expansive, and justice-oriented. He stuck to ideal principles, but was sensitive to cultural relativity, always ready to rethink the meaning of his principles for new issues or circumstances. He treasured the ecumenical movement and his work for it, hoping for achievements that did not occur. He wanted social ethics to develop into a coherent discipline, yet admitted that his work reflected the field's issue-oriented eclecticism. He blended theology, social science, and philosophy, drawing on disciplines holding a relative autonomy, which he anchored by sticking with personal idealism. Muelder sustained his core positions and went through no phases, representing Boston personalism better than it had ever been, until lightning struck in Montgomery, Alabama.

7

Whiteheadian Ordering

God and Creativity

The only vital school of liberal theology in North America is the one founded on the organic philosophy of Alfred North Whitehead. It has been such for the past fifty years, overcoming its aborted beginning, obscure jargon, and ambiguous entanglement in the Chicago school. Whiteheadian thought is the dominant type of process theology, though not the only type. It nearly sprouted in 1930 as the second generation of the Chicago school, but faltered. In 1945, two years before White-head died, Whiteheadian theology got a second chance at Chicago and acquired a name, "process theology."

The school of Whitehead has a genius founder in Whitehead, a brilliant cofounder in Charles Hartshorne, a successor relationship to the first and second generations of the Chicago school, and many renowned theologians, notably Daniel Day Williams, Bernard E. Meland, Schubert Ogden, John B. Cobb Jr., David Ray Griffin, and Catherine Keller. It became a school as the third generation of the Chicago school, featuring a scholastic cast of mind. Then Meland and Cobb differently broke the mold in the early 1970s, opening the way to feminist, ecological, and sort-of postmodern process theologies. Meland, reflecting that he embodied three Chicago school generations, plus two kinds of White-headian theology, observed puckishly in 1962: "In ways I find it difficult to explain, I find that, to myself, I am the Divinity School. Its history is the history of my own theological pilgrimage."[1]

The first theologians of the Chicago school were Shailer Mathews and George Burman Foster, who said that theology had to become as modern as possible. Mathews identified modernism with the scientific method, identified liberalism with two groups he liked but rejected—Unitarians and religious humanists—and self-identified as a modernist evangelical, prizing "evangelical" as a banner word. Then he and Foster converted to history of religions historicism just after it emerged. A modernist theology, they agreed, had to be fully historicist, whether or not it remained evangelical by upholding any normative gospel claims. Both grappled with the "whether or not" throughout their careers. Mathews translated Christian doctrines into the language of evolutionary process, functional patterns, value theory, and cultural progress. Foster wavered on the upshot of modernist-as-possible, sometimes with an echo of Herrmann versus Troeltsch. At times, Foster was a forceful proponent of going all the way with the naturalistic worldview of modern science. At other times he said that science does not grasp what matters in religion—inspiration, personality, spiritual power—and religion is pointless without a real God.[2]

The Chicago theologians became a school by shucking off Foster's double-mindedness. Mathews, Gerald Birney Smith, Edward Scribner Ames, and Shirley Jackson Case opted wholly for making theology modern, empirical, and naturalistic. They projected buoyant self-confidence in taking this tack, keeping their inner doubts in-house and keeping philosophy to a minimum. Philosophy got in the way of finding the facts, so the Chicago school founders debated whether they needed any philosophy at all. They settled on the pragmatism of William James and John Dewey.

Ideas are true according to their practical usefulness. Concepts are habits of belief or rules of action. Ideas are like knives and forks, enabling useful action. Every Chicago school founder prized scientific method as the way to determine what works, but James also taught that consciousness is a nonentity better replaced by functional realities of experience. Those who cling to consciousness, James said, "are clinging to a mere echo, the faint rumor left behind by the disappearing 'soul' upon the air of philosophy." The pragmatic alternative is the reality of experience, which is relational. Instead of fixing on atomistic units of experience, empiricism should study experience as a flowing, immediate continuity. Life is a continuous flux or stream of experiences lacking distinct boundaries. Radical empiricism, in James' conception, focused on the relational flow of experience. Because life flows together and onward in a stream of experiences that are continually overlapping, the relations that exist between things are as real and as directly experienced as the things themselves. The relations that connect experiences are themselves experienced relations.[3]

James said that radical empiricism consists of a postulate, a statement of fact, and a generalized conclusion. The postulate is that philosophers should debate only about things that are definable in terms drawn from experience. The statement of fact is that all relations between things, whether conjunctive or disjunctive, are equally matters of direct particular experience as the things themselves. The generalized conclusion is that parts of experience hold together by relations that are themselves parts of experience. Rationalistic idealists such as F. H. Bradley, J. M. E. McTaggart, and Josiah Royce taught that experience as immediately given has no conjunctive structure; experience is disjunctive, torn apart from reason and truth. They disclosed the hidden wholeness of things by interpreting the world's separate things as shapes of Spirit. The dialectic of the Hegelian truth relation reunites parts of reality in paired categories of subject and object, knower and known, thought and being, and reason and experience.[4]

James countered that the truth relation has a definite content and everything in it is experienced. The whole nature of the truth relation can be told in positive terms—he was not a materialist. To be true, ideas must *work* functionally, and they do. Since James did not believe in the infinite, personal, Creator God of Christianity or the deity of Christ, he did not count himself a Christian. But he had a religious sensibility of a liberal Protestant type, and he and Dewey were good at befriending liberal theologians. The Chicago school debated through its first generation how much it should wager on full-fledged radical empiricism, which opened the door to process theology.

At Union Theological Seminary and Boston University, theologians claimed that modern Christianity did not break continuity with historic Christianity. At Chicago, theologians said modernity was a revolution, breaking continuity. Foster said it with rollicking brilliance in *The Finality of the Christian Religion* (1905). Smith said it for twenty years in articles expounding the agenda of the Chicago school. A truly modern theology does not proceed by assuming religious norms from the Christian past. Like Troeltsch, the early Chicago school emphasized the sociocultural development of Christianity and the relation of its teaching and practices to other religions. Mathews said doctrines are best understood as sociohistorical products of culturally shaped world-views or "social minds." Science deserves its superior standing in modern consciousness, as James and Dewey contended; thus, knowledge in the field of religion must be attained by disciplined empirical reflection on experience, especially the experience of external relations. Methodolog-ically, the early Chicago theologians were empiricists and historicists, with caveats from Foster. Ontologically, they were religious naturalists, though Foster zigged and zagged about the transcendent reality of God. Epistemologically, they embraced the pragmatic empiricist doctrine that knowledge is best attained by observing objects and making inferences about what they do.

"Religion," they taught, following James, is a collective name, like "government." There is no single essence of religion. Religion is a name for the many ways in which people engage in religious practices. Some ways are good, progressive, intelligent, and morally healthy, and many are none of these things. When Mathews spoke carefully, especially to academic audiences, he remembered that he was a historicist, employing "social process" as a signifier for the kingdom faith. On other occasions he spoke of Christ's kingdom as an ongoing historical project. The dif-ference mattered to every Chicago theologian, but not as much as the truism proclaimed in both cases: modern Christianity grafts the ideals of Jesus into the ongoing social process as history moves forward to its consummation as the reign of God.[5]

The best Chicago theologian of the first generation was a doctoral protégé of Foster, Douglas Clyde Macintosh. He had meant to study with Foster and Dewey at Chicago for a year (1905–1906) before taking his doctorate under James at Harvard, but Dewey moved to Columbia Uni-versity and Macintosh surprised himself by sticking with Foster. Macin-tosh started with Foster's vestigial left-Ritschlian personalism, moved to Hegelianism, and balked at moving to the pragmatism of his teachers. On the one hand, it was a short step from Ritschlian practical reason to Jamesian pragmatism, as Foster said. On the other hand, Macintosh never accepted that metaphysical reasoning was passé in theology. All religious claims make tacit assumptions about reality, and all make state-ments about a reality of some kind. Macintosh wrote his dissertation on this topic, accepting the Ritschlian value-judgment theory of religion, but construing theology as a theory of religion. For thirty-three years he taught at Yale, reconstructing Ritschlian value theory, on Chicago school terms, as a theory of reality.[6]

Macintosh developed a realistic monist epistemology and an ethical intuitionist moral theory, both of which were so complex that one of his early students at Yale, Reinhold Niebuhr, was dissuaded from pursuing a doctorate. Yet the complex theoretical superstructure supported an ingeniously simple argument. Every science, Macintosh reasoned, assumes that its object exists and can be known. Chemistry assumes the existence of matter and psychology assumes states of consciousness. Theology has the same right, as a working hypothesis, to assume *that* God is, without assuming *what* God is. Religious experience is the working material of theology, but the point is to describe the divine Object known through experience. Theology attends to that which is apprehended in religious experience. In the spirit of James' defense of the will to believe, Macintosh said there ought to be a God to give spiritual meaning and moral direction to life. In that case, there may be a God, because science is compatible with the notion of an indwelling, divine mind at work in nature and history. Thus, at least as a tentative conclusion, there *must* be a God if one is to have a morally healthy, rational existence. Concisely, "we have a moral right to believe as we must in order to live as we ought."[7]

In his early career Macintosh featured his moral optimism—faith in the cosmos joined to moral obligation. First he argued for moral optimism; then he argued that God exists. In the 1930s he stopped appealing to moral optimism as a form of apologetics, because young people had no optimism. Macintosh switched to saying that moral optimism is a fruit of Christian faith, not its basis. But he never recanted the Jamesian right to believe, or his belief that pessimism and Christian faith are enemies. A pessimistic theology is a reactionary absurdity. Macintosh had a two-level house—a normative theology built on empirical foundations—held together by ethical intuition: it is reasonable to believe in the conservation of values, and if we judge that the value-conserving factor in life is good and enhances personality, we are warranted in surmising that God is good and personal.[8]

Macintosh never tried to operate without a metaphysic and did not waver about God's objectivity; thus he was a forerunner of what became second-generation Chicago school theology. Every liberal theology resting on religious experience confronted the problem that experience is subjective. Mathews emphasized structure and process for this reason, playing down experience, a variation on the tack that Wieman later took aggressively. Macintosh agreed that the subjectivity of experience is a problem for theology. But appealing to experience, he implored, is indispensable. Rightly construed, theology is precisely the fallible attempt to understand the objective aspects of subjective experiences. Religious experience is unavoidably subjective, so the conditions under which theology operates are also unavoidably subjective. But empirical theology is objective in a twofold sense: it submits to scientific tests of verification, and its divine referent is an objective reality. Empirical theology studies how God affects us when we attend to God, pray to God, surrender to God, and carry out God's will. To lose the divine referent is to be utterly lost.[9]

Back at Chicago, Macintosh's teachers debated this verdict to the end of their careers. The first generation ran from 1900 to 1928. The founders taught that the social gospel exemplified good religion whether or not Jesus taught a version of it and that God is a representation of religious ideals and/or the mystery of the personal character of natural process. Ames conceived God as the idealization of select aspects of the world. God is functional as the idealization of love and creativity. Foster tacked back and forth between Ames and Troeltsch, in the former mode comparing God to Uncle Sam, in the latter mode imploring that religion is pointless without a real metaphysical God. Mathews anticipated emergent theism without making an ontological claim for it, construing "God" as an interpretive pattern, a name for the personality-evolving reality of the cosmos. This interpretive pattern, he reasoned, expresses "an experienced relationship with an objective environment." The environment is an aspect of a dynamic relation in which human subjects play a role. Mathews ignored the post-Kantian puzzles that his conceptualism took him into, since Kantian idealism had derailed previous liberal theologies. He had little patience for epistemological theorizing, including the implications of his own. As long as one bears in mind, he argued, that God is an instrumental pattern, it is legitimate to employ personal metaphors in speaking of divine reality: "For God is our conception, born of social experience, of the personality-evolving and personally response elements of our cosmic environment with which we are organically related."[10]

For most of his career, Smith was the Chicago school's truest believer that science is the salvation of theology. He wrote programmatic articles for Chicago school journals—*American Journal of Theology, Biblical World, Journal of Religion*—declaring that theology had to become as scientific as chemistry, or at least sociology. But every social science took its own path, taking no interest in theology, and by the mid-1920s Smith felt keenly that little had come of his agenda articles. He took a slightly mystical turn, admitting that theology needed to be more religious than he previously said, and he chafed at Mathews for resting too comfortably with an answer. His last word on the God-subject was that more studies were needed to determine whether God is anything more than the representation of religious ideals.[11]

Smith arrived at the latter impasse just before the first generation ended. Chicago theologians had debated for nearly thirty years how far they should take their commitment to religious naturalism, whether God should be conceived as a cosmic reality, and what came of construing God as an analogical expression for an idealized concept of the universe. In 1926 Whitehead published *Religion in the Making*. The Chicago theologians read it with total bafflement. The book was advertised as a primer in religion, but the Chicago theologians could not understand a single page of it. Ames and Case dismissed it as completely unintelligible. Smith reported that he felt some affinity with it, but could not explain why. Mathews confessed, "It is infuriating, and I must say embarrassing as well, to read page after page of relatively familiar words without understanding a single sentence." With his typical wry humor, however, Mathews added that perhaps the problem was not with Whitehead. Did anyone claim to understand this purported genius?[12]

Yes, there was one American expert on Whitehead—Henry Nelson Wieman, who taught philosophy at Occidental College. Wieman had earned a doctorate under Ralph Barton Perry and W. E. Hocking at Harvard, cutting his intellectual teeth on James, Dewey, Perry, Hocking, and Henri Bergson. He scoffed that James wrote brilliantly entertaining books that never plunged below the surface, unlike Dewey, a better pragmatist. In the 1920s, while teaching at Occidental, Wieman studied the emergent evolutionists, especially Samuel Alexander, C. Lloyd Morgan, and Alfred North Whitehead. The Chicago theologians, learning of his existence, asked him to lecture about Whitehead. Wieman told them that Whitehead's thought was perfectly intelligible and extremely important. Serious religious thinking has to be metaphysical, but modern theology must not take its bearings from Plato and Aristotle, or Kant and Hegel, or Newtonian physics. Whitehead's organicism showed the way for modern theology. It was essentially relational, dynamic, and open-ended; it theorized about the really existing natural world of empirical process, not about imaginary beings; it was grounded in the new theories of emergent evolution, relativity, and gestalt psychology; and it proved that the universe exists only by virtue of its order, which is aesthetic and loving.

Whitehead showed that the existence and nature of God are revealed in the inherent structure of physical nature. Meland later recalled, "It was as if shuttered windows in one's own household had been swung open, revealing vistas of which one had hitherto been unmindful."[13]

Wieman joined the Chicago faculty, awkwardly at first. He was a hybrid like Hocking and Hartshorne—trained in philosophy, yet driven by religious questions and committed to a philosophical approach to them. He respected his new colleagues for pioneering an empirical, naturalistic, pragmatic approach to theology, but could not fathom why they took so much interest in history, and he chided them for letting go of God's objective reality. History doesn't matter, because history doesn't prove anything. It doesn't matter how many Isaiahs there were or whether Paul left his cloak at Troas. What matters is, What is it all about? Why is theology worth caring about? Wieman said liberal theology was too sentimental. It shrank from defending God's existence and tried to make itself attractive by appealing to social concerns. That strategy was a loser; it drove the strong and intelligent people away from religion. Meland later recalled that Wieman seemed like the Chicago theologians, except for being "strangely and tantalizingly unlike them." Wieman put it sharper: "I felt strangely out of place and in a very alien intellectual atmosphere, despite the most exceptional kindness toward me by almost all the faculty."[14]

Most of the founders were a kindly bunch, evincing the niceness of church culture even as they stirred controversy in the churches for liberalizing Christian doctrine. Mathews endured constant attacks from fundamentalists; his position as Dean of the Divinity School and leadership role in the American Baptist Church made him a special target. But the Divinity School *was* drifting into mere religious humanism, exactly as conservatives charged. By the mid-1920s the school's evangelical origins had faded precipitously, its intellectual creativity was eroding, and students caught that their teachers were demoralized and confused. Wieman offered a bracing alternative, vowing to make theology tough-minded again. Religion is pointless without God, but science negates traditional ways of conceiving God's existence. Wieman argued that whatever else the word "God" may mean, at bottom it designates the "Something" upon which human life depends for its welfare and growth. It cannot be doubted that such a Something exists: "The mere fact that human life happens, and continues to happen, proves that this Something, however unknown, does certainly exist."[15]

God is as certain as the external world, and as real as a toothache. Liberals like Smith made everything uncertain, but Wieman said the modern age needed certainty above all. At bottom, there were two possibilities about this Something. Either the universe is a single organic unity that has indivisibly created and sustained human life, or some of its sustaining conditions are more crucial than others. The first view is pantheistic; the second is theistic. In either case, God is the name for the undeniable Something of supreme value in life. Minimally defined, God's existence is a metaphysical deduction, but as a real object of knowledge, God must be studied scientifically, the true method of knowing.

Science judges the truth or falsity of metaphysical propositions. Wieman was dead serious that only science yields knowledge. Any discipline that claims to know something has to develop a scientific method that adequately examines its data. Human beings were amply acquainted with food, light, sound, and motion long before they understood anything about these things scientifically. Because experience is more complex than light, sound, and motion, psychology lagged behind physics as a science. Theology lagged further behind because religious experience is exceedingly complex and theologians only recently began to accept the scientific imperative. Wieman had the Chicago spirit, but shorn of its historicism and philosophical ambivalence. Empirical theology needed to move beyond mere acquaintance knowledge of God, to real knowing.[16]

His rationalism was unyielding. To Wieman, the cognitive meaning of religion was consuming and religiously sufficient. He did not lack feeling, or religious feeling, but stressed that sentimentality is a deadly enemy of religion, "a dry rot that destroys religion at its roots." Anything evocative is problematic. Wieman allowed that aesthetic factors prevail in music, poetry, worship, and other forms of art. But there is only one proper way to use words—to designate an object, not to evoke a sentiment. It galled Wieman that liberal preachers emoted in their sermons about love, the community of faith, the cross, the Word of God, and the Spirit of Christ, hoping to get by on sentiment. He admonished, "These are dangerous words and should be rarely used." To use a word for the sake of the sentiment attached to it is dishonest. Designative language is clear and concrete. Evocative language indulges and obscures, transferring loyalty from the proper objects of faith to words that designate them. The early Wieman already exuded the laboratory flatness that later consumed him, but early Wieman had a Whiteheadian sense of aesthetic totality. Religion deals with the concrete fact in its totality, he reasoned, so theologians must be willing to wrestle with obscurity, unlike chemists and physicists. Religion is loaded with mystery that even the most rigorous empirical theology cannot avoid. Good theology, however, keeps mystery talk to a minimum, making theology as designative and empirical as possible.[17]

Like Macintosh, Wieman proposed to understand religion scientifically as the process by which human beings seek adjustment to God, and he grieved at the plague of irrationalism sweeping European theology. But Macintosh radiated evangelical piety, moral feeling, and personal theism. Wieman was indifferent to churchly religion, having become a philosopher of religion after watching a sunset across the Missouri River during his senior year of college. He never passed through an evangelical phase, a phase in which the Bible interested him, or a Ritschlian phase. Wieman told students that the Bible is "a vastly over-rated book." Calling it "the 'inspired Word of God' and all the rest of the hullabaloo has given it a false prestige." God, he reasoned, is the complex environmental nature that yields the greatest good when human subjects adjust rightly to reality. God may be more than this definition, but in the wrestle of religion with truth, it is best to work with the God that is known. Facts are more important than any cherished belief, the world is not a nice place, "and God is not a nice God." Wieman stressed that God can be terrible even when God is good. Whitehead said religion is "what the individual does with his own solitariness," the transition "from God the void to God the enemy, and from God the enemy to God the companion." Wieman treasured this statement for burning the sentimentality out of liberal religion. True religion, he argued, is about adjusting to God, not achieving human ideals. The object of religious experience is within religious experience, not in the transformation of society. Religion is the art and theory of introspection. It begins in the wounding experience of the void, deepens with the experience of God as the enemy, and matures in the experience of God as the companion of one's living. Wieman stressed the necessity of the enemy stage. Bad religion is sentimental, or dogmatic, or both, clinging to illusions in which God is never the enemy. The true God is the ultimate fact of life with which human beings must struggle.[18]

This was a hard-edged rendering of Whitehead. Tennyson asserted poetically that a little flower in a crannied wall contains the inner reality of God and humanity; Whitehead agreed that everything that exists involves in its existence the totality of all being. Each particular thing in existence is what it is because all the rest of being is what it is. Tennyson's flower "prehends" all being; the universe is "concreted" in the flower; God is the principle of concretion, though not in the pantheistic sense. Wieman emphasized that on Whitehead's terms, God is not simply another name for the existing world in its totality. God is the sustaining character that the universe displays, the aesthetic order of being. God is less and more than the total concrete world of existing things—less because God excludes evil, and more because God transcends the existing world as the power that shapes and pervades the world. The idea that God transcends all being, Wieman argued, must be eliminated from theology, but God's creative power over the world of abstract forms is rightly described as transcendent.[19]

Whitehead grew up in Kent, England; his father was an Anglican cleric and schoolmaster; and Whitehead's career had three phases. From 1885 to 1914 he explored the logical foundations of mathematics; from 1914 to 1924 he worked principally on the philosophy of natural science, especially theoretical physics; and from 1925 until his death in 1947 he concentrated on metaphysics. Institutionally these phases corresponded with his teaching career at Trinity College, Cambridge (1885–1910), where he collaborated with his student Bertrand Russell on the principles of mathematics; at the Imperial College of Science and Technology at University College, London (1914–1924), where he taught philosophy of science and served as dean of the Faculty of Science; and at Harvard University (1924–1937), where he joined the faculty at the age of sixty-three and developed his speculative philosophy.

Methodologically his system had strong parallels to Heidegger's phenomenology, taking immediate human experience as his point of departure, in Whitehead's case as a panexperientialist. Whitehead taught that perceiving, valuing, and remembering are structural clues to the interpretation of experience, and feeling is the essential clue to being. Like Bergson, Alexander, and Morgan, Whitehead rejected the mechanistic view of nature as a machinelike system of pushes and pulls. Things are complexes of motions that possess within themselves their own principle of motion. Evolution contains a *nisus* (striving) toward higher levels of novel emergence, and each entity is related to all others in a living organic universe. In the mid-1920s Whitehead dropped his atheism, describing God as the source of cosmic order. Wieman was his first American proponent, helping to create an American audience for Whitehead's forthcoming system, *Process and Reality* (1929). From the beginning Wieman had a few caveats. He disliked that Whitehead had Anglican admirers in England, which suggested that his thought could be hijacked by neo-supernaturalists. Whitehead overplayed the aesthetic as a designative category for religious experience, and Wieman never liked Whitehead's idea that God is a concrete entity. To Wieman, Whitehead's God made far more sense as the principle constituting the concreteness of things.[20]

Then *Process and Reality* confirmed Wieman's misgivings and created new ones. Whitehead described the fundamental units of reality as "actual entities" or "actual occasions" that realize some value and pass out of existence in the process of being succeeded by similar entities. Actual entities are experiencing subjects. The internal constitution of the fundamental things that make up the universe *is* their experience. Like the monads of Leibnizian philosophy and the energy quanta of post-Newtonian physics, Whitehead conceived actual entities as complex, active, interdependent units. Building on Leibniz's relation of "perception" to "apperception," he coined the term "prehension" to designate the process by which an actual entity grasps another entity as an object of its experience. The coming-into-being of the subject must be accounted for, and all actual entities are simultaneously the subject that experiences and the "superject" of its experiences. *Process and Reality* developed a temporal panexperiential theory of reality. Against the notions that a stable subject has experiences and matter has no feeling, Whitehead developed the idea of a self-creating subject.[21]

Creative process includes the becoming of new subjects as well as the appearance of new patterns among things. Whitehead described the becoming of an actual entity as a "concrescence," the merging of various aspects of experience into a unity. He delineated two kinds of actual entities, which he called "God" and "actual occasions." Every actual occasion originates physically, but God's prehensions are underived, constituting God's primordial nature. The universe is "a creative advance into novelty." Not only does no one cross the same river twice. No thinker thinks twice, or, more broadly, "no subject experiences twice." Locke described time as a perpetual perishing, but didn't think it through. Even Kant's first analogy of experience wrongly assumed that substance is permanent. Whitehead reasoned that forms are permanent, not substance: "Forms suffer changing relations; actual entities 'perpetually perish' subjectively, but are immortal objectively." That is, in the process of passage, actual entities lose their subjective immediacy, but gain objectivity as forms.[22]

Process and Reality famously described God as an order in the process of creativity, distinguishing between the primordial and consequent natures of God. God is a concrete actual entity that envisages pure potentials, which Whitehead called "eternal objects." God and the world are both in the grip of the creative advance into novelty, the ultimate metaphysical ground. Every self-actualizing subject possesses the power to actualize or negate the life-enhancing aim of God's primordial nature. As a primordial reality, God is "the unlimited conceptual realization of the absolute wealth of potentiality." God lures God's subjects to make creative, life-enhancing choices, but God does not infringe the freedom of the moral agent to make choices: "He is the lure for feeling, the eternal urge of desire."[23]

God's primordial nature constitutes the universe of creative possibilities, while God's consequent nature consists of the accumulated actualization of the choices of self-actualizing entities. God's primordial nature is conceptual and does not change, but God's consequent nature is derivative and conscious, and thus changes along with the creative advance of the world. Whitehead reasoned that the two natures interact through the "weaving of God's physical feelings" in God's consequent nature upon the concepts of God's primordial nature. The reality of God is shaped by the interaction of God's originating conceptual experience and God's conscious, physical, consequent experience: "He does not create the world, he saves it; or, more accurately, he is the poet of the world, with tender patience leading it by his vision of truth, beauty, and goodness."[24]

Wieman's first review of *Process and Reality* was generally positive, celebrating that Whitehead's system was better than all others. But Wieman hedged from the beginning, troubled by Whitehead's metaphysical cast, especially his reworked Platonist concepts, which invited neo-supernatural appropriation. English Anglican theologian Lionel Thornton provided an example in *The Incarnate Lord* (1928), describing the incarnation as the culmination of evolutionary process. Wieman shuddered that Whitehead already had mainstream theological admirers. Moreover, sooner or later a better system would come along, making Whitehead's system obsolete. Wieman did not know where Whitehead erred, but he said the system undoubtedly contained serious errors. His deeper misgivings showed through the caveats. Didn't Whitehead's claim to empiricism amount to window-dressing? Wasn't his system essentially a castle of abstractions?[25]

For two years Wieman stewed over these questions. Whitehead dealt exclusively with ideas, building one idea out of another, but Wieman believed that ideas should be used as tools of thought, not as ends. His favorite image was that ideas should be torches that light the way, not suns and stars that one venerates as objects of belief. *Process and Reality* was a brilliant work—"the most magnificent achievement of constructive imagination that modern times can show"—but also a "wholly ground-less" feat of speculation. Nothing in it was based on empirical demon-stration: "There is no evidence whatsoever to support it." For example, the theory that God has a consequent nature was pure speculation—true only as a form of imaginative symbolism or mythmaking. The fact that Whitehead did not regard his system as a mythical construct showed the danger of metaphysical abstraction, for the "new metaphysics" simply replaced the dogmatism of classical theism with a new myth, while refus-ing to acknowledge its mythical basis. Wieman said Whitehead's system was "infected with error through and through." It was not empirically based and thus had no means to correct its empirical errors.[26]

This did not mean that Whitehead's system was no better than others from an empirical standpoint. Wieman appreciated that Whitehead did not run ahead of science when he explicated God's primordial nature and that he did not conceive God as a transcendental power working behind the natural process. God's primordial reality is the fact of mutual support within the creative process, the ordering power that presses for harmony and the flourishing of life. The consequent God, however, was another matter. It was not essential to Whitehead's system; Wieman said it was more like a dome and spire. Whitehead added the consequent God because religious feeling asks for it, mostly to deal with the problem of evil. Life requires a process of selection, and selection is both the measure of evil and the means by which evil is evaded. Whitehead explained, "The evil of the world is that those elements which are translucent so far as transmission is concerned, in themselves are of slight weight; and that those elements, with individual weight, by their discord, impose upon vivid immediacy the obligation that it fade into night."[27]

Lacking the consequent God, everything in the universe is destined to silence. All virtue, beauty, and tragedy eventually sink into nothing-ness. Creativity drives on relentlessly, swallowing everything in the fading past. The past is not completely lost, because living things retain parts of the past and growth occurs, but the life process is awesomely destructive and wasteful. The powers of consciousness and value have little force by comparison. So Whitehead added the consequent God: all values are preserved in an everlasting consciousness that grows with the rising and perishing of life. Wieman sympathized, disapproved, and offered an improvement. If Whitehead had to speculate a consequent God, he might have stopped with the fact that values are conserved in life, and to some degree, values grow. In this way, he would not have sailed past the scientific world picture: "But the human heart cries for more, as it views the continuous perishing of so much that is superbly precious. It cries for more and Whitehead yields to the appeal."[28]

Wieman sometimes yielded too, especially when he wrote about prayer and the spiritual life. But mostly he stuck to empirical description and analysis, practicing what he prescribed: track the flow of experience, correct your errors, don't project your ideas and feelings onto God, and discover what God is doing in the world. He welcomed Mathews and Macintosh to this work, but judged that both were prone to personalized projection. From 1927 to 1947 Wieman's voice prevailed at Chicago, and for decades afterward his thought defined one wing of the process school. He remained more deeply Whiteheadian than he acknowledged, retaining Whitehead's ideas that events are the fundamental elements of reality, duration is real and factual, and objects are aspects of events, but in the language of a simpler materialism. The later Wieman described God as the source of human value, but rarely referred to God, explaining that what matters is the growth of value, not what it is called.[29]

By the late 1940s his two most distinguished disciples, Meland and Daniel Day Williams, felt keenly that Wieman's approach was sterile and exhausted. Meland said Wieman lacked any notion of faith as a judgment on reason; Williams pointed to Wieman's simplistic epistemological positivism as the culprit. Bernard Loomer, concurring that Wieman's theology smacked too much of Dewey, instrumentalism, and a laboratory atmosphere, said the Chicago school should have stuck with Whitehead. On these grounds they pulled it toward Whitehead and Hartshorne, contending that Wieman exaggerated Whitehead's deficiencies. Admittedly, Whitehead was not empirical by positivist standards, but neither was Wieman, who focused on relational patterns of events, and neither was James, who pioneered the focus on relational fluidity. Wieman's supposedly stringent empiricism was loaded with philosophical assumptions; only a lapsed Whiteheadian would describe empirical "patterns" of events and their religious meaning in his fashion, theorizing a vision of reality. But he did it with borrowed pieces of something great, Whitehead's full-fledged metaphysic.[30]

Hartshorne and Dipolar Theism

The Whiteheadian turn developed slowly before it occurred swiftly. Williams joined the Chicago Theological Seminary faculty in 1939, and Loomer and Meland joined the Divinity School faculty in 1942 and 1945. Meland earned his doctorate under Smith in 1929, Williams earned master's degrees at Chicago and Chicago Theological Seminary in 1933 and 1934, and Loomer earned his doctorate under Wieman in 1942. The Federation of Theological Schools played a key role in consolidating the Whiteheadians by fusing the Divinity School, Chicago Theological Seminary, Meadville Theological School, and Disciples Divinity House. In 1945 Loomer was appointed dean of the Divinity School, which gave the Whiteheadians further leverage to build a school. Loomer's influence at Chicago was immense. A demanding teacher and intense classroom performer, he specialized in line-by-line readings of *Process and Reality*, and students pored over his unpublished dissertation on Whitehead. Outside the classroom Loomer was charming, informal, and gregarious, renowned for his saucy humor, but he made enemies who found him obnoxious and bullying, all of which entered local lore about the cult of Whitehead.[31]

Hartshorne stood at the center of the Whitehead renaissance, always eager to boost Whitehead's reputation. With characteristic modesty he noted that his favorite philosophers—Plato, Descartes, Leibniz, Whitehead, and Peirce—were mathematicians, and he was not. Hartshorne took over Whitehead's idea that the universe consists of events composed of aesthetic feeling. He stressed that there is no evidence that the universe consists of dead matter or that mind and matter are equally ultimate realities. He believed that physics would eventually grow into an elementary branch of comparative psychology or sociology, and the natural sciences into branches of natural history, once scientists gave up on dead matter. German psychologist Gustav T. Fechner harmed the reputation of panpsychism by claiming that even rocks have souls. Whitehead averted unwelcome company by eschewing the term, but Hartshorne said there was no reason to eschew the correct term. He and Whitehead distinguished between composite units of experience bearing psychic life and mere aggregate entities that do not. Molecules and atoms possess some degree of feeling; rocks do not.[32]

In *Beyond Humanism* (1937) Hartshorne said that Leibniz nearly put philosophy on the right track concerning matter, but he tried to combine panpsychism with determinism and Aristotelian substance, both holdovers from medieval theology. Schopenhauer grasped that every atom contains a germ of psychic life, but his atheism stopped him from recognizing the role of creation in nature and the necessity of an ordering ground; plus, Schopenhauer wrongly denied that intelligence is essential to will. Hartshorne taught that James, Bergson, Alexander, Whitehead, and Albert Einstein were forerunners of a coming transformation of consciousness, and Peirce, the genius of American pragmatism, preceded all of them by distinguishing among feeling-quality, reaction, and meaning as aspects of experience. Yellowness belongs to feeling, conflict belongs to reaction, and awareness belongs chiefly to meaning. To Peirce these categories were psychic because mind is a unity of feeling, striving, and meaning. Hartshorne explained, "The doctrine of sympathy, which Peirce was one of the first to hold, is that all feeling feels other feeling, all reaction has an object which itself is reactive, and all meaning means other meaning, as well as reactions and feelings. Since the three categories exhaust experience, we could have no other predicates with which to clothe objects; and that we have objects at all is due entirely to the sympathetic duality or immanent sociality of experience."[33]

Hartshorne won a respectful hearing in his field, but got his best students at the Divinity School. He took an appointment at the Divinity School in 1943 after his first work of religious philosophy, *Man's Vision of God and the Logic of Theism* (1941), won favorable reviews from theologians. Carving a third way between classical theism and atheistic humanism, Hartshorne argued that theism conceives God as absolutely perfect and unsurpassable, atheism denies that any being is perfect or unsurpassable, and the best alternative is absolute *and* relative *and* panentheist. God is perfect in some respects and not in others, unsurpassable by others, and surpassable by Godself. Hartshorne resisted the choice between limiting God's power and limiting God's goodness, countering that divinity means the sharing of suffering, not the privilege of escaping it. "God is love" is the most important thing ever said about God, notwithstanding that theologians rarely said so.[34]

Hartshorne criticized wobbly aspects of Whitehead's system, but embraced what he called the role of "a warm partisan." Much like Brightman toward Bowne, Hartshorne admired Whitehead, clarified muddled aspects of his thought, and revised key aspects of his system. Unlike Whiteheadian philosophers William Christian and Victor Lowe, Hartshorne did not fix on establishing the correct interpretation of Whitehead. He took Whitehead's system as the point of departure for his own philosophy, not for settling debates about Whitehead's meaning. Sometimes he was too modest: "My primary aim has always been to arrive at truth through Whitehead, or to make truth accessible to others through him, more than to ascertain or communicate the truth about Whitehead." Sometimes he acknowledged that his vocation was to teach the ideas of Peirce, Whitehead, and himself. Hartshorne's kindly generosity and his close identification with Whitehead made it difficult for many readers, even his students, to recognize his originality.[35]

He was more rationalistic than Whitehead, his rationalism deepened in his later career, and he disagreed with Whitehead about eternal objects and the nature of divine reality. Whitehead's eternal objects served as potentialities for actual entities, supplying to each experience its subjective aim. Hartshorne accepted only select aspects of this idea because it smacked too much of Platonic forms. He allowed that a mathematical object such as Planck's constant might qualify as an eternal object, accepted that human beings prehend that God possesses eternal ideas, and accepted that this prehensive grasping allows human subjects to grasp the ideas. He objected that the idea of creative process is more coherent without a realist theory of universals, and that Whitehead failed to explain which ideas are eternal in God and which are acquired by God or human beings through the creative process. Moreover, Whitehead begged the question whether the object "red" must be conceived as being absolutely independent from "yesterday" or "today" in all possible stages of cosmic development. With Peirce, Hartshorne believed that only extremely general abstractions such as "quality" are timeless or eternal in their relevance. Overall, Whitehead's doctrine of eternal objects was a subset of his theory of mental prehension, and both were too Platonist.[36]

More important, Hartshorne rejected Whitehead's idea that God is an actual entity whose being is always in process of becoming through God's consequent experience of the world. Whitehead's description of the laws of process conflicted with his claim that God influences the world through God's everlasting coming-into-being. If God is an always-becoming concrescence, and actual occasions must perish before they can be prehended by subsequent occasions, how does God act in the world? In *Process and Reality*, Whitehead said that data are available only after the internal existence of the entity has vanished. Whiteheadian philosopher A. H. Johnson asked Whitehead in 1936 how it is possible for God to provide data for other entities if God never perishes. Whitehead replied that this was "a genuine problem" he had not attempted to solve.[37]

Hartshorne's solution personalized Whitehead's God and dropped Whitehead's idea of God as an everlasting concrescence. God, he argued, is a personal society of divine occasions. Each of the divine occasions unifies the present moment and is prehended by succeeding occasions. Sometimes Hartshorne said he merely clarified Whitehead's muddled idea of God, correcting Whitehead's actual entity description, which made God analogous to a momentary experience of an individual. Since Whitehead's God was not a succession of deities, and Whitehead's actual entities did not change (they merely became), and Whitehead's God did change with the acquisition of new prehensions, Hartshorne judged that Whitehead could not have meant that God is like a single member of a sequence of actualities. Whiteheadian theism makes sense, even on Whitehead's terms, only if God is conceived as a society of actualities. Whitehead's God was vaguely impersonal and not clearly active in the world. Hartshorne developed his dipolar concept of God, which he later called dual transcendence, to defend Whitehead's distinction between the primordial and consequent natures of God. Eventually it became the centerpiece of Hartshorne's position—a full-fledged theory of dipolarity combining his opposition to mere abstract eternality and mere concrete temporality, which also combined his opposition to abstract theistic absolutism and mechanistic materialism.[38]

Classical theism conceptualized divine reality as eternal, not temporal; active, never passive; wholly actual, never potential; necessary, not contingent; independent, never dependent; spiritual, not material; simple, not a compound; absolute, not relative to anything; causative, not effected by causes; and impassable, not affected by human feelings. Augustine, Aquinas, Calvin, and Leibniz took for granted these attributes and their negations. In *The Divine Relativity* (1948), Hartshorne countered that God orders the universe by taking into God's life all existing currents of feeling. God is irresistibly influential because God is distinctly open to influence. Why should God be less divine if God is acted upon by the world, subject to change, and truly personal? Hartshorne called for a decision against Greek eternalism and classic renderings of Genesis. A God that really has social relations and is constituted by relationships would be relative and personal: "Just as giving up what is metaphorical in 'substance' or in 'cause' does not mean giving up the human person, or the essential interconnectedness of the process, so it need not, and I think could not, mean giving up the divine person and the divine influence promotive of a measure of world order."[39]

Hartshorne believed that theology needed to wring as much as possible out of empiricism, and he respected Mathews, Macintosh, and Wieman for creating an empirical theology. He especially admired Macintosh, "a rare combination of intellectual integrity and generosity toward the thought of others." But religious truths, he argued, are fundamentally metaphysical, not empirical. Truth statements about God belong to metaphysics, not to empirical science. If God is the measure of all actual and possible truth, divinity is not a mere fact or a mere symbol. God is a necessary reality of a metaphysical kind.[40]

American logician Morris R. Cohen argued that the law of contradiction does not preclude the existence of contrary determinations in an entity. There is such a thing as a "necessary co-presence and mutual dependence of opposite determinations," which Cohen called the "law of polarity." Logical coherence requires only a distinction of aspects between polarities, such as physicists managed in conceiving light as corpuscular and a set of waves. Hartshorne applied Cohen's polar principle to the relation of absolute and relative. Categories such as simplicity, being, and actuality have no reality except in correlation with complexity, becoming, and potentiality. As usual he cited forerunners, notably Plato, Heraclitus, Schelling, Fechner, Peirce, Whitehead, James, Brightman, Nicholas Berdyaev, Martin Buber, and Radhakrishnan. Hartshorne reasoned that God is like an individual person in possessing an individual essence and a collection of accidents. That which is in God is not always in God's essence. God's being contains non-ultimate forms of being, but they are contained as accidents and never as wholes, like a large building containing small parts. In God's being, each pole and its categorical contrary contains a supreme case, such as an actuality that includes all actuality, or a potentiality that includes all potentiality.[41]

This was the core idea of divine polarity: God is a supreme being whose being contains both the supreme unity and the supreme diversity, the supreme cause and the supreme effect, the supreme actuality and the supreme potentiality. Hartshorne accepted the classical equation of God with being as such, for God's essence is to exist. God cannot be without existence, and existence cannot be without God. But God's becoming is not negated by, or inferior to, God's being. Other beings, Hartshorne acknowledged, are contingent products of becoming, but "we should think of God as qualifying becoming essentially." In God, being and becoming inhere in a single reality; God is the supreme being whose being is inherently in process. God has no beginning, which would be a process independent of God, and no end, for God is the power of being within process as such. Hartshorne denied that God's necessary existence is contradicted by the affirmation that God experiences change. On the dipolar model, necessary existence is the unlimited capacity to adjust, not something that precludes needing to adjust. Theism has only bad choices if contingency is inferior to necessity, or potentiality and actuality are mutually exclusive. Dipolar thinking offers deliverance from bad choices by affirming that God's being contains all contrasts *and* that only the ultimate polarities inhere in God's essential character.[42]

The latter principle was crucial; otherwise God's being would include evil. Hartshorne reasoned that moral evil is not an ultimate or universal category—animals are not capable of moral evil—and moral wickedness is not in God's essential character. On the other hand, evil in the sense of suffering is an ultimate category; thus, God contains suffering, and God suffers. Hartshorne insisted that his few words about sin and evil said just enough about both subjects, and he left it to theologians to go on about God's suffering; Berdyaev was his favorite on the latter subject. Hartshorne's subject was the nature of divine reality. Five questions were essential to him: Is God eternal? Is God temporal? Is God self-aware? Does God know the world? Does God include the world?

Hartshorne categorized religious thinkers on this fivefold grid. Plotinus and Wieman were one-factor thinkers, as Plotinus described divine reality as the eternal beyond consciousness and knowledge, and Wieman said yes to temporality. Aristotle propounded a two-factor doctrine, describing divine reality as eternal consciousness, and Alexander espoused a conditional three-factor doctrine, describing divine reality as wholly temporal but emergently conscious and knowing the world. Classical theism is a three-factor doctrine: God is eternal, self-aware, and knows the world. Spinoza and Royce affirmed four factors: divine reality is eternal, conscious, knows the world, and includes the world so far as the world is affirmed as real.[43]

This scheme was geared to demonstrate that modern panentheism offers the most inclusive, robust, and affirmative doctrine of God. Hartshorne rendered James and Brightman as limited panentheists for describing divine reality—sometimes with dipolar logic—as eternal, temporal, conscious, and partly exclusive of the world. James never considered that divine experience could be both inclusive and distinctive, while Brightman qualified God's inclusiveness to preserve God's individuality. Hartshorne said full-fledged panentheism is a better idea, because it applies dipolar logic to all the categories, affirming that God is eternal, temporal, conscious, knows the world, and includes the world. God grows in perfection while representing the absolute maximum of perfection that is possible at any given time. God is not merely the totality of concrete actualizations, as in Whitehead's doctrine of the consequent nature. God is the *personal order* of the sequence of concrete actualizations. Hartshorne's theological followers pressed hard on the difference, but he left theology to them, concentrating on the logic of perfection and the ontological proof of God's existence.[44]

Hartshorne was emphatic that metaphysical arguments merely demonstrate God's existence. Metaphysics has nothing to say about God's concrete actuality at any given moment. God's existence is necessary, and is therefore logically provable, but God's actuality is contingent, and therefore must be known, as far as possible, through science and personal experience. Religion is about the love of God known concretely, and experience is the source of our knowledge of God. Hartshorne could laugh at the limits of metaphysical reason and himself. His absentmindedness was legendary; sometimes he had to ask people which way he had been walking in order to figure out whether he had already eaten lunch or taught a class. Ontologically, Hartshorne was a panexperiential idealist, but epistemologically he was a realist who, like Whitehead, claimed to fit his philosophy to empirical evidence.

His Chicago theological protégés, notably Loomer, John B. Cobb Jr., and Schubert Ogden, drew confidence from Hartshorne's rationalism, finding it an antidote to fashionable theologies of the time. Another protégé, Daniel Day Williams, though closer to Hartshorne personally, was more ambivalent about his legacy. On the one hand, Williams lauded Hartshorne extravagantly for demonstrating the superiority of dipolar panentheism. On the other hand, Williams worried that Hartshorne set off a gusher of hyperrationalism that overidentified process theology with scholastic arguments. Having rebelled against Wieman's cold empiricism in his early career, Williams was wary of trading one scholastic mentality for another. He said process theology needed to blend metaphysical panentheism with a robust experiential theology speaking the language of love, faithfulness, and hope. In 1954, two years into a book manuscript that exemplified his prescription, Williams succeeded Tillich at Union Theological Seminary. Very late in his career, in 1968, it was finally published, *The Spirit and the Forms of Love*. By then the next generation had surged ahead, conceiving process theology as an emphatically scholastic enterprise. Williams and Meland were forerunners of another kind of process theology, but Meland surpassed his friend in making the case.[45]

Bernard E. Meland: Mystical Naturalism and the New Metaphysics

For thirty years Mathews was the representative Chicago theologian. He served as dean of the Divinity School for twenty-five years, played leadership roles in the Northern Baptist church and the Federal Council of Churches, and buoyantly embraced the public responsibilities of a movement figure. Meland, the next person to exemplify the Chicago school in such a comprehensive fashion, was a private figure by comparison, brooding and reflective. He joined Hartshorne, Loomer, and Williams in espousing the new metaphysics, but did so in ways that linked him to Mathews, Smith, and Wieman. He was a product of the first generation as a protégé of Mathews and Smith. He boosted Wieman's status in the second generation by forming a partnership with him. In his later career, Meland spoke for generation three, and pointed beyond it. He was capable of writing direct, clear, even snappy sentences, especially when he wrote on socio-ethical subjects. But Meland wrote mostly in a murky, ruminating, elusive style that his colleague, theologian Joseph Sittler, aptly likened to a fog-producing mist.[46]

He was born in 1899 in Pullman, Illinois, a Chicago suburb near the Pullman Car Works, where his father worked as a cabinetmaker and inside finisher of Pullman railroad cars. Meland's parents emigrated to the United States from Norway in their youth, with little schooling; Meland later emphasized that they did not represent the stereotypical immigrant story of finding greater opportunity in America: "My father really stepped backward in the economic and social scale when he arrived in this country." Struggling against privation and illness, "we were people on the margin. By the severest kind of economy we could manage to keep out of debt for a time, but the worker's pay in those days was meager in comparison with costs."[47]

Two youthful influences contributed to Meland's reflective, aesthetic, mystically tinged personality. The first was the "quiet love of nature" that he developed while laboring on farms: "It was a companion to me—this vast expanse of earth." The second was his family's Lutheran heritage. Though Meland went along with his family's conversion to Presbyterianism in 1910, he believed his early Lutheranism made an imprint on him. Religiously, he never stopped feeling at home in Lutheran sacramentalism, "despite all the intellectual somersaulting I have gone through." He had similar feelings about his working-class background, which made him averse to middle-class Protestantism.[48]

For several years after high school Meland worked at clerical jobs and flirted with becoming a forest ranger. In 1920 he enrolled at Park College and tried to retain the evangelical near-fundamentalism in which he had been raised. In 1923 he graduated from college, now espousing the social gospel, and still considering forest conservation. Meland read books by Rauschenbusch and Mathews, caught the anti-war fervor of the mid-1920s social gospel, and became a social gospel progressive. He enrolled at McCormick Theological Seminary and joined the Presbyterian youth movement, giving speeches on "War Is Sin" and "Toward a Christian Social Order." Later he recalled, "We were out to save the world and to remake the church. Naturally I had frequent occasions to proclaim my cause and to decry the state of things." He met Reinhold Niebuhr, then in his pacifist social gospel phase, and gained the reputation of a spellbinder: "As a boy orator, I wowed them!"[49]

But Meland soon wearied of movement activism. He worried that his "seige of barnstorming" was rhetorically overheated and half educated; later he called it "the effervescence of a superficial mind." He didn't like thinking of himself as a shallow exhibitionist. If he was going to be a liberal, why did he have to be a revival version of one? Reading James and Royce, Meland began to imagine himself as an intellectual. Royce's *Religious Aspect of Philosophy* made a strong impression, and in 1925 Meland transferred to the University of Chicago Divinity School, where he was chagrined to discover that he had the wrong intellectual hero; the Chicago pragmatists looked down on Royce. More embarrassment ensued. Meland swelled with pride and delight when Mathews greeted him warmly—"Meland, I like what you're doing!" Then he realized that Mathews was speaking of his barnstorming. Meland was too embarrassed to tell the dean he had enrolled at the Divinity School to get off the activist circuit. Determined to reinvent himself, he devoured stacks of books, treated the Divinity School as his monastery, and reveled in the Gothic seclusion of Swift Hall. Later he allowed that he might have overreacted to movement shallowness. Meland took five courses from Mathews, never quite fathoming his enthusiasm for sociology, and eleven courses from Smith, who was in crisis.[50]

Smith was ambitious, fiercely honest, skilled at critical analysis, and disillusioned. He took a nature-mystical turn in reaction to disillusion, which Meland welcomed, feeling overdosed on sociology from Mathews. Meland cherished Smith's critical acumen, and worried that Smith was troubled: "Something that he could not communicate, or that he would not do so, seemed to hover about, giving an overtone of sadness to whatever conclusions he might come." Smith seemed to yearn for the evangelical liberalism of his seminary days, or an alternative to it. In the late-1920s he pondered a fusion of naturalistic mysticism and Wieman's objectivism, taking a fatherly interest in Wieman. At the same time, Meland mediated Wieman's awkward relationships with senior faculty. Smith did not dispute Wieman's judgment that the Chicago school was floundering, and he confirmed Meland's sense that it lacked religious feeling. When Meland won a fellowship to Marburg in 1928, Smith encouraged him to study under Frederick Heiler and Rudolf Otto.[51]

Mathews and Wieman cautioned Meland that Otto's mysticism was out of control, but Meland was deeply impressed by Otto: "Here was a presence. The great *Das Heilige* was all that you had expected him to be." Heiler, a Lutheran convert from Roman Catholicism, taught Meland that worship and prayer are central concerns of theological study. Otto stressed the religious importance of silence and the parallels between Eastern and Western mysticism, teaching that the object of religion is transmoral and transrational. To Meland, the mystically oriented liberalism of Otto and Heiler was about real things, while the Barthian ascendancy seemed a reactionary throwback, a bantering of words from another century. Meland could not imagine taking the Barthians seriously. The liberal tradition remained full of promise, and it had no competitors. He later recalled that at the time he was "fixed and complacent . . . in the grooves of an unreconstructed liberalism."[52]

But Meland puzzled over the conflicting agendas of his Chicago teachers. Mathews claimed that he and Wieman took the same approach to theology and the entire Chicago school was conceptualist. Meland realized that both claims were wrong. The differences between Mathews' emphasis on imaginative conceptualization and Wieman's realism were far-reaching. Mathews and Ames conceived God in social scientific categories as the idealization of social values; Wieman said God is either really something or nothing worth bothering about; Smith wavered between these views without committing himself. Smith did not affirm or deny that God is cosmically real, and he worried that every Chicago theologian shortchanged spiritual experience. Meland felt closest to Smith, at the time and later. Meland's early theology was conceptualist in the mode of Mathews and Ames, but in the 1930s he was widely viewed as a Wieman protégé, and he viewed himself as an advocate of Smith's mystically tinged naturalism. While studying in Germany, shortly before he returned to Chicago in 1929 to take his doctoral exams, Meland received a telegram from Mathews offering a teaching position at Central College in Fayette, Missouri. Upon returning to Chicago, Meland learned that Smith had died. Losing Smith cut Meland deeply, causing him to regard his own work as the continuation of his teacher's.[53]

Meland taught at Central College, a Southern Methodist school, for seven years, ignoring annual appointment controversies over his orthodoxy that absorbed college trustees and the local Methodist conference. As a doctoral student he had waded more than he liked in the shallow waters of pragmatism and social science; as a young academic he turned to poetry, literature, art, and philosophy, giving himself to mystical and aesthetic values "of which the pragmatic faith is unaware." Meland later recalled that these pursuits carried him "more and more into [a] profounder orientation of religion, more mystical in quality, more sensitive and wistful before ideas that reach us through Christian tradition." Ironically, his alliance with Wieman began during this period. Meland had overlapped with Wieman only long enough to take one course with him, but he liked Wieman's colorful rhetoric of "concrete abundance," "undefined awareness," and "rich fullness," and he was grateful to Wieman for helping him complete his doctorate.[54]

From the beginning there were key differences between them. Wieman disliked Meland's mystical aestheticism, and Meland disliked Wieman's cold behaviorism, imploring Wieman to express his mystical impulse. Meland judged that liberal Protestantism was spiritually weak, especially at worship, because it harbored an anti-mythical prejudice. Vital religion requires ritual, and ritual is essentially dramatized myth. But Protestantism lacked the crucial element of devotional drama. Meland invoked Otto's cardinal rule: religion is about the experience of the holy. A religion that cannot dramatize its myth cannot sustain itself as a living faith. Otto and Tillich were right about that: to renew itself spiritually, liberal Protestantism had to rethink one of its deepest prejudices.[55]

On divine reality, however, Meland knew only two credible options: Mathews/Ames conceptualism and Wieman objectivism. He worried that both were spiritually cold. The former construed God as a conceptual symbol and the latter construed God as a singular "Something." The conceptual option was colder, yet Meland favored it because Wieman's monism seemed impossibly simplistic to him. Meland reasoned that God is a vast and unfathomably complex community of activities that cannot be known as a singular concrete anything. Even if the pluralistic elements of life are construed as harmonious, reality "gives the effect of a *community of activities*, rather than a single behavior." To isolate God's nature as any single datum is to distort the diversity of empirical evidence of divine reality, as James argued in *The Varieties of Religious Experience*. God is a single object of thought only for the imagination, not for experimental science.[56]

In 1934 Meland and Wieman coauthored a book, *American Philosophies of Religion*, published two years later. The experience confirmed to Meland that he and Wieman were moving in opposite directions, but in one respect it strengthened Wieman's influence over him. Wieman convinced Meland that his position was the simplistic one because it did not account for the reality of unifications. Unities are corporate actualities, Wieman argued, not simply works of the imagination. Like the early Chicago school, Meland still conceived relations and structures in Kantian terms as functions of the mind. Wieman convinced him to take seriously the later James' idea of experienced relations and Whitehead's idea of the structure of events: relations and structures are real, factual data in experience, not merely functions of mind. They are given realities to be described, not merely imagined.

Meland turned a corner upon absorbing the difference. He began to speak of the Whiteheadian "creative factor" in the universe as the "Creative Order," his favorite God-term, though Meland coined several others. Creative Order signified a non-supernatural but "more-than-human" creative reality that includes human beings and extends beyond their efforts. Meland adopted Whitehead's language about the "weaving" of God's (consequent) physical feelings upon God's (primordial) concepts: the Creative Order weaves and shapes all existence toward "a richer integration of activity," growing "toward increasing organic unity." Years later, Meland rued the irony that Wieman converted him to radical empiricism just before Wieman lapsed into a neo-Kantian instrumentalism.[57]

American Philosophies of Religion was published just as Meland joined the faculty of Pomona College in Claremont, California. The book distinguished between two kinds of supernaturalism (traditional and neo-supernatural), three kinds of idealism (absolute, mystical, and personal), three kinds of romanticism (philosophical-ethical intuitionist, theological-ethical intuitionist, and aesthetic naturalist), and four kinds of naturalism (evolutionary theist, cosmic theist, religious humanist, and empirical theist). Wieman and Meland classified Tillich and Niebuhr as neo-supernaturalists; Royce and Hocking as absolutist idealists; Rufus Jones as a mystical idealist; Bowne and Brightman as personalists; Macintosh and Eugene Lyman as philosophical intuitionists; William Adams Brown, Walter Marshall Horton, Henry P. Van Dusen, and John C. Bennett as theological intuitionists; John E. Boodin and (young) Robert L. Calhoun as evolutionary theists; Whitehead and F. S. C. Northrop as cosmic theists; Max C. Otto, Roy W. Sellars, A. Eustace Haydon, and Walter Lippmann as religious humanists; and Ames, Dewey, Mathews, Smith, Meland, and Wieman as empirical theists.

The progress motif was built into the book's structure, beginning with traditional supernaturalism, moving progressively through idealism, romanticism, and naturalism, and culminating with the empirical theist version of religious naturalism, which unfolded in almost-alphabetical order with Ames and Dewey (humanistic theism), Mathews (conceptual theism), Smith and Meland (mystical naturalism), and Wieman (naturalistic theism). Meland wrote the culminating chapter, listing himself alongside Smith, but did not describe his own contribution to mystical naturalism. Basically he conveyed his own thought through Smith, explaining that if Smith had lived to develop his position, he would have said that human beings are at home in the universe, which contains a Creative Order that sustains and promotes life.[58]

Meland defended Wieman from two kinds of criticism. Humanists charged that Wieman was a closet humanist who gave the name "God" to select human functions; traditional theists charged that Wieman reduced God to an impersonal process; Meland's defense of Wieman on these points was also a self-defense. But Meland's misgivings about Wieman's position were already gnawing at him. Though Meland described himself as a mystical naturalist, Wieman wanted to lump him with various "aesthetes in religion." This title offended Meland: "I made no apologies for my aesthetic interests and inclinations, but to be called an *aesthete in religion* was enough to arouse my fighting, Nordic blood."[59]

At Pomona College he taught history and philosophy of religion, deepening and broadening his aesthetic and cultural interests. Meland read widely in cultural anthropology and puzzled over the religious "what" that links psychology of religion, philosophy of religion, sociology of religion, and theology. Each discipline describes religion in its own image. Sociology describes religion as a phenomenon of group spirit; philosophy of religion describes it as a pre-philosophical response to perennial truth questions; psychology of religion describes it as therapeutic compensation or neurosis. Meland reasoned that if religion exists, there must be something more fundamental to it than these descriptions. Human consciousness is a novel structure that transcends physiological and psychical structures. But is religion an elemental human function? Is the religious response as constitutive to human being as breathing?[60]

Meland labored on a book manuscript that said yes, arguing that religion is about the human impulse to cherish and sustain life. Religion, "attachment to life," is an essential psychical condition of the human organism. Meland had the same problem in writing this book that John Cobb experienced a generation later; having been trained narrowly in Chicago school modernism, he lacked the languages, historical training, and scholarly breadth to range outside it. Meland also realized his focus on appreciative consciousness might reflect merely a Western way of thinking about religion. He did not claim to find the essence of all religions; it was enough to say that "attachment to life" is a clue to understanding human beings in diverse cultural contexts. Religion, he proposed, is essentially aspirational outreach—the various affections, commitments, and experiences of faith and hope constituting the religious response. Meland never finished the manuscript, but its arguments pervaded his subsequent work.[61]

His reading and reflection on the appreciative consciousness gave him a new sense of integration: "It was as if a consciousness not my own had impelled me in various directions in preparation for a fuller grasp of the problem at which I was working. Quite involuntarily the words seemed to form in my mind, 'I have found my voice!'" Now he realized why James, Bergson, Whitehead, and Wieman spoke to him. It began with the worldview issue and moved to something more. To Plato the changing character of the world of experience was evidence of its unreality. Ideas are real because they do not change; God is an intermediary being who rescued the rational souls of human beings from the world of flux. Rationalist consciousness began with Aristotle, who removed the stigma of unreality from the world of experience, but kept the static worldview. Aristotle identified God with Plato's Supreme Good and theorized a mathematical concept of universal order. Western thought was variously Platonist or Aristotelian until modern philosophy finally questioned its static assumptions. Kant was a breakthrough figure, theorizing the powers of mind and the moral consciousness, until James came along;

Meland routinely shortchanged Schelling and Hegel. Hegelian unfolding never happened, or somehow didn't matter, to judge from Meland and his Chicago teachers. According to Meland it was James and Bergson who dismantled the idea of a static order, conceiving the world process as fundamentally creative, which broke the hegemony of Aristotelian rationalism and Kantian idealism. Meland's "something more" was appreciative consciousness—the living reality on which the new worldview rested.[62]

In the new metaphysics, the keywords were interaction, creativity, adjustment, flux of experience, and empirical reality. To the appreciative consciousness, Meland said, God is a reality within the world process, and human beings seek fulfillment in it. Meland seized on Whitehead's claim that the new metaphysics began in 1904, when James argued that "consciousness" refers to a function, not an entity. The key to the new metaphysics was its focus on process, which Meland described as "the story of *emergents* and *transitions* and *fulfilments*." Whatever spiritual meaning there may be in life must be found in and through the material world. The language of consciousness, though differently construed than in the Kantian tradition, was still indispensable to it: "The tendency to shunt off metaphysical problems, so evident in pragmatism and humanism, has given way in Wieman's thought to a fresh and forthright empirical approach to the whole of objective reality as it impinges upon man's world." This was Meland's point of departure. For twenty years Meland avoided taking sides between Wieman and Whitehead, touting the superiority of the new metaphysics while pleading for the right to be imprecise in his formulations.[63]

The right to be vague became an important principle to him, for Jamesian reasons, as a point of difference from Wieman, and as a fact about the condition of liberal theology. Meland said it was no longer possible for a liberal theologian to write as clearly and luminously as William Newton Clarke did in *An Outline of Christian Theology* (1899): "What William Newton Clarke and others of his day possessed as a guiding principle in theology we, today, lack. The extreme straining of our thinking, the perplexed look upon our faces as we grope through the dark of our minds for sure ideas, not to mention the troubled look of our listeners, is evidence enough that the central light is not there. Here and there sure voices speak out boldly as if this light had come to them; but the divergence of views, and their speaking to substantiate them, betray the uncertainty of their vision." In Clarke's time, idealism ruled in philosophy, the conflicts between spirit and matter appeared to be resolved, theology made its peace with evolutionary theory, historical criticism was presumed to be friendly to liberal theology, and Ritschlian theology spurned metaphysical speculation and mysticism: "Thus there arose a period of clarification in Christian thought which has hardly been equaled before or since."[64]

Certainly not since; Meland observed in 1943: "Our time has been the complete revocation of this simplified worldview." Relativity theory revolutionized physics; empiricism seemed too simplistic; metaphysics and mysticism made comebacks; gestalt psychology expanded psychology's object; and two world wars crushed the optimism of the social gospel, sending "the concept of *progress* spinning through space, a guiding star of another day, fallen and devoid of light." Meland believed he possessed the key to the next phase of theological reconstruction: "That *God is the Creativity*, shaping our future." Creativity is forward-looking and forward reaching, and every human life is a channel of it.[65]

He won the theology chair at Chicago in 1945 shortly after Loomer became dean, highly self-conscious of the situation in liberal theology. Meland treasured liberal theology for bridging the chasm between supernaturalism and naturalism, and he loved the old liberals, regularly teaching courses about them: "There is something glorious about the theological era stretching from the time of Horace Bushnell to the closing years of Walter Rauschenbusch." The social gospel liberals saved Christianity by harmonizing it with science and modern society; however, they did not make Christian thinking integral with modern thought. Meland said he felt the difference constantly in Mathews' classroom—the tension between Mathews' gospel faith and his modernism. Somehow the two sources of his thought never fused together.[66]

The old liberal goal of integrating Christianity with the best of modern knowledge was still right, but no one had done it. Good theology, Meland argued, takes seriously the import of human emergence as a limiting condition of consciousness and a means of transcendence. Modern theology needed to go beyond liberalism, but the way beyond it was *through* its defining resolve to integrate Christianity and modern experience, not by reverting to supernatural revelation—the make-believe throwback of every version of neo-orthodoxy.[67]

This was an argument for third-generation Chicago school reconstruction. Meland spent the rest of his career pursuing it, but never quite in the way he proposed, because the war changed him. The deaths of former students weighed heavily on him, Hiroshima and Nagasaki repulsed him, and Meland was horrified by we-win celebrations. Instead of calling for repentance or the hanging of bomb makers, he observed, triumphal preachers lifted their voices "in praise of these miracle workers who could bring the war to a close in one fell swoop—or, should we say, two!" It disgusted Meland that church religion exploited the moment: "Imagine! This is where we, who are religious leaders, come in! Now our entrance has every possibility of being pathetic. We have some age-old phrases saved up for just such a time as this. And we are not averse to engaging in mumbo-jumbo if we can be on parade."[68]

Meland pondered what it would take to regain a spiritual culture, now that America had given itself to the lust for wealth and dominance. He implored churches to stand against commercialism and imperialism, renewing the habits of contemplative thought and practice. Religion, to be religious, has to nurture imagination and creativity, but American religion was overwhelmingly literalistic, destroying imagination. Meland lamented that even his favorite theological tradition was literalistic. Liberal empiricism got rid of metaphysics and mysticism, reducing religion to ethical awareness, and historical criticism reduced the Bible to oral and literary fragments. In *Seeds of Redemption* (1947), Meland said theology needed to recreate the imaginative capacities, perceiving the truth spoken in biblical myth.[69]

Seeds of Redemption marked a shift of emphasis from mystic naturalism to a chastened post-liberalism that puzzled over the problem of faith and reinterpreted Christian symbols. Meland reflected that the great social gospel liberals were eminently sane. Clarke, Mathews, and even Rauschenbusch winced at displays of strong feeling, seeking to make Christianity respectable. Liberals erred in straining out the paradoxes of biblical faith and hope, though Meland lamented that Kierkegaardian dialectics came into theology via Barth, a thinker entranced by dogma. Whatever the neo-orthodox theologians got right, all retreated to authority religion; Meland said the same thing was true of Catholic neo-Thomism. American Christianity and society needed the same thing, to fulfill the promise of America's spiritual culture. The spirit of a culture is in its living hopes and aspirations. In America it was the pulsating life of an active nation and its wealth of diverse voices "singing of America's dream." Meland wrote very little about racism, except to say it was America's greatest evil and had to be rooted out of American culture, otherwise America was lost.[70]

Declaiming in prophetic mode was hard for him, and his later books reverted to foggy theology. In 1949 Meland belatedly settled the question of his relationship to Wieman and Whitehead. As always he began with the crisis of liberal theology, stressing that Niebuhr became famous and many others won tenure by ridiculing it. Meland yearned for the days when theologians did not sneer at liberal idealism, humanism, and modernism. He scrounged for a hopeful word in *The Reawakening of Faith* (1949), for the first time clearly choosing Whitehead over Wieman. Meland said Whitehead compared to Augustine and Thomas Aquinas for reorienting Christian thought. Whitehead showed that experience is continuous and the meanings of the past persist in emergent events. Christian faith, on this telling, is the inheritance of Christian insights upon experience that persist into the presently emerging culture.[71]

Meland charged that Wieman epitomized the faults of modernism, being prejudiced against the past and consumed with a narrow rationalism. Thus his work was spiritually deflating. The great religious thinkers struggle with the problem of faith, but Wieman took little interest in faith. His instrumental empiricism had no feeling for religious feeling, and Wieman had little tolerance for the Jamesian fringe of conscious awareness. James taught that good empiricism tolerates a certain vagueness of thought in exploring the subtleties of relation. To Meland, this was the crucial difference between James and Dewey, and Wieman unfortunately sided with Dewey.[72]

Meland knew that his work was elusive and prone to musing. During his student days, upon deciding to leave the Presbyterian youth movement, he spoke with movement leader Stanley High, who tried to dissuade him. High said that philosophy and theology retreated into ambiguity, but "what we need is clarification and communication." Years later Meland reflected that High pursued a rewarding career as an ecumenical leader and communicator, "while I have submerged myself in philosophy and theology and am becoming more and more ambiguous and incommunicable." He tried to write constructive theology and a history of American liberal theology, but got blocked, musing, "There is too much of the subjectivist speaking in me. Or, to put it differently, the inner landscape of memory and brooding, with its coloring and circuitous paths, make too great a claim upon me to permit a propositional faith."[73]

Meland greatly disliked what he called "the cultic tone" of the Whiteheadian school that surrounded Loomer and Hartshorne at Chicago. It seemed to him that Loomer, Hartshorne, and their doctoral students magnified Whitehead's least attractive characteristic, his overreaching scholasticism. It should be enough, Meland believed, to say that events are primary, there is a "matrix of sensitivity" out of which all events emerge, reality is social, relations are dynamic, and the interaction of structures (emergence) makes for a progression from lower to higher complexes of events. Theologically, if the structure of experience is a living complex of relations and meanings, faith is a social energy. Meland turned to cultural anthropology to explain what that meant: "In any culture, long before there are explicit attitudes of faith assuming theological refinement, there is a fabric of inexpressible meaning in living which provides a depth of incentive and of uncanny commitment to the ultimate ground of one's being and destiny."[74]

This was the root of his insistence that liberal theology had to rethink its prejudice against myth. Tillich and Niebuhr, building on Bergson's distinction between conceptual knowledge and intuition, described myth as a mode of discourse expressing dimensions of experience that cannot be expressed in another way. Meland supplemented Tillich and Niebuhr with cultural anthropology, arguing that myths express a matrix of feeling that is the source of every culture's poetry, song, art, and religious ritual. Myth is the creative drama of spiritual meaning. Culture is the bearer of the movement of Creative Passage within experience. Neo-orthodoxy, though essentially backward, was right to insist that myth is a vehicle of God's Word. Liberal theology, though right to disavow authority religion, was wrong to whittle down the Christian myth to fragments of the Christian ethos. The latter fault, Meland said, was killing liberal Christianity—a tragedy for Western culture.[75]

It started with Schleiermacher, whose focus on spiritual feeling threw out speculative ideas. Every liberal theology afterward was a whittling strategy. The Ritschlian school banked on strategic neo-Kantianism and historicist social religion, and the Chicago school completed the secularizing thrust of the Ritschlian school. Meland declared, "The liberal church has a theological task on its hands which amounts to a major reconstructive effort. It has delayed this task too long. By persisting in the same course it has become the foil of reactionary thought and, within its own ranks, has steadily lost prophetic power. The reconstruction must go deeper than a reappraisal of premises. Its feeling orientation must change radically to accord with the feeling context of all vital existence today and of creative meaning in our time."[76]

Meland could imagine a liberal Christianity that emphasized the mythic symbolism of the Christian narrative of sin, repentance, forgiveness, and redemption without lapsing into neo-supernaturalism. At least, he had an idea of it. Rightly understood, faith is aligned with the myth-ical consciousness as a form of psychical energy. Instead of abandoning the myth to conservatives, "the liberal is called upon to bring the art and literature of an informed imagination, the philosophic acumen of the liberated mind, and the ethically awakened conscience into the service of extending this Christian criticism of man's life into the whole of culture." Meland took from Barth and Kierkegaard the theme that Spirit cannot be sought and is never achieved, while lamenting that Barth had no artistic sense of this spiritual truth. We experience the transcendent good in all occasions of repentance, forgiveness, and love. Once "an intrusion of spirit" occurs, it changes the matrix of thought and feeling.[77]

This was Meland's baseline. Salvation is the renewal of creative good in human subjects. It is the same process of symbolization as the indi-vidual's process of maturation, except at a deeper level of personal con-sciousness "feeding at the level of spirit." To be saved is to be opened to the creative working of spirit through commitment to the good that Christ personifies. Meland was very short on belief-statements about God and Christ, but he affirmed that God is a temporal structure "of infinite goodness and incalculable power," divine reality is evidenced by acts of redemption, forgiveness, and love, and Christ is the revealer of God and mediator of God's redeeming work. Christ, Meland argued, is more than a memory to individual Christians; he is *the* mythic figure of the West, "the persisting structure of sensitive meaning which works at the level of cultural institutions and creative effort, pointing men to the real energy of grace in their midst."[78]

Meland had a strong sense of cultural decline. It pained him to com-pare the social gospel heyday to the corrupt banality of the 1950s. He tried to believe it was not too late, as he put it in 1957, "to repossess this formative power of the Christian mythos as a counterpart of the Chris-tian ethic." Mostly he did not believe it, even as churches set attendance records. By the early 1960s he no longer claimed there was still time to transform America's spiritual culture; grudgingly he scaled back to smaller ambitions. Meland loathed the mediocrity of church religion, but the fashionable 1960s-talk about religionless Christianity was pitifully absurd to him, foolish wordplay leading nowhere. A better Christianity began with healthy congregations.[79]

He retired from the Divinity School faculty in 1964, teaching part-time afterwards for four years. Meland tried to write a history of Ameri-can liberal theology, but the scale and complexity of the project defeated him. He opted for essays on method, which yielded a book in 1976, *Fallible Forms and Symbols*. As usual he lined out his intellectual tradition, now adding Schleiermacher, Otto, and Tillich, and dropping Bergson and Niebuhr. Meland said he agreed with Schleiermacher, Otto, and Tillich that religion is about ultimate concerns, but he rejected their appeal to the numinous, which smacked of a transcendent realm. Immediacy and ultimacy flow together in lived events. Every occurrence of awareness contains a sensitive and creative "More" on its fringe, and every event is a novel individual concretion.[80]

Emphatically, he was still a process theologian, but he could not write for *Process Studies* because this flagship Whiteheadian journal, founded by Cobb and Lewis Ford, only accepted scholastic articles. Meland did not believe that Whitehead's system literally described reality or that Whitehead systematized everything worth saying by James and Bergson. Meland lamented that Whitehead specialized in conceptual argument and most Whiteheadians were more rationalistic than Whitehead. James didn't just *say* that perceptual flux is the living nexus of the real; he wrote like he believed it. Certainly, James employed concepts, but he used them instrumentally to pose questions or to relate one track of experience to another, not to literally describe reality. Meland did not doubt that James would have poked holes into Whitehead's system, like he did to Hegel and Royce. All abstract conceptual systems falsify the total import of the always-changing nexus of events.[81]

James was a necessary corrective to Whitehead, and especially to Whiteheadians. Meland interpreted *Process and Reality* as an aesthetic imaginative vision, not a conceptual description of reality based on rational necessity. But he acknowledged that the problem of excessive rationalism in Whiteheadian thought began with Whitehead, not with Hartshorne. James' formative imagery came from psychology; Whitehead's came from physics, especially the energy-field. Thus his philosophy had a cosmological bent inviting external, rationalistic systematization. Whitehead's vision was "magnificent," Meland said—the best such resource available to theologians. But to treat it as the true theory of reality was to "profane" its visionary character "and forfeit the creative stimulus of its imaginative venture."[82]

Meland pressed the difference just as Hartshorne's protégés, Cobb and Schubert Ogden, turned Whiteheadian thought into an ascending theological school. It pained him that Cobb and Ogden were thoroughgoing demythologizers in theology and advocates of Hartshornian metaphysical clarity and certainty. Meland said the sharpest disagreements in theology tend to occur between likeminded theologians. Barth and Emil Brunner had nearly the same theology, but clashed over small differences; the differences between Niebuhr and Tillich had a similar significance. Meland could see much of himself in Ogden's early work, and he respected Ogden's commitment to Whiteheadian metaphysics. But Ogden's exaltation of the scientific worldview smacked of Newtonian rationalism, he was oblivious to the creative aspects of myth, and he demonstrated "a degree of confidence in the formulations of human reason comparable to that of Professor Hartshorne, which I am unable to share."[83]

Hartshorne's rationalism overpowered his Jamesian recognition that natural phenomena are too complex to permit precise measurement. Meland said that logic and observation, though indispensable, "stand under the judgment of the very realities to which they attend." Put differently, and more provocatively, logic and observation appeal to the realities of life as metaphors. They do not define or describe the truth that is given; they are merely words that listen for it. Meland believed that Whitehead perceived the difference, but his system exuded confidence in his categories. The later Whitehead may have believed that his categories described the reality to which they pointed; Meland lamented that orthodox Whiteheadians certainly believed it: "By the time Whiteheadians begin to distribute this new crop of fundamental notions, process thinking takes on the air of a new rationalism. Thus the demon dogmatism begins to plague us again."[84]

Meland had not become a liberal or even a Whiteheadian to replace one dogma with another. He declared that he was "a rebel among process theologians, protesting this very tendency to close the gap between manageable and unmanageable aspects of experience." Rationalistic process theology subsumed the Christian story of redemption under the idea of creativity. So had Meland, until he published *Fallible Forms and Symbols*. Now he realized that redemption includes experiences of renewal and hope that creativity does not cover. Meland stretched his naturalism as far as it could go toward salvation by grace, describing salvation as the reception of a good not one's own. Similarly, "emergence" effectively translates much of the meaning of revelation, but is not a satisfactory substitute for it. Whiteheadians had to stop claiming that their concepts closed the gap between Christian images and reality.[85]

The Chicago school had generations beyond the generation of Loomer and Meland, but its reign at Chicago ended with Loomer and

Meland. Loomer taught until 1965 at Chicago, where his doctoral students included Cobb, Don Browning, Gabriel Fackre, Seward Hiltner, Peter Homans, Tom Lawson, Howard Parsons, Preston Roberts, Valerie Saiving, John Spencer, and Edgar Towne. In 1965 Loomer moved to the Graduate Theological Union in Berkeley, California, where he attracted his usual mixture of admirers and critics. By then, Divinity School dean Jerald C. Brauer had established that Chicago would not be hiring another generation of Whiteheadians. Brauer broke the school mentality at Chicago, diversifying the faculty ecumenically and ideologically, which isolated Meland in his last years there.

In 1966, editing a conference volume on empirical theology, Meland observed that the Divinity School was in a transitional phase. Clearly, empirical theology had been dethroned at Chicago, but Meland couldn't figure out what was taking its place. "Ecumenical" was not a substantive answer, all four of the Divinity School's recent theologians (Langdon Gilkey, the late Joseph Haroutunian, Brian Gerrish, and Joseph Sittler) were difficult to categorize, and all leaned closer to neo-orthodoxy than to Chicago liberalism. Uncertain what to say about them, Meland said they represented "an interim of reaction and reassessment," having succeeded a "vigorous and highly productive" group. Wherever the Divinity School was going, his kind of theology was still being pursued "intensively in other seminaries and universities." It still existed in many places where Chicago graduates taught, even though, as Meland regretted, Brauer regarded it as merely one menu option.[86]

Meland became a lonely figure even in his group. He was kindly and shy, but had blasted the Whiteheadian school during its takeoff. His line on myth seemed reactionary to liberals, and nobody said that Whitehead mattered because he conjured some great metaphors. Even Williams believed that Meland's critique of Whiteheadian scholasticism was overwrought. But Meland lived long enough to see the tide turn in his direction. There was an inkling of it in Valerie Saiving's early work, before feminist theology existed. Cobb's conversion to environmentalism in 1969 opened the door to ecological, feminist, and eco-feminist process theologies, transforming process theology itself. Cobb went through a decade-long rethinking of his essentialism, structuralism, and anthropocentrism, moved by liberation theology and the ecological crisis to give up his scholastic conception of Whiteheadian theology. In 2007, when Cobb issued a second edition of his classic scholastic work, *A Christian Natural Theology* (1965), he explained that he still espoused the same "basic argument," but had to find new ways of expressing it. Often he found himself treading the middle ground between rationalist Whiteheadians Lewis Ford and David Ray Griffin and feminist-metaphorical White-headians Marjorie Suchocki and Catherine Keller. When Meland died in 1993, the latter wing was growing and the rationalist wing was not. This trend continued, yielding a Whiteheadian school best known for its myth-creative feminism, environmentalism, and interreligious theology.[87]

Sometimes Meland said that process categories are true; more often he claimed merely that they are meaningful; in both cases he appealed to experience, history, cultural anthropology, and the natural sciences as warrants for his claims, not the coherence of Whitehead's system. Meland never took a clear position on the relation of the process categories to experience. If the metaphysical concept of concretion or emergence is true, is it true on the basis of its conceptual coherence, or its expression of experience? Is it metaphysically true to say that events are primary, reality is social, relations are dynamic and real, and emergence is interactive and progressive? Or are these statements merely intimations of experience? Meland never clarified what falsification meant for him, which was not good enough for the Whiteheadians who built the process school. Cobb, Ogden, and Griffin built the school on their claims to metaphysical clarity and truth. Their philosophical confidence was their strength. Eventually they found themselves in a different kind of school, but it would not have happened the other way around.

In the 1960s and early 1970s, Meland seemed nothing like a harbinger of the Whiteheadian future. He just seemed lonely and hard to explain. "God the problem" was sharply debated in theology, partly as a response to the "death of God" theologies of the mid-1960s. This debate featured arguments in analytic philosophy and scholastic Whiteheadian thought that were foreign to Meland, so he steered clear of it. Yet his position distinctly cut a path between the camps that defined this discussion. Meland's naturalistic theism was fully naturalistic concerning experience and the exclusion of transcendental ideas, and it was firmly theistic in holding fast to the grace of nature and the imaginative discovery of given possibilities of value.[88]

God, to Meland, was "a temporal structure of infinite goodness and incalculable power." He believed that God's creative and redemptive activity could be tracked in history; God is the creative energy in history that enables people to be good and sensitive. Meland never accepted Wieman's belief that a single source of value is at work in the universe.

To Meland, the goal was a pluralistic and radical-empiricist path between Wieman's monism and Loomer's pantheistic identification of God with all processes in their totality. Attending to God's reality was deeply important to Meland, though his principled naturalism made him reluctant to say much about God. His theology, as Tyron Inbody observes, was ironic on this account.[89]

Meland's idea of God was constructivist in the sense that he conceived all ideas of divine reality as constructs of the human imagination. It was radical empiricist, not Kantian, in conceiving God as something more than a construct of the mind. It was synthetic, not analytical, in defining God contemplatively as a religious symbol, not cognitively as an abstract object. As a religious concept, Meland reasoned, God is "a collective representation of certain sustaining relations having cosmic implications." The religious idea of God is a synthetic concept uniting the multiplicity of experience. Empirically, God is a plurality of activities, not a single object, but religiously, God is the object of devotion and worship that represents the hidden wholeness of things. Against Kantian conceptualism, Meland argued that God is wholly constitutive within the structure of creative process, but against rationalistic Whiteheadians, he contended that the philosophy of creative process is equally as much an imaginative construction as Kantian dualism.[90]

Thus Meland cut a path between Wieman and Hartshorne, Hartshorne and Ames, and Ames and Wieman, applying the theory of structured relations to divine reality. He coined the Chicago school's most evocative descriptions of divine reality, and revised some of Whitehead's, while straining not to claim more about God than he knew: "Creative Order," "Creative Matrix," "Matrix of Sensitivity," "Sensitive Nature within Nature," "Depth of Mystery," "Cosmic Presence and Intent," "Ultimate Efficacy within relationships," and "Ultimacy as Creative Passage." Meland opposed Wieman's veiled absolute—the monist belief in the divine ground and unity of goodness—and Loomer's pantheistic claim that God includes evil. Thus he resisted Wieman's lingering idealism while regarding Loomer's over-the-line pantheism as a nonstarter.[91]

Meland recognized that the creative matrix is ambiguous as a datum of human understanding, aesthetically ambiguous, and perhaps morally ambiguous: "We do not understand this silent working of a creative God in our midst if we think of it as wholly beneficent. Growth involves destruction if it is to be creative." Even if reason is able to make meaningful and truthful statements about reality, as he believed, the deep ambiguity of life is daunting. Meland brooded that "living is suffering," dissonance is real and pervasive throughout existence, and "there is no human life of any depth or vigor that is without its tragic sense." Life is not an inspiring melody that ultimately resolves its variations in a pleasing and familiar chord. It is more like "the complex interweaving of themes in a symphony, in which the advancing mood of fate is ever pressing hard upon the opposing mood of triumph."[92]

To be sure, Meland's symphony analogy still implied that life is ultimately coherent. But his thought was shot through with tragic feeling. Despair was a real possibility for Meland, something to be fought off. His answer to despair was faith, not the certainty of value. Faith as trust was precarious and real to Meland; it was the basis of his religious outlook. To many rationalist Whiteheadians—though never to Cobb, even before Cobb rethought his theology—faith was a given as the pursuit of value. To Meland, faith was existential, and not given; it was about the struggle for meaning in existence. Rationality is capable of attaining only a modicum of intelligibility within a swirling maze of experience and events that flash and topple around us, "seemingly absurd, many of them, fraught with anxious moments and enigmatic instances." Even this modicum merely allays *the mind's allegiance to despair.* Only faith can temper the threat of despair that presses upon any person who takes to heart the terrible suffering and tragedy of life.[93]

Some of Meland's protégés shared his blend of aesthetic and ethical impulses—especially William Dean, Tyron Inbody, John Spencer, and Douglas Sturm. Often they disagreed about what he said. At a 1978 American Theological Society conference, four Chicago school experts on Meland's thought—Larry Greenfield, Philip Hefner, Joe Pickle, and Edgar A. Towne—were each convinced that none of the others had rightly interpreted him. This outcome was in Meland's spirit, who often claimed that nobody understood him. In its movement-building days, the process theology movement seemed to leave him behind, and only his former students remembered him. A generation later, a different kind of process theism found a forerunner in his richly aesthetic and complex thinking.[94]

Neo-Hegelian Theonomy
Religious Socialism as Theology

Paul Tillich came closer than anyone to synthesizing the post-Kantian, Hegelian, neo-Marxian, existential, and theological concerns of this book. He was steeped in Kant, Hegel, and Schelling, writing two dissertations on Schelling before he marched off to the hellish horror of World War I. After the war he careened from Prussian nationalism and militarism to democratic socialism, developing a profound theology of religious socialism. Philosophically he remained a disciple of Schelling and Hegel, but could no longer appropriate them the same way, leaning on Marx and Kierkegaard for correction. Theologically he remained the protégé of Martin Kähler, sharply critical of what the Ritschlian school did to liberal theology, without repudiating Hegel, Schelling, and Schleiermacher. Marxist theory was powerfully enabling for Tillich, but it also rationalized what he got wrong, especially about ethical idealism and the sheer moral necessity of battling for justice.

He was born in 1886 in a parsonage in Starzeddel, a walled, feudal-like village in East Elbia, Prussia, near Berlin, where his father Johannes Tillich was the first Lutheran pastor in a family of musicians and manufacturers. Johannes Tillich exuded Prussian dignity and authority, prized Greek philosophy and things intellectual, rose to parish superintendent in Schönfliess when Tillich was five years old, and was gifted musically. A promotion in 1900 took the Tillich family to Berlin. In both places Tillich befriended children of the landed nobility, far above his family's modest economic status, learned Latin from his father, and was raised to regard the Social Democratic Party as a criminal enterprise.

Tillich always portrayed his father as strict and overbearing, notwithstanding that Johannes Tillich's letters to him were kindly, sensitive, philosophically sophisticated, and sympathetic, plus parental and theologically orthodox. Tillich said very little about his rigidly Calvinist mother, Mathilde Tillich, except that he adored her and was crushed when she died of cancer at the age of forty-three. He said he lost her during his preadolescence, although he was seventeen when she died. Tillich exaggerated the time of his maternal loss and his father's severity for similar reasons. He was sensitive, deeply admired and loved his parents, and had to justify why he desperately strove to overcome his father's influence over him. Barth and Tillich's closest friend, Richard Wegener, similarly judged that the key to Tillich was his consuming need to free himself from the Grand Inquisitor.[1]

As a teenager Tillich withdrew as often as possible into romantic reverie, preferring imaginary worlds. He pored over Kant and Fichte during his last year of *Gymnasium* training before retracing his father's theological itinerary for a semester at Berlin, a semester at Tübingen, two years at Halle, and a year at Berlin. He started at Berlin in 1904, plunging into Schelling's transcendental philosophy. At Tübingen he tramped through hills and woods, enthralled by landscapes, cloud formations, flowers, forests, and the sea, savoring experiences of the finite blurring into the infinite. Schelling's nature romanticism caught Tillich before he noticed Schelling's sense of the demonic. He also studied Schleiermacher's theology and thrilled at the poets of German Romanticism, Hölderlin, Novalis, and Rilke, ranking Goethe lower. For the rest of his life Tillich said he was a pagan as far as trees were concerned.

Philosopher Fitz Medicus trained Tillich in German idealism, especially Fichte, but the great teacher in Tillich's life was Halle theologian Martin Kähler, then near the end of his long battle against the nineteenth century. Kähler began his career as a Goethe enthusiast before fixing on the Lutheran doctrine of justification. He taught that modern theology pursued a pointless enterprise, the quest of the historical Jesus, and that justification by grace through faith applies to doubters as well as sinners, a godsend notion for Tillich. Historical criticism, Kähler said, yields no dependable knowledge of Jesus of Nazareth, so faith cannot be founded on so-called historical facts. The New Testament Gospels are testimonies of faith, not source material for historical knowledge. The Gospels present a picture of Jesus Christ as a figure who made an impression of divinity on the apostles. What they experienced can be grasped only in faith.

These ideas later linked Tillich to Barth, Brunner, and Bultmann. Another Kähler principle was more important yet to Tillich: all serious doubt contains faith in the truth as such. Tillich said he could not have become a theologian lacking this teaching. Whoever doubts in good faith actually affirms God and is justified. Kähler taught that God is not a being among other beings, as though God were an object. To speak of God as the Supreme Being is stupid. Kähler described God as the unconditioned that conditions everything else, borrowing a phrase from German idealism, and described himself as a lonely biblical theologian perched between orthodoxy and shallow Ritschlian liberalism. Every one of these ideas played a prominent role in Tillich's theology, and many readers thought he originated them. Tillich told his father that the theological titans at Berlin were dwarfs compared to Kähler.[2]

His course work completed in 1908, Tillich prepared for ordination exams while considering whether to become an academic. He earned his doctorate in philosophy in 1910 from the University of Breslau, where he never studied but submitted a dissertation on Schelling's philosophy of religion, and his licentiate in theology in 1912 from Halle, where he wrote a dissertation on Schelling's mysticism and guilt consciousness. Schelling expressed Tillich's sense of nature as the finite expression of the infinite ground of all things. The first dissertation combined Schelling's metaphysic of potencies with a Schelling-like survey of the history of religion, and the second one mapped out the differences between grounding religion in mystical experience of God and the experience of guilt. Tillich geared his theology to Schelling's metaphysical idealism while expecting to spend his career teaching philosophy.[3]

He prized his training, never exuding Barth's subsequent need to put down his teachers. Shortly before Germany went to war, Tillich applied to Halle for a faculty position and served briefly as a pastor. He married his first love, Margarethe Wever, who had two children with Wegener after Tillich went off to war as an army chaplain. Characteristically, Tillich never held it against either of them. He befriended Wegener in 1909 and looked up to him. Tillich entered the war as a shy intellectual, a monarchist, a churchy Lutheran, and a typical German patriot, steeped in the authoritarian ethos of Wilhelmine Prussia. He knew almost nothing about the working class, women, or himself, preaching nationalistic war theology. Later he recalled that he was thirty years old before he lost "my enthusiasm for uniforms, parades, maneuvers, history of battles and ideas of strategy."[4]

The war burned a hole in Tillich's psyche that showed for the rest of his life. For four years he endured bayonet charges, battle fatigue, nervous waiting, the disfigurement and death of friends, and mass burials at the western front with the Seventh Division. He also endured two nervous breakdowns. Germany expected to race through Belgium and knock out France before taking on Russia; instead it blundered into four years of horror in France. For two years Tillich teamed with a Catholic chaplain at the front lines in northeast France, conducting worship services under trees, in caves, and in trenches, all under fire. His first exposure to heavy fire occurred at the end of October 1915, at the battle of Tahure. The invading Germans sustained heavy losses. Tillich preached about patriotic self-sacrifice, courage, loyalty, eternal life, and divine sovereignty. He surprised himself by winning the trust of working-class soldiers. He devoured art books at the front and toured art museums on leaves, craving beauty. The battle of Champagne in 1915 seared him permanently. Tillich ministered all night to the wounded and dying as they were brought in, "many of them my close friends. All that horrible, long night I walked along the rows of dying men, and much of my German classical philosophy broke down that night."[5]

It seemed to him that the world was ending. The battle of Verdun in May 1916 was the worst of the war, with slaughter on both sides totaling 700,000 deaths. Tillich wrote to his father that unimaginable hell raged all around him. Verdun caused his first nervous breakdown. A friend sent a picture of herself sitting on a lawn, clothed in a white dress. Tillich said it was inconceivable to him that something like that still existed. He had a breakthrough in the French forest, reading Nietzsche's *Thus Spoke Zarathustra*. Nietzsche's ecstatic affirmation of life and his searing assault on Christian morality thrilled the traumatized chaplain. Tillich allowed himself to imagine a life after the hell of war, partied and caroused on leaves like a typical soldier, and endured the "turnip winter" of 1917, when Germans survived on turnips. In April 1918 he had a second breakdown after a bloodbath and asked to be discharged. The army turned him down and Tillich rallied again, grateful not to miss the end of the war and the German revolution, which he witnessed at the Spandau Military Base in Berlin. Though still a nationalist, he sympathized with the rebelling workers, believing that Germany needed a social revolution. He studied political theory, discarded his church ethic, and careened rapidly to radical socialism, though Tillich never quite joined the Independent Social Democratic Party (USPD), which broke off from the pro-war Social Democratic Party (SPD) during World War I. He later recalled that he entered the war a dreaming innocent and emerged from it a wild man.[6]

Religious Socialism as Crisis Theology

The only kind of theology that deserved to be written had to address the abyss in human existence. Tillich felt engulfed by the abyss that the later Schelling merely glimpsed. He told his friend Emanuel Hirsch in 1918 that the later Schelling's "gloomy power" spoke to him more than Schelling's early romanticism. Elsewhere he recalled, "The experience of the four years of war tore this chasm open for me and for my entire generation to such an extent, that it was impossible ever to cover it up." The war, he said, caused a "personal *kairos*" for him. Tillich hung out with Berlin's sprawling café society of musicians, actors, painters, writers, and intellectuals, teaching as a *Privatdozent* at the University of Berlin. Released from army service on January 1, 1919, he wore his army grays and Iron Cross to his first class. That year Tillich's first published speech, "On the Idea of a Theology of Culture," expounded what became his signature thesis: religion is the substance of culture and culture is the form of religion.[7]

He found a group of likeminded intellectuals that he dubbed "the *Kairos* Circle." The core members were minister and social worker Karl Mennicke, theologian Günther Dehn, socialist economists Eduard Heimann and Adolf Löwe, and legal theorist Arnold Wolfers. They founded a journal, *Blätter für religiösen Sozialismus* (*Leaves for Religious Socialism*), contending that Germany's socialist parties were stuck in dogmatic ideologies and bygone battles, including knee-jerk hostility to religion, and too much fixation with economic policies. The churches and socialist parties were deeply flawed, so uniting them was pointless. Something new had to break through. Tillich made a Kähler move to express what it was, renewing a biblical term with rich connotations and no recent history: *kairos*.[8]

Kairos, the "right time," as distinguished from *chronos*, formal time, conveyed the crucial point. Tillich loved the Greek recognition that time as the richly significant moment—kairos—needed its own word, distinct from time as temporal succession. This recognition enabled the Greek language to express the dynamism of Hebrew religion and early Christianity, as in the gospel idea that the kairos of the Logos incarnate did not come until the moment of the fullness of time (kairos). Tillich conceived the kairos as the moment in time when the eternal breaks into the ambiguous relativity of existence and creates something new—a variation on the Schelling-Hegel theme that every living thing contains in its deep essence the conflict between a present and a becoming form. The conflict between our intuition of a becoming form and the existing form moves life forward, never without dangers and risks. The kairos has an ultimate sense and a special sense, plus a twofold sense as the right time of a becoming form and a break against treating any envisaged possibility as an absolute. In its ultimate sense, the Tillichian kairos was the center of history, the interpretive key to the whole of history and its parts. In its special sense it was a decisive force in a given situation, the coming of a new "theonomy" that fuses the sacred with critical rationality. Some things are possible only in particular times; all great turning points in history reflect the one eternal kairos that confers meaning on the whole of history; and all possibilities contain idolatrous dangers.

The kairos, thus conceived, complemented Tillich's ideas of the religious nature of culture, the demonic, the "Protestant principle," the Unconditioned, and the dialectic of heteronomy and autonomy. Religion is the substance of culture in the sense of signifying the incarnation of faith in a given culture. The sacred is the life *in* the profane, for nothing can live outside the sacred power of its origin. Everything in life is subject to idolatrous corruption—the demonic attribution of absoluteness to something finite, relative, and corruptible. The glory of Protestantism is the Protestant principle that legitimizes rigorous criticism of everything and thereby serves as a brake against idolatry. The Unconditioned is the meaning that is the foundation of all meaning-fulfillment. It cannot be proved and it does not "exist," for if it existed in the temporal order, it would not be Unconditioned. It can only be pointed to. Tillich wrote systematic essays about all these concepts except the Unconditioned and sprinkled them into a book, *Das System der Wissenschaften* (1923). Bold new directions, he said, were suddenly possible in Germany, plus new forms of idolatry. The old order was gone and discredited, and bourgeois culture went down with it. The socialist and communist movements were products of the same spiritually bankrupt culture that these movements opposed. Europe needed a liberating religious socialism that synthesized and transcended the heteronomous consciousness of the authoritarian past and the autonomous consciousness of individualistic bourgeois modernity.[9]

The kairos socialists were for radical change without revolutionary romanticism or utopianism. They were realists, by their lights, who dared to imagine a completely different world. In 1923, defining the basic principles of religious socialism, Tillich said dialectical mediation is a spiritual necessity, not merely a political one. The sacramental consciousness has a sense of the holy, it consecrates matter or concepts as divine, and it conceives history as myth, construing everything in life in relationship to sacred symbols of faith. Its power radiates through sacred myths that confer meaning upon past and present, humankind and nature, and individual and community, the latter through family, soil, tribe, cult, class, nation, and/or political system. The rational consciousness, by contrast, is based on form and law as directed toward the right (*das Richtige*), not the holy. Rationality judges even the holy according to critical standards of right, demystifying the world relentlessly, as in Kantian criticism. Religious socialism, to Tillich, was dialectical and prophetic, uniting the mythological and critical interpretations of history: "It has the holy, but only as it permeates law and form; it is free from sacramental indifference, but it does not succumb to rational purgation."[10]

Religious socialism wards off the demonic elements of mythic sacramentalism by embracing rational, liberal, and democratic elements. At the same time it opposes the sterile materialism and soulless autonomy of the bourgeoisie that socialist movements strangely borrowed. To Tillich, this did not mean that heteronomy and autonomy were equally problematic. Religious socialism began as a struggle against injustice, dehumanization, inequality, and authoritarianism. As such it was never less than ethical and prophetic. When religious socialists confronted a choice between defending liberal democracy and upholding their religious traditions, they had to defend liberal democracy. Tillich loathed that church leaders sneered at the Weimar Republic for reactionary reasons. He had a similar feeling about left-wing anti-liberalism, which tragically drove Germany's best political hope, the USPD, into the Communist Third International. By 1922 the only political vehicle for democratic socialists was the SPD, which welcomed the rump-USPD leftovers. Tillich insisted that the road to religious socialism runs through liberal democracy. Illiberal socialism, even for an interim, did not tempt him.

Bad forms of Marxism treat democracy and liberal rights as superfluous. Tillich said Marx's critique of commodity fetishism was the best part of Marxism, which Tillich theologized as a critique of spiritual death. Capitalism strips nature of its sacramental power by commodifying all existence: "The more a thing becomes a commodity, the less it exists in an eros-relation to the possessor and the less intrinsic power it possesses. In this inner emptiness, however, the thing becomes the object of the subjective eros and of the subjective will to power." The sacramental relationship to nature provides a brake on natural human desires for pleasure and domination. Capitalism, Tillich argued, eliminates the brake. Anything that the subjective will to power or desire for dominance takes from nature, it loses for itself.[11]

Tillich conceived the class struggle as an expression of the demonic character of capitalism, not as a given of human nature to be tolerated. He faulted the Socialist parties for treating socialism as a counter-concept to capitalist economics. Socialists had to stop saying that socializing the economy is the essence of socialism. To Tillich the goal of socialism was theonomy, replacing the subjective will to power with a liberating religious ethos. Socialism as mere counter-capitalism rationalized alternative forms of hubris, power worship, and dehumanization. Religious socialism applied the anti-authoritarian principle of radical democracy to everything, accepting the democratic constitutional state "as a universal form" and filling this form with the divine good. Socialism, Tillich said, is essentially and emphatically a struggle for justice. As such it cannot be pacifist or anarchist, because gains toward justice must be defended. Neither does true socialism romanticize the proletariat, because every working-class community abounds with vulgar tastes and prejudices that socialism must overcome.[12]

Tillich's Berlin period inspired his signature ideas. He studied art, literature, psychoanalysis, and politics, caroused bohemian cafés and dance clubs, and indulged himself sexually, even after remarrying. He thrived on his new friendships and interests, sexual and otherwise, rationalizing that he could not fulfill his potential if he did not satisfy himself erotically. Hirsch implored Tillich to curtail his promiscuity, or failing that, choose philosophy over theology, before he became a scandal for theology. Tillich told his friend that he liked his new life. In 1924 he wrote in *Blätter für Religiösen Sozialismus*, "I have come to know the Bohéme; I went through the war; I got involved in politics; I became fascinated by the art of painting, and, in the course of this winter, with greatest passion by music." Tillich's second wife, Hannah Gottschow, shared his sexual lifestyle during their years in Germany, but not after they were exiled to the United States. He was sexually promiscuous for the rest of his life, which Hannah Tillich bitterly regretted after they moved to America and he assiduously kept secret.[13]

In 1924 he made a career move to Marburg, lacking any chance of promotion at Berlin. Tillich felt stifled at Marburg, where Rudolf Otto was ailing, Heidegger was frosty, Tillich barely knew Bultmann, and the community reeked of quaint small-town provincialism. He caught Heidegger during his *Being and Time* period, absorbing Heidegger's description of human beings as the unique type of being through whom Being (the primordial ground) presents itself to be known. Tillich adopted Heidegger's language about the "thrown" character of human "being-there" (*Dasein*) and the perils that attend the self's coming-to-awareness of its arbitrarily given ("thrown") existence. He took over Heidegger's notion that the authentic self faces up to one's nothingness and becomes a caretaking being-toward-death by changing the form of one's totalized givenness. Authentic existence, Heidegger argued, is the way of death-accepting courage and care for the world. Tillich channeled Heidegger, Nietzsche, and Kierkegaard whenever he wrote about existentialism.

But he had to live in a city, preferably one with likeminded friends. In 1925 Tillich moved to Dresden Institute of Technology, rescued by his friend Richard Kroner, a wealthy post-Kantian idealist who admired Tillich's thought while believing it was too close to Schelling to be Christian. The Dresden Institute, though lacking accredited university status, got Tillich out of Marburg. He published a breakthrough book, *The Religious Situation* (1926), calling for a "faithful realist" revolt against bourgeois civilization. In much of European art, philosophy, and science, Tillich said, the revolt was happening. The expressionist and post-expressionist movements in painting, the Nietzschean and Bergsonian philosophies of life, the Freudian discovery of the unconscious, and Einstein's revolution in physics exuded a fundamental openness to the Unconditioned. Tillich favored expressionist painting for the rest of his life, prizing its subversive disruption of appearances. *The Religious Situation* lamented that theology was not similarly creative. He felt alienated from the church, bristling at Barth's popularity among church theologians.[14]

Tillich tried to be nice to Barth, but Barth protested that Tillich's Unconditioned was a "frosty monster" rolling over everything in the spirit of Hegel and Schleiermacher. Tillich countered that Barth's theology was merely a sophisticated form of otherworldliness. In essence Barth offered the God of Pauline supernaturalism as the answer to modern religious needs. This prescription, Tillich said, even in Barth's able rendering of it, was neither credible nor even cognizant of its religious elements. Barth's religion of faith was still religion, notwithstanding his polemics against religion, and its otherworldly appeal to revelation brushed aside modern challenges to belief. If theologians wanted to say something worthwhile, they had to become philosophers of culture as well as theologians. Tillich put it sharply in 1929: "Revelation is revelation to me in my conscious situation, in my historical reality."[15]

He won a following for this message in the Hofgeismar Circle, a group of young socialists that challenged the SPD from the left. In 1928 Tillich, Heimann, Löwe, and Mennicke joined eighty religious socialists and young socialists for a three-day conference at Heppenheim-on-the-Bergstrasse, near Heidelberg. Ethical socialist writer Hendrik de Man urged the group to make a clean break with Marxism, contending that socialism would never attract many followers as long as it bore the albatross of Marxist materialism, determinism, and atheism. Tillich and Heimann replied that this seemingly attractive position lacked something indispensable, Marxian dialectic. Did the gathered socialists see the coming of the gestalt in the seething tensions of the proletarian situation? Did they believe the new order was struggling to emerge in the existing proletarian movement? That was Marxian dialectic. Tillich and Heimann said it was far superior to non-dialectical morality *and* the mechanical dialecticism of vulgar Marxism. This argument yielded a new version of the defunct kairos circle journal, renamed *Neue Blätter für den Sozialismus*, adding "new" and dropping "religious." Tillich's first issue appeared in January 1930, four months after he began teaching at the University of Frankfurt. He kept it going on a monthly basis until June 1933, reaching a circulation of 3,000.[16]

Winning the philosophy chair at Frankfurt was Tillich's academic breakthrough, at the age of forty-three. It thrilled him to land at Frankfurt, where he joined Max Horkheimer's Frankfurt Institute for Social Research. The Frankfurt Institute Marxists contended that orthodox Marxism over-relied on a base-superstructure reductionism that screened out existential and cultural factors. Marxism, on this telling, was a magnificent tradition of social criticism needing to be saved from scholastics determined to make it small and manageable. Tillich urged the Frankfurt Marxists not to repress religious questions. Socialism, he argued, is the self-expression of the oppressed, providing meaning for subjected people, and meaning is ultimately religious, pointing to the Unconditioned that transcends all specific contexts. A person's religion is whatever concerns her ultimately. Nobody fights for justice lacking faith and ultimate concerns. Thus socialism is incomprehensible without its religious dimension. Many heard this only as backward religiosity and/or political naiveté. Even Tillich's friends said he lived in his head. Harold Poelchau claimed that Tillich sustained a childlike optimism right up to his firing. Dehn was stunned in 1932 when Tillich gave a lecture never mentioning the political crisis, enraptured by his own ideas. These impressions entered the lore about Tillich, notwithstanding that precious few academics had more on their record to convict them when the Nazis took over.[17]

In October 1931 Tillich lectured on socialism at Wolfers' German Academy of Politics, feeling his way toward a book. The following July he witnessed a right-wing riot on the Frankfurt campus, replete with storm troopers and Nazi students beating up leftist and Jewish students. By then Tillich was dean of the philosophical faculty. He flushed with anger, dragged the injured students to safety, and made an outraged speech against the Nazi students, demanding their expulsion. This reaction sealed his fate in Germany, although Tillich had no inkling of it, still believing that cultured Germany would not turn fascist. Later that summer, vacationing in the mountains of Sils Maria, Switzerland, along with Hannah Tillich, Löwe, Karl Mannheim, and Adolf Grimme, Tillich wrote *The Socialist Decision*.[18]

True socialism was the salvation of Europe, he argued, but it needed new answers. The Nazis were gaining and Tillich had joined the SPD as a sign of his political seriousness. He placed himself between the older generation of crusty SPD politicos and the younger generation of socialists that quoted de Man, wrote for *Neue Blätter*, and made Tillich feel middle-aged. The older generation still dominated the socialist movement, stuck in mechanistic materialism, while the younger generation renounced nineteenth-century positivism and the grotesque socialism of the Soviet Union. Tillich said there was a case to be made for progressive Marxian socialism: "It holds fast to Marxism and defends it against the activism of the younger generation; but it rejects the form in which the older generation took it over from the nineteenth century. It goes back to the real Marx and to a concept of dialectic in which necessity and freedom are conjoined."[19]

The Socialist Decision acknowledged that religious socialists had a hard time convincing socialists to give up their anti-religious animus. In Germany the early socialist movement naturally allied itself with the bourgeois parties that opposed the state church. Plus, socialists truly

believed that scientific socialism abolished the need for religion. Then
the bourgeois parties made their peace with religion, but the socialist
movement never did. All of this had to be overcome, beginning with confessions of sin by the churches. As usual Tillich insisted he was not being
idealistic. Socialism was pointless as idealism; it had to emerge from
existing liberation movements. He saw no hope for religious socialism
in the Catholic Church, because the Vatican crushed every wellspring of
the critical spirit within theological education and the clergy. As long as
dogmatic clericalism dominated the Catholic Church, Catholic socialism
was impossible.[20]

At every key turn, Tillich addressed the questions of what he
took from Marx and whether religious socialism worked better without Marxism. The first question was always complicated for him and
the second was not: no. Tillich acknowledged that Engels/Kautsky
economic materialism was very problematic, and Marx contributed
mightily to the problem. There was no denying that orthodox Marxism denigrates all ideas, artistic and literary creations, spiritual values,
moral intuitions, and love and feeling as superstructural rationalizations of economic interests. But Tillich said orthodox Marxism was
never an adequate summary of Marx's complex thought, and the recent
publication of the early Marx's grappling with Hegel—*The Economic
and Philosophical Manuscripts of 1844*—clarified his purpose and meaning. Marx was routinely interpreted as teaching that spirit (*Geist*) is
causally dependent on economics. Tillich countered that spirit is not a
thing, and neither is economics. Economics is infinitely complex and
multifaceted, involving the direction and quality of needs, modes of
production and social relationships, scales of enterprise, and virtually
every aspect of human being. Economics cannot be isolated and made
the cause of something intrinsic to it, spirit.[21]

Neither is spirit anything in itself. Spirit is always the spirit of
something, "the spirit of a being that, through spirit, achieves self-
understanding." Marx grasped this connection between being and consciousness, taking from Hegel that the unity of being and consciousness is
lost when being is conceived as a discrete cause from which spirit follows
as a discrete effect. Tillich put it bluntly: "There is no such being and
no such spirit." Human being is always a twofold unity of being and
consciousness in which the positing of subject or object as a discrete factor is nonsensical. This does not mean that false consciousness does not
exist. Tillich bypassed scholarly debates about the variously contradictory

things that Marx said about ideology, cutting to the point: the idea of false consciousness makes sense only in connection with the idea of a true consciousness—a consciousness united with the new being. False consciousness willfully thwarts the movement toward liberation. Religious false consciousness is false for being reactionary, not for being religious.[22]

The religion issue exemplified that socialism needed new answers. Historically, liberalism played the leading role in dissolving the communal bonds to land, social rank, ethnicity, race, religion, and patriarchy, but in every case the socialist movement became the executor of the dissolving powers of liberalism. Tillich stressed that Social Democracy carried through the liberal attack on privilege and inequality, even as socialism defined itself fundamentally against the bourgeois principle of class rule. To be sure, socialism had special problems concerning the politics of community, beginning with its deeply contradictory relationship to liberalism. Socialism was the greatest ally of liberalism and its greatest enemy, a contradiction plaguing every socialist party. Moreover, socialists had huge disadvantages in the electoral arena. They could not compete with the right-nationalist parties in appealing to the bonds of soil, race, memory, and nation, and they had no apparent substitute for the liberal belief that unfettered capitalism creates social harmony and prosperity.

In fact, Tillich said, socialism is more deeply opposed to liberalism than to right-nationalist conservatism, paradoxical as that sounded. Socialists reject both parts of the liberal view that capitalism creates social harmony because free markets conform to natural law. Tillich implored that socialists could not give ground on this twofold principle and still be socialist. The concessions had to tilt the other way, conceiving socialism as a politics of community, with all its perils. Even to lean in this direction was to ensnare the socialist movement in feudal ideologies that buttressed the class rule of aristocrats by appealing to the powers of origin. Tillich moved straight to the issue of national community, urging that socialism had to get its bearings by beginning there. Traditional socialist internationalism is liberalism taken seriously, transcending national limitations in the name of an international ideal of humanity. Tillich agreed that internationalism is the ideal, "in the last analysis." Socialists must put humankind above the nation and defend international law. But socialists could not afford to ignore that socialism depends for its realization "on national powers of origin." He implied that the SPD ignored it for too long. To suggest that Social Democrats flunked the patriotism test before 1914, or during the war, or in 1919, or in the 1920s, was perilous and wrong, but Tillich went there anyway, grasping at straws in a desperate situation. He could have faulted the SPD for exalting its partisan self-interest above the cause of democracy, but he opted for a larger concession. German Social Democracy, he said, belatedly learned that the "concrete community of place, race, and culture" always trumps the abstract appeal of transnational proletarian solidarity.[23]

Finally the socialist movement recognized that it could not actualize itself if it did not actualize itself nationally. Socialists had never believed in the free market rationale for liberal internationalism, and now that rationale lay in ruins. Dissolving the bonds of origin did not lead to a united humanity. It led to permanent economic warfare and wars of empire. Tillich said socialists had to accept the nation as a power of origin, much as it pained them to do so. They needed to do it emphatically as socialists, recognizing that the nation is the most important and powerful weapon of domination ever placed in the hands of capital. Socialism had no future if it did not embrace this contradiction. It had to be internationalist in opposition to national imperialism and nationalist in opposition to the liberal and previously socialist ideology of international citizenship. The SPD, Tillich said, had rightly moved in this direction. It put the nation first in the German revolution, the civil war, the battle against inflation, and the coal-industry battle against France in the Ruhr Valley. These patriotic policies tore the party apart in the 1920s and nearly killed it. Tillich noted that right-wing parties never demonstrated similar self-denial for the nation. He said it strongly, charging that right-wing demagoguery on this point was "demonic in the most negative sense of the word."[24]

That alone would have condemned him after the Nazis took over. Tillich finished *The Socialist Decision* in November 1932, a month after he attended one of Hitler's rallies, which he found terrifying and disgusting. He ended the book by imploring that proletarians could not succeed by themselves. There had to be a coalition of proletarian, religious, and liberal forces; otherwise the right-nationalists would prevail. Even right-nationalists were not beyond the pale, if approached correctly. Right-romanticism expressed a legitimate protest against the bourgeois evisceration of the powers of origin. Religious socialists sympathized with this reaction and channeled it to better ends. Tillich later admitted that he grasped the emotional power of Nazi mythology because he felt it personally. One reason he wrote the book was to overcome the mythical romantic element in himself. *The Socialist Decision* came off the press just as Hitler became chancellor in January 1933. No review was published, but nasty articles impugning Tillich's loyalty appeared. Nationalist students marched in torchlight parades opposing toleration of the un-German spirit, rehearsing for the book burnings that began in May. On April 13 the government issued its first list of enemies of the state, under two categories. The first category consisted of Communists, Socialists, other left-wing intellectuals, and others deemed politically suspect. The second consisted of Jews.[25]

Tillich, Horkheimer, Löwe, Mannheim, and two legal scholars, Hermann Heller and Hugo Sinzheimer, were purged from Frankfurt immediately. Every week there were new dismissals. The roll of famous Jewish intellectuals and artists was staggering, headed by Bertholt Brecht, Ernst Cassirer, Albert Einstein, Wassily Kandinsky, Wolfgang Köhler, Thomas Mann, Erwin Panofsky, Max Reinhardt, Karl Ludwig Schmidt, and Bruno Walter. Most were purged for being Jews, although Tillich was less singular as a gentile than he sometimes claimed, being joined by Dehn, Mennicke, Klee, and sociologist Alfred Weber.[26]

In May, Union Theological Seminary president Henry Sloane Coffin attended a meeting at Columbia University that discussed the fate of the purged academics. Coffin knew hardly anything of Tillich, but H. Richard Niebuhr had translated *The Religious Situation*. Reinhold Niebuhr urged the Union faculty to offer refuge to Tillich; that summer every Union faculty member agreed to a five percent salary reduction to fund a position. Tillich balked and grieved at the thought of leaving Germany to teach anywhere in America, much less a seminary. His doctoral student Theodor Adorno pleaded with him that staying in Germany was not worth getting killed. Tillich tried to get his job back, until the secret police came to a friend's home in Dresden to arrest Tillich. Then he relented to being rescued by Union, at the age of 47, identifying with Abraham in Genesis 12:1: "Now the Lord said to Abram, 'Go from your country and your kindred and your father's house to the land that I will show you.'" He also described Niebuhr as "my savior."[27]

Tillich's American Career

Tillich's American career has no parallel in modern religious thought. He achieved spectacular success in a nation lacking an intellectual culture by his standards and in which he was an exile. He never learned much about American theology or politics, never felt comfortable at Union Seminary, and fretted for years that he could not write his system outside

Germany. His early attempts to explain himself in an American context were unsuccessful, and much of the Union faculty doubted that he belonged at Union or any seminary. Then he attained fame far beyond anything that was possible anywhere else, aided by American friends who published collections of his essays, transcribed his classroom lectures into the three-volume *Systematic Theology*, and put his needs above their own. The crowning irony of his ironically famous American career was that his system had to be translated into German.

Returning to Germany in 1948, Tillich gave numerous lectures and was warmly received as long as he stayed off the topic of German guilt. The self-pity of his German friends disturbed him, especially their refusal to admit any moral responsibility for the fate of the Jews. He reasoned that their feeling of guilt was so great they were forced to repress it. Tillich carefully considered several teaching offers, but returned to Union, having become an American. His acclaimed essay collection *The Protestant Era* was published in 1948, as was his sermon collection, *The Shaking of the Foundations*. He told a friend that harvest time had come for him. His *Systematic Theology* unfolded the concepts about religion, God, Christ, and myth that he refashioned from Schelling, Hegel, and German mysticism, employing a correlation method that moved from existential questions to Christian answers. The questions came from the modern cultural situation and the answers were reinterpreted Christian symbols. Tillich said that claiming to speak out of revelation or faith alone is not credible because every theologian is both committed and alienated: "He is always in faith *and* in doubt; he is inside *and* outside the theological circle. Sometimes the one side prevails, sometimes the other; and he is never certain which side really prevails."[28]

The Christian answer is the theologian's ultimate concern, but no formulation of it is infallibly correct or culturally unconditioned. Religion is ultimate concern, which is unconditional, "independent of any conditions of character, desire, or circumstance." Idolatry is precisely to treat anything that is conditioned as absolute. This was the core critique of religion that Tillich shared with Barth, except Tillich did not exempt Christianity from the category of religion. Rightly conceived, theology gives itself only to the unconditioned; thus, the object and first formal criterion of theology is that which concerns us ultimately: "Only those propositions are theological which deal with their object in so far as it can become a matter of ultimate concern for me."[29]

A worthy ultimate concern must determine our being or not-being; nothing that does not possess the power of threatening or saving one's being deserves to be an ultimate concern. "Being," for Tillich, did not refer to existence in time and space, for existence is constantly threatened and saved by things and events that fall short of ultimacy. Being is the "whole of human reality, the structure, the meaning, and the aim of existence." True religion is about cosmic meaning, the saving of the whole that is threatened. It is unconditionally concerned about that which conditions human existence beyond the conditions that indwell and surround human beings.[30]

Just as Schleiermacher described true religion before making an argument for Christianity as the best example of true religion, Tillich described the criterion of good theology before making an argument for Christianity as the best theological answer. Like other theologies, Christian theology is *logos* of *theos*, a rational interpretation of religious rituals, symbols, and myths. But Christian theology is founded on the transcendent claim that the Logos entered history in and through the life of a human being, Jesus. The essential Christian affirmation is that the divine logos, the mind of God, was uniquely revealed in the event of Jesus as the Christ. Tillich emphasized that Christianity is distinctively concrete and universal. It makes a claim about Jesus that is more concrete than any mystical vision or metaphysical principle, yet no vision or principle is as universal as the logos, "which itself is the principle of universality." Compared to the logos, everything else is particular, including the half-God Arian theology that nearly captured Christianity in the fourth century. Tillich was grateful that the Athanasian party prevailed, because Arian theology sold short the universality and concreteness of the Johannine confession that the Word became flesh and dwelt among us.[31]

Tillich derived his theological norms from four sources—the Bible, church history, history of religions, and culture—while rejecting the liberal convention that personal experience is a theological source. He conceived experience as the medium through which the sources speak to the theologian. One experiences the power of the sources before analyzing them. Experience is receptive, not productive, for the productive power of experience is limited to the transformation of what is given to it. True reception intends only reception. If it intends something else, such as transformation, it falsifies that which is received. Tillich reasoned that the event of Jesus Christ is both infinite in its meaning and the defining event of Christianity; thus it is the criterion of religious experience. Experience is a vehicle for theology, not an independent source, for the event of Jesus as the Christ is given to experience, not derived from it.[32]

Here the idealist emphasis on the creativity and primacy of experience must be held in check. If a univocal unity existed between the (regenerated) human spirit and the divine Spirit, it would be appropriate to conceive experience as an independent source of theology. But Tillich was a non-Pietist Lutheran on this point. The mystical and holiness traditions made exorbitant claims for regenerated experience, and liberal idealists had a similar tendency to obscure the eschatological aspect of the Christian vision of divine-human unity, reading themselves into the incarnation of Christ. The linchpin of Tillich's Christology was the "new being" in Christ, but he had a resolutely Lutheran sense of the not-yet of divine-human unity: every Christian remains a sinner. Revelation may occur through saints just as it formerly occurred through prophets and apostles, but revelation always comes *to* the saints and *against* their nature, not from them: "Insight into the human situation destroys every theology which makes experience an independent source instead of a dependent medium of systematic theology."[33]

Tillich's theory of myth was as influential as his enormously influential rendering of religion as ultimate concern, though few Americans realized that he got it from Schelling. Like Schelling, Tillich said that myth is an essential component of human life and thought, and symbols convey the mythical truths of religion. Myths are not merely prescientific explanations of events in the world; they are constellations of symbols that express humanity's relation to that which concerns human beings ultimately. Even science is myth-creative inasmuch as it employs concepts such as "evolution" that are transcendent to things. By its nature, myth (like science) seeks to unify creation, or at least make it intelligible, under a single conceptuality. The key to myth is its unifying impulse, but myth is true only in broken form. Tillich explained that pure unbroken myth is always a history of the gods. Hebrew monotheism cracked the mythical unity of religion and science: God was transcendent; his name was not to be spoken; he lived even if his nation died; a gap opened between the transcendent realm and the natural world.[34]

But the breaking of mythological consciousness enhances the value of myth as an aspect of thought, allowing its true character to emerge. Even in its broken state, the mythical imagination seeks to find the hidden wholeness of reality. Tillich argued that broken myth is precious to theology precisely in its meaning-seeking drive to reunify the world.

The world of things described by science is related to its unconditioned ground, the unconditioned transcendent is interpreted from the viewpoint of modern knowledge, and the unifying impulse of religion is restored in the broken symbol. In other words, science becomes myth-creative out of its need to theorize that which transcends the world of things, theology accepts the authority of science to explain the physical world, and theology relates all such knowledge to the religious transcendent. Myth, in its drive to unify these fields of experience, participates in and points to the unconditioned.[35]

Because symbolism is the language of faith, myth is intrinsic to every act of faith. Tillich cautioned that this does not make it beyond criticism. All mythical speech must be demythologized by modern knowledge before it can be useful for theology. Demythologizing, to the extent that it breaks and de-literalizes religious myth, is an indispensable aspect of theology. On the other hand, any demythologizing strategy that negates myth is terribly wrong, because it silences the experience of the Holy, depriving religion of its language. Myth and symbol are ever-present forms of human consciousness. One can replace a myth by another myth, but myth itself is constitutive to the spiritual life.[36]

The test of a myth or a symbol is whether it expresses the spiritual realities in which it participates and to which it points. Tillich taught that symbols differ from signs inasmuch as symbols participate in the reality to which they point. Symbols and signs both point beyond themselves to something else, but symbols participate in the meaning and power of the reality for which they stand. A symbol opens up the deepest dimension of the human soul and reality, which is the ultimate power of being. It radiates the power of being and meaning of that for which the symbol stands. It is true to the extent that it expresses the inner necessity that it carries for consciousness. In other words, it is true to the extent that it reaches its Unconditioned referent: "The only criterion that is at all relevant is this: that the Unconditioned is clearly grasped in its Unconditionedness. A symbol that does not meet this requirement and that elevates a conditioned thing to the dignity of the Unconditioned, even if it should not be false, is demonic."[37]

Tillich became so famous for these arguments that his friend Wilhelm Pauck struggled with a guilty conscience, believing that he or Tillich should explain how much Tillich owed to Schelling. Pauck's enduring guilt about it later impeded him from completing the second volume of his intellectual biography of Tillich. In 1952 Tillich's bestselling *The*

Courage to Be lauded Kierkegaard, Nietzsche, Heidegger, and novelist Franz Kafka for showing the existential courage to accept despair. The best existentialists were courageous, he argued, because they roared for life without deflecting its negativity and tragedy. Depth psychology, in Tillich's American career, took over the role that religious socialism played in his early career. He made a spectacular success, but bristled when Americans misconstrued his shift as a change of mind. Unlike Niebuhr, Tillich remained a socialist and a neo-Marxist for the rest of his life. In 1945 he explained what happened: "I once believed that with the categories of religious socialism I could lead a fundamental change in Christian theology. But since then my hopes are confined to giving the American people a well-worked-out theology which they have never had. In 1920 it was different, then I wanted to inaugurate a new period of Christianity."[38]

He wrote fourteen explicitly Marxist essays during his American career, usually after a magazine editor asked. Always he said that neo-Marxian religious socialism remained central to his thinking. He had not really changed, despite becoming famous for writing about other things. In 1949 Tillich wrote an autobiographical article for the *Christian Century* that the editors titled, "Beyond Religious Socialism." Tillich hated the title, later explaining, "If the prophetic message is true, there is nothing 'beyond religious socialism.'" Even his view of Marx had not changed, hard as that was to say at the height of McCarthyism. Tillich still admired the "prophetic, humanistic and realistic elements in Marx's passionate style and profound thought" and still rejected the "calculating, materialistic, and resentful elements in Marx's analysis, polemics, and propaganda." The Cold War, he allowed, snuffed out his guilty feeling that he should involve himself in political issues. It created a bipolar world that crushed any possibility of a theonomous third way between capitalism and Communism, making politics small and depressing. The tragedy of the fascist catastrophe gave way to the tragedy of Cold War dualism: "I lost the inspiration for, and the contact with, active politics."[39]

That failed the test of the courage to be, as Tillich very well knew. Pauck and James Luther Adams said Tillich felt compelled in his American career to express his enduring Marxian socialist convictions in alternative ways. Both told stories about Tillich avoiding involvements that might have gotten messy. Pauck said Tillich had an extreme case of career ambition; Adams said Tillich folded on Communism and racial injustice because he didn't want to lose his white American audience.

Then Tillich found an enormous audience by writing about anxiety and existentialism. Retiring from Union Seminary in 1955, he taught at Harvard for five years, won national celebrity, and finished his career at the University of Chicago Divinity School, where he died in 1965. He left behind, in my view, the intellectually richest theological thinking of the twentieth century. And he evoked a contentious literature on his neo-Marxian legacy.[40]

Robert Fitch, Alistair MacLeod, Clark Kucheman, and Dennis McCann said that Tillich's Marxism harmed his legacy. Terence O'Keefe, Walter Weisskopf, Ronald Stone, Guy Hammond, James Champion, and Donnelly debated if and why Tillich dropped his commitment to religious socialism in 1934 or at some point afterward, usually 1948. My reading is that Tillich marshaled his signature ideas in his early career and refashioned them in different ways throughout his career.[41]

He remained the same kind of neo-Marxian religious socialist just as he remained the same kind of post-Kantian idealist and existentialist. His luminous book *Love, Power, and Justice* (1954) perfectly distilled his neo-Hegelian religious socialist worldview, without naming it. His politics were always there, which he never denied when asked, even as Union students passed through his classroom with no clue that he had ever been politically active. When pressed on the subject, Tillich said that a faithful church inspires prophetic criticism and that he did not give up the kairos idea after World War II yielded the void of the Cold War.[42]

The kairos idea enabled him to experience the void of the post–World War II situation as sacred—interpreting the moment in the light of the eternal. Tillich said that proclaiming the kairos in this context demanded patient waiting in a vacuum, not transformative action. He was mindful that Barth said the same thing in 1920, but Tillich stressed the difference: Barth gave up the very idea of a concrete kairos, viewing the relation of the eternal to the temporal as a permanent crisis. Tillich did not regret having risked something in the 1920s and 1930s, even as he railed against utopianism. Neither did he believe there was only one kairos, the mistake of orthodox Lutheranism.[43]

As for Marxism, the interpretive options are profuse, and Tillich was far from alone in trying to strip the dogmatism and utopianism out of Marx. Marx bore ample responsibility for orthodox Marxism, which turned dialectical materialism into a doctrine of metaphysical materialism. Tillich persistently criticized Marx on this ground while insisting that orthodox Marxism contradicted Marx's revolutionary call to the proletariat and his obvious moral passion. The prophetic ethical passion *within* Marxism, Tillich said, is genuine dialectics—the very thing that drew him to Marx and made him some kind of Marxist. Marx said things that smacked of determinism, but that didn't make determinism more defining or fatal in Marxism than in Christianity.[44]

Very late in his career and life, after he moved from Harvard to Chicago, Tillich offered four rules for interreligious dialogue and three arguments for a Christian theology of religions. The rules were that each participant must respect the value of the other's religious conviction, be able to represent her own religious perspective with conviction, presuppose a common ground that makes dialogue and conflict possible, and be open to criticism of one's perspective. Tillich did not claim that all religions are fundamentally alike; in Troeltsch's fashion, he judged that only two religions—Christianity and Buddhism—aspire to universality, and Buddhism contains nothing like the social, political, and personal symbol of the kingdom of God. There is no analogy in Buddhism for the liberal, democratic, and socialist offshoots of Christianity. Buddhism has a strong sense of compassion, but no will to transform social structures; it is about salvation from reality, not transformation of reality. Tillich commended dialogues that identify commonalities, but the purpose of dialogue is not merely to identify commonalities.

The three ideas on which Tillich based his theology of religions were geared to his claims about idolatry, the Unconditioned, ultimate concern, Hegelian dialectic, and the logos: (1) Rightly understood, Christian faith transcends religion and non-religion; it is not one religion among others. (2) The Hegelian principle of dialectical participation—things and the universe are nonidentical but united by participation—is better than the Eastern principle of identity that things and the universe are one, though Tillich acknowledged that the Eastern principle (especially in Japanese Buddhism) affords a keener sense of the religious significance of nature. (3) Eastern wisdom, like every form of wisdom, belongs to the self-manifestations of the logos. Thus, if Christ is rightly called the incarnation of the logos, all forms of Eastern wisdom must be included in the interpretation of Jesus as the Christ.[45]

This scheme turned on Tillich's identification of Christ with the universal principle of divine self-manifestation. Johannine theology, he argued, saved the early church from turning Christ into the property of a factional party. The church fathers grasped the universality of the logos idea, teaching that the Logos is present in all religions and cultures.

Christianity began to think of itself as one (embattled) religion among others only after Islam emerged in the seventh century. Christianity became obsessively exclusive, lost its universalistic self-confidence, and thereby lost its inclusiveness as a religion of Spirit. A few pre-Enlightenment theologians tried to recover it, notably Nicholas of Cusa, Faustus Socinus, and Boehme, which led to the Enlightenment project of judging all religions by the same rational criterion. The Enlightenment faith in reason created the philosophy of religion, in which Christianity was subsumed under the universal concept of religion.[46]

This story had the appearance of recovery and progress, but Tillich cautioned that Enlightenment religion produced a faulty universality. Enlightenment Christian universalism led straight to humanistic relativism, in which Christianity became the exemplar of the species religion. This was a dead end, despite the great names associated with it: Kant, Schleiermacher, Hegel, Schelling, and Troeltsch. The giants of liberal theology subsumed Christianity under the concept of religion, construing Christianity as the best realization of religion, but their concept of religion was a Christian-humanist construct of their making. Troeltsch, struggling with this problem, gave up his claim to universality, coining an ism that didn't catch on, "Europeism"—Christianity is the ideal religion for Western civilization.

Tillich did not claim that he improved on the liberal icons, but he justly claimed to make a beginning. The better idea was a non-parochial understanding of religion and a conception of Christianity that transcends religion and non-religion. Liberal theology tried to find a home for religion in moral reason (Kant), religious feeling (Schleiermacher), metaphysical knowledge (Hegel), and the community of faith (Ritschl). Tillich said the best home for religion is everywhere. Religion is the dimension of depth in every function of humanity's spiritual life; it should not be reduced to one function of the human spirit. The Bible pictures no temples in the kingdom, where God is all in all. The way forward is not to relinquish one's religious tradition for the sake of a universal concept that is not universal and is merely a concept: "The way is to penetrate into the depth of one's own religion, in devotion, thought and action. In the depth of every living religion there is a point at which the religion itself loses its importance, and that to which it points breaks through its particularity, elevating it to spiritual freedom and with it to a vision of the spiritual presence in other expressions of the ultimate meaning of man's existence."[47]

Universally, if the Holy is experienced, three movements or elements are present. Tillich employed a familiar dialectic to describe them. The founding element is the experience of the Holy within the finite, which he variously called the sacramental basis of religions or, within Christianity, the "Catholic substance." Universally, in everything that exists, the Holy appears in a special way. The second element is the critique of idolatry, the "demonization of the sacramental," which can take the form of mysticism or, in modern Christianity, the Protestant principle. Mysticism and the Protestant principle similarly militate against absolutizing any expression of the Ultimate: "The Holy as the Ultimate lies beyond any of its embodiments." The embodiments of the Holy are needed, but are secondary to the Ultimate itself. The third constitutive aspect of the experience of the Holy is the ethical or prophetic element. Justice is a universal principle that transcends every particular religion; denying justice in the name of the Holy is always demonic. Religion without justice becomes a party to evil, while religion without the sacramental and mystical-critical elements becomes moralistic and eventually secular.[48]

Tillich's theology of religions thus rephrased his original theology of religious socialism. In 1965, near the end of his life, in his last public appearance, he offered a name, smacking of Hegel, for the unity of the three elements, "the religion of the concrete spirit." The inner aim of religion, Tillich argued, is to become the sacramental-mystical-prophetic religion of the concrete spirit. The entire history of religions is a struggle to realize it, the fight of the Unconditioned against religion within religion. Harnack, claiming that Christianity embraces everything within the history of religions, caught a glimpse of this idea, but he cared only about Culture Protestantism. Tillich's last word was a plea for the universalism of concrete spirit: "The universality of a religious statement does not lie in an all-embracing abstraction which would destroy religion as such but in the depths of every concrete religion. Above all, it lies in the openness to spiritual freedom both from one's own foundation and for one's foundation."[49]

These ideas radiated distinctly across the field of theology and beyond it. Among the theological giants that arose between the two world wars and toppled the Ritschlian school, Tillich stands out for influencing the entire field of theology *and* for shaping how nontheological scholars of religion viewed religion *and* for reaching a vast public audience. His strategy was a form of soft imperialism that imposed a "religious" consciousness on many who didn't want it; Tillich delighted in telling his Frankfurt school atheist friends that they were religious without knowing it. He made religion make sense to vast audiences that did not belong to a religious community or were on their way out. He recalled of his chaplaincy during World War I: "If I used Biblical language to the soldiers, it meant nothing to them—they were about to die, and yet the Bible had nothing to say to them. I preached sermons, therefore, that never used any of the language of the Bible. They were a little mystical, a little poetical, and also had a touch of common sense, and they had an effect." The bestsellers of his later career used a similar strategy to great effect.[50]

Tillich told his audiences that good philosophy struggles between skepticism and faith and between demonic and divine forces. No worthwhile philosopher settles for mere analysis. All creative philosophers struggle with the mystery of existence, caught between the possibilities of affirming and negating life. Schelling and Hegel were his favorites, in that order, but Tillich allowed that both soared too high on too much hubris. Tillich regretted that the logical side of Hegel's work droned the same noise in the same rhythm. He prized the other Hegel—the philosopher of life who wrote *Phenomenology* and delivered sprawling, probing, opinionated lecture series on religion, art, nature, history, and the history of philosophy. Modern anthropologists studied bones and culture but not the human spirit; Hegel, commendably, grappled with the human spirit.[51]

Tillich does not get his due in books on the Frankfurt school because he was insistently a theologian within it and the scholarly gatekeepers of the Frankfurt legacy do not want theologians. He perceived Hegel's under-recognized influence on Marx before it became fashionable to say that Marx was not a dogmatic materialist. He caught Marx's Hegelian humanism before J. P. Mayer and Siegfried Landshut—contributors to Tillich's journal *Neue Blätter*—published, in 1932, Marx's previously unknown *Economic and Philosophic Manuscripts of 1844*. Throughout his career, Tillich believed that Marx was a secular prophet and existentialist, albeit with a problematic utopian impulse, and that Marx's dialectical and humanist tropes are more important than the economic arguments of *Capital*.[52]

In his Frankfurt years, Tillich's Marxism rested on the centrality of the proletarian struggle, the critique of commodity fetishism, the suspicion of ideological taint in bourgeois thought, the unmasking of ideological distortion, and the prophetic condemnation of exploitation and oppression. That is, it was essentially political. In his later career he deepened his debt to critical theory, largely as compensation for losing even an imagined political context, and he relied more heavily on onto-logical and psychoanalytic arguments. The most deeply Marxist piece he ever wrote, "The Class Struggle and Religious Socialism," appeared in 1929, just before he moved to his academic nirvana at Frankfurt. It rang brilliantly with what matters about Marxism, which later caused Tillich to bury it.

Marxism, he said, is "primarily a reality and only secondarily an idea." What is real is the raising of the oppressed from abjection and oppression "to a powerful consciousness of meaning." The existential real-ity of proletarian uplift outstrips every intellectual rendering of it. Marx-ism as an idea, whatever it is, is much less important than the Marxian reality. To Tillich the reality of the proletarian revolution was a religious achievement marking a breakthrough toward universal human dignity, not merely a struggle for political power and a socialized economy. To conceive socialism as a religious phenomenon is to view socialism "as a genuine revelation of the human situation of our time." Radical versions of Christian socialism were right to theologize the proletarian movement as a struggle for the kingdom of God.[53]

In 1950 Adams included this article in the first draft of *The Protestant Era*. Tillich was aghast, imploring Adams it would ruin him in Amer-ica: "You can't publish that! Oh, no, no, it's too Marxist." Adams oblig-ingly eliminated it from a reader that otherwise reflected Tillich's early thought. Tillich's discussion of the kingdom of God in volume three of *Systematic Theology*, published near the end of his life, rambled with faint echoes of religious socialism minus any reference to the proletariat, for which he substituted a depoliticized euphemism, "the bearers of history." Tillich knew his early writings said it better. In 1929 he said that Chris-tian theology needed Marxism as a preventive to rendering the kingdom ethic as mere utopianism, notwithstanding that Marxism had its own utopia problem: "Religious socialism must recognize the inevitability of the class struggle and disclose its demonic character. Its task cannot be to call for socialism without a class struggle. To do so would be to betray the real situation of the proletariat, to withdraw from reality. Religious socialism would then become utopianism, a utopianism that would be no better for its religious sanction."[54]

He felt the ambiguity of his situation before he suddenly lost every-thing that mattered to him. Was he wasting his time hanging onto liberal Protestantism, as his Frankfurt friends told him? Tillich had a profound and subsequently haunting answer. Protestantism, he said, is only Protestant when it transcends its confessional status. Protestantism and socialism could have developed differently, so the enmity between them was not inevitable. However, to the extent that socialism expresses the proletarian situation, it challenges Protestantism to discover its true nature in the Protestant principle—the creative power of criticism expressing the relation between the Unconditioned and the conditioned. The power that grasps us in the state of faith is not a God-object. It is the power that points us to the infinite and inexhaustible depth of our being, criticizing every form of religious pride and secular self-sufficiency. It says that the human situation is basically distorted because human beings arrogantly make gods of themselves, their desires, and their products. Human beings are unities of body and soul, but this biblical truism became so alien to the churches that they had to learn it from the socialist movement.[55]

Tillich appreciated that liberal Protestantism respected science and modern criticism and espoused a humanistic ideal of personality. But the liberal Protestant emphasis on individual reason and morality yielded little self-criticism of its idolatrous elements. Schleiermacher's religion of consciousness is edifying mostly to middle-class churchgoers. Liberal Protestantism had no chance of fusing with the oppressed as long as it identified religious feeling with the sphere of consciousness. Tillich judged that depth psychology was like socialism in recovering lost worlds of meaning and vitality. It was no coincidence that psychoanalysis spread in the same Protestant nations that suffered massive breakdowns of the conscious personality through war, trauma, loss, and destruction. Religion has to get to the subconscious basis of desires and choices. Liberal Protestantism was too rationalistic and isolating to do it.[56]

Tillich never forgot that he began as a traumatized German militarist staggering into a new world, though it took him longer than he said to let go of Prussian chauvinism. He carefully veiled to American audiences the extent of his dependence on Hegel and Schelling, and he shrewdly cut through these entanglements by scapegoating Ritschlian liberalism. The Ritschlian school, he would say, fatefully severed love from justice and power by reducing love to emotion. It banished ontology from theology and lived off culture religion, a mere husk. Occasionally Tillich remembered that a better theology would not have prevented Germany from invading Belgium and France. The remedy to bad liberalism, in any case, was to restore the Trinitarian holism of love, power, and justice, building upon Hegel's ontology of love.[57]

Ontology asks the simple, slippery, confounding question of what it means to be, describing structures that are common to everything that participates in being. Tillich said these structures must exist because being is undeniable, and thus it must have connected and conflicting forces. He loved the saying of Heraclitus that the logos of being is the power that keeps the world going, and the saying of Xenophanes that Mind is the divine power that swings the wheel of being. He absorbed the Aristotelian principle that the universal eros drives everything toward the pure actuality that moves the world as the object of love, not as a cause. With Augustine, Boehme, Schelling, and Schopenhauer, Tillich held together the concept of will as a marker of power and the logos of being that preserves the element of justice. With Augustine and Hegel, he said that love is greater than power and justice.[58]

If love were merely an emotion, it could not be commanded. Tillich embraced Hegel's dictum that the love commandment to love your neighbor as yourself, correctly understood, fulfills the law. Life is being in actuality. Love is the moving power of life, the desire to reconcile the estranged. Being is the power of being to endure and overcome nonbeing, which is not actual without the love that drives all that is toward all from which it is estranged. Tillich stressed the Hegelian point that separation cannot be ontologically ultimate, for that which is *essentially* separated cannot be united. Estrangement is a falling away from original oneness; whatever is absolutely estranged from me can only destroy me. Tillich ran through love as eros, *epithymia*, *philia*, and New Testament *agape*, cautioning that agape is not the highest form of love. Agape is the sacrificial depth of love—love cutting the whole of life and all other forms of love. Agape is love cutting into love in the same way that revelation "is reason cutting into reason." Like Hegel, Tillich wished that "self-love" could be banished as a concept, or at least construed as a metaphor. Self-affirmation, selfishness, and self-acceptance are important realities, but none qualify as self-love, for love is the drive to unify the separated, and every self is a unity of self-consciousness.[59]

Tillich has influenced me more than any other philosophical theologian, and Niebuhr is the social ethicist that I constantly think through, with, and against. Their affinities outnumbered their differences; they differed from each other chiefly over the role of philosophy in theology; and Tillich made far better use of philosophy. But my leading regrets about Tillich are the same ones I hold about Niebuhr. Both opted out of solidarity movements for social justice and postcolonial liberation. Both ridiculed social gospel socialists and religious idealists who battled in solidarity movements. Both basked in the applause of the American empire. And both justified these positions in their later careers with Marxist reasons. First they burdened Christian socialism with Marxist requirements and expectations. Then they had an excuse to drop Christian socialism (Niebuhr after 1945) or do almost nothing for it (Tillich). Both theologians defended the American empire whenever it had an interest at stake in the so-called Third World, and both were scathing in ridiculing ethical socialists who battled for "lost" causes.

The figures who pulled the ecumenical movement into global solidarity struggles for social justice and postcolonial reordering were the scorned religious idealists who never accepted Niebuhr's framework: Mordecai Johnson, Benjamin E. Mays, Howard Thurman, Martin Luther King Jr., Pauli Murray, Myles Horton, Walter Muelder. It's the left wing of the black social gospel and its white allies. Those who stuck with social gospel radicalism did not believe that struggles for justice were optional depending on their success or that the welfare state eliminated the need for economic democracy. Quitting the struggle was not an option for them, and thus not considered.[60]

9

Struggling for Liberation

Breaking White Supremacy and Sexism

Every form of liberation theology begins in solidarity with oppressed people, privileges their experiences, views the world from their perspectives, and calls for liberation from domination and dependence. And every liberationist discourse grapples with the haunting verdict of black lesbian feminist poet Audre Lorde that the master's house will never be sundered by using the master's tools. Lorde may have been right, but her own brilliant tool-wielding was evidence to the contrary, as was the pioneering liberationism of W. E. B. Du Bois, Martin Luther King Jr., and Rosemary Radford Ruether. Du Bois was steeped in Harvard, Emerson, Hegel, James, the University of Berlin, and later, Marx, using all to sunder the master's house. The key to King's incomparable greatness was his capacity to bridge audiences and movements lacking any history of dealing with each other. Ruether employed the the tools of her training to co-found feminist liberation theology and theorize the relationships of feminism to other forms of liberation.

Philosophically, Du Bois and King had Hegel, Marx, and numerous post-Kantian personal idealists and Christian socialists in common. Both employed Christian and post-Kantian arguments about the universality of human dignity and both were rooted in the hybrid character of African American culture, refusing to conceive black life in competitive relation to European or Euro-American life. Hegel's influence on Du Bois showed through in Du Bois' signature claim that he was a doubly conscious striver prevented by a racist veil and caste system from attaining true self-consciousness. On similar grounds, plus Hegel's influence on personalist theory, King described Hegel as his favorite philosopher, citing Hegel's concept of God's revelatory cunning in history and his holism. Ruether, though late to adopt a philosophical perspective, gravitated to Whitehead upon realizing that she needed a philosophical basis for her claims about divine reality and eco-feminism. Liberationist criticism begins with harm and critique, yielding a fierce desire to understand, as exemplified by Du Bois, King, and Ruether.

Du Bois was born in Great Barrington, Massachusetts, in 1868. He loved his mother, Mary Silvina Burghardt Du Bois, but later seethed that she and her family pushed his father, Alfred Du Bois, out of their life. Alfred Du Bois was born in Haiti, descending from free people of color and a wealthy physician of French Huguenot origins, Dr. James Du Bois. Du Bois eventually met his stern, mannered, austere grandfather Alexander, but had no memory of his father, who left when he was an infant. In *Darkwater* (1920) Du Bois introduced Alfred Du Bois with Homeric imagery: "Alfred, my father, must have seemed a splendid vision in that little valley under the shelter of those mighty hills. He was small and beautiful of face and feature, just tinted with the sun, his curly hair chiefly revealing his kinship to Africa." In this telling, Alfred Du Bois was romantic, kindly, dashing, and a dreamer, albeit unreliable: "He yielded and flared back, asked forgiveness and forgot why, became the harshly-held favorite, who ran away and rioted and roamed and loved and married my brown mother."[1]

Alfred Du Bois, however, almost certainly committed bigamy when he married Mary Burghardt, and he never contacted his son after fleeing, despite living in New England into the late 1880s. Du Bois obscured his father's lack of interest in him by misstating his age, whereabouts, and longevity. In *Darkwater* he claimed to remember "urgent letters" from his father telling them to join him in New Milford, "but mother no longer trusted his dreams, and he soon faded out of our lives into silence." In *Dusk of Dawn* (1940) he remembered differently that his father, "a light mulatto, died in my infancy, so that I do not remember him." In *The Autobiography of W. E. B. Du Bois* (1968) he said his father lived with him for "a few years" before moving to Connecticut "to build a life and home for mother and me." The later Du Bois absolved his father of any blame, claiming that his mother's clannish, rustic family got rid of Alfred because he had cultured manners and was not black enough.[2]

Mary Du Bois rented a dilapidated house near the railroad tracks, two blocks from a stretch of saloons and prostitution, which she shared with a similarly destitute white family. She struggled with depression and rarely said a word. Then she moved next to the railroad station, suffered a stroke, and coped with a lame leg and a withered hand. Yet Du Bois idealized his childhood because he had a twofold thesis about the meaning of his life: One, he was an outsider who understood the dominant society from within and without. Two, lacking "the problem," he would have enjoyed the perks of his brilliance and not bothered with social justice activism. As it was, his very being was a problem in racist America, so he was compelled to deal with it. Idealizing his youth buttressed both aspects of this self-interpretation.

Great Barrington, a Republican Anglo-Saxon town of five thousand, had fifty African Americans. Du Bois received good schooling and had plenty of friends, black and white. In the world of adults, he noticed, whites and blacks kept more or less to themselves, whites had the good jobs, and blacks were pretty much restricted to day labor, farming, and house service. Moreover, Great Barrington definitely had something against the incoming Irish and South Germans that labored in the mills. But Du Bois experienced almost no racial discrimination in his youth. He despised the Irish and South Germans just like his white friends, annexing "the rich and well-to-do as my natural companions. Of such is the kingdom of snobs!"[3]

He lacked any sense of being a racial other until the age of ten, when a girl visiting the town refused to exchange visiting cards with him: "Then it dawned upon me with a certain suddenness that I was different from the others; or like, mayhap, in heart and life, and longing, but shut out from their world by a vast veil." Du Bois may have lost his innocence that suddenly, on the edge of puberty, like many others. But years later he seemed to place this incident during high school, recalling that in high school he "began to feel the pressure of the 'veil of color.'" In any case Du Bois caught the great break of his life in high school.[4]

His high school principal, Frank Hosmer, came from the milieu of New England, Congregationalist, abolitionist families that ran the American Missionary Association (AMA) and the Freedmen's Bureau. In later life he served as president of a missionary college in Hawaii, returned to Massachusetts to serve in the state legislature, and died in 1918 from overwork in the Red Cross. Hosmer told Du Bois he was intellectually gifted, so he should study algebra, geometry, Latin, and Greek. Du Bois later reflected that had he lacked a principal who cared about him, he would have trained for a trade and thought nothing of it. In the late 1870s Du Bois followed his mother from the Episcopal Church to the Congregational Church, also attending the African Methodist Episcopal Zion Church. These churches were important social outlets for him; he loved the prose of the King James Bible and impressed churchgoers with his Greek. Du Bois absorbed New England Puritanism at a deep level, especially the conviction that truth is a moral absolute transcending mere data. He never stopped believing that liberty is the conformity of one's will to moral duty. Shortly after Du Bois graduated from high school, his mother died of a stroke, liberating him from having to care for her: "Now it was the choking gladness and solemn feel of wings!" Du Bois was brainy, self-absorbed, and eager to fly, though not without a "half-guilty feeling." He vowed to study at Harvard, but accepted the aid of local Congregationalists who got him into Fisk University in Nashville, Tennessee.[5]

Fisk opened in 1866 on the site of a Union army hospital, where three officers of the AMA pledged to build a school. On its first day two hundred former slaves enrolled; within a month there were six hundred; by the end of the year it had a thousand students. Clinton B. Fisk, a Freedmen's Bureau official and former Union army colonel, ran the school in its early years, directing teachers from the AMA and the Freedmen's Bureau. Fisk was thoroughly New England in some ways, producing Afro-Saxons, or Black Puritans. But most of Du Bois' classmates were otherwise very different from any Afro-Americans he had known in New England. Some were wealthy sons or daughters of white planters; a few came directly from farming backgrounds; most were children of preachers, barbers, undertakers, physicians, or privileged domestic servants. Some had faced mobs and witnessed lynchings, and nearly all were steeped in the South's lexicon of racial insult and exclusion.

Du Bois began to realize what it meant for blacks lacking his unusual background to be black in America. Outside the Fisk campus, the slightest contact with a white person could bring danger. Fisk drew him into a black world, mostly gratefully, although emotional Southern black worship frightened him: "A sort of suppressed terror hung in the air and seemed to seize them—a pythian madness, a demoniac possession, that lent terrible reality to song and word." Absorbing the "wail and groan and outcry," Du Bois knew he would never be black in that way; New England reticence and intellectualism were too deep in him. For a while he stuck with placid Congregational orthodoxy, until Fisk imposed apologetics on him, which backfired. Du Bois spurned the special pleading of George Frederick Wright's *The Logic of Christian Evidences* (1880), which claimed to reconcile natural science and Christian orthodoxy. The book seemed as ridiculous to him as Fisk's anti-dancing moralism. In 1888 he gave a graduation address praising Bismarck for forging a nation out of bickering peoples, contending that black Americans needed similar leadership. Then he entered the Harvard class of 1890 with third-year status, having received a scholarship aimed at diversifying Harvard's ingrown white New England constituency.[6]

He had expected to go to Harvard, and his mettle prevailed. Du Bois studied under William James, Josiah Royce, Hegelian moral philosopher George Herbert Palmer, social gospel theologian Francis Greenwood Peabody, and historian Albert Bushnell Hart, taking especially to Peabody and James. He decided that he believed in will, ideals, and the power of spirit backed by Spirit divine, not traditional theism. Du Bois believed especially in the power of ethical will, an idea shared by James, Royce, Palmer, Peabody, and Hart, with a range of religious inflections. He moved up to the doctoral program, studying under Hart, economist Frank W. Taussig, and sociologist Edward Cummings. Hart was a New England idealist and German-trained historian who kept these identities strictly compartmentalized. Moral propaganda had its place, but not in academic scholarship. Hart loathed imperialism on ethical grounds, but academic history had to be purged of every kind of propaganda and cheerleading. He told Du Bois that British historicism, though entertaining, was loaded with British hero worship, moralism, and colonial pretension. The Germans pioneered serious, critical, respectable, academic history, a model to be followed. Du Bois absorbed Hart's historiography, plus two years of German historiography first hand at the University of Berlin, studying under political historian Heinrich von Treitschke and economists Adolf Wagner and Gustav von Schmoller.

He was enthralled by Germany: "I dreamed and loved and wandered and sang." Du Bois felt liberated from racial hostility and caste, although he noticed that Germans denigrated Jews and Poles. He thoroughly enjoyed himself, catching a glimpse of life's beauty, and had sexual relationships that would have been unthinkable in the United States. He loved German Romanticism, especially Goethe and Beethoven, absorbed lectures on post-Kantian idealism and Socialism, and felt overwhelmed by the latter, surprised that Socialism was so complicated. His German teachers, however, turned out to be less restrained than Hart by academic rules. Wagner and Schmoller lionized the German welfare state and army, and Treitschke cheered for German imperialism. German academics, it turned out, did not conceal their romantic nationalism and colonizing ambitions. Du Bois did not blame them, writing in his journal: "These are my plans: to make a name in science, to make a name in literature and thus to raise my race. Or perhaps to raise a visible empire in Africa thro' England, France, or Germany." He did not think it was grandiose to see a future emperor in the mirror, though he puzzled at what to call this ambition: "I rejoice as a strong man to run a race, and I am strong—is it egotism—is it assurance—or is it the silent call of the world spirit that makes me feel that I am royal and that beneath my scepter a world of kinds shall bow."[7]

By that optic it was no big deal for him to brush off Treitschke's slur against "mulattoes" like himself, because Du Bois was a romantic authoritarian like Treitschke. He wanted desperately to complete his doctorate at Berlin, but his money ran out and Du Bois had to settle for Harvard, becoming the first black American to earn a Harvard Ph.D., in 1895. He later recalled that upon finishing his blissful two years in Europe he went to Paris for a last look, spent his last dollar, took passage to the United States in steerage, and maddeningly found himself "suddenly back into 'nigger'-hating America!"[8]

Du Bois, on black dignity and humanity, was fully Du Bois from the beginning, although that included a taken-for-granted patronizing view of Africa. Then it took him many years to shed his romantic authoritarianism and elitism. It happened mostly by adopting a socialist vision of radical, multiracial, economic democracy. Meanwhile the Hegelian influence showed through in his introduction to a national audience in August 1897. Du Bois' article "Strivings of the Negro People," published in *Atlantic Monthly*, introduced the magazine's audience to a bracing, unimagined black intellectualism. Six years later it was the stunning opening chapter of *The Souls of Black Folk* (1903).

Du Bois surely had in mind Hegel's insight about the sociality of consciousness and power when he famously expounded on the double consciousness of African Americans, although he never explicitly said so. There are traces of the double-consciousness idea in other thinkers who influenced Du Bois, especially Emerson, James, and Johann Gottfried von Herder, although Du Bois did not mention them either, and James had not yet published his two-selves idea when Du Bois wrote "Strivings of the Negro People." Du Bois knew Hegel's idea that self-consciousness exists only in being acknowledged: self-consciousness comes out of itself when it encounters another self-consciousness, finding itself in an *other* being, and superseding the other in doing so. Du Bois entered the national picture by posing a double-minded question of his own: What does it feel like to be treated as a problem? He told *Atlantic Monthly* readers he heard this unasked question every day. It lay behind the awkward self-justifying remarks of white strangers, such as, "I know an excellent colored man in my town," or, "I fought at Mechanicsville," or, "Do not these Southern outrages make your blood boil?" The real question, Du Bois said, was seldom asked or answered. What was it like, for a black American like him, to be "born with a veil, and gifted with second-sight in this American world—a world which yields him no true self-consciousness, but only lets him see himself through the revelation of the other world"? The veil shut the Negro out from the world of the others.[9]

Emerson's concept of double consciousness underwrote Emersonian spirituality. Every self possesses a doorway to the sacred realm through its own spiritual nature. Double consciousness is the dichotomy between a grubby, calculating, sensate lower self and the higher self of a reflective soul. To Emerson the idea of double consciousness was transhistorical, generically human, and potentially redemptive. To Du Bois the double consciousness of the black American was gritty, social, historical, and problematic. It was the experience of being compelled to look at one's self "through the eyes of others, of measuring one's soul by the tape of a world that looks on in amused contempt and pity." Du Bois had never felt otherwise, "save perhaps in babyhood and in Europe." In America he felt his duality as an American and a Negro—"two souls, two thoughts, two unreconciled strivings; two warring ideals in one dark body, whose dogged strength alone keeps it from being torn asunder." This struggle to forge his double self into a better, truer, self-consciously integral self was the key to African American existence: "The history of the American Negro is the history of this strife." It raged through every version of the hopeless debate between nationalism and integration, in which black Americans argued about which of their selves to give up. The answer was not to Africanize America, "for America has too much to teach the world and Africa." Neither did he believe in bleaching his black soul "in a flood of white Americanism," for he was certain that "Negro blood has a message for the world." The answer was to be allowed to be fully a Negro and an American, and thus "a co-worker in the kingdom of culture."[10]

Du Bois struck gold by projecting his struggle with marginality and duality onto all African Americans. Emerson worried that Americans, lacking a culture of their own, lived parasitically off European culture. Americans needed to unleash their inward spiritual capacities to create a beautiful culture based on genuine self-knowledge—something their outward American freedom enabled them to do. Du Bois shared this idea of culture as a commonwealth of value and aspiration and its American ideal of self-creation and individuality. The very end of human striving is to be a coworker in creating a cultural commonwealth. But white America was deeply problematic for blacks, a "race" that Du Bois described repeatedly as backward and undeveloped. *Atlantic Monthly* was not the place to linger over the meaning of "Negro blood" or how many races existed. Du Bois settled for a half sentence describing the Negro as a "seventh son" of the world preceded by "the Egyptian and Indian, the Greek and Roman, the Teuton and Mongolian." He boasted that the spirituals were the only true American music and no group surpassed black Americans in espousing the Declaration of Independence. Black Americans, Du Bois acknowledged, needed practical education more than ever; he did not dispute Booker T. Washington on this point. But above all they needed "the broader, deeper, higher culture of gifted minds and pure hearts." Black Americans needed to share in the commonwealth of (elite) culture, which began by aspiring to it. To secure the vote was a matter of "sheer self-defense." Beyond that, Afro-Americans needed work, culture, and liberty flowing together, "each growing and aiding each, and all striving toward that vaster ideal that swims before the Negro people, the ideal of human brotherhood, gained through the unifying ideal of Race." This ideal of race, he asserted, did not bring blacks into opposition with whites. It operated "in large conformity to the greater ideals of the American Republic, in order that some day on American soil two world-races may give each to each those characteristics both so sadly lack."[11]

Later that year, in 1897, addressing the newly founded American Negro Academy, Du Bois lingered over Negro blood and races—entangling race with nationality and offering a table of the ostensible races. Black Americans, he said, were inclined to "minimize race distinctions," since race was used against them every day. Du Bois sympathized, but countered that race is terribly important. In fact, race is the most important thing of all: "The history of the world is the history, not of individuals, but of groups, not of nations, but of races, and he who ignores or seeks to override the race idea in human history ignores or overrides the central thought of history." So, what is a race? Du Bois started with a mushy sociohistorical answer that answered nothing: "It is a vast family of human beings, generally of common blood and language, always of common history, traditions, and impulses, who are both voluntarily and involuntarily striving together for the accomplishment of certain more or less vividly conceived ideals of life."[12]

It was hard to say what that meant, so Du Bois offered a twofold table of the races, appealing to Darwinian biologist Thomas H. Huxley and German ethnographer Friedrich Ratzel for at least the first category. There were at least two primary races, and possibly three—"the whites and Negroes, and possibly the yellow race." And there were eight historic races—"the Slavs of eastern Europe, the Teutons of middle Europe, the English of Great Britain and America, the Romance nations of Southern and Western Europe, the Negroes of Africa and America, the Semitic people of Western Asia and Northern Africa, the Hindoos of Central Asia, and the Mongolians of Eastern Asia." Du Bois had to know what was wrong here. Biological science was belatedly dubious about the first category, and the second category was a hopeless mess of groups lacking parallelism with the first category. If there were eight historic races, why did Native Americans not count as a race? If the English counted as a race, how could the Spanish be left out? All that Du Bois could say was that historians would judge which groups mattered enough to be deemed an historic race and which ones belonged to "minor race groups." Racial distinction, he reasoned, surely began with physical differences, but there were spiritual and psychical differences that cut deeper than physical characteristics. In that case, race and nationality could not be disentangled. The Teutonic nations, for example, were united first by racial identity and common blood, but the emergent commonalities of history, law, religion, habits of thought, and a conscious striving together for certain ideals were more important.[13]

However that sorted out, African Americans were despised and brutalized in America. Even if no one could say what, exactly, a race was, white Americans had no trouble picking out one for the worst abuse. Thus Du Bois told the American Negro Academy it was desperately needed: "We need race organizations: Negro colleges, Negro newspapers, Negro business organizations, a Negro school of literature and art, and an intellectual clearing house for all these products of the Negro mind." Reprising his double-consciousness thesis, he said that black Americans were Americans by virtue of their birth, citizenship, political ideals, language, religion, and nothing else: "Farther than that, our Americanism does not go." African Americans were Negroes in everything else that mattered. They gave their country its only original music and fairy tales, and its only pathos and humor amid America's "mad money-getting plutocracy." America's eight million blacks, Du Bois declared, were "the advance guard of the Negro people." If they took their "just place in the van of Pan-Negroism," the Negro race as a whole would advance and Afro-Americans would insure their future as a race in America.[14]

Two things needed to happen in America, he argued. First, African Americans had to overcome their own "immorality, crime, and laziness." Second, white Americans had to permit "a more impartial selection of ability in the economic and intellectual world." Du Bois declared that black Americans would either conquer their vices or be destroyed by them: "We are diseased, we are developing criminal tendencies, and an alarmingly large percentage of our men and women are sexually impure. The Negro Academy should stand and proclaim this over the housetops, crying with Garrison: *I will not equivocate, I will not retreat a single inch, and I will be heard*."[15]

The academy loudly acclaimed this appeal to racial solidarity and idealism, taking in stride Du Bois' insulting rhetoric of disease, venality, and backwardness. No one objected that his fixation with lifting up a male elite was similarly problematic or that his blend of neo-Lamarckian social theory and Hegelian idealism was dubious. Herbert Spencer was the commanding thinker of the age when Du Bois began his career. One could not be a philosopher, natural scientist, or social scientist without mastering Spencer's fusion of Darwinian natural selection, Lamarckian development, Malthusian population theory, early thermodynamics, laissez-faire economics, and libertarian politics. Spencer coined the phrases "social Darwinism" and "survival of the fittest." Like Charles Darwin he ranked human groups hierarchically from the "savage" to the "civilized." Unlike Darwin he said that Darwinian natural selection, though important, is not the main mechanism for generating biological diversity. Spencer taught that every individual's biological development (ontogeny) recapitulates the entire evolutionary development (phylogeny) of its species. The environment acts directly on organisms, yielding new races, and the survival of a race depends on its interaction with its environment. If there is a one-to-one correspondence between phylogeny and ontogeny, such that ontogeny repeats forms of the ancestors, the characteristics of "less developed races" must exist within the more advanced races.[16]

Life is a continuous process of development from incoherent homo-geneity (protozoa) to coherent heterogeneity. Races are real and hierarchi-cally ordered, with traits that can be measured. Any political intervention that impedes this natural process is harmful. The foremost biologist of the late nineteenth century, Ernst Haeckel, also a social Darwinist, pro-nounced that the hierarchical ordering of the races was obvious, intelli-gence was obviously the key distinguishing factor, Africans were obviously at the bottom of the human order, and any policy that helped the unfit to survive was odious. White people, he claimed, had an unbroken his-tory of superiority; in fact, the Caucasian "Mediterranean man" was the only species (excepting the Mongolian) to have arisen above nature to the status of civilization: "The Caucasian, or Mediterranean man (*Homo Mediterraneus*), has from time immemorial been placed at the head of all the races of men, as the most highly developed and perfect."[17]

Du Bois later recalled that he felt the power of Spencer's system. Social scientists sought to discover social laws correlating with Spencer's physical laws. Albion Small, the founding chair of sociology at the University of Chicago and founder of the *American Journal of Sociology*, countered that sociology needed to operate inductively and historically. Du Bois was mindful of the lag between the regnant neo-Lamarckian theory and what he later called "actual scientific accomplishment," although in 1897 he did not know how this story would turn out. That year he scrounged for as much consolation as he could find in the regnant picture, telling the American Negro Academy that the "same natural laws" governed the development of all races. If this meant that biology determined so-called "racial temperaments," Du Bois was prepared to admit that such temper-aments existed, as long as he got to interpret them.[18]

Small contended that Spencerian sociology was too theory-laden and deductive, analogizing from chemistry and genetics to social processes. Meanwhile biologists admitted they could not find a determinant of racial difference and basis of racial classification. Huxley and French anthropol-ogist Paul Broca focused on skin color, but got nowhere. Others including Broca pressed hard on facial angles, jaws and skull size, to no avail, as Caucasians alone included every possible head shape. For a while Huxley, Broca, Haeckel, and Friedrich Müller believed that human hair must hold the answer, but that got nowhere too. Then early twentieth-century biology refuted the strong version (one-to-one correspondence) of reca-pitulation theory and social science turned away from neo-Lamarckian explanations. Had Du Bois launched his career a decade later, he would have eschewed neo-Lamarckian explanations of "race," which might have tempered his racial romanticism. But that is speculative and not what happened, and scholars have clashed over Du Bois' culpability in treating race as a biological category, and/or adopting a sociohistorical theory of race with a biological component, and/or legitimizing essentialist notions of racial temperament.[19]

Du Bois was influenced by the central European nationalists he read at Fisk, Harvard, and Berlin, which caused him to conceive black nationalism in European terms. He also absorbed Hegel's concept of world history as the struggle of the spirit of freedom to realize itself through specific historical peoples. Hegel traced the self-realization of Spirit through six historic peoples—the Chinese, Indians, Persians (culminating with Egyptians), Greeks, Romans, and Germans. Du Bois added to this scheme the Negro as a "seventh son" born with a veil and second sight. In Haitian vodou, the seventh son is the fortunate one, born with the gift of prophecy. Du Bois took up Hegel's trope that North America represented the future. History is about the struggle for freedom, he argued, North America played the leading role in it, and black Americans played the leading role in the North American struggle. Booker Washington's small-bore capitalism was too individualistic and compromised to be liberating; Du Bois needed a theory with greater scope and ambition. Historian Joel Williamson puts it aptly: "Out of slavery and out of the later striving of black folk for whiteness in an oppressive white world came a rising sense of black soul."[20]

Hegelian idealism, on this reading, helped Du Bois affirm the white culture that was in him. He refused to disparage the ideal of freedom, the politics of civil rights, or the intellectualism that he got from white culture. The two warring ideals within him were Hegelian antimonies, clashing toward breakthrough. Black Americans had begun to move toward self-consciousness in struggling for freedom. Du Bois believed that when black people knew their souls, they would know God truly as the divine Spirit of freedom and accept their whiteness; then History would move forward. Du Bois had a vision of blacks and whites joining together to create a nation based on human equality and freedom. It was a Christian vision in which black churches had a crucial role to play, although Du Bois believed from college onward that intellectually Hegel expressed what was true in Christianity, in a higher form.

Literary critic Henry Louis Gates says that double consciousness was a singularly illuminating metaphor for the psychology of citizenship faced by all African Americans. Political historian Lawrie Balfour says it was a trademark rhetorical device marking Du Bois' experience as a symbol of uplift and a member of an oppressed caste. Philosopher Robert Gooding-Williams argues that Du Bois used this idea to criticize the failings of black leaders. Philosopher Cornel West commends Du Bois for fixing on the dialectic of black self-recognition—in-but-not-of—but says that Du Bois oversimplified the cultural predicament of black Americans. Sociologist Lawrence Bobo and political theorist Adolph Reed say we should stop talking about double consciousness because it didn't explain anything (Bobo), or it smacked of nineteenth-century Lamarckianism (Reed), and Du Bois dropped it anyway. Historian Ernest Allen Jr. says it was merely a tactic to ease the fears of Talented Tenth achievers that their success in the white world would be discredited. Literary critic Paul Gilroy, in his early work, described double consciousness as the key to everything that matters—the dialectic of fulfillment and transfiguration. But the later Gilroy said it is too nineteenth century to matter anymore, because it cannot handle the postmodern experience of cultural multiplicity and multiple identities. Political historian Terence L. Johnson describes double consciousness as the key to Du Bois' theorizing of black sorrow, despair, and hope, contending that his construal of hope amid suffering and despair should be as deeply inscribed in liberal thought as the principles of liberty and opportunity. Social ethicist Eboni Marshall Turman says that Du Bois left a problematic legacy for black moral agency by pathologizing black embodiment. An "is" that only "is" insofar as it is established by an other is toxic for black selves under the furious attempts of white supremacy to maintain its dominance.[21]

All these arguments have a point to make, and those of Balfour, West, Johnson, and Turman are especially valuable to me. The double-consciousness trope was creatively enabling for Du Bois. The dialectic of recognition is a reality, whether for good or not. Sustaining hope amid suffering and despair is a high calling. And any argument that makes black bodies invisible or secondary is not liberating. The double-consciousness trope endures partly because it mirrors what we say about race—a social invention, yet terribly real and embedded in psyches, social structures, and communal legacies. Double consciousness was a truth of Du Bois' experience and a source of creativity in him. He fashioned an alternative to the draining debate between nationalists and integrationists by affirming his tortured double consciousness. African Americans had to stop arguing about which of their selves to give up, opting for a robust, full-bodied struggle for radical democracy. However, when Du Bois said that black bodies are gifted with second sight, he was thinking like Emerson—privileging powers of mind over embodiment as a mechanism of resistance. That is problematic for every embodied self that struggles with the problems of identity and communal belonging under the continued fury of white supremacy to maintain its dominance.

The nationalist tradition said that separatism of some kind is the only salvation for black Americans. Du Bois refused to believe that, so he was willing to link arms with white liberals in founding the NAACP in 1909. By then he was the intellectual hero of the protest-activist wing of the black social gospel. The NAACP had plenty of liberals, black and white, for whom capitalism was a name for the freedom principle. Du Bois offended both groups every time he editorialized about the ravages of capitalism. Until World War I he recycled conventional socialist critiques of capitalist inequality and commercialism. But after Europe plunged into war in 1914, Du Bois leaned on John Hobson's argument that capitalism is imperialist, not merely unjust and corrupting.

Hobson was a British anti-imperialist and ethical socialist who argued that a new kind of imperialism emerged in the 1880s, one driven by economic competition for new markets and the discovery of natural riches in Africa. He wrote about this historical turn as it occurred, publishing ten books before he wrote *Imperialism* in 1902. Hobson said that modern capitalism was unsustainable without exploiting colonized markets. He made moral arguments, condemned British racism, stressed that politics matters, influenced Christian socialists, and compelled his readers to absorb that the new imperialism was harder to combat than the old one. Du Bois sharply amplified Hobson's argument that the vicious plunder of Africa relied on the equation of color with inferiority. The European powers took an important lesson from the British and American slave trades: the pillage and rape of Africa could be called something else if black people were less than human.[22]

Western movements for democracy and "progress" played crucial roles in accelerating the flow of finance capital to far-off lands, thus ratcheting up the clash of empires. Democracy was supposed to be the answer to the terrible problems of inequality, exploitation, and oppression. The ship of state was supposedly launched on the great tide of democratic expansion. Yet as democracy spread, so did the rule of might, regardless of which party won office. Democracy and imperialism grew together, unless—what? In England, the Labour Party became the vehicle of the ethical socialist and Christian socialist answer. In the United States, Du Bois would have stuck with the Socialist Party if Socialist leader Eugene Debs had been willing to fight for racial justice. But Debs said that socialism is the cure for racism, so he had no special message about racism; achieving socialism would abolish racism. The sophistry of that tack galled Du Bois, driving him out of the Socialist Party, though he supported Debs and Norman Thomas in their subsequent presidential campaigns.

He did not sneer at the democratic faith of radical liberals and socialists, because he shared it. Du Bois was a progressive who believed in radical democracy. But he cautioned that the seemingly paradoxical wedding of democracy and imperialism was not really puzzling. White workers were asked to share the spoils of exploiting people of color. The chief exploiter role that passed from the merchant prince to the aristocratic monopoly to the capitalist class now belonged to the democratic nation. Du Bois said the only solution to this miserable picture was for democratic socialism to reach all the way to the poor and excluded, not stopping with white workers. Socialism and the unions had made a beginning. The capitalist class would yield to the unions as long as it found new markets to exploit. Under modern capitalism the national bond was not based on something flimsy like patriotism, loyalty, or ancestor worship. It was based on the wealth that creates a middle class and flows to the working class. But most of this new wealth rested on the exploitation of Asians, Africans, South Americans, and West Indians. Du Bois believed the old capitalist exploitation was fading, and it was not the reason why Germans and Britons were slaughtering each other. Socialism was advancing in Germany and Britain, while both nations took for granted their right to rule and exploit nonwhite peoples. World War I was about which group of white nations would do so.

Du Bois acknowledged that Japan did not play along, because Japan demanded white treatment without allying with white nations. China, too, was increasingly independent, complicating the Western domination of China. But everything depended on how far the logic of democracy extended. If progressive movements accelerated the imperial logic of modern capitalism, the only solution was to universalize democracy. If the movements for liberalism, unionism, anti-imperialism, and socialism were to create a decent world, they had to struggle for democracy everywhere, not just at home. Du Bois implored, "We must go further. We must extend the democratic ideal to the yellow, brown, and black peoples." First the movements for democratic socialism had to win power wherever they existed. Then they had to fulfill the universalism of their creed; otherwise socialism was the worst form of hypocrisy. Du Bois believed that for the rest of his life.[23]

For forty years he was the intellectual hero of the protest-activist wing of the black social gospel. Reverdy Ransom, James R. L. Diggs, Richard R. Wright Jr., Robert Bagnall, George Frazier Miller, and Byron Gunner were prominent social gospel clerics in the Du Bois orbit. They contended that black churches had to join the struggle against white oppression and for comprehensive social justice; it was not enough for churches to help blacks survive a hostile society. Du Bois could be blistering about religious orthodoxy because he said it stunted human souls. In 1940, speaking at the commencement ceremony of his former employer, Wilberforce University, Du Bois excoriated the school's Christian legacy as "childish belief in fairy tales, a word-of-mouth adherence to dogma, and a certain sectarian exclusiveness." Wilberforce's tradition of religious orthodoxy, he charged, was "a miserable apprehension of the teaching of Christ." Welcome to your commencement! But Du Bois had a passionate religious spirit, a keen appreciation of Jesus, and a lover's quarrel with the black church.[24]

His writings were strewn with religious images, even after he supposedly dropped religion for Marxism. *The Souls of Black Folk* famously invoked "our spiritual strivings" and lauded the spirituals. *Darkwater* began with Du Bois' social gospel "Credo," conjured a black baby Jesus in his essay, "The Second Coming," conjured an adult black Jesus in his scathing essay, "Jesus Christ in Texas," and ended with a "Hymn to the Peoples" in which the Buddha walked with Christ. The later Du Bois drifted into the pro-Communist Left, the only political movement that strongly defended the rights of black Americans, and in the 1950s he became an outright Communist. Yet even the later Du Bois wrote about saving "the tattered shreds of God." His spiritual sensibility came through to many readers. They caught that a religious, arguably Christian passion lay behind Du Bois' furious attacks on unworthy ministers and church dogmatism.[25]

Even at Wilberforce, lashing the university for hiding behind miserable orthodoxy, Du Bois stumped for social gospel religion, telling the graduates it was not too late to mobilize the churches for social change. By 1940 that was an echo of what the younger Du Bois had hoped the church would become under the sway of the social gospel. In the early twentieth century he was a critical booster, taking for granted that the movement for black liberation had to be religion-friendly. Nothing compared to the black church as a source of inspiration, hope, solidarity, identity, belonging, entertainment, moral language, and transcendent meaning. Any movement worth building had to share in the life of the black church, speaking its language of hope and redemption. The black social gospel was founded on that conviction and fired by it.

Long before Martin Luther King Jr. burst onto the national scene in Montgomery, Alabama, there was a tradition of black social gospel leaders that struggled to abolish Jim Crow and the mania of racial lynching, refuting the racist culture that demeaned their human dignity. They showed that progressive theology could be combined with social justice politics in black church contexts. They refused to give up on the black churches, even as a chorus of black and white intellectuals contended that black churches were hopelessly self-centered, provincial, insular, anti-intellectual, and conservative. King's role models were black social gospel leaders who came of age in the 1920s: Benjamin E. Mays, J. Pius Barbour, Mordecai Johnson, and Howard Thurman. Their role models were the black social gospel founders.

The Personalist Socialist Radical King

King became the star of the civil rights movement by inspiring and uniting coalitions that had never existed previously. He inspired and united through the power of Christian love, his preaching artistry, and his almost superhuman magnanimity. He became a global icon by electrifying the March on Washington in August 1963 with his hopeful "I Have a Dream" vision of a free and equal American society. But the King of the Dream moment was already exhausted and fighting off despair. Afterwards he got only more so, until the end. King was more angry and radical in 1960 than in 1955, more in 1965 than in 1960, and more at the end, in 1968, than ever. In his last years he was more angry and radical than anyone around him, grieving that white supremacy still reigned in American society.

He keenly understood that he was the most hated person in America, and why. King compelled white Americans to confront the hostility for black Americans that they variously displayed and covered up. White Americans needed to confess their racism, relinquish their sense of racial entitlement, and build a culture of atonement for 246 years of chattel slavery and 100 years of racial segregation. No mere political movement would make that happen. In 1963, shortly after "I Have a Dream," King began to say that America was deeply sick and no mere reform movement would save it. The slaying of four church girls in Birmingham, Alabama—Addie Mae Collins, Denise McNair, Carole Robertson, and Cynthia Wesley—drove him to near-despair. He fought off everworsening depression and exhaustion, accepting reluctantly that no other life was in store for him. The movement *was* his life, and he didn't expect to reach the age of forty.

He was raised in a Southern, Baptist, clerical version of the black social gospel that he fortified at two graduate seminaries before beginning his ministry in Montgomery. King's maternal grandfather Alfred Daniel Williams took over tiny Ebenezer Baptist Church in Atlanta in 1894, moved his growing congregation several times, and died in 1931 of a heart attack. King's maternal grandmother Alberta Williams convinced Ebenezer to replace her husband with her son-in-law, Martin Luther King Sr., which left her intact as First Lady of the congregation. King Senior was rough-hewn and strong-willed, having come from rural poverty to claw his way to an education at Morehouse College. As a youth his classmates taunted him for smelling like the mules he tended. Then he endured snickering that he preached in his father-in-law's church and lived in his mother-in-law's house. Ebenezer was bankrupt when King Senior took over in January 1932, padlocked by a court order. He built it into a thriving congregation that straddled the line between a class church and a mass church, emphatically in the emotional preaching style of a mass church. King Senior raised his three children in middle-class privilege in the same hovering, raging, loving style that he ruled Ebenezer.[26]

He epitomized the authoritarian-entrepreneurial black Baptist preacher, raising money with bluster and daring. King Senior resurrected Ebenezer so quickly that by the end of his first year, he was Atlanta's highest paid black pastor. In 1934 he attended the Baptist World Alliance Congress in Berlin. His name was Michael King, and his three children were Christine, Michael Luther Jr. ("Little Mike") and Alfred Daniel ("A. D."); Little Mike was born in 1929. King Senior, enthralled at visiting Martin Luther's homeland and consorting with Baptist leaders, returned to a gala reception at Ebenezer. In a burst of emotion he honored the occasion by changing his name to Martin Luther King, adding that Little Mike would heretofore be named Martin Luther King Jr. Family and friends called the two Martin Luther Kings "Big Mike" and "Little Mike," which eventually morphed into "Daddy King" and "M. L."[27]

Daddy King, though pugnacious and domineering, always keeping the deacons in line, was also winsome, vibrant, and careful. He rebuked Jim Crow effrontery on the rare occasions that he failed to avoid white people, refusing to be addressed as "Boy." Being addressed by one's first name was also problematic in Jim Crow America, so black Americans often chose not to have one, opting for initials. Daddy King told his children to avoid whites; otherwise he did not talk about them or racism. To him, segregation was evil, white racism was a mystery best left to God, and there was nothing else to talk about concerning race. In the pulpit and at home he oscillated between cajoling and yelling, tirelessly admonishing about how to behave. His famous son, not coincidentally, never barked at anyone until very near the end of his life.

King absorbed the evangelical piety and social concerns of his parents. He got a more intellectual version of both things at Morehouse College, where Mays influenced him as president. He moved on to Crozer Seminary in Chester, Pennsylvania, where he read the canon of American liberal theology: *The Vicarious Sacrifice*, by Horace Bushnell; *An Outline of Christian Theology*, by William Newton Clarke; *Christian Theology in Outline*, by William Adams Brown; *Christianity and the Social Crisis* and *A Theology for the Social Gospel*, by Walter Rauschenbusch; and *A Philosophy of Religion*, by Edgar Brightman. King studied Clarke's textbook with particular care, identifying with Clarke's evangelical liberalism. He wrote papers that embraced Schleiermacher's Christology and affirmed that the kingdom of God "will be a society in which all men and women will be controlled by the eternal love of God." King said the social gospel was right in conceiving economic justice as an essential aspect of gospel teaching: "I am a profound advocator of the social gospel."[28]

Rauschenbusch converted King to social gospel socialism, a vision of economic democracy. King's storied encounter with Howard University president Mordecai Johnson, a Rauschenbusch protégé, occurred during King's second year at Crozer, at Fellowship House in Philadelphia. Johnson gave one of his customary bravura talks commending the anti-imperial nonviolence of the Gandhi movement. Hearing it from white Fellowship of Reconciliation (FOR) leader A. J. Muste had brought out King's incredulity. Hearing it from a black social gospel leader enthralled King: "His message was so profound and electrifying that I left the meeting and bought a half-dozen books on Gandhi's life and works." According to King, he relinquished his belief that "love your enemies" applies only to individual relationships.[29]

King misrepresented how and when he embraced Gandhian nonviolence, and he seriously understated the importance of his church and familial background. It took a great deal of scholarly deconstruction in the 1980s and 1990s to get a better account of both things. This revisionist corrective acquired ballast from the discovery that King's writings contained unacknowledged borrowings that fictionalized his past and that much of his academic work was plagiarized. On the one hand, these revelations reinforced the new emphasis in King scholarship on the distinctly Southern black church style of King's religious thinking and preaching. On the other hand, they inspired exaggerated claims about his lack of intellectual sincerity and accomplishment.

King scholars Keith Miller and David Garrow deprecated King's graduate education, claiming it was not much of an education and King never cared about academic theology anyway. Miller said King dismissively threw off "his professors' strange, artificial tongue and their ivory-tower theological formalism." Garrow said King pretended to learn what his professors at Boston University pretended to teach. David Levering Lewis followed suit, declaring that the revelations about King's plagiarism shockingly refuted Lewis' biography of King: "Who he was simply escaped me." Now Lewis had a different picture: "A picture emerges of King the young graduate student tooling about Boston on dates in his green Chevrolet, cavalierly submitting essays and dissertation chapters that were mosaics of the works of others, and of smug professors willfully indulging a bright enough degree candidate who, his studies completed, would return to the South to serve his people." Richard Lischer said the real issue was that King struggled falteringly for much of his career to hold together black church evangelicalism (good) and white liberalism (mostly bad). In the cross fire of scholarly overreactions, it became hard to say that King might have been complex and sincere all along while taking some shortcuts.[30]

It is wrong to say that King glided blithely through graduate school without caring about the theology he learned. King studied Rauschenbusch and Niebuhr intently, fashioning his Christian socialism. He took for granted throughout his career that the social gospel at its best was socialist, as evidenced by Rauschenbusch, Johnson, Niebuhr, J. Pius Barbour, and Walter Muelder. King learned the liberal tradition by reading theologians—Rauschenbusch, Clarke, Brown, and L. Harold DeWolf—who took sin and evil very seriously, contrary to standard caricatures of these thinkers. All wrote profusely about sin as badness, pride, selfishness, perversity, and tyranny, and all expounded a social gospel idea of the kingdom of God. King's papers demonstrated real intellectual engagement, and he struck everyone who knew him in Boston as a serious and engaged scholar. On the other hand, King's knowledge of Gandhi was patchy and thin when the Montgomery boycott began. FOR stalwarts Bayard Rustin and Glenn Smiley, upon rushing to Montgomery, asked King how much he knew about Gandhian nonviolence. King did not say what he later claimed, that he had studied Gandhi intently for years. He told the Gandhian activists he knew very little.[31]

At Crozer and Boston University, King knew just enough about Gandhian strategy to feel attracted to it. At the level of this feeling he struggled with the implications of Niebuhrian realism. Christian socialism had to combine the best parts of Rauschenbusch, Niebuhr, and Gandhi, as Johnson did. But all of that was theoretical to King as a graduate student, and not what he mostly thought about, because his question was how he should think about God and human beings.

J. Pius Barbour, King's pastor during his Crozer years, combined the same intellectual planks that later marked King, playing a crucial role in passing them to King. Barbour was rooted in Southern black Baptist religion, modernized by liberal theology and historical criticism, and influenced by Brightman's personalism, Niebuhr's realism, Rauschenbusch's socialism, and Wieman's naturalistic behaviorism. Like Johnson, Barbour conceived social gospel socialism as a critique of capitalist exploitation and a vision of economic democracy. He organized his sermons in thesis-antithesis-synthesis fashion, sometimes announcing in advance what the synthesis would be. He expounded Brightman's theory of moral laws from the pulpit, excoriated adulterous ministers, instructed Crozer students in raconteur fashion, and blasted idealistic sentimentality, sometimes citing Niebuhr or Wieman on the latter theme.[32]

King's fascination with Wieman began in Barbour's living room and was reinforced at Crozer. In both places he heard much about Chicago school naturalism versus Boston school personalism, while contemplating doctoral study. He applied to Boston University and Edinburgh University while grappling with Brightman's *Philosophy of Religion*, which confused and inspired him. King said he was amazed that debates about God's existence and nature were so complex. He didn't know what to think, but found the subject consuming. Then Boston University admitted him and King's confusion became clarifying. He liked Brightman's contention that critically interpreted experience is the privileged source of religious knowledge. He welcomed the opportunity to study philosophy under Brightman, choosing Boston over Edinburgh, and New England over Scotland: "How I long now for that religious experience which Dr. Brightman so cogently speaks of throughout his book. It seems to be an experience, the lack of which life becomes dull and meaningless. As I reflect on the matter, however, I do remember moments that I have been awe awakened; there have been times that I have been carried out of myself by something greater than myself and to that something I gave myself. Has this great something been God? Maybe after all I have been religious for a number of years, and am now only becoming aware of it." In that mood he enrolled at Boston University to become a theologian.[33]

King ventured carefully into Boston, wearing tailored suits and cultivating the ponderous, detached, pipe-wielding air of a philosopher. He organized a discussion group for black students called the Dialectical Society, which met once per week over a potluck supper, presenting formal papers. King kept it determinately philosophical, avoiding politics, race, piety, and emotion. He fended off challenges to his leadership, employing his genial charm. Two African American students, George Thomas and Douglas Moore, disliked the avoidance of race and politics, but King had no political interests at the time and his academic work absorbed him. King's roommate Philip Lenud later recalled, "He was just a born pacifist. People would just take advantage of him because he was so good-natured." Classmate Cornish Rogers added that King was a ringleader for Southern black students who tended to be uncomfortable with white classmates: "He was just a very amiable person, and he liked folks, he liked parties, and he was fairly well off because he had a good salary, and he lived in an apartment and not on campus as we did, and he had his own car and a closet with a lot of very expensive clothes in it. He was like a prince."[34]

To all he seemed a model graduate student, long on intellectual ambition and eager to move through his program. Brightman was ailing, but DeWolf was kindly, direct, exacting, and eager to help students. In his first year King took three courses with DeWolf on systematic theology, plus DeWolf's courses on personalist theory and New Testament theology. Having come for Brightman and philosophy, King got a pulpit-ready version of personalist theology and philosophy from a Brightman protégé.

In the classroom DeWolf taught that Bowne improved on the impersonalism of absolute idealism, which was strong for being metaphysical and idealist, but unacceptably monist. Absolute idealism was strong in accounting for the unity of mind, but didn't account for error and evil. If error and evil are incomplete goods that are actually good when viewed in light of the whole—which is impossible—one might as well claim that good is incomplete evil. DeWolf persuaded King that the problems of epistemological dualism are acceptable by comparison. Personalist theory explains error and evil without attributing either to the Absolute, it has a real doctrine of creation, and King embraced DeWolf's double-aspect interactionist idea of the self—a person is an intrinsically conscious self in and for itself, but as viewed by others, a person is a system of processes.[35]

King took Brightman's second-year course on Hegel, but Brightman died shortly after the semester began. That left King stranded in philosophy without a doctoral advisor, so he made the obvious move to DeWolf and the School of Theology, taking three more courses with DeWolf. Through Peter Bertocci, Brightman's successor, King embraced Hegel's idea that truth is the whole and, with caveats, Hegel's dialectic. King habitually thought in triads yielding a synthesis. A Christian philosophy, he reasoned, must be expansive and holistic, reflecting the universality of Christianity. Above all, King loved the same thing in Hegel that caught Du Bois—the notion that Spirit uses the passions of partly unsuspecting individuals to fulfill its aims of self-consciousness and freedom. King invoked this defining Hegelian idea for the rest of his life.[36]

Though King took no courses from Muelder, he studied and cited Muelder's writings, agreeing that Reinhold Niebuhr's Christian realism was strongest as a critique of liberal sentimentality, but fatally flawed: "There is one weakness in Niebuhr's ethical position which runs the whole gamut of his writings. This weakness lies in [the] inability of his system to deal adequately with the relative perfection which is the fact of the Christian life." King followed Muelder in objecting that Niebuhr dropped essential Christian questions of salvation. How do human beings develop spiritually? How does personality actualize Christian values? What is the significance of self-sacrificing love in human nature and history? King observed, "All these problems are left unsolved by Niebuhr. He fails to see that the availability of the divine *Agape* is an essential affirmation of the Christian religion."[37]

There is such a thing as redemptive energy that transcends individual and collective egotism. To King, dropping the language of spiritual regeneration was not an option. Moreover, Muelder emphasized self-sacrificial love (agape), drawing on Anders Nygren's theological analysis of love. King never ceased invoking Nygren, often mystifying audiences that puzzled over why it mattered so much to him. Straightforwardly he applied agape to atonement theology, contending that forensic theory is "based on a false view of personality." Merit and guilt belong to individuals and cannot be transferred from one person to another; it is immoral to punish one person for the sins of another; and orthodoxy compounds its immorality by making God the obstacle to human redemption: "Christ's death was not a ransom, or a penal substitute, or a penal example; rather it was a revelation of the sacrificial love of God intended to awaken an answering love in the hearts of men."[38]

King was a personalist down the line, with no exceptions. Against Barth's "deification of revelation," King said that revelation and reason are complementary; without reason, revelation "remains a bundle of nothing." Against Barth and Niebuhr on original sin, King said there is no single essential sin. Guilt and merit are inalienable in individuals, and sin happens whenever human beings misuse their free will. Against the Catholic doctrines of papal primacy and the infallibility of the church, King replied, "All of this strikes me as erroneous and unhistorical." Jesus may have organized the disciples, "but to say that Christ consciously organized the Church and made Peter the first Pope is [to] push the record to false proportions." Invoking DeWolf's distinction between the spiritual church and the organized church, King affirmed, "The true Church is the spiritual Church. If there are any claims to infallibility it is here. It is in the spiritual church that we witness the kingdom of God on earth."[39]

Many of King's papers at Boston University and Crozer Seminary contained extensive unattributed passages. To some degree his faulty citation practices reflected his boundary situation as a product of the oral culture of black church preaching, which expressed religious authority by synthesizing the words of many voices. King grew up in a folk culture that viewed speech and ideas as communal property shared via repetition, imitation, and call-and-response, but he knew that his graduate papers violated basic academic standards. Unfortunately his dissertation repeated the same practices, copying extensive sections of others' works, including a review of Tillich's *Systematic Theology* by Raphael Demos and especially a 1952 Boston University dissertation on Tillich by Jack Boozer.[40]

As an academic text King's dissertation was seriously flawed, but that does not negate its value as a window on the religious worldview that undergirded his ministry and activism. The parts that King wrote were indistinguishable from the parts he took from others. He had serious and defining intellectual and spiritual concerns. He wanted very much to be a religious intellectual like Mays, Johnson, Barbour, and Morehouse theologian George Kelsey. He had chewed over Tillich versus Wieman in classrooms and Barbour's living room. He had pulled the Dialectical Society into his Tillich and Wieman project, pressing the question of divine personality. To King, studying at the bastion of personalist thought renewed the question on a weekly basis: Did his teachers have a persuasive alternative to the differently impersonal theologies of Tillich and Wieman? But if they were wrong about the divine ground of human personality and dignity, what theology should he preach?

King committed to a dissertation topic shortly before he accepted a call to Dexter Avenue Baptist Church in Montgomery, Alabama. It evaluated the theologies of Tillich and Wieman from a personalist perspective, making no attempt to relate King's theological convictions to his experience as a black American. James Cone later observed incredulously that it was "as if the black experience in the white world had nothing to contribute to King's critique of Tillich and Wieman or any other thinker or idea in Euro-American history." King stuck to the view that he urged upon the Dialectical Society: they needed to produce academic work making no mention of race, showing the academy they could do it. King and classmate Major Jones vowed to write dissertations belonging to the realm of race-transcending theory, where philosophical theologians supposedly dwelt.[41]

Tillich and Wieman established God's existence by definition and refused the attribution of personality to God. God is the ground or power of being that cannot be denied unless one denies the reality of being itself (Tillich), or God is the something of supreme value that cannot be denied unless one denies the reality of the good (Wieman). King argued that personal idealism has better concepts of God and personality. Tillich and Wieman identified personality with limited human personality, asserting that God transcends the limitations of personal existence. King countered that only human personalities are limited in the manner of creatures: "Personality as such involves no necessary limitation. It means simply self-consciousness and self-direction." Applied to God, the idea of personality implies no limitation. Moreover, the idea of divine personality is the necessary presupposition of the idea that God is good. King favored Wieman's emphasis on divine goodness over Tillich's emphasis on divine power, but Wieman's axiology had no theological foundation, and both theologians were wrong to accentuate one pole of God's being. God is good, King cautioned, only if God is personal. The reciprocal union of heart, will, and intellect described in Scripture "is possible only between personal beings. Only the personality of God makes possible the union of communion with him." Lacking freedom and intelligence, there is no such thing as goodness. Wieman's theorizing about goodness and love was merely abstract, not genuinely ethical, for goodness and love are attributes of personality.[42]

King espoused a quantitative pluralism, recognizing the manifold realities of sense experience, and a qualitative monism, affirming that reality has a unifying ground in God's being: "Neither swallows the other." On one side, personal idealism safeguards individuality against every type of ultimate monism; on the other, it advocates a basal monism that fends off every type of ultimate pluralism. King entered the ministry confident in his theological and philosophical basis. He had studied two powerful theological minds that opposed his belief in divine personality and came out believing in it more than ever. Grounding himself in personalist thought strengthened his religious convictions. The fact that King gave a misleading rendering of his story invited scholarly deconstruction after he was gone, which came with a vengeance. Academics derided his conviction that personal idealism gave him an intellectual foundation. Miller observed, "Today almost no one prizes, studies, or even remembers Personalism for itself." David L. Chappell said that personalist ideas do not matter because King's personalism did not differentiate him "from thousands of preachers nobody has ever heard of."[43]

This scholarly fashion usually plays up Niebuhr's influence on King, which overlooks that Niebuhr's rendering of biblical theology was thoroughly personalist. Niebuhr set (his own) biblical theology against classical and modern conceptions of the self, contending that Scripture construes human beings as created, finite, irreducible unities of body and spirit. Pointing to Niebuhr does not negate the significance of personalism, though it does get a crucial thing right: Niebuhr persuaded King that coercive violence is unavoidable in all struggles for justice. Chappell and Taylor Branch say that King was Niebuhrian on this point all along, and Garrow says he turned that way after moral suasion failed in 1962. I believe that King was Niebuhrian on this point all along *and* that he remained dead serious about embracing Gandhian nonviolence as a way of life, not merely a tactic. He said so emphatically until the end, disbelieving that he had to choose between nonviolence and recognizing it was coercively violent.[44]

Debates over this point have wrongly pushed out of view King's understanding of what mattered to him theologically. He had distinct theological beliefs that undergirded and enabled him, exactly as he said. King insisted that his belief in personality divine and human was his mainstay in a turbulent world. It mattered to him greatly that there was a modern, progressive, justice-oriented theological perspective that centered on his most cherished belief. This perspective blended black church religion, liberal theology, Christian philosophy, and racial justice and social justice militancy like nothing else: "This personal idealism remains today my basic philosophical position. Personalism's insistence that only personality—finite and infinite—is ultimately real strengthened me in two convictions: it gave me metaphysical and philosophical grounding for the idea of a personal God, and it gave me a metaphysical basis for the dignity and worth of all human personality."[45]

God is the personal ground of the infinite value of human personality. This two-sided credo had a negative corollary confirming King's deepest feeling: if the worth of personality is the ultimate value in life, America's racial caste system was distinctly evil. Evil is precisely that which degrades and negates personality. The purpose of Jim Crow was to humiliate, exclude, and degrade the personhood of African Americans, but King's family and church taught him he was "as good as anybody." No philosophy supported these convictions more powerfully than the one that King absorbed and embraced as a graduate student.

The notion that King dumped his graduate school theology after he became a movement leader has a hard time accounting for the fact that he preached from the same barrel of sermons throughout his career. From the beginning he riffed on them differently in different contexts, constantly revising and improvising his stock sermons. Some were already staples for him when he arrived in Montgomery. By the end of his first year in Montgomery, almost the entire corpus existed. Each had set pieces that King inserted into other sermons as the occasion demanded or the Spirit moved him. Churchgoers and movement veterans would cheer as soon as he got rolling on one, much like a singer performing a medley of her hits. "I Have a Dream" was one of them three years before the March on Washington. "I've Been to the Mountaintop" was a staple from January 1957 onward, which he used whenever he was especially down or anxious. King's favorite sermon, "The Three Dimensions of a Complete Life," was already his favorite when he gave it as a trial sermon at Dexter Church. It won plaudits and the job at Montgomery. He gave it many times and every year afterward, notably at Purdue University in 1958, addressing the first National Conference on Christian Education of the newly formed United Church of Christ, and at St. Paul's Cathedral in London in 1964, on his way to accept the Nobel Peace Prize. He kept giving it until the end, which meant, for King, that he never stopped composing it.

The movement that swept him to prominence in December 1955 would not have caught fire without him. King's distinct brilliance lit up the Montgomery, Alabama, bus boycott on its first night and sustained it against enraged opposition. The torrent of hate and death threats that he received nearly broke him, compelling him to decide whether he was willing to follow Jesus to the cross. He had a moment of illumination in his kitchen in January 1956, when he realized that nothing less than the cross lay before him, and he had to rely on the love and grace of God. Then he personally linked the fledgling, theatrical, church-based movement in the South to the venerable, institutional, mostly secular movement in the North. Rustin and Smiley rushed to Montgomery, linking King to their networks in FOR, the Socialist Party, In Friendship, War Resisters League, and other New York–based organizations.

King bonded closely with Rustin and Rustin's white Old Left ally, Stanley Levison. They briefed King for meetings, arranged speaking engagements, ghosted his articles and books, handled the press, linked him to their networks, and convinced him to create a new organization led by Southern black preachers. By August 1957 the new organization had a name, the Southern Christian Leadership Conference (SCLC), and a slogan, "To Redeem the Soul of America." It was stocked with powerhouse preachers who deferred to King: Fred Shuttlesworth, Ralph Abernathy, and Joseph Lowery. Later King added Wyatt Walker, James Bevel, Hosea Williams, and C. T. Vivian, eventually putting Andrew Young in charge of corralling them.

King rightly figured that the movement needed a church-based organization dedicated to spreading protest wildfire. The NAACP was too formal, membership-based, and consumed with marching through the courts to light a fire. The SCLC founders grasped their advantage over the NAACP. White racists did not fear black preachers the way they loathed the NAACP. The SCLC was designed to seize on this advantage and to avoid competition with the NAACP.

All the founders except Ella Baker, a black organizer allied with Rustin and Levison, conceived SCLC as a King-centered operation that

guarded King's back. Baker wanted SCLC to be a grassroots organization devoted to long-term community organizing. She clashed with the
founding clerics over this issue and their sexism. All the SCLC clerics
were sexists, disrespecting every woman who worked for the SCLC for
the next dozen years. Baker kept SCLC going during its tenuous early
years, but was never accorded the respect of a leader. She ended up as a
mentor to the Student Nonviolent Coordinating Committee (SNCC),
which went on to replicate the male-domination story. Dorothy Cotton
cracked the inner circle of the SCLC staff in 1960 as education director, getting similar treatment as Baker. Diane Nash was SNCC's indispensable leader during the sit-in and Freedom Ride movements, yet even
during her moment of national renown she was pushed out of the way
at spotlight time by male headliners. King had no feminist impulse to
correct these abuses or even acknowledge there was a problem, and he
hurt his devoted spouse Coretta Scott King by breaking his marital vows.

Rustin, Levison, and Baker were veterans of the Old Left who fondly
remembered how the Congress of Industrial Organizations (CIO) used
strikes, boycotts, and marches to make gains for economic justice. They
were chastened by this history, because the Old Left strategy of fusing
anti-racism with trade unions and socialism failed in the 1930s and 1940s.
Black Southerners were forced to find allies among Northern liberals and
leftists, not Southern white workers. The three movement veterans were
strategic in basing SCLC on the Southern black church, notwithstanding
that Rustin was a gay Quaker socialist based in New York, Levison was
a New York Jew and former Communist, and Baker's childhood North
Carolina experience of the black church made her averse to authoritarian
preachers. The SCLC governing board and staff greatly disliked that King
relied on Old Left outsiders, but he was adamant about needing them. He
took in stride that they came with Old Left baggage; it was one of God's
mysteries why so many Communists and so few white liberals had cared
about black Americans. King treasured Rustin and Levison for devoting
themselves wholly to the movement without making demands on him
and without playing roles in SCLC.[46]

King's socialism was a unifying factor for the movement veterans that
he united. He believed that politics is a struggle for power among predatory rivals, and Christian socialists needed to be realistic about the clash
of interests. Publicly espousing democratic socialism, however, would
have yielded only turmoil and vilification for King. Every insider in his
New York socialist network was intimately acquainted with this problem

and wanted King to finesse it. Since they were open about being socialists, they were Red-baited constantly, especially by Communists who lied about their own politics and by reactionaries who equated social democracy with Communism. Rustin carefully shielded King from the socialist label as he ghostwrote articles for King and linked him to Rustin's allies.

In the late 1950s King's fame soared to dizzying heights while he puzzled and stewed over what to do with it. He talked about Gandhian disruption without causing any. He enlisted Gandhian Methodist cleric James Lawson to train SCLC in nonviolent resistance, but shuddered at imagining the human carnage. Then the student sit-in explosion of 1960 and the Freedom Rides of 1961 pushed King into actual Gandhian disruption. SCLC struck hard in April 1963 in Birmingham, Alabama, where a gusher of marching children helped King let go of some of his fear of getting children killed. The Birmingham campaign led to the March on Washington, the golden moment of August 1963. It also led in September to the slaying of the four church girls in Birmingham, nearly crushing King. He began to say that America was deeply sick.

SCLC campaigned in St. Augustine, Florida, in 1964 and Selma, Alabama, in 1965, which elicited vicious beatings and the civil rights bills of 1964 and 1965. King knew he was always in danger because he brought too much violence to the surface to be spared. He preached about it as though heading toward Golgotha. After the Civil Rights Act passed in 1964, King endured stupid questions about why there still needed to be a civil rights movement and why he seemed angry. In the summer of 1964 he told journalist Alex Haley that his biggest mistake was that he overestimated the spiritual integrity of white Southern ministers. The essence of Pauline Christianity, he said, is to rejoice at being deemed worthy to suffer for the divine good: "The projection of a social gospel, in my opinion, is the true witness of a Christian life."[47]

Haley asked if black churches did better at projecting a social gospel, and King hedged on "no." It was hard to mobilize black ministers, because they shunned movements they did not organize, and most had no experience with movement activism. Many just wanted to preach about heaven. King stressed the difference, however, between the situations of the white and black churches. White churches were not oppressed, while black churches were subjected to the worst brutality ever inflicted on Christian churches anywhere. There was no basis of comparison.[48]

Haley asked how one could be militant and nonviolent at the same time; King said this was like realism and idealism. A seeker of justice *must* be realistic *and* idealistic, holding to both in tension. Nonviolence is a healing sword, "a weapon fabricated of love." Haley observed that many whites believed the civil rights movement had gone far enough and should cease. King's response was blistering: "Why do white people seem to find it so difficult to understand that the Negro is sick and tired of having reluctantly parceled out to him those rights and privileges which all others receive upon birth or entry in America? I never cease to wonder at the amazing presumption of much of white society, assuming that they have the right to bargain with the Negro for his freedom. This continued arrogant ladling out of pieces of the rights of citizenship has begun to generate a *fury* in the Negro."[49]

The fury in King was evident to anyone willing to see it. He observed that "abysmal ignorance" about racial justice prevailed among white Americans, and three groups were especially significant. One was the whole class of "bigots and backlashers" that attacked the civil rights movement. Another group, woefully ignorant public officials, discharged their responsibilities without recognizing the harm they caused, because it never occurred to them to listen to black people. The third group was the hardest to take—"enlightened" types who gave nauseating counsel about proceeding gradually: "I wonder at men who dare to feel that they have some paternalistic right to set the timetable for another man's liberation."[50]

The Selma campaign marked four turning points. It led to the Voting Rights Act of 1965, turned King into the political leader of millions of white Americans, marked the end of King's influence over Black Power militants, and marked the end of King's willingness to confine SCLC campaigns to the South. Every day King was asked if the movement was over. This galling question steeled his resolve to take the struggle North, where very few of his lieutenants wanted to go. In the North, racism was structural and threefold in every city. Segregated housing led to segregated schools, and segregated housing and schools handicapped black Americans in the job market.

King dragged SCLC to Chicago and was battered viciously. This time there was no national political victory that redeemed the battering, just as Watts and Detroit exploded in rioting and Black Power became a rallying cry. King agonized over all of it and the war in Vietnam. Until he got pelted with rocks in Chicago, King refused to say that white Americans never intended to integrate their schools and neighborhoods. Then he said it bitterly, observing in 1966 that American racism was distinctly vicious.

King told an SCLC retreat at Frogmore, Georgia, that its victories were superficial: "The white man literally sought to annihilate the Indian. If you look through the history of the world this very seldom happened." This, he warned, was what black Americans were up against—a genocidal impulse fueled by the pervasive white American belief in white superiority. By that optic, the current talk about a backlash was superficial.[51]

King sympathized with the Black Power movement because it instilled something (racial pride) and sought something (real power) that were both desperately needed. But the Black Power ideology currently in vogue, he said, had three fatal problems: it was nihilistic and separatist, and these things combined to justify violence. SCLC had to stand for power as the capacity to achieve a positive and creative purpose. It could not wave off the problem of how things were heard. King wanted to say that America needed a strong dose of democratic socialism, but he settled for saying it to movement insiders. He believed that getting rid of the class system was essential and that SCLC needed to become an outright anti-poverty organization, demanding a minimum guaranteed income.[52]

For two years King opposed the war in Vietnam, modulated how and where he said it, and agonized over his posture. The civil rights establishment and his closest aides, notably Rustin and Levison, implored him not to join the anti-war movement. Becoming an anti-war leader would alienate President Johnson, most of the Democratic Party, and probably the Ford Foundation. If King lost influence in civil rights to become one leader among others in a radical anti-war movement, what good was that? King wrestled with this question until January 1967, when he resolved to risk everything. The Riverside address of April 4, 1967, dramatically expounded his reasons for doing so.

King declared at Riverside Church that Vietnam was a recycled colonial war and failing to oppose it had become a form of betrayal. Nine years of French colonial aggression backed by the United States after Vietnam declared its independence in 1954 led to America taking over the colonizer role. He ridiculed America's liberator self-image, lamenting that the United States was on the wrong side of anti-colonial movements throughout the world. America was rich, privileged, short on compassion, and morbidly afraid of Communism. Thus the first modern nation had become the world's foremost counterrevolutionary power. "I am convinced that if we are to get on the right side of the world revolution, we as a nation must undergo a radical revolution of values." Americans, King charged, prized profit, property, and machines above human beings. This warped value system defeated all attempts to overcome "the giant triplets of racism, materialism, and militarism." America needed to stop tolerating extreme inequality in the United States, stop pillaging nations in the Third World, and stop presuming its right to bully and invade weaker nations. To put it positively, America needed a spiritual awakening to its own revolutionary democratic ideals—"a true revolution of values."[53]

King said he could not continue to speak for nonviolence if he did not speak against the most violent force in the world—his own government. He evoked a bitter outpouring of editorial condemnation in reply, which fueled the takeoff of a skyrocketing anti-war movement. Viewed politically, King's timing was perfect for embracing and boosting the anti-war movement. But King judged himself in politics by the standard of righteousness, and thus did not congratulate himself for shrewd timing. It gnawed at him that he dithered for two years. He told SCLC, "My name then wouldn't have been written in any book called *Profiles in Courage*. But now I have decided. I will not be intimidated."[54]

The burden of holding fast to nonviolence weighed heavily on King. Thus he declared repeatedly that he believed in nonviolence more than ever, it was a faith and way of life for him, and he would never retreat from it. He said so emphatically in his last book, *Where Do We Go from Here: Chaos or Community?* (1967). King excoriated the white American view of America as "a middle-class Utopia" committed to fair play and racial harmony, which he called "a fantasy of self-deception and comfortable vanity." Contrary to most white Americans, American society was only slightly less racist and repressive than before the Montgomery boycott: "It is an aspect of their sense of superiority that the white people of America believe they have so little to learn." Most white Americans were unwilling to do anything to abolish racism that cost them anything, so the backlash raged with impunity, ending King's refusal to call it a backlash.[55]

Until Gandhi came along, King said, all revolutions were based on love and hate: hope in the expectation of freedom and justice, and hate for oppressors. Gandhian nonviolence was more revolutionary than all previous revolutions because it rested on hope and love, breaking the cycle of revenge. King implored readers that despair never sustained any revolution for long. This was "the ultimate contradiction of the Black Power movement." It snuffed out the flame of hope in the name of revolution, ignoring that a revolution stripped of hope inevitably "degenerates into an indiscriminating catchall for evanescent and futile gestures."[56]

No oppressed group can be liberated without integrating, or integrate without being liberated, because power has to be shared in a just society. The sharing of power is the very definition of a just society. King reached for a way of describing his commitment to nonviolence that settled the questioning about it. He believed that most black Americans agreed with him about nonviolence, but even if they did not, he believed in it. He was committed to molding a consensus about nonviolence and took no interest in being a consensus leader. The latter type merely searched and represented, conforming to whatever happened to be. King was nothing like that; for him it was convictional leadership or bust, and his conviction was a burning fire in him: "Occasionally in life one develops a conviction so precious and meaningful that he will stand on it till the end. That is what I have found in nonviolence."[57]

Where Do We Go from Here was King's best book—eloquent, practical, timely, judicious, and visionary, featuring his trademark blend of reformist common sense and liberationist militancy. It spoke to the moment with passion, but evoked little response at first, until the response turned scathing, perfectly symbolizing the moment. Reviewers ridiculed King as a has-been dreamer who no longer mattered. Newark and Detroit erupted in flames, King took an early exit from a radical conference in Chicago at which he was berated, and SCLC conducted bruising debates over its mission. Marian Wright, a lawyer working for the NAACP Legal Defense Fund in Mississippi, had an idea that King liked—marching poor people from Mississippi to Washington, D.C., to stage sit-ins. King's lieutenants objected that poverty was an abstraction and squatting in the nation's capital would go badly. He took their rebuttals personally; their fractiousness no longer seemed creative to him.[58]

They had to march on the nation's capital to spark a new generation of protest against denigration and oppression. King put it dramatically in a Christmas sermon, making his usual vow to endure suffering, respond to violence with soul force, and love the oppressors. But now he said it by counterposing the dream and the nightmare, invoking four nightmares. He saw his dream turn into a nightmare when four young girls were murdered. He saw the nightmare again in the vicious poverty gripping urban black American neighborhoods. He saw it again as black Americans set fire to their own neighborhoods. He saw a fourth nightmare rage out of control as America ravaged Vietnam. King lived on the edge of despair while refusing to give up hope: "Yes, I am personally the victim of deferred dreams, of blasted hopes, but in spite of that I close today by saying I still have a dream, because, you know, you can't give up in life."[59]

Erecting a city of the poor would show he had not given up. King said they had to find a way to dramatize what poor people were up against. He wished he could do it without protesting and going to jail, because he was tired of both. He wanted to talk about democratic socialism, but that was out of play. All he could do was stand with the poor and dramatize their situation. This was the best way to expand the civil rights movement into a human rights movement that showcased the struggles of oppressed peoples across racial lines.

Near the end he was accustomed to being more radical than everyone around him. In his last weeks King doubled down on the path of public sacrifice, dragging others along. He launched the Poor People's Campaign at the lowest point of his life, topping his previous forays into risky, controversial, chaotic protest. King would not be shamed into reverting to middle-class politics. Now he outflanked even Bevel, his usual barometer of going too far. King had to stand with the poorest of the poor and afflicted; otherwise he was not really a follower of Jesus. He bulled forward, bearing his cross, enduring one sleepless night after another, and rousing himself with sermonic riffs about the view from the mountaintop. He closed his last sermon, on April 3, 1968, with the mountaintop run. The previous year, he put it hauntingly to the SCLC staff: "When I took up the Cross, I recognized its meaning. The Cross is something that you bear, and ultimately that you die on."[60]

Every King sermon was a gloss on his vision of a beloved community. Freedom is participation in power, and the goal of the movement was to transform the lack of power of black Americans into creative, vital, interpersonal, organized power. All can be free, but only if all are empowered to participate. Freedom and integration go together to build the beloved community, a universal goal embracing all peoples. King epitomized the black social gospel at its best and most radical, which made him the first in the line of what came to be called, shortly after his death, liberation theology.

After he was gone he left an incomparable legacy and an immense void. King's reputation among white Americans climbed ever higher, putting a national holiday in reach. People who had spurned or reviled him while he lived now claimed to admire him; many "forgot" having reviled him. To win the iconic status he deserved, he had to be domesticated, and was. The memory of King taking the struggle to Chicago, railing against capitalism and the Vietnam War, espousing a version of black radicalism, and organizing a Poor People's Campaign faded into an unthreatening idealism. King became safe and ethereal, registering as a noble moralist. The civil rights movement was reduced to a reform movement for individual opportunity—safe, admirable, and quintessentially American. It became hard to remember why, or even that, King was the most hated person in America during his lifetime.

But I am speaking now of the King that prevailed in popular culture. In the social justice movements that carried on what King cared about, the real King was not forgotten. Often this memory was the main thing that kept us going, during and after the heyday of the movements for liberation theology. James Cone and J. Deotis Roberts pioneered forms of black liberation theology; Gustavo Gutiérrez, Juan Luis Segundo, and José Míguez Bonino pioneered Latin American liberation theologies respectively in Peru, Uruguay, and Argentina; and Mary Daly and Rosemary Radford Ruether developed the first liberation theologies focused on the liberation of women. Liberation theology was always about construing the world from the perspective of a specific oppressed community or people. Thus it raised new questions for religious thought and sometimes asked how different struggles for justice should relate to each other. To Ruether, the latter question was never optional.[61]

Feminist Liberation Theology: Rosemary Radford Ruether

My first encounter with Ruether occurred in 1974, during my first semester of divinity school, when she spoke at Boston College. To me she was already a theological star: prolific, brilliant, radical yet perfectly sane, and the leading feminist theologian. Her books had exciting titles exuding revolutionary anticipation—*The Radical Kingdom, Liberation Theology, Religion and Sexism*—and at Boston College she polled the audience on provocative titles for her next collection, which became *New Woman, New Earth*. Feminist theology, she declared, was the "next great revolution" in theology and religion; I remember thinking that "next" seemed surprisingly modest, since the revolution was well underway.

Fifteen months later she was the featured speaker at a University Christian Movement conference that I organized in Cambridge. The church hall was packed with students from local congregations and divinity schools, and Ruether expounded on women as "the first and final proletariat," admonishing a dissenter that "God created a world, not a church." None of my professors at Harvard would have drawn such a large or politically active crowd. She seemed supremely confident in herself and her message, exhorting women not to settle for whining; feminism was a revolution, not a pity party. Ruether roared against sexism, racism, militarism, and other oppressive isms, sometimes breaking a heavy feeling in the air with a caustic expletive. For many of us it was thrilling just to be in the same room with her.

She teased me about studying at a school that had no feminist theologians, and I agreed that Harvard's lack of one was incredible. How could it be that Harvard Divinity School had no place for feminist criticism? How could Harvard possibly justify not teaching feminist theology or scholarship? Several years passed before it occurred to me that Ruether could not have been as confident as she seemed. For feminist theology barely existed anywhere in the mid-1970s, and even Ruether, for all her books and speaking engagements, had almost no experience of teaching it.

She was born to a cultured, humanistic, Catholic mother and an Anglican, Republican, Virginia gentleman father who died when she was twelve. After an early childhood in Georgetown, Ruether spent her adolescent years in California, where her role models were women. She credited her mother Rebecca Cresap Ord Radford, her mother's friends, and Scripps College as the formative influences on her. From her mother, as Ruether later stressed, she inherited a "sense of secure self-confidence" in her ability and a more cosmopolitan Catholicism than the "ghettoized" type in which Mary Daly grew up. At Scripps, a Claremont, California, college featuring a humanities core curriculum, she majored in classics, which set her on the path to religious studies.[62]

Ruether's undergraduate professors taught her to understand Christianity as an alien development within the ancient Mediterranean world that ultimately became the preserver of its legacy. Her favorite teacher, classicist Robert Palmer, regarded Christianity as a poor replacement for the humanism and splendor of classical culture. Others denigrated Catholicism as inferior to classical culture and Protestantism. In four years of college Ruether rarely peered beyond the fifth century, absorbing the outlook of her teachers, though she also reacted against them, discovering an unexpected loyalty to her mother's church. Near the end of her doctoral studies at Claremont Graduate School it occurred to her that her undergraduate teachers had not taken her seriously. Scripps professors took for granted that they taught future wives and society matrons, not scholars. This realization filled Ruether with a "profound sense of betrayal," pushing her toward feminism.[63]

Well into her college career she was clueless about politics. In 1956, while her college friends supported Adlai Stevenson for president, Ruether didn't know if she was a Democrat or Republican. Two years later she married Herman Ruether, a political scientist whose liberal politics rubbed off on her. Then her involvement in campus ministry drew her into the civil rights and anti-war movements. Ruether later recalled that she gravitated swiftly to the Left as soon as she thought about such issues. Intrigued by biblical prophecy, which she studied in the context of Mediterranean religious history, she formed three conclusions: the only scholarship worth reading was liberal Protestant; biblical monotheism was commendably ethical, unlike the pagan theophanies of the gods; and Protestant scholarship was too much like the Bible in denigrating pagan religions. Ruether liked the prophets, but not their polemic against Baalism; she admired that Catholicism synthesized the religious heritages of the ancient world. Vatican II helped her decide to stay in the Catholic Church; meanwhile she wrote a dissertation on Gregory of Nazianzus, the Cappadocian monk and bishop of Constantinople who defended Nicene orthodoxy at the Council of Constantinople in 381. Ruether argued that Christianity mistakenly turned monasticism into a lifelong vocation of a spiritual elite of celibates, unlike the Asian model.[64]

Her involvements in movement politics shaped her entire theological career. Ruether missed Freedom Summer, but the following summer, in 1965, she worked as a Delta Ministries activist in Beulah, Mississippi. The following year she began her teaching career at Howard University, where she taught from 1966 to 1976, and threw herself into Washington, D.C.'s church-based anti-war movement, getting arrested at pray-ins: "One lived in a constant atmosphere of political awareness that made any other part of the country appear asleep."[65]

By 1968 she was already a prolific essayist, with little hint of a feminist perspective. Ruether's first post-dissertation book, *The Church Against Itself* (1967), contended in the "secular city" spirit of the time that the church as triumphant colossus and sacramental fortress was disintegrating. To make its way in the new world the church had to learn to live with "radical cultural insecurity." Her first glimmer of feminist consciousness was a protest against the Catholic prohibition of artificial contraception, in 1964. As a graduate student with three children, Ruether experienced the church's command as a psychological impossibility. In effect, the church told her to abandon her vocational dream in order to bear an unlimited number of children, "a demand that I scuttle my interests, my training, and in the last analysis, my soul." The church's moral rigor in this case did not serve a worthy moral value, she said. It evoked merely her "weariness and disgust."[66]

Ruether witnessed the clash between integrationist liberals and black power radicals that defined the shifting politics of racial justice, but treaded lightly in faculty meetings and class. Her status at Howard was tenuous simply by virtue of being a white female professor and lacking female students. It grew more complex and tense as she identified with the feminist uprising of the late 1960s. Along with Daly, Letty Russell (Yale Divinity School), and Beverly Harrison (Union Theological Seminary), Ruether was a founder of feminist theology, but she and Russell came to feminism through New Left politics, criticizing the sexism they experienced in it. More than anyone except Daly, Ruether inspired a feminist movement in theology through her writings and speaking engagements. But her scholarship and activism were on her time, for at Howard she could not teach feminism or even talk about it: "Every time I raised the issue, I was accused of being racist." The issue of sexism, at Howard, had to be raised by black feminists; meanwhile "it was clear my feminist work needed to happen somewhere else." Thus Ruether moved in 1976 to Garrett Evangelical Theological Seminary.[67]

In her early years at Howard she labored over a massive manuscript on the roots of Jewish messianism in Near Eastern kingship and New Year rituals. Ruether's publisher rejected it, partly because her account of the Canaanite origins of messianic ideas offended a peer reviewer, and she never published it. Yet her research for the book proved to be a wellspring for many years, fueling her writings on Christology, anti-Semitism, goddess religion, and political theology. Ruether made her early renown as a critic of Western dualism. By 1970 she had a signature lecture on this theme that inspired and framed much of the feminist theology movement. Judith Plaskow and Carol Christ, who heard it as graduate students at Yale, later remembered it as "almost miraculous." Ruether's definitive version, published in 1972, described sexism as a by-product of the breakdown of tribal culture.[68]

Tribal culture, she said, mythologized a holistic worldview. The earth goddess and sky god played complementary roles, as did females and males. The salvation of the individual was not divorced from that of the community or the renewal of the earth. New Year's festivals celebrated the annual death and resurrection of the cosmos; the king (personifying the community) played the role of the dying and rising god; his female counterpart (a virgin and mother, and wife and sister) rescued the dying god from the netherworld. At the end of the celebration the two united to form the divine child of the new year's life. This communal sense of a sacred cosmos began to break down in the first millennium B.C.E., partly as a consequence of imperial invasions that swept the peoples of the Mediterranean into alien civilizations. To the extent that the religions of the earth survived, they became private cults for individuals. Renewing earth and society was no longer the point. Salvation became otherworldly and individual; nature became an alien reality; individuals imagined that their bodies were foreign to their true selves; the idea of a heavenly escape to a true home displaced the idea that the earth is humanity's home.[69]

Ruether construed early Christianity as a synthesis of the Hebrew and classical myths of redemption. The Hebrews clung to their tribal identity against a succession of imperial powers, claiming the land as a divine legacy, interpreting the earth festivals as historical events in their communal journey, and looking forward to a renewal of earth and society in a messianic age. They also repressed the feminine imagery of the old religions, aside from symbolizing Israel as the bride of Yahweh, divorcing the cycle of death and resurrection from the sacred cosmos. Death and resurrection were refigured as historical wrath and redemption. Classical philosophy further alienated the individual from the world, viewing the body as an obstacle to clear knowledge and moral integrity. Christianity absorbed the Platonist myth of liberation to an eternal otherworld. In Christianity the old myths of the new year and the virgin-mother goddess, the historical consciousness of Israel, and the anti-feminine spirituality of late antiquity were refashioned, synthesizing the best and worst of late classical civilization. Accenting the downside, Ruether remarked, "What we see in this development is a one-sided expression of the ego claiming its transcendental autonomy by negating the finite matrix of existence."[70]

In language that hadn't quite caught up to her vision of feminist transformation, she implored that "women must be the spokesmen for a new humanity arising out of the reconciliation of spirit and body." The crucial challenge and "secret power of the women's revolution" was to liberate women from patriarchal oppression without buying into the "masculine ethic of competitiveness." Unlike men, Ruether explained, women typically cultivate an ethic of "communal personhood" that allows them to participate in the success of others instead of viewing others as threats to their own success. The revolution that was needed, and occurring, achieved women's liberation without losing women's superior capacity for community.[71]

By 1971 feminist theology was hot enough that Harvard Divinity School wanted to teach it, if only on an occasional basis. Ruether, having never taught it herself, welcomed the opportunity to do so as a one-year visiting professor. Later she put it more caustically, recalling that Harvard was willing to patronize feminists as visiting lecturers, but "never to embrace" them as members of its club. Ruether's first experience of teaching feminist theology was bruising. She shook her head at the faculty: "These scholars had kept their eyes determinedly averted from the collapse of the society around them, never allowing it to impinge upon or question their segregated mental world." At the same time she had troubling encounters with radical feminist students, for whom Daly represented the real thing.[72]

Daly raged against universal patriarchy, described feminism as the ultimate revolution, and was well on her way toward repudiating Christianity. Ruether later recalled of her encounter with Daly-feminism: "To be concerned about class and race was seen as distracting from 'pure' feminism. The influence of Mary Daly was evident here." Radical feminists responded to Ruether's politicized feminism "in a slightly pitying manner, as though I was 'still back in the sixties.'" Her research on patristic anti-Judaism was even more incomprehensible: "Anti-Semitism was not even a fad become passé for them. It simply did not make any sense at all." Judaism held no interest except as the grandfather of "patriarchal misogyny." For Ruether the experience was chastening: "I came to realize how faddish 'social' theologies are apt to be." It also clarified what kind of feminist she wanted to be, stressing the interrelationships between feminism and other justice causes.[73]

In her early years at Garrett, Ruether stewed over the lack of a systematic text in feminist theology, devising makeshift course packs. Meanwhile she wrote the first feminist systematic theology, *Sexism and God-Talk*, published in 1983. For twenty-five years it was the only work of its kind. Ruether described her critical principle as "the promotion of the full humanity of women," identifying five sources of feminist theology: (1) the Bible, especially its prophetic-liberating stream; (2) marginalized Christian traditions such as Gnosticism and Quakerism; (3) primary themes of classical Christianity; (4) non-Christian "Near Eastern" and

Greco-Roman religion and philosophy; and (5) critical post-Christian perspectives such as liberalism, Romanticism, and Marxism. All were sexist, so all had to be judged by the feminist critical principle. Feminist theology is a type of liberation theology in which women are included in the prophetic norm: "Feminism sees what male prophetic thought generally has not seen: that once the prophetic norm is asserted to be central to Biblical faith, then patriarchy can no longer be maintained as authoritative."[74]

Ruether's version of feminist theology appealed to the prophetic-liberating stream of biblical religion, like other liberation theologies, expounding four themes: God favors the oppressed, domination is repugnant, a new age of peace and justice is coming, and oppressive ideologies must be abolished. In political terms, feminist liberation theology advocates a social order founded on the principles of freedom, equality, cooperation, and ecology. Ruether stressed that feminist theology is not based on "unprecedented ideas," as it deepens the ethical conscience of biblical religion by applying the prophetic-liberating principle to women: "Feminist theology makes explicit what was overlooked in male advocacy of the poor and oppressed: namely, *women* of the oppressed. This means that the critique of hierarchy must become explicitly a critique of patriarchy. All the liberating prophetic visions must be deepened and transformed to include what was not included: women."[75]

Ruether's development of these themes virtually defined the mainstream of feminist liberation theology in its first generation. She supported liberal feminism to a point, but blasted its middle-class biases. She incorporated the radical feminist emphasis on transformations of consciousness, but rejected its Gnosticism and separatism. In Daly's type of feminism, Ruether said, "the history of women becomes a trail of crucifixions, with males as the evil archons of an anticosmos where women are entrapped." Radical feminists sought an alternative world "within their inner selves," engendering a new language of inner transformation that broke apart the dominant language of patriarchy: "They escape together through the holes rent in the fabric of patriarchal ideology into a separate and higher realm of female interiority." This was a rerun of Gnosticism, Ruether said, except that in Daly's version, feminism was built "on the dualism of a transcendent spirit world of femaleness over against the deceitful anticosmos of masculinity."[76]

To Ruether it was one thing, and absolutely needed, to condemn male domination; it was something else to dehumanize all males. Separatism reversed the logic of misogynistic patriarchy, treating women as normative humanity and males as defective humans. This strategy was no more liberating or life-affirming than its enemy, since it projected moral responsibility for all the world's evils onto an alien group: "Such enemy-making of men would ultimately subvert the whole dream of a women's culture based on mutuality and altruism. The very process of projecting the negative part of their own psychic potential onto males, and failing to own these themselves, would tend to make such women's groups fanatical caricatures of that which they hate." Ruether cautioned that to dehumanize the other is to dehumanize oneself, since "one duplicates evil-making in the very effort to escape from it once and for all, by projecting it on the 'alien' group."[77]

Her alternative blended elements of liberal, socialist, and radical feminism, prophetic Christianity, and ecological holism. Sometimes Ruether distinguished between liberal feminism (women and men share the same essential humanity), romantic feminism (valorizing distinct feminine qualities), and her integrative third way, which did not ghettoize women's concerns (as in romanticism) or keep racial and class hierarchies intact (as in liberalism). In other contexts she espoused a dialectical synthesis of liberal, socialist, and radical feminisms. Liberalism, she argued, rightly upholds the doctrine of a common human nature and its derivative principle of equal rights for all people, but it wrongly settles for a reform politics of equal opportunity gains for middle class and professional women. Building on Zillah Eisenstein's *The Radical Future of Liberal Feminism*, Ruether said the liberal feminist pursuit of social equality is unattainable on liberal terms. Liberal demands for federally funded childcare, parental leave, flextime, work sharing, and comparable worth are not viable without structural changes in the direction of democratic socialism. The liberal demand for equality cannot be achieved on liberal terms.[78]

Ruether denied that gender oppression or any other form of oppression is more fundamental than the others. To radical feminists of the wave-two, "sisterhood is powerful" generation, feminism was a revolution of consciousness proclaiming that gender oppression is the fundamental evil everywhere. Ruether countered that gender is a fundamental organizing variable in social structure, culture, and personal life. Any feminism that fails to attack patriarchy as a social system will fail to liberate women from the shackles of male domination, but the ideal is to integrate the liberal concern with equal rights, the democratic socialist commitment to distributive justice, and the radical emphasis on gender feminism. Each perspective is deficient by itself, and each is necessary and generative to the extent that it remains open to the liberating capacities of other perspectives.[79]

Ruether stressed that her theology mined the central tradition of the scriptural witness, the one by which biblical faith "constantly criticizes and renews itself and its own vision." By claiming the Bible's prophetic-liberating stream as a norm for criticizing Christianity and patriarchy, feminist theology operates in the same fashion as other liberation theologies, stripping away layers of ideology and dogma. Christ is the symbol of a new humanity and representative of God's Word, the manifestation of the self-emptying of God, the "kenosis of patriarchy." The dynamic relationship between Redeemer and redeemed is intrinsic to Christianity, for Christ's identity continues as the symbol of liberated humanity. Christic personhood continues in the struggles of faithful people: "Redemptive humanity goes ahead of us, calling us to yet incompleted dimensions of human liberation."[80]

Sexism and God-Talk was vague and evasive about how Ruether believed the God symbol should be construed. Then she adopted Whitehead's answer in her book *Gaia & God* (1992), replete with Whitehead's dipolar concepts. Ruether endorsed Whitehead's idea of a divine matrix that lures its subjects to make choices creating new life-giving possibilities: "The reality of God is thus shaped through interrelation with self-actualizing entities. God not only lures and offers new life, but also suffers, experiencing the pain of destructive choices as well as the pleasure of good choices."[81]

Again she argued for an integrative perspective, rejecting eco-feminist theologies that replaced a monotheistic, transcendent, male-identified religion with a multicentered, immanent, female-identified one. Ruether said feminist theology needed a more imaginative alternative to androcentric monotheism than simply its reversal, "something more like Nicholas of Cusa's paradoxical 'coincidence of opposites,' in which the 'absolute maximum' and the 'absolute minimum' are the same." In physics the distinction between matter and energy does not hold at the subatomic level; matter is conceived as energy moving in defined patterns of relation. At the level of the absolute minimum, Ruether wrote, the appearance of physical something morphs into a void-like web of relationships in which the universe is interconnected: "As we move below the 'absolute minimum' of the tiniest particles into the dancing void of energy patterns that build up the 'appearance' of solid objects on the macroscopic level, we also recognize that this is also the 'absolute maximum,' the matrix of all interconnections of the whole universe." She shared Whitehead's fascination that a creative order exists: "Thus what we have called 'God,' the 'mind,' or rational pattern holding all things together, and what we have called 'matter,' the 'ground' of physical objects, come together."[82]

Ruether's eco-feminism connected the meaning of human living to these absolutely minimal and maximal worlds, "standing between the dancing void of energy" that underlies the atomic structure of all entities in the universe. To seek religious meaning in a possibly meaningless world is to commune with the universe as heart to heart. Human beings are connected to all living creatures past, present, and future through matter and consciousness; thus all creatures are linked to Gaia, the living and sacred earth/organism. To bear compassion for all living things is to break down the illusion of otherness with the power of spirit: "Surely, if we are kin to all things and offspring of the universe, then what has flowered in us as consciousness must also be reflected in that universe as well, in the ongoing creative Matrix of the whole."[83]

In her later career she traveled widely in support of eco-feminist and social justice causes, writing extensively on the plight of Palestinians and helping women's groups in a variety of contexts to "legitimize their questions," as she put it. Routinely Ruether was lauded as the most influential and accomplished feminist theologian of her generation. Letty Russell called her friend "a very wise woman" and partner in "the work against racism and in subversion of church hierarchy." Theologian Susan A. Ross said Ruether's books endured as theological landmarks because they stressed the interrelatedness of oppressions, criticized the Christian tendency to "totalize and dualize," repudiated the "insidious misogyny" of Christianity, and featured strong historical research. Jewish liberationist Marc H. Ellis commended her opposition to Christian anti-Semitism and solidarity with Palestinians. Brazilian eco-feminist Ivone Gebara called her an "intellectual for our contemporary time committed to justice with love." Religious historian Rosalind Hinton, Ruether's former student, noted that Ruether's writings were always timely and relevant because they were rooted in her global activism. Every Ruether book had a community behind it.[84]

Ruether was the epitome of a scholar-activist, contextualizing feminism in global communities. The coming of wave-three feminism, however, swiftly dated her to the generation of feminists that cut their intellectual teeth on poststructuralist theory, the rise of womanism, and queer theory. Ruether grew accustomed to seeing herself dismissed as an old-fashioned liberal, especially for her rendering of Christianity's usable past. Among feminists schooled in poststructuralist criticism, the problem was repeatedly described as Ruether's essentialist theological method, reformist theological agenda, and essentialist feminism. Ruether was criticized for extending the method of liberation theology to feminism and for operating with old-fashioned categories of experience and binary sexuality. Sometimes critics added that she over-politicized theology and/or showed little spiritual feeling or religious belief.

Mary McClintock Fulkerson said Ruether's gender criticism was "a kind of 'me, too' theory" that reproduced the heterosexual binary of liberal essentialism, and her rendering of experience wrongly implicated women's experience "in a realm prior to language." Ellen T. Armour said Ruether's writings were structured "by an assumed feminine identity" to which distinctions of race and class were mere additions. By casting patriarchy as the father of oppression, Ruether added to the oppression experienced by women of color and poor women, conceiving race and class as further means of subjecting and dividing the objects of the father's attention, women. Delores Williams said Ruether was a primary culprit of the white feminist universalization of white women's experience, which obscured the racism and privileges of white feminists. To Williams virtually everything that Ruether said about feminism privileged the beliefs of white feminists, including her claim that "encountering the divine as goddess" was a point of unity for feminists throughout the world. Williams countered, "This is exactly the problem. The 'divine as goddess' is a concern emphasized in *white* feminist theology." Daphne Hampson described Ruether as a classic "golden thread" essentialist who privileged her version of a "sacred history" of liberating praxis; moreover, "one is hard pressed to see how hers is a theology, as opposed to simply a political agenda for the liberation of people." Sheila Greeve Davaney described Ruether as a guardian of the liberal experientialist school that "enhanced the credence of its norms by providing them with an ontological or divine foundation." Kwok Pui-lan judged that Ruether's essentially reformist approach to theology gave "too much power to the theological categories established by the patriarchal tradition."[85]

Elisabeth Schüssler Fiorenza pressed hard against Ruether's method and theology, charging that she idealized prophetic Christianity to the point of obscuring its oppressive elements. Rather than subject prophetic religion to historical and ideological criticism, Ruether appealed to it as an interpretive pattern abstracted from biblical history, playing down the patriarchal character of biblical prophecy and its repression of goddess religion. Schüssler Fiorenza said it was pitifully inadequate for Ruether to claim that biblical prophecy "can be used in the interest of feminism." Worse yet, because it was false, Ruether spoke of transforming the sexist tradition of biblical prophecy into a feminist liberating tradition. Just because the Bible promotes freedom and social justice doesn't mean it implicitly supports women. According to Schüssler Fiorenza, Ruether's approach fell short even of liberalism, being essentially a neo-orthodox attempt to rescue biblical religion from its feminist critics. Feminist theology needed something else, Schüssler Fiorenza contended: a radical feminist hermeneutic incorporating "Wicca's feminist spiritual quest for women's power."[86]

Ruether gave short shrift to critics of her religious temperament. She took no interest in calibrating her spiritual tone to that preferred by unsympathetic critics, and she preferred to have a major biblical tradition on her side than to spurn any such connection to the biblical witness or other forms of liberation theology. But she took sharp exception to the charge of essentialism. It galled her, she said, to be lumped repeatedly with Daly as an essentialist who excluded the claims of race and class: "There is a group of scholars that is very competitive within the academy and are making their careers by critiquing all that came before them as essentialist without making any distinctions between scholars' work. Some have not even read much of my work. They don't have an understanding of how we got started. Race and class were central to what we were doing and then we added a gender critique."[87]

She stressed that the founding Christian feminists began in the civil rights movement and the New Left. "We did not start with a univocal 'woman' and then seek to add race and class difference." The founders conceived race, class, and gender as interconnected variables creating multiple differences. They did not espouse Daly-type essentialism or even liberal essentialism: "Mary Daly wasn't even around. She was in Europe studying Catholic theology and Thomism and trying to become a Catholic theologian." Ruether protested that her legacy was "distorted by these claims of essentialism." Perhaps the generation of feminists that came after her, which was trained in the academy, universalized its own experience, "but that is what we were fighting against. Men were universalizing their experience and white people were universalizing their experience. We were not going to do it too. That is what we were critiquing."[88]

Admittedly, early feminist theology was white, but that was because there were no women of color in the field. Ruether observed that when African American women began to enter the field in the early 1980s, the discourse changed. Having come to the academy from activist movements, she and her Christian feminist colleagues deserved better than to be remembered wrongly, especially by a generation that belonged to the academy and spoke the language of French deconstruction: "I don't think our legacy is fairly contextualized yet." Sometimes she said it ruefully: "It's telling that so many people thought they had to trash me in order to have something to say. If they were really making an advance, why was it necessary to distort what I said?"[89]

Ruether deserved a more accurate remembering, though she failed to grasp the harm that white feminist, global sisterhood rhetoric inflicted on women of color and the generation of feminists schooled in postmodern theory. Some told stories of being gruffly treated by her on their way up. But many also told stories of her modeling feminist scholar-activism, bustling to conferences and speaking engagements, holding advising meetings in the car on her way to the airport. Ruether exemplified the feminist maxim that "Everything is related," leaving a legacy of activist scholarship that invited others to use it for movements still to come.

10

Rethinking Relationality

Theologies of Becoming

Every theology is a response to its time, and ours is the age of postmodern fragmentation, difference, deconstruction, neoliberal globalization, poststructuralism, and nihilism. No theologian of the past half century has won a large following comparable to Schleiermacher or Tillich. The few theologians to make a public splash have focused on specialized concerns or written in a popular trade-market style. No theologian who writes in the broadly visionary style of Schleiermacher or Tillich has won a significant audience. Even the idea of systematic theology has become passé. Four theologians of the late twentieth and early twenty-first centuries are especially important to me for rethinking, in a religious philosophy vein, what it means to be entangled and related in a postmodern context: David Tracy, Peter C. Hodgson, Edward Farley, and Catherine Keller. None are renowned beyond the guild of academic theology, but all have responded creatively to the postmodern situation in religious thought.

Tracy launched a new era of Catholic theology by treating Catholic and Protestant theologians as conversation partners, after which he branched into wider interreligious conversations. Hodgson and Farley developed complementary theologies as Vanderbilt colleagues that reran the choice between Hegel and Schleiermacher, mediated by the phenomenology of Edmund Husserl and Martin Heidegger. Keller, the leading feminist theologian of wave three, which she calls wave four, began her career by playing up the implicitly feminist and ecological aspects of

Whitehead's thought and resisting postmodern fragmentation. Then she decided that mining the postmodern aspects of Whitehead's thought is more fruitful, drawing upon the same deconstructionist critics and classic mystical theologians who caught the later Tracy.

Catholics were latecomers to liberal theology, post-Kantian idealism, and process thought because the Vatican condemned modern theology and prescribed an official philosophy, Thomism. Three papal encyclicals—*Testem benevolentiae* (1899), *Lamentabili Sane* (1907), and *Pascendi Dominici Gregis* (1907)—crushed the first wave of theological modernism in the Catholic Church. Afterward the church hierarchy policed strict versions of Catholic orthodoxy and scholastic Thomism. The theologians who paved the way to the reforms of Vatican II (1962–1965) had to risk papal censure. Some were silenced, notably French Dominican Yves Congar, French Jesuits Henri de Lubac and Pierre Teilhard de Chardin, and American Jesuit John Courtney Murray. Scholastic Thomism was distinctly problematic for reformers. Belgian Jesuit Joseph Maréchal cracked it open by construing the Thomist analogy of being within Kant's transcendental framework. German Jesuit Karl Rahner developed Maréchal's approach into an exploration of being within consciousness, synthesizing Thomas, Kant, Maréchal, and Heidegger in his doctoral dissertation, *Spirit in the World* (1937), the basis of Rahner's transcendental Thomism. In the footsteps of these pioneers, a modernizing tradition of Catholic theology developed during and after Vatican II; Swiss theologian Hans Küng was its most prominent exponent. In the mid-1970s a second stage of post–Vatican II theologizing began, bearing few traces of the long estrangement between Catholicism and Protestantism. David Tracy was its symbol.[1]

Revisionist Theology, Catholic Imagination, and Postmodern Openness: David Tracy

Born in Yonkers, New York, in 1939, Tracy began his preparatory seminary training at the age of thirteen, feeling called to parish priesthood, and his major seminary training at St. Joseph's Seminary in Dunwoodie, New York, where America's first experiment in Catholic modernism was aborted in the early 1900s. Tracy's early academic interests were literature and history, not theology. His intellectual hero was poet T. S. Eliot, until Kierkegaard and Catholic apologist John Henry Newman similarly captivated him. Scholastic theology was boring by comparison. Ordained as a diocesan priest in Bridgeport, Connecticut, in 1963, Tracy studied under

Canadian Jesuit theologian Bernard Lonergan at the Gregorian University, where the excitement over Vatican II convinced him that theology could be interesting. Ecumenical theologians flocked to Rome, people talked about theology in the streets, and Tracy admired Lonergan. He later recalled: "It was thrilling, it was really a wonderful period. But I never liked scholastic theology, at least in its official version." In 1969 he completed his doctoral dissertation on Lonergan's interpretation of Thomas. Tracy taught at Catholic University for two years before joining Langdon Gilkey and Paul Ricoeur at the University of Chicago; Gilkey later recalled, "We had David pegged as the next Lonergan or maybe Rahner, but to our delight he became a little more like us."[2]

Rahner and Lonergan were the major theorists of transcendental Thomism, respectively leading its Continental post-Kantian and Anglo-American wings. Maréchal argued that scholastic Thomists wrongly stripped Kant of his attempt to establish the metaphysical foundations of scientific knowledge. Heidegger, Rahner's graduate mentor at Freiburg, made a similar argument about neo-Kantian interpretations of Kant, refracted through Heidegger's ontology. Rahner contended that Thomas, Kant, Maréchal, and Heidegger differently grappled with the problem of comprehending being as such. He founded transcendental Thomism on the claim that being is best understood by investigating the being that occurs within consciousness. Human beings are embodied spirits whose being is fundamentally ordered toward and grounded in God, pre-apprehending the divine. Lonergan made a similar argument with a different method drawn from the philosophy of science. In *Insight: A Study of Human Understanding* (1957), he argued that the foundation of every form of inquiry is discoverable by analyzing the dynamic structure of one's own experience, insight, judgment, and decision. In *Method in Theology* (1972), he delineated eight functional specializations in theology, philosophy, and science: research, interpretation, history, dialectic, foundations, doctrines, systematics, and communication. Lonergan broke each specialization into four levels that corresponded to his analysis of consciousness, proposing a universal method based on self-appropriation, "a normative pattern of recurrent and related operations yielding cumulative and progressive results." Theology, he argued, is like science in being open-ended and heuristic, featuring distinct operations that relate to each other. These relations form a pattern that describes the most fruitful way of proceeding, the operations can be repeated indefinitely, and they yield cumulative and progressive results.[3]

Tracy embraced his teacher's belief that the crucial problem in theology is to develop the best method. His first book, *The Achievement of Bernard Lonergan* (1970), explained Lonergan's method of "horizon" analysis and theological method, declaring, "In its starkest terms, the theological problem is this: Can the theologian determine a basic pattern for all the patterns of related and recurrent operations involved in the theological task? Can he determine a fundamental theological method which will allow all practitioners to collaborate systematically with one another? Can he ground that pattern in a transcendental method which is not open to fundamental revision?" Tracy agreed with Lonergan that theology must be collaborative and interdisciplinary. Lonergan believed that his method cut across confessional and ideological differences, and he hoped that "theologians of different allegiance" would adopt it. In his later career he wrote sparingly about doctrines, but Lonergan's theology was conservative by post–Vatican II standards. Seven years after he retired from the Gregorian in 1965, Lonergan noted in *Method in Theology* that he retained "quite conservative views on religious and church doctrines."[4]

That was a key difference between Lonergan and Tracy. Addressing the International Lonergan Congress of 1970, Tracy broke Lonergan's foundational theology into two parts. The first was methodological, delineating and integrating the disciplines through a theory of human consciousness and functional specialization. The second was the epistemological/metaphysical grounding of the entire enterprise as a *theo*logical project. Tracy argued that Lonergan's theory of understanding was a major achievement, but his metaphysical foundation simply assumed the truth claims of Catholic doctrine. That was unacceptable, putting religious doctrines outside the pale of critical interrogation. Theology, Tracy said, must be ambitious like Lonergan, but critical of its doctrinal inheritance. Specifically, it must be Christian, revisionist, panentheist, critical in the sense of open-ended inquiry, modern in the sense of holding fast to the morality of knowledge, and postmodern in the sense of criticizing Enlightenment individualism and rationalism. Good theology is a genuinely public discourse driven by the liberating, public character of critical reason. To that end Tracy devoted his breakout book, *Blessed Rage for Order* (1975).[5]

Tracy took for granted the postmodern critique of the autonomous, rational achiever of Enlightenment. No self is autonomous, reason is pervaded by interest, and idealism is illusory. But that does not negate the morality of knowledge, a phrase that Tracy adapted from theological scholar Van Harvey, signifying the willingness to follow the evidence. Tracy said the morality of knowledge leaves room in principle for the overthrow of any method, paradigm, or conclusion that does not hold up to critical scrutiny, and theologians are not exempt from it. To be sure, most theologians are committed to Christianity; until the modern age all theologians were believers by definition. But a modern theologian does not have to be a believer; what is binding is the morality of knowledge. One cannot do serious work in theology without providing appropriate forms of evidence for one's claims.[6]

The modern theologian, though still a theologian, addresses more publics and is judged by stiffer tests of credibility than theologians of previous ages. Liberal theology reconciled theology with modernity, navigating between orthodox overbelief and secular disbelief. Now theology had to move into the postmodern age and condition. In the spirit of Lonergan's imperatives—"Be attentive, be intelligent, be rational, be responsible, develop, and, if necessary, change"—Tracy said theology needed to move beyond modernity while remaining "in fundamental fidelity to the critical exigencies of the liberal period." He affirmed that applying such criticism to liberalism is the greatest tribute that could be made "to the deepest demands of the liberal spirit."[7]

By his reckoning there were five types of contemporary theology: orthodox, liberal, neo-orthodox, radical, and revisionist. Orthodoxies were anti-modern, establishing religious norms by external authority. Liberal theology, epitomized by Schleiermacher, embraced the values of modernity. There were many kinds of neo-orthodoxy, but all criticized liberalism within the liberal framework. Commendably, Karl Barth and Rudolf Bultmann recovered the existential truths in biblical symbols; not commendably, they placed fundamental claims outside the reach of criticism, and the later Barth often regressed from neo-orthodoxy to orthodox dogmatism. Tracy described neo-Thomism and transcendental Thomism as Catholic forms of neo-orthodoxy, rating Rahner as the best Catholic neo-orthodox theologian. Jürgen Moltmann's political theology and Gustavo Gutiérrez's liberation theology were also types of neo-orthodoxy, basically politicizing the neo-orthodox approach. Tracy placed death-of-God theologians Thomas Altizer and William Hamilton in the radical camp and placed himself in the revisionist camp along with Gilkey, Canadian Catholic theologians Gregory Baum and Leslie Dewart, and the Whiteheadians.[8]

He defined the revisionist approach more generously and openly than the other models, since this was his group. Historically it was the idea of an alternative to the other models; systematically it was the attempt to compare and reconcile "the principal values, cognitive claims, and existential faiths of both a reinterpreted post-modern consciousness and a reinterpreted Christianity." Tracy identified with Meland's yearning for a postliberal theology that moved through and beyond liberalism and modernity, standing for the "radical continuation" of modern critical theory, symbolic interpretation, and praxis. Revisionists held the same ideal as the liberal tradition—to interpret Christianity in the light of modern knowledge and circumstances—but Tracy did not want to call it updated liberalism, contending that revisionists had "new methodological and substantive resources."[9]

Revisionist theology had two principal sources: Christian texts and common human experience and language. It correlated these two sources by unveiling the religious dimension in experience, conceiving theology as hermeneutics, and employing a metaphysical theory that shaped and ventured truth claims. Following Hans-Georg Gadamer, Tracy conceived hermeneutics as the interpretive mediation of past and present, an improvement on historical criticism, which construed the meaning behind the text. Gadamer and Ricoeur said the text perceives and shapes reality, requiring hermeneutical refection. Tracy adopted Ricoeur's method of ascertaining the meaning in front of the text, the mode of being in the world it discloses for readers. In Tracy's version this method culminated with metaphysical analysis because theology deals with all experience as such, not just confessional traditions. Religion is about all that is. One's concept of God must cohere with one's basic understanding about reality, necessitating philosophical validation and refinement. Moreover, if religious experience includes an ultimate dimension or horizon, as Gilkey and Tracy contended, metaphysical analysis is needed to adjudicate the adequacy of religious claims.[10]

On religion Tracy appropriated the Schleiermacher-Otto-Tillich tradition of discerning religious dimensions of existence and the Weber-Durkheim-Peter Berger-Clifford Geertz tradition of identifying religion with reality-constructing social functions. Religion expresses limits to ordinary experience, such as finitude and contingency, and discloses fundamental structures of human existence, such as basic beliefs in order, value, or the fundamental trust that life is worth living. On the religious dimensions of science, Tracy employed Lonergan's analysis of self-transcendence: the key to authentic living is to allow oneself a continually expanding horizon. Scientists confront limit issues whenever they inquire about the basic character of the universe or ask whether their purposes are worthwhile. On the religious dimensions of morality, Tracy employed Stephen Toulmin's analysis of moral argument and Schubert Ogden's theory of faith. Toulmin said there is no moral answer to the question of why one should be moral; the logic of the question is religious because of its limit-character. Ogden, extending Toulmin, argued that all religious language is re-presentational, providing symbolic forms expressing the faith that life is worth living. On the religious dimensions of everyday life, Tracy pointed to the limit-experiences of illness, guilt, anxiety, and mortality, as well as the "self-transcending" experiences of love, joy, creativity, and reassurance.[11]

At the metaphysical level Tracy surprised many readers by opting for Whitehead instead of Lonergan or Rahner. Tracy said that only process theology explicates the scriptural metaphor "God is love" without negating it. Thomas, Tracy argued, described "God is love" as an analogy of improper attribution; the process categories of dipolarity, internal relations, and becoming express in conceptual form the tensive meanings of the originating metaphor of love divine. That was slightly misleading concerning Thomas, who denied that the attribution of God's love is metaphorical or improper. Thomas taught that an attribution is proper if its formal meaning implies no incompleteness, and that love and joy have this character. But Tracy had a real difference at stake. Thomas conceived love in God as a "joining force" in God's self-relation; to Tracy and the Whiteheadian school, love in God was also the relation between God and God's creation in mutual reciprocity.[12]

Citing his favorite process theologian, Ogden, Tracy said that all Christians probably trust at some level that God is affected by their doings: "They live as if, to use the expression of one process theologian, God really were Pure Unbounded Love struggling, suffering, achieving with humanity." To Tracy and Ogden, Whiteheadian theism allowed Christians to say *and mean* that God is pure unbounded love. One cannot mean it, Tracy warned, if one says that God is not really (*relatio entis*) but only notionally (*relatio rationis*) affected by human actions. It is better to say that God is absolute as the one whose existence depends on no other being and relative as the one whose actuality is relative to all other beings. Analogously and really, God is supremely perfect in God's abstract absoluteness and relativity; only God is relative to and affected by all others. Tracy did not ask why the will to relate is loving necessarily. It was enough to say that God is actually loving by virtue of being eminently social, temporal, and related.[13]

Faith, as Tracy rendered fundamental theology, was simply the belief that serves to justify or warrant a theological conviction. Religious claims must be tested by a metaphysical criterion (coherence and accordance with experience) that has no particular relation to Christianity; theology discloses that common experience contains traces of the divine; and theology is exactly like sociology, history, and chemistry in accepting the morality of scientific knowledge. Tracy was no positivist; he affirmed that evidence is theory-laden and that theories interpret culturally conditioned perceptions, not objective or provable facts. His case for the primacy of scientific morality rested on its critical logic in following evidence.

In theory he distinguished the tasks of fundamental, systematic, and practical theology. Fundamental theology defends the possibility of religious claims being true, systematic theology interprets the meaning of specific beliefs, and practical theology examines the implications of beliefs for particular social and historical contexts. Many theologians used "dogmatic" and "systematic" interchangeably, but Tracy avoided the term "dogmatic." Many Catholic theologians defined fundamental theology as method, apologetics, and criteriology, but Tracy reasoned that each type of theology should have its own method. The first half of *Blessed Rage for Order* spelled out the method of fundamental theology, understood as the criteria of truth, and the second half carried out the method. The logical connection between the scientific community and the community of faith was left to systematic theology, as well as the meaning of faith in a distinctly Christian sense of the term. Thus Tracy's method excluded historical matters and apologetics, and his constructive section restricted Christology to a form of re-presentative limit-language. In both cases it was novel to limit the frame of discourse to analyzing "texts" or "the Christian fact" apart from the historical theological meanings of the Scriptures, tradition, Christian community, and gospel. His constructive section adhered so closely to the spirit and rules of his method that numerous reviewers of *Blessed Rage for Order* and its sequel, *The Analogical Imagination*, judged that both books were consumed with method. Moreover, despite stressing that his subject was theological pluralism, Tracy ignored black and feminist liberation theologies, overlooked the major Latin American liberationist who could not be dismissed as neo-orthodox (Juan Luis Segundo), and did not ask the basic liberationist questions: Whose experience? For whose interest? How do we select the aspects of experience that have religious pertinence?[14]

Blessed Rage for Order was the first U. S. American theological work to fuse modern Catholic and Protestant theologies into a single agenda, and was widely praised for its ambitious and erudite contribution to that agenda. But it also raised questions about Tracy's project and direction. Jesuit theologian Avery Dulles protested that Tracy's method of correlation merely Christianized a secular worldview: "I doubt whether anyone is likely to become a Christian simply in order to have his secular faith elucidated or expressed by better symbols." Cobb, Gordon Kaufman, and Farley judged that Tracy made no original argument of his own, merely assembling the arguments of others. Cobb stressed Tracy's dependence on Ogden; Kaufman wished that Tracy had developed his own position; Farley complained, "Where one might have expected an argument, what occurs is an exposition of a literature." Farley tried to imagine how Tracy would deal with "a clear-cut piece of doctrinalized tradition" such as the Trinity or the assumption of Mary; the gap between method and dogmatics was very wide in his case. Harvey Cox lamented that Tracy's pluralistic horizon did not include North American liberationists.[15]

Van Harvey doubted that Tracy's hermeneutical borrowings from Ricoeur, Gadamer, and Ian Ramsey were compatible with the metaphysical realism of process thought, and he wished that theological liberals would stop pleading that unfaith is an ontological impossibility. Perhaps Tillich, Gilkey, Ogden, and Tracy experienced something like the unity of living and value, but contingent secularists like him did not. Other reviewers puzzled that a Catholic theologian had almost nothing to say about ecclesiology, while liberationists did not appreciate Tracy's claim that they merely reworked neo-orthodoxy to support radical politics. For years afterward Tracy was described as epitomizing the kind of theologian who universalized his own white, male, privileged, highly academic experience. Some reviewers suggested that a final verdict on his fundamental theology had to wait for his systematic theology.[16]

Tracy puzzled over the problem of moving from fundamental to systematic theology. It didn't help when reviewers claimed that *Blessed Rage for Order* lacked any constructive theology. He confessed that he had only "hints and guesses" about how to proceed: "Frankly, I've gone back to the drawing board." He vowed to "clear my own head on what an adequate model for a Christian systematics might be."[17]

For a while he settled on the "Catholic analogical imagination," especially the ideas that human beings are more good than bad, reality is ultimately trustworthy despite ignorance and sin, reason is the way to find the order of things, and the reign of God is about love, not fear and abasement. Tracy lauded the First Vatican Council for beginning the Catholic turn from deductive proof making. Instead of proving the mysteries of faith in scholastic fashion, Vatican I described theology as the analogous but real understanding (*intelligentia*) of Christian mystery. Analogies find the crucial median between univocal and equivocal claims. Traditional Thomism, canonized by sixteenth-century theologian Thomas de Vio (Cardinal Cajetan) and defended by Reginald Garrigou-Lagrange, espoused a one-doctrine idea of analogical understanding based on Aristotelian substance. But other schools of Thomism contended that Thomas privileged the act of existing, not Aristotelian substance. Existential Thomists Etienne Gilson and (Anglican) Eric Mascall, and participation Thomists Cornelio Fabro and Louis-Bertrand Geiger, argued that analogies are true or false on proportional terms. Rahner made a Heidegger-like move from the analogy of being to the analogy of *having* being, which made human subjectivity in relation to divine being the focus of analogical usage. David Burrell said there was a linguistic basis in Thomas for distinguishing between two kinds of analogical usage. Analogies refer either to one focal meaning (attribution) or to an ordered relationship among different uses (proportionately). Tracy appropriated Rahner and Burrell, stressing that every school develops analogies from nature to understand the relationships of Christian concepts to each other.[18]

In other words, modern Catholic thought about analogy was very much like modern Protestant thought about metaphor. Tracy recalled that scholastics and Enlightenment rationalists denigrated metaphor in favor of literal meaning and analogy in favor of univocal usage. To a significant degree, twentieth-century religious thought was about the renewal of metaphor and analogy. The meaning of an analogy changes through interaction; good analogies and metaphors illumine the obscured dimensions of the familiar, evoking what Aristotle called similarity in dissimilarity. The emergent meanings of analogies are not poor substitutes for real meanings; rather, analogies relate all other usages to the focal meaning of a given subject. To Tracy the Catholic analogical imagination was the key to renewing Christianity in a world of secular challenges and religious pluralism. It focused on similarities, but in a dialectical fashion that emphasized similarities within difference.[19]

The book version of this argument, *The Analogical Imagination* (1981), delineated three publics that theology occurs within and addresses: society, academy, and religious community. Tracy argued that systematic theology is fundamentally hermeneutical and the best analogy for theological meaning and truth is art—another enterprise that modernity overly privatizes. The best way to do theology in its three contexts is to decipher the common human experiences of meaning and truth in the production and reception of a classic. For Christians, he said, the most pertinent classic is the Christian tradition. Like all classics, the religious classic makes a disclosure claim about the meaning and truth of reality, describing an experience of the whole as the self-manifestation of an ultimate power. The language of authentic religious experience is about real, incomprehensible mystery, not certainty and clarity, using the language of liberation, wholeness, and salvation to articulate its convicting experience.[20]

Once again Tracy developed a method in part one that he exemplified theologically in part two, arguing that the church's memory of Jesus lives through Christian history as a presence that shapes Christian experience. Previous modern generations, he said, had a dominant question that framed how the Christ event was experienced, but his generation was too pluralistic to have a singular framework. Liberationists pointed to the breakdown of the colonial era and the identities of the oppressed, but Tracy was not a liberationist. Tillich pointed to modern meaninglessness, but cultural pluralism shredded Tillich's claim that cultures have a religious dimension. Tracy's leading candidate for *the* issue was "the uncanny," a Freudian term for the sense of "not-at-homeness" in the world. Implicitly, *The Analogical Imagination* affirmed that Tracy had a home in Catholicism, but he warned against "those bogus affirmations, those principles of domination, those slack feelings which tempt us beyond mere error and even illusion to the final distortions of indecency."[21]

Once again he was lauded for his synthetic complexity and blasted for belaboring method at the expense of content. Lutheran theologian Ted Peters bemoaned the half-page sentences featuring "dependent clauses, parenthetical allusions to a half-dozen great systems of thought, and Tracy's desire to exhaust an idea each time he mentions it." Still, Peters said, *The Analogical Imagination* amply rewarded the struggle to read it. Cobb worried that Tracy's "monumental" work did not allow a diversity of perspectives to redefine what theology should be; in particular the insights of feminists and liberationists made no impact on the "overall structure" of Tracy's theology. Catholic theologian T. Howland Sanks judged that Tracy was strong on methodological prescription and theological conversation, but weak on doctrinal content; his book described an adequate Christology but "does not actually do this himself." Baum praised Tracy for offering a remarkable tour through "realms of spirit and understanding," while lamenting that he did not privilege the struggles of oppressed people for liberation.[22]

Burrell disliked Tracy's rhetorical effusiveness, criticized his neglect of the Trinity and creation, dismissed process theology as "philosophical gas" and "a useless shuffle," and was unmoved by "the whole." He appreciated that Tracy said nice things about the value of tradition, but sharply attacked the "double-decker character" of his project. Tracy was confused, and therefore confusing, Burrell said. He did not write systematic theology, contrary to his claims; he only wrote about it. The closest that he came to doing theology was in the footnotes.[23]

Tracy replied to his critics, both friendly and harsh, that the second parts of his books really were constructive theology—a new kind that took seriously the pluralism of contemporary culture, religion, scriptural forms, and the Christian tradition. Later he wished he had published the second parts of both books as separate works; it was discouraging to see his theologizing repeatedly dismissed. Tracy allowed that his work was short on sacramental theology and overly fixed on books. On the other hand, he denied that his theology merely talked about manifestation without manifesting anything, for theology-as-hermeneutics conceives truth *as* manifestation.[24]

The Analogical Imagination was the second volume of a projected trilogy on fundamental, systematic, and practical theology, but Tracy's mixed genre proved confusing to readers, and the book on practical theology went unwritten. He wanted to write a methodological section that developed the relationship of theory and practice, followed by a constructive section that correlated theory/practice to theology, principally the Spirit and church. But the task of relating social science and ethics to theology defeated him. He reported, "I may never be ready to attempt that third volume," regretting his inability to figure out "the most complex task of all." Still later he regretted having created an expectation: "It's a very difficult discipline—practical theology. Very difficult."[25]

He stopped writing big books, switched to the essay format, and stewed over misrepresentations of his work. *Blessed Rage for Order* laid the hermeneutical groundwork for the hermeneutical model of theology as conversation that he developed in *The Analogical Imagination*. Both were revisionist texts, though his emphasis on the classic somewhat muted his modernism. In the 1980s Tracy remained an advocate of historical consciousness, pluralism, modernity, scientific rationality, correlation method, public theology, process theology, panentheism, the religious classic, a Catholic tradition concept of the apostolic witness, the analogical imagination, theology as hermeneutics, and interpretation as conversation.[26]

But he made two significant shifts. The first, his postmodern/interreligious turn, began in the early 1980s and considerably widened the scope of his thought. The second, his mystical-prophetic turn, emerged in the early 1990s but was prefigured by the implicit distancing from modernity that Tracy introduced in *The Analogical Imagination*. Though he denied that his resort to Gadamerian retrieval was a conservative tack, Tracy opened his thought to new sources and perspectives, especially Buddhism, mysticism, deconstruction, postmodern cultural criticism, liberation theology, and comparative theology. His Gadamerian idea of theology as interpretive conversation and retrieval made room for the hermeneutics of suspicion and critique. He still believed in the central importance of modernity, but also believed that postmodernism was more than a fad: "There is a dark underside to modern thought, including modern theology. Anyone who sees this problem at all is likely to attempt one or another form of postmodern theology."[27]

In 1987 he published an essay collection, *Plurality and Ambiguity*, reprising a trademark theme: interpretation is the key to understanding and conversation is the key to interpretation. Tracy argued that classical modes of argument often interrupt genuine conversation, language is often a fragmenting force, and dialogue with the other in late modernity is often disrupted by the terror of otherness. Religion—"the most pluralistic, ambiguous, and important reality of all"—can be a sign of resistance and hope, or oppression. Philosopher Richard Rorty, who made a splash as a postmodern gadfly, told readers to forget about religion, because postmodern maturity changed the subject. Tracy took this judgment seriously, but held out for the analogical imagination: "Anyone who can converse can learn to appropriate another possibility." Every authentic conversation holds the possibility of mutual transformation.[28]

Western and Eastern Christianity both change when they hold genuine conversations, and the same thing happens when Christians and Buddhists converse. Tracy observed that interreligious conversation usually relies on analogies, which are indispensable and terribly limited, taking conversation only so far. The analogical imagination recognizes and articulates that differences are genuinely different "but also similar to what we already know." On a personal level, it dares to enter "that unnerving place" of risking one's identity and security by facing the claims of the other. Thomas Merton, the Trappist monk and author who became a Christian Buddhist, was an exemplar to Tracy. Cobb became another exemplar by founding a Christian-Buddhist dialogue at the American Academy of Religion. Tracy remarked, "The profound Buddhist insight into the self's need to stop its compulsive clinging to all false securities has caused some Christian theologians to realize that even the most refined concepts of theism can function as fatal evasions of Ultimate Reality."[29]

He grew fond of saying that religion should never be boring. Fundamentalism, scholasticism, hyperrationalism, and positivism are boring because they obsess over clarity, certainty, and control. Religion, on the other hand, is about otherness, difference, and the disturbing: "It is not more of the same." *Plurality and Ambiguity* signaled that Tracy's interests were shifting to the mystics and prophets. Kierkegaard attacked Christendom; Teresa of Avila wrote about mystical experience while cautioning against ecstasies and visions; John of the Cross described the dark night of the soul; Tracy suggested that real religion is a sign of hope and resistance, containing its own hermeneutic of suspicion: "As long as human beings question their most profound joys and their deepest anxieties, they remain open to the need for some enlightenment, some emancipation. The alternative is yet another superfluous vote in the endless plebiscite conducted by the unrelenting enforcers of more of the same."[30]

He found a helpful forerunner for interreligious conversation in William James, who combined an "instinct for plurality" with a strong sense of unity-amidst-diversity. James looked to the saints and mystics for clues to the mystery of life, without claiming that only the "sick-soul" types are interesting. He was generous with mild healthy-minded movements, like mind cure and liberal Protestantism, and with very healthy-minded thinkers like Emerson and Walt Whitman. In *Varieties of Religious Experience*, James evaluated religious experience by three criteria: "immediate luminousness," coherence with existing knowledge, and individual and social consequences. Tracy acknowledged that James had little sense of the role of language in producing experience and did not anticipate postcolonial judgments that "religion" is a Western invention. With a bit of postmodern tweaking, however, James was still useful.

Immediate luminousness might be translated as suggestive possibility, a Heidegger/Gadamer category suggesting openness to mutual transformation through engagement with the other. Coherence with science still matters, assuming that science is hermeneutical, and so is the Jamesian emphasis on individual and social consequences, though James was too individualistic.[31]

After pondering for a while which dialogue he should join, Tracy chose Buddhism because it seemed radically other to Christianity and there was an active group to join. He concentrated on the Mahayana Buddhism of Nagarjuna, especially the modern Kyoto school, expecting that his knowledge of Hegel and Whitehead would be helpful. Instead he found deeper affinities with Jacques Derrida and Gilles Deleuze. The "strangely metaphysical, yet anti-metaphysical" character of much Buddhist thought resembled Heidegger's critique of the West's onto-theo-logical fixation, Derrida's attack on logocentrism, and the deconstructionist rejection of the "self" as a ground for understanding "reality." Tracy acknowledged that it was "deeply disorienting" to think of the self as an illusion, ultimate reality as nothingness, and—pervading no-self and emptiness—a codependent origination as describing all reality. What did that have to do with his decisions to become a Catholic priest and theologian? Moreover, it wasn't even correct to speak of a Buddhist doctrine of the no-self: "Rather there is a realization of emptiness and dependent co-origination and thereby no-self through such practices as Zazen meditation and occasional glimpses of this non-doctrinal truth."[32]

Deconstructionism gave him clues to Kyoto school Buddhism, but both were far from his Catholic notions of ego, self, and subject. Tracy got his bearings from the apophatic stream of Neoplatonist Christian mysticism, especially Meister Eckhart (1260–1328) and Jan Ruysbroeck (1293–1381). Eckhart, a German Dominican theologian, combined a rigorous intellectualism and radical detachment; Tracy found him the closest Christian analogue to Buddhism. Ruysbroeck, a Flemish priest and prior of a small religious community, fashioned a Trinitarian interpretation of Eckhart's "Godhead beyond God." Unlike the love mysticism of Bernard of Clairvaux, John of the Cross, and Teresa of Avila, Eckhart prized radical detachment above all. He taught his students to break through the world of particulars to reach the ground of reality where God and the soul are one. For him "nothingness" was virtually a God-term and "abstractedness" (*Abgeschiedenheit*) the highest virtue. He famously insisted that even the names Father, Son, and Spirit are inappropriate for the "Godhead beyond God," though Tracy judged that Ruysbroeck better perceived the trinitarian manifestation of Eckhart's radically indistinct, no-thing, God beyond God.[33]

Eckhart was ambiguous about whether such transcendental terms as One and *Esse* should be applied to the Godhead or the Father-Source, but Ruysbroeck emphasized that all language for God is inadequate *and* that the Godhead beyond God necessarily manifests itself to Christians as the self-manifesting Trinity. The negative way demands the negation of all names for God, but God's wisdom in the Logos and love in the Spirit are central clues to the divine mystery. The Son is the self-manifestation of the Father as Logos; the Spirit is the relationship of divine self-manifestation. To Ruysbroeck the economic Trinity of expression was the main clue to the ontological Trinity.[34]

Tracy questioned whether Christianity was ready for Eckhart's God beyond God, and whether Buddhist compassion could be united to prophetic justice. But he believed in the mystical way of negation as a way to a transcendent spiritual awareness, and stressed that Eckhart came closer to Buddhism than any Christian theologian. To Tracy the goal was to move beyond Eckhart in something like the way that Ruysbroeck prefigured, to a "fully mystico-prophetic" theology uniting spiritual transformation and historical engagement. Transformed by the self-manifestation of divine mystery, the mystical prophet returns to history to struggle for justice and love. "We cannot finally stay with the Buddhist," Tracy cautioned. The goal of interreligious dialogue is mutual transformation, exactly as Cobb contended after Cobb stopped believing, in the late 1970s, that religions have comparable essences.[35]

Tracy believed in confronting otherness and seeking mutual transformation; on the other hand, the otherness of Buddhism is extremely daunting, negating all talk of commonality and complementary affinity. No strand of Christianity comes close to the Buddhist doctrine of transience; not even Whiteheadian theism approximates the Buddhist world of radical relationality. For Buddhism there is no circumference or order. Ultimate reality is emptiness. At times Tracy seemed to question whether he made the right decision in selecting the most radically "other" tradition. Moreover, the Kyoto school was merely one form of otherness; dialogues within traditions are often as problematic as interreligious dialogues, and Tracy emphasized that the candidates for interreligious conversation are impossibly profuse. Christianity alone is impossibly profuse. Tracy reflected, "There are now many 'others' who do theology in ways very different, even conflictually other, from my own white, male, middle class, and academic reflections on a hermeneutics of dialogue and a praxis of solidarity. They bespeak critiques, suspicions, and retrievals of the Christian heritage which I too need to hear far better than I have to date."[36]

That made the present age an extraordinary time to be a theologian. Grateful to belong to a church with a two thousand-year tradition, Tracy appreciated his opportunity to participate in its struggle to become "a polycentric, a truly world church." The inability of the present age to name itself intrigued him. For some, the age of modernity and the bourgeois subject continued; others waited for the restoration of traditions leveled by modernity; others embraced postmodernity and the death of the subject. Tracy welcomed the deconstructionist slaying of the self-grounded modern self. He did not mourn the demise of the autonomous reasoner who built the foundations of the world out of his or her rationality. Derrida, Deleuze, and Foucault were right to favor the dissenters, hysterics, mystics, and avant-garde artists; Tracy was all for replacing the *status quo* with the *fluxus quo*. But postmodern criticism, he said, is terribly short on prophetic-ethical seriousness, parading a spirit of carnival frivolity, "nihilism with a happy ending." Tracy yearned for a different kind of postmodern religiosity, "a mystical-prophetic theology with many centers."[37]

In 1992 he began to imagine a new trilogy reflecting his conversion to mystical prophecy. Volume one, *This Side of God*, would deal with God, volume two with Christ, and volume three with Spirit; Tracy pushed aside his file on practical theology. He still valued the ism approach to theology, reading new books on theism, atheism, pantheism, and panentheism, and still believed that panentheism is the best way to conceptualize God's relationship to the world. But he no longer believed that concepts are the best way to approach the question of God. The modern debate about God focuses on what is possible and actual. Modern theology from Schleiermacher onward links God with possible or actual concrete experiences, making arguments about God's possibility or actuality by appealing to experience, reason, or imagination. Hermeneutic theologies deal with the possible; empirical and process theologies make claims about what is actual; in both cases, theology is about human attempts to comprehend divine existence.[38]

Tracy mused that the mystics he liked did not make arguments about a comprehensible God. Neoplatonist Christian mysticism was God-centered, not epistemology-centered, insisting on the incomprehensibility of whatever God is. Tracy resolved to start there, with Dionysius, Eckhart, Ruysbroeck, Marguerite Porete, and Nicholas of Cusa. Taking his central cue from the apophatic mystical tradition and Derrida's late-life interest in it, Tracy turned against the modern attempt to persuade about the actuality or possibility of divine reality. A second stream of Christian theology complemented this diagnosis by emphasizing the hiddenness of God; Tracy called it the prophetic tradition. Here the major theologians were Luther, Calvin, and Pascal, especially Luther. Both traditions can be intensified or generalized, Tracy reasoned. The mystic tradition is meditative, associated with wisdom, and when generalized moves into a metaphysical or aesthetic mode. The prophetic tradition is apocalyptic and/or focused on the cross, suffering, and negativity, and when generalized becomes ethical or ethical-political.[39]

These categories were an echo of the distinction between manifestation and proclamation, which Tracy correlated with the mystical and prophetic traditions. Manifestation correlates with myth, ritual, sacrament, and wisdom, but always carries the danger of degenerating into a self-absorbed, clerical, totalized system. Thus the prophetic critique of domination and oppression is indispensable in Judaism, Christianity, and Islam, shattering the uniformity of domination systems. The wisdom tradition in its most intense form is apophatic, or mystical; the prophetic tradition in its most intense form is apocalyptic, especially when prophecy fails. Tracy observed that prophecy generalized becomes social ethics, as occurred under modernity and liberal Protestantism. Thus Catholics are usually less troubled than Protestants about the demise of modernity. Prophecy secularized is social activism, as in the social gospel; wisdom secularized is the aesthetic faith depicted in Iris Murdoch's novels, in which art is the form of the good.[40]

Modern theology, Tracy argued, was flawed from the beginning by the scholastic distinction between theology and spirituality. This flaw became a fatal separation in Protestant theology, yielding theologians lacking any spiritual practices. Then Catholic theology took a similar path after it modernized. Tracy lauded a handful of exceptions on both sides, citing Anglicans Austin Farrer and Rowan Williams, and Catholics Rahner, Lonergan, Gutiérrez, and Hans Urs von Balthasar, as theologians who combined intellectual sophistication and spiritual depth. Balthasar wrote grand-scale works explicating the erasure of spirituality thesis. Farrer mined scriptural texts with a spiritual sensitivity to symbols and images. Tracy said he sought to be that kind of theologian.[41]

For twenty-five years and still counting, he stewed over the first volume of his new trilogy, occasionally carving articles and lectures from it, deflecting queries about its publication. Gradually Tracy surmised that the God-centered alternative to epistemological actuality or possibility is impossibility and that his mystical-prophetic perspective had much to gain from postmodern reflection on fragmentation. Modern theology, philosophy, and culture conceived history as a linear schema with a single telos, Western modernity. God was part of the schema, either as something fairly important or an important missing part. But what if history is jagged, labyrinthine, and radically interruptive? What if the ideological and socioeconomic schema underlying modernity is imperialist and implausible? Tracy pointed to massive suffering, "the reality of the others and the different." He did not believe that a consoling ism-God does anything significant. God enters history "as an awesome, often terrifying, hope-beyond-hope . . . the unpredictable, liberating, Hidden God."[42]

His theological exemplars were the "relentless theological radicals" of divine incomprehensibility (Eckhart) and divine hiddenness (Luther). Luther taught that God is revealed through the hiddenness of suffering and the cross. The hidden God is the crucified God (*deus crucifixus*) who suffered for our sake on Calvary and was humiliated (*deus incarnatus*, *deus absconditus in passionibus*). Whatever is to be known about God must be gleaned from the godforsaken agony of God incarnate on the cross. But Luther had a second way of thinking about divine hiddenness that Tracy, following religious historian B. A. Gerrish, called "Hiddenness II." In his famous response to Erasmus in *On the Bondage of the Will*, Luther distinguished between the will of God that is revealed and preached in history and the hidden God that is unknown. The hidden God must be left alone, he said. Since God in God's own nature is unknown to us, the hidden God is not our concern: "We have to do with Him as clothed and displayed in His Word, by which He presents Himself to us. That is His glory and beauty." God does many things that God's Word does not reveal, and God wills many things that the Word does not show that God wills. Thus Luther counseled that "we must keep in view His Word and leave alone His inscrutable will; for it is by his Word, and not by His inscrutable will, that we must be guided."[43]

Tracy stressed that Luther's two ideas of divine hiddenness are strikingly different, if not contradictory; both are unsettling and extreme; and Hiddenness II is "literally awe-ful" in its metaphors of power, energy, abyss, chasm, chaos, and even horror. Sometimes Luther described the

God of Hiddenness II as a frightening, impersonal force of sheer power. This was the religious background to Otto's very Lutheran description of God as numinous and holy, and Tillich's dialectic of the God beyond God (though Tillich also credited Eckhart). Tracy stood against liberals like Ritschl, who dismissed Hiddenness II as a medieval throwback, and dogmatists like Barth, who criticized Luther for destroying God's unity. Though Luther's theologizing about Hiddenness I was more deeply theological and christological, it was wrong to dismiss Hiddenness II or domesticate Luther's ambivalent ideas about God's ambivalent hiddenness by harmonizing them.[44]

Reprising a favorite theme that he now fashioned differently, Tracy played up the different theological strategies and perspectives of the Gospels. The Gospel of John, long his favorite, is a meditation on the salvation of the world by divine love. Matthew reflects the struggle of the early Jewish-Christian community to organize itself and its beliefs. Luke is a realistic narrative that shows the development of the gospel from Judaism to Jewish-Christianity to universal Christianity. Mark eschews doctrinal and narrative embellishment, shows a tragic sense of life, presents an interruptive view of history, portrays Jesus as crying out in godforsaken agony on the cross, and offers a startlingly brief account of the resurrection hope. Mark's apocalyptic sense of history and stark portrayal of a crucified God comes closest to Luther's theological sensibility. Tracy moved in the same direction, though he still preferred the Fourth Gospel.[45]

Luther recovered the theology of the cross and rightly feared the divine inscrutability, but he appropriated these truths in merely personal terms. The existential and dialectical theologies of neo-orthodoxy rebelled against liberal sentimentality and idealism, but usually looked for God's hiddenness in the estrangement of the alienated modern self. Tracy believed that praxis is the key to a better theology, appropriating liberationist, interreligious, and postmodern currents. A mystic-prophetic theology of praxis would understood the cross as "the revelation of God in hiddenness, in suffering and struggle, in the endurance and the joys of those individuals and groups too often effectively designated non-persons by the dominant culture: the oppressed and marginalized in all history, in every society, in every church."[46]

His signature categories became otherness, difference, marginality, incomprehensibility, hiddenness, impossibility, transgression, excess, and fragmentation. Tracy appreciated the Neoplatonist understanding of love as overflow and emanation, and the modern preoccupation with interrelation, but favored the postmodern understanding of love as sheer excess and transgression. The relational schemes of Hegel and Whitehead seemed tepid by comparison. Certain strands of love mysticism, apophatic mysticism, and Eastern thought, he said, supported his preference. Hinduism uses an excess of forms to refer to divine reality; Buddhism and negative theology take the opposite tack of exploring formlessness; Tracy pointed to the affinity between apophatic mysticism and the religiously musical postmodernism of Derrida, John Caputo, and Mark C. Taylor. All were critics of the desire for totality, opposing the claims of system and dogma. The later Derrida moved in this direction, interpreting the mystics as pointers to a "question mark" hovering between God and the Void. Tracy wanted Derrida's followers to claim their implied ethic of resistance to tyranny and injustice. His own project was to gather the fragments of his various sources into a vision of mystical-prophetic engagement.[47]

He planned to discuss Christology, Trinity, anthropology, justification, and sanctification in his second volume, leaving the Spirit and theology of world religions for volume three. Tracy mused that if he finally wrote the book on practical theology that had been too hard for him, it would be harder than ever. He told me, with characteristic humility, it had been an act of "hubris" to think he could write it. In the past he had not believed that theology and spirituality must be integrated; now this was his main subject. Volume one, *This Side of God*, still unpublished in 2019, is on the spirituality of apophatic religion: if God is best described as hidden or incomprehensible openness, to experience God is to "let go" into the open. History and nature are openings into the "gracious void" of the divine mystery, not systems that contain God.[48]

Gracious, kindly, and famously owlish in his personal habits, Tracy became somewhat reclusive in his later career at Chicago on account of poor health. Repeatedly he revised *This Side of God*, always judging it was not quite ready for publication. For years the manuscript described God as the gracious void, until Tracy decided that was too Christian. He settled on "the open," contending that to experience "the open," the sheer giftedness of life, one should practice a spiritual discipline, but the practices are only a preparation. The divine mystery either breaks into one's awareness or doesn't. In his early career Tracy believed that apocalyptic is embarrassing and the second coming is a negligible symbol from a bypassed world. By his late career he believed that the second coming, whatever it is, has to be as important as the incarnation, cross, and resurrection. Without changing a single major position in his theology, he became a very different kind of theologian.[49]

Shapes of Freedom and Presence: Peter Hodgson and Edward Farley

Tracy had plenty of late twentieth-century company in preferring the term "revisionist" over liberal, which paralleled the triumph of "progressive" over liberal in politics, although all three terms are problematic. "Liberal" carries excessive historical baggage, "progressive" smacks of the discredited Progressive belief in progress, and "revisionist" is too passive and squishy. Peter Hodgson felt acutely the problems of these categories, while feeling least conflicted about "revisionist." He and his colleague Edward Farley belonged to the theological generation that had to rethink what it believed after neo-orthodoxy crashed. Hodgson took a circuitous route to neo-Hegelian theology, Farley drew deeply from the well of Husserlian phenomenology, and both characterized their differences as a rerun of Hegel versus Schleiermacher, which ironically reflected that Hegel and Schleiermacher were much alike.

Hodgson's theological career was unexpected and Farley's was not. Hodgson was born in 1934 in Oak Park, Illinois, grew up in Memphis, moved to Baltimore during high school, earned his college degree in history at Princeton, and was surprised to like theology, specifically Tillich's *The Protestant Era*. Farley was born in 1929 in Louisville, grew up Presbyterian, and graduated from Centre College and Louisville Presbyterian Theological Seminary. Hodgson took his graduate training at Yale Divinity School, then in its golden age under theologians H. Richard Niebuhr, Robert C. Calhoun, Hans Frei, Julian Hartt, George Lindbeck, James Gustafson, and Claude Welch, and New Testament scholars Paul Meyer, Paul Minear, and Paul Schubert. Farley took his doctoral training at Union Theological Seminary under Daniel Day Williams and Wilhelm Pauck, graduating in 1957.[50]

Yale and Union were bastions of American neo-orthodoxy, which customarily played down its liberal elements in Reinhold Niebuhr's fashion, but Calhoun and Williams were unapologetic liberals. Hodgson learned of F. C. Baur in Schubert's classroom, wrote a dissertation on Baur under Frei's direction, and debated Hegel versus Barth with Frei. Frei liked Baur's emphasis on God's self-mediation in the world, but cautioned Hodgson against Baur's reliance on Hegel; Barth was better for spurning speculative philosophy. Hodgson, however, was drawn to Baur, partly because he did not like Barth's biblical authoritarianism and Christocentrism. Perhaps Baur offered a better basis for neo-orthodoxy? With that question in mind, Hodgson defended Baur's synthesis of historicism and Hegelian speculation, claiming that Baur was not as Hegelian as his reputation, and graduated in 1963. Many years later he took it back: "I now see that Baur's version of Hegel is very close to Hegel's version of himself, in other words that Baur represents a middle Hegelian position vis-a-vis the left-wing and right-wing distortions that Hegel himself anticipated and attacked."[51]

In 1963 the Baltimore Presbytery ordained Hodgson to the Presbyterian ministry, despite objections that his neo-orthodoxy was too liberal; the same year he began his academic career at Trinity University in San Antonio, Texas, where he taught for two years before moving to Vanderbilt. The "new hermeneutics" of Ernst Fuchs and Gerhard Ebeling, appropriating the later Heidegger, was the newest fashion in theology. Heidegger described language as the primal voice of being, "that event in which for the first time being as being is disclosed to man." Ebeling applied Heidegger's emphasis on the creative primal character of language to theology, seeking to recover the "language event" behind the theological formulations of early Christian preaching, which required a new quest of the historical Jesus. To Hodgson the "new hermeneutic" thesis that language is the site of presence and transformation showed the way beyond Yale neo-orthodoxy. The new hermeneutic was not just a method; it was the process in which language itself speaks.[52]

He adopted Ebeling's notion that Jesus is significant as the "word event" of faith, creating a new world through a new language. Language is a gathering power expressing the event of being itself. Human beings have presence and life to the extent that they participate in the presence and life of God; Jesus is the agent of a new humanity and the "absolute anticipation" of the consummation of humanity; to be faithful in the way of Jesus is to participate in the kingdom of God. Hodgson's book explicating this argument, *Jesus—Word and Presence*, was published in 1971. In 1969 he plunged into civil rights activism, befriending James Lawson and black liberationist Gayraud Wilmore, and welcomed Farley to the Vanderbilt faculty. Hodgson underwent a second theological education from 1969 to 1974. In 1971 he teamed with Lawson to teach a course on theology and the black experience, which yielded Hodgson's book *Children of Freedom: Black Liberation in Christian Perspective* (1974). Then he wrote *New Birth of Freedom* (1976), construing theology as an act of solidarity with movements for Third World, African American, and women's liberation.[53]

Hodgson acknowledged that he could not do black theology, feminist theology, or Third World theology. All he could do as a middle-class, white, American, Protestant, male academic was take up the essentially Christian and American struggle for freedom as a descendant of the white American males who enslaved blacks, pulverized the Native American population, and subjugated women. He described racism as a primordial example of idolatry, "the apotheosis of one's own race and the negation of others." Hodgson supported court-ordered busing to achieve racially integrated schools, observing that anti-busing freedom talk was really a defense of class and race privileges. White flight from Nashville and other communities repelled him, revealing "the 'radical' character of prejudice and the need for a fundamental 'turning' of perspective before the racial problem can be solved." He argued that civil rights integration and black power separatism had complimentary contributions to make, but neither was the ultimate answer. What was needed was the kind of rainbow movement for social justice that Du Bois and the later Malcolm X espoused.[54]

Hodgson reasoned that his solidarity work should produce constructive theologizing about freedom. Drawing on Heidegger, Hegel, and Ricoeur, he analyzed Marxist, Freudian, existential, behaviorist, technological, and countercultural perspectives, developing a phenomenological analysis of structures of freedom. The essential structures were autonomy (subjective freedom), community (intersubjective freedom) and openness (transsubjective freedom). Freedom, he argued, being essentially triadic, does not exclusively emphasize the autonomous ideals of self-determination or self-fulfillment, the community of free production, or the openness of emancipated spirit. Bondage is a distortion of human freedom and desire—idolatry. It is not the logic of being, the work of an evil god, a tragic conflict between the life and death instincts, the repression of libidinal desire, or the factors of production. The interior act of bondage, otherwise called sin, is objectified and reinforced by oppressive subjective, intersubjective, and transsubjective powers.

Bondage always possesses an internal-external dynamic. Hodgson reasoned that liberation cannot be achieved merely by removing the demons of psychic terror or the objective conditions of estrangement or oppression. Liberation is the actualization of freedom, which requires psychic emancipation, a transformed community of the free, and a transformative openness to the future. True communion is reciprocally co-intentional. Members will the good for each other and put themselves at the disposal of each other. The actualization of divine love is the "new birth of freedom" in which each person exists for the sake of the other.[55]

Hodgson was sincere, quiet, skilled at phenomenological analysis, and shy, plus amply aware that he was an outsider to liberation theology. Several reviewers made the latter point in ways that cut him deeply. Theologian Letty Russell said Hodgson's work was "deductive and propositional," not liberationist, skewing liberationist themes "by putting them into a schematic framework." Basically he offered "a correlation of white, western issues raised by intellectual non-believers, with biblical answers to the meaning of freedom." Theologian Frederick Herzog blasted Hodgson for perfecting the liberal trivialization of liberation theology. In the real thing, Herzog said, praxis gives rise to thought, beginning with an act of solidarity with the oppressed. Hodgson began with Schleiermacher's phenomenology of religious experience, appropriated Heidegger, skimmed off the top of liberation theology, and fashioned the result as an all-inclusive liberation perspective. Herzog said Hodgson was a typical liberal, prizing academic credibility, not Christian praxis: "Theological schools are enclaves of self-perpetuating intellectual elites reversing the order of God's priorities."[56]

Many academics would have shucked off the harsh reviews and moved on to the next book, reasoning that theologians needed to reckon with Hegel, Heidegger, and maybe Husserl. Hodgson burned with shame at being criticized justly. He later recalled, "I felt isolated, an out-of-place academic liberal, a white male who lacked a community of discourse and practice that might have contextualized and funded his work." To find his voice, he had to start over, writing from where he lived and thought, which he called "a bridge between enlightenment and liberation, modernity and postmodernity, my first and second theological educations." Hodgson retained his left-liberationist commitments, but had to find a way to write as himself.[57]

He acquired a conversation partner in Farley, who taught in his early career at DePauw University and Pittsburgh Theological Seminary and moved to Vanderbilt in 1968 while Hodgson was on sabbatical at Tübingen. Farley's early books had a neo-orthodox bent, but at Vanderbilt he developed a revisionist approach that steered through the phenomenology of Schleiermacher and Husserl. In 1975 he published a signature work, *Ecclesial Man: A Social Phenomenology of Faith and Reality*, which was rooted in two intuitions: (1) Something actually happens in Christianity and other faiths that shapes and propels human life in particular directions. If something happens, it can be studied as a factual datum. The convictions that faith possesses about reality arise in concrete interrelations that can be studied for clues about the way things are. (2) Determinate communities of faith possess insights that are religiously true beyond their historical and cultural circumstances.[58]

These intuitions led Farley to Husserl's phenomenological tightrope between metaphysics and anti-metaphysics. Theologically, Farley returned to the "essence of Christianity" tradition of Schleiermacher and Harnack, with a difference, since the old liberals did not seriously doubt that faith apprehends a distinct reality. To Farley this was the consuming question, something deeper than finding the best method. Does faith apprehend realities that transcend a mere phenomenal status? The old liberalism, though rightly defining its subject as the essential content of Christianity, evaded the problem beneath the problem, taking for granted that faith apprehends distinct realities through linguistic and historical phenomena.[59]

Gilkey and Lonergan interpreted Husserl's phenomenology as a philosophical psychology excluding metaphysical claims. Farley said that was not right. Husserl described the transcendental realm as a mirror of the structures of the world, but he was not a realist or an idealist. He did not construe reality as the outward things, facts, or relations that make an impression on consciousness *or* construe reality as the projection of powers of mind. Husserl's early theorizing on the intentional nature of consciousness dealt with consciousness as such, and its acts. The transcendental consciousness is structured by the nature of the object of perception. Farley allowed that Husserl's focus on the intersubjective character of subjectivity led him to conceive the transcendental realm as worldly. More importantly, Husserl said the transcendental realm reflects the very structure of the lifeworld, including intersubjectivity.[60]

Farley might have mystified fewer readers had he said outright that Husserl was a transcendental idealist. But not saying it was important to Farley, because Husserl stopped short of full-fledged ontology, aside from occasional side remarks. He studied the transcendental realm in which ontological essences are constituted (phenomenology), not the essences of determinate regions of being (ontology). To Husserl it was enough to show that the transcendental subject intrinsically has a world and reflects it. He described universal structures of the world as such, not mere meanings, unveiling what Farley called "certain strata of reality, thus, laying the groundwork for other enterprises." Farley applied Husserl's method to the realities apprehended by Christian faith, arguing that Christianity's founding apprehensions were pre-reflective and mediated through the distinct sociality of the Christian community.[61]

The early Farley contended that modern doubt began with theological leaders. By the mid-1970s he believed that the loss of religious reality occurred first in the community of faith, which theologians subsequently reflected. Theologians would not have taken Feuerbach or atheistic positivism seriously had they belonged to vibrant communities of faith. Farley said the matrix of apprehension always contains three elements: language, existence, and intersubjectivity. Faith apprehends its realities through myths and doctrines that are themselves rooted in stories and images. Existence is the universal structure of the lifeworld (transcendental existence) and the lifeworld in its concreteness (historical existence) through which redemption occurs. Intersubjectivity is the co-intentionalities that lie beneath conscious interaction.[62]

Husserlian phenomenology, to Farley, distinctly made sense of the religious apprehension of the world, showing that Christianity is best understood as a particular community of faith (ecclesia) through which there occurs a "modification of human existence toward redemption." "Ecclesia" was Farley's term for the ideal of the church or its essential meaning. Faith apprehends its realities in a faith-world, ecclesia. Like Husserl, Farley said all apprehensions are a structure of present and "appresent" realities. We experience more than what is directly perceived; appresentation is the intuition of components of an object that are copresent with presented realities and necessary to perceiving objects as unities. It is not quite a direct intuition, but a sense of something indirectly presented. Since the perceiving subject is grounded upon transcendental intersubjectivity, the co-intentionalities that lie beneath conscious action and all forms of concrete existence possess appresented realities. The realities of faith are not accessible apart from the mediating sociality of the Christian community. Faith is a determinate reality that correlates with the mediating sociality of ecclesia and the transcendental, fallen, and redemptive realities of human life.[63]

Farley reasoned that Husserl's jargon-laden prose evoked a needed "linguistic shock." If faith reshapes actuality, it is appropriate to blend novelty, mystery, and concreteness in linguistically unconventional ways: "I may not do this very well, but it is a writing style that comes with the cognitive style of explorations of this sort." He did not believe that all theologians should adopt his preference for Husserl; Farley leaned toward the view that theologians should be philosophical pluralists. Every philosophy is merely one way of doing philosophy. Hodgson later recalled of Farley, "Because of his learned and sophisticated arguments, he could be quite intimidating. He was five years my senior and I always regarded him with awe but greatly appreciated him as a colleague."[64]

In 1975 they played founding roles in a landmark Vanderbilt venture, the Workgroup on Constructive Theology. Organized to celebrate Sallie McFague's inauguration as dean at Vanderbilt, the group's original Vanderbilt members included McFague, Hodgson, Farley, historical theologians Eugene TeSelle and Jack Forstman, and philosopher of religion Robert C. Williams. Other early members included Carl Braaten, David Burrell, CSC, John B. Cobb Jr., Langdon Gilkey, Julian Hartt, Gordon Kaufman, David Kelsey, Robert H. King, Walter Lowe, Schubert Ogden, George W. Stroup, David Tracy, and Robert R. Williams. Later the group addressed its white maleness problem, adding Sheila Briggs, Rebecca S. Chopp, M. Shawn Copeland, Dawn DeVries, James H. Evans Jr., Elisabeth Schüssler Fiorenza, Mary Gerhart, Catherine Keller, Linda Mercadante, Marianne Sawicki, Marjorie Suchocki, Kathryn Tanner, Susan Brooks Thistlethwaite, and Sharon Welch. Later there were third and fourth generations, and each produced a textbook. Farley and Hodgson wrote the original book's much-cited chapter on Scripture and tradition.[65]

At the time Farley was thinking a great deal about Scripture and tradition. *Ecclesial Man* was the prolegomenon to the prolegomenon of his constructive theology. His next book, *Ecclesial Reflection: An Anatomy of Theological Method* (1982), was the prolegomenon. Farley spent the late 1970s and early 1980s puzzling over what theology should do if it cannot establish what is true by citing Scripture. The Farley/Hodgson chapter previewed the argument of *Ecclesial Reflection*, defining "Scripture" in the history-of-religions sense as the normative writings of a religious faith. The authors stressed that this term has a more determinate meaning in classic Judaism, Christianity, and Islam: Scripture is a divinely inspired deposit of revelation safeguarded by an authoritative tradition. This second meaning they called "the Scripture principle," which originated as the solution to the dispersion of the Jewish people after the Babylonian Exile. The Diaspora Jews, stripped of their land, temple, and priesthood, preserved a socioreligious identity by creating the synagogue and written Torah. The Torah became the site of a divine communication from a past

age. It was purportedly true in all its details, securing the identity of a
dispersed people by containing symbolic references to the nation, land,
and temple. The Scripture principle, despite the Jewish belief in salvation
history, was backward looking. Since the nation was dispersed, there
could be no new revelation to the people as a whole. The locus of Jewish
identity shifted to the sacred text and its teaching.[66]

Farley and Hodgson said the Jewish Scripture principle was secured
by the principles of secondary representation (authoritative transmission
of the original deposit), leveling (shifting the religious identity from the
contents of a message to the whole of the contents and the textual vehicle itself), and immutability (the revelation is absolute, not provisional
or contextual). Christianity took over this construct, despite being very
different from Judaism. In Christianity the primary internal threat was
a multiplicity of theologies within a culturally diverse religion, not cultural assimilation. The early church had its own writings, but no canon;
Christianity fixed on Jesus, contradicting the leveling principle; and
Christianity relativized Jewish Scripture, contradicting the immutability principle. None of this stopped Christianity from employing its
own Scripture principle, until biblical criticism and liberal theology dismantled it. The authors said the Christian house of authority was truly
demolished, notwithstanding that multitudes still tried to live in it. In
its place Farley and Hodgson argued that Scripture should be construed
functionally: God is active in biblical imagery through the shaping of
identities. David Kelsey and James Barr were pioneers of this approach,
but they made only a beginning.[67]

That was the preview version. *Ecclesial Reflection* ran much longer,
opening with a Foucault-like archaeology of the strata beneath the biblical house of authority. Reviewers routinely described it as devastating.
Farley traced the historical development of the Scripture principle, elaborated its fundamental axioms and identity claims, and recounted the
modern deconstruction of dogma. He said the idea of salvation history
depends on a monarchical image of God's relation to the world that leads
to a morally disastrous religious triumphalism and chauvinism. Theology
as citation should no longer exist. Argument by authority and proof text
should be things of the distant past. The fact that both were prevalent
in churches was a terrible problem that fostered "obscurantism, dualisms
in the human self, superstition, sexism, reality denial, [and] legalism as
a unifying piety and mindset." To precritical believers, Farley observed,
the debate over authority does not take place on Christian ground; there

is no Christianity apart from the house of authority. In Farley's terms, the way of authority is a priori to the essence of Christianity. But that was precisely what he did not believe, "at least in the sense of ecclesiality."[68]

To quit the house is to leave behind the foundations on which it was built: "salvation history, identity, canon, inspiration, sacred Scripture, infallibility, and the rest." Farley said it is better to make a clean break from authority religion than to liberalize the ideas of canon or inspiration. His alternative conceived theology as "ecclesial reflective inquiry" that critically interprets pre-reflectively apprehended realities of faith. Theology does not determine or originate the realities it explicates. It does not establish religious realities, but is founded by them. To fail in theology is to fall short of bringing to expression the realities that attend the ecclesial community. The first theological task is hermeneutical; the second is normative and ontological; the third applies the ecclesial universals to concrete contexts, reflective praxis.[69]

But Farley never got to praxis, which was not an option for Hodgson. In mid-career Farley wrote books that grieved over the fragmentation of theological education and the trivialization of theology, proposing that theology should return to its roots in holistic wisdom, until he decided that theology was hopelessly fragmented and no reform movement would save it. The later Farley teetered on religious Stoicism, emphasizing tragedy, relativism, and apophasis. He declined to speak of divine attributes, preferring Karl Jaspers' concept of ciphers—deep symbols that arise "with appresentations of redemption."[70]

Ciphers, he argued, refer to divine Creativity and indirectly describe it. Because redemption actually occurs, the ciphers or symbols of Creativity can be distinguished. Farley favored the symbols of Redeemer, Creativity, and the Holy, which correlated with the three redemptive transformations of founding, love, and justice. Spirit is the divine name that signifies the convergence of each triunity. The bespeaking of God begins with redeeming transformations of evil that occur in the spheres of human agency, the interhuman, and the social. Creativity founds individual agents, turns the accusing face of alienation into a relation of reconciling love, and is the inclusive criterion of justice. Farley did not mean there are three redemptions, and he did not believe that God is personal. Redemption in any sphere influences the other spheres. The symbols of redemption do not converge into one of the spheres; they express how the interplay of redemption within the spheres applies to Creativity—a cipher naming that to which ciphers refer. Farley could have said that the three symbols of redemption converge to appresent God as personal, but to him that smacked of synthesizing the symbols into a referent. Farley had Tillich's aversion to any suggestion that God is an object. To speak of God as a person, or as personal in the Hegelian sense, is to revive the hoary impression that God is a specific entity.[71]

Creativity is expressed in the symbols of empowerment, eternity, and aim. Empowerment takes place in the work of founding, reconciling love, and justice. Eternity is the sufficient and inclusive divine time, not timelessness. Aim is the bent of creativity away from idolatry, alienation, and subjugation. Farley reasoned that if being is conceived as process or activity, not substance or structure, the Catholic identification of God with being is justified. On the other hand, mystical theology deserves the last word in cautioning against any identification of God with being, creativity, or anything else. Creativity, the cipher, refers but does not directly describe, while Creativity itself evades direct description. Farley described the Holy as "the cipher that shatters all ciphers." Even the metaphors of otherness (ineffability, unfathomable depth) are inadequate ciphers for the Holy. They are merely the best we can do. Many reviewers said Farley's later theology was too stripped-bare. Theologian Wendy Farley, assessing her father's work, rightly said that he commendably stripped theology of sovereignty models and monarchical imagery. For feminist reasons, ecological reasons, worldview reasons, and spiritual reasons, Christianity must break free from the logic of divine omnipotence.[72]

The later Farley had a deeper affinity with Hegel than he acknowledged, although he never gave up his claim to Schleiermacher and Husserl. He grasped that Hegel's theology was a tragic process theodicy much like his own, but Farley played down his proximity to Hegel because there were bad parts of Hegel to negotiate and his friends Hodgson and Robert R. Williams specialized in Hegel. Williams taught philosophy of religion at the University of Illinois at Chicago. Hodgson found his voice as a theologian by doing painstaking editorial scholarship on Hegel. Both were Hegelians in a fashion that enabled Farley to keep a comfortable distance.

Hodgson's beginning was the key to his later career. His bruising experience as a liberation theologian sent him back to the nineteenth century, specifically, Hegel's religion lectures of 1821, 1824, 1827, and 1831. The first and second German editions, compiled by Philipp Marheineke in 1832 and 1840, were based on students' lecture notes. There was no reliable edition in any language, the English editions were especially poor, and in 1976 Hodgson began to fantasize about producing an alternative "to the outmoded translation of an outmoded edition of a work of seminal importance for the whole of modern theology, philosophy of religion, and religious thought."[73]

His first pass settled for a new translation of the outmoded Lasson edition of volume three, which was published by Scholars Press in 1979. But that was a stopgap; meanwhile Hodgson met Walter Jaeschke, a member of the editorial staff of the Hegel Archive at Ruhr University in Bochum, West Germany, which was preparing a critical edition of Hegel's works. In 1981, with Jaeschke's assistance and the help of a National Endowment for the Humanities grant, Hodgson plunged more deeply, preparing a new English translation and edition of the entire three-volume work. By 1988, working with Robert F. Brown and J. Michael Stewart, he had published the three volumes, plus a one-volume edition based on Hegel's lecture series of 1827.[74]

This project was consuming and formative for Hodgson. Had he realized how taxing it would be, he might not have ventured into it. As it was, by 1988 he was eager to write constructive theology. His editorial work was a refuge from disappointment, but during his middle career, which stretched into the 1990s, Hodgson became seriously depressed and addicted to alcohol. He later recalled, "Ironically, I seemed to be doing creative work while escaping from reality. Perhaps 'futility' was knocking at the door, which I attempted to slam shut, and I also shut myself off from healing resources for too long." Immersed in Hegel, he took comfort in scholarly achievements while struggling with personal afflictions. Hodgson readily quoted from memory the reviews that derided him for wrapping the sword of liberation in the "cotton balls" of German Romanticism. By the mid-1980s, Hegelian idealism was, for him, "a cannon ball that propelled me into a fresh engagement with my own context."[75]

He wrote a book on the church, declaring that liberation theology and the new consciousness of world religious pluralism signaled the advent of "a new cultural and theological paradigm." Hodgson commended the liberationist insistence that all theology arises out of particular situations. North American liberal Protestantism no longer played a central role in society and culture, going down with the bourgeois culture it accommodated, along with its ideals "of individuality, private rights, technical rationality, historical progress, the capitalist economy, the absoluteness of Christianity, and so on." The surge of the political and evangelical right was a response to the fall of modernity, as was postmodern nihilism. To

Hodgson, Hegelian sublation expressed a powerful truth in this situation. Annulling and preserving is a simultaneous process. Theology needed to repudiate the false and oppressive aspects of Western Christianity while preserving its true and liberating aspects: "Perhaps the special responsibility of First World theology is to contribute all that it can to the resources for the new vision of humanity emerging from the Third World, from the underside of history—a side that must also become our side as we make the passage."[76]

He still believed in the fusion of liberalism and liberation that fired his early work, but felt less awkwardly self-conscious about saying so. Teaching about new visions of the church was an emancipating factor; participating in the Workgroup was another; Hegel was the biggest enabler. Hodgson embraced Hegel's idea that the divine Spirit and the common Spirit of the ecclesial community are the same thing: "God in the modality of Spirit *is* the redemptive, transfigurative power that indwells and constitutes a new human intersubjectivity, an intersubjectivity shaped by the paradigmatic love of Christ, which is an 'infinite love in infinite anguish.'" Citing Gutiérrez, Ruether, Leonardo Boff, and other liberation theologians, Hodgson described the church as "an anticipatory sign and sacrament of the realm or kingdom or rule of God—the basileia vision of Jesus, the vision of a new realm brought into being by God's saving and transformative rule, the productive ideal of a new way of being communally human in the world and before God, a liberated communion of free subjects, a realm of freedom imaged in the ecclesia of freedom."[77]

His breakthrough work was a Hegelian theology of history, *God in History: Shapes of Freedom* (1989). Hodgson described God and history as correlative realities that come together at the point of liberating and transfiguring praxis: "God is present in history in the many shapes of freedom, among which there is for Christians a paradigmatic gestalt, the shape of love in freedom associated with Jesus' proclamation and crucifixion." The aim of history, though never achieved, is approximated in many ways, marshalling the shapes of freedom into "a nexus of communicative freedom."[78]

He cautioned that Hegelian sublation is a difficult process. Simultaneous annulling and preserving is always contested on all sides, and the agents of transformation must be wary of hubris. Hodgson said it would be an "absurd pretension" for anyone to claim to be better than Augustine, Thomas, Calvin, Schleiermacher, or Barth at comprehending God's relation to history. The best that anyone can do is to think creatively in response to one's time. His Hegelian proposal was that "God" and "history" are co-constitutive categories. God is in history and history is in God, though the "in" of coinherence is not symmetrical, since God does not depend on history in the way that history depends on God. To be free is to shape activity. Human beings come into contact with the ultimate ground of all things through their partial, open-ended, always fallibly interpreted experiences of freedom. God is manifest in history through the shapes that freedom takes. Thus God and history come together at the point of emancipating and transfiguring praxis.[79]

Hodgson took over Hegel's idea that the world process, especially world history, is an essential moment in the divine life. God is self-mediated through the world, becoming a concrete Spirit (*Geist*). The dialectic of identity-difference-mediation applies to God's self-relation, which includes the world; Hegel's God is absolute through difference and relationship. Hodgson admired Whitehead and felt a particular kinship with Cobb, but chose the good parts of Hegel over Whitehead and Cobb. Hegel sustained the classic distinction between the immanent and economic trinities by distinguishing between the inward and outward moments of divine mediation. Hodgson explained, "The dialectic of identity-difference-mediation within the divine life is the condition of possibility for there being a world that is different from God yet constitutive of God (just as God is constitutive of it)."[80]

Throwing out the bad parts of Hegel started with repudiating his conceit that he was the last word in philosophy. Nineteenth-century left-Hegelians rightly accused right-Hegelians of systematizing the bad parts of Hegel and distorting what he said. On the other hand, the left-Hegelians ended up as atheists. Hodgson, having devoted ten years of editorial labor to the very lectures that fueled the left-right blowout, vowed to hold "as far as possible" to the Hegelian middle. He took no interest in making Hegelianism safe for Christian orthodoxy, just as he disliked the left-Hegelianism that turned Hegel into an atheist. Hegel showed the way forward in theology, if joined to liberationist commitments on postmodern terms. Hodgson fashioned Hegel's concept of history as the progress of the consciousness of freedom to a postmodern context, replacing Hegel's progressivism with a vision of many "partial, fragmentary, always ambiguous histories of freedom" that struggle against forces of domination.[81]

The quasi-Hegelian Barth devoted a key section of his doctrine of God to "The Being of God as the One Who Loves in Freedom." Hodgson took this description as a model of Trinitarian figuration, fixing on "One," "love," and "freedom." God is the One whose identity is self-constituting. God enters the world and suffers in and for it as love. God as freedom preserves and overcomes the difference between God and world. Hodgson explained that freedom is "precisely presence-to-self in, through, and with otherness; it is intrinsically communal, social, synthetic." He preferred "One" and "love" to the symbols of Father and Son, retaining Spirit as the richest symbol of the divine life as a whole. Hegel's dialectic of identity-difference-mediation is the logical structure, which correlates with Hodgson's description of God as One-love-freedom, which correlates with the figures God-World-Spirit. "Spirit" is the name for the intersubjective presence of God—the third figure of the divine Trinity—but it also symbolizes the entire Trinitarian process of mediation: "To say that God is Spirit is to say that God is the Free One, or, more precisely, 'the One who loves in freedom.'"[82]

Hegel described the relationship between "Father" and "Son" as being too childlike to sustain the entrance of Spirit. The picture God, Hegel said—the divine abstractedness—was given up in the death of Christ and reborn in the unity of "Father and Son" as concrete, worldly love or Spirit. Thus Hegel anticipated Ricoeur's statement that the idol of the "father" had to die to recover the non-idolatrous truth buried in the symbol. Hodgson updated what that means: "What must be dispossessed, of course, is the patriarchal father figure who both threatens and consoles, evoking the most archaic forms of religious feeling: the fear of punishment and the desire for protection." The logic of de-patriarchal annulment and retrieval is in the Bible, especially the transformation of the Father to the figure of the in-breaking *basileia* in the teaching of Jesus. Modern Christianity took a further step by recovering repressed female imagery for God. Hodgson suggested that the next step might be to completely relinquish the father figure, allowing God the Father to die for the sake of others—"the very antithesis of the primitive father figure." Some way of speaking of God must be found "that transcends distinctions of sex as well as those of class, position, nation, and race." Meanwhile he invoked the generic name "God," noting that it may derive from an Indo-European term (*ghau*) that means to "call out" or "invoke." God is the One whom believers invoke as the unity and power of the world;

the word "designates the oneness, the unity, the holiness, the sublimity, the aseity of God."[83]

The language of Father and Son is irretrievable, but not the language of Spirit. Hodgson argued that the dualistic connotations of disembodied "spirit" are hangovers from Neoplatonism, not fatal defects. Hegel's idea of Spirit mediates the unity of reason and nature, body and soul, male and female, and God and world, overreaching these distinctions and leveling the hierarchies derived from them. Just as Christ is the figure of God's objective presence in history, the Spirit is the figure of God's intersubjective and eschatological presence. As intersubjective presence, the Spirit is the ground of the freedom of humankind, but as eschatological presence, the Spirit is the "quintessence of divine freedom, of God's being in-and-for-itself."[84]

Whiteheadian theology, by comparison, turns God into something bland and shapeless. Hodgson did not say it contentiously; he prizes the Whiteheadian tradition—especially Ogden's idea that divine action is something between individual personal agency and generalized influence—and Cobb's emphasis on transformation and creative synthesis. But Ogden was vague about the difference between historical and nonhistorical divine action, and Cobb was vague about what it means to say that God lures or persuades. Hodgson's alternative blended Hegel, liberation theology, and postmodern criticism. Instead of describing God's efficacious presence in the world as a lure, uniform inspiration, abstract ideal, or individual action, he conceived divine action as a pattern or gestalt that guides and shapes history: "God is present in specific shapes or patterns of praxis that have a configuring, transformative power within historical process, moving the process in a determinate direction, that of the creative unification of multiplicities of elements into new wholes, into creative syntheses that build human solidarity, enhance freedom, break systemic oppression, heal the injured and broken, and care for the natural."[85]

A pattern is more specific, configuring, and dynamic than a generalized influence or presence. Moreover, describing God's action as a structuring gestalt avoids the problems of supernatural personification. Hegel appropriated Goethe's idea of gestalt to designate a complex, plural unity that is both transpersonal and interpersonal. The idea of a plural infinite gestalt or individual totality is closely related to Hegel's concept of the infinite as a multiple unity. In *Phenomenology* Hegel described consciousness as a plural unity that relates itself to its object and distinguishes itself from it, engendering increasingly complex yet focused cases of reduplicated relation. He historicized the concept of gestalt, using the shapes of spirit (*Gestalten des Geistes*) to designate stages in the history of spirit. Like Troeltsch, Hodgson took over the Hegelian idea of the shaping of creative syntheses in historical existence. But stronger than Hegel and Troeltsch, Hodgson argued that the divine idea emerges in history as a liberating gestalt, not a principle or ideal. God appears and works in the shapes of freedom.[86]

Freedom is the substance of spirit and goal of history. This does not mean that configurations of freedom constantly occur, for if history is a process of random configurations, freedom is diminished. The history of freedom can possess a purpose and still be open-ended. Hodgson stood on the claim that human beings have a responsibility to enhance and expand freedom; thus history, like art and love, has a *telos* that can be characterized as an "open wholeness." The universal responsibility to expand freedom has a teleological character: "Through this continuing shaping process, certain matrices of historical practice may be built up that provide a basis for further enhancements and expansions of freedom; and these matrices, if they can be joined together and sustained, may constitute a trajectory of the history of the praxis of freedom." We no longer conceive the world as a total design or assume a fulfilling end of historical existence. But we can and must believe "that the shaping power or gestalt of God is present in every moment of the process—in the building up, the preservation, and the breaking down of shapes of freedom, as well as in the transition to new shapes, new cultural configurations."[87]

William Jones, in his landmark book *Is God a White Racist?* (1973), contended that the oppression of blacks cannot be reconciled with the claim that a good and omnipotent God exists. Thus he rejected orthodox Christianity and black liberation theology, espousing a religiously tinged humanism. Hodgson replied, "In my view, the only way to refute Jones would be to argue that African Americans have experienced and continue to experience the liberating power of God *in and through* their unfinished emancipatory struggle." Hodgson aligned himself with Cone on this point, observing that Jones rejected Cone's liberation theology on the ground that it is impossible to prove that the *decisive event* for blacks has occurred. To Jones, either God intervenes supernaturally to liberate oppressed people or God is not a liberating God.[88]

Hodgson claimed, mistakenly, that Cone's refusal of this either-or "demonstrates a liberal sensibility," not grasping the depth of Cone's contempt for liberal theology. But Hodgson rightly said that liberal theology can be conceived as a type of liberation theology: "African American theology helps to teach us that there is no triumphal march of God in history, no special and privileged history of salvation, but only a plurality of partial, fragmentary, ambiguous histories of freedom. What is shaped in history are fragile syntheses of values and praxis that achieve momentary, relative victories over chaos and tyranny through a process of confrontation and compromise."[89]

No synthesis lasts for long. History consists of continuities and discontinuities that cannot be patched, as Hodgson said, "into an overarching linear teleology." Hegel was not wrong to describe history as the progress of the consciousness of freedom, because advances in consciousness do occur, as in the struggles of the movements for racial justice, feminism, ecology, and the rights of gay, lesbian, bisexual, transgender, and queer persons. But nearly always there is a backlash, and in U.S. American history there is always a backlash. Hodgson put it mildly, observing that breakthroughs for liberation can be "suppressed by reactionary practices."[90]

He taught theology in that spirit, always in Hegelian triads. The book version of Hodgson's introduction to theology course, *Winds of the Spirit* (1994), divided theology into triads of the emancipatory, ecological, and dialogical, which correlated with freedom, love, and wholeness, which correlated methodologically with interpreting, contextualizing, and revisioning, which were grounded in the dialectic of God/the One, World/Love, and Spirit/Freedom. He compared theology to sailing—making contact with "powerful, fluid elements" over which one has little control. The elements are symbolized by wind and water, and the enterprise lacks any foundation other than itself. Like a sailboat without an external prop or secure port, theology relies on "the structural integrity and interplay of its component parts, which enable it to float and sail." It does not discover its spiritual truths as existent abstractions. Rather, theology creates truth, value, and beauty through the interaction of ship and elemental forces. On occasion the ship has to be docked for repairs and refitting. Theology is drawn and driven by the many winds of the Spirit and the prevailing wind that is God's Spirit. Because theology sails into regions of deep mystery, and because the bond between the human and sacred realms is broken, the indirect language of metaphor and symbol is indispensable to theology. Theology speaks the language of faith, but it cannot rest with its symbols, for symbols give rise to thought, seeking intelligibility. Thus the theologian must "saturate the symbols of faith with intelligibility."[91]

That put him in the line of revisionist "radical liberals" who rethink Christian claims in light of critical questions raised by modern and postmodern experience. The purpose of dialogue, he argued, "is precisely for communication, enlargement of horizons, newly configured wholeness in the midst of irreducible difference and recalcitrant diversity." The challenge of religious pluralism is like the problem of historical purpose. Every answer is partial and problematic, but the prize deserves to be struggled for. The eros for wholeness is constitutive of the divine good. The only unity worth having is complex, dialectical, and "seething" in its diversity. It is an active unity-in-diversity—an open, dynamic, and relational whole, like God.[92]

Hodgson's later work has a deep continuity with his early work, but the later books are better for engaging feminism, liberation theology, the ecological crisis, interreligious theology, and postmodern criticism. In his retirement he regrets that theology is no longer a field that supports broad visionary thinking: "Theology has become balkanized, split into various factions and interests, each pursuing its own agenda, generally tolerant of but not especially interested in what others are doing." Theologians, he believes, should not accept that conflicts are given "and visions are passé." He ended his career yearning for theology to risk more for reconciliation. But he also said he gave thanks for the deconstruction of "my old identity as a white middle-class liberal male."[93]

Feminist Whiteheadian Poststructural Becoming: Catherine Keller

Catherine Keller, though shaped by many of the same concerns as Tracy, Farley, and Hodgson, approaches all of them differently, first on account of being female, second on Whiteheadian grounds, and subsequently as a Whiteheadian poststructuralist. Raised in a seminomadic family long on intellectual brilliance and emotional turbulence, she moved too many times to be able to remember her past, lacking places for memory. Keller describes her childhood as a "perpetual geographic motion" that took her to Heidelberg and Wellesley, graduating from neither. In 1977 she graduated from Eden Theological Seminary and in 1984 earned her doctorate at Claremont under Cobb, "a source of inspiration for other tramps, I hope." From the beginning she wrote dense, expansive, multivocal, richly evocative, poetic prose, contending in her first book, *From a Broken Web* (1986), that a separate self and misogyny go together in Western culture, being "the most fundamental assumptions of our culture."[94]

Odysseus is the model of the self as epic hero; Marduk slaying the primeval goddess Tiamat shows the misogynist underpinnings of the separate self; Aristotle rationalized the separate self; the transcendent Christian God turned self-ism and sexism into cultural norms; and psychoanalysis re-mythologized the unrelated, achieving individual. Keller stressed that the separate self is nearly always male, fearful of merger and self-loss, and thus fearful of women. To females Western culture offers the "soluble" or connective self, which is problematic in a patriarchal context, but not lacking redemptive elements. She advocated feminist relation, not the dominance of the domesticated mother or defeat of individual differentiation: "Most of us have grown up in intimate connection with mothers whose creative energies, trapped in domesticity, pose an overpowering emotional threat." To be relational is saving only as a feminist transformation of consciousness and culture through which women and men outgrow "this covert and culturally ramified matriphobia."[95]

Freudian psychoanalysis, fixing on the Oedipus myth, caused immense harm. Keller prefers the object-relations revision of psychoanalytic theory; her early appropriation of it accepted its binary sexual ordering: human beings fundamentally seek relationship, not (Freudian) homeostatic equilibrium, and women normally assume the role of primary caretakers in families because girls do not have to break with their mothers to define themselves sexually. Boys are forced to define themselves negatively, as *not* like their primary love object; girls experience themselves as being essentially related to the object-world. Keller followed Nancy Chodorow and Dorothy Dinnerstein in contending that the centrality of mothering to emotional development leaves males feeling separate. Angry at lost relation, males become hostile and dominating toward females. The male psyche breaks into a dyadic structure of self versus female other, while the female psyche develops into a continuous and relational structure of self-mother-male other. The consequences are bad for males and disastrous for females. Women, Keller said, perpetuate the vicious cycle of sexism by mothering.[96]

Western theism, metaphysics, and common sense similarly perpetuate sexism. To be an individual is to be an enduring self-identical substance, essentially separate from others, "except God, with whom matters simply reverse themselves." Western subjectivity, Keller argued, is a reflexive experience of oneness against the many, making normative selfhood "a game of one and two" that echoes in both monist and dualist ontology. The idealization of the autonomous hero is the logical and historical outgrowth of conceiving God as ultimately separate and unchanging. Augustine worked himself into "bizarre contortions" over the Trinity because the Western church had a deep psychic need to curb God's relationality. By hypostatizing the divine spirit of love as a separate substance, Augustine preserved God's independence from the world, disposing of relation by reifying it.[97]

Like most Whiteheadians, Keller commends William James on relational flux and the experience of relation, and she prizes Whitehead's advance on James, who lacked any account of the interdependence of the different streams of experience. But Keller argues that too many Whiteheadians proceed as though psychoanalysis never happened; moreover, James' idea of the fringe of consciousness is no substitute for the elusive unconscious probed by psychoanalysis. Lacking a theory of the unconscious, there is no way to explain personal identity through time on a non-substantialist basis. Keller says that James made a good beginning by focusing on the flow and plurality of self-identity. Then Whitehead improved on James by turning "change" into becoming, recognizing that "change" still implies a static doctrine of substance. An individual that changes remains the same subject underlying its changes. Whitehead fashioned a Jamesian insight into a radically relational metaphysic in which individual entities do not have feelings; they become through feeling. The subject, and thus the capacity for feeling, emerges by feeling the world. To come into being is to feel one's way into being, both consciously and unconsciously. Every individual is a pulse of experience that gains its selfhood through feelings that make the self what it becomes.[98]

One's experience comes into being by feeling the feelings of one's world. To Keller this is the crucial Whiteheadian claim: "I *am* this 'throb of experience'; I *am* the complex unity of feeling that rises up at this moment in response to my feelings of the plural world." Her first book argued that women generally have more "natural sympathy" than men with Whiteheadian theory because of its emphasis on feeling. Feeling connected to others and the world, women find that Whitehead makes sense of their experience. But women usually learn the arts of empathy "for wrong reasons and deleterious ends," acquiescing in their oppression. Over-conforming to the feelings of others, women slip into "derivative, ultimately self-sabotaging modes of external relations, neither triumphantly independent nor widely connective." The Greeks described non-civic selfhood as "idiocy." Keller reflected, "Woman has been the household idiot. In her domestic captivity she endures both a depriving privacy and a confining connectivity."[99]

Keller is deeply influenced by Mary Daly and persuaded that her unified self was a hangover from Thomism. "I almost became a Christian Mary Daly," she recalled to me, "but I rethought where that leads." As a tactic, Daly's separatism was "strategically indispensable." As an ideology, it was sexism in reverse. The early Keller described her feminist theology as a fusion of Whitehead's vision of creative relation with Daly's passion for liberation: "Without continuously and explicitly antipatriarchal work on itself and its real worlds, process thought will not and cannot advance the realization of its own vision. Because it is a metaphysic of feeling, process thought must be *felt*; because feeling is what actualizes the possible, process thought is useful only inasmuch as it gets concretely actualized in life, in relations, in culture." She called it a post-patriarchal ethic of "attunement" to interconnectedness and a "webbed vision" of body and soul as entire societies, affirming differentiation *and* connection, freedom *and* relation: "Divining my own desire I make connection with yours; divining each others', we sense our own; and often only your divination of my truth divulges it to me."[100]

She was critical of Daly's separatism and apocalypticism, but also critical of feminists who got ahead by spurning Daly. Then Keller took a similar two-handed approach to the book of Revelation. In *Apocalypse Now and Then* (1996), she cautioned against merely rejecting apocalyptic. The master script contains a "hidden transcript" of resistance to oppression; moreover, the apocalypse is not an event looming on the horizon, but a "multidimensional, culture-pervading spectrum of ideological assumptions, group identities, subjective responses, and—perhaps most interesting of all—historical habits." Even those who reject apocalyptic, she cautioned, live within it: "We are *in* apocalypse: we are in it as a script that we enact habitually when we find ourselves at an edge, and we are in it as the recipients of the history of the social and environmental effects of that script."[101]

Retro-apocalyptic takes Revelation literally; crypto-apocalyptic internalizes apocalyptic without believing in it; anti-apocalyptic rejects all forms of preoccupation with the end of the world; Keller was counter-apocalyptic, stressing the relational link between past text and present situation. Mere rejection of apocalyptic is a self-contradictory form of it, announcing the end of the end. Apocalyptic is repugnant *and* a source of liberating inspiration. Appropriating Julia Kristeva's concept of the *abject*—the site of simultaneous attraction and repulsion—Keller worked at the edge of the fragile borders of identity where boundaries are blurred, compulsion and hope are intertwined, and revelation occurs despite being subjected to criticism. She was against closing the world via apocalyptic and against closing the text via anti-apocalyptic. Counter-apocalyptic, she said, disarms the apocalyptic imagination and sustains its justice-demanding intensity, the former by echoing and parodying its polarities, and the latter by reclaiming "its courage in the face of impossible odds and losses."[102]

Kristeva identified three phases of feminism. The suffragists through Simone de Beauvoir, struggling to be included as equals in history, were stage one. The generation of radicals represented by Daly and Luce Irigaray were stage two. Stage-three feminists, Kristeva's generation, reentered history on their terms, defying everyday sexism. Kristeva was anti-apocalyptic and secular, but her scheme had an apocalyptic pattern: three intersecting ages converging to form a new age. In the United States, Keller noted, stage-three feminism was poststructuralist, anticosmological, and censured any discourse about nature. Keller judged that if feminism had gone through three stages thus far, a fourth was needed; she called it "eco-social feminism."[103]

In the United States, wave imagery prevailed. Keller fondly recalled that wave two broke into theology in 1973 with "Daly's blast of the trumpet." *Beyond God the Father* offered feminist theory as apocalyptic oracle, describing Christianity as a plot to purge the world of women. Five years later, Daly's *Gyn/Ecology* construed Armageddon as a feminist holy war "waged by Wholly Haggard Whores" to liberate female spirit. By embracing the imagery of apocalyptic war and deliverance, Daly surrendered "to the mesmerism of the book she debunks, indeed to its most lethal fantasy." Opening the scroll of feminist martyrs, "she bathes herself in the rhetorical blood of the Lamb and launches the final crusade." Keller never forgot what she owed to Daly. In fact, whenever she read Daly, she struggled not to be sucked "into the vortex of her truth rhythms." But Keller regretted Daly's air of absolute certainty, her peevish refusal—"like an apocalyptic warrior refusing to be shamed"—to deal with racism, and the influence of her separatism. Wave-two feminists embarrassed the movement with universal claims that did not speak for women of color and did not anticipate the critique of binary ordering advanced by queer theory and poststructuralist feminism. Stung by womanist criticism and informed by poststructuralist theory, wave-three feminists declared that essentialism, not patriarchy, is the root of evil. Keller recalled, "We had been eager to hear men denouncing other men as sexist. Now white feminists got points from each other for denouncing other feminists as racist."[104]

Certainly it was good that white feminists acknowledged their racism. But it seemed to Keller that much of the ensuing feminist confessing and denouncing of white supremacy was merely a pitch for being recognized as morally blameless, changing nothing. Moreover, it was not a good thing to herd together "gender, sex, nature, position, ground, horizon, project, social justice, end, purpose, identity, cosmology, and anything reminiscent of spirit" as essentialist evils. In its identity-politics versions, wave-three feminism was too narrow. In its poststructuralist versions, it yielded a profusion of incommensurable gestures. Keller held out for a relational, cosmological, counter-apocalyptic feminism, construing identity as a "fluid matrix of multiple mutualities." Apocalypse, she warned, cannot be rejected without being committed. Like Cobb she conceived divinity as the lure that invites multiple realities into a new togetherness. Taking clues from Hegel and Whitehead, she moved from eschatology to pneumatology, describing Spirit as the relation of relations that exists as the intersubject of multiple narratives. Spirit is the "infra-relation" of our crisscrossing stories, "twining together like the code of the genetic double helix."[105]

She was too influenced by poststructuralist criticism to say much about the reality that lures the cosmos toward good relation. Keller liked Catholic theologian Elizabeth Johnson's sisterly renaming of God as "She Who Is," but cautioned that Johnson committed "enthusiastic overreach." Feminist theologians had to guard against surrendering to the transcendental signified. Replacing "Logos" with the "Sophia" of biblical Wisdom feels good, but it lifts the Spirit out of finite reality. To Keller the Spirit as the relation of relations made sense only as the "immanently signified." Hers was a vision of "finite, spirit-filled mutualities locally congregating," not a new heaven and a new earth. She could believe in finitude without end, understood as the eternal preservation of creation in God, and hoped for "a critical mass of spirit in history." But transcendence construed as something beyond the process of transformation immanent within relations was out of play.[106]

Hodgson regretted that Keller became timid and qualified when she talked about God. If God is the all-encompassing mystery, he argued, "discourse about God demands boldness, risk, perhaps even recklessness on the part of theologians." Even on Whiteheadian terms, it is wrong to describe God merely as the matrix of life. Whitehead transformed oppositions into relations, which implies "difference, otherness, transcendence." Hodgson wanted Keller to describe God boldly as "the wind-force that sweeps across and through the matrix, ordering, structuring, transforming it, creating wave-like patterns in the swirling chaos, making of it a maze of signification, of distinctions and relations." Neo-evangelical theologian Miroslav Volf went further, objecting that Keller had no concept of transcendent presence or redemption. Employing a phrase of Barth's, Volf declared that Keller's spider-Spirit was "too *pauvre* for a god" and that her cultural approach to theology was similarly impoverished.[107]

To others, Keller set the standard for postmodern feminist theology. Mary Grey declared that Keller's "challenging, exhilarating, even daring book" offered an unparalleled critique of the self-destructive cultural enactment of a text. Elizabeth A. Say lauded Keller's dense, poetic, and rigorous style, urging readers to "let Keller guide us to an affirmation of hope." Tina Pippin admired Keller's edgy attitude and skill, but wished she would let go of apocalyptic.[108]

Keller pays close attention to trends in the field. Some theologians lose their creative edge if they read other theologians; Keller is the opposite. Jürgen Moltmann is a favorite interlocutor. She likes his eschatological, ecological, democratic socialist, theopassionist, panentheist, and proto-feminist planks and dislikes his faith in heavenly eternity. Keller allows that Moltmann does not get distracted from the struggle for human flourishing, but his belief in life after death smacks of leftover supernaturalism to her; she doubts that he would sustain his cheerful serenity if he did not believe in it. To her, theology has little future worth having if it requires such a faith.[109]

In the late 1990s she worried that feminist theology paraded too much the mood and style of poststructuralist criticism. Broadsides against essentialism were obligatory, epitomized in "a certain trendy drift of thinking" that casually lumped realism and relation under the dreaded category of essences. Keller called it "sucking at the breast of poststructuralist theory" and "drinking father's milk through female authors." Schüssler Fiorenza blasted Rita Nakashima Brock and Carter Heyward for prizing relationality as a feminist value, admonishing that feminist Christology "must not be conceptualized in personalistic, individualistic terms as connectedness between individuals. Rather it must be articulated in sociopolitical categories." According to Schüssler Fiorenza, relational feminist theology was a project of "elite white ladies." Keller replied that women of color usually preferred relational complexity and the name "women's movement" to the politicized, de-biologized feminism of Schüssler Fiorenza, whose chief example of white-lady essentialism happened to be Brock. Keller was incredulous at this attack on her friend: "Unless race is a more shifting and disembodied category than even postmodern gender, Brock was still a Japanese and Hispanic American, with a powerful identification with women of color, when I last heard."[110]

This howler, to Keller, was a symptom of anti-essentialism run rampant, fitting Schüssler Fiorenza's trendy assurance that language does not refer to the world. Keller implored her colleagues to stop embarrassing feminist theology. "Christian feminism is left looking rather foolish: clinging to social-ethical criteria which have lifted feminist discourse beyond white women's interest, it buys into the antisociality of postmodern individualism at the same time." The antisocial milk of French deconstruction, she implored, is a poor substitute for relational bonds and solidarity. Ontologically, it rests on the separate self of patriarchy. Relational feminism does not claim that women are naturally more connective than men, and it is not "a pretext for return to Victorian femininity or to the mother's breast." To come of age, she said, is to outgrow the androcentric language of separation and independence, "outgrowing late-adolescent revolts against mom as well as dad."[111]

But believing that precluded Keller from inveighing against the poststructuralist tide. Her friend and Whiteheadian ally David Griffin rebuked the irrationality and nihilism of "destructive postmodernism," contending that Whitehead launched a constructive form of postmodernism that did not denigrate reason or common sense. Keller winced at Griffin's polemics; by 2002 she was willing to say so, urging Whiteheadians not to recycle it. Griffin was right, she said, to defend process thought from unjust criticism, and right that ethical engagement is better than the ironic detachment of deconstructionists. Nonetheless, "some of us within the process trajectory have outgrown the terms and tenor" of anti-deconstruction polemics. Griffin condemned postmodern irrationality without engaging Derrida, Deleuze, Foucault, Irigaray, and Kristeva; he overgeneralized Rorty's ironic frivolity; and it was not good policy to make wholesale judgments against a creative, many-sided style of theory. Keller said it was just as perilous for Whiteheadians to dismiss deconstructionists as the other way around: "Without each other, each might lose the world."[112]

Griffin said he was not a foundationalist and neither was Whitehead. To Keller this was a welcome first step. Griffin's Whitehead broke the logic of Cartesian and Lockean foundationalisms by reuniting thought and embodiment: if we learn to think with our bodies, we become open to the interrelatedness of their worlds. Keller cheered that Cobb took a second step by playing down aspects of Whiteheadian thought that are not useful. Keller took a third step by reading even Whitehead's "most stubbornly rationalist language" as strategically deconstructionist. Whitehead, she observed, read the great Western metaphysicians very carefully. He probed for cracks in Plato, Aristotle, Locke, Descartes, Leibniz, and Spinoza, driving his categories, wedge-like, into the fissures of their systems. Much like deconstructionists, Whitehead debunked the false certainties and systematic closures of Western philosophy. He taught that overstatement is the chief failing of philosophers, cautioning that even science cannot be pursued "in watertight compartments." His scheme was actually a deconstructionist-like exposure of the fissures in Western metaphysics without losing the capacity to speak of nature, worldview, cosmos, universe, and totality.[113]

On this telling, Whitehead opposed the same things that poststructuralists oppose, but unlike them he rightly risked metaphysics, melting the unchanging reality of being into "the turbulent flow of an endless Becoming." Keller implored that there is no alternative to speaking about nature and the world: "We cannot always be coy. We need to think as bodies very concretely about our earth context and with our communities. We need operable language, theological and cultural, with which to confront the hegemony of a transnational economy bent on consuming world, earth, and community." She claimed that process thought, being linked to religious communities, evinces "a robust capacity" to influence social movements, while poststructuralist theory rarely gets beyond the university classroom.[114]

Process thought is about writing the connections, while poststructuralism is about tracing the differences. Seeking to do both, Keller began to think of herself as "a cross-dressing process-poststructuralist," contending that the poststructuralist language of difference can be spoken in "thick" ways that allow for Whiteheadian connective "folds." Deleuze, invoking a term coined by James Joyce, described a "chaosmos" that grounds the production of events. Events occur in a chaotic multiplicity not lacking a screen-like ground that "intervenes" in the production of events. Keller welcomed this glimmer of a poststructuralist discourse with Whiteheadian folds; Deleuze's "chaosmos" is much like Whitehead's categoreal grid of process. The poststructuralist animus against foundationalism is a healthy impulse, but "grounding" and "founding" are not the same thing, for Whitehead's fixation with grounding is, at its best, postmodern: "Our constructions do not need to turn the dense ecology of that which precedes and supports us into a substructure, substratum, and substance." On the other hand, she argued, the poststructuralist rhetoric of absence, chaos, and undecidability vibrates "with extrahuman rhythms." There is a "depth" in the "face" of postmodernism that is "the chaos of creation itself."[115]

This was the theme of *Face of the Deep* (2003), which explored the "face of the other" (Levinas) and "depth/surface" (Derrida, Deleuze) for the theology of creation. Beginning with a gloss on a subordinate clause of the Bible's opening sentence (what happened to the chaos of Genesis 1:2?), Keller rejected *creatio ex nihilo* and "tehophobia," advocated *creatio ex profundis* and "tehophilia," surveyed "orthodoxies of nothing" from Irenaeus to Barth, analyzed literary and theological treatments of the primal chaos, appropriated Derrida, Deleuze, and Whitehead on the relation of depth and surface, and developed a *tehomic* theology from the Hebrew word for ocean, deep, or abyss in Genesis 1:2: "The earth was a formless void (*tohu va bohu*) and darkness covered the face of the deep (*tehom*), while a wind from God (*ruach Elohim*) swept over the face of the waters."[116]

She had begun *in media res*, conceiving relationality as a process that has no beginning. Then she moved to apocalypse as the production of endlessly dis/closive events. Now Keller further deconstructed linear time by rejecting the idea and theologies of origin. The Beginning, she said, and all beginnings, do not lie back, like origins; they open out, or are cut open. The universe is pushed out infinitely by a strange dark energy lacking a center. It expands endlessly at a speed that appears to be accelerating. Galaxies lace together like a circulatory system: "The nonlinear geometry of chaos is figured everywhere." Contrary to the "dominology" of patristic and classical Christian theology, the Beginning of Genesis is not the absolute Beginning created from nothing, but a beginning-in-process, "an unoriginated and endless process of becoming: *genesis.*" Creation is about "beginning" (events in relation that are always relative, contested, and historical), not "origin" (which is absolute).[117]

Keller said she would believe in creation as becoming even if the Bible opposed her. As it is, Genesis is like most of the ancient world in assuming that the universe was created from some uncreated Other, a primal chaos that a creator molded to order. *Creatio ex nihilo* became Christian orthodoxy only because Christian theologians refused to accept the constraint on God's power implied by Genesis 1:2. Eleventh-century French biblical and Talmudic scholar Rashi described verse two as a dependent clause; Keller, agreeing, said Genesis does not signify a linear sequence. "In beginning" (*bereshit*) fashions a subordinate clause, not a summary announcement; following Rashi and others, she interpreted verse two as an elaborate parenthesis; only verse three is an independent clause. In Rashi's translation: "At the beginning of the Creation of heaven and earth when the earth was without form and void and there was darkness . . . God said . . ." This version accents the prior existence of chaos, disrupting the flow of commandment and fulfillment. In context and in form, Keller observed, "the chaos is *always already there*." She liked nineteenth-century scholar Hermann Gunkel's rendering of the Spirit of God "vibrating upon the face of the waters," which suggests the fluttering oscillations of chaos theory.[118]

Every attempt to discover an absolute origin brings us to the boundaries of language, an infinite regress, "originating conditions that have themselves originated." Derrida called it "the bottomless," denying that the "bottomless play of the signifier" has any depth; Keller countered that the face of this bottomless play signifies the Deep. Her theology of becoming was an alternative to the being of *ex nihilism* and the nonbeing of nihilist flux: becoming as beginning, "the topos of the Deep." Unlike Moltmann, who assumed creatio ex nihilo, Keller did not distinguish between God's "making" and "letting be." In Genesis, Elohim makes by letting be. What matters is whether the future is construed as wide and opening. Moltmann retained an absolute origin and future, transferring the foundational force of creatio ex nihilo to the promise of eternal life. Keller countered that God is concomitant with creation, not prior to it.[119]

She stressed that the Deep of Genesis traces to Babylonian mythology. In the Enuma Elish, Tiamat, the oceanic, saltwater, primal chaos, lay in primordial bliss with Apsu, the sweet-water abyss, creating the universe from their mingling waters. Later Marduk slew his grandmother Tiamat and stretched out her oceanic carcass to form the world. The hero's slaughter of the first goddess sanctified Babylon's imperial politics, lifting war over cosmic creation; eventually "Tiamat" migrated into Hebrew as "tehom." The Priestly writer's understanding of Babylonian warrior matricide is unknown, but Genesis 1 takes over the watery, female Deep of Babylonian myth without demonizing it. Orthodoxies eradicate the chaos of creation out of fear of the depth—"tehomophobia." Creation theology, a better idea, is depth loving ("tehomophilia"). Barth's tehomophobia was unusual only in its bluntness: "Nothing that is good can come out of *tehom*." Keller countered that a theology of radical becoming has to be feminist, because "the He-God powers every ontotheology." We have a grave problem, Yahweh is Marduk's nephew, and the problem cannot be solved by getting rid of God, because atheism does not address most of the problem: "Only at the theological depth sounded by the tehomic tropes will feminism as theology and theology as feminism continue to become. The relationism of feminist theology requires an ever wider scale of iterative differences."[120]

This was a vision of originary indeterminacy generating order upon "the face" of chaos, not in opposition to it. Keller called it "apophatic panentheism," blending negative theology and Whitehead. If "God" is not the founding word, and "God creates" is not the original act and fact, and it really makes no sense to begin sentences with "God is" or "God does," as though "God" identifies something, how should the divine "whatever" be marked off from the impersonal flux of the cosmos? Keller's mystical-leaning answer assumed Whitehead's dialectic of possibility becoming actuality, especially Joseph Bracken's notion of a divine matrix blending Whiteheadian creativity and Eckhart negative theology. "God" is actualized as the difference of the bottomless ground of creativity from itself. God emerges against the ground of creativity as the divine matrix by which better possibilities are chosen. The "en" of panentheism asserts the crucial line of difference between the divine and cosmic, but the line can never be drawn. Keller explained, "For is not the line always already smudged? The smudge, the flux, 'is' the *en*, the overlap, of divinity with world, of world with divinity." The cosmos unfolds "in" the divine and the divine unfolds "in" the cosmos under many names, including Elohim, Sophia, Logos, and Christ.[121]

Panentheism brought out the apologist in Keller, who said it retains "what all theism desires: a 'Thou' different enough and intimate enough to love and to be loved." It was birthed by orthodox Christian fathers, but disowned by orthodoxy. Thus it contains the parts of classical theism that spiritually sensitive people still desire. The divinity of panentheism is a God of life, "the life of the world, the spirit of a chaosmos in which death circulates through every living process, decision always cuts, and choice marks every birth, consciously or spontaneously." Keller stressed her novelty. Feminists looked past the theology of creation, and many liberals and liberationists assumed creation out of nothing. Cobb and Griffin anticipated her to some extent, but they described a creation from chaos only in passing, developing a theology of nature, not creation. *Face of the Deep* was the first full-orbed theology of creation from a tehomic perspective.[122]

Reviewers noted, mostly in appreciation, that the book was original, suggestive, and profusely multivocal in style and content. Laurel Schneider called it "deliberately lush, dripping, and surprising, like a rain forest." Schneider had regrets, wishing for "less flash and more pause; less gesture toward justice and more of its messy realization; less crowding of voices and texts and more calm boldness in her own voice." She also wished for a clearer idea of God, but judged that *Face of the Deep* was a brilliant landmark. Jonathan Baxter questioned whether Keller gave away too much of the Christian tradition in order to "wrestle a blessing" for tehom, but concluded that her book successfully articulated "a *spirited* return for the becoming of theology." B. Jill Carroll worried that Keller's tehomic vs. ex nihilo rhetoric set up its own fixed dualism, and she wearied of "strange coinage, hyphenated and spliced words, and subversive turns of phrase." But *Face of the Deep*, besides being smart and witty, made a strong case that the God of orthodoxy "was a simple imposter too estranged from the cosmos." Douglas Sturm agreed that Keller's book was mind stretching, important, and distinctively polyphonic. He also lingered over the problems of style and imagined audience: "Sometimes abstruse and obscure, sometimes playful and poetic, always serious, the text assumes a special kind of reader." Keller, he observed, wrote for a select audience with highly specialized intellectual skills, but the book's message deserved a wider audience.[123]

Keller felt keenly the problem of modern theology that fuses the problems of audience and style. In the eighteenth century, theology entered the path of doubt, and doubt has grown worse. She mused that theology struggles with a double bind. To the extent that theologians work on the cutting edge of their discipline, they lose their traditional constituencies in religious communities, thereby losing the basis of any progressive religious praxis. To the extent that they write in and for religious communities, they are sucked into "the dogmatic drag, the vortex of swirling symbols and insecure institutions." Even the most "forward-looking" theologies are plagued and disoriented by this problem: "We tumble off the timeline of progress."[124]

For most of her career she fretted over this double bind; at the end of *The Face of the Deep*, she vowed to see it heretofore as an opportunity. Keller tired of the question whether a theologian should have more to say about God; there is no shorthand answer that dispels the expectation or puzzlement behind the question. She took no interest in standing at the ancient gate or church door, "ready to receive refugees from secular modernity." That strategy leads to drowning from dogmatic drag. The better option is to break free of theology's colonizing past, reinvent theology for new audiences, and embrace the postcolonial situation in which theology finds itself. Theologians must learn to dwell in the in-between of the divine and the world, subverting "the dispiriting dominologies of antiquity and (post)modernity." They should try to speak meaningfully to eco-warriors, feminists, liberationists, and anti-globalization activists, plunging into the deep ocean of divinity, tracing the unfolding creation of life from its depths without apologizing for declining liberal churches or seminaries.[125]

That helped her get clear about why she is a theologian and what she feels compelled to say about God. Influenced by the same deconstructionists as Tracy, especially Derrida's later reflections on apophasis and the im-possible, and the same Neoplatonic mystics as Tracy, in her case especially Nicholas of Cusa, Keller took deconstructionist criticism where it did not want to go, into outright theological reflection on the "cloudy edges" of the impossible. Derrida, cautioning against the idea of possibility, said that to theorize the possible "is to be already there and to paralyze oneself in the in-decision of the non-event." To be there already is to be left with nowhere to go. To Tracy, deconstruction rendered ism theology as beside the point, but Keller lingered over apophatic panentheism and the impossible, intrigued by Derrida's exaltation of the "more than possible, the most impossible *possible*." Near the end of his life Derrida said his favorite nickname for God was *posse ipsum*, possibility itself. That led Keller to a sustained grappling with the first theologian to describe God as *posse ipsum*, Nicholas of Cusa.[126]

Nicholas was born in Kues, Germany, in 1401, earned a doctorate in canon law at the University of Padua in 1423, and spent his entire career trying to reform and unite the Roman Church as a canon lawyer, diplomat, theologian, and bishop. He was trained in scholastic and humanistic learning, but mostly self-taught in theology and philosophy, influenced especially by the sixth-century Greek mystic Dionysius the Areopagite, also called Pseudo-Dionysius. Nicholas declined academic posts to remain in church administration, defended the authority of the council over the pope at the Council of Basel in 1433, and switched to the papal party after the council. In 1437 he served as a papal legate to Constantinople, seeking unity with the Greek Church; on the journey home he wrote *De Docta Ignorantia* (1440, *On Learned Ignorance*), a stunning meditation on the "knowing ignorance" that precludes all certain claims about God. Nicholas served as a papal delegate to Germany for ten years, was elevated to cardinal in 1448 and named bishop of Brixen in 1450, and wrote philosophical works in his later career.[127]

He was perhaps the most brilliant thinker in the entire line of Neoplatonist mystical theology running from Gregory of Nyssa to Dionysius to Meister Eckhart to the anonymous fourteenth-century Middle English author of *Cloud of Unknowing* to the sixteenth-century Lutheran mystic Jacob Boehme. Keller offered a brisk genealogy of this tradition, working up to Nicholas via Gregory of Nyssa, Dionysius, and *Cloud of Unknowing*. She stressed that Nicholas was steeped in a tradition of negative theological "cloud-writing" about "the numinous dark," which countered the Thomist identification of God with Being. Positive theology, supremely in Thomas, sublimates the negative into the positive, prizing its rational balance. Negative theology, before and after Thomism, is a critique of what came to be called onto-theology, emphasizing contradiction and irresolution. Eventually Catholic theologians like Nicholas were obligated not to say that Thomism wrongly blocked theologians from their true referent, the being-less Beyond. Yet Nicholas culminated the tradition of negative, mystical, apophatic theology by pressing his verdicts that the universe is boundless and God is unfathomably enfolded in all that is.[128]

Nicholas anticipated, by a century, the discovery of Copernicus that the universe is infinite and the earth is moving. He gets less credit than he deserves in history of science textbooks because his subject was God, and he was more radical than Copernicus, who pictured a heliocentric universe. *On Learned Ignorance* argued that the universe is boundless, with no fixed center: "There are no immobile and fixed poles in the sky." He went on to write, among other books, two luminous works of mystical theology bound by the strictures of *On Learned Ignorance*. *The Vision of God* (1453), in the form of a prayer, argued that God seen is identically God seeing. To see God is nothing else or less than for God to see the one who is gazing; my individuated reality is a contracted image of God through my relation to divine reality. In his famous ninth chapter, Nicholas expounded on the enfolding/unfolding dialectic of *On Learned*

Ignorance, picturing God inside the wall of paradise that symbolizes the coincidence of opposites. There are three stages in the spiritual journey, he wrote. Outside the wall, reason grasps that things are enfolded in God and the same things are unfolded in the created universe. Christ stands at the entrance of the wall, the second stage, where enfolding and unfolding coincide, disclosing the coincidence of opposites. Inside the wall, the third stage, God's presence is utterly transcendent, unspeakable, and conceptually unknowable. *The Vision of God* favored "the oppositeness of opposites" as the best name for the unfathomable God, oppositeness without oppositeness. *On the Not Other* (1462), revisiting this question, said it is best to think of God as the Not Other, because God is not other than anything that God creates and sustains in being, yet God is utterly not like all the finite others of our experience.[129]

Keller made puckish asides about exalting a fifteenth-century hierarch who excelled at church politics, kept his orthodox credentials intact, and did not question the Neoplatonic One. Nicholas is, among other things, a tantalizing symbol of the Christian possibility that was lost after the Protestant Reformers blasted Renaissance humanism. He believed that his brand of knowingly ignorant mystical theology should be a feature of theology and the church's teaching. That was not to be. Keller returns to where Nicholas left off: the idea that God cannot be separated from the world is itself apophatic, as Nicholas said: "We see most truly this indivisibility is not apprehensible by any name nameable by us or concept formable." Moreover, "not other" is another discursive apophasis that is also an "experimental kataphasis," a conjectured affirmation. *The Vision of God*, she says, hurtles through the centuries as "an illicit grammatology of divine potentiality." Moreover, Nicholas went on to fuse *posse* and *est* as a new name for God, *possest*, "possi-being." Keller does not gild the lily, acknowledging that Nicholas never quite broke with Thomism on the doctrine that God is pure actuality. Nicholas reasoned that actuality and potentiality coincide in God, for God is free of all opposition. He left room for the possibility that God has the potency to develop into something other than God, and his intensely abstruse dialogues with Dionysius yielded tortuous sentences defying comprehension. But Nicholas clearly taught that divine possibility finds actualization in the world of others, contrary to Thomism.[130]

Keller delights that Nicholas settled at the end on possibility itself, *posse ipsum*, as his favorite name for God. Nothing that is can be without first being possible. The same thing holds true for anything to be doable.

"Possibility itself" names the ultimate condition of the possibility of any activity. Keller acknowledges that Nicholas did not try to prove God's existence and did not believe in trying. Still, "if we identify that *posse* as 'God,' then there is no doubt of its reality." Nicholas settled on the view that *posse ipsum*—"that than which nothing can be more capable, prior, or better"—is much better than the alternatives, such as *possest*. *Posse* is a nominalized verb meaning "able to do." On Nicholas' terms, Keller stresses, "possibility itself" is not a claim about God's ability to do anything or everything. Nicholas believed, like Whitehead, that nothing is known outside of relation and God is infinitely implicated in the world. Thus, the can-do meaning of "possibility itself" is about *our* ability to do. Keller explains, "Once we admit that our free action is preceded by the possibility of that action, we are living evidence of that *posse ipsum*—the power of our ability, which is being offered as the name and utterly visible sign of God."[131]

She plays up the affinity between Nicholas and Whitehead, describing both as experimental theorists of a non-oppositional binary dynamic—God is creating and creatable: "One can say of both that the creating is by 'attraction' or by 'calling,' therefore by communication rather than manipulation, and that the being created of God is the event of being moved by the moving manifold." The upshot of these iterating passives is that in our feelings of God, God feels us. But Keller allows that only Whitehead said that. Nicholas did not believe that God receives something from creatures, and he never gave up the Neoplatonic One. Yet for Nicholas, as for Whitehead, the enfolding of creatures in God makes us non-separable from, though not identical with, the maximum. Nicholas-style enfolding resembles what Whitehead called "a tenderness which loses nothing that can be saved," the integration of everything savable in God's consequent nature. Nicholas sang hymns of praise to the God of (Renaissance) freedom and the divine indwelling: "Sweetness of every delight, you have placed within my freedom that I be my own if I am willing. Hence unless I am my own you are not mine." In the divine cloud, he said, he found "a most astonishing power," seeing in God's absolute face "the natural face of all nature." Whitehead, in Keller's telling, fashioned a metaphysic that better fit the feeling and dipolar panentheism of Nicholas, and better grounded the Hegelian idea that the divine self-actualization is a becoming.[132]

Hegel construed the divine becoming as the actualization of a determinate dialectic, temporalizing the Neoplatonic One that he and

Nicholas took over from Christian orthodoxy. According to Keller, Whitehead improved on both by theorizing that creativity drives God's becoming in response to the becoming of the world. The divine becoming is the actualization of an indeterminate creativity. The many become one, and are increased by one, but this one is just one among many others. It unfolds as a singular event by enfolding in the universe. Keller recognizes that Whiteheadian theism is distinctly prone to objectification, erecting a new metaphysical scholasticism. She enlists apophatic mystics to guard against it, following the example of Whiteheadian philosopher Roland Faber. But Whiteheadians wager everything on the Whiteheadian one and many; the differences between rationalist and metaphorical Whiteheadians dissolve on this point. Whether God is a real entity, as in Whitehead, or a real society of occasions, as in Hartshorne, or a metaphor of our infinite entanglement, as in Keller, Whiteheadians unite in giving up the onto-theological God whose Being is the One. Deconstruction, as Keller says, is heir to the Nietzsche-Heidegger-Levinas announcement that that God is dead.[133]

The Hegel-Whitehead difference that matters, on this view, is that Hegel conceived the Trinity as a dynamic and intersubjective way to save the Neoplatonic One. Whiteheadians are done with that renovation project, whatever they say individually about the Trinity. What matters, Keller says, "what might matter endlessly, is what we earth-dwellers now together embody. Not what we say *about* God but how we *do* God." What matters is our collective God-making, *theopoiesis*. The divine complication appeals to its own explication—"its unfolding, its getting *done*." It is an entangled-becoming defying conceptual explication, something like the Whiteheadian urge of desire urging a certain kind of practice: "Contemplative even in its most activist, most affirmative, most gender-queerclassraceabilitypluralistecopolitical unfoldings." All such language will pass, but "its entanglements may not."[134]

11

In a Post-Hegelian Spirit

Divine Becoming and Discontent

Realistic theologies are keyed to what is said to be actual, reading knowledge of God and the aims of ethical action from the given. Idealistic theologies are keyed to claims about truths transcending actuality. I am opposed to lifting realistic actuality above idealistic discontent, even as I acknowledge that idealism poses the greater danger. A wholly realistic theology would be a monstrosity, a sanctification of mediocrity, inertia, oppression, domination, exclusion, and moral indifference. Christianity is inherently idealistic in describing the being or movement of spirit as the ultimate reality and in holding to transcendent moral truths. But an idealistic theology lacking a sense of tragedy, real-world oppression and exclusion, and the danger of its own prideful intellectualism would be worse than the worst theological realism. The only kind of idealism that interests me is liberationist—privileging the critique of oppression, linking tragedy with the struggle for justice, expressing idealistic discontent, and admitting what it does not know.

Religious thinkers rely on metaphors, symbols, and/or analogies to signify things beyond our grasp. Some rely on poetic metaphors, creating new meanings by saying one thing to mean something else. Some are radically metaphoric in the Kantian sense of constructing worlds, whether or not they acknowledge it. Some are radically Kantian in the sense of claiming to reflect the very method and powers of mind. Some claim that analogies steer better than symbols between univocal and equivocal claims, or that symbols and analogies share this work in complementary fashion. Metaphors, symbols, and analogies convey invisible worlds of meaning. I take for granted, with Augustine, Eckhart, Nicholas, Boehme, Calvin, Barth, Tillich, David Tracy, Edward Farley, and Catherine Keller, that anything I understand is not God, *and* that religious thinking should be fired by a passion for truth. Thus I do not spurn metaphysical audacity, for faith is a form of daring.

The great "I AM" of Exodus 3:14, God telling Moses, "I AM WHO I AM. . . . Say to the Israelites, 'I AM has sent me'" (NRSV) is a sign of the identity of thought and being, the keystone of idealism. The self-naming of God with a verb identifies God with self-expressive movement, an inference heightened in the alternative NRSV translation, "I will be what I will be." Hegel caught the non-anthropomorphic divine of Exodus 3:14 by theorizing the self-reflection of Spirit as thought and being united *in Spirit*. This was a move beyond traditional Western metaphysics, an onto-theology of a new category—fluid, spiraling, self-realizing Spirit. God's being is the self-revealing and self-realizing process of differentiation and reconciliation, Spirit. Being-in-itself externalizes itself in being-for-itself and returns in the Spirit as being-in-and-for-itself. Being is an abstraction from becoming, and Christianity is about the gift of love divine poured out in differentiation, suffering, death, and reconciliation.

Hegel, however, was notoriously proud and overreaching, compelling theologians who followed his lead to scale back his intellectualism. Tillich's corrective fused the classic Thomist identification of God with being itself to a form of post-Kantian idealism chastened by Marx on one side and Kierkegaard on the other. But this solution to a deadly problem lost Hegel's intersubjective dynamism. Tillich's ontology operated on the polarity of self and world. His career had nearly ended when he realized that he did not improve on Hegel by casting aside the fluid language of being-as-becoming Spirit. Whitehead recovered Hegel's relational dynamism by conceiving creativity, not God, as metaphysically ultimate. Whitehead's God is a being, an actual entity that lures the universe into ever-greater complexity, novelty, value, order, and beauty. But what sort of God is not ultimate and is not free to be terrible?[1]

Religious idealism from Augustine to Jonathan Edwards fixed on the participation of all knowledge in the movement of divine self-knowledge. Kant and Fichte cast idealism in Cartesian terms by making a revolutionary claim about the agency of the human knower. The mind is active in producing experience. A subject becomes a subject by the act of constructing itself objectively to itself, but a subject is not an object except for itself. Kantian idealism became "post-Kantian" by pursuing what it means to think that subject and object are identical on the level of mind, each involving the other. Schelling, Schlegel, and Coleridge variously expanded on the transcendental ego of Kant and Fichte, still conjuring a supersensible entity. Hegel transformed the I-am-I monism of Kant and Fichte by construing the I as existing concretely in self-recognition in others. Spirit is the intersubjective gestalt of the world, not a gestalt of consciousness. Thus Hegel risked onto-theology of a new kind. His *Phenomenology of Spirit* was exactly what its title ambitiously promised, a phenomenology daring to be a noumenology. Philosophy and theology folded together *if* the divine-human relation is best construed as reciprocal self-recognition in the other. Our groping knowledge of the absolute *is* its self-knowledge.

Subjective idealism, the idea that there is no reality without self-conscious subjectivity, renders the ideal as spiritual or mental ideality, as contrasted with the material or physical. Immediate objects of perception are the ideas of the perceiving subject; thus, all that we know are our own representations, not reality itself. To the extent that Kant was a subjective idealist, he had an affinity with Berkeley, who subjectivized Plato's idealism by extending Locke's analysis of the secondary qualities of matter to the primary qualities of matter. Locke said the material universe is a system of material bodies mechanically interacting in space and that its operation depends on primary qualities of matter—solidity, figure, extension, motion, and number. Ideas arise in the mind through a process of mechanical stimulation in the sense organs. Some ideas represent to the mind real things, other ideas such as sound and color have no real counterpart in physical reality, and we are aware only of our own ideas. Berkeley noted that these claims do not fit together. If Locke was aware only of his own ideas, how did he know that the universe is a vast machine? If blue and sound depend on the existence of mind, how did Locke know that big or small, round or square, or solid or fluid would still exist if mind disappeared? Berkeley countered that Locke did not know any such thing, because matter is not real; only mind is real. Knowledge is the apprehension of a succession of ideas, not something governed by actual self-existing matter, which is merely an idea. Knowledge is ideational as a succession of feelings.

Berkeley recognized that knowing has a relational aspect, requiring sensations *and* mental relations. But he failed to think it through, reducing space and substance to mere feelings, which defied the rock-bottom empirical sense of matter as something occupying space. Kant corrected Berkeley's failure by showing that relations and sensations require powers of mind. Even to describe things as bundles of sensations, as Berkeley did, implied that the bundles are as constitutive in things as the sensations. Thus Kant labored over his bundled categories of quantity, quality, relation, and modality, improving on Berkeley's subjective idealism even if, as I believe, he is not best interpreted as a subjective idealist. Space is made up of relations, a meaningless notion without a mind that relates one thing to another *and* for which things are related—holding together both terms of a relation. The relation between two points is not *in* either point by themselves; the relation is in the "between."

Many post-Kantians assumed Kant's affinity with Berkeley while developing their own forms of subjective religious idealism, notably Rudolf H. Lotze and Rudolf Eucken in Germany, Andrew Seth Pringle-Pattison and Hastings Rashdall in England, and Borden Parker Bowne, George H. Howison, and Albert C. Knudson in the United States. To them, Kant's idealism bound the Kantian forms of experience to the transcendental subject, the precondition of the forms. The knowing subject employs its categories of understanding to intuit objects of sense data, and the ideal or the rational is subjective. Religious post-Kantian subjectivists usually stressed the Berkeleyan point that there is nothing in matter that does not imply mind. A thing exists for "another," but a consciousness exists for itself; the very being of a mind consists in being itself conscious. A mind, unlike a thing, is not made what it is by being experienced by another mind; it is what it is for itself. Since matter is unintelligible without mind, it must never have existed without mind. Ultimately, for those who completely dropped Kantian modesty, nothing exists except minds and their experiences. But since matter as a whole does not exist merely for our minds, which know only a tiny bit of the universe, there must be a Mind that knows the whole.[2]

Objective versions of religious post-Kantian idealism were the same thing flipped over, usually following Hegel, Schelling, or Schlegel. Philipp K. Marheineke, Karl Rosenkranz, and Karl Ludwig Michelet in Germany; A. E. Biedermann in Switzerland; Edward Caird, C. C. J. Webb and William Temple in England; and Josiah Royce, W. E. Hocking, and Edgar S. Brightman in the United States took this tack. They, too, said there must be a Mind that knows the whole; some kind of unity must underlie the diversity of things. But they construed the ideal as normative, not substantive. Reality conforms to the archetypes of an intelligible structure. Everything is a manifestation of the ideal, an unfolding of reason. In Kantian terms, objective idealism detaches the forms of experience from the transcendental subject, applying the forms to being as such. The ideal or the rational is archetypal and structural, as it was for Plato and Leibniz. The neo-Kantian Marburg school of Hermann Cohen, Friedrich Albert Lange, Paul Natorp, and Ernst Cassirer, despite its anti-metaphysical temper, inadvertently boosted the objective idealist tradition by defending the "pure thought" of Kant's transcendentalism and ethics. They described the Kantian forms of experience as regulative *and* as constitutive of nature itself. Like the religious objective idealists they spurned, the Marburg neo-Kantians construed the Kantian categories as bridges between the dualism of subject and object.[3]

Mixed forms of subjective and objective idealism, then and now, usually hold fast to Kant's emphasis on self-conscious subjectivity while affirming that the Kantian categories bridge Kant's dualistic epistemological agnosticism. Mixture interpretations of Kant are either patchworks or attempts to reconcile his contradictions. In my view, the starting point for interpreting Kant should be what he said about transcendental idealism: truth consists in the conformity of objects to concepts. How far Kant took conceptualism is a question that yields very different renderings of him. I believe that he tried to hold together both kinds of idealism without resolving his ambiguous doctrine of ideas. But however the Kant question is settled, *both* kinds of idealism claim that reality depends on the ideal or the rational. Subjective idealism renders the categories as objects within experience, making them primarily psychological. Objective idealism renders the categories as the conditions of experience, making them primarily epistemological.

Everything that Kant said about transcendental idealism was subjective idealist, which did not unify the manifold of intuition or make sense of beauty, organic relations, and the wholeness of nature. Thus he employed a doctrine of intellectual intuition in the *Critique of Pure Reason*, re-invoked it in the *Critique of Judgment*, and treated it with such restraint in both cases that textbook renderings of Kant left it aside. Kant was skittish about intellectual intuition because the more he relied on it, the less he felt he was in rational control. To follow through takes some daring, as does Kant's principle that all human beings should be treated as ends in themselves, on which Kant grievously did not follow through.

Kant made room for the possibility of freedom by limiting causality to a law of the mind, and he made room for the actuality of freedom by insisting on the actuality of the moral law. Moral activity is impossible lacking free moral subjects. Kant connected the principles of the intellectual world and the sensible world through practical reason and the subordination of everything to freedom. The moral law is simple, absolute, and sublime, discernable to anyone who universalizes the moral question. To actually do the right thing, however, we have to fight off the radical evil within us. Kant was deeply earnest about the moral obligation to fight off radical evil, the one thing that assured him of his freedom. His wayward protégé, Fichte, was equally consumed by it, shunning sociality because it felt like a threat to his moral freedom and rationality. Liberal theology eventually acquired an exaggerated reputation for discarding the language of sin and evil, and many liberals during the Progressive Era believed in human perfectibility, which made liberalism ridiculous to the generation that lived through World War I and the Depression. Liberal theology, however, began with the Kantian recognition that "original sin" is a mythological marker of something terribly real—the universal human propensity for badness, selfishness, egotism, and will to power.

Kantian ethics, in theory, condemned every denial of the humanity of another human being. Every person's humanity—the matrix of capacities that directly and indirectly permits rational self-conscious activity—must be recognized as an end in itself. Two centuries past Kant, we still have no better foundation for human rights theory and policy than Kant's affirmation of respect for humanity as such construed as a universal moral obligation. On Kantian terms, this affirmation is an exercise of practical reason yielding a cosmopolitan ethical result. Every version of the Golden Rule expounded in the Confucian, Buddhist, Jewish, Muslim, and Christian religions implies a duty of reciprocal respect for the human dignity of others. Kant's fusion of the moral duty to treat every human being as an end to a doctrine of universal moral obligation laid the groundwork for doctrines of human rights that grapple with cultural difference and repudiate Kant's conceits about white European superiority.

Kantians and post-Kantians, religious and secular, should have managed not to denigrate the humanity of everyone who was not white, European, male, and a property owner. Liberal theology and secular liberalism capitulated to conventional bigotry because neither had any history that was not complicit in slavery, racism, imperialism, nationalism, misogyny, and class oppression. But there is a double standard in this area that routinely stigmatizes idealists unfairly; Reinhold Niebuhr spent most of his career exploiting it. We hold idealists to a higher ethical standard than realists, skeptics, conservatives, materialists, and nihilists because idealists implore us to believe that ethical ideals are real and necessary. Kant's idealism is an invitation to moral censure, but at least he set himself up for it. The universal aspiration that marked Christianity from its beginning is similarly ambiguous. It yielded all manner of overreaching imperial Christianities, yet Paul and the early Logos theologians were not wrong to aim beyond provincial mythologies. The idea that there is such a thing as an individual person, and the corollary that this person has sacred dignity, came from Christianity. These ideas did not come from anywhere else, which is not to say that they should be set aside for coming from Christianity.

When Kant pleaded for a hearing after the first *Critique* was ignored, his foes were commonsense realists determined to dismiss his argument as a hodgepodge of Berkeleyan solipsism and scholastic obscurantism. Kant could not defeat them, or even win a hearing, without battling for the thing-in-itself on his terms—which changed dramatically between the first and second editions of the first *Critique*. He wanted a doctrine of the transcendental object that did not leave him exposed to ridicule. But his attempt to provide discursive content for the unknowable thing-in-itself yielded hopeless contradictions not worth the trouble, so he ripped the transcendental object out of most of the second edition, leaving vestiges of it elsewhere, unwilling to rewrite the entire book.

The idea of intellectual intuition had a similarly patchy and conflicted role in Kant's work because he realized how easily it might veer out of rational control. His interpretation of reason in the first two critiques deepened the contradictions of subjectivity by placing the conflicts between autonomy and heteronomy, freedom and determinism, reason and sensibility, a priori and a posteriori, universality and particularity, objectivity and subjectivity, obligation and inclination, and form and matter *within* individual human subjects. The first *Critique* had the germ of Kant's idea of intellectual intuition in his section on the Transcendental Deduction, but the first *Critique* was mostly about the limits on human knowing within the bounds of sense. The second *Critique* stressed that the Enlightenment valorization of autonomy turned even universality—something previously imposed only internally—into something legislated internally. The third *Critique* mediated Kant's binary oppositions by developing the idea of intellectual intuition, a form of inner teleology in which means and ends are internally and reciprocally related.

Each means and end becomes itself in and through the other, and neither can be itself apart from the other. In a work of art, Kant said, an interplay takes place between the whole and the parts: "The parts of the thing combine of themselves into the unity of a whole by being reciprocally cause and effect of their form. For this is the only way in which it is possible that the idea of the whole may conversely, or reciprocally, determine, in its turn the form and combination of all the parts, not as cause—for that would make it an art product—but as the epistemological basis upon which the systematic unity of the form and combination of all the manifold contained in the given matter become cognizable for the person overestimating it."[4]

There is a type of unity that promotes and sustains differences. The inner reciprocity of parts and wholes is a kind of teleology, a form of internal purposiveness. This idea launched the post-Kantian revolution that threw off Kant's restraints. Kant teetered on the edge of the limit of reason as he construed it, believing that he ascertained where the boundary existed, but reason drove him over the edge, at least on "regulatory" terms—the ground of his postulated moral deism and his idea of inner teleology. Post-Kantians, variously dispensing with the thing-in-itself, caught the radical upshot of inner teleology: there is a Kantian basis for intellectual intuition and the principle of constitutive relationality. Identity is differential, not oppositional. Mechanistic philosophy does not account for the inwardly reciprocal purposiveness in aesthetic judgments. Kant tried to hold off the post-Kantian revolution by cautioning that his theory of beauty was a regulative idea resting on the dichotomy between inward and outward purpose. Perhaps it described the way things really are, and perhaps it didn't. Surely it was purposive, but external purpose was something else.

Post-Kantian Romantics, Hegelians, and religious idealists replied that intellectual intuition does not submit to Kantian confinement. The Romantics stressed that works of art figure reconciliation as an unrealizable idea; thus, art deepens the oppositions it seeks to overcome. Romantic idealism was about transforming the world into a work of art, completing the Kantian revolution and the French Revolution. Schlegel, naming the Romantic eruption, said that Romantic poetry is progressive and universal, fusing poetry and prose, inspiration and criticism, and art and nature; all good poetry is romantic. Religious post-Kantians cited Schleiermacher and a host of Mediating theologians on the primacy of feeling and the constitutive role of purpose in thought, especially the higher forms of thought.[5]

Perhaps one has to be a post-Kantian to claim, as I do, that Kant truncated his own idea of intellectual intuition because it scared him, threatening his rational control. Heidegger, however, rendered a similar judgment, contending that Kant was frightened by the presentational anarchy of the imagination. Heidegger explained in *Kant and the Problem of Metaphysics*, "In the radicalism of his questions, Kant brought the 'possibility' of metaphysics to the abyss. He saw the unknown. He had to shrink back." Heidegger allowed that Kant was frightened by the transcendental power of the imagination; more important, during the period that Kant revised the first *Critique* for its second edition, "pure reason as reason drew him increasingly under its spell." Kant's strenuous wrestling with the problem of the transcendental object drew him into a daunting dance with the abyss from which all determination emerges—a groundless ground indistinguishable from nothing. He "awoke," in Heidegger's image, to the necessity of searching for finitude in the pure thinking agent itself, not in the determination of finitude through sensibility. Otherwise, Kant's moral necessity was not really pure, being conditioned by something. On Heidegger's account, Kant inaugurated the line of groundless transcendental thought in which Husserl bracketed the question of real existence for phenomenology and Heidegger explored how Being confers its beingness upon beings by a process of "lighting up." Mark C. Taylor aptly notes the postmodern upshot of Kant's transcendentalism: "Such an unfathomable ground is the no-thing on which every foundation founders."[6]

The post-Kantian revolution carried out Kant's revolution of imagination, the turning of consciousness inward into self-consciousness. If Kant was right about the inner teleology of judgment, self-consciousness itself must be self-reflexive. The apprehending subject of self-consciousness turns back on itself by becoming an object to itself. Self-as-subject and self-as-object relate to each other reciprocally, each becoming itself through the other. Fichte, Schelling, and Hegel were the first to follow through on Kant's reconstruction of subject-object identity. Fichte's original edition of *Wissenschaftslehre* (*Science of Knowledge*, 1794) was subjective idealism with a vengeance, inflating the I=I into a gigantic transcendental egoism swallowing everything. Ten years later he flipped the same book into an argument for the priority of being over the ego, but it didn't matter, because Fichte had dramatized the lure and danger of subjective idealism. Thus he was remembered for surrendering to subjectivity. Schelling said that some form of transcendental objective idealism—which changed with every book he poured out—was the answer to the impasse contained in Kant and carried out by Fichte. Nature is an organic product of consciousness tending toward the realization of reason. Philosophy rightly theorizes the movement from the pure subjectivity of self-consciousness to objectivity or nature, conceiving duality as a division within a fundamental Neoplatonic unity marked by two parallel sciences, philosophy of nature (*Naturphilosophie*) and science of knowledge (*Wissenschaftslehre*).[7]

Hegel drifted confusedly as Schelling shot to the top of the field; it took Hegel several years just to comprehend what this discussion was about. Hegel was a Romantic only briefly, during his reunion with Hölderlin in Frankfurt from 1797 to 1800, but he found his core idea during this period, from Hölderlin: love. Christianity, Hegel wrote, is essentially about love divine, God overcoming human estrangement from God and neighbor. Jesus brought love divine into the world and changed the God that humans rightly worship. The power of love, Hegel argued, is that of spirit working on spirit: "The outgoing of the divine is only a development, so that, in annulling what stands over against it, it manifests itself in a union with that opposite."[8]

This was the Christian germ of Hegel's dialectic. Hölderlin encouraged Hegel to find his own way by holding to his truth, letting go of his presumption that he had to run everything through Fichte's philosophy. That liberated Hegel's inner Aristotle, leading him to refashion Aristotle's doctrine of final causation, just as Schelling's embrace of Spinoza liberated Hegel from Kant's fixation with the boundary between finitude and the infinite. Hegel fixed from the beginning on self-return and union, leading many to interpret him as denying that love treasures the existence of the beloved as other. I shall make a contrary argument, without denying his emphasis on self-return. But whether or not Hegel fell short on this point, his breakthrough was immensely significant for religious thought. Hegel's philosophy began as a neo-Kantian theology of love, morphed into a phenomenology of the structures of life, and evolved into a phenomenology of the spiraling intersubjective gestalt of the world, Spirit.

Ultimately, Hegel argued, the principle of subject-object identity is not about the self-knowledge of a finite subject. It is about the self-knowing of the divine within a finite subject in mutual and reciprocal recognition. If God is the absolute "I AM" or "I will be what I will be," reality is the self-thinking of loving, self-sacrificing, suffering, reconciling Spirit. Love is an ontological principle *and* a social-intersubjective principle. The divine comes to know itself through us in interplays of reciprocal recognition, creating a liberating community of freedom. Spirit empties itself into the world of sensuous particularity in its creation of the world as an experience of itself. Divine intersubjectivity occurs through dialectical spirals of self-revealing, self-realizing differentiation and reconciliation, bringing all that exists into being.

Perhaps Hegel rehabilitated classic onto-theology by modernizing Logos theology, as right-Hegelian theologians have argued since the beginning of the Hegel school. Perhaps he fashioned a panlogical closed system that left no room for freedom and real subjectivity, as in right-Hegelian interpretations pro and con. Heidegger, however, analyzing Hegel's concept of experience, pressed the implication of Hegel's claim that science itself is an appearance when it makes an appearance. Hegelian appearance, Heidegger observed, is the authentic presence itself, the eschatological here-yet-not-realized coming of the absolute. The Hegelian absolute, in its will to be with others, is being present; in itself, it is for itself; for the sake of the coming, "the presentation of knowledge as phenomenon is necessary." Heidegger stressed that presentation turns toward the will of the absolute: "The presentation is itself a willing that is, not just a wishing and striving but the action itself, if it pulls itself together within its nature." If the presentation is the willing action itself, the Hegelian absolute is not the stable Logos of a closed system. It is an infinitely restless will that wills itself in willing all that emerges as phenomena and wills everything that wills itself.[9]

Taylor, employing Jean-Luc Nancy's language of Hegelian restlessness, draws a straight line from Kant's description of the inconceivability of freedom to Hegel's infinite restlessness to Heidegger's account of the groundless ground of Being. Heidegger taught that the only thing we comprehend about whatever the ground of being may be is its incomprehensibility. Freedom is incomprehensible because it transposes the inquirer into the realization of Being, "not in the mere representation of it." Taylor and Nancy similarly construe Hegel's restless negativity as the upshot of Kantian freedom and the first recognition of postmodern groundlessness. Nancy describes Hegel as the "inaugural thinker of the contemporary world"—the first to acknowledge that the world finds itself in its struggle with suffering by way of its restlessness, "not in the solace of edifying discourses that do nothing but pile on more testimony to its misery." Hegel paved the way to Heidegger and postmodernism by theorizing the restlessness of the negative.[10]

Nancy's Hegel is the modern world's inaugural witness to the sheer misery and restlessness of life, without divine presence or reconciliation. The Hegelian subject is not a self to itself—an agent that synthesizes representations or holds an interior personality. It is that which dissolves all substance, "every instance already given, supposed first or last, founding or final, capable of coming to rest in itself and taking undivided enjoyment in its mastery and property." It is an act, being what it does. It conceives itself, grasps itself, and relates itself to itself, becoming immanent and infinite in the finite realm of the world, the only world that exists. In the restlessness of its immanence, the Hegelian subject becomes the spirit of whatever the world becomes—the passage of negativity or transformation, not a point. Nancy notes that Hegel did not begin with a principle or a foundation, being devoted to the movement of truth. To think is to make an infinite subject's decision to grapple with infinity itself, refusing to rest with any finite form of being. Hegel's philosophy is a praxis of sense, not a system of propositions. To begin with anything other than an infinite subject's decision to grapple with infinity is to assume a derived beginning from somewhere else. Hegel does not begin or end; his thought is "an upsurge in the course of the given, a rupture, nothing that could be posited as such." To Hegel there is only "the full and complete actuality of the infinite that traverses, works, and transforms the finite."[11]

Nancy turns aside the warhorse objection that Hegel presupposed the Whole that his system claimed to discover. Hegel did not play with readers, even if he presupposed the absolute—the absolute *real* of manifestation that negates all posited things. To be in the absolute is purely to be. The conjunction of thought and being, philosophy's oldest concern, is also philosophy's most serious concern, yielding whatever is to be said about the conjunction of freedom and necessity. The Hegelian difference of being relates to itself through itself as the power of the negative, the infinite act of relating to itself. Nancy's Hegel has nothing to do with spiritual community, mystical unity, panentheism, Eckhart, or Boehme, notwithstanding that Hegel said otherwise. Becoming is merely the condition of every thing, not a process that leads to something else; the infinite restlessness of becoming detaches each thing from its determination. Thought, being separate from things and restless, is the ordeal of separation, including the separation of things from judgments, concepts, and significations. On this account Hegel divorced thought from the realm of identity and subjectivity. The Hegelian self is pure negativity, "being unto the ordeal of being." It is being that does not found itself or sustain itself—sense left to its own infinite return to same, a naked infinity of singularities, none of which achieves reconciliation with the whole. It is precisely that which does not find itself except as nothingness: self-negation, negativity for itself.[12]

Though Nancy derides the Hegel who wrote "sentimental or hackneyed" peons to love divine, he acknowledges that Hegel connected love to power, describing love as the truth of struggle. Hegel, Nancy insists, did not care about subjectivity or anything religious; to suppose otherwise is to misunderstand him. The truth of Hegelian desire is to *be* other, caring nothing for communion, relation, mutuality, aspiration, sexuality, or voracity. On this telling, Hegelian thought finds in love the precision and acuity that active singularity demands—the recognition of desire by desire: "It is recognition of one put-out-of-itself by one put-out-of-itself." There is no Hegelian object of desire, for the Hegelian subject *is* desire of the subject. Love, far from being the loving recognition of one by the other, is the alteration of each one—my desire that the other recognize me as the desiring "infinite becoming-self that I am."[13]

I do not dispute that this is a legitimate way to interpret Hegel, and I acknowledge that the idea of love treasuring the existence of the other is difficult to extricate from Hegel's predominant language of self-return. Nancy's restlessly negative Hegel is a successor to the left-Hegelians of the 1830s who first liberated Hegel from Christianity, the Kojève and Frankfurt school traditions that renewed neo-Marxism, the psychoanalytic neo-Hegelianism of Kojève protégé Jacques Lacan and his school, and the Lacanian writings of the early Žižek, who argued in the 1990s that Hegel propounded a logic of difference closely resembling that of Derrida. Neither is Hegelian atheism something owned by left-Hegelians or postmodernists. Atheistic forms of absolute idealism have existed since David Friedrich Strauss sabotaged his academic career in Germany and J. M. E. McTaggart headed one wing of British Hegelianism. In both cases, however, an enormous amount of theory, first-person commentary, and lecture exposition must be set aside to construe Hegel as a shredder of religious community, spiritual feeling, subjectivity, and God. One has to press hard on a thesis of cunning subterfuge, or take for granted somebody's version of this explanation, as Nancy does. Hegel himself grappled intensely with Christian symbols and developed a process theodicy. He presided over a burgeoning theological school and prized his alliances with religious idealists. If he actually propounded a vision of nihilistic undoing, his cunning and mendacity were colossal.

Improving on Kant: Post-Kantian Religious Idealism

Post-Kantian religious idealists of Hegel's time and for generations afterward usually caught his religious seriousness, whether or not they were Hegelians. They said that Kant's religion was the real problem for religious thought, because Kant aimed too low. Kant reduced religion to moral control, but true religion is not about grasping something. It is openness to the mystery of the whole and a sense of its infinite nature. Religion is about awe, dependence, freedom, worship, appreciation, mystery, and the Spirit of the whole—the hidden wholeness of things. A stream of post-Kantians protested that Kant replaced the soul with dubious substitutes. In effect, Kant had five egos. One ego was empirical and bound by causation. Another ego was the transcendental unity of apperception, a logical point of reference marking a more or less collected self's perception of links between itself and the world of appearances. Another ego was an unknowable thing-in-itself. Another ego was the goal of knowledge, a transcendental ideal. Kant's fifth ego was the moral ego that posits its own freedom. Supposedly this was more modest and rigorous than the idea of a soul, but how could it be modest to have five egos?

Many post-Kantian idealists preferred to conceive the soul as a knowable first principle, though not as a substance. The U. S. American personal idealists through whom I ran this argument in chapter 6 were linked to similar post-Kantian traditions led by Ullmann, Rosenkranz, Dorner, Otto Pfleiderer, and Ernst Troeltsch in Germany and by Caird, Pringle-Pattison, Rashdall, and Temple in Britain. My discussion built up to Brightman and Walter Muelder, and favored them, because their religious idealism was robustly dynamic, holistic, social, interreligious, and ethical—improving on Hegel and conveying why personality matters. But even the less compelling forms of post-Kantian religious idealism rightly fixed on the argument that activity is essential to being. The knowing subject and the subject's activity are one. There is no thought without a thinker, no activity without an agent, and no consciousness without a subject. The soul is real as a self's self-consciousness of its unity and self-identity. The Kantian categories are the preconditions of experience that make experience possible; they cannot be imported into the mind from without. But against Kant, if the categories of thought do not apply to things-in-themselves, these things cannot be affirmed at all.[14]

These religious idealists, though enormously influential in the late nineteenth and early twentieth centuries, fought rearguard battles in theology over Kant's legacy, because Kant supposedly delegitimized metaphysical theology. On Kant's authority, religious thinkers in the traditions of Kant, Schleiermacher, Ritschl, Herrmann, Barth, most of the American social gospel, the early Chicago school, and others took leave of metaphysics, at least as a theological enterprise. Many American theologians turned away from epistemology too, although Kant's authority could not be claimed for that resort. Somehow they just knew things, and if they felt obligated to claim a philosophy, it came from William James and John Dewey. Most social gospel theologians, the early Chicago school, Reinhold Niebuhr, and the entire Niebuhr school took this tack. The religious idealists who kept post-Kantian theory alive had to contend against neo-Kantian Ritschlians who reduced theology to historicism and ethics, and against pragmatists who reduced philosophy to tool sharpening, value theory, and social criticism. They did so—especially Brightman and Muelder—by rethinking the best parts of post-Kantian theory, refusing to have no epistemology.

When Kant described practical reason and aesthetic judgment, he gave an important role to the power of will. When he described pure theoretical reason, he had room only for rules of mind through which the mind construes the world. But these rules do not unify the self or the world of appearances. The Kantian categories place a tenuous subject among isolated things and events. There were Romantic and absolute idealist versions of this objection, but the personal idealists pressed it hardest, to their credit. Some conceived will or purpose as a category of thought on the same plane as causality, negation, existence, or necessity. Others argued that will is a factor in pure reason even though it does not play a definite role in elementary experience. Most events do not require a purpose in the way that every event has a cause and takes place in time. But will is indispensable to reflection and is constitutive of it. The higher forms of thought require will; there is no reflective reason without it. Even if purpose is hidden to intuition, it is revealed to reflection and is in it.

Kant's doctrine of the thing-in-itself and his compartmentalization of will were similar kinds of mistakes, as the personal idealists justly protested. The thing-in-itself has no content and it fails the tests of the categories. It is not in space or time; it is not one or many; it is not a cause or an effect. Therefore it yields nothing except a brake on knowing. More important, the deepest, most direct, and most certain knowledge that reason possesses is the reflective self's knowledge of itself—which Kant excluded by restricting pure theoretical reason to knowledge of phenomena. British and North American post-Kantians did not invoke Kant's authority when they rejected his ostensible dualism, because the objective idealist reading of Kant was very slow to reach Britain and North America.

Modern theology developed under the shadow of German idealism, yielding ironically contrary traditions flowing from the same Kantian/post-Kantian wellspring. From the beginning, liberal theology touted its autonomy, always claiming to break away from the house of authority—living and breathing in the sunlight of freedom, reason, and the good. Yet the dependence of liberal theology on idealism belied its defining claim to autonomy. All four of its major German liberal traditions grappled with this problem, and all had ample histories in Britain, the United States, and other nations boasting schools of liberal religious thought.

Kant refuted the prejudice of the French Enlightenment against religion, showing that German *Aufklärung* was compatible with good religion, as defined by reason: moral duty, a moral guarantor, and the immortality of the soul. He grieved at the lack of progress in his field, metaphysics, which compared poorly to the achievements of Newtonian physics and mechanistic philosophy. Eventually Kant decided that his field did not understand reason itself. Thinking rigorously about thinking drove him to a novel idealism that accepted the triumph of scientific rationality *and* saved modern thought from its mechanistic disbelief in freedom. Scientific rationality and free-willed moral values are compatible as long one holds fast to the necessary distinctions between phenomena and noumena, knowledge and faith, fact and value, and subject and object. Kant's relegation of religion to moral faith spared the theologians who followed him from having to worry about conflicts between science and religion.

Schleiermacher compartmentalized with equal zeal, protecting the autonomy of his theology, with a better understanding of religion than Kant. The monist spirit of Goethe, Spinoza, and the early Schelling pervaded Schleiermacher's theology, which he denied, insisting that his full-fledged, post-Kantian, objective idealism was just his philosophy. Theology is something else: reflection on faith. Ritschl embraced both of these compartmentalization strategies, adopting Kant's trademark distinctions plus Schleiermacher's rendering of Christianity as the experience of redemption. All were bulwarks against Hegel and owning up to a religious philosophy, and all were compatible with historicizing Christianity as a Jesus movement devoted to the kingdom of God. Ritschl's faith in historicism compensated for his compartmentalizing strategy, claiming that historical criticism yields assured results supporting the Christ of faith. Historical criticism recovers the original character of Christianity in the early church's apostolic circle of ideas, interpreting the results from the inside perspective of faith. Or, in Harnack's version, it yields the simple and sublime religion of Jesus himself, stripping away the church layers of Christ-legend.[15]

Two prominent Ritschlians, Herrmann and Troeltsch, poked holes in Ritschlian certainty from opposite standpoints, accentuating compartmentalization (Herrmann) and repudiating it (Troeltsch). Herrmann said historical knowledge is merely probable and never saved anyone. Only faith is saving, through grace, and faith is a distinct kind of knowledge. Theology should have nothing to do with historical apologetics, philosophical theories, or any kind of apologetics. Troeltsch replied that Herrmann was right about historical relativism and wrong about everything else. Historical relativism cannot be avoided, with or without the principle of personality that Troeltsch featured, wavered on, and eventually dropped. Troeltsch pioneered the idea of deriving a liberal theology from a history of religions analysis, although he failed to produce one. Tellingly, both Herrmann and Troeltsch insisted that he was the true successor of Schleiermacher and the other was hopelessly wrong. Herrmann pointed to Schleiermacher's faith-alone fideism and his argument about the autonomy of theology. Troeltsch played up Schleiermacher's Romanticism, liberal idealism, and attention to world religions, conjecturing that Schleiermacher would have disavowed insider-fideism had he lived to see what Herrmann did with him.[16]

The Ritschlian school gave liberal theology its heyday of clarity, self-confidence, and dominance, producing inside and outside forms of historicism that made permanent contributions to modern theology. It also set up liberal theology for a devastating repudiation. On neo-Kantian grounds the Ritschlian school delegitimized the very idea of a Christian ontology of love, leaving liberal Protestant theology with a shallow choice between Nietzschean will-to-power and Culture Protestant morality. Nietzsche repudiated Christian love and its renunciation of power as sickly, sacrificial, herd-following hypocrisy. Liberal Protestant theology readily accepted this antinomy, identifying power with loveless compulsion and God with ethical love. The upshot was an ethical theism lacking a sense of the infinite divine mystery and any concept of the necessary relationships among love, power, and justice. Tillich put it aptly, with a touch of disgusted polemic: "God as the power of being was discarded as a pagan invasion. The Trinitarian symbolism was dissolved. The kingdom of God was reduced to the ideal of an ethical community. Nature was excluded because power was excluded. And power was excluded because the question of being was excluded." Ritschlian liberalism touted its emphasis on social religion as a defining strength, but its moralistic basis yielded shallow forms of social religion lacking concepts of justice and power aside from whatever got imported from without.[17]

Three kinds of theology flowed from Kant's critical idealism and moral religion: (1) Kantian and Ritschlian theologies that repudiated metaphysical reasoning beyond the Kantian framework of epistemology and method, (2) post-Kantian theologies that reconstructed Western metaphysics within or beyond the Kantian frame, and (3) the Schleiermacher approach of trying to have it both ways. The transcendental Thomist variation on type two, discussed in chapter 10, brought Catholic thinkers into this discussion. Joseph Maréchal accepted Kant's starting point in the immanent object, without accepting intellectual intuition. Karl Rahner applied the phenomenology of Husserl and Heidegger to the Thomist analogy of being, exploring the being of consciousness. Bernard Lonergan moved away from Rahner's reliance on Heidegger, grounding transcendental Thomism in scientific studies of the structures of consciousness. In the 1950s and 1960s, Rahner and Lonergan played major roles in keeping onto-theology alive, in both cases on theologically neo-orthodox terms. On my reading, Hegel pioneered the most capacious and radically hospitable form of type-two religious idealism—an intersubjective phenomenology and ontology of being *as* becoming—despite magnifying the worst conceits of the Enlightenment.

Hegel cannot be cleaned up for most philosophy departments if the heart of his project was onto-theology, or if any theology besides anti-theology was even a sideline for him, so his religious commitments are usually ignored by philosophers or explained as something else. One variation of the anti-theology option is to claim that his theological positions were heterodox, so at least his theology wasn't Christian. Many have said so, usually with supportive quotes from a theological conservative. Cyril O'Regan commendably lines out the "heterodox" influences on Hegel, emphasizing Eckhart, Boehme, Joachim of Fiore, and more problematically, Valentinian Gnosticism. The latter reference is problematic because Hegel did not cite Gnostics favorably and he rejected the spirit-matter dualism of Gnostic theology. O'Regan made an important contribution by detailing what the discussion of Hegel's "heterodoxy" should be about, in O'Regan's case armed with a subtle understanding of the history of Christian thought. But usually the label terminates discussion among philosophers and other nontheological critics. One would never know, to read customary dismissals of Hegel's "heterodoxy" or his supposed anti-theology, that liberal, neo-orthodox, ecumenical, liberationist, and postmodern theologians conceive Christianity as a fluid, contested, and revisable subject, appropriating Hegel's so-called "heterodoxy" on panentheism, the Trinity, theo-passionism, divine temporality, and social ontology.[18]

Hegel and Schelling revolutionized the Kantian revolution by developing Kant's notion of the intersubjective universal forms of experience, making the unconditioned or in-itself the real subject-object of philosophy. They broke open the very assumption about divine reality that Nietzsche denounced as an enemy of freedom and subjectivity, that Heidegger rejected in liberating being from the metaphysical God, and that Levinas rejected in dissociating God from being. Hegel turned his post-Kantian ontology of love into a theology of intersubjective Spirit fitting his discovery of social subjectivity. God is the intersubjective whole of wholes—spiraling relationality that embraces all otherness and difference. God's infinite subjectivity is an infinite intersubjectivity of holding differences together in a play of creative relationships not dissolving into sameness.

The notion that Hegel fashioned a closed system is an example, as Žižek wonderfully put it, of shooting too fast. In 1981 General Wojciech Jaruzelski declared martial law in Poland, suppressed the Solidarity union movement, and instituted a 10:00 p.m. curfew; anyone walking the streets after curfew was shot. One soldier killed a pedestrian at 9:50, explaining that the victim lived too far away to make it home by 10:00, so why wait? The Hegel stereotype similarly shoots too fast, making a presumption about Hegelian reconciliation that is not Hegelian, based on a presumption about absolute knowing that is not Hegelian, both prematurely.[19]

But Hegel was also the worst of the religious idealists. He threw away the two greatest strengths of the idealistic tradition: its emphasis on ethical subjectivity and its insistence that all thinking about God is inadequate, a mere pointer to transcendent mystery. He had overreaching confidence in his concepts, to put it mildly, leaving little or no room for apophatic theology, the intuition of God as the holy unknowable mystery of the world. He recycled racist and pro-colonial conventions with casual conceit, drifting in his later career to the stuffy political right. And he provided an ample textual basis for the many right-Hegelians, existentialists, textbook authorities, and others who construe him as a panlogical totalitarian.

Hegel's intellectualism spurned the emphasis on feeling, willing, and ethical struggles for justice that define and fuel religious idealism at its best. He shunned the types who burned for social justice, finding them boorish company, while his esteem for Prussian civilization became inflated to the point of self-parody. He appeared to sublimate God and selves into a logical concept that seemed to drain both of personality. He ridiculed Schleiermacher for theologizing about mere feeling, an overkill exaggeration that confirmed impressions of "seemed to." He invited the impression that nature is insignificant, which lost the nature-romantic feeling of Schlegel, Schelling, Schleiermacher, and Coleridge. Hegel took for granted that philosophy is a superior mode of knowing, he wrongly assumed that religion has a unitary history, he claimed that Christianity is the "consummate religion," and he legitimized Europe's colonial ambitions, all of which rolled into his mythology of European superiority. Everything that critical theory and postcolonial criticism are about has some root in Hegel—for good, for ill, and never lacking moral ambiguity.

Hegel, Postcolonial Criticism, and Neo-Hegelian Critical Theory

Philosophy of Right located the science of right within the science of mind, tracking the development of Spirit through Oriental, Greek, Roman, and Germanic civilization. Mind, Hegel argued, especially will, is the logical structure of right, and freedom is both the substance of right and its goal. Free will is a logical concept, through which Hegel deduced the world's historical movement. Beginning with immediacy is abortive by definition. Otherness becomes immediacy by turning upon itself, transforming the opposite into its immediate—otherness reduplicated.

Hegel improved on social contract theory by refusing to conceive his singular willing subject as the basic atom from which society is constructed. His rights-bearing subject had to find its determinacy for itself in the movement of society and history. *Philosophy of Right* grounded the right to property in an exchange relation of reciprocal recognition between two willing subjects, not in mere possession. Marx cut his teeth on Hegel's theory of sociality and civil society, and Jürgen Habermas grounded his theory of communicative rationality on it. But Hegel conceived the common will as a fusion of differing particular wills—the state as the realization of the ethical idea. He described the state as "absolutely rational" and the "actuality of the substantial will," and thus an "unmoved end in itself." Freedom achieves its "highest right" through the state, which holds priority over the rights and freedoms of individuals, though Hegel cautioned against putting it that way, since the highest freedom of every individual is indistinguishable from the duty of individuals to be members of the state.[20]

Philosophy of Right, to be sure, had liberal planks. Hegel advocated freedom of the press and public opinion, criticized Plato for curtailing individual freedom, and made arguments for trial by jury and two-house parliamentary government. He said the state acquires international legitimacy by passing from an independent constitutional organism to a global phenomenon bound by international law. But *Philosophy of Right* reeked of comfort and self-satisfaction, abounding in privileged admonitions to do one's duty and not make trouble. Hegel conferred logical superiority on a state capitalist version of bourgeois ideology, topped off in the Prussian case by a constitutional monarchy. Then he ludicrously claimed that history reached its zenith in the Germanic civilization of Northern Europe: "This is the absolute turning point; mind rises out of this situation and grasps the infinite positivity of this its inward character, i.e., it grasps the principle of the unity of the divine nature and the human, the reconciliation of objective truth and freedom as the truth and freedom appearing within self-consciousness and subjectivity, a reconciliation with the fulfillment of which the principle of the north, the principle of the Germanic peoples, has been entrusted."[21]

Hegel was the first to escalate ordinary Enlightenment conceit to the claim that Europe was the center and end of the entire planet's history. Oriental civilization, Hegel said, created strong, natural, magnificent, patriarchal, theocratic communities, but lacked the rights and spirit of individual personality. The Greeks unified the finite and infinite, but suppressed it in caves, traditional imagery, and the dim recesses of memory. The Romans were adept at differentiation, but sundered the ethical life into private self-consciousness on one side and abstract universality on the other. Only in Germanic civilization did the two realms of the spirit and its world plunge into infinite grief and achieve reconciliation. When Hegel cast his gaze across the Atlantic Ocean, he saw nothing but gradations of backwardness and weakness. He told students that even the animals and fauna were inferior in America. Hegel allowed that "America" was "the country of the future" and its world-historical importance was yet to be revealed, but North and South America were still too backward and weak to matter. In both cases the "dregs of European society" conquered native peoples, destroyed their cultures, and established poor imitations of superior European societies that were far from reaching Enlightenment status. Meanwhile the German state organically unified substantive knowing and willing, Germanic religion unified the representation of its truth with its ideal essentiality, and Germanic philosophy unified the free comprehension of truth with the state, the natural world, and the ideal world.[22]

This vainglorious assertion of Germanic superiority occurred barely fifty years after the Industrial Revolution made it imaginable. Argentine/Mexican liberationist philosopher Enrique Dussel presses the point that European dominance was "just a few decades old" when Hegel proclaimed that the Spirit developed along the shores of the Mediterranean, seeped into Southern Europe, survived the "Middle Ages," and reached its highest development in the Northern climes of the modern Germanic and Anglo-Saxon nations. Hegel somehow overlooked that his lens was provincial and very new, distorting what he said about ancient subjects.[23]

This conceit coincided strangely with his acute hermeneutical sensitivity. Hegel had a sophisticated concept of philosophical mediation as being on the same level, dialectically, as the truth it explicates. His mediating hermeneutic was constructive and integrationist, not a destructive external operation conducted after the fact, which made him a better interpreter of ancient texts and early Christian theology than rationalist scholars of his time. But when Hegel held forth about world history, he projected European hegemony backward onto his skewed version of its purported Greek and Christian origins. Dussel stresses that Hegel's colonizing logic obscured that modernity began with the discovery of the New World. Granted, the free cities of medieval Europe in which modernity germinated were tremendously creative. "But modernity as such was 'born' when Europe was in a position to pose itself against an other, when, in other words, Europe could constitute itself as a unified age exploring, conquesting, colonizing an alterity that gave back an image of itself." This colonized other, Dussel observes, was actually covered up, not discovered. It was concealed by European aggression and dominance as the backward nonentity that Europe already presumed. Modernity, as a concept, was born in 1492: "The moment of origin of a very particular myth of sacrificial violence, it also marks the origin of a process of concealment and misrecognition of the non-European." Then the same presumption, occlusion, and violence infected the entire discourse of modernity.[24]

Modernity began when the Mediterranean millennium crumbled. Portugal and Spain opened Europe to the west, Russia opened Europe to the east, and the previously dominant Arab world was enclosed. Spain and Portugal gave way to the British Empire, placing Europe at the center. Dussel describes the discourse of modernity as a succession of proto-Cartesian "I" claims. "I conquer" savaged the Aztec and Inca civilizations, and all of North and South America. "I enslave" swept Africans into chattel slavery. Descartes, Spinoza, Kant, and Hegel successively rendered the Cartesian I as the manifestation of divinity on earth. Nietzsche, proclaiming the death of God, defended the Western conqueror. In fact, Europe died because it deified itself. Kierkegaard said the I opens the world of the subject, and Heidegger said it opens the world of being; Dussel counters that the doyens of existentialism and phenomenology unfailingly fetishized their own world. Even the neo-Marxian Frankfurt school of Max Horkheimer and Theodor Adorno, the best of the European tradition, conjured an ontology of the European center. Dussel argues that Marx was right in claiming that criticism begins with the criticism of religion: "Liberation is possible only when one has the courage to be atheistic vis-à-vis an empire of the center, thus incurring the risk of suffering from its power, its economic boycotts, its armies, and its agents who are experts at corruption, violence, and assassination."[25]

Dussel contrasts his liberationist standpoint to the ideal of cosmopolitan inclusion and reform espoused by Hegel's modernizing children, notably Habermas and Charles Taylor. Liberation ethics, on Dussel's account, challenges the order created by capitalism and imperialism in the form of "a constitutive questioning, one that opens a world from itself, its own road from within itself. It is a metaphysical, transontological praxis—liberation properly so called." Liberation is defiantly anarchic, being the act by which subaltern communities express or realize themselves; however, anarchism is a "reprehensible" form of utopianism, providing no model for the stage after revolutionary destruction. Dussel construes liberation as a double movement, a denial of something denied by the dominant order. To be liberated is to leave the prison (denying the denied) and to affirm the indigenous history that preceded the prison and endures outside it. Liberationist and postcolonial theorists have a role to play in liberation, but "only the praxis of oppressed peoples of the periphery, of the woman violated by masculine ideology, of the subjugated child, can fully reveal it to us."[26]

Cultural anthropologist Walter D. Mignolo builds on Dussel's pioneering work, noting that Hegel organized Kant's cosmopolis on a temporal scale that relocated the spatial distribution of Asia, Africa, America, and Europe in a chronological order supposedly marking the direction of history. Suddenly, the entire planet was said to live in different temporalities, "with Europe in the present and the rest in the past." Time became a fundamental concept of colonial reality. The present was modern and civilized, the past was traditional and uncivilized, and people were closer to nature the longer ago they lived. Colonialism transposed geography into chronology and time into a colonizing tool, separating Europe from its own past, now marked as the Middle Ages. Then modern Europe established itself as the present by creating, in Diana Hugh's phrase, "the otherness of the past and the past of the other." Geopolitically, Mignolo observes, the transposition of geography into chronology was a fateful achievement, serving "as the justification of the ideology of progress and, in the twentieth century, of development and underdevelopment."[27]

Romance studies scholar Bruno Bosteels observes that the ravages of capitalism and colonialism should at least trigger a bad conscience among Hegel's successors: "The question then becomes whether there are not also elements within Hegel's method and system, no doubt starting with the very notion of bad conscience as unhappy consciousness, that would enable the recognition of the non-European. Even the project of a universal history might not be beyond salvage." Intellectual historian Susan Buck-Morss contends that such a project is salvageable *and* imperative. The universal story of freedom struggle that must be told rips the historical facts about freedom out of the self-centered stories told by the victors: "The project of universal freedom does not need to be discarded but, rather, redeemed and reconstituted on a different basis."[28]

It begins by telling the stories concealed by colonial and other forms of oppressive power. It ratchets to a higher level by refashioning Hegel's project, philosophy of history, now looking for philosophical truth in traces of nonidentity. Bosteels reflects that such a project raises error, failure, and alienation into a new principle, the opposite of Hegel's fiction.

Postcolonial theorist Gayatri Chakravorty Spivak puts the latter point sharply, cautioning that any critique of the Hegelian morphology from within must commit a "mistaken" reading of its own "because it attempts to engage the (im)possible perspective of the 'native informant,' a figure who, in ethnography, can only provide data, to be interpreted by the knowing subject for reading." There is no correct scholarly model for this undertaking: "It is, strictly speaking, 'mistaken,' for it attempts to transform into a reading position the site of the 'native informant' in anthropology, a site that can only *be* read, by definition, for the production of definite descriptions. It is an (im)possible perspective." Spivak takes no interest in searching for Hindu contemporaries of Hegel who reacted to Hegel. By the late nineteenth century, India had pro-Hegelian versions of the *Gita*, "and these will come from Indian 'nationalists.'" Kant and Hegel might have made better use of their information, but the deeper problem was insuperable.[29]

Any attempt to incorporate non-Europeans into Hegel's scheme founders on two devastating facts: non-Europeans were not historical subjects to Hegel, and they are lost to us, even as objects of the anthropological gaze. Bosteels cautions that the subaltern cannot be fitted to a global logic. A truly global history lets the subaltern speak in ways that do not fit any logical scheme. Spivak explains, "The historian must persist in *his* efforts in this awareness, that the subaltern is necessarily the absolute limit of the place where history is narrativized into logic. It is a hard lesson to learn, but not to learn it is merely to nominate elegant solutions to be correct theoretical practice."[30]

This is the upshot of the postmodern interpretation of Hegel pioneered by Žižek and amplified by Nancy. Now Hegel is construed, as Bosteels observes, as a thinker of nonidentity, "or even of alterity, albeit in spite of himself." Instead of subsuming the particular under an empty universal, the postmodern Hegel is a theorist of pure singularity—the event—and of encounter. Instead of correlating the status quo with the positivity of the infinite, the postmodern Hegel invites us to throw ourselves "into the most extreme experience of self-divestiture." Catherine Malabou, a protégé of Derrida, similarly reads Hegel as a protodeconstructionist by focusing on Hegel's discussions of temporality and the formation of a concept, which she calls "plasticity." Moreover, Malabou addresses the counterfactual subject that Nancy avoids: the Hegelian state. Hegel reversed Rousseau, she argues. Rousseau grasped that in modern states, the desire of the self for recognition requires a subjective individual component and an objective political community. Hegel united Rousseau's divided subject by reconciling the subject and the political community through the state, conceiving the general will as the language of a linguistic community preceding the individual will *and* the political community. The Hegelian state synthesized the political languages of contracts and individual self-expression with a shadowy religious language uniting the particular and the universal. This religious dimension of the state, Malabou argues, is the Hegelian ground of having faith in one's self and the other. Without God there is no forgiveness and no assurance of the value of one's being.[31]

Adorno, throughout his career, and Derrida, in his later career, similarly grasped that we are never done with Hegel. Adorno caught the significance of Hegel's grappling with negativity, division, and nonidentity, cautioning readers not to rush to Hegel's speculative reconciliation, although he acknowledged that Hegel was ultimately a theorist of identity and reconciliation. Adorno fled Nazi Germany in 1934, lived in London and New York, coauthored *Dialectic of Enlightenment* with Horkheimer, and returned in 1949 to Frankfurt, where he mentored Habermas, who grew up during the Nazi era. Habermas was sixteen years old when World War II ended. The revelations of the Nuremburg Trials shocked him to his core, driving him to his first intellectual passion: the Frankfurt school of Adorno, Horkheimer, and Herbert Marcuse.[32]

As a student in the 1950s, Habermas lived intellectually in the 1920s, enthralled by Georg Lukács' *History and Class Consciousness* (1923). He studied the history of German thought to understand how Germany had fallen into fascism. He mastered Kant, Fichte, Schelling, Hegel, and Marx, interpreting Marx through Lukács. In 1953 Habermas read Heidegger's reissued *Introduction to Metaphysics* (1935, 1953) and was stunned at Heidegger's fawning allusion to the "inner truth and greatness" of the Nazi movement. Habermas called out Heidegger for an explanation; Heidegger's silence confirmed Habermas' conviction that German philosophy had failed when it mattered. Habermas studied American pragmatism and democracy, especially Charles Sanders Peirce, George Herbert Mead, and John Dewey, completed his doctoral dissertation at Bonn in 1954 on Schelling's idealism, and wrote his first book on the historical development of civil society. He came early to his signature idea that certain basic structures, rules, and categories are presupposed by reason and communicative action. His first attempt to construct a systematic framework for an interdisciplinary social theory, *Knowledge and*

Human Interests (1968), mixed a Kantian transcendental argument with a neo-Hegelian argument about the universal conditions of communicative action. On the one hand, Habermas said that reason self-reflectively grasps the universal conditions of theoretical knowledge. On the other hand, he described self-reflection as the liberation of the subject from its dependence on hypostatized powers of reason.[33]

Knowledge and Human Interests was essentially epistemological, assuming a Cartesian/Kantian/Husserlian focus on consciousness. Habermas played up the logical connections between his twin concepts of self-reflection, not yet believing there was a crucial choice to be made between them. Then he decided that his Kantian transcendentalism was a barrier to understanding human rationality as communicative action. Though Habermas retained Kant's desire to establish the universal conditions of reason, he dropped its a priori reasoning about puzzles of consciousness, taking his famous "linguistic turn." To make progress in philosophy, and hopefully to change the world, he focused on the public, empirical, world-changing concept of reason pioneered by Hegel and Marx: self-reflection as emancipation.

One side of his work focused on the dilemmas of the modern state. Habermas argued in *Legitimation Crisis* (1973) that the state is constantly in crisis because it cannot meet the demands of modern society to simultaneously solve problems, advance democracy, and support cultural identity. In this situation, he said, philosophy cannot be the sole basis of normative reflection that it was for Kant; philosophy must work in tandem with social science. Habermas' next work, *Sprachpragmatik und Philosophie* (1976), later folded into an English book titled *Communication and the Evolution of Society* (1979), expounded his groundbreaking program of "universal pragmatics"—a reconstruction of the universal conditions of understanding through a philosophy of language, speech act theory. Habermas argued that communicative action is a distinct type of social action oriented to mutual understanding. Other types of social action such as conflict, competition, and strategic angling are derivatives of communicative action, geared to success or some utilitarian end. Communicative action cares only about reaching understanding (*verständigungsorientiert*). Anyone who acts communicatively must raise universal validity claims and believe that such claims can be validated.[34]

In this telling, there are four types of validity claims—comprehensibility, truth, truthfulness (sincerity), and normative rightness—and all are at least implicit in every speech act. To make a universal validity claim is to utter something understandably, give the hearer something to understand, make oneself understandable, and achieve an understanding with another person. Habermas stressed that his model of communicative action replaced the Cartesian focus on a single subject of consciousness with a dialogical focus on a speaker and hearer who are oriented to a mutual reciprocal understanding. Whenever a breakdown in communication occurs, we should adopt a level of discourse and argument in which we justify the validity claims that have been called into question. Only the best and truest arguments should prevail: "The goal of coming to an understanding is to bring about an agreement that terminates in the intersubjective mutuality of reciprocal understanding, shared knowledge, mutual trust, and accord with one another."[35]

He was willing to be a guardian of universal rationality against the upsurge of postmodern attacks on universal everything. Habermas' two-volume *Theory of Communicative Action* (1981) developed a critique of modernity and a reconstructive theory of it. He recounted how reason was embodied in the modern political realm, which established republican forms of government and the importance of civil society, and in the economic realm, which established a social space for the free pursuit of individual self-interests. He explored the rise of modern bureaucracy, Max Weber's critique of the iron cage, and the Frankfurt school contention that Marx was wrong about the emancipating future of scientific-technological progress. Habermas argued that the Frankfurt school brought critical theory to a dead end by charting the repressive triumph of instrumental reason over all spheres of life. The subjective forces that Marx believed would overthrow capitalism were colonized in every sphere of modern life, rationalizing the "lifeworld"—Habermas' conceptual complement to communicative action. He introduced this concept in volume one, developed it in volume two, distinguished it from a system, and integrated it with his two-level social theory—an analysis of communicative rationality as the rational potential built into everyday speech and a theory of modern society. Habermas contended that modern rationality is worth saving, but not the one-sided version of it that colonizes the lifeworld and deflated the Frankfurt school.[36]

Systems, on his account, are predefined modes of coordination in which nonlinguistic media are dominant and the demands of communicative action are minimized. Markets and bureaucracies, for example, are structured contexts in which money or institutional power drives most of the coordinating action. In lifeworld contexts, by contrast, consensual modes of coordination hold sway. Civil society is a theater of lifeworld contexts: families, schools, civic associations, neighborhoods, religious communities, and other sites where people have to acquire the skills of cooperative rationality. Habermas describes the lifeworld as the constellation of contexts, resources, and dimensions of action that enable agents to cooperate on the basis of mutual understanding. He inspired an academic industry of commentary by making a subtle, complex, painstaking, sometimes polemical case for the importance of communicative rationality. Habermas claims that philosophers never got over the trauma of their failure to solve the riddles of subjectivity, so philosophy still abounds in Cartesian conceptions of self, language, and society. Meanwhile, social science is usually too large or too small, recycling large-scale theories that don't explain very much and micro-studies that don't try to explain very much. Habermas made a target of himself by pressing both points.[37]

Above all, he stirred controversy as a critic of the postmodern upsurge. In *The Philosophical Discourse of Modernity* (1985), Habermas took aim at both streams of postmodern theory deriving from Nietzsche's attack on subject-centered reason. The Heidegger/Derrida line is about being and language, while the Georges Bataille/Michel Foucault line is a critique of power. Habermas rejects the ontological dichotomy between Being and beings that grounds the Heidegger/Derrida dichotomy between worldview structures and whatever appears within these worlds. Heidegger hypostatized the aspect of language that discloses worlds, crafting a linguistic historicism wrapped in a vaguely religious language about the "destining of Being" and "truth-occurrences." Habermas argues that the entire Heideggerian tradition wrongly separates meaning from validity, undercutting propositional truth and the value of discursive argument. Philosophy should discern the dialectical interdependence between historically shaped understandings of the world and the experiences and practices that are possible within the world. Heidegger, however, ignored the reciprocal connection between propositional truth and truth-as-disclosure, reducing propositional truth to truth-as-disclosure.[38]

Habermas judges that Heidegger's vaunted overcoming of metaphysics is really a hyper-temporal foundationalism that refuses to engage or even describe concrete historical reality. Empirical arguments and discursive reasoning are disdained as low-class, consigned to the realm of the ontic. Derrida's aesthetic play with language extended this mentality, obliterating the genre distinction between philosophy and literature. Against Derrida, Habermas distinguishes between the communicative action of everyday discourse and poetic discourse. In some contexts the poetic function of language predominates, but in others it plays a subordinate role, contrary to Derrida's grammatology, which says nothing about the capacity of language to solve problems. Derrida was consumed by the capacity of language to create a world. Habermas concedes that Derrida actually studied language (unlike Heidegger), and he dismissed the later Heidegger's "network of metaphors." But Derrida spurned the role of communicative action in science, law, economics, political science, and ethics, recycling from Heidegger "the familiar melody of the self-overcoming of metaphysics," which yielded the baleful deconstructionist trope that philosophy is just a form of writing.[39]

Habermas renders the other postmodern tradition more favorably because Bataille and Foucault did not mystify "Being" and Foucault inaugurated a field of research. Bataille investigated things excluded from the world of utilitarian efficiency, which he called the "other of reason," while Foucault unmasked the struggle for power in all forms of knowledge. Both fixed on Nietzsche's idea that reason is a disguised and perverted servant of the will to power; the aim of criticism is to expose the power that reason serves. Thomas McCarthy notes that Habermas respects Foucault for his creative research agenda, which amplified the Frankfurt school project of discerning power claims in theoretical and practical reason. To the extent that Foucault's genealogical unmasking can be described as a transcendental historiography supplementing Marxian criticism and the sociology of knowledge, Habermas finds it useful.[40]

But Habermas protests that Foucault went far beyond this description, destroying under a fancy cover, "deconstruction." Unlike Kant, Hegel, and Marx, who critiqued reason rationally, Foucault attacked reason in the name of a destructive rhetorical "other" of reason. Habermas confesses that reading Foucault is "irritating" to him. Foucault played a double game without acknowledging it—employing genealogy as an empirical analysis of the technologies of power underlying social science *and* as a transcendental analysis of scientific discourse. He used genealogy to get around the problems of meaning, validity, and value that he spurned as holdovers from the Enlightenment, but did not escape the contradiction of using reason to criticize reason. Meanwhile he invented an anti-humanist glossary to substitute for the loss of meaning, validity, and value. Habermas puts it sharply: "Foucault's dramatic influence and his iconoclastic reputation could hardly be explained if the cool facade of radical historicism did not simply hide the passions of aesthetic modernism. Genealogy is overtaken by a fate similar to that which Foucault had seen in the human sciences: To the extent that it retreats into the reflectionless objectivity of a nonparticipatory, ascetic description of kaleidoscopically changing practices of power, genealogical historiography emerges from its cocoon as precisely the *presentistic, relativistic, cryptonormative* illusory science that it does not want to be."[41]

Habermas justly protests that flattening modern society and culture to power is one-sided. Modern law and ethics are tools of domination *and* emancipation; their normalizing function is not oppressive-only. What we need is a dialectic that recognizes the bad, the good, the ambiguous, and their interrelation. Hegel offered the first workable framework for the problem of modern society by separating the political sphere of the state from civil society. Moreover, he rightly conceived reason as a healing power of unity and reconciliation.

Habermas commends Hegel for integrating the opposition between modernity and antiquity into a theory of society: in civil society, each member is one's own end, but no member can attain one's ends except through contact with others. Every particular end assumes the form of universality through its relation to other people and is attained along with and through the welfare of others. Hegel's ethic of reconciliation was, and is, the right project. On the other hand, Hegel's institutionalism went far overboard, reflecting his Prussian comfort. The early Hegel had an ethical intersubjective concept of communicative reason, but the later Hegel elevated the state to the reality of the substantive will. He grew so crusty that he snorted against the reform movement in England and bound the individual will to the institutional order, prizing the higher subjectivity of the state over the subjective freedom of the individual. Habermas is more Hegelian than the later Hegel: "A different model for the mediation of the universal and the individual is provided by the *higher-level intersubjectivity of an uncoerced formation of will* within a community existing under the constraints toward cooperation." Free and equal persons should achieve a coercion-free consensus that bears the stamp of universality and retains the right of appeal. Habermas calls philosophy back to the Young Hegelian moment when Marx criticized philosophy for changing nothing, after which philosophers turned to Nietzsche, Heidegger, and irrationalism. The remedy is to conceive reason as communicative action and achieve the cooperative order of a fully realized social democracy.[42]

Many have adopted this proposal as a point of departure, notably Kenneth Baynes, Seyla Benhabib, Nancy Fraser, Hille Haker, Axel

Honneth, David Ingram, Christopher Latiolais, and Rudolf Siebert. Fraser and Honneth are especially significant for conceiving justice as struggles over both economic redistribution and cultural recognition, with the difference that Honneth conceives recognition as fundamental and redistribution as derivative, whereas Fraser conceives the two categories as cofundamental. Fraser's subsequent work added a third dimension, arguing that political representation is also a cofundamental dimension of justice. All theorists in the Habermas tradition of critical theory grapple with the Hegel-like dilemmas that Habermas poses for interpreters and translators. His book *Die Einbeziehung des anderen* describes a fragile and fragmented process of drawing in and taking regard, negotiating between cultural differences and republican principles, but the English translation, *The Inclusion of the Other*, suggests an accomplished fact of inclusion. Debates over this suggestion are tellingly fractious, interrogating the political limits of conversation, how given communities are excluded from conversation, and whether cosmopolitan ordering is just an updated version of assimilation. The ideal is always to conceive civil society as a pluralistic sphere in which citizens define the terms of their common life, conducting inclusive democratic arguments about collective norms, social policies, and political decisions. This ideal practically invites suspicion as a balm for the bad conscience of liberals or a ploy by managers and corporations to preserve the dominant order.[43]

Sharon Welch's work in feminist social ethics luminously exemplifies the push and pull of conversation, liberation, and needing to work together, in her case in three career phases. In her early career she combined a sisterhood-is-powerful version of radical feminism with Foucault's deconstruction. In her second phase she accepted black feminist critiques of white feminist essentialism, combined Habermas and liberationist criticism, and formulated a feminist ethic of risk. In her third phase she pulled back from liberationist criticism, contending that progressives must relearn how to support leaders and work together.[44]

Her first book, *Communities of Solidarity and Resistance* (1985), was published just before she dropped theology. Welch treasured liberation theology for its witness against oppression, but rejected its claims to truth. James Cone contended that non-liberationist understandings of the gospel are heretical; Welch replied that all such contentions smack of special pleading. As a female oppressed by every version of Christian orthodoxy, she wanted nothing to do with the language of orthodoxy/heresy. Moreover, her oppressor status as a white American made her doubly skeptical of liberationist truth claims, because she knew from personal experience that Christianity blends easily with structures of oppression. It was naïve and dangerous, she argued, to say that only liberation theology is "truly" Christian. To take that line is to claim an exception from the contingent temporality of theological discourse, which is not credible even for something as admirable as liberation theology.[45]

Liberation theology, to Welch, was a valuable form of the revolutionary strand in Christianity. She identified with its radical consciousness and praxis, not its appeal to Christian norms, reasoning that liberationist faith is true if it liberates oppressed persons. Nothing is added to the truth of liberationist claims by claiming continuity with biblical or dogmatic norms. Welch disclaimed any interest in the question of unbelief. To her, the feminist movement and parts of the peace movement were liberating because they were "intrinsically relative" enterprises devoted to the abolition of domination: "I find in sisterhood a commitment to liberation and an openness to different ways of understanding and reaching liberation." She did not see much liberation under Christian auspices: "In sisterhood there is freedom from a self-securing that requires absolutizing one's perspective. In the Christian tradition, however, I find a pathological obsession with security, an obsession that impels the denial of difference (thus concern with heresy and essences), an obsession that leads to a blinding Christian triumphalism, an obsession that receives symbolic expression in the concept of the sovereignty of God."[46]

On feminism, Welch invoked Mary Daly: sisterhood is the ultimate revolution. On morality, she invoked Foucault: all forms of moral discourse contain rhetorical strategies to gain power. Liberation theology is liberating *when* it acknowledges its drive for emancipating power *without* making dogmatic ethical claims. Welch said the language of universal values is repugnant because it reeks of privilege and masks its struggle for control. Every language of universality is an instrument of privilege and domination. One needs a privileged education to learn about ontological categories and universal values; universal languages are spoken by ruling groups precisely to avoid having to relinquish their power. When token exceptions from excluded groups speak a supposedly universal language, they negate their own dignity. The category of "equal rights," for example, masks discrimination and rewards token exceptions. Welch declared, "It would be an act of the greatest folly for me to criticize sexism on the grounds of universally recognized values such as equality, the nature of moral persons, or any other determination of what characterizes the human, and thus women, as such." It seemed absurd to "use the very categories that masked my oppression in order to denounce it." She said the rhetoric of equal rights was not much of an ally in the struggle for feminist gains. What mattered were particular acts of resistance to male domination. Feminism moved forward when women raised their voices, refused to be treated as sexual objects, and smashed patriarchal assumptions.[47]

In her second phase Welch let go of Christian theology, gravitated to social ethics and women's studies, and sought to formulate a feminist ethic. She stopped talking about feminist sisterhood after reading black feminist and womanist critiques of white feminism. "Risk" became her central theme. Following womanist ethicist Emilie Townes, Welch conceived social ethics as the study of social structures, processes, and communities, especially "socially shared patterns of moral judgments and behavior." If the shared social structures and patterns of morality are immoral, how does one get to something better? Welch's ethic of community and solidarity stressed the necessity of taking risks, the lack of a feminist ethic of conflict, and the indispensability of community. Feminist ethics, she argued, puts a premium on accountability and respect, not on intellectual justification and universality. To be accountable is to confront the existence of harm and inequality of power. Townes described accountability as "a respect-filled communal dialogue with a trans-class base." Welch added that to be respectful is to recognize the dignity, equality, and independence of others.[48]

That led her to Habermas, needing an account of how respectful communities share principles, rules, and customs, and how multiple communities speaking different moral languages might interact. Welch adopted Habermas' argument that cultivating public conversations among diverse communities requires an ethic of communicative action. At the same time she rejected his method of prescribing liberal norms of civility and rationality, forbidding privileged claims and appeals to authoritative traditions, and seeking a pluralistic consensus. Welch argued that the communicative model is liberating only if it rests on prior commitments to solidarity and concrete justice-making actions. It is not very transformative merely to join an ongoing conversation, and solidarity is a better goal than consensus. Moreover, it is disrespectful to require participants from oral cultures to relinquish their traditions. Human beings are more than rational actors; mere agreement is less important than mutual transformation toward liberation: "When mutual transformation occurs, there is the power of empathy and compassion, of delight in otherness, and strength in the solidarity of listening to others, bearing together stories of pain and resistance."[49]

Welch reasoned that a feminist ethic should move "from critique to action and back to critique." Lacking a basis in action, critique devours the critic's hope and energy. Mere criticism leads to numbness, a cynical despair at the futility of caring or seeing: "Without working with others on projects geared toward social change, it is impossible to maintain the vision and energy necessary to sustain long-term work." Middle-class people who hang back from justice struggles are prime candidates for cynical despair. The numbness of middle-class privilege is a deadening by-product of the luxury of being able to avoid oppressed and excluded people. Disengagement leads to cynicism, a distorted form of rage reflecting the vicious cycle of disengagement. Cynics view victims merely as victims. Engaged activists, Welch argued, see larger realities and opportunities: "As long as critique occurs in the context of work for justice, it is possible to experience the essential factor in maintaining resistance—love for oneself, for the oppressed, and for those working against oppression."[50]

She acknowledged that early white feminism universalized the experiences of privileged white women in the name of "women's experience." Daly, Rosemary Ruether, and many others described patriarchy as the fundamental form of oppression and women's liberation as a universal cause, an account sharply rejected by Audre Lorde, Jacquelyn Grant, and Katie Cannon. But Welch implored that the poststructuralist denigration of personal experience is not a corrective. There is such a thing as referring to experience hermeneutically as a process or discursive strategy, eschewing essentialist presumptions. Moreover, the appeal to experience is a staple of womanist and Latina literature. Rejecting experience as a hermeneutical category does not solve any of the conflicts of interpretation and interest that exist within liberation movements. What is needed is an ethic of criticism that accepts the inevitability of conflict between and within liberationist movements.[51]

Welch had one more adjustment to make, which occurred during her tenure as president of Meadville Lombard Theological School. Her stewardship of a Unitarian Universalist seminary and her sympathetic support of Barack Obama's presidency gave her second thoughts about the activist cast of her work. I shared conference platforms with Welch at which I lamented that Obama was wasting a crisis opportunity and she replied that progressives must learn how to support reasonably good leaders. She surprised herself by telling audiences that Reinhold Niebuhr now made sense to her, and not just as a sellout. If one is responsible for leading a progressive institution and ensuring its survival, what sense does it make to rattle on about breaking the system? Later she wrote a book version, summarizing her argument in the title, *After the Protests Are Heard* (2019). Welch describes a cascade of hopeful experiments in community economics, recommending a "try everything" attitude. She says that protest activism has its place, but gains for justice are concretized by institutions, and institutions do not succeed in our fragmented, postmodern, media- and market-saturated society without leaders who hold them together and depend on a certain amount of supportive, slack-cutting good will. To undermine whatever progressive institutions we happen to have is reactionary, not liberating.[52]

Hegel, Marx, Tillich, Love, Power, and Justice

My commitment to a Christian socialist idealism that emphasizes struggle and tragedy, accepts liberationist criticism, and shares the pluralist concern with working together shapes what I take from Hegel and Tillich. Hegel is both alien to me and distinctly the thinker with whom I am never done. Marx and Kierkegaard scored against Hegel by emphasizing the situation of the knower, but both were one-sided compared to Hegel, not even trying to stand for reconciliation. Levinas scored against Hegel by railing against the constraints of ontology and upholding the priority of the ethical, but anti-ontology is still a form of ontology, mirroring what it repudiates, with no basis for claiming to know anything. Levinas repeated Kierkegaard's experience of mirroring what he denounced, which was, at bottom, the very commitment of philosophy to find the truth. Hegel had a better idea by relating God and the world dialectically, preserving unity and difference with a tragic sensibility that caught the infinite love-anguish of Calvary. Tillich caught some of Hegel's best tropes while assuming too much the right-Hegelian reading of Hegel and the Marxian critique of ethical idealism.

Tillich folded Hegel's analysis of love, anguish, and power into a theory about the unity of love, power, and justice, conceiving each as an integral moment of a whole. The power of being is its capacity to affirm itself against inner and external nonbeing. A self becomes powerful by absorbing nonbeing in self-affirming fashion. To conquer separation is to gain power, and love is the power that unites the separated. Thus love is the foundation of power, not its negation. Whatever makes reunion impossible is against love. Love is compelled to destroy whatever is against love, employing compulsory power when necessary. Tillich described this compulsion and destruction as the tragic aspect of love—love participating in the negation of whatever opposes love. If being is the power of being, and the power of being is actualized as the negation of negation, justice is the power of being actualizing itself. The same structures and dynamics of self-actualization that underlie love and power underlie justice. Justice preserves the independence and integrity of whatever is reunited. Justice is immanent in power, since no power of being lacks an adequate form, "but whenever power of being encounters power of being, compulsion cannot be avoided." The test of whether compulsion serves or violates justice is whether it serves or violates the intrinsic claim of a being to be recognized as what it is within the context of all others.[53]

Tillich appreciated that late nineteenth-century neo-Kantians resisted mechanistic materialism by resorting to value theory, carving out a refuge based on self-standing values. But values are not self-standing; all values come from a time and place, lacking a privileged standpoint to judge existence. Thus the neo-Kantian strategies got thinner and thinner. Tillich exuded Hegel's ambition for theology while leaving behind Hegel's excesses. In Christ, Tillich affirmed, God separated God's self from God's self; in the Spirit, God reunites God's self with God's self. This symbolic affirmation points to what matters in Christianity, that God "is not dead identity but the living ground of everything that has life." The essential unity of love, power, and justice is recoverable only through the divine ground in which these realities are united and become integral in human existence. The power of God is that God overcomes estrangement, not that God prevents it. The cross is the symbol of love divine, participating in the destruction of whatever acts against love.[54]

German idealism conveyed what Tillich loved in Lutheran hymnody, Boehme's Lutheran mysticism, and Rilke's poetry. It asserted the principle of identity without grasping its basis, until Kant explained that theoretical knowledge cannot be explained by pointing to the realm of things and that idealism is best conceived as a philosophy of freedom. Thought and being come together as the principle of truth, yielding a philosophy of freedom that fixes on human creativity and subjectivity, asks questions, recognizes absolute demands, appreciates nature and art, and probes for meaning in social movements. The correspondence between reality and the human spirit is in the concept of meaning, where objective and subjective spirit form a unity. Tillich insisted that philosophy has no other basis. If philosophy is a worthy enterprise, it has to be idealistic: "Whenever idealism elaborates the categories that give meaning to the various realms of existence, it seeks to fulfill that task which alone is the justification of philosophy."[55]

But Tillich rendered Hegel and Schelling as system essentialists. On this telling, Hegel and Schelling believed that their categories described reality as a whole, although the later Schelling caught what was wrong with essentialist systems, grasping that reality is the manifestation *and* contradiction of pure essence. Moreover, Tillich said, "human existence itself is an expression of the contradiction of essence." Knowledge of pure essence must wait for contradictions within existence to be recognized and overcome.[56]

That was still a Hegelian way of putting it, appropriating Marx's rejoinder that every vision and concept of harmony is untrue under the conditions of the class struggle, and Kierkegaard's rejoinder that every such vision and concept is untrue under the conditions of sinful human finitude. To Tillich the paradoxical truth of Marxian criticism was intelligible from the Christian standpoint of Kierkegaard and Luther: the greatest possibility of obtaining a truth not tainted by ideology occurs at the point of despair, in the estrangement of human beings from their essential nature.[57]

Tillich had plenty of company in believing that ethical socialism is pointless and that Marxism works better without Marx's utopianism. His unfounded optimism on the second point played a major role in getting the first point wrong. Tillich rightly perceived that Marx's utopianism was the key to almost everything he got wrong about the immanent collapse of capitalism, the inevitability of proletarian revolution, and the anarcho-syndical paradise of the future. Thus he stripped Marxism to reverse-Hegelian dialectic, figuring that a Marxism shorn of utopian expectation and dogmatism would be more credible. But Marxism was not an otherwise solid worldview with a utopian husk, or a substitute for ethical struggle.

Marx's revolutionary expectation took the place of God, ethical claims, anthropology, the state, and prosaic politics. Believing in the inevitability of the revolution and its utopian promise relieved Marx of needing to bother with messy anthropological and political questions, let alone religious questions. Tillich rationalized that Marx preserved the creative meaning of Hegel's dialectic; thus his unfortunate eschatology could be shucked off. For a while, in the 1930s, Tillich and Niebuhr agreed about that. But Marx did not preserve the creative meaning of Hegel's dialectic. He stripped a mechanistic interpretation of the dialectic to economic determinism, casting off Hegel's obsession with the divine and human spirit of freedom. Overthrowing the capitalist system of production and exchange would somehow transform everything and everybody. To Marx this "somehow" contained no miracle, as Tillich called it. It was as inevitable and materially determined as the self-destruction of capitalism.

Neo-Hegelian Theology

Hegel's concept of the absolute idea, though caricatured as a grandiose fiction, in fact restated Aristotle's principle that the knower and the known have a transparent relationship. In a crucial sense, the thinker and the thinker's thoughts are one. The absolute idea is a logical abstraction, the scheme or form of self-consciousness. Hegel's idea of absolute Spirit, on the other hand, is metaphysical, dealing with facts of existence. Here lies the crucial Hegelian puzzle. Did Hegel fuse the categories of logic and metaphysics, unfolding his logic *as* a metaphysic? Did he identify reason with experience, or leave room for a relation of corresponding reciprocity between them? On the closed-system interpretation, Hegel taught that nature is the logical idea in the form of otherness, whether or not he claimed to describe anything that actually occurred.

Hegel did not, in fact, claim to describe anything factual, just as he did not conceive the idea as being factually antecedent to nature and Spirit. Hegel's system is an abstraction, not a description of a factual process. Nature and the thought determinations comprising the absolute idea are abstractions existing within the life of Spirit. The hard question is whether he closed the gap between logic and metaphysics. Hegel learned from Fichte, Schelling, and Hölderlin to extend Kant's analysis of predication: thinking and difference are reflections, respectively, of what they are not—being and identity. The identity of thought and being discloses the capacity of reason to ground itself. The absolute is the result of the self's cancellation of the finite, the negation of the negation—a successive overcoming of finite determinations. This progression culminates in the appearance of the absolute idea, in which reason realizes its absolute other as itself and releases itself into nature, the other of the idea.

Schelling and Hegel got that far together, tracking the reflexive unfolding of reason. Post-Kantian idealism is founded on the dialectical experience of thought. But Hegel ostensibly went on to derive the actual world of existence from the logic of the concept, claiming that reason concerns itself with the in-itself of things. This in-itself is not the fact that things exist, nor even their being; to Hegel it was the concept, the essence (*Wesen*). Schelling protested that according to Hegel the nature of human beings and of plants remains the same whether or not people or plants exist on earth. On this telling, Hegel did not bridge the chasm between thought and nature; he leaped across it with sparkling metaphors of deduction. The later Schelling boasted that he never believed he could leap across the chasm. He, too, was an absolute idealist who loved Spinoza, but he never claimed that philosophy deals only with the essence of things. Moreover, though Schelling dropped his early Romanticism, he continued to say that philosophy is like poetry and art in needing the voice of feeling and that Hegel's logic overwhelmed nature and subjectivity.[58]

Post-Kantian idealism was about thought reflecting what it is not—being—as itself, even as thought appears not to be itself. Knowledge depends on movement, not being read off from any particular thing. But Schelling stressed that logic can only deliver a reflection of thought, contrary to Hegel, for whom reason sought to know itself in being to the point where contradictions ceased and Spirit is self-realized. Schelling countered that the virtual world of the concept and the actual world of existence, though inseparable, cannot be demonstrated to reflect each other. There must be a slight asymmetry in the identity of thought and being in which the expansive force of thought—the ideal—is slightly stronger than the contractive force of being. Identity is the *condition* of divine revelation through creation, the divine lure of desire that thrives in the interplay of contrary forces.

That was very close to Hegel's actual position, but Schelling charged that Hegel's system, despite featuring movement, had no real *other* to the necessity of reason. Thus it had no real God, no actual chain of events, no real opposition, no real freedom, and no God that freely relates to the world. It was not even correct to speak of real history or development in Hegel's system, because Hegel had no room for a future that is not already contained in the concept. Schelling acknowledged that Hegel said contrary things in his lectures on religion, where he Christianized his system by allowing the absolute spirit to freely create a world and to "externalize itself with freedom into a world." The later Hegel, on this telling, set reason free in order to build up a theological school. But Schelling judged that Hegel never quite worked up to the Christian God. His proof was that Hegel never said that at the creation of the world Hegelianism was an impossible thought. Thus his system inadvertently showed why Christian thinking must begin with, not work up to, the Christian God.[59]

Schelling hammered Hegel on his weakest point, he did so in the name of post-Kantian freedom and subjectivity, and he sealed his ostensible victory by exaggerating Hegel's panlogical system, inspiring Kierkegaard to escalate the same argument. Kierkegaard's many successors charge that Hegel wrongly domesticated the space between the finite and the infinite; today the leading exponent of this claim is Irish Catholic philosopher William Desmond. In *Hegel's God* (2003) Desmond says that the Christian God wholly transcends nature and humanity, but Hegel construed God's transcendence entirely in terms of human self-transcending. Hegel's God is self-creating and immanent—a self-determining being in which the relating to an other that occurs is purely a self-completing immanence, or holism, closing the middle space between the finite and the infinite. Desmond coined a name for this Hegelian process, "sublationary infinitism." Hegelian theology, in his account, is an erotic of self-creation lacking agape and the creation of a genuinely other world. Logically it leads to post-religious humanism, exactly as the original left-Hegelians claimed, although Desmond chides that today's postmodern Hegelian atheists are "blandly bourgeois" by comparison: "The humanists of the revolutionary Left have been overtaken by the humanists of postreligious persuasion for whom the critique of religion is not the basis of all critique; it is just an embarrassment."[60]

Desmond says that "pious" Hegelians read Hegel too innocently, yielding a simplistic Hegel who defended Christianity; "impious" Hegelians read Hegel too suspiciously, yielding a simplified Hegel who was out to destroy Christianity; the point of convergence for both groups is Hegel's immanent God, construed either as pantheism or atheism; and the truth is that Hegel contrived a modern semi-Christian religion that prized the state as "the more ultimate ethical community than the religious community of spirit." Desmond renders Hegel's logic as S(S-O)—the subject is the relation of subject and object, the basis of Hegel's pantheistic religion. He protests that postmodern interpreters trawl through Hegel's works in search of terms like *entlassen* to make Hegel come out postmodern, loosening the logic of self-return. According to Desmond, Hegel taught that I begin and end with myself, being in relation to myself when I relate to an object. To be sure, he allows, Hegel spoke occasionally about the divine idea releasing the other "to exist as a free and independent being," and sometimes Hegel wrote of divine love. But the language of self-return predominates in Hegel's work, because Hegelianism is about coming to self in one's other.[61]

I concur with Desmond that Hegel featured self-return language, his religion of the state was highly problematic, he made equivocal claims that sparked the left-right split in early Hegelianism, and there "is no uncontroversial way of reading Hegel." But Desmond completely misses the significance of triple mediation in Hegel's logic. Like most interpreters who describe a closed-system Hegelianism, Desmond sees only one, not three, and he wrongly dismisses the importance of Hegelian *entlassen*, the German equivalent of Latin *absolvere*—to loosen or let go. In Hegel's logic, each of the three elements of universality, particularity, and individuality mediates the other two. We are not left with a forced choice between identity and difference. Everything rational preserves identity and difference through mediation. Desmond contends that Hegel subordinated the economic Trinity to the immanent Trinity and thus erased God's real relations to the world. Nothing is outside Hegel's God, so God's relations to the world are epiphenomenal to God's ideal self-relations. Hegel's God is a counterfeit double, a self-doubling of the pantheist One. Many have said so, similarly pushing aside what Hegel said he believed: monism is wrong, pantheism is impossible, letting go occurs, and the economic Trinity of God, world, and real relations is primary. Desmond charges that Hegel eliminated the asymmetry between the transcendent God of Christianity and the created world of finite humanity. But Christian theology has debated from its beginning how the relation of God to the world should be conceived if God is everywhere and every person bears the image of God.[62]

Hegel's rendering of the economic Trinity *was* novel and arguably heterodox—two points in his favor, on my view. Hodgson notes that to Hegel, God's logical self-othering—the immanent Trinity—is a *condition* of empirical relations. Others affect God without negating God only if God is inwardly complex. The economic Trinity subsumes or includes the immanent Trinity, the opposite of orthodox Christianity, such that history is constitutive of the divine life, not a sideshow. Hegel sought to give difference its due by replacing abstract identity with recognition. As Hodgson says, "The Hegelian totality is the very antithesis of sameness, of totalitarian hegemony." Hegel's triad of logic-nature-spirit has no absolute primacy, no founding, and no grounding. Each element of his triadic mediation assumes the middle position and is mediated by the others, and the third term is never the same as the first. Hegel posited no master syllogism and no single order among the members of a dialectical relation. "Totalizing" is precisely what he repudiated when he spurned Schelling's philosophy of identity, "the night when all cows are black."[63]

Hegel's God is the luminosity in which colors are discriminated. He employed the terms "totality" (*Totalität*) and "integral whole" (*Ganzheit*) interchangeably, conceiving totality *as* an integral whole. God is the Spirit as totality because the holistic Trinity is a spiral of concentric relations: Father within Son within Spirit. Hodgson notes that Hegel reversed the orthodox Trinitarian procession—rendering the spiral through the Son into the Spirit—to move away from the abstract Supreme Being. Hegelian "totality" is about differentiation, color, concreteness, and wholeness. It is not pantheist because Hegel's concept of God as the totality as Spirit did not even refer to the empirical world as such. God, to Hegel, is the essence upon which everything depends for its existence, *and* this essence is internally concrete as subject and spirit. God is an abiding unity in which differences subsist. Sometimes Hegel smacked of Buddhist emptiness in saying it, as in his 1827 religion lectures: "God is not alongside things, in the interstices, like the God of Epicurus; instead God is actual in the things, but then the things are not actual. This is the ideality of things." He implored his students not to call it pantheism—the "feeble thinking" in which one concludes that the things are God. Spinoza, never feeble, was not a pantheist, because this term conveys the terrible misunderstanding that the *All* should be construed "as a collective totality [*Allesheit*], not as universality [*Allgemeinheit*]." God is the All that remains utterly one as the negativity of the finite, not the apotheosis of the finite.[64]

Absolute spirit, in Hegel's thought, is not a totalizing concept, and neither is absolute knowledge. The absolute of the concluding chapter of *Phenomenology* is not absolutely established or closed in the fashion of definitive metaphysics. Hegel did not say that divine omniscience is imputed to human wisdom. To him, absolute knowledge was philosophical eros, the restless desire for wisdom and love of it, a point stressed by Williams, Hodgson, Stephen Crites, and Andrew Shanks among the religious neo-Hegelians, and by Žižek, Taylor, Malabou, and Nancy. Shanks describes absolute knowing as "ideal know-how," the "very fullest possible truth-as-openness," knowing *how* to discern creative thought. The purpose of *Phenomenology* was to clear away attitudes that block fresh thought.[65]

Hegel had no concept of a static absolute; his self-transformative logic rendered the absolute as radically relative and dynamic. Barth and Levinas, equating the absolute with anti-relative absoluteness, contended that God is only God as the Wholly Other not-something of radical exteriority, the other side of the abyss between finite and infinite, and creature and Creator. But the infinite of Wholly Other transcendence is another finite, limited by its own exteriority. The Hegelian infinite, a whole encompassing otherness, is actually infinite. To know being at all, as Hegel showed in every chapter of *Science of Logic*, is to know being as infinite.

On apophasis, Hegel is problematic at best, owing to the arrogance problem. But there is a basis for contending that Hegel's fluid dialectic left unnoticed room for divine mystery and non-knowing. G. R. G. Mure lined it out in *A Study of Hegel's Logic* (1950), and Williams developed it in *Recognition: Fichte and Hegel on the Other* (1992), showing that Hegel's logic did not completely sublate empirical reality. The Hegel of the closed transcendental system identifies thought and sense as thought: Hegelian subjectivity is monolithic and his system *is* the logic. On this reading, the other is what Feuerbach charged—merely *thought* of the other. But if Hegel did not construct a closed system, he did not wholly identify reason and sense. Thought has a relation of reciprocity to experience. On this interpretation, Hegel conceived the relationship between the science of logic and the philosophies of nature and spirit as corresponding, not identical. His categorical structure may have been a logical mill, but the system was open to the contingencies of the empirical realm. Schelling was right that Hegel never bridged the gap between his logic and his philosophies of nature, spirit, and politics. But that is a weakness only if the ideal is a closed system. Hegel's logical other and empirical other were not the same thing, contrary to a great many books on Hegel.[66]

Hegel construed God as the inexhaustible creativity by which potential differences within divinity are released, creating a world, and by which the divine ideality actualizes itself. Divine creativity is expansive and nothing is outside it—the opposite of Levinas' doctrine that the divine withdraws from the world to leave space for separated beings. Far from eliminating subjectivity, Hegel insisted that substance is not understood until it becomes subject. Far from displacing the really existing lifeworld, Hegel said the lifeworld is real as subject-relative. Far from inflating Kant's transcendental ego, Hegel argued that ideality and reality interact, yielding Spirit. I respect Levinas' resolve to ward off all worldviews that undercut the primacy of ethical action, which he shared with Fichte. But Levinas had consuming Eurocentric conceits of his own, despite living into the 1990s, and Fichte became a raving nationalist—unlike Hegel, who spurned nationalists and anti-Semites. Hegel was neither the state absolutist imagined by Levinas and Karl Popper, nor the triumphal optimist immortalized in textbooks. Supposedly, Hegel taught that freedom is progressively achieved in history and evil gradually disappears. This interpretation, though not entirely wrong, misses Hegel's crucial emphasis on tragedy in history and his anti-theodicy of God's death.[67]

Hegel taught that history is a slaughterhouse, evil is a permanent possibility, international liberal democracy is the best we can do in a brutal world, and God saves the world through tragedy, suffering, and death. His philosophy was a proto-Lutheran theodicy of reconciliation. Luther accentuated the Pauline theme that God self-reveals through suffering and brokenness, not through overpowering force. Good theology, Luther said, approaches everything through what is seen in the suffering and God-forsakenness of Christ: "Because men do not know the cross and hate it, they necessarily love the opposite, namely, wisdom, glory, power, and so on." To be a theologian, one must construe the manifest things of God through suffering and the cross. Hegel, while leaving behind Luther's medieval supernaturalism, agreed that the cross is the lens by which God's relation to the world should be conceived. We are saved by the suffering love of divine grace, not by a nonexistent moral world or the moral order secured by Kant's divine guarantor. Hegel perceived the beauty in the terror of Calvary, where God and death united in divine love. Calvary is rightly construed as a death in God, love divine self-sacrificing in an historical figure. Reconciling cognition is nothing without the actual suffering of the world. Religious consciousness does not start with its inner life, uniting within itself the thought of the divine with existence: "This God is sensuously and directly beheld as a Self, as an actual individual man; only so *is* this God self-consciousness."[68]

World history is a slaughterhouse in which the innocent and the good are annihilated, and history advances to higher stages of development in which the advanced nations possess rights not recognized in lower civilizations. The best and worst of Hegel converged in explicating this theme. He did not teach that might makes right or that progress abolishes evil. Hegel taught that where reconciliation occurs, history becomes a theodicy. He put it plainly in *Lectures on Natural Right, 1817–1818*: "World history is this *divine tragedy* where spirit rises up above pity, ethical life and everything that in other spheres is sacred to it." Wherever nations and peoples have been laid low and afflicted, they *had* to be laid low and afflicted: "World spirit is unsparing and pitiless. Even the finest, highest principle of a people is, as the principle of a particular people, a restricted principle, left behind by the advancing spirit of the age." Hegel liked Schiller's claim that world history is the court of judgment, although Schiller focused on individuals, not historical epochs. Judgment, Hegel argued, is immanent in each moment of history; it is not reserved to the eschatological end. Moreover, there is no world court to judge the nations. Conflicts are settled by war; the only "beyond" of conflict and war is the world spirit, not a court. Hegel put it with a brutality akin to seventeenth-century Calvinism: "No people ever suffered wrong; what it suffered, it deserved. The court of world judgment is not to be viewed as the mere might of spirit."[69]

To say that no people ever suffered wrong, deserving what it suffered, is unspeakably repugnant. It speaks badly for Hegel and the audience he flattered that he went on in this mode without being compelled to say what he did not mean. He did not mean that compassion and moral sorrow for oppressed and vulnerable people are unjustified. Hegel chose a brutal way of expressing his tragic view of history: world history is a divine tragedy, spirit rises above ethical feeling and moral duty, and this rising above the afflicted is part of the tragedy that inheres in every advance in the struggle for freedom and justice. Hegel reads very differently, as Williams says, when his emphasis on the tragedy of life is not screened out. Lutheran theologian Eberhard Jüngel, stressing Hegel's moral recognition of tragedy, argues that Hegel's theology is the antithesis of "might makes right" brutality and realpolitik. Hegel taught that God is spirit, spirit is free, and the mission of world spirit in history is to realize its freedom. Hegel's God is the surge of desire for freedom and justice, albeit through world history as the court of judgment, and colored by Hegel's Eurocentric conceits.[70]

Hegel's justification of God was so suffused with tragic feeling that it qualifies as theodicy only as the negation of it. To Hegel, world history was a theodicy to the extent that the divine achieves reconciliation with tragedy and evil within history. Reconciliation occurs with the negative, but does not eliminate it. Duty conquers by subduing its enemies, but love conquers by overcoming hostility, and love is greater than duty and right. Hegel argued that even the love commandment pales by comparison, for love itself declares no imperative: "It is no universal opposed to a particular, not unity of the concept, but a unity of spirit, divinity. To love God is to feel one's self in the 'all' of life, with no restrictions, in the infinite." Oneness with God is a harmony, not a universal, for the particular in a harmony is in concord, not discord. The early Hegel and the later Hegel said the same thing about love: "Love your neighbor as yourself" does not commend loving your neighbor as much as yourself, for self-love is a meaningless concept. The love commandment is that one should love the other as the creature that one is, recognizing a life similar to one's own.[71]

Jüngel presses the upshot that world historical reflection becomes a theodicy for Hegel only if, but also whenever, reconciliation occurs. In that case, as Williams says, theodicy on Hegel's terms becomes an event of cognitive discernment, not a universal structure or a law of progress as in conventional readings of Hegel. Reconciliation occurs in spite of tragic disaster and in the midst of it. Hegel, putting it evocatively, famously said that reason "is the rose in the cross of the present." There is wonder, delight, and beauty in the present, because subjective freedom has its ground in the divine, but it is situated in the world of Calvary. Hegel implored against the "shallow and irreligious" construal of Christ's suffering and death "as merely historical, as a happening; for it is divine history (*gottliche Geschichte*)." Jüngel and Lutheran theologian Wolfhart Pannenberg fault Hegel for claiming that reconciliation occurs with and to the negative, not in spite of it as Christians are supposed to believe. But Hegel did not say that the tragic and negative are validated by the reconciling final purpose of the whole. He denied emphatically that he legitimized evil in the whole.[72]

Calvary as divine history is the abyss in which everything vanishes, the death of God. Hegel insisted that the death of God is the negation of every orthodoxy, theodicy, and philosophy of religion, an abyss devouring everything that belongs to finitude, including finite reflection. It negates the concept of God, compelling a new experience of the absolute—not a cheap atheism—amid the utter devastation of loss. Only God's self-communicating and sacrificial Spirit can experience death and come back from it. In *Phenomenology* Hegel said the Spirit endures death and maintains itself in it: "It wins its truth only when, in utter dismemberment, it finds itself." In the religion lectures he amplified Luther's claim that the death of God is the death of death, describing Calvary as the abolition of the understanding by reason. In both places Hegel cited Johannes Rist's passion hymn of 1641, "O Traurigkeit, O Herzeleid," expounding its stunningly "monstrous" picture of a dying God that is simultaneously the highest love. Calvary portrays the unity of the divine and the human at its peak, sacrificial love that gives up "all that is one's own." Life is contradiction and the resolution of contradiction; God is the supreme exemplification. Nothing is alive without contradiction, and the life of spirit does not shrink from death. The very union of God and death supremely exemplifies God's love: "The death of Christ [is] the vision of this love itself—not for or on behalf of others, but precisely *divinity* in the universal identity with other-being, death."[73]

James Cone, in his searing work *The Cross and the Lynching Tree*, commended Niebuhr for perceiving the strange beauty in the horror of Calvary. Niebuhr said the cross is the "supreme symbol of divine grace," bearing a "terrible beauty" that can only be expressed poetically: "Christianity is a faith which takes us through tragedy to beyond tragedy, by way of the cross to victory in the cross." Cone observed that Niebuhr had the rare theological imagination to grasp why the cross matters: "The cross is the burden we must bear in order to attain freedom. . . . One has to have a powerful religious imagination to see redemption in the cross, to discover life in death and hope in tragedy."[74]

The line of black social gospel ministers running from Reverdy Ransom, Adam Clayton Powell Sr., Mordecai Johnson, and Howard Thurman to Martin Luther King Jr. had a religious imagination of this kind, conveying the terrible, sublime, redemptive power of the cross without trying to explain it in a theory. Cone observed, "The more black people struggled against white supremacy, the more they found in the cross the spiritual power to resist the violence they so often suffered." The crucifixion of Jesus placed God among a persecuted, tyrannized, tortured, and crucified people. Black Americans, like Jesus, were stripped, paraded, mocked, whipped, spat upon, and tortured to death. Just as Jesus was a victim of mob hysteria and imperial violence, African Americans were victims of mob hysteria and white racism. The cross and the lynching tree both struck terror in the heart of the subject community.[75]

Precious few ministers of any race or denomination condemned lynching from the pulpit or drew out the connection between lynching and the cross. Niebuhr was not one of them, but Niebuhr at his best—his profound rendering of the cross as a symbol of God's judgment on human sin and God's loving forgiveness—drew on a Lutheran tradition of theologizing that Hegel expressed with singular force.

The first Hegelian school privileged the logical mill and the providential progress motif, playing down the tragic and heterodox aspects of Hegel's thought. It felt compelled to show that Hegel's religious philosophy was compatible with Christian orthodoxy. This compulsion heightened after left-Hegelians said the aim of Hegel's thought was to abolish Christianity. Theological interpreters of Hegel always have this overdetermined legacy of system orthodoxy versus atheistic dismissal to overcome. It takes a great deal of digging and refuting to recover the parts of Hegel that still matter for theology. Hegel was the first philosopher to construe the death of God as a theological concept—God realized as Spirit through the negation of the negative. Like Whitehead and Hartshorne, Hegel expounded a process theodicy of God salvaging what can be salvaged from history. But Hegel's tragic sense of the carnage of history cut deeper, lingering at Calvary.

Process Theodicy in a Whiteheadian Key

Whitehead, in *Religion in the Making*, described evil as suffering, loss, and the feeling that accompanies loss: "The common character of all evil is that its realization in fact involves that there is some concurrent realization of a purpose toward elimination." In *Process and Reality* he elaborated, "The ultimate evil in the temporal world is deeper than any specific evil. It lies in the fact that the past fades, that time is a perpetual perishing. Objectification involves elimination." Evil is something built into the world, the losses that come from the process of becoming and the feelings caused by loss. Black feminist theologian Thandeka, though trained in process theology at Claremont, judges that Whitehead's rendering of evil is too weak and neutral to register the unjust distribution of oppression: "Process thought does not make a distinction between suffering endemic to the entire human race and suffering which is meted out by one ethnic group to another." On this account, she says, it is not amenable to liberationist appropriation, for Whitehead's God has "the manners of an English gentleman," but the God of the oppressed has "the hard-edged rage of random injustice, awesome power, inexplicable suffering and steadfast love."[76]

Thandeka, caught between her Unitarian Universalist disbelief in a powerful God and her liberationist sensibility, concludes that Whiteheadian theism is not the answer because its fixation with beauty and reason is not liberating for oppressed people. Womanist theologian Monica Coleman, similarly steeped in Whitehead, presses for a different verdict while conceding that Whiteheadian thought must be supplemented with other ideas and commitments. Since Whitehead did not address systemic oppression or the politics of justice, process theologians must employ other sources on these subjects, for "one of God's ideals for the world is justice." But Coleman argues that two Whiteheadian ideas promote the transformation of social structures: God shares in human suffering, and God and the world are interdependent. The latter idea is a bulwark against racist dualism and otherworldliness. Coleman cautions that binary models of liberation mirror the same pattern of dualistic ordering as the racism they oppose. Whitehead's process ontology accounts for the multivalent reality of oppression. If God is only for the oppressed, God must puzzle over persons who are oppressed and oppressors simultaneously. Coleman argues that a God who resists oppression does not "accept or despise" one person more than another or switch sides depending on the momentary situation: "God resists the oppressive activity and calls each party to justice in their future actions. God calls the world around these people to enact justice in their lives."[77]

Coleman's use of "call" language is another revising strategy, personalizing the lure of becoming, which renews an old argument in Whiteheadian theory over Whitehead's God. Whitehead argued that actual occasions must perish before they can be prehended by subsequent occasions *and* that God is an actual entity whose being is always in process of becoming through God's consequent experience of the world. The former doctrine, Whitehead's account of the laws of process, contradicts what he said about God. Data are available only after the internal existence of the entity has vanished, and God never perishes. But if God never perishes, how is it possible for God to provide data for other entities?

By the mid-1930s Whitehead recognized the problem, without trying to solve it. Even if one accepts his position on paradoxical terms, it is hard to see how God can be said to act in the world. Whiteheadian process is about actual occasions perishing before they are prehended by subsequent occasions, but Whitehead said that God is an always-becoming concrescence. Hartshorne reasoned that Whitehead's cosmology needs a better concept of God. It cannot be that God is an actual entity analogous to a momentary experience of an individual, for on that account, God is a succession of deities. Surely Whitehead didn't mean that. Moreover, if God is a never-completed single entity, God can never experience satisfaction. Hartshorne responded by personalizing Whitehead's God and dropping the idea that God is an everlasting concrescence. God is a personal society of divine occasions, and each of the divine occasions unifies the present moment and is prehended by succeeding occasions. Since Whitehead's actual entities do not change (they merely become), and Whitehead's God changes by acquiring new prehensions, Hartshorne judged that Whitehead's God makes sense only as a society of actualities. God is not a single member of a sequence of actualities, God acts in the world, and God is not the vaguely impersonal deity or succession of deities described by Whitehead.[78]

Hartshorne developed his dipolar concept of God to defend Whitehead's distinction between the primordial and consequent natures of God; later he called it dual transcendence. This idea became the centerpiece of his system, combining his opposition to mere abstract eternality and mere concrete temporality, which also combined Hartshorne's opposition to abstract theistic absolutism and mechanistic materialism. *The Divine Relativity* (1948) disputed the classic conceptions of divine reality as eternal, not temporal; active, never passive; wholly actual, never potential; necessary, not contingent; independent, never dependent; spiritual, not material; simple, not a compound; absolute, not relative to anything; causative, not affected by causes; and impassable, not affected by human feelings. Hartshorne denied that God is less divine if God is acted upon by the world, subject to change, and personal. God orders the universe by taking into God's life all existing currents of feeling. God is irresistibly influential because God is distinctly open to influence. A God that really has social relations and is constituted by relationships would be relative and personal. To Hartshorne it was self-sabotaging to save the God idea by settling for an impersonal something. We should not relinquish the idea of personal identity merely because we recognize that "substance" is metaphorical and consciousness is successive. Logically speaking, divine personality is analogous to human personality, and too much is at stake to fold on this point.[79]

The dipolar idea, as differently rendered by Whitehead and Hartshorne, was enabling in both cases. Both expounded dipolar concepts of God influencing and being influenced, and not changing and changing. Whitehead tried to account for both kinds of dipolarity under the primordial/consequent distinction, describing God under the primordial category as unchanging and as influencing the world, and under the consequent category as changing and as influenced by the world. He reasoned that the initial aims through which God influences the world come from God's primordial nature alone, but he also said the primordial nature is an abstraction lacking actuality. That contradicted his metaphysical principle that only actualities provide explanatory reasons. By treating a mere abstraction in God as an actuality, Whitehead violated his principle that God must not be treated as an exception to metaphysical principles. Hartshorne's correction, besides conceiving God as an ordered society of occasions of experience analogous to a human soul, corrected Whitehead's overreliance on the primordial/consequent distinction. God's initial aims are acts of God's entire being in the moment. God's consequent nature is simply the abstract principle that each new moment requires what Hartshorne called "a new Consequent State of deity." The idea of God's consequent nature is an abstraction from the process by which God apprehends all events that have just occurred and unifies them into a divine satisfaction.[80]

Whiteheadians have long debated Whitehead versus Hartshorne on this subject, with Schubert Ogden and Edgar Towne defending Hartshorne, William Christian and Marjorie Suchocki defending Whitehead, David Ray Griffin espousing a synthesis, the later John Cobb switching from Hartshorne to Whitehead, Lewis Ford developing a futurist alternative, and Donald Sherburne claiming that Whiteheadian theory works better without God. The early debate revolved in scholastic fashion around the apparent contradictions in Whitehead's system. Much of the later debate has revolved around Cobb's contention that Whitehead's suggestion of two ultimates—creativity and God—offers a better basis for Christian dialogue with Buddhism than Hartshorne's insistence on the necessity of a single ultimate. Cobb argues that Whiteheadian creativity is equivalent to Buddhist emptiness, or dependent origin. The Whiteheadian language of flux, order, and substance-less process supports Cobb's aim of mutual transformation, fixing on the similarity between Buddhist *pratityasamutpada* and Whiteheadian concrescence, the assimilation of shards of experience into a unity. For a while Cobb argued that Whitehead's two ultimates offer the best basis for achieving agreement between Buddhists and Christians. Later he said there are three ultimates: an indeterminate ground, a divine-entity God, and the concrete totality of the world.[81]

Whiteheadian theory, however, assigns God's relations in dyadic fashion to terms outside God's self, either as external absoluteness or internal relativity. It has no concept of divine self-relatedness, apart from world-relatedness. Whiteheadian theory has no basis for distinguishing between the operations of the divine Word and Spirit. To wring a doctrine of the Holy Spirit out of Whitehead, one must construe the Spirit as particular providence for particular occasions. The Holy Spirit, on this rendering, is God's love for the world, which Whitehead distinguished from the primordial nature of God that provides the initial aim of all occasions. But Whitehead and Hartshorne had no doctrine of the Trinity, for the usual Enlightenment rationalist reasons and because Whiteheadian theory is fundamentally dyadic. The Whiteheadian God is not moved by ideal subjectivity to enter the suffering and otherness of the world and return to God's self. Many liberal theologians prefer Whitehead to Hegel on precisely this point. I take the contrary view that liberal theology does not get stronger by eliding the Trinity.

Hegel inspired nineteenth-century schools of Mediating and Hegelian theology that reconceived divine immutability within a holistic process ontology. Calvary is the divine history through which substance becomes subject. Various kenosis theologies of the nineteenth century were marked by Hegel's influence while resisting his process ontology. Kenotic theologians Gottfried Thomasius and W. F. Gess taught that God self-divested God's power during the period of the incarnation and for the sake of the incarnation. Mediating theologian Isaak August Dorner countered that the kenotic interpretation of Philippians 2:6 undermines Christian salvation by de-actualizing the divinity of the Logos, a rerun of the Arian mistake. Dorner, the crucial link in modern theology, besides Herrmann, between Schleiermacher and Barth, played this role by mining Hegel's theological creativity.[82]

Barth drew the godforsaken death of Christ on the cross into his concept of God, refashioning the claims of Luther, Hegel, and Dorner about a divine Logos and a death in God. Hans Urs von Balthasar, influenced by Barth and Hegel, traced the self-surrendering suffering and death of Christ into the inner mystery of God's Trinitarian being, an idea later appropriated by Rahner, Jüngel, Pannenberg, Moltmann, and American Lutheran theologian Robert Jenson. If Hegel is impossibly heterodox, it is difficult to explain his immense ecumenical legacy.[83]

God, Mind, and the World

This legacy includes the major Anglican theologian of the twentieth century, William Temple, whose personal example and thinking drew me into the Episcopal Church when I was in my late twenties. Temple was a neo-Hegelian philosophical theologian, a theorist of economic democracy, and an Anglican bishop who ended his career as archbishop of

Canterbury. He was spiritually deep, eloquent, and ethically sincere, a light to many. To me he remained a model after I moved from solidarity organizing and parish ministry to the academy. I puzzled that theologians of my generation did not read him. One of my early books, *The Democratic Socialist Vision* (1986), made a case for his relevance.[84]

Temple's early books, written on the side while he became a clerical and ecumenical leader, fashioned Anglican logos theology in Hegelian terms. Spirit is the nature of the Supreme Reality that created all things, a real source and cause of process. The will of Christ is one with the will of God and expressive of it, but not identical with it. Will and personality are ideally interchangeable terms. Love divine creates and calls out from created things the love that all things were created to be and to express.[85]

Temple expounded these themes as an Oxford fellow and cleric on his way to a global stage as an ecumenical leader. From 1932 to 1934 he gave the Gifford Lectures, titled *Nature, Man and God* (1934), lacking any trace of Barth's polemic against philosophical theology. Crisis theology did not suit Temple's temperament or reasoned faith, and it ignored the real world described by science. Yet he felt deeply the crisis of capitalist civilization, which caused him to change his philosophical position. Marxism, he acknowledged, spoke powerfully to the Depression generation. It was so relevant that "only a Dialectic more comprehensive in its range of apprehension and more thorough in its appreciation of the interplay of factors in the real world, can overthrow it or seriously modify it as a guide to action." A new dialectic was needed, which Temple called dialectical realism. To make his idealistic perspective make sense to a generation that no longer believed in progress or idealism, he had to find a realistic basis for it that drew upon "the inter-play of factors in the real world." He found it by appropriating Whitehead's organic naturalism.[86]

Temple appreciated that Whitehead's twofold basis in evolutionary theory and relativity theory yielded a conception of life and the universe as dynamic and interconnected. It seemed to Temple that a great dialectical movement of thought—Cartesianism—was finally passing away in the world-historical crisis of the 1930s. Modern thought, lured into a tunnel by Descartes, approached a phase of Hegelian antithesis. Every dominant thesis has inertia and the impression of common sense going for it; the antithesis is a protest against the limitations of the thesis; once the antithesis is worked out and its shortcomings exposed, it gives way to a synthesis. The modern thesis was the Cartesian project of beginning with radical doubt, which Temple called "academic doubt," since

Descartes did not really doubt that the world was out there or that he was distinct from his kitchen.[87]

Descartes set modern philosophy down the path in which Berkeley abolished the material world and Hume claimed he didn't have a mind, just a flux of ideas caused by nothing, held by nothing, and merely happening. Temple said the Hegelian school came closest to reuniting reason and experience, but it shared the customary philosophic sin of conceiving cognition as the original form of apprehension. Having been trained by Edward Caird at Oxford, Temple took for granted that Hegel was in the Cartesian line and culminated it. Though Temple still believed in the priority of Spirit, he no longer believed in the logical priority of the subject in the subject-object relation of knowledge. He reasoned that one does not have to uphold the primacy of Spirit as Subject of knowledge to uphold a spiritual worldview. In fact, it is important not to say that the mind begins with itself and its ideas before apprehending the external world through construction and inference.[88]

Idealism had to be corrected by organic evolutionary theory. Temple took no position on the nature of the physical structure of reality; Whitehead's panexperientialism was one possibility. What mattered was that whatever it is, it preceded consciousness. Whether or not all existence is organic, the organic principle is the means by which all apprehensions of the world must be understood and placed. Experience precedes consciousness even if Whitehead overstretched in describing all actions and reactions of physical entities as experience. The mind discovers beauty and extension in the world, which are there in the initial datum, but an object apart from knowledge is not exactly what it is for knowledge, which rules out conventional realism. Temple's view, dialectical realism, conceived the subject-object relation as ultimate in cognition; neither the subject nor the object is reducible to the other. All apprehension is of objects and is interpretive from the beginning: "Thus we are led to the view that thinking is grounded in the process of adjustment between organism and environment and is indeed an extension of that process." Thought expands by adjusting to wider environments: "Intellectual growth is a perpetually fuller responsiveness to the truth of the environment; aesthetic growth to its beauty; moral growth to its goodness; religious growth to its spiritual character expressed in all of these."[89]

The mind *emerges* through the process of apprehensions and adjustments that it apprehends. The fact that the world gives rise to minds that apprehend the world, Temple argued, tells us something important about the world—there is a deep kinship between mind and the world. The world has a relation of correspondence to mind, something that every rational being experiences in discovering oneself to be an occurrence within the natural process with which one recognizes kinship. But mind and matter are related dialectically. Matter does not generate thought, nor does thought generate matter; the world of matter, always a relative flux of forms, lacks a self-explanatory principle, while mind has the principle of purpose or rational choice. Since there is no materialist explanation for the emergence of mind, and because mind contains a self-explanatory principle of origination, it is reasonable to believe that mind contains the explanation of the world process: "The more completely we include Mind within Nature, the more inexplicable must Nature become except by reference to Mind." Put differently, if mind is part of nature, nature must be grounded in mind; otherwise nature could not contain it.[90]

The world process as such stands in need of explanation. Here Temple took leave of Whitehead, whose explanation—the primordial nature of God—does not explain anything. Whitehead said that relevant novelty without God is impossible, but he did not explain how, *with* God, novelty is possible. The primordial nature of God is merely a name for something desired as essential, an explanation for the initiation of the flux. Temple argued that unless God is something other than the ground of possibility, it does not help to say that God is the ground of possibility. That has no more explanatory value than to say that the ground of possibility is the ground of possibility. Temple acknowledged that Whitehead said beautifully poetic things that sound like Christian theology. The primordial God might be construed as an impersonal stand-in for Eternal Word, creativity as an impersonal substitute for Father-Creator, and the consequent God as an impersonal stand-in for Holy Spirit. But it was hard to see, after Whitehead excluded personality from his description of organism in process, how he could justify his end-of-the-book description of God as "the great companion—the fellow-sufferer who understands."[91]

Temple conceived the world process as the medium of God's personal action and God's active purpose as the determinant element in every actual cause. To half believe in God, he said, is pointless. The concept of divine personality must be taken "in bitter earnest," conceiving God's purposive Mind as the immanent principle of the world process. Temple drank deeply from Whitehead without giving up God's eternal perfections. God's saving purpose is unchanging because it is perfectly good and persists through time. But God is neither changing nor unchanging, because God does not persist through time; God eternally is.[92]

In the end, Temple's dialectical realism was an adjustment, adding an organic evolutionary plank to his neo-Hegelian synthesis. The world has an immanent reason, a Logos. If this principle is impersonal, it is a principle of logical coherence. If it is personal, it is purposive, moral, spiritual, and a principle of variation, for personality, whether human or divine, is immersed in the world process at the level of immanent reason. Beyond the flux of the world process, however, "there is the personality itself, transcendent, and, in proportion to its completeness of integration, unchangeable." God immanent is a principle of adjustment, but God transcendent "is the eternally self-identical—the I AM." This dialectic, Temple urged, not Whitehead's scheme of God and world, is at the heart of things. God transcendent is the eternal I AM, while in God immanent, God is self-expressed and the world is implicit.[93]

All existence is a medium of revelation. If there is an ultimate reality that is the ground of everything else, and this reality is not personal, there can be no special revelation; there can be only the uniform procedure of general revelation. But if there is a personal ultimate reality that is the ground of everything else, all existence is revelation and there is a ground for expecting special revelation. If *any* occurrence is revelatory, there cannot be any occurrence that is not revelatory. Temple put it in epigram fashion: "Only if God is revealed in the rising of the sun in the sky can He be revealed in the rising of a son of man from the dead; only if He is revealed in the history of Syrians and Philistines can He be revealed in the history of Israel; only if He chooses all men for His own can He choose any at all; only if nothing is profane can anything be sacred."[94]

Revelation is the full actuality of the relationship between nature, humanity, and God. Everything is revelatory, but not everything equally reveals the divine character. Temple described revelation as the "coincidence of event and appreciation," the apprehension by a mind arising out of the world process of the process for what it is—the self-expression of the divine mind. Contrary to centuries of church doctrine, revelation is not the communication of doctrine. The church construed revelation as propositional because Greek and scholastic theologians wrongly elevated conceptual thinking above revelatory experience. Temple countered bluntly, "There is no such thing as revealed truth." Revelation is like beauty in existing objectively and being revelatory only when apprehended by discerning minds.[95]

The world was going to hell, but the answer was not in the swirl of redemption theologies propounded by Continental Protestants. To give up on a theology of manifestation and explanation meant that theologies could only speak past and against each other. There had to be a basis for renewing philosophical theology. Hegel was still helpful, but the Hegelian theology that Temple absorbed at Oxford under Caird contributed to the fall of idealism by fixing on its ideas about mind and denigrating the external world of existing things. The long reign of post-Kantian idealism ended after the natural sciences took over the academy and philosophy turned positivistic. Temple realized why it fell from its high perch and why it needed help from Whitehead.

Post-Kantian idealism was never refuted, nor surpassed by a richer philosophy. It faded from fashion, replaced by trends that shrank what philosophy is about. In theology the school of Whitehead filled the void by differently founding a theology of manifestation. It made a real advance by doing so, building on the greatest metaphysical system of the twentieth century. Whiteheadian theology became the leading type of liberal theology and the one indispensable school of thought for progressive theology as a whole. Cobb and Griffin showed the relevance of process thought to ecology and interreligious dialogue, inspiring a profusion of Whiteheadian theologies by Keller, Coleman, and many others. The Whiteheadian school has played the leading role among theologians in battling a powerful reductionist tide in the academy and popular culture, refashioning the longtime debate with dead matter materialists.

Dualist theories of mind and matter violate the principle of continuity and fail to explain how such radically different things as mind and matter can causally influence each other. They also violate the principle of the conservation of energy—that the energy of the universe has remained constant since the big bang. Materialist theories, both dogmatic and emergent, do not explain the unity of experience, the unity of bodily behavior, and the reality of freedom. If there is no mind, how do we possess a unified conscious experience? How can I orchestrate different physical actions at the same time? How can a personal center of consciousness be a wholly material being?[96]

Whiteheadian panexperientialism is a distinct version of the third possibility that minds are real but thoroughly natural. The unsolved dilemmas of the dualist and materialist theories indicate that something is wrong with the assumptions of both camps. As Griffin observes, dualists and materialists do not know that the basic units of nature have no experiential features; they simply assume an early Enlightenment worldview. Griffin aptly counters that naturalizing a really existing mind synthesizes the best parts of the regnant theories. If experiences are actual things and all actualities have experience, the aspect of the world that we know most directly—our own conscious experience—is not supernatural or anomalous. Mind and matter go all the way down. Dualism and materialism commit Whitehead's fallacy of misplaced concreteness, failing to recognize that their basic notions are abstractions.[97]

Whiteheadian theory replaces the substantialist premises of dualism and materialism with the categories of organic process, contending that experiences have spatial extension and bodies endure through time. It avoids the dualistic problems of discontinuity and interaction between ontologically dissimilar entities, while accounting for the reality of experience, freedom, and the unity of experience and behavior. It does not have to solve the impossible problem of drawing a line between experiencing and non-experiencing individuals, and it does not have to explain how non-experiencing entities or processes generate experience. It offers a naturalistic, qualitatively monist form of realism that takes consciousness seriously and regards everything in the world as real in some way.

However, Whiteheadians emphasize their ostensible break from religious idealism, believing that this claim should enhance their standing in the secular academy, which has never happened. Whitehead's system is about God's prehension of all finite occasions, lacking any special category for individual persons or God's prehension of them. We enjoy the illusion of continuity merely as a by-product of the rapidity of succession. Some Whiteheadians, notably Griffin, construe the soul as a distinct series of partly self-caused events differing from the events that constitute the brain. The Whiteheadian "self," on this rendering, is a series of relational occasions, the most that Griffin can wring out of Whitehead. Whiteheadians convey a queasy ambiguity on this subject, insisting on their break from the post-Kantian tradition even as they contend that nature is like human subjects, to be a person is to experience and be experienced, we cannot trust our reason if we are not free, every person bears the sacred likeness of God, and God is the soul of the world.

These signature Whiteheadian affirmations are straight out of post-Kantian religious idealism, with or without the dubious claim that the academy will surely embrace Whitehead sooner or later. Whitehead's lure for creative transformation is another way of naming Hegel's creative self-othering of Spirit. Griffin, Cobb, Keller, and Coleman convey idealistic feeling about consciousness and freedom when they turn to this subject, pressing for the logical upshot of a radical claim about experience: it makes more sense to say that all actualities have experience than to claim that experiences are not actual things. Somehow it must be possible to fuse the materialist truism that all actual things are physical to the dualist truism that mind and brain are distinct and interact. Since the scientific picture of reality finds no place for consciousness or freedom, something has to be wrong with it. Whiteheadian theory offers compelling clues and metaphors about what it is.

Some Whiteheadians are content to say that Whitehead devised a compelling myth, and others press for scholastic clarity and certainty. The rationalistic impulse is valuable to the extent that it keeps metaphysical questions in play, provides conceptual frameworks and arguments, makes "best possible" theoretical claims, sustains intellectual ambition, and enables interreligious and interdisciplinary conversation. It is problematic when it overreaches, brandishing claims to metaphysical certainty and proofs of God's existence. Whiteheadian theory has a serious problem with the second law of thermodynamics, because Whitehead said the universe is increasingly creative and complex. But no cosmology fits with everything we know, which is vastly exceeded by everything we don't know. The Whiteheadian school deserves enormous credit for grappling creatively with big questions and having the audacity to be a school. The Whiteheadian picture of the world giving rise to minds that apprehend the world suggests a deep kinship between mind and the world—one that deepens the idealistic emphasis on will, purpose, subjectivity, and feeling.

To begin with the divine self-giving is to begin in faith with that which transcends faith and draws it forth. Every way of describing the coming together of God and the world is inadequate. Spirit is my privileged concept for it because Spirit is the ultimately inclusive ultimate, the category of identity in reality. Spirit is everywhere as identity, love, inner unity, meaning, purpose, and reality; it can be personal or impersonal; and it is always *of* something. Its underlying idea is the power of life itself, the association of life with breath that underlies the words for spirit in Semitic and Indo-European languages: *ruach* (Hebrew), *pneuma* (Greek), and *spiritus* (Latin). In the Bible the images of breath, wind, fire, light, and water give materiality to this notion of an immaterial life force. God's vibrating breath/wind/spirit swept over the face of the aboriginal waters in creation and breathed life into human beings. Spirit equals breath, and breath equals life, the aliveness and power of your life. Thought and being unite in self-giving and self-realizing Spirit—the spiraling, relational, holistic soul of the world that wills creative transformation and suffers to overcome evil.

The categories of identity, love, and purpose imply some level of self-consciousness, and thus personality. Love makes you care, makes you angry, throws you into the struggle, keeps you in it, and helps you face another day, willing the flourishing of all without exception.

Notes

Preface

1 Gary Dorrien, *Economy, Difference, Empire: Social Ethics for Social Justice* (New York: Columbia University Press, 2010).

2 Walter Rauschenbusch, *Christianity and the Social Crisis* (New York: Macmillan, 1907).

3 James Cone, *Black Theology and Black Power* (New York: Harper & Row, 1969); Cone, *A Black Theology of Liberation* (Philadelphia: J. B. Lippincott, 1970).

4 Dieter Henrich, "Formen der Negation in Hegels Logik," in *Seminar: Dialektik in der Philosophie Hegels*, ed. Rolf-Peter Horstmann (Frankfurt: Suhrkamp, 1978), 213–29; Henrich, *Between Kant and Hegel: Lectures on German Idealism*, ed. David S. Pacini (Cambridge, Mass.: Harvard University Press, 2003); George Rupp, *Christologies and Cultures: Toward a Typology of Religious Worldviews* (The Hague: Mouton, 1974); Gary Dorrien, *The Making of American Liberal Theology: Crisis, Irony, and Postmodernity, 1950–2005* (Louisville: Westminster John Knox, 2006).

5 Gary Dorrien, *The Democratic Socialist Vision* (Totowa, N.J.: Rowman & Littlefield, 1986); Dorrien, *Reconstructing the Common Good* (Maryknoll, N.Y.: Orbis Books, 1990); Dorrien, *Soul in Society: The Making and Renewal of Social Christianity* (Minneapolis: Fortress, 1995).

Chapter 1

1 Friedrich Nietzsche, *Thus Spoke Zarathustra*, trans. R. J. Hollingdale (Harmondsworth, UK: Penguin, 1973); Nietzsche, *On the Genealogy of Morals*, trans. Walter Kaufman and R. J. Hollingdale (New York: Vintage, 1967); Martin Heidegger, *The End of Philosophy*, trans. Joan Stambaugh (London: Souvenir Press, 1975); Heidegger, *Identity and Difference*, trans. Joan Stambaugh (New York: Harper & Row, 1969); Emmanuel Levinas, *Otherwise than Being or Beyond Essence*, trans. Alphonso Lingis (The Hague: Martinus Nijhoff, 1981).

2 Albion W. Tourgée, "Shall White Minorities Rule?" *Forum* 7 (1889): 144–55; W. D. P. Bliss, *What Is Christian Socialism?* (Boston: Society of Christian Socialists, 1890); George D. Herron, *The New Redemption: A Call to the Church to Reconstruct Society according to the Gospel of Christ* (Boston: Thomas Y. Crowell, 1893); Herron, *The Christian Society* (Chicago: Fleming H. Revell, 1894); Vida D. Scudder, *Socialism and Character* (Boston: Houghton Mifflin, 1912); W. E. B. Du Bois, "The African Roots of the War," *Atlantic Monthly* 115 (1915): 707–14; John A. Hobson, *Imperialism* (London: Allen & Unwin, 1948 [1902]); Stewart Headlam, *Christian Socialism* (London: Fabian Society, 1892). For a detailed rendering of this argument, see Dorrien, *Social Democracy in the Making*.

3 Immanuel Kant, "Of the Different Human Races" (1777), in *The Idea of Race*, ed. Robert Bernasconi and Tommy L. Lott (Indianapolis: Hackett, 2000), 11–19; Kant, "Lecture Advertisement" (1775), in *Akademie-Ausgabe of Kant's Gesammelte Schriften* (Berlin: G. Reimer, 1910–), 2:429; Friedrich Schleiermacher, *Über die Religion: Reden an die Gebildeten unter ihren Verächtern* (Hamburg: Felix Meiner, 1958); Schleiermacher, *On Religion: Speeches to Its Cultured Despisers*, trans. Richard Crouter (Cambridge: Cambridge University Press, 1993); Schleiermacher, *On Religion: Addresses in Response to Its Cultured Critics*, trans. Terrence Tice (Richmond: John Knox, 1969), 48–49, 64; G. W. F. Hegel, *Lectures on the Philosophy of World History*, trans. H. B. Nisbet (Cambridge: Cambridge University Press, 1984), 171–90, "barbarism" and "great," 174.

4 Hegel, *Lectures on the Philosophy of World History*, trans. Nisbet, "the surplus," 165; "what has," 171.

5 Dorrien, *Social Ethics in the Making*, 6–59; Dorrien, *New Abolition*; Dorrien, *Breaking White Supremacy*.

6 Victor Shea and William Whitla, eds., *Essays and Reviews: The 1860 Text and Its Reading* (Charlottesville: University of Virginia Press, 2000).

7 Julius Kaftan, *Dogmatik* (Freiburg: J.C.B. Mohr, 1897); Theodor Häring, *Zur Versöhnungslehre, eine dogmatische Untersuchung* (Göttingen: Vandenhoeck & Ruprecht, 1893); Martin Rade, *Die Wahrheit der christlichen Religion* (Tübingen: J.C.B. Mohr, 1900); Ferdinand Kattenbusch, *Von Schleiermacher zu Ritschl. Zur Orientierung über den gegenwärtigen Stand der Dogmatik* (Giessen: Ricker, 1892); Friedrich Loofs, *Leitfaden zum Studium der Dogmengeschichte* (Halle: M. Niemeyer, 1889); Max Wilhelm T. Reischle, *Christliche Glaubenslehre in*

Leitsätzen für eine akademische Vorlesung, 2nd ed. (Halle: M. Niemeyer, 1902); Reischle, *Die Frage nach dem Wesen der Religion Grunglegung zu einer Methodologie der Religionsphilosophie* (Freiburg: J.C.B. Mohr, 1889).

8 F. C. Baur, *Das Christenthum und die christliche Kirche der drei ersten Jahrhunderte* (Tübingen: L. F. Fues, 1853), 133; Horton Harris, *The Tübingen School: A Historical and Theological Investigation of the School of F. C. Baur* (Grand Rapids: Baker Book House, 1990), 101–12; Otto Ritschl, *Albrecht Ritschls Leben*, 2 vols. (Freiburg: J.C.B. Mohr, 1892, 1896); Albert Temple Swing, *The Theology of Albrecht Ritschl*, trans. Alice Mead Swing (New York: Longmans, Green, 1901), 10–22; Rolf Schafer, *Ritschl* (Tübingen: Mohr, 1968); Philip Hefner, "Albrecht Ritschl: An Introduction," in Albrecht Ritschl, *Three Essays*, trans. and ed. Philip Hefner (Philadelphia: Fortress, 1972), 1–50; Peter C. Hodgson, *The Formation of Historical Theology: A Study of Ferdinand Christian Baur* (New York: Harper & Row, 1966), 62, 67, 277.

9 Albrecht Ritschl, *Die Entstehung der altkatholischen Kirche* (Bonn: Adolph Marcus, 1850); Hodgson, *Formation of Historical Theology*, 214–17; Harris, *Tübingen School*, 108.

10 Rolf Rendtorff, "Die jüdische Bibel und ihre antijüdische Auslegung," in *Auschwitz—Krise der christlichen Theologie: Eine Vortragsreihe*, ed. Rolf Rendtorff and Ekkehard Stegemann (Munich: Christian Kaiser, 1980), 99–116; Lou H. Silberman, "Wellhausen and Judaism," *Semeia* 25 (1982): 75–82; Martin Luther, "The Babylonian Captivity of the Church," in *Martin Luther's Basic Theological Writings*, ed. Timothy F. Lull (Minneapolis: Fortress, 1989), 267–313; Paul A. de Lagarde, *Gesammelte abhandlungen* (Leipzig: F. A. Brockhaus, 1866); Lagarde, *Librorum Veteris Testamenti canonicorum* (Göttingen: Prostat in aedibus Dieterichianus Arnoldi Hoyer, 1883); Lagarde, *Onomastica sacra* (Hildesheim: G. Olms, 1887); Lagarde, *Schriften für das deutsche Volk* (München: J. F. Lehmann, 1934 [1878]).

11 F. C. Baur, *Ausgewählte Werke in Einzelausgaben*, 5 vols., ed. Klaus Scholder (Stuttgart: Friedrich Fromann Verlag, 1963–1975), 1:313; Baur, *Die christliche Gnosis, oder die christliche Religions-Philosophie in ihrer geschichtlichen Entwicklung* (Tübingen: C. F. Osiander, 1835); Albrecht Ritschl, "Theology and Metaphysics," in *Three Essays*, 151–217.

12 Albrecht Ritschl, *The Christian Doctrine of Justification and Reconciliation*, ed. H. R. Mackintosh and A. B. Macaulay (Edinburgh: T&T Clark, 1902), quote 205.

13 Ritschl, *Christian Doctrine*, 3.

14 Ritschl, *Christian Doctrine*, 1–2.

15 Ritschl, *Christian Doctrine*, 13; Ritschl, "Instruction in the Christian Religion," in *Three Essays*, 232–40.

16 Agnes von Zahn-Harnack, *Adolf von Harnack*, 2nd ed. (Berlin: Walter de Gruyter, 1951 [1936]); Martin Rumscheidt, "Harnack's Liberalism in Theology: A Struggle for the Freedom of Theology," in *Adolf von Harnack: Liberal Theology*

at Its Height, ed. Martin Rumscheidt (Minneapolis: Fortress, 1991), 9–41; Wilhelm Pauck, "Adolf von Harnack," in *A Handbook of Christian Theologians*, ed. Dean G. Peerman and Martin E. Marty (Cleveland: World Publishing, 1965), 86–111; *Adolf von Harnack: Christentum, Wissenschaft und Gesellschaft*, ed. Kurt Nowak, et al. (Göttingen: Vandenhoeck & Ruprecht, 2003); Karl Barth, *Protestant Theology in the Nineteenth Century* (Valley Forge: Judson Press, 1973), 656.

17 Adolf Harnack, "The Evangelical Social Mission in the Light of the History of the Church," delivered at the Evangelical Social Congress, Frankfurt, May 17, 1894, in Harnack and Wilhelm Herrmann, *Essays on the Social Gospel*, trans. G. M. Craik, ed. Maurice A Canney (New York: G. P. Putnam's Sons, 1907), 3–91; Adolf von Harnack, *What Is Christianity?* (1900), trans. Thomas Bailey Saunders (Philadelphia: Fortress, 1957), 8–10.

18 Harnack, *What Is Christianity?* 20; Wilhelm Pauck, *Harnack and Troeltsch: Two Historical Theologians* (New York: Oxford University Press, 1968), 33–34; Harnack, "The Present State of Research in Early Church History," in Rumscheidt, *Adolf von Harnack*, 182–93; David Friedrich Strauss, *The Life of Jesus Critically Examined*, 3 vols., trans George Eliot from the 4th German ed. (London: Chapman Brothers, 1846).

19 Harnack, *What Is Christianity?* 30, 51–52; Harnack, "The Two-Fold Gospel in the New Testament," in Rumscheidt, *Adolf von Harnack*, 146–54.

20 Harnack, *What Is Christianity?* 56.

21 Adolf Harnack, *History of Dogma*, vol. 1, trans. Neil Buchanan (Boston: Little, Brown, 1905), 41–136; Harnack, *What Is Christianity?* 190–245.

22 *An die evangelischen Christen im Auslande* (September 4, 1914), and *An die Kulturwelt* (October 4, 1914), cited in Rumscheidt, "Harnack's Liberalism in Theology," 25; "Declaration of Professors in the German Reich" (October 23, 1914), Humanities Web Documents, www.humanitiesweb.org; "Manifesto of Ninety-Three German Intellectuals to the Civilized World" (October 3, 1914), Humanities Web Documents, www.humanitiesweb.org. The latter document is often misdated, as on this site.

23 Gustav Ecke, *Die theologische Schule Albrecht Ritschls und die Evangelische Kirche der Gegenwart* (Berlin: Reuther & Reichard, 1897); Johannes Rathje, *Die Welt des freien Protestantismus: Ein Beitrag zur deutsch-evangelischen Geistesgeschichte, dargestellt an Leben und Werk von Martin Rade* (Stuttgart: Ehrenfried Klotz Verlag, 1952), 102–3.

24 Wilhelm Herrmann, *Faith and Morals*, trans. Donald Matheson and Robert W. Stewart (New York: G. P. Putnam's Sons, 1904); Robert T. Volkel, *The Shape of the Theological Task* (Philadelphia: Westminster, 1968); Daniel Deegan, "Wilhelm Herrmann: A Reassessment," *Scottish Journal of Theology* 19 (1966): 188–203; Claude Welch, *Protestant Thought in the Nineteenth Century*, 2 vols. (New Haven: Yale University Press, 1972, 1985), 2:44–45; Friedrich August Gottreu Tholuck, "Theological Encyclopedia and Methodology," *Bibliotheca Sacra* 1 (1844): 194–95, 565–66; Karl Barth, "The Principles of Dogmatics

according to Wilhelm Herrmann," in *Theology and Church: Shorter Writings, 1920–1928*, trans. Louise Pettibone Smith (New York: Harper & Row, 1962), 238; Barth, appendix to *Karl Barth-Rudolf Bultmann Letters, 1922–1966*, trans. Geoffrey W. Bromiley (Grand Rapids: Eerdmans, 1981 [1971]), 153.

25 Wilhelm Herrmann, *Die Metaphysik in der Theologie* (Halle: M. Niemeyer, 1876); Herrmann, *Die Religion im Verhältnis zum Welterkennen und zur Sittlichkeit* (Halle: M. Niemeyer, 1879); Herrmann, "Der evangelische Glaube und die Theologie Albr. Ritschls," in *Gesammelte Aufsätze*, ed. F. W. Schmidt (Tübingen: Mohr, 1923), 1–25; Hermann Timm, *Theorie und Praxis in der Theologie Albrecht Ritschls und Wilhelm Herrmanns* (Gütersloh: Gerd Mohn, 1967), 98.

26 Wilhelm Herrmann, "Kants Bedeutung für das Christentum" (1884), in *Schriften zur Grundlegung der Theologie*, ed. Peter Fischer-Appelt (München: Chr. Kaiser, 1966), 1:104–22; Herrmann, "Hermann Cohens Ethik" (1907), "Die Auffassung der Religion in Cohens und Natorps Ethik" (1909), and "Der Begriff der Religion nach Hermann Cohen" (1916), in *Schriften zur Grundlegung der Theologie*, 2:88–113, 206–32, 318–23; Herrmann, "Die Auffassung der Religion in Cohens and Natorps Ethik," in *Gesammelte Schriften*, ed. Friedrich Wilhelm Schmidt (Tübingen: Mohr, 1923), 377–405; Herrmann, *Ethik*, 5th ed. (Tübingen: Mohr, 1913), 90–96; Theodor Mahlmann, "Das Axiom des Erlebnisses bei Wilhelm Herrmann," *Neue Zeitschrift für systematische Theologie* 4 (1962): 11–18; Peter Fischer-Appelt, *Metaphysik im Horizont der Theologie Wilhelm Herrmanns* (Munich: Chr. Kaiser, 1965); Paul Natorp, *Religion innerhalb der Grenzen der Humanität*, 2nd ed. (Tübingen: Mohr, 1908).

27 Ernst Troeltsch, "Historical and Dogmatic Method in Theology," trans. Ephraim Fischoff (1898), in *Religion in History*, ed. James Luther Adams (Minneapolis: Fortress, 1991), 10–32, "takes a mile," 10.

28 Wilhelm Herrmann, *The Communion of the Christian with God: Described on the Basis of Luther's Statements*, trans. J. Sandys Stanyon (Philadelphia: Fortress, 1971), 36–37, 59–60; see Herrmann, "Der evangelische Glaube und die Theologie Albrecht Ritschls," 11–25; Herrmann, "Der geschichtliche Christus der Grund unseres Glaubens" (1892), in *Schriften zur Grundlegung der Theologie*, 1:149–85.

29 Herrmann, "Albrecht Ritschl, seine Größe und seine Schranke," in *Festgabe von Fachgenossen und Freunden A. von Harnack zum seibzigsten Geburtstag dargebracht*, ed. Karl Holl (Tübingen: Mohr, 1921), 405–6; Herrmann, "Die Absolutheit des Christentums und die Religionsgeschichte: Eine Besprechung des gleichnamigen Vortrags von Ernst Troeltsch" (1902), in *Schriften zur Grundlegung der Theologie*, 1:193–99.

30 Herrmann, *Communion of the Christian with God*, lxv–lxvi, 5, 19–49; on the theme that Christian faith requires the historical fact of Jesus, see Wilhelm Herrmann, "Warum bedarf unser Glaube geschichtlicher Tatsachen?" (1884), in *Schriften zur Grundlegung der Theologie*, 1:81–103.

31 Herrmann, *Communion of the Christian with God*, lxvii, 7, 17, 14–15, 51; on Pietist accounts of faith, see Wilhelm Herrmann, *Dogmatik* (Stuttgart: Friedrich Perthes, 1925); for the English edition, see Herrmann, *Systematic Theology*, trans. Nathaniel Micklem and Kenneth A. Saunders (New York: Macmillan, 1927), 34–36, 43–47.

32 Herrmann, *Communion of the Christian with God*, 45, 46.

33 Herrmann, *Communion of the Christian with God*, 69–70, 71–72; G. E. Lessing, *Lessing's Theological Writings*, ed. Henry Chadwick (London: Adam & Charles Black, 1956), 12–13; Ludwig Feuerbach, *The Essence of Christianity*, trans. George Eliot (New York: Harper & Row, 1957 [1841]).

34 Herrmann, "Die Lage und Aufgabe der evangelischen Dogmatik," in *Gesammelte Aufsätze*, quote 118–19 (repr. in *Schriften zur Grundlegung der Theologie*, 1:1–89); Herrmann, "The der Gegenwart," in *Communion of the Christian with God*, 74–75; Herrmann, "Warum bedarf unser Glaube geschichtlicher Tatsachen?" 94–101; Herrmann, *Christlich-protestantische Dogmatik* (1906), in Paul Hinneberg, ed., *Die Kultur der Gegenwart: Ihre Entwicklung und ihre Ziele* (Berlin: Druck und Verlag von B. G. Teubner, 1909), 1:4:2, 129–80, in Herrmann, *Schriften zur Grundlegung der Theologie*, 1:298–358; see Herrmann, "Der evangelische Glaube und die Theologie Albr. Ritschls"; Herrmann, "Die religiöse Frage in der Gegenwart" (1908), in *Schriften zur Grundlegung der Theologie*, 2:114–49; Karl Barth, "Principles of Dogmatics," 247–48. Herrmann's first edition *Der Verkehr des Christen mit Gott* was published in 1886; revised editions were published in 1892, 1896, 1903, 1908 (5th and 6th eds.), and 1921. The J. Sandys Stanyon–R. W. Stewart second English edition was based on the fourth German edition.

35 Herrmann, "Die Absolutheit des Christentums und die Religionsgeschichte," 193–99; Herrmann, *Christlich-protestantische Dogmatik*, 1:4:2, 604–24; Herrmann, "Der Widerspruch im religiösen Denken und seine Bedeutung für das Leben der Religion" (1911), in *Schriften zur Grundlegung der Theologie*, 2:233–46; James M. Robinson, *Das Problem des Heiligen Geistes bei Wilhelm Herrmann* (Marburg: K. Gleiser, 1952), 16–22; Ernst Troeltsch, "Half a Century of Theology: A Review" (1908), in *Ernst Troeltsch: Writings on Theology and Religion*, trans. and ed. Robert Morgan and Michael Pye (Louisville: Westminster John Knox, 1990), "the agnostic," "subjective," and "firm," 58, 66, 75; Troeltsch, "The Significance of the Historical Existence of Jesus for Faith" (1911), in *Ernst Troeltsch*, "obscure" and "almost," 191–92.

36 Wilhelm Herrmann, "Die Bedeutung Der Geschichtlichkeit Jesu Für Den Glauben: Eine Besprechung des gleichnamigen Vortrags von Ernst Troeltsch" (1912), in *Schriften zur Grundlegung der Theologie*, 2:282–89. See Herrmann, "Die Lage und Aufgabe der evangelischen Dogmatik in der Gegenwart," 95–96, 126–38; Herrmann, *Systematic Theology*, 21. These lectures were published shortly after Herrmann's death by Martin Rade in the form in which Herrmann last presented them, during the winter semester of 1915/16.

37 Herrmann, *Systematic Theology*, 26–29, 35–37; Friedrich Schleiermacher, *The Christian Faith*, ed. H. R. Mackintosh and J. S. Stewart (Edinburgh: T&T Clark, 1968), 142–256; Herrmann, "Die Lage und Aufgabe der evangelischen Dogmatik in der Gegenwart," 106–22; Herrmann, "Hermann Cohens Ethik," 108–9.

38 Wilhelm Herrmann, "The Moral Teachings of Jesus," in Harnack and Herrmann, *Essays on the Social Gospel*, 175–85, 206–25; Herrmann, *Systematic Theology*, 44; Johannes Weiss, *Die Predigt Jesu vom Reiche Gottes*, 2 vols. (Göttingen: Vandenhoeck & Ruprecht, 1900); W. Wrede, *Das Messiasgeheimnis in der Evangelien* (Göttingen: Vandenhoeck & Ruprecht, 1901).

39 Herrmann, "Die Auffassung der Religion in Cohens und Natorps Ethik," in *Schriften zur Grundlegung der Theologie*, 2:208.

40 Daniel Day Williams, *God's Grace and Man's Hope* (New York: Harper & Brothers, 1949), quote 22; Lloyd Averill, *American Theology in the Liberal Tradition* (Philadelphia: Westminster, 1967), 23.

Chapter 2

1 See Ludwig Ernst Borowski, *Darstellung des Leben und Charakters Immanuel Kants* (Königsberg: F. Nicolovius, 1804; Bruxelles: Culture et civilization, 1968); Reinhold Bernhard Jachmann, *Immanuel Kant geschildert in Briefen an einen Freund* (Königsberg: F. Nicolovius, 1804); Ehregott A. Christian Wasianski, *Immanuel Kant in seinen letzten Lebensjahren* (Königsberg: F. Nicolovius, 1804).

2 Heinrich Heine, *Zur Geschichte der Religion und Philosophie in Deutschland* (Hamburg: Hoffmann und Campe, 1868), reprinted in Heine, *Lyrik und Prosa*, 2 vols., ed. Martin Greiner (Frankfurt: Büchergilde Gutenberg, 1962), 2:461.

3 Two major biographical works on Kant superseded the literature in this field, providing a richer account of Kant's life and character: Karl Vorländer, *Immanuel Kant: Der Mann und das Werk*, 2 vols. (Leipzig: Felix Meiner, 1924); and Manfred Kuehn, *Kant: A Biography* (Cambridge: Cambridge University Press, 2001).

4 G. W. Leibniz, *Discourse on Metaphysics, Correspondence with Arnauld, and Monadology*, trans. George Montgomery (LaSalle, Ill.: Open Court, 1902), 5–7, 14–15, 18–19; Leibniz to Arnauld, October 6, 1687, in *Discourse on Metaphysics*, 211–35; Leibniz, *New Essays on Human Understanding*, trans. Peter Remnant and Jonathan Bennett (Cambridge: Cambridge University Press, 1982).

5 Gottfried W. Leibniz and Christian Wolff, *Briefwechsel zwischen Leibniz und Christian Wolff* (Hildesheim: G. Olms, 1860); Christian Wolff, *Gesammelte Werke* (Hildesheim: G. Olms, 1962); see Johann D. Walch, *Kontroversstücke gegen die Wolffsche Metaphysik* (Hildesheim: G. Olms, 1724); Ulrich Ricken, *Leibniz, Wolff und einige sprachtheoretische Entwicklungen in der deutschen Aufklärung* (Berlin: Akademie-Verlag, 1989); Joachim Birke, *Christian Wolffs Metaphysik und die zeitgenössische Literatur-und Musiktheorie* (Berlin: Walter de Gruyter, 1966); Erich Riedesel, *Pietismus und Orthodoxie in Ostpreußen*

(Königsberg: Ost-Europa Verlag, 1937), 39; Peter C. Erb, ed., *Pietists: Selected Writings* (New York: Paulist Press, 1983); Richard Benz, *Die Zeit der Deutschen Klassik, 1750–1800* (Stuttgart: Reclam, 1953); Hajo Holborn, *A History of Modern Germany, 1648–1840* (New York: Knopf, 1968). For a modern edition of Wolff's famous speech at Halle on Chinese philosophy that got him in trouble, see Wolff, *Oratio de Sinarum philosophia practica / Rede über praktische Philosophie der Chinesen*, ed. Michael Albrecht (Hamburg: Felix Meiner, 1985). On the Pietist battle against Wolff, see Max Wundt, *Die deutsche Schulphilosophie im Zeitalter der Aufklärung* (Hildesheim: G. Olms, 1964), 230–64.

6 See Kuehn, *Kant: A Biography*, 56–60; Riedesel, *Pietismus und Orthodoxie in Ostpreußen*, 138–39; Vorländer, *Immanuel Kant*, 1:5–9; Hartmut Böhme and Gernot Böhme, *Das Andere der Vernunft: Zur Entwicklung von Rationalitätsstrukturen am Beispiel Kant* (Frankfurt: Suhrkamp, 1983), 475–95.

7 See Benno Erdmann, *Martin Knutzen und seine Zeit: Ein Beitrag zur Geschichte der Wolfischen Schule und Insbesondere zur Entwicklungsgeschichte Kants* (Leipzig: Voss, 1876); Christian August Crusius, *Kleinere philosophische Schriften* (1737; Hildesheim: G. Olms, 1987); Crusius, *Weg zur gewissheit und Zuverlässigkeit der menschlichen Erkenntnis* (1744; Hildesheim: G. Olms, 1969); Erb, *Pietists: Selected Writings*, 97–215; Erich Beyreuther, *Geschichte des Pietismus* (Stuttgart: Steinkopf, 1978).

8 See Frederick C. Beiser, "Kant's Intellectual Development: 1746–1781," in *The Cambridge Companion to Kant*, ed. Paul Guyer (Cambridge: Cambridge University Press, 1992), 26–27; Ernst Cassirer, *Kants Leben und Lehre* (Berlin: Cassirer, 1921), 22–58; A. Drews, *Kants Naturphilosophie als Grundlage seines Systems* (Berlin: Mitscher and Röstell, 1894); Isaac Newton, *Philosophiae Naturalis Principia Mathematica* (1689; for an English translation, see *Sir Isaac Newton's Mathematical Principles of Natural Philosophy and His System of the World*, trans. Florian Cajori [Berkeley: University of California Press, 1934]).

9 David Hume, *Enquiries concerning Human Understanding and concerning the Principles of Morals*, ed. L. A. Selby-Bigge and P. H. Nidditch, 3rd ed. (1748, 1751; Oxford: Clarendon, 1975); Hume, *A Treatise of Human Nature*, ed. L. A. Selby-Bigge and P. H. Nidditch (1739, 1740; Oxford: Clarendon, 1978); Francis Hutcheson, *A System of Moral Philosophy in Three Books*, 2 vols. (Glasgow: R. & A. Foulis, 1755); Immanuel Kant, *Gesammelte Schriften*, 29 vols., ed. Königlich PreuBischen Akademie der Wissenschaften und Deutsche Akademie der Wissenschaften (Berlin: G. Reimer und Walter de Gruyter, 1900–1995), 1:8–12; Alexander G. Baumgarten, *Metaphysica* (Hildesheim: G. Olms, 1982); Baumgarten, *Ethica philosophica* (Hildesheim: G. Olms, 1969); Frederick C. Beiser, *German Idealism: The Struggle against Subjectivism, 1781–1801* (Cambridge, Mass.: Harvard University Press, 2002), 44–47; Leibniz, *Discourse on Metaphysics*; G. W. Leibniz, *Theodicy*, trans. E. M. Huggard (LaSalle, Ill.: Open Court, 1985); Kuehn, *Kant: A Biography*, 91–92.

10 See Immanuel Kant, *Novo dilucidatio*, in *Gesammelte Schriften*, 1:460–510; Beiser, "Kant's Intellectual Development," 34–35.

11 Kuehn, *Kant: A Biography*, 112–16.

12 Immanuel Kant, *Observations on the Feeling of the Beautiful and Sublime*, trans. John T. Goldthwait (1764; Berkeley: University of California Press, 1991), quotes 77, 79, 81.

13 Kant, *Observations on the Feeling of the Beautiful and Sublime*, 45–75.

14 Kant, *Observations on the Feeling of the Beautiful and Sublime*, 103–4, 109–10.

15 Kant, *Observations on the Feeling of the Beautiful and Sublime*, 97, 110–11; David Hume, "Of National Characters" (1748), reprinted in Hume, *Essays and Treatises on Several Subjects*, 2 vols. (Edinburgh: Bell and Pradfute, 1825), 1:521–22.

16 See Kuehn, *Kant: A Biography*, 144–58; Jachmann, *Immanuel Kant geschildert in Briefen an einen Freund*, 152–55, 185.

17 Immanuel Kant, *Die falsche Spitzfindigkeit der vier syllogistischen Figuren*, in *Gesammelte Schriften*, 2:42–59; Kant, *The One Possible Basis for a Demonstration of the Existence of God*, trans. Gordon Treash (New York: Abaris Books, 1979).

18 Anselm, *Basic Writings: Proslogium, Monologium, Gaunilon's Reply on behalf of the Fool, Cur Deus Homo*, trans. S. W. Deane, 2nd ed. (LaSalle, Ill.: Open Court, 1962), 53–55.

19 Descartes, third and fifth *Meditations*, in *The Philosophical Works of Descartes*, trans. Elizabeth S. Haldane and G. R. T. Ross, 2 vols. (Cambridge: Cambridge University Press, 1931), 1:157–71, 179–85; G. W. Leibniz, *Monadology*, in *Discourse on Metaphysics; Correspondence with Arnauld; Monadology*, tr. George Montgomery (Lasalle, Ill.: Open Court, 1988), 251–72, quote 260.

20 Kant, *One Possible Demonstration*, 57–61, quote 57; Immanuel Kant, *Critique of Pure Reason*, trans. Norman Kemp Smith (New York: Macmillan, 1929), 505, A599/B627. In citations of Kant's first *Critique*, "A" refers to the first edition (1781) and "B" refers to the second edition (1787). Smith's text is based on the second edition, but Smith also folded into the text passages and sections that Kant omitted from the second edition.

21 Immanuel Kant, *Untersuchhung über die Deutlichkeit der Grundsätze der natürlichen Theologie und der Moral*, Prize Essay for Berlin Academy, 1764, in *Gesammelte Schriften*, 2:276–86; Kant, *Dreams of a Spirit-Seer Illustrated by Dreams of Metaphysics*, trans. E. F. Goerwitz (New York: Macmillan, 1900); Kant, *Theoretical Philosophy, 1755–1770*, trans. David Walford and Ralf Meerbote (Cambridge: Cambridge University Press, 1992), 299–311; Kant, *Bemerkungen zu den Beobachtungen über das Gefühl des Schönen und Erhabenen* (1764), in *Gesammelte Schriften*, 20, 44; Beiser, "Kant's Intellectual Development," 40–41; Jean Jacques Rousseau, *The Discourses and Other Early Political Writings*, ed. and trans. Victor Gourevitch (Cambridge: Cambridge University Press, 1997), 3–28, 113–88; Rousseau, *The Social Contract and Other Later Political Writings*,

ed. and trans. Victor Gourevitch (Cambridge: Cambridge University Press, 1997).

22 Immanuel Kant, *De mundi sensibilis atque intelligibilis forma et principiis*, in *Theoretical Philosophy*, 405–15; Kant, *Critique of Pure Reason*, 10, Axiv.

23 Kuehn, *Kant: A Biography*, quote 212; see Kant, *Theoretical Philosophy*, 388–416.

24 Kant, *Critique of Pure Reason*, 65, A19.

25 Kant, *Critique of Pure Reason*, 111, B102/A77.

26 Kant, *Critique of Pure Reason*, 113–14, A80/B106.

27 Kant, *Critique of Pure Reason*, 120–28, A84–95/B117–29.

28 See Kant, *De mundi sensibilis atque intelligibilis forma et principiis*, 405–15; Kuehn, *Kant: A Biography*, 243–44.

29 H. J. Paton, *Kant's Metaphysic of Experience*, 2 vols. (London: Allen & Unwin, 1970 [1936]), 2:547. On the differences between Kant's rendering of the Transcendental Deduction in the first and second editions of the *Critique of Pure Reason*, see Norman Kemp Smith, *A Commentary to Kant's Critique of Pure Reason*, 2nd ed. (London: Macmillan, 1962 [1923]), 284–91.

30 Kant, *Critique of Pure Reason*, 151–52, B130–31.

31 Kant, *Critique of Pure Reason*, 182–83, A141–B181/A142.

32 H. A. Prichard, *Kant's Theory of Knowledge* (Oxford: Clarendon, 1909); P. F. Strawson, *The Bounds of Sense: An Essay on Kant's Critique of Pure Reason* (London: Metheun, 1966); Jonathan Bennett, *Kant's Analytic* (Cambridge: Cambridge University Press, 1966); Robert Paul Wolff, *Kant's Theory of Mental Activity* (Cambridge, Mass.: Harvard University Press, 1963).

33 Hermann Cohen, *Kants Theorie der Erfahrung* (Berlin: F. Dümmler, 1885); Paul Natorp, *Philosophie, ihr Problem und ihre Probleme; Einführung in den kritischen Idealismus* (Göttingen: Vandenhoeck & Ruprecht, 1911); Ernst Cassirer, *Kant's Life and Thought* (New Haven: Yale University Press, 1981); Karl Ameriks, *Kant and the Fate of Autonomy* (Cambridge: Cambridge University Press, 2000); Graham Bird, *Kant's Theory of Knowledge* (New York: Humanities Press, 1962); Henry Allison, *Kant's Transcendental Idealism* (New Haven: Yale University Press, 1983); Allison, "Transcendental Idealism: The Two Aspect View," in *New Essays on Kant*, ed. Bernard den Ouden and Marcia Moen (New York: Peter Lang, 1987), 155–78; Arthur Collins, *Possible Experience* (Berkeley: University of California Press, 1999); Beiser, *German Idealism*, 6.

34 Hans Vaihinger, "Die transcendentale Deduktion der Kategorien in der Ersten Ausgabe der Kritik der reinen Vernunft," in *Philosophische Abhandlungen* (Halle: M. Niemeyer, 1902), 24–98; Smith, *Commentary to Kant's Critique of Pure Reason*.

35 Ralph Walker, *Kant* (London: Routledge, 1978); Sebastian Gardner, *Kant and the Critique of Pure Reason* (London: Routledge, 1999); Beiser, *German Idealism*.

36 G. W. F. Hegel, *The Difference between Fichte's and Schelling's System of Philosophy*, trans. H. S. Harris and Walter Cerf (Albany: State University of New York

Press, 1977); Hegel, *Faith and Knowledge or the Reflective Philosophy of Subjectivity in the Complete Range of Its Forms as Kantian, Jacobian, and Fichtean Philosophy*, trans. Walter Cerf and H. S. Harris (Albany: State University of New York Press, 1977); Ernst Behler, "Friedrich Schlegel und Hegel," *Hegel-Studien* 2 (1963): 203–50; Walter Benjamin, *Der Begriff der Kunstkritik in der deutschen Romantik* (Bern: Francke, 1920).

37 Beiser, *German Idealism*, 25.

38 Kant, *Critique of Pure Reason*, quote 346, A370.

39 Kant, *Critique of Pure Reason*, 439, A491/B519; Strawson, *Bounds of Sense*, 235–63; Karl Ameriks, *Kant's Theory of Mind: An Analysis of the Paralogisms of Pure Reason* (Oxford: Clarendon, 1982), 255–94.

40 Kant, *Critique of Pure Reason*, 349–50, A376–77; 359, A393; 67–70, B37/A23–A25/B40; Beiser, *German Idealism*, 69–71.

41 Kant, *Critique of Pure Reason*, 67–70, B37/A23–A25/B40; 79–80, A38/B55; 268–69, A251–52; 269, A252; 339–40, A359; Beiser, *German Idealism*, 69–71.

42 Smith, *Commentary to Kant's Critique*, 406–7; J. N. Findlay, *Kant and the Transcendental Object: A Hermeneutic Study* (Oxford: Clarendon, 1981), 195–225.

43 Kant, *Critique of Pure Reason*, 270–72, B309/A255–B311.

44 Christian Garve, "Kritik der reinen Vernunft von Immanuel Kant," *Zugaben zu den Göttinger gelehrte Anzeigen* 3 (1782): 40–48; Garve, "Kritik der reinen Vernunft von Immanuel Kant," *Allgemeine deutsche Bibliothik* (1783): 838–62; Immanuel Kant to Johann Schultz, August 26, 1783, in Kant, *Briefe, Akademie Ausgabe*, ed. R. Reicke (Berlin: G. Reimer, 1912), 10:350–51.

45 Immanuel Kant, *Kant's Critical Philosophy for English Readers*, trans. John P. Mahaffy and John H. Bernard, vol. 2, *Prolegomena to Any Future Metaphysic* (1783; London: Macmillan, 1889), quotes 8, 11.

46 Kant, *Prolegomena*, quotes 7, 4.

47 Immanuel Kant, *Critique of Practical Reason*, trans. Lewis White Beck (Indianapolis: Bobbs-Merrill, 1956), 3–5, "the keystone," 3; see Kant, *Critique of Practical Reason*, in *Practical Philosophy*, trans. and ed. Mary J. Gregor (Cambridge: Cambridge University Press, 1996), 133–271.

48 Kant, *Critique of Pure Reason*, 18, Bx; 319–20, A328/B385–A329/B386; 474–76, A550/B578–A553/B581.

49 Kant, *Critique of Pure Reason*, 525–27, A631/B659–A635/B663, quotes 526, 526–7; see Kant, *Lectures on Philosophical Theology*, trans. Allen W. Wood and Gertrude M. Clark (Ithaca, N.Y.: Cornell University Press, 1978), 28–31.

50 Immanuel Kant, *Foundations of the Metaphysics of Morals*, trans. Lewis White Beck, with critical essays edited by Robert Paul Wolff (1785; Indianapolis: Bobbs-Merrill, 1969); Kant, *Critique of Practical Reason*, trans. Beck; Kant, *Religion within the Limits of Reason Alone*, trans. Theodore M. Greene and Hoyt H. Hudson (1793; Chicago: Open Court, 1934); or Kant, *Religion within the Boundaries of Mere Reason and Other Writings*, trans. and ed. Allen Wood and George di Giovanni (Cambridge: Cambridge University Press, 1998).

51 Kant, *Critique of Pure Reason*, 29, Bxxx.

52 For the kept-separate view, see Allen W. Wood, *Kant's Moral Religion* (Ithaca, N.Y.: Cornell University Press, 1970); for the illegitimate-substitution view, see Smith, *Commentary to Kant's Critique*, 637–41; and Lewis White Beck, *A Commentary on Kant's Critique of Practical Reason* (Chicago: University of Chicago Press, 1960); for the changed-his-mind view, see Erich Adickes, *Kants Opus Postumum, dargestellt und beurteilt* (Berlin: Reuther & Reichard, 1920), 769–85.

53 Kant, *Critique of Pure Reason*, 646–7, A822/B850–A823/B851, quote 646, A823/B851; Kant, *Critique of Practical Reason*, trans. Beck, 4–7.

54 Kant, *Critique of Pure Reason*, 650, A828/B856.

55 Kant, *Critique of Pure Reason*, 650, A828/B856.

56 Kant, *Critique of Pure Reason*, 650, A828/B856; Kant, *Lectures on Philosophical Theology*, 121–31.

57 Kant, *Critique of Pure Reason*, 651, A830/B858; Kant, *Religion within the Boundaries of Mere Reason*, 169–70, 6:174–76; Allen W. Wood, "Rational Theology, Moral Faith, and Religion," in Guyer, *Cambridge Companion to Kant*, 396–97.

58 Kant, *Religion within the Boundaries of Mere Reason*, 164, 6:168; 166, 6:171; 170, 6:174; Kant, *Foundations of the Metaphysics of Morals*, 19–25, 44, quote 44.

59 Kant, *Religion within the Boundaries of Mere Reason*, 160–61, 6:163–64.

60 Kant, *Religion within the Boundaries of Mere Reason*, 52–73, 6:29–53.

61 Kant, *Religion within the Boundaries of Mere Reason*, 52–55, 6:29–32.

62 Kant, *Religion within the Boundaries of Mere Reason*, quote 79, 6:60.

63 Kant, *Religion within the Boundaries of Mere Reason*, quote 80, 6:61; G. E. Lessing, "The Education of the Human Race," in *Lessing's Theological Writings*, trans. Henry Chadwick (London: Adam & Charles Black, 1956), 82–98.

64 Kant, *Religion within the Boundaries of Mere Reason*, 190–91, 6:200–202.

65 Christian Garve, *Abhandlung über die Verbindung der Moral mit der Politik* (Breslau: Korn, 1788); Garve, "Kritik der reinen Vernunft von Immanuel Kant," *Zugaben zu den Göttinger gelehrte Anzeigen*, 40–48; Garve, "Kritik der reinen Vernunft von Immanuel Kant," *Allgemeine deutsche Bibliothik*, 838–62; A. Stern, *Ueber die Beziehung Garves zu Kant* (Leipzig: Denicke, 1884); J. A. Eberhard, *Neue Apologie des Sokrates* (Berlin: Voss, 1772); J. G. H. Feder, *Ueber Raum und Causalität* (Frankfurt: Dietrich, 1788); Frederick Beiser, *The Fate of Reason: German Philosophy from Kant to Fichte* (Cambridge: Harvard University Press, 1987), 165–72, quote 172; Kuehn, *Kant: A Biography*, 250–54.

66 Friedrich Heinrich Jacobi, *Ueber die Lehre des Spinoza in Briefen an Herrn Moses Mendelssohn* (Breslau: G. Lowe, 1785), in *Werke*, 6 vols., ed. F. H. Jacobi and F. Köppen (Leipzig: Fleischer, 1812), 4:1–47; and Jacobi, *F. H. Jacobi: The Main Philosophical Writings and the Novel "Allwill,"* ed. and trans. George di Giovanni (Montreal: McGill-Queen's University Press, 1994); Thomas Reid, *An Inquiry into the Human Mind, on the Principles of Common Sense*, 3rd ed. (Dublin: R. Marchbank, 1779); Reid, *Essays on the Intellectual Powers of Man* (1785), in

The Works of Thomas Reid, ed. Sir William Hamilton (Edinburgh: MacLachlan and Stewart, 1872), 1:255–59; Beiser, *Fate of Reason*, 165–67; S. A. Grave, *The Scottish Philosophy of Common Sense* (Oxford: Oxford University Press, 1960).

67 Reid, *Essays*, 1:255–59; G. A. Tittel, *Ueber Herr Kants Moralreform* (Frankfurt: Pfahler, 1786); Tittel, *Kantische Denkformen oder Kategorien* (Frankfurt: Gebhardt, 1787); Heinrich Weber, *Hamann und Kant: ein Beitrag zur Geschichte der Philosophie im Zeitalter der Aufklärung* (München: C. H. Beck, 1904); Beiser, *Fate of Reason*, 167–72; Manfred Kuehn, *Scottish Common Sense in Germany, 1768–1800: A Contribution to the History of Critical Philosophy* (Montreal: McGill-Queen's University Press, 1987).

68 Johann Schultz, *Erläuterungen über des Herrn Prof. Kants Kritik der reinen Vernunft* (Königsberg: Dengel, 1784); Karl Leonhard Reinhold, *Brife über die kantische Philosophie* (Leipzig: G. J. Göshen, 1790); Reinhold, *Über das Fundament des Philosophischen Wissens* (Hamburg: Felix Meiner, 1978 [1791]); Reinhold, *Über die Möglichkeit der Philosophie als strenge Wissenschaft* (Hamburg: Felix Meiner, 1978 [1790]); Kuehn, *Kant: A Biography*, 329–34; Johann Gottfried Herder, *Against Pure Reason: Writings on Religion, Language, and History*, trans. and ed. Marcia Bung (Minneapolis: Fortress, 1993); Herder, *Metacritique* (1799) and *Calligone* (1800), in *Werke*, 3 vols., ed. Wolfgang Pross and Pierre Penisson (München: Carl Hanser, 1984–1985); Herder, *Outlines of a Philosophy of the History of Man*, trans. T. O. Churchill (London: J. Johnson, 1880); Friedrich Heinrich Jacobi, *Werke*, 2 vols., ed. Friedrich Roth and Friedrich Köppen (Darmstadt: Wissenschaftliche Buchgesellschaft, 1976), 2:299–308; Jacobi, *Wider Mendelssohns Beschuldigungen betreffend die Briefe über die Lehre des Spinoza* (Leipzig: Göschen, 1786).

69 J. G. Hamann, "Metakritik über den Purismum der reinen Vernunft," in *Sämtliche Werke, Historisch-Kritische Ausgabe*, 7 vols., ed. J. Nadler (Vienna: Herder, 1949–1957), 277–87; English edition in Hamann, *Writings on Philosophy and Language*, trans. Kenneth Haynes (Cambridge: Cambridge University Press, 2007), 205–18.

70 Hamann, *Writings*, quotes 208, 210; Hamann, *Schriften zur Sprache*, ed. J. Simon (Frankfurt: Suhrkamp, 1967); Beiser, *Fate of Reason*, 38–43.

71 Immanuel Kant, "Beantwortung der Frage: Was ist Aufklärung?" *Berlinische Monatsschrift* 4 (1784): 481–94; Kant, "An Answer to the Question: What Is Enlightenment?" trans. James Schmidt, in *What Is Enlightenment? Eighteenth-Century Answers and Twentieth-Century Questions*, ed. James Schmidt (Berkeley: University of California Press, 1996), 58–64, quotes 58, 59.

72 Kant, "What Is Enlightenment?" quote 63.

73 Kant, "What Is Enlightenment?" quotes 62, 63.

74 Johann Georg Hamann to Christian Jacob Kraus, December 18, 1784, trans. Garrett Green, in Schmidt, *What Is Enlightenment?* 145–48, quotes 147, 148.

75 Carolus Linnaeus, *Systema naturae per regna tria naturae, secundum classes, ordines, genera, species, cum characteribus, differentiis, synonymis, locis*, 3 vols. (Hale: Curt, 1760–1770), 1:20–24; Georges Cuvier, *Le Régne animal*, 5 vols.

(Paris: Deterville Libraire, 1829–1830), 1:180; Kant, "Different Human Races," 11.

76 Kant, "Different Human Races," 12, 16, 19; Kant, "Lecture Advertisement," 2:429; J. Kameron Carter, *Race: A Theological Account* (Oxford: Oxford University Press, 2008), 83.

77 Kant, "Different Human Races," 20–22; Kant, *Menschenkunde*, in *Gesammelte Schriften*, quotes 25:2:1187–88, cited in Carter, *Race*, 90–91.

78 Immanuel Kant, *Reflexionen*, in *Gesammelte Schriften*, quote 25:878, cited in Carter, *Race*, 92; see Mark Larrimore, "Sublime Waste: Kant on the Destiny of the 'Races,'" in *Civilization and Oppression*, ed. Cheryl J. Misak (Calgary: University of Calgary Press, 1999), 103–14.

79 Kant, *Reflexionen*, 878; Immanuel Kant, *Anthropology from a Pragmatic Point of View*, trans. Victor Lyle Dowdell, ed. Hans. H. Rudnick (Carbondale: Southern Illinois University Press, 1978), "the two most," 226.

80 Kant, *Anthropology*, quotes 226, 229.

81 Kant, *Anthropology*, quote 101.

82 Kant, *Anthropology*, 102; see Carter, *Race*, 105; Sara Eigen and Mark J. Larrimore, eds., *The German Invention of Race* (Albany: SUNY Press, 2006).

83 Kant, *Religion within the Boundaries of Mere Reason*, quotes 130, 132.

84 See Jonathan M. Hess, *Germans, Jews, and the Claims of Modernity* (New Haven: Yale University Press, 2002); Michael Mack, *German Idealism and the Jew: The Inner Anti-Semitism of Philosophy and German Jewish Responses* (Chicago: University of Chicago Press, 2003).

85 Kuehn, *Kant: A Biography*, quote 340; Immanuel Kant, "On the Common Saying: 'This May Be True in Theory, but It Does not Apply in Practice'" (1793), in *Kant's Political Writings*, ed. Hans Reiss, trans. H. B. Nisbet (Cambridge: Cambridge University Press, 1970), 61–92.

86 Kuehn, *Kant: A Biography*, 378–80, quote 379.

87 Immanuel Kant, "Perpetual Peace: A Philosophical Sketch," in Reiss, *Kant's Political Writings*, 93–108.

88 Kant, *Critique of Practical Reason*, trans. Beck, 4–5, 8–9; see Mark C. Taylor, *After God* (Chicago: University of Chicago Press, 2007), 108–9.

89 Kant, *Critique of Pure Reason*, Bxxiii, 25. A clearer translation reads, "And no principle can be taken with certainty in *one* relation unless it has the same time been investigated in its *thoroughgoing* relation to the entire use of pure reason." Immanuel Kant, *Critique of Pure Reason*, trans. and ed. Paul Guyer and Allen Wood (Cambridge: Cambridge University Press, 1998), Bxxiii, 113–14.

90 Henrich, *Between Kant and Hegel*, "feedback," 51; Henrich, "The Basic Structure of Modern Philosophy," *Cultural Hermeneutics* 22 (1974): 1–18; Henrich, "Fichte's Original Insight," trans. David Lachterman, in *Contemporary German Philosophy* (University Park: Pennsylvania State University Press, 1982); Henrich, "Self-Consciousness: A Critical Introduction to a Theory," *Man and World* 4 (1971): 2–28.

91 Henrich, *Between Kant and Hegel*, 51–52.

92 Immanuel Kant, *Critique of Judgement*, trans. James Creed Meredith (Oxford: Oxford University Press, 1973), 3–39; Kant, *What Real Progress Has Metaphysics Made in Germany since the Time of Leibniz and Wolff?* trans. Ted Humphrey (New York: Abaris Books, 1983), 157. See Kant, *Critique of the Power of Judgment*, trans. Paul Guyer and Eric Matthews (Cambridge: Cambridge University Press, 2000); Henrich, *Between Kant and Hegel*, 52–53.

93 Kant, *Critique of Practical Reason*, trans. Beck, 3–4.

94 Henrich, *Between Kant and Hegel*, 59.

Chapter 3

1 Friedrich D. E. Schleiermacher, *Aus Schleiermachers Leben in Briefen*, 4 vols., ed. Wilhelm Dilthey (Berlin: G. Reimer, 1858–1863); for an English edition of volumes 1 and 2, see Schleiermacher, *The Life of Schleiermacher as Unfolded in His Autobiography and Letters*, 2 vols., trans. Frederica Rowan (London: Smith, Elder and Company, 1860), 1:1–6; Martin Redeker, *Schleiermacher: Life and Thought*, trans. J. Wallhauser (Philadelphia: Fortress, 1973), 6–9.

2 *Life of Schleiermacher*, 1:6–10; Friedrich Schleiermacher to Georg Reimer, April 30, 1802, in *Life of Schleiermacher*, quote 1:283–84.

3 Friedrich Schleiermacher to Gottlieb Schleiermacher, January 21, 1787, in *Life of Schleiermacher*, 1:46–47, 49.

4 Gottlieb Schleiermacher to Friedrich Schleiermacher, February 6, 1787, in *Life of Schleiermacher*, 1:50–53, quotes 50, 52.

5 Friedrich Schleiermacher to Gottlieb Schleiermacher, undated, in *Life of Schleiermacher*, 1:56–58, quotes 56, 57.

6 Gottlieb Schleiermacher to Friedrich Schleiermacher, March 19, 1787, in *Life of Schleiermacher*, 1:62–63, quote 63; 1:14; Keith W. Clements, introduction to *Friedrich Schleiermacher: Pioneer of Modern Theology*, ed. Keith W. Clements (Minneapolis: Fortress, 1991), 17–18.

7 *Life of Schleiermacher*, 1:78–125; Friedrich Schleiermacher, *Schleiermacher's Soliloquies: An English Translation of the Monologen*, trans. Horace Leland Friess (Chicago: Open Court, 1957), quote 74.

8 *Life of Schleiermacher*, 1:133–42; Johann Wolfgang Goethe, *Collected Works*, ed. Victor Lange, Eric Blackall, Cyrus Hamlin, vol. 9, *Wilhelm Meister's Apprenticeship* (Princeton: Princeton University Press, 1994).

9 Friedrich Schleiermacher to Charlotte Schleiermacher, February 12, 1801, in *Life of Schleiermacher*, "her colossal," 1:249; *Life of Schleiermacher*, "he had," 1:140.

10 Friedrich Schlegel, *Philosophical Fragments*, trans. Peter Firchow (Minneapolis: University of Minnesota Press, 1991), quotes 31–32; Schlegel, *Dialogue on Poetry and Literary Aphorisms*, trans. Ernst Behler (University Park: Pennsylvania State University Press, 1968); Theodore Ziolkowski, *German Romanticism and Its Institutions* (Princeton: Princeton University Press, 1990), 260–61.

11 Friedrich Schleiermacher to Charlotte Schleiermacher, October 22, 1797, in *Life of Schleiermacher*, 1:58–162, quote 159; see Schleiermacher to Charlotte Schleiermacher, November 21, 1707, in *Life of Schleiermacher*, 1:162–64.

12 Friedrich Schleiermacher to Charlotte Schleiermacher, December 31, 1797, in *Life of Schleiermacher*, 1:188, 165–69, quotes 167–68; Friedrich Schleiermacher to Henriette Herz, February 15, 1799, in *Life of Schleiermacher*, 1:188.

13 Friedrich Schleiermacher to Henriette Herz, March 3, 1799, in *Life of Schleiermacher*, 1:193–94, quote 194; Schleiermacher, *Über die Religion*; for English editions, see Schleiermacher, *On Religion: Speeches to Its Cultured Despisers*; Schleiermacher, *On Religion: Addresses in Response to Its Cultured Critics*.

14 Schleiermacher, *On Religion: Addresses in Response to Its Cultured Critics*, quotes 39, 40.

15 Schleiermacher, *On Religion: Addresses in Response to Its Cultured Critics*, 48.

16 Schleiermacher, *On Religion: Addresses in Response to Its Cultured Critics*, quotes 53, 54, 55.

17 Schleiermacher, *On Religion: Addresses in Response to Its Cultured Critics*, quotes 55–56, 58.

18 Schleiermacher, *On Religion: Addresses in Response to Its Cultured Critics*, quotes 84; see 68, n. 4; Benedict de Spinoza, *On the Improvement of the Understanding; The Ethics; Correspondence*, trans. R. H. M. Elwes (New York: Dover Publications, n.d.).

19 Friedrich Schleiermacher, "Über sein *Glaubenslehre* an Herrn Dr. Lücke, zwei Sendschreiben," *Theologische Studien und Kritiken* 2 (1829): 255–84 and 481–532; for an English edition, see Schleiermacher, *On the Glaubenslehre: Two Letters to Dr. Lücke*, trans. James Duke and Francis Fiorenza (Atlanta: Scholars Press, 1979), quotes 50–51.

20 Schleiermacher, *On Religion: Addresses in Response to Its Cultured Critics*, 48.

21 See Robert R. Williams, *Schleiermacher the Theologian: The Construction of the Doctrine of God* (Philadelphia: Fortress, 1978), 25; Gary Dorrien, *Word as True Myth*, 13–22.

22 Kant, *Anthropology*, 9–129; Kant, *Critique of Judgement*, 204–27; Ameriks, *Kant's Theory of Mind*, 84–123.

23 Schleiermacher, *On Religion: Addresses in Response to Its Cultured Critics*, quote 79; see Schleiermacher, *Soliloquies*, 10–25; Richard R. Brandt, *The Philosophy of Schleiermacher: The Development of His Theory of Scientific and Religious Knowledge* (New York: Harper & Brothers, 1941), 105–44; Williams, *Schleiermacher the Theologian*, 4–7; Edmund Husserl, *Ideas: General Introduction to Pure Phenomenology*, trans. W. R. Boyce Gibson (New York: Humanities Press, 1976), 41–47.

24 Schleiermacher, *On Religion: Addresses in Response to Its Cultured Critics*, 82.

25 Schleiermacher, *On Religion: Addresses in Response to Its Cultured Critics*, 82, 79.

26 Schleiermacher, *On Religion: Addresses in Response to Its Cultured Critics*, 162–63.

27 Schleiermacher, *On Religion: Addresses in Response to Its Cultured Critics*, 146–47, 154–62, quotes 162, 146.

28 Schleiermacher, *On Religion: Addresses in Response to Its Cultured Critics*, 207–71, quotes 208, 209, 233.

29 Schleiermacher, *On Religion: Addresses in Response to Its Cultured Critics*, 48.

30 Schleiermacher, *On Religion: Addresses in Response to Its Cultured Critics*, 48, 49.

31 Schleiermacher, *On Religion: Addresses in Response to Its Cultured Critics*, 49.

32 Schleiermacher, *On Religion: Addresses in Response to Its Cultured Critics*, 63–64.

33 Friedrich Schleiermacher to Eleanore Grunow, June 8, 1802, in *Life of Schleiermacher*, 1:293–95, quote 295.

34 Friedrich Schleiermacher, *Grundlinien einer Kritik der bisherigen Sittenlehre* (Berlin: Realschulbuchhandlung, 1803); Schleiermacher to Eleanore Grunow, August 12, 1802; August 19, 1802; August 26, 1802; September 10, 1802, in *Life of Schleiermacher*, 1:302–3, 303–8, 311–14, 319–24; Redeker, *Schleiermacher*, 70–71.

35 Friedrich Schleiermacher to Ehrenfried and Henriette von Willich, October 11, 1805, in *Life of Schleiermacher*, 2:22.

36 Friedrich D. E. Schleiermacher, *Hermeneutics: The Handwritten Manuscripts*, ed. Heinz Kimmerle, trans. James Duke and Jack Forstman (Atlanta: Scholars Press, 1986), 41–65; Friedrich Schleiermacher to Charlotte von Kathen, June 20, 1806, in *Life of Schleiermacher*, 2:36; Redeker, *Schleiermacher*, 77–78.

37 Friedrich Schleiermacher to Henriette Herz, November 21, 1806, in *Life of Schleiermacher*, 2:40.

38 Henriette von Willich to Friedrich Schleiermacher, March 1807; April 28, 1807; n.d., and Friedrich Schleiermacher to Henriette von Willich, March 20, 1807; April 1807; May 8, 1807; n.d., in *Life of Schleiermacher*, 2:44–54.

39 Franz Kade, *Schleiermachers Anteil an der Entwicklung des preussischen Bildungswesen von 1808–1818* (Leipzig: Quelle & Meyer, 1925); Friedrich Schleiermacher, *Gelegentliche Gedanken über deutsche Universitäten im deutschen Sinne* (Berlin: Realschulbuchhandlung, 1808); Redeker, *Schleiermacher*, 91–96.

40 Friedrich Schleiermacher, *Brief Outline on the Study of Theology*, trans. Terrence N. Tice (Atlanta: John Knox, 1977), 19–114, quote 19.

41 James Gillman, *The Life of Samuel Taylor Coleridge* (London: W. Pickering, 1838); James D. Campbell, *Samuel Taylor Coleridge: A Narrative of the Events of His Life* (London: Macmillan, 1894); E. K. Chambers, *Samuel Taylor Coleridge: A Biographical Study* (Oxford: Oxford University Press, 1938); Lawrence Hanson, *The Life of S. T. Coleridge, the Early Years* (New York: Russell & Russell, 1962); Rosemary Ashton, *The Life of Samuel Taylor Coleridge: A Critical Biography* (Oxford: Blackwell, 1996); Richard Holmes, *Coleridge: Early Visions, 1772–1804* (New York: Pantheon Books, 1999). This section on Coleridge contains highly condensed summaries of my discussion in Dorrien, *Kantian Reason and Hegelian Spirit*, 119–45.

42 Samuel Taylor Coleridge, *Poems on Various Subjects* (London: C.G. and J. Rob-insons; Bristol: J. Cottle, 1796); Coleridge to Joseph Cottle, February 1796, in *Collected Letters of Samuel Taylor Coleridge*, 6 vols., ed. Earl L. Griggs (Oxford: Oxford University Press, 1956–1971), 1:185; *The Watchman*, ed. Lewis Patton (Princeton: Princeton University Press, 1970); William Wordsworth and Samuel Taylor Coleridge, *Lyrical Ballads, 1798* (London: Oxford University Press, 1969); see Coleridge, *Poetical Works*, ed. Ernest Hartley Coleridge (Oxford: Oxford University Press, 1969); Wordsworth, *Poetical Works*, ed. Thomas Hutchinson (Oxford: Oxford University Press, 1936).

43 Samuel Taylor Coleridge to George Fricker, October 4, 1806, in *Collected Letters of Samuel Taylor Coleridge*, quote 2:1189; Holmes, *Coleridge: Early Visions*, 205–75; Molly Lefebure, *The Bondage of Love: A Life of Mrs. Samuel Taylor Coleridge* (New York: Norton, 1987), 113–18; Norman Fruman, *Coleridge, the Damaged Archangel* (New York: G. Braziller, 1971); Thomas MacFarland, *Coleridge and the Pantheist Tradition* (Oxford: Oxford University Press, 1969); Oswald Doughty, *Perturbed Spirit: The Life and Personality of Samuel Taylor Coleridge* (Rutherford, N.J.: Fairleigh Dickinson University Press, 1981); Richard Holmes, *Coleridge: Darker Reflections, 1804–1834* (New York: Pantheon Books, 1998), 1–106; J. D. Boulger, *Coleridge as Religious Thinker* (New Haven: Yale University Press, 1961), 219–20.

44 Samuel Taylor Coleridge, *The Friend*, 2 vols., ed. Barbara E. Rooke (Princeton: Princeton University Press, 1969), 1:277; 2:116–21, 141–47; *Collected Letters of Samuel Taylor Coleridge*, 3:120–280; Holmes, *Coleridge: Darker Reflections*, 145–96, 356–58; Walter Scott, *The Lady of the Lake* (Cambridge: Riverside Press, 1883 [1810]); George Gordon Byron, *The Bride of Abydos: A Turkish Tale* (London: J. Murray, 1813); Coleridge to John Morgan, May 14, 1813, in *Collected Letters of Samuel Taylor Coleridge*, 3:489–90.

45 Samuel Taylor Coleridge, *Biographia Literaria, or, Biographical Sketches of My Literary Life and Opinions*, 2 vol. set, vol. 7 of *The Collected Works of Samuel Taylor Coleridge*, ed. James Engell and W. Jackson Bate (Princeton: Princeton University Press, 1983), 1:5–88; William Wordsworth, *The Prelude: The Four Texts (1798, 1799, 1805, 1850)*, ed. Jonathan Wordsworth (Harmondsworth, UK: Penguin, 1995).

46 Coleridge, *Biographia Literaria*, quotes 1:304–5.

47 Coleridge, *Biographia Literaria*, 1:153–59.

48 Coleridge, *Biographia Literaria*, 1:160–64; Giordano Bruno, *De la causa, principio e uno in Dialoghi italiani*, 3rd ed., ed. G. Aquilecchia (Florence: Sansoni, 1958); Nicholas of Cusa, *Philosophisch-Theologische Schriften*, ed. Leo Gabriel, 3 vols. (Vienna: Herder, 1967); F. W. J. Schelling, *Ideas for a Philosophy of Nature as Introduction to the Study of This Science*, trans. Errol E. Harris and Peter Heath, 2nd ed. (Cambridge: Cambridge University Press, 1988 [1803; 1st ed. 1797]); Schelling, *System of Transcendental Idealism*, trans. Peter Heath (Charlottesville: University Press of Virginia, 1978 [1st German ed., 1800]).

49 Coleridge, *Biographia Literaria*, 2:234–48.

50 Reviews of *Biographia Literaria* in *New Annual Register* 38 (1817): 145; *British Critic* 8 (1817): 460–61; John Wilson, *Blackwood's Magazine* 2 (1817): 3–18; William Hazlitt, *Edinburgh Review* 38 (1817): 488–515, reprinted in *Coleridge: The Critical Heritage*, ed. J. R. de J. Jackson (London: Routledge, 1970), 294–387; see also reviews in *Literary Gazette* 29 (1817): 83–85; *M Mag* XLIV (1817): 153–60; *American Monthly Magazine and Critical Review* 2 (1817): 105–14; *New Monthly Magazine* 8 (1817): 50.

51 Samuel Taylor Coleridge, *Aids to Reflection*, vol. 9 of *The Collected Works of Samuel Taylor Coleridge*, ed. John Beer (Princeton: Princeton University Press, 1993), quote 107.

52 Samuel Taylor Coleridge to Thomas Clarkson, 1806, in *Collected Letters of Samuel Taylor Coleridge*, 2:1198.

53 Coleridge, *Aids to Reflection*, 216–36, quote 202.

54 Peter Allen, *The Cambridge Apostles: The Early Years* (Cambridge: Cambridge University Press, 1978); James Marsh, "Preliminary Essay," in Coleridge, *Aids to Reflection*, ed. James Marsh (Burlington, Vt.: Chauncy Goodrich, 1829), 12–52; P. Carafiol, "James Marsh's American *Aids to Reflection*: Influence through Ambiguity," *New England Quarterly* XLIX (1976): 27–45; Anthony J. Harding, "James Marsh as Editor of Coleridge," in *Reading Coleridge*, ed. W. B. Crawford (Ithaca, N.Y.: Cornell University Press, 1979), 223–51; editor's introduction to Coleridge, *Aids to Reflection*, 1993 ed., cxvi–cxxii; *Coleridge's American Disciples: The Selected Correspondence of James Marsh*, ed. John J. Duffy (Amherst: University of Massachusetts Press, 1973), 75–154.

55 Ralph Waldo Emerson, October 9, 1829, in *The Journals and Miscellaneous Notebooks of Ralph Waldo Emerson*, vol. 3, *1826–1832*, ed. William H. Gilman and Alfred R. Ferguson (Cambridge, Mass.: Harvard University Press, 1963), 164; Coleridge, *Aids to Reflection*, 1829 ed., quote 257; Emerson, sermon of February 14, 1830, in *Journals and Miscellaneous Notebooks*; February 11, 1830, "Every man makes his own," 3:179; Emerson, March 2, 1830, in *Journals and Miscellaneous Notebooks*, "the most elevated conception," 3:182.

56 Emerson, July 15, 1831, in *Journals and Miscellaneous Notebooks*, "God in us," 3:273; Emerson, July 29, 1831, in *Journals and Miscellaneous Notebooks*, succeeding quotes 3:279. Emerson used the latter material in his sermon of July 31, 1831, in *Journals and Miscellaneous Notebooks*.

57 Ralph Waldo Emerson, "The Over-Soul" (1841), in *Essays of Ralph Waldo Emerson* (Cambridge, Mass.: Harvard University Press, 1987), "simplest," 173; Emerson, *Journals and Miscellaneous Notebooks*, 3:260; Emerson, October 27, 1833, in *Journals and Miscellaneous Notebooks*, 3:301.

58 Ralph Waldo Emerson, September 3, 1833, in *The Journals and Miscellaneous Notebooks of Ralph Waldo Emerson*, vol. 4, *1832–1834*, ed. Alfred R. Ferguson (Cambridge, Mass.: Harvard University Press, 1964), quotes 4:83–84.

59 Frederic Henry Hedge, "Coleridge," *Christian Examiner* 14 (1833): 109–29; Ralph Waldo Emerson to Edward Bliss Emerson, December 22, 1833, in *Letters*

of Ralph Waldo Emerson, vol. 1, ed. Ralph L. Rusk and Eleanor Tilton (New York: Columbia University Press, 1939), "an unfolding" and "living," 401–2.

60 Margaret Fuller journal entry in the editor's introduction to *The Transcendentalists: An Anthology*, ed. Perry Miller (Cambridge, Mass.: Harvard University Press, 1950), quote 35; Frederic Henry Hedge, "Antisupernaturalism in the Pulpit," *Christian Examiner* 52 (1864): 145–59, in *An American Reformation: A Documentary History of Unitarian Christianity*, ed. Sydney E. Ahlstrom and Jonathan S. Carey (San Francisco: International Scholars Publications, 1998), 419–31; Hedge, *Reason in Religion* (Boston: Roberts, 1865), 218–19.

61 Friedrich Schleiermacher, *Der christliche Glaube nach den Grundsätzen der evangelischen Kirche im Zusammenhange dargestellt*, 2 vols., 2nd ed. (Berlin: G. Reimer, 1830 [1821]); for the English edition, see Schleiermacher, *Christian Faith*.

62 Friedrich Schleiermacher, *Die Weihnachtsfeier: ein Gespräch* (Halle: Schimmelpfennig und Kompagnie, 1806); Schleiermacher, *Dialektik, Auftrag der preussichen Akademie der Wissenschaften auf Grund bisher unveröffentlichen Materials*, ed. Rudolf Odebrecht (Leipzig: J. C. Hinrichs, 1942), 260–87; Schleiermacher, *Dialectic, or, The Art of Doing Philosophy*, trans. Terrence N. Tice (Atlanta: Scholars Press, 1996), quote 17. This text is based on lecture notes by one of Schleiermacher's students, August Twesten; the English edition contains excerpts only.

63 Schleiermacher, *Dialectic*, quote 38.

64 Schleiermacher, *Christian Faith*, quote viii.

65 Schleiermacher, *Christian Faith*, 12–13.

66 Schleiermacher, *Christian Faith*, 14, 31–34.

67 Schleiermacher, *Christian Faith*, 16.

68 Schleiermacher, *Christian Faith*, 374–89.

69 Schleiermacher, *Christian Faith*, 259–68, 425–38, quote 435.

70 Schleiermacher, *Christian Faith*, 31–38.

71 Schleiermacher, *Christian Faith*, quotes 52, 57.

72 Schleiermacher, *Christian Faith*, 60–62, quotes 60, 62.

73 Friedrich Schleiermacher, "Christ Our Only Savior," in *Servant of the Word: Selected Sermons of Friedrich Schleiermacher*, trans. Dawn DeVries (Philadelphia: Fortress, 1987), 29–30; Schleiermacher, *Introduction to Christian Ethics*, trans. John C. Shelley (Nashville: Abingdon, 1989).

74 Schleiermacher, "Christ the Liberator," in *Servant of the Word*, 55–56.

75 Schleiermacher, *Christian Faith*, 262. This emphasis on the double character of Christian experience is slighted in Richard R. Niebuhr's otherwise discerning study of Schleiermacher, *Schleiermacher on Christ and Religion* (London: SCM Press, 1965). Niebuhr invents the term "Christo-morphic" to suggest that Schleiermacher's system as a whole is shaped by Christology.

76 Schleiermacher, *Christian Faith*, 261.

77 Christlieb Julius Braniss, *Über Schleiermachers Glaubenslehre: Ein kritischer Versuch* (Berlin: Duncker & Humblot, 1821), 197; Johann Friedrich Ferdinand

Delbrück, *Erörterungen einiger Hauptstücke in Dr. Friedrich Schleiermachers christliche Glaubenslehre* (Bonn: Adolf Marcus, 1827), 190; Heinrich Gottlieb Tzschirner, *Briefe eines Deutschen an die Herren Chateaubriand, de la Mannais und Montlosier über Gegenstände der Religion und Politik* (Leipzig: Johann Ambrosius Barth, 1828), 28, 33; Isaaco Rust, *De nonnullis, quae in theologia nostrae aetatis dogmatica desiderantur* (Erlangen: Kunstmann, 1828), 65–69; Karl Gottlieb Bretschneider, *Grundansichten* (Leipzig: Johann Ambrosius Barth, 1828), 65–69; Georg Friedrich Wilhelm Hegel, "Vorwort zur Hinrichs' *Religionsphilosophie*," in *Berliner Schriften, 1818–1831*, ed. Johannes Hoffmeister (Hamburg: Felix Meiner, 1956).

78 Schleiermacher, *On the Glaubenslehre*, 36.

79 Ferdinand Christian Baur, *Primae rationalismi et supranaturalismi historiae capita potiora* (Tübingen: Hopferi de l'Orme, 1827); Heinrich Johann Theodor Schmid, "Uber das Verhältnis der Theologie zur Philosophie," *Für Theologie und Philosophie* 1 (1828): 16–73; Schleiermacher, *On the Glaubenslehre*, 37–38, 43–47.

80 Bretschneider, *Grundansichten*, 15; Schleiermacher, *On the Glaubenslehre*, 38–39.

81 Schleiermacher, *On the Glaubenslehre*, 47–51, quote 51.

82 Schleiermacher, *On the Glaubenslehre*, quotes 52, 53.

83 Schleiermacher, *On the Glaubenslehre*, 53–60.

84 Schleiermacher, "Christ Our Only Savior," 34.

85 Johann Gottfried Eichhorn, *Einleitung in das Neue Testament*, 2nd ed., 3 vols. (Leipzig: Weidmannischen Buchhandlung, 1810–1820); Johann David Michaelis, *Einleitung in die göttlichen Schriften des Neuen Bundes*, 2 vols. (Göttingen: Jandenhoeck, 1777); Wilhelm Martin L. de Wette, *A Critical and Historical Introduction to the Canonical Scriptures of the Old Testament from the German of Wilhelm Martin Leberecht de Wette*, 2 vols., trans Theodore Parker (Boston: Charles C. Little & James Brown, 1843); Christian Hartlich and Walter Sachs, *Der Ursprung des Mythosbegriffes in der modernen Bibelwissenschaft* (Tübingen: Mohr, 1952); Friedrich Schleiermacher, *The Life of Jesus*, trans. S. Maclean Gilmour, ed. Jack C. Verheyden (Philadelphia: Fortress, 1975), 36–42, 455.

86 Redeker, *Schleiermacher*, quote 213.

87 *Friedrich Schleiermachers Briefwechsel mit J. Chr. Gass*, ed. Wilhelm Gass (Berlin: G. Reimer, 1852), Gass quote 195; Karl Barth, *Protestant Theology in the Nineteenth Century: Its Background and History* (London: SCM Press, 1972), Neander quote 425.

88 G. W. F. Hegel, *Lectures on the Philosophy of Religion*, 3 vols., ed. Peter C. Hodgson, trans. R. F. Brown, Peter C. Hodgson, and J. M. Stewart (Berkeley: University of California Press, 1984–1987), 1:271–76, 395.

89 Richard Crouter, "Hegel and Schleiermacher at Berlin: A Many-Sided Debate," *Journal of the American Academy of Religion* 48 (1980): 19–43; Crouter,

"Rhetoric and Substance in Schleiermacher's Revision of *The Christian Faith* (1821–1822)," *Journal of Religion* 60 (1980): 285–306.

Chapter 4

1 For representative works, see Frederick Copleston, *A History of Philosophy*, 8 vols. (Westminster, Md.: Newman Press, 1963), 7:159–247; Friedrich W. J. Schelling, *The Grounding of Positive Philosophy*, trans. Bruce Matthews (Albany: State University of New York Press, 2007); Stanley Rosen, *G. W. F. Hegel: An Introduction to His Science of Wisdom* (New Haven: Yale University Press, 1974); Jacques Derrida, *Glas*, trans. John P. Leavey Jr. and Richard Rand (Lincoln: University of Nebraska Press, 1986).

2 Bruno Bauer, *Kritik der evangelischen Geschichte der Synoptiker*, 3 vols. (Leipzig: O. Wigand, 1841–1842); Alexandre Kojève, *Introduction to the Reading of Hegel*, ed. Raymond Queneau and Allan Bloom, trans. James H. Nichols Jr. (New York: Basic Books, 1969); Jean Hyppolite, *Genesis and Structure of Hegel's Phenomenology of Spirit*, trans. Samuel Cherniak and John Heckman (Evanston, Ill.: Northwestern University Press, 1974); Herbert Marcuse, *Reason and Revolution: Hegel and the Rise of Social Theory* (Boston: Beacon Press, 1960); Jean-Paul Sartre, *Critique of Dialectical Reason*, trans. Alan Sheridan-Smith (London: NLB, 1976).

3 Terry Pinkard, *Hegel's Phenomenology: The Sociality of Reason* (Cambridge: Cambridge University Press, 1994); Rolf-Peter Horstmann, *Ontologie und Relationen* (Königstein: Athenäum-Hain, 1984); Judith Butler, *Giving an Account of Oneself* (New York: Fordham University Press, 2005); Charles Taylor, *Hegel* (Cambridge: Cambridge University Press, 1975); Merold Westphal, *History and Truth in Hegel's Phenomenology*, 3rd ed. (Bloomington: Indiana University Press, 1998).

4 Quentin Lauer, SJ, *Essays in Hegelian Dialectic* (New York: Fordham University Press, 1977); Henrich, *Between Kant and Hegel*; Rupp, *Christologies and Cultures*; Andrew Shanks, *Hegel and Religious Faith: Divided Brain, Atoning Spirit* (London: T&T Clark, 2012); John W. Burbidge, *Hegel on Logic and Religion* (Albany: State University of New York Press, 1992); Martin J. De Nys, *Hegel and Theology* (London: T&T Clark, 2009).

5 Stephen Houlgate, *An Introduction to Hegel: Freedom, Truth, and History* (Oxford: Blackwell, 2005); Robert Stern, *Hegelian Metaphysics* (Oxford: Oxford University Press, 2009).

6 Slavoj Žižek, *The Sublime Object of Ideology* (London: Verso, 1989); Jean-Luc Nancy, *Hegel: The Restlessness of the Negative*, trans. Jason Smith and Steven Miller (Minneapolis: University of Minnesota Press, 2002); Taylor, *After God*; Catherine Malabou, *The Future of Hegel: Plasticity, Temporality and Dialectic*, trans. Lisabeth During (London: Routledge, 2005).

7 Theodore Ziolkowski, *Das Wunderjahr in Jena* (Stuttgart: Klett-Cotta, 1998); *Evolution des Geistes: Jena um 1800*, ed. Friedrich Strack (Stuttgart: Klett-Cotta,

1994); Karl Obenauer, *August Ludwig Hülsen* (Erlangen: Junge und Sohn, 1910); Ernst Behler, *Frühromantik* (Berlin: Walter de Gruyter, 1992); Rudolf Haym, *Die romantische Schule* (Berlin: R. Gaertner, 1870); F. W. J. Schelling, *Vom Ich als Princip der Philosophie* (1795), in *Sämtliche Werke*, 14 vols., ed. K. F. A. Schelling (Stuttgart: Cotta, 1856–1861), 1:151; Schelling, *Philosophy of Nature*; F. W. J. Schelling: *Briefe und Dokumente*, ed. Horst Fuhrmanns (Bonn: Bouvier, 1962–1975), 2:51–52; G. W. F. Hegel to Friedrich W. J. Schelling, December 24, 1794, in *Hegel: The Letters*, trans. Clark Butler and Christiane Seiler (Bloomington: Indiana University Press, 1984), 28–29; Beiser, *German Idealism*, 349–64; Karl Rosenkranz, *Georg Wilhelm Friedrich Hegels Leben* (Darmstadt: Wissenschaftliche Buchgesellschaft, 1963), 3–7; J. G. Fichte, *The Science of Knowledge*, trans. Peter Heath and John Lachs (1794; Cambridge: Cambridge University Press, 1982).

8 Benedict de Spinoza, *The Ethics*, in *Works of Spinoza*, 2 vols., trans. R. H. M. Elwes, Bohn Library Edition (London: George Bell and Sons, 1883), 2:45–271, quote 45; F. W. J. Schelling, *System der gesammten Philosophie* (1804), in *Sämtliche Werke*, 6:147–48, quote 148.

9 H. S. Harris, *Hegel's Development: Toward the Sunlight, 1770–1801* (Oxford: Oxford University Press, 1972), 57–72; Terry Pinkard, *Hegel: A Biography* (Cambridge: Cambridge University Press, 2000), 15–17.

10 Schelling, *On the World Soul* (1898), in *Sämtliche Werke*, 2:459; Schelling, *Philosophy of Nature*; Schelling, *System of Transcendental Idealism*.

11 G. W. F. Hegel to F. W. J. Schelling, November 2, 1800, in *Hegel: The Letters*, 63–64; Hegel, *Fichte's and Schelling's Systems of Philosophy*.

12 F. W. J. Schelling, *The Unconditional in Human Knowledge: Four Early Essays (1794–1796)*, trans. Fritz Marti (Lewisburg, Pa.: Bucknell University Press, 1980); 90–95; Schelling, *System of Transcendental Idealism*; F. W. J. Schelling to J. G. Fichte, October 3, 1801, in *Briefe und Dokumente*, 2:348–56; G. W. F. Hegel to F. W. J. Schelling, November 2, 1800, in *Hegel: The Letters*, 63–64; Hegel, *Fichte's and Schelling's Systems of Philosophy*.

13 Schelling, *Unconditional in Human Knowledge*, quote 92; Schelling, *Darstellung meines Systems der Philosophie* (Stuttgart: Frommann-Holzboog, 2009 [1801]); see Schelling, *On the World Soul*, 2:459; Otto Pöggeler, "Philosophy in the Wake of Hölderlin," *Man and World* 7 (1974): 158–76; Pinkard, *Hegel*, 79–81.

14 G. W. F. Hegel, *Phenomenology of Spirit*, trans. A. V. Miller (Oxford: Oxford University Press, 1977); Robert Pippin, "You Can't Get There from Here: Transition Problems in Hegel's *Phenomenology of Spirit*," in *The Cambridge Companion to Hegel*, ed. Frederick C. Beiser (Cambridge: Cambridge University Press, 1993), 52–53.

15 Gary Dorrien, *Kantian Reason and Hegelian Spirit*, 179–84; Rudolf Haym, *Hegel und seine Zeit: Vorlesungen über Entstehung und Entwicklung, Wesen und Wert der Hegelschen Philosophie* (Berlin: R. Gaertner, 1857), quotes 243–44; Theodor Haering, "Die Entstehungsgeschichte der Phänomenologie des Geistes," in

Verhandlungen des dritten Hegelkongresses, ed. B. Wigersma (Tübingen: Mohr, 1934), 118–38; Otto Pöggeler, "Zur Deutung der *Phänomenologue des Geistes,*" *Hegel-Studien* 1 (1961): 255–94; Pöggeler, "Die Komposition der *Phänomenologie des Geistes,*" in *Materialien zu Hegels Phänomenologie des Geistes,* ed. Hans Friedrich Fulda und Dieter Henrich (Frankfurt: Suhrkamp, 1973), 329–90; Pöggeler, *Hegels Idee einer Phänomenologie des Geistes* (Freiburg: Karl Alber, 1973), 231–98; Walter Kaufmann, "Hegel's Conception of Phenomenology," in *Phenomenology and Philosophical Understanding,* ed. Edo Pivcevic (Cambridge: Cambridge University Press, 1975), 229, 220; Kaufmann, *Hegel: Reinterpretation, Texts, and Commentary* (Garden City, N.Y.: Doubleday, 1965), 133–58; Kaufmann, "The Hegel Myth and Its Method," in *Hegel: A Collection of Critical Essays,* ed. Alasdair MacIntyre (Notre Dame: University of Notre Dame Press, 1976), 21–60; Michael N. Forster, *Hegel's Idea of a Phenomenology of Spirit* (Chicago: University of Chicago Press, 1998); Robert Stern, *Hegel's Phenomenology* (London: Routledge, 2001); Robert D. Winfield, *Overcoming Foundations: Studies in Systematic Philosophy* (New York: Columbia University Press, 1989); Klaus Hartmann, "Hegel: A Non-Metaphysical View," in *Hegel: A Collection of Critical Essays,* 101–24; Quentin Lauer, SJ, *Hegel's Concept of God* (Albany: State University of New York Press, 1982); Cyril O'Regan, *The Heterodox Hegel* (Albany: State University of New York Press, 1994); Alan M. Olson, *Hegel and the Spirit: Philosophy as Pneumatology* (Princeton: Princeton University Press, 1992); Jon Stewart, "The Architectonic of Hegel's *Phenomenology of Spirit,*" in *The Phenomenology of Spirit Reader: Critical and Interpretive Essays,* ed. Jon Stewart (Albany: State University of New York Press, 1998), 441–77; Pippin, "Hegel's *Phenomenology of Spirit,*" 52–85.

16 Kant, *Metaphysical Foundations of Natural Science,* trans. E. B. Bax (1786; London: George Bell, 1883), 119.

17 Hegel, *Phenomenology of Spirit,* quotes #16, 9; #17, 10; #20, 11; #21, 11, 12.

18 Hegel, *Phenomenology of Spirit,* #22, 12.

19 Hegel, *Phenomenology of Spirit,* #25, 14.

20 J. N. Findlay, *Hegel: A Re-Examination* (New York: Macmillan, 1962), 34–57, quote 57; Robert C. Solomon, "Hegel's Concept of *Geist,*" in *Hegel: A Collection of Critical Essays,* 125–49.

21 Solomon, "Hegel's Concept of *Geist,*" "some sort," 125; "fundamentally," 126; "one ego," 148; Robert C. Solomon, *In the Spirit of Hegel: A Study of G. W. F. Hegel's Phenomenology of Spirit* (New York: Oxford University Press, 1983), "very" and "anti-religious," 27.

22 H. F. Fulda, "Der Begriff des Geistes bei Hegel und seine Wirkungsgeschichte," in *Historisches Wörterbuch der Philosophie,* ed. Joachim Ritter, Band III (Stuttgart: Schwabe and Company, 1971), 191–93.

23 Robert Pippin, *Hegel's Idealism: The Satisfactions of Self-Consciousness* (Cambridge: Cambridge University Press, 1989), 35–41, 163–71, 175–88, quote 39.

24 Hegel, *Phenomenology of Spirit,* #50, 29; see Robert R. Williams, *Recognition: Fichte and Hegel on the Other* (Albany: State University of New York Press),

141–60; H. S. Harris, "The Concept of Recognition in Hegel's Jena Manuscripts," *Hegel-Studien Beiheft* 20 (1979): 229–48; Heinz Röttges, *Dialektik und Skeptizismus: Die Rolle des Skeptizismus für Genese, Selbstverständnis und Kritik der Dialektik* (Athenäum: Hain Verlag, 1986), 149–56; Westphal, *Hegel's Phenomenology*, 135–40; Ludwig Siep, *Anerkenung als Prinzip der praktische Philosophie* (Freiburg: Karl Alber, 1979).

25 Hegel, *Phenomenology of Spirit*, #146, 88–89.

26 Hegel, *Phenomenology of Spirit*, #147–48, 89–90.

27 Hegel, *Phenomenology of Spirit*, #166–77, 104–11; #167, 104–5.

28 See Dieter Henrich, "Hölderlin und Hegel," in *Hegel im Kontext* (Frankfurt: Suhrkamp, 1967), 26–27; Williams, *Recognition*, 144–46; Jean Hyppolite, "Life and the Consciousness of Life in the Jena Philosophy," in *Studies on Marx and Hegel*, ed. and trans. John O'Neill (New York: Harper & Row, 1969), 6–7.

29 Hegel, *Phenomenology of Spirit*, #178–96, 111–19.

30 Hegel, *Phenomenology of Spirit*, #194, 117; #196, 118–19.

31 Karl Marx, "Economic and Philosophic Manuscripts of 1844," in *Karl Marx: Selected Writings*, ed. David McLellan (Oxford: Oxford University Press, 1977), quote 101; Friedrich Nietzsche, *On the Genealogy of Morals*, in *Basic Writings of Nietzsche*, trans. Walter Kaufmann (New York: Modern Library, 1968), 460–92; Martin Buber, *I and Thou*, trans. Walter Kaufmann (New York: Scribner's, 1970); Simone de Beauvoir, *The Second Sex*, trans. H. M. Parshley (New York: Vintage, 1989), 64–65; Frantz Fanon, *Black Skin, White Masks* (New York: Grove Press, 1967); Kojève, *Introduction to the Reading of Hegel*; Georg Lukács, *The Young Hegel*, trans. R. Livingstone (Cambridge: MIT Press, 1976); Marcuse, *Reason and Revolution*; Hyppolite, *Hegel's Phenomenology of Spirit*.

32 Kojève, *Introduction to the Reading of Hegel*, 56–57; Sartre, *Critique of Dialectical Reason*; Hyppolite, *Hegel's Phenomenology of Spirit*, 172–77.

33 John Edward Toews, *Hegelianism: The Path Toward Dialectical Humanism, 1805–1841* (Cambridge: Cambridge University Press, 1985), 203–369; David McLellan, *The Young Hegelians and Karl Marx* (New York: Macmillan, 1969); Marcuse, *Reason and Revolution*, 251–87.

34 Hartmann, "Hegel: A Non-Metaphysical View," 101–24; Terry Pinkard, *German Philosophy, 1760–1860: The Legacy of Idealism* (Cambridge: Cambridge University Press, 2002), 236–42; Pinkard, ed., *Rediscovering Hegel* (The Hague: Dordrecht, 1995); Alan White, *Absolute Knowledge: Hegel and the Problem of Metaphysics* (Athens: University of Ohio Press, 1983); Tom Rockmore, *Cognition: An Introduction to Hegel's Phenomenology of Spirit* (Berkeley: University of California Press, 1997); Pippin, *Hegel's Idealism*, 16–41, 175–260; "as if he," 7; Taylor, *Hegel*, "is posited," 538.

35 For interpretations of Hegel that construe his metaphysic of becoming as a Kantian critique and a post-Kantian reconstruction, see Dieter Henrich, *Der Ontologische Gottesbeweise* (Tübingen: Mohr, 1960), 192; Robert R. Williams, *Tragedy, Recognition, and the Death of God: Studies in Hegel and Nietzsche* (Oxford: Oxford

University Press, 2014), 162–63; Robert Wallace, *Hegel's Philosophy of Reality, Freedom, and God* (Cambridge: Cambridge University Press, 2005), 100.

36 Hegel, *Phenomenology of Spirit*, #676–83, 411–16.

37 Hegel, *Phenomenology of Spirit*, #684–757, 416–58; #758, 458–59.

38 Hegel, *Phenomenology of Spirit*, #761, 460–61.

39 Hegel, *Phenomenology of Spirit*, #763, 462.

40 Hegel, *Phenomenology of Spirit*, #770, 465.

41 Hegel, *Phenomenology of Spirit*, #781–87, 473–78.

42 Hegel, *Phenomenology of Spirit*, #788–808, 479–93.

43 G. W. F. Hegel, *Encyclopedia of the Philosophical Sciences*, part 1, *Logic*, trans. William Wallace (Oxford: Oxford University Press, 1965), 113–22, quote 116.

44 G. W. F. Hegel, *Science of Logic*, trans. A. V. Miller (London: Allen & Unwin, 1969), quote 25.

45 Hegel, *Science of Logic*, quote 43.

46 Hegel, *Science of Logic*, 82–105.

47 Hegel, *Science of Logic*, 105–6.

48 Hegel, *Science of Logic*, 105–56, quote 105; see Henrich, "Formen der Negation in Hegels Logik," 213–29; John M. E. McTaggart, *A Commentary on Hegel's Logic* (Cambridge: Cambridge University Press, 1910; repr., New York: Russell & Russell, 1964), 13–21; John Burbidge, "Hegel's Conception of Logic," in *Cambridge Companion to Hegel*, 86–101; Burbidge, *On Hegel's Logic: Fragments of a Commentary* (Atlantic Highlands, N.J.: Humanities Press, 1981).

49 J. M. E. McTaggart, the authority beyond numerous textbook renderings of Hegel's ostensible thesis-antithesis-synthesis, described it as "the one absolutely essential element in Hegel's system." Everything in Hegel's system "depends entirely" upon it, he taught. Robert C. Solomon, avenging decades of textbook renderings, leaps to the antithesis, that "Hegel *has no method* as such—at least, not in the *Phenomenology*." McTaggart, *Commentary on Hegel's Logic*, 1; Solomon, *In the Spirit of Hegel*, 21.

50 Hegel, *Science of Logic*, quote 107.

51 Findlay, *Hegel: A Re-Examination*, 72.

52 Pinkard, *German Philosophy*, 252; Henrich, "Formen der Negation in Hegels Logik," 213–29; Robert Brandon, "Some Pragmatist Themes in Hegel's Idealism: Negotiation and Administration in Hegel's Account of the Structure and Content of Conceptual Norms," *European Journal of Philosophy* 7 (1999): 164–89.

53 G. W. F. Hegel, *Encyclopedia of the Philosophical Sciences*, part 2, *Philosophy of Nature*, trans. A. V. Miller (Oxford: Oxford University Press, 1970); Hegel, *Encyclopedia of the Philosophical Sciences*, part 3, *Philosophy of Mind*, trans. William Wallace (Oxford: Oxford University Press, 1971); Hegel, *Phenomenology of Spirit*, #309–46, 185–210.

54 G. W. F. Hegel, *Philosophy of Right*, trans. T. M. Knox (Oxford: Oxford University Press, 1952), quote 32.

55 J. F. Fries, *Wissen, Glaube und Ahndung* (Jena: J. C. G. Göpferdt, 1805); Pinkard, *Hegel*, 431–56; Hegel, *Berliner Schriften*, 575–602.

56 Hegel, *Philosophy of Right*, 5–6.

57 Hegel, *Philosophy of Right*, quote 10.

58 Günther Nicolin, *Hegel in Berichten seiner Zeitgenossen* (Hamburg: Felix Meiner, 1970), Fries quote 221; Pinkard, *Hegel*, 457–63; see Shlomo Avineri, *Hegel's Theory of the Modern State* (Cambridge: Cambridge University Press, 1972); Z. A. Pelczynski, ed., *Hegel's Political Philosophy: Problems and Perspectives* (Cambridge: Cambridge University Press, 1971).

59 G. W. F. Hegel to Edouard-Casimir Duboc, July 30, 1822, in *Hegel: The Letters*, quotes 493–94; Hegel, *Lectures on the History of Philosophy*, 3 vols., trans. E. S. Haldane and Frances H. Simson (London: Kegan Paul, Trench, Trübner & Co., 1892–1896); Hegel, *Philosophy of Nature*, 3 vols., trans. M. J. Petry (London: Allen & Unwin, 1970); Hegel, *Aesthetics: Lectures on Fine Art*, 2 vols., trans. T. M. Knox (Oxford: Oxford University Press, 1975); Hegel, *The Philosophy of History*, trans. J. Sibree (Buffalo, N.Y.: Prometheus Books, 1991).

60 Hegel, *Lectures on the Philosophy of Religion*; G. W. F. Hegel to Carl Daub, May 9, 1821, in *Briefe von und an Hegel*, 2:262; Hegel to H. W. F. Hinrichs, April 4, 1822, in *Briefe von und an Hegel*, 2:303, cited in Hodgson, editorial introduction to Hegel, *Lectures on the Philosophy of Religion*, 1:3.

61 Hodgson, editorial introduction to Hegel, *Lectures on the Philosophy of Religion*, 1:2; see Philip M. Merklinger, *Philosophy, Theology, and Hegel's Berlin Philosophy of Religion, 1821–1827* (Albany: State University of New York Press, 1993), 1–16.

62 Hegel, *Lectures on the Philosophy of Religion*, 1:83, 86–87.

63 Hegel, *Lectures on the Philosophy of Religion*, 1:88.

64 Hegel, *Lectures on the Philosophy of Religion*, 1:91.

65 Hegel, *Lectures on the Philosophy of Religion*, 1:130.

66 Hegel, *Lectures on the Philosophy of Religion*, 1:126–27.

67 Hegel, *Lectures on the Philosophy of Religion*, 1:128.

68 Hegel, *Lectures on the Philosophy of Religion*, "an established," 1:160; G. W. F. Hegel, foreword to H. F. W. Hinrichs, *Die Religion im inneren Verhältnisse zur Wissenschaft* (Heidelberg, 1822), i–xxviii; reprinted in *Beyond Epistemology: New Studies in the Philosophy of Hegel*, ed. Fredrick G. Weiss, trans. A. V. Miller (The Hague: Martinus Nijhoff, 1974), 227–44, dog quote 242.

69 Hegel, *Lectures on the Philosophy of Religion*, quotes 1:312, 283, 347; *Meister Eckhart: Die deutschen und lateinischen Werke*, ed. J. Quint (Stuttgart: W. Kohlhammer, 1936), 1:201, 2:252; *Meister Eckhart: Teacher and Preacher*, ed. Bernard McGinn (New York: Paulist Press, 1986), 270.

70 Hegel, *Lectures on the Philosophy of Religion*, 1:349–50.

71 Hegel, *Lectures on the Philosophy of Religion*, 1:375–77.

72 Hegel, *Lectures on the Philosophy of Religion*, 1:378–79.

73 See Karl Philipp Moritz, *Anthousa; order, Roms Alterthümer* (Tübingen: Niemeyet, 2005 [1791]); Georg Friedrich Creuzer, *Symbolik und Mythologie der alten Völker, besonders der Griechen,* 4 vols. (Leipzig: Heyer und Leske, 1819–1823); editorial introduction to Hegel, *Lectures on the Philosophy of Religion,* 2:4–12.

74 This description summarizes Peter Hodgson's detailed account in the editorial introduction to Hegel, *Lectures on the Philosophy of Religion,* 2:13–15.

75 Walter Jaeschke contends that Hegel had Jewish religion in mind in his discussion of "light religion" in *The Phenomenology,* not Persian religion. See Walter Jaeschke, *Die Vernunft in der Religion: Studien zur Grundlegung der spekulativen Religionsphilosophie* (inaugural diss., Ruhr-Universitätm, 1985), 288–95; cited in Hodgson, editorial introduction to Hegel, *Lectures on the Philosophy of Religion,* 2:15, 21.

76 Hegel, *Lectures on the Philosophy of Religion,* 2:423–54.

77 Hegel, *Lectures on the Philosophy of Religion,* 2:432, 434, 436.

78 Hegel, *Lectures on the Philosophy of Religion,* 2:438–39.

79 Hegel, *Lectures on the Philosophy of Religion,* 2:439–40.

80 Hegel, *Lectures on the Philosophy of Religion,* 2:443–45, quote 445.

81 Crouter, "Hegel and Schleiermacher," 19–43; editor's note to Hegel, *Lectures on the Philosophy of Religion,* 2:444.

82 Hegel, *Lectures on the Philosophy of Religion,* 3:163, 170.

83 Hegel, *Lectures on the Philosophy of Religion,* 3:178–80, quote 178.

84 Hegel, *Lectures on the Philosophy of Religion,* 3:178–81; 3:351–54; Hegel, *Science of Logic,* 575–622.

85 Hegel, *Encyclopedia of the Philosophical Sciences,* 1:274–75.

86 Hegel, *Lectures on the Philosophy of Religion,* 3:183–84.

87 Hegel, *Lectures on the Philosophy of Religion,* 3:186–88.

88 Hegel, *Lectures on the Philosophy of Religion,* 3:192.

89 Hegel, *Lectures on the Philosophy of Religion,* 3:192–93.

90 Hegel, *Lectures on the Philosophy of Religion,* 3:194, 214–15.

91 Henrich, "Hölderlin und Hegel," "once," 27; "the event," 28; Williams, *Recognition,* "a community," 80. I am using Williams' translation of the Henrich quotes.

92 Hegel, *Lectures on the Philosophy of Religion,* 3:125; see 3:326.

93 Hegel, *Lectures on the Philosophy of Religion,* 3:219.

94 Hegel, *Lectures on the Philosophy of Religion,* 3:220; see Eberhard Jüngel, *God as the Mystery of the World: On the Foundation of the Theology of the Crucified One in the Dispute between Theism and Atheism,* trans. Darrell L. Guder (Grand Rapids: Eerdmans, 1983), 63–100; Jürgen Moltmann, *The Crucified God: The Cross of Christ as the Foundation and Criticism of Christian Theology,* trans. R. A. Wilson and John Bowden (New York: Harper & Row, 1974), 203–19, 253–54; O'Regan, *Heterodox Hegel,* 199–200; Williams, *Tragedy, Recognition, and the Death of God,* 297–98.

95 Hegel, *Lectures on the Philosophy of Religion,* 3:220–22.

96 Hegel, *Lectures on the Philosophy of Religion*, 3:232–33.

97 See Toews, *Hegelianism*, 71–94; editor's note to Hegel, *Lectures on the Philosophy of Religion*, 3:232.

98 G. W. F. Hegel to Friedrich August Gottreu Tholuck, July 3, 1826, in *Hegel: The Letters*, 519–20, quote 520; see Tholuck, *Die speculative Trinitätlehre des späteren Orients: Eine religionsphilosophische Monographie aus Handschriftlichen Quellen der Leydener, Oxforder und Berliner Bibliothek* (Berlin: F. Dümmler, 1826); Tholuck, *Die Lehre von der Sünde und vom Versöhner, oder, Die wahre Weihe des Zweiflers* (Hamburg: Friedrich Perthes, 1839 [1823]).

99 Hegel to Tholuck, July 3, 1826, in *Hegel: The Letters*, "does not," 520.

100 G. W. F. Hegel to Karl Sigmund von Altenstein, April 3, 1826, in *Hegel: The Letters*, 531–32.

101 G. W. F. Hegel to Edouard-Casimir Duboc, April 29, 1823, in *Hegel: The Letters*, 489–500; Hegel, *Encyclopedia of the Philosophical Sciences*, 1:72; editor's note to *Hegel: The Letters*, 497; Hegel, *Lectures on the Philosophy of Religion*, 1:178–80, quote 180.

102 Karl Daub, *Judas Ischariot, oder das Böse im Verhältnis zum Guten*, 2 vols. (Heidelberg: Mohr & Winter, 1816–1818); Daub, *Theologumena: sive doctrinae de religione Christiana, ex nautra Dei perspecta, repetendae, capita potiora* (Heidelberg: Mohr & Zimmer, 1806); Daub, *Lehrbuch der Katechetik* (Frankfurt: August Hermann, 1801); Philipp K. Marheineke, *Die Grundlehren der christlichen Dogmatik* (Berlin: Duncker & Humblot, 1819); Marheineke, *Christliche Symbolik, oder historischkritische und dogmatischkomparative Darstellung des Katholischen, Luterischen, Reformirten und Socianischen Lehrbegriffs* (Heidelberg: Mohr & Zimmer, 1810); Carl Friedrich Göschel, *Von den Bewwisen für die Unsterblichkeit der menschlichen Selle im Lichte der spekulativen Philosophic* (Berlin: Duncker & Humblot, 1835); Kasimir Conradi, *Unsterblichkeit und Ewiges Leben: Versuch einer Entwicklung des Unsterblichkeitsbegriffs der menschlichen Seele* (Mainz: F. Kupferberg, 1837); Marheineke, *Die Grundlinien der christlichen Dogmatik als Wissenschaft* (Berlin: Duncker & Humblot, 1827); Karl Rosenkranz, *Encyklopädie der theologischen Wissenschaften* (Halle: C. A. Schwetschke und Sohn, 1831); Daub, *Die dogmatische Theologie jetziger Zeit oder die Selbstsucht in der Wissenschaft des Glaubens und ihrer Artikel* (Heidelberg: Mohr, 1833).

103 David Friedrich Strauss, *The Life of Jesus Critically Examined*, trans. George Eliot, ed. Peter C. Hodgson (Minneapolis: Fortress, 1972); Feuerbach, *Essence of Christianity*; Karl Marx, "Theses on Feuerbach," in *Karl Marx: Selected Writings*, 156–58.

104 G. W. F. Hegel, review of Carl Friedrich Göschel, *Aphorismen über Nichtwissen und absolutes Wissen im Verhältnisse zur christlichen Glaubenserkenntnis* (Berlin: Dunker & Humblot, 1829), reprinted in Hegel, *Sämtliche Werke*, vol. 20, ed. Herman Glockner (Stuttgart: Frommon, 1968), 276–313; Hegel, *Berliner*

Schriften, 324–29; Nicolin, *Hegel in Berichten seiner Zeitgenossen*, 638–82; *Hegel: The Letters*, 668–77.

105 Göschel, *Aphorismen*, 160; Toews, *Hegelianism*, 90; editor's note to *Hegel: The Letters*, 537.

106 Hegel, review of Göschel, *Aphorismen*, 276–77; Hegel, *Berliner Schriften*, 324–29; G. W. F. Hegel to Carl Friedrich Göschel, December 13, 1830, in *Hegel: The Letters*, 543–44; Göschel to Hegel, December 31, 1830, in *Hegel: The Letters*, 545.

107 Nicolin, *Hegel in Berichten seiner Zeitgenossen*, quotes 474, 476; Toews, *Hegelianism*, 89; Pinkard, *Hegel*, 660.

108 Dorothee Sölle, *Christ the Representative* (Minneapolis: Fortress, 1967); Andrew Shanks, *A Neo-Hegelian Theology: The God of Greatest Hospitality* (London: Routledge, 2016), 25–29.

109 G. W. F. Hegel, *Lectures on the Philosophy of World History*, vol. 1, *Manuscripts of the Introduction and the Lectures of 1822–1823*, ed. and trans. Robert F. Brown and Peter C. Hodgson (Oxford: Clarendon, 2011), quote 457.

Chapter 5

1 Merleau-Ponty quote in Tarmo Malmberg, "Godard ja dialektinen filosofia," in *Etunimi Jean-Luc*, ed. Jukka Sihvonen and Simo Alitalo (Sauvo: 1986), 47; and Mauri Yia-Kotola, "The Philosophical Foundations of the Work of Film Director Jean-Luc Godard," in *Mediapolis: Aspects of Texts, Hypertexts, and Multimedial Communication*, ed. Sam Inkenin (Berlin: Walter de Gruyter, 1999), 150.

2 Karl Marx, "The Difference between Democritus' and Epicurus' Philosophy of Nature" (Ph.D. diss., University of Jena, 1841), in *Karl Marx: Selected Writings*, 11–16; Marx, *Writings of the Young Marx on Philosophy and Society*, ed. L. Easton and K. Guddar (Garden City, N.Y.: Doubleday, 1967); Leszek Kolakowski, *Main Currents of Marxism: Its Rise, Growth and Dissolution*, vol. 1, *The Founders*, trans. P. S. Falla (Oxford: Clarendon, 1978), 81–146; Mary Gabriel, *Love and Capital: Karl and Jenny Marx and the Birth of a Revolution* (New York: Little, Brown, 2011), 11–69; Max Beer, *Life and Teaching of Karl Marx* (New York: International Publishers, 1929), 2–19.

3 David McLellan, *Karl Marx: His Life and Thought* (New York: Harper & Row, 1973), 44; Karl Marx, "On the Freedom of the Press," in *Karl Marx: Selected Writings*, 17–18; Marx, "The Leading Article of the *Kölnische Zeitung*," in *Karl Marx: Selected Writings*, 18–20; Marx, "Communism and the *Augsburg Allgemeine Zeitung*," in *The Karl Marx Library*, vol. 1, *On Revolution*, ed. Saul Padover (New York: McGraw-Hill, 1971), 3–6; Heinrich Gemkow, *Friedrich Engels: A Biography* (Dresden, Germany: Verlag Zeit im Bild, 1972), 38–55; Tristram Hunt, *Marx's General: The Revolutionary Life of Friedrich Engels* (New York: Henry Holt, 2009), 19–24; Terrell Carver, *Friedrich Engels: His Life and Thought* (London: Macmillan, 1989), 16–22.

4 Karl Marx, *A Contribution to the Critique of Political Economy*, trans. S. W. Ryazanskaya (New York: International Publishers, 1999 [1st German ed., 1859]), 22; Marx, "Contribution to the Critique of Hegel's *Philosophy of Right*" (1843), in *The Marx-Engels Reader*, 2nd ed., ed. Robert C. Tucker (New York: Norton, 1978), 16–25, "just as," 20. See Avineri, *Hegel's Theory of the Modern State*, 115–54; R. N. Berki, "Perspectives in the Marxian Critique of Hegel's Political Philosophy," in *Hegel's Political Philosophy*, 199–219.

5 Marx, "Economic and Philosophic Manuscripts of 1844," "great achievement" and "nothing but," 97; Marx, "For a Ruthless Criticism of Everything Existing" (1843), in *Marx-Engels Reader*, "I am speaking," "dogmatic," and "one-sided," 13; "new principles," 14; "its dream," 15; Friedrich Engels, *The Condition of the Working Class in England* (1845), in *Collected Works of Karl Marx and Friedrich Engels* (New York: International Publishers, 1975), 4:295–596.

6 Marx, "Theses on Feuerbach," 157–58, and *Marx-Engels Reader*, 144–45.

7 Karl Marx and Friedrich Engels, *The Holy Family* (1845), in *Karl Marx: Selected Writings*, 131–55; "all treatises," 132; "Critical Criticism," 133.

8 Karl Marx and Friedrich Engels, *The German Ideology* (1845), in *Karl Marx: Selected Writings*, 159–92; "the rule," 159; "the wretchedness," 160; "as individuals," 161.

9 Marx and Engels, *German Ideology*, "life is not," 164; "each can become," 169.

10 Karl Marx and Friedrich Engels, *The Communist Manifesto*, in *Karl Marx: Selected Writings*, "specter," 221; Marx, "Articles for the *Neue Rheinische Zeitung*," in *Karl Marx: Selected Writings*, 271–76.

11 Marx and Engels, *Communist Manifesto*, "prelude," 246; Karl Marx, "Address to the Communist League" (1850), in *Karl Marx: Selected Writings*, 277–85; Marx, "Speech to the Central Committee of the Communist League" (1850), in *Karl Marx: Selected Writings*, 298–99; "Declaration of the World Society of Revolutionary Communists" (1850), in Christine Lattek, *Revolutionary Refugees: Socialism in Britain, 1840–1860* (London: Routledge, 2006), "the aim," 61.

12 Karl Marx, *Capital: A Critique of Political Economy*, trans. from the third German edition by Samuel Moore and Edward Aveling (Chicago: Charles H. Kerr, 1906), 1:15–20, "they had managed," 1:20; "foreign," 1:16. Marx completed essential portions of the second and third volumes before his death, but these volumes were completed and published by Engels. I use the Kerr edition of volume one out of longtime familiarity, and on occasion I will reference the same passages in the Penguin edition of volume one translated by Ben Fowkes, *Capital: A Critique of Political Economy* (London: Penguin, 1990). For volumes two and three I will refer to the Penguin edition: *Capital*, trans. David Fernbach (London: Penguin, 1992, 1991).

13 Marx, *Capital*, 1:24–25, "that mighty," "the demiurgos," and "the ideal," 1:25. For the Penguin edition translated by Fowkes, see 1:102–3.

14 Marx, *Capital*, 1:25–26, "peevish" and "the rational," 1:25; "is in its," 1:26; Karl Marx, "Critique of Hegel's *Philosophy of Right,*" in *Karl Marx: Early Texts*, trans. David McLellan (Oxford: Basil Blackwell, 1971), 61–72; Marx and Engels, *German Ideology*, 159–91.

15 Marx, *Critique of Political Economy*, 19–23, "to anticipate," "real," and "on which arises," 20.

16 Marx, *Critique of Political Economy*, "natural relations" and "capital is," 213; Marx, "Economic and Philosophical Manuscripts of 1844," 75–112; Karl Marx, *Grundrisse: Foundations of the Critique of Political Economy*, trans. Martin Nicolaus (London: Penguin, 1973), 83–111.

17 David Ricardo, *On the Principles of Political Economy and Taxation: Works and Correspondence of David Ricardo*, ed. Piero Sraffa (Cambridge: Cambridge University Press, 1951); Marx, *Capital*, 1:80–83, "a very queer," 1:81; "social things," "no connection," 1:83.

18 Marx, *Capital*, "the fantastic" and "this I call," 1:83; "and this one," 1:149.

19 Marx, *Capital*, 1:567; John Stuart Mill, *Principles of Political Economy*, 2 vols. (1848; 7th ed., London: Longmans, Green, Reader, and Dyer, 1871), 1:252–55.

20 Marx, *Capital*, 1:567–90, "phenomenal," 588; "natural," 589; Adam Smith, *An Inquiry into the Nature and Causes of the Wealth of Nations* (1776), 2 vols. (Chicago: University of Chicago Press, 1976), 1:450–73.

21 Marx, *Capital*, "this antagonism," 1:533.

22 Marx, *Capital*, "first," "it is," and "by a few," 1:837; "effrontery," 1:701; "despotism," 1:702.

23 W. E. B. Du Bois, "Marxism and the Negro Problem," *Crisis* 40 (1930): quote 103–4.

24 Søren Kierkegaard, *The Concept of Dread*, trans. Walter Lowrie (Princeton: Princeton University Press, 1957), 29; Kierkegaard, *Papers and Journals: A Selection*, trans. Alastair Hannay (Harmondsworth, UK: Penguin, 1996), quote 382.

25 For postmodern readings of Kierkegaard, see Louis Mackey, *Points of View: Readings of Kierkegaard* (Tallahassee: Florida State University Press, 1986); Roger Poole, *Kierkegaard: The Indirect Communication* (Charlottesville: University of Virginia Press, 1993); Poole, "The Unknown Kierkegaard: Twentieth-Century Receptions," in *The Cambridge Companion to Kierkegaard*, ed. Alastair Hannay and Gordon D. Marino (Cambridge: Cambridge University Press, 1998), 66–72; Mark C. Taylor, *Altarity* (Chicago: University of Chicago Press, 1987); Taylor, *Journeys to Selfhood: Hegel and Kierkegaard* (Berkeley: University of California Press, 1980); Taylor, *After God*.

26 Søren Kierkegaard, *The Point of View for My Work as an Author: A Report to History*, trans. Walter Lowrie (New York: Oxford University Press, 1939), 78; Walter Lowrie, *Kierkegaard* (New York: Oxford University Press, 1938), 8–15; Alastair Hannay, *Kierkegaard: A Biography* (Cambridge: Cambridge University Press, 2001), 30–39; Joakim Garff, *Søren Kierkegaard: A Biography*, trans. Bruce H. Kirmmse (Princeton: Princeton University Press, 2005), 3–9; Hans Lasson

Martensen, *Af mit Levnet*, 3 vols. (Copenhagen: Gyldendal, 1882–1883), 1:78–79, reprinted in *Encounters with Kierkegaard: A Life as Seen by His Contemporaries*, ed. Bruce H. Kirmmse, trans. Bruce H. Kirmmse and Virginia R. Laursen (Princeton: Princeton University Press, 1996), 196; Kirmmse, *Kierkegaard in Golden Age Denmark* (Bloomington: Indiana University Press, 1990); Lowrie, *A Short Life of Kierkegaard* (Princeton: Princeton University Press, 1942), 22–26; Søren Kierkegaard, entry of May 19, 1838, in Kierkegaard, *Journals and Papers*, 7 vols., ed. and trans. Howard V. Hong and Edna H. Hong (Bloomington: Indiana University Press, 1967–1978), 5:5324.

27 Søren Kierkegaard, journal entry of August 1, 1835, in *Papers and Journals*, quote 32*; see The Journals of Kierkegaard*, trans. Alexander Dru (New York: Harper Torchbooks, 1959), 44–48; Niels Thulstrup, *Kierkegaard's Relation to Hegel*, trans. George L. Stengren (Princeton: Princeton University Press, 1980), 14–38.

28 Søren Kierkegaard, *The Concept of Irony, with Continual Reference to Socrates*, trans. Howard V. Hong and Edna H. Hong (Princeton: Princeton University Press, 1989).

29 Søren Kierkegaard, *Either/Or*, 2 vols., ed. and trans. Howard V. Hong and Edna H. Hong (Princeton: Princeton University Press, 1987); Kierkegaard, *Fear and Trembling; Repetition*, ed. and trans. Hong and Hong (Princeton: Princeton University Press, 1983); Kierkegaard, *Prefaces: Light Reading for Certain Classes as the Occasion May Require, by Nicolaus Notabene*, trans. William McDonald (Tallahassee: Florida State University Press, 1989); Kierkegaard, *Concept of Dread*; Kierkegaard, *Stages on Life's Way*, trans. Hong and Hong (Princeton: Princeton University Press, 1988); Kierkegaard, *Eighteen Upbuilding Discourses*, ed. and trans. Hong and Hong (Princeton: Princeton University Press, 1990).

30 Søren Kierkegaard, *Philosophical Fragments, or, A Fragment of Philosophy, by Johannes Climacus*, trans. David F. Swenson and Howard V. Hong (Princeton: Princeton University Press, 1962); Kierkegaard, *Concluding Unscientific Postscript to Philosophical Fragments*, trans. David Swenson and Walter Lowrie (Princeton: Princeton University Press, 1941).

31 Kierkegaard, *Philosophical Fragments*, quotes 3, 6, 7.

32 Kierkegaard, *Philosophical Fragments*, quote 14.

33 Kierkegaard, *Philosophical Fragments*, 16.

34 Kierkegaard, *Philosophical Fragments*, 17.

35 Kierkegaard, *Philosophical Fragments*, 22.

36 Kierkegaard, *Philosophical Fragments*, 43, 45.

37 Kierkegaard, *Philosophical Fragments*, quotes 46, 64.

38 Kierkegaard, *Philosophical Fragments*, quote 68.

39 Kierkegaard, *Philosophical Fragments*, quote 130.

40 Kierkegaard, *Philosophical Fragments*, quote 139; see M. Jamie Ferreira, "Faith and the Kierkegaardian Leap," in *Cambridge Companion to Kierkegaard*, 207–34.

41 Kierkegaard, *Concluding Unscientific Postscript*, quotes 235, 236, 19.

42 Kierkegaard, *Concluding Unscientific Postscript*, quotes 3, 4; see Niels Thulstrup, commentator's introduction to Kierkegaard, *Philosophical Fragments*, xciv.

43 Kierkegaard, *Concluding Unscientific Postscript*, 18–33, quote 33.

44 Kierkegaard, *Concluding Unscientific Postscript*, 99–100; Friedrich A. Trendelenburg, *Logische Untersuchungen* (Berlin: G. Bethge, 1840); Trendelenburg, *Die logische Frage in Hegel's System* (Leipzig: F. A. Brockhaus, 1843); Trendelenburg, *Elementa logices Aristoteleae* (Berlin: G. Bethge, 1844); Merold Westphal, *Becoming a Self: A Reading of Kierkegaard's Concluding Unscientific Postscript* (West Lafayette, Ind.: Purdue University ress, 1996), 87–89.

45 Kierkegaard, *Concluding Unscientific Postscript*, 103; Hegel, *Science of Logic*, 25–29, 43–64.

46 Kierkegaard, *Concluding Unscientific Postscript*, quote 107.

47 Kierkegaard, *Concluding Unscientific Postscript*, quote 142.

48 Kierkegaard, *Concluding Unscientific Postscript*, 150.

49 Kierkegaard, *Concluding Unscientific Postscript*, quote 176; see C. Stephen Evans, *Kierkegaard's "Fragments" and "Postscript": The Religious Philosophy of Johannes Climacus* (Atlantic Highlands, N.J.: Humanities Press, 1983); Evans, *Passionate Reason: Making Sense of Kierkegaard's Philosophical Fragments* (Bloomington: Indiana University Press, 1992).

50 Kierkegaard, *Concluding Unscientific Postscript*, 176.

51 Kierkegaard, *Concluding Unscientific Postscript*, "fantastic," 176; "essentially," 177.

52 Kierkegaard, *Concluding Unscientific Postscript*, 177–83, quotes 182.

53 Kierkegaard, *Concluding Unscientific Postscript*, 190.

54 Kierkegaard, *Concluding Unscientific Postscript*, 199–200.

55 Kierkegaard, *Concluding Unscientific Postscript*, quotes 205, 216, 219.

56 Kierkegaard, *Concluding Unscientific Postscript*, 223–24, 292–93, quote 292; Hamann, *Sämtliche Werke*; Jacobi, *Wider Mendelssohns Beschuldigungen*; Jacobi, *F. H. Jacobi*; Jacobi, *David Hume über den Glauben, oder, Idealismus und Realismus* (1787; New York: Garland, 1983). Ronald Green, in *Kant and Kierkegaard: The Hidden Debt* (Albany: State University of New York Press, 1992), argues that Kierkegaard was essentially a Kantian who concealed his debt to Kant. This thesis fastens on Kantian differences with Hegel that are certainly there in Kierkegaard, but Green glosses over the very point of Kierkegaard's polemic, to buttress his case for the very anti-Kantian religion of Religiousness B.

57 Kierkegaard, *Concluding Unscientific Postscript*, 493–519.

58 Søren Kierkegaard, *The Book on Adler*, trans. Howard V. Hong and Edna H. Hong (Princeton: Princeton University Press, 1998); George Pattison, *Kierkegaard: The Aesthetic and the Religious* (London: Macmillan, 1992); Sylvia Walsh,

Living Christianly: Kierkegaard's Dialectic of Christian Existence (University Park: Pennsylvania State University Press, 2005).

59 Søren Kierkegaard, *Upbuilding Discourses in Various Spirits*, trans. Howard V. Hong and Edna H. Hong (Princeton: Princeton University Press, 2005); Kierkegaard, *Works of Love*, trans. Howard V. Hong (New York: Harper & Row, 1962); Kierkegaard, *Christian Discourses*, trans. Walter Lowrie (London: Oxford University Press, 1940); Kierkegaard, *The Moment and Late Writings*, ed. and trans Hong and Hong (Princeton: Princeton University Press, 1998); Wanda Warren Berry, "The Heterosexual Imagination and Aesthetic Experience in Kierkegaard's *Either/Or, Part One,*" in *International Kierkegaard Commentary*, vol. 3, *Either/Or 1* (Macon: Ga.: Mercer University Press, 1995); Berry, "Kierkegaard and Feminism: Apologetic, Repetition, and Dialogue," in *Kierkegaard in Post/Modernity*, ed. Martin J. Matustik and Merold Westphal (Bloomington: Indiana University Press, 1995), 110–24.

60 Karl Barth, *Der Römerbrief* (Bern: G. A. Baschlin, 1919); Philipp Bachmann, "Der Römerbrief verdeutscht und vergegenwärtigt: Ein Wort zu K. Barths Römerbrief," *Neue kirchliche Zeitschrift* 32 (1921): 518; Emil Brunner, "*The Epistle to the Romans*, by Karl Barth: An Up-to-Date, Unmodern Paraphrase," in *The Beginnings of Dialectic Theology*, ed. James M. Robinson, trans. Louis De Grazia and Keith R. Crim (Richmond: John Knox, 1968), 63; Adolf Jülicher, "A Modern Interpreter of Paul," in *Beginnings of Dialectic Theology*, 72; Barth, *Epistle to the Romans*, 6th ed., trans. Edwyn C. Hoskyns (Oxford: Oxford University Press, 1975 [1933]).

61 Karl Barth, "The Christian's Place in Society," in *The Word of God and the Word of Man*, trans. Douglas Horton (Gloucester, Mass.: Peter Smith, 1978), 282–83.

62 Barth, *Epistle to the Romans*, quotes 36.

63 Barth, *Epistle to the Romans*, quotes 39, 42.

64 Barth, *Epistle to the Romans*, quotes 98–99, 105.

65 Barth, *Epistle to the Romans*, quotes 108–9, 116.

66 Barth, *Epistle to the Romans*, quotes 141–42, 225.

67 Karl Barth, "Preface to the Second Edition," in *Epistle to the Romans*, 10.

68 Emil Brunner, *The Theology of Crisis* (New York: Scribner's, 1929); Brunner, *Wahrheit als Begegnung* (Zurich: Zwingli-Verlag, 1938); Friedrich Gogarten, "Between the Times," in *Beginnings of Dialectic Theology*, 277–82; Fritz Buri, *Theologie der Existenz* (Stuttgart: Paul Haupt, 1954); Buber, *I and Thou*; Gabriel Marcel, *Being and Having*, trans. Katharine Farrer (Glasgow: The University Press, 1949); Emmanuel Levinas, *Totality and Infinity: An Essay on Exteriority*, trans. Alphonso Lingis (Pittsburgh: Duquesne University Press, 1969), "egoist's," 305; Levinas, "Transcendence and Height" (1962), in *Emmanuel Levinas: Basic Philosophical Writings*, ed. Adriaan T. Peperzak, Simon Critchley, and Robert Bernasconi (Bloomington: Indiana University Press, 1996), "absolutely," 30; Eberhard Jüngel, "Von der Dialektik zur Analogie: Die Schule Kierkegtaards und der Einspruch Pertersons," in *Barth-Studien* (Gütersloh: Gerd Mohn, 1982), 127–79.

69 Karl Barth, *Die christliche Dogmatik im Entwurf, I: Die Lehre vom Worte Gottes. Prolegomena zur christlichen Dogmatik* (Munich: Chr. Kaiser, 1927); Barth, *Church Dogmatics*, vol. 1, bk. 1, *The Doctrine of the Word of God*, trans. G. T. Thomson (Edinburgh: T&T Clark, 1936).

70 Karl Barth, *Church Dogmatics*, vol. 2, bk. 1, *The Doctrine of God*, ed. G. W. Bromiley and T. F. Torrance (Edinburgh: T&T Clark, 1957), 257–321; Barth, *Protestant Theology*, 1973 ed., quote 396.

71 Barth, *Protestant Theology*, 1973 ed., quotes 409, 413.

72 Barth, *Protestant Theology*, 1973 ed., 414.

73 Barth, *Protestant Theology*, 1973 ed., 414–15.

74 Barth, *Protestant Theology*, 1973 ed., quote 419.

75 Barth, *Protestant Theology*, 1973 ed., quotes 419.

76 Barth, *Protestant Theology*, 1973 ed., quotes 420; see Barth, *Doctrine of God*, 297–321.

77 Levinas, *Totality and Infinity*, "the perception," 74; "the nakedness," 74–75; "the same," 102.

78 Levinas, *Totality and Infinity*, "ancient" and "whence came," 102; "the most," 196.

79 Levinas, *Totality and Infinity*, "he posits" and "it becomes," 196; "the finitude" and "the relation," 197.

80 Steven G. Smith, "Reason as One for Another: Moral and Theoretical Argument in the Philosophy of Levinas," in *Face to Face with Levinas*, ed. R. Cohen (Albany: State University of New York Press, 1986), 53–54; Williams, *Recognition*, 299.

81 Steven G. Smith, "Dialogue with Emmanuel Levinas," in *Face to Face with Levinas*, "I am," 22.

82 Williams, *Recognition*, 298–99; Jacques Derrida, "Violence and Metaphysics," in *Writing and Difference*, trans. Alan Bass (Chicago: University of Chicago Press, 1978), "Levinas is," 99; Hegel, *Geschichte der Philosophie, Hegel Werke, Theorie Werkausgabe* (Frankfurt: Suhrkamp, 1971), 18:299, cited in Williams, *Recognition*, 299; Smith, "Dialogue with Emmanuel Levinas," "He answers," 56.

83 Williams, *Recognition*, 300–301.

84 Gilles Deleuze, *Difference and Repetition*, trans. Paul Patton (New York: Columbia University Press, 1994), 42–50, "contradiction," 44.

Chapter 6

1 Borden Parker Bowne, *Metaphysics* (New York: Harper & Brothers, 1898); Bowne, *Theism* (New York: American Book, 1902); Bowne, *Personalism* (Boston: Houghton Mifflin, 1908); Bowne, *The Essence of Religion* (Boston: Houghton Mifflin, 1910); Dorrien, *Making of American Liberal Theology: Imagining Progressive Religion*, 370–92.

2 Albert Cornelius Knudson, *The Philosophy of Personalism: A Study in the Metaphysics of Religion* (New York: Abingdon, 1927); Knudson, *The Doctrine of God* (New York: Abingdon, 1930); Edgar S. Brightman, *The Problem of God* (New York: Abingdon, 1930); Brightman, *Personality and Religion* (New York: Abingdon, 1934); Brightman, *A Philosophy of Religion* (New York: Prentice-Hall, 1940); Brightman, *Person and Reality: An Introduction to Metaphysics*, ed. Peter A. Bertocci, Janette G. Newhall, and Robert S. Brightman (New York: Ronald Press, 1958); Dorrien, *Making of American Liberal Theology: Making Christianity Modern*; *The Boston Personalist Tradition in Philosophy, Social Ethics, and Theology*, ed. Paul Deats and Carol Robb (Macon, Ga.: Mercer University Press, 1986).

3 Borden Parker Bowne, *The Philosophy of Herbert Spencer* (New York: Nelson & Phillips, 1874), 11–13; Bowne, "Herbert Spencer's Laws of the Unknowable," *New Englander* 32 (1873): 1–34; Bowne, "The Philosophy of Herbert Spencer," *Methodist Review* 56 (1874): 510–14.

4 R. Hermann Lotze, *Microcosmos: An Essay concerning Man and His Relation to the World*, 2 vols., trans. Elizabeth Hamilton and Emily E. C. Jones (Edinburgh: T&T Clark, 1888); Lotze, *Grundzüge der Religionsphilosophie* (Leipzig: G. Hirzel, 1884); Lotze, *Metaphysik* (Leipzig: Felix Meiner, 1912); Lotze, *Logik* (Leipzig: Weidmann'sche Buchhandlung, 1843); Borden Parker Bowne, "Ulrici's Logic," *New Englander* 33 (1874): 458–92; Bowne, "Philosophy in Germany," *Independent* 32 (1874): 4–5; Bowne, "The Materialistic Gust," *Independent* 26 (1874): 2–3; Hermann Ulrici, "Review of Bowne's *Philosophy of Herbert Spencer*," *Zeitschrift für Philosophie und philosophische Kritik* 66 (1875): 160–64; Francis J. McConnell, *Borden Parker Bowne: His Life and His Philosophy* (New York: Abingdon, 1929), "that is nothing," 37; "Ephraim," 91.

5 Borden Parker Bowne to Kate M. Bowne, May 31, 1909, in K. M. Bowne, "An Intimate Portrait of Bowne," *Personalist* 2 (1921): 5–15, "in any" and "strong," 10; Rufus Burrow Jr., *Personalism: A Critical Introduction* (St. Louis: Chalice Press, 1999), 27–32.

6 T. H. Green, *Works of T. H. Green*, 3 vols., ed. R. L. Nettleship (London: Longmans, Green, 1885–1888); Green, *Prolegomena to Ethics* (Oxford: Clarendon, 1883); F. H. Bradley, *Appearance and Reality: A Metaphysical Essay* (Oxford: Oxford University Press, 1893); Bradley, *Essays on Truth and Reality* (Oxford: Oxford University Press, 1914); Bernard Bosanquet, *Psychology of the Moral Self* (New York: Macmillan, 1897); Bosanquet, *The Principle of Individualism and Value* (London: Macmillan, 1912); Bosanquet, *The Value and Destiny of the Individual* (London: Macmillan, 1913); Richard B. Haldane, *The Pathway to Reality*, 2 vols. (London: J. Murray, 1903, 1904); J. M. E. McTaggart, *Studies in the Hegelian Dialectic*, 2nd ed. (New York: Russell & Russell, 1964 [1896]); John Caird, *The Fundamental Ideas of Christianity* (Glasgow: James MacLehose, 1899); Edward Caird, *The Evolution of Religion*, 2 vols. (Glasgow: James MacLehose, 1894).

7 Andrew Seth [Pringle-Pattison], *Hegelianism and Personality* (Edinburgh: W. Blackwood and Sons, 1887); Seth, *Scottish Philosophy, a Comparison of the Scottish and German Answers to Hume* (Edinburgh: W. Blackwood and Sons, 1885); James Ward, *Naturalism and Agnosticism*, 2 vols. (London: Macmillan, 1909); C. C. J. Webb, *God and Personality* (London: Allen & Unwin, 1919); Hastings Rashdall, *Philosophy and Religion* (London: Duckworth, 1910); Josiah Royce, *The Religious Aspect of Philosophy: A Critique of the Bases of Conduct and of Faith* (Boston: Houghton Mifflin, 1885); George H. Howison, *The Limits of Evolution, and Other Essays concerning the Metaphysical Theory of Personal Idealism* (New York: Macmillan, 1901).

8 Borden Parker Bowne, *Theory of Thought and Knowledge* (New York: Harper & Brothers, 1897), "the unity," 105; Arthur Schopenhauer, *The World as Will and Representation*, 2 vols., trans. E. F. J. Payne (New York: Dover, 1966); Schopenhauer, *Essays and Aphorisms*, trans. R. J. Hollingdale (London: Penguin, 1970).

9 Bowne, *Theory of Thought and Knowledge*, "it is only," 108.

10 Bowne, *Personalism*, "a purely," 257.

11 Bowne, *Personalism*, 268–77.

12 Bowne, *Theism*, 224–25.

13 Francis J. McConnell, "Bowne and Personalism," in *Personalism in Theology: A Symposium in Honor of Albert Cornelius Knudson*, ed. Edgar S. Brightman (Boston: Boston University Press, 1943), "hole" image, 24; William James to Borden Parker Bowne, August 17, 1908, appendix A in *Representative Essays of Borden Parker Bowne*, ed. Warren E. Steinkraus (Utica, N.Y.: Meridian Publishing, 1980), 189–90; W. E. Hocking, "The Metaphysics of Borden Parker Bowne," *Methodist Review* 105 (1922): 371–74; McConnell, *Borden Parker Bowne*, 76–78, 274–80.

14 McConnell, *Borden Parker Bowne*, "now let us," 93; Borden Parker Bowne, *Studies in Christianity* (Boston: Houghton Mifflin, 1909), 3–83.

15 Bowne, *Studies in Christianity*, "ignorant," 40; "texts have been," 71.

16 Bowne, *Studies in Christianity*, 132–67.

17 Bowne, *Studies in Christianity*, "if we wish," 155.

18 Bowne, *Studies in Christianity*, "there can," 157.

19 Bowne, *Studies in Christianity*, "the method," 159; Dorrien, *Making of American Liberal Theology: Imagining Progressive Religion*.

20 Albert C. Knudson, *The Doctrine of Redemption* (New York: Abingdon, 1933).

21 Bowne, *Theism*, "Christianity has been," 299; "by making," 300.

22 Editorial, "The Acquittal of Professor Bowne," *Christian Advocate* 89 (1904): 571; George Elliott, "The Orthodoxy of Bowne," *Methodist Review* 38 (1922): 399–413; Harmon L. Smith, "Borden Parker Bowne: Heresy at Boston," in *American Religious Heretics: Formal and Informal Trials* (Nashville: Abingdon, 1966), 148–87; John Miley, *Systematic Theology*, 2 vols. (New York: Hunt & Eaton, 1893), 2:155–94; Bowne, *Studies in Christianity*, "when the inferior," 366.

23 Bowne, *Studies in Christianity*, "questions," 382; "modern," 371.

24 George A. Coe, *A Syllabus of Eight Lectures on Education in Religion and Morals* (Evanston, Ill.: Northwestern University Press, 1904); Henry Churchill King, *Theology and the Social Consciousness* (New York: Hodder & Stoughton, 1902); George Burman Foster, *The Finality of the Christian Religion* (Chicago: University of Chicago Press, 1906).

25 Ernst Troeltsch, *Gesammelte Schriften*, 4 vols. (Tübingen: Mohr, 1912–1925); Troeltsch, *Meine Bücher* (1922), in *Gesammelte Schriften*, 4:3–18; Troeltsch, "Die 'kleine Göttinger Fakultät' von 1890," in Hans-Georg Drescher, *Ernst Troeltsch: His Life and Work*, trans. John Bowden (Minneapolis: Fortress, 1993), 11–12; Troeltsch, "Historical and Dogmatic Method in Theology" and "The Dogmatics of the History-of-Religions School," trans. Walter E. Wyman Jr. (1913), in *Religion in History*, 11–32, 87–108.

26 Ernst Troeltsch, "Christianity and the History of Religion," in *Religion in History*, quotes 78.

27 Troeltsch, "Christianity and the History of Religion," 78–83; Ernst Troeltsch, "Geschichte und Metaphysik," *Zeitschrift für Theologie und Kirche* 8 (1898): 1–69; Troeltsch, "Historical and Dogmatic Method in Theology," 21; Lotze, *Microcosmos*; Lotze, *Grundzüge der Religionsphilosophie*.

28 Ernst Troeltsch, *Die Absolutheit des Christentums und die Religionsgeschichte* (Tübingen: Mohr, 1902); English edition, *The Absoluteness of Christianity and the History of Religions*, trans. David Reid (Louisville: Westminster John Knox, 2005), quotes 45, 47.

29 Troeltsch, *Absoluteness of Christianity*, 48–59.

30 Troeltsch, *Absoluteness of Christianity*, 67–94; Heinrich Rickert, *Die Grenzen der naturwissenschaftlichen Begriffsbildung. Eine logische Einleitung in die historischen Wissenschaften* (Tübingen: Mohr, 1902); Rickert, *Kulturwissenschaft und Naturwissenschaft* (Tübingen: Mohr, 1921); Rickert, *Zur Lehre von der Definition* (Tübingen: Mohr, 1915).

31 Troeltsch, *Absoluteness of Christianity*, quote 98; Ernst Troeltsch, *Glaubenslehre*, ed. Gertrud von le Fort (Berlin: Duncker & Humblot, 1925); English edition, *The Christian Faith*, trans. Garrett E. Paul (Minneapolis: Fortress, 1991), 12–24.

32 Ernst Troeltsch, "Political Ethics and Christianity," 1904 address to the Evangelical Social Congress, trans. James Luther Adams, reprinted in *Religion in History*, 173–209; Max Weber, *The Protestant Ethic and the Spirit of Capitalism*, trans. Peter Baehr and Gordon C. Wells (German ed., 1905; New York: Penguin, 2002).

33 Ernst Troeltsch, "Die Bedeutung des Protestantismus für die Enstehung der modernen Welt," April 1906 address to the Ninth Congress of German Historians, Stuttgart; amplified edition published under the same title in *Historische Zeitschrift 97* (1906): 1–66; English edition, Troeltsch, *Protestantism and Progress: The Significance of Protestantism for the Rise of the Modern World*, trans. J.

Montgomery (1912; Philadelphia: Fortress, 1986); Troeltsch, *Wesen der Religion und der Religionswissenschaft* (1906), in *Gesammelte Schriften*, 2:452–99; Troeltsch, *Die Trennung von Staat und Kirche, ders Staatliche Religionsunterricht und die theologischen Fakultät* (Tübingen, 1907); Troeltsch, "Luther und die moderne Welt," in *Das Christentum*, ed. P. Herre (Leipzig), 69–101, and Troeltsch, *Gesammelte Schriften*, 4:202–54; Troeltsch, *Die Bedeutung der Geschichtliichkeit Jesu für den Glauben* (Tübingen, 1911); Troeltsch, *The Social Teaching of the Christian Churches*, 2 vols., trans. Olive Wyon (first English ed., New York: Macmillan, 1931; first German ed., Troeltsch, *Die Soziallehren der christlichen Kirchen und Gruppen*, in vol. 1 of *Gesammelte Schriften*; Louisville: Westminster John Knox, 1992).

34 Troeltsch, *Social Teaching of the Christian Churches*, 2:688–784.

35 Troeltsch, *Social Teaching of the Christian Churches*, 2:1011–12, quote 1012.

36 Troeltsch, *Social Teaching of the Christian Churches*, 2:1005; Ernst Troeltsch, *Nach Erklürung der Mobilmachung* (Heidelberg: Carl Winters Universitätsbuchhandlung, 1914), 5–7; Troeltsch, *Das Wesen des Deutschen* (Heidelberg: Carl Winters Universitätsbuchhandlung, 1915), 30–32; Troeltsch, *Unser Volksheer* (Heidelberg: Carl Winters Universitätsbuchhandlung, 1914), 4–6.

37 Ernst Troeltsch, *Der Historismus und seine Probleme* (Berlin: R. Heise, 1924), and Troeltsch, *Gesammelte Schriften*, quote 3:677.

38 Troeltsch, *Der Historismus und seine Probleme*, 765–67; Ernst Troeltsch, *Der Historismus und seine Überwindung: Fünf Vorträge* (Berlin: R. Heise, 1924); English edition, Troeltsch, *Christian Thought: Its History and Application*, ed. F. von Hügel (New York: Meridian Books, 1957 [1923]), 123–36, 218–22; see Robert Rubanowice, *Crisis in Consciousness: The Thought of Ernst Troeltsch* (Tallahassee: Florida State University Press, 1982), 62–98.

39 Troeltsch, *Der Historismus und seine Probleme*, in *Gesammelte Schriften*, 3:702–20, quotes 708, 710; Troeltsch, *Christian Thought*, 121–44.

40 Troeltsch, *Der Historismus und seine Probleme*, 3:728–29.

41 Albert Cornelius Knudson, "A Personalistic Approach to Theology," in *Contemporary American Theology: Theological Autobiographies*, 2 vols., ed. Vergilius Ferm (New York: Round Table Press, 1932), "an instinctive," 1:219; Elmer A. Leslie, "Albert Cornelius Knudson, the Man," in *Personalism in Theology*, 1–4; Leslie, "Albert Cornelius Knudson: An Intimate View," *Personalist* 35 (1954): 357–68.

42 Knudson, "Personalistic Approach to Theology," quotes 223.

43 Albert C. Knudson, "Bowne as Teacher and Author," *Personalist* 1 (1920): 5–14, "he had," 7; "first," 8; "he saw," 6; Knudson, "Personalistic Approach to Theology," "it brought me," 223; Leslie, "Albert Cornelius Knudson, the Man," "it was" and "I have felt," 8.

44 Edgar S. Brightman, "Bowne: Eternalist or Temporalist," *Personalist* 28 (1947): 257–65, "made him seem," 257; Hinkley G. Mitchell to Albert C. Knudson, November 17, 1905, and Mitchell to Knudson, February 8, 1906, Albert

C. Knudson Papers, Boston University School of Theology Archives, Mugar Library, Boston University; Albert C. Knudson, *The Old Testament Problem* (Cincinnati: Jennings and Graham, 1908). Brightman recounted his encounters with Bowne to Jannette E. Newhall, his longtime assistant and colleague; see Newhall, "Edgar Scheffield Brightman: A Biographical Sketch," *Philosophical Forum* 12 (1954): 12.

45 Leslie, "Albert Cornelius Knudson, the Man," "destined," 11; Francis J. McConnell, *The Diviner Immanence* (New York: Methodist Book Concern, 1906); George Albert Coe, *The Religion of a Mature Mind* (Chicago: Fleming H. Revell, 1902); John Wright Buckham, *Personality and the Christian Idea* (Boston: Pilgrim Press, 1909); Buckham, *Mysticism and Modern Life* (New York: Abingdon, 1915); George A. Gordon, *Ultimate Conceptions of Faith* (Boston: Houghton Mifflin, 1902).

46 Edgar Sheffield Brightman, "Religion as Truth," in Ferm, *Contemporary American Theology*, 1:55–56; Brightman, "The Criterion of Religious Truth in the Theology of Albrecht Ritschl" (Ph.D. diss., Boston University, 1912), 106–7; Newhall, "Edgar Sheffield Brightman," 9–21.

47 Edgar S. Brightman, "The Unpopularity of Personalism," *Methodist Review* 104 (1921): 9–28, "an air," 10; Brightman, "Personalism and the Influence of Bowne," *Personalist* 8 (1927): 25–32.

48 Brightman, "Unpopularity of Personalism," "for much," 13; Brightman, "Why Is Personalism Unpopular?" *Methodist Review* 104 (1921): 524–35.

49 Brightman, "Why Is Personalism Unpopular?" "the clergy," 535.

50 Edgar S. Brightman, "The Tasks Confronting a Personalistic Philosophy, Part 1," *Personalist* 2 (1921): 162–71, quote 165.

51 Brightman, "Tasks Confronting a Personalistic Philosophy, Part 1," "open-minded," 165; Edgar S. Brightman, "The Tasks Confronting a Personalistic Philosophy, Part 2," *Personalist* 2 (1921): 254–66; Samuel Alexander, *Space, Time, and Deity*, 2 vols. (New York: Humanities Press, 1920); C. Lloyd Morgan, *Emergent Evolution* (London: Williams and Norgate, 1923); Morgan, *Life, Mind, and Spirit* (New York: Henry Holt, 1925); Alfred North Whitehead, *The Concept of Nature* (Cambridge: Cambridge University Press, 1964 [1920]); Whitehead, *Science and the Modern World* (New York: Macmillan, 1925); Brightman, *An Introduction to Philosophy* (New York: Henry Holt, 1925); Brightman, *Immortality in Post-Kantian Idealism* (Cambridge, Mass.: Harvard University Press, 1925); Brightman, *Religious Values* (New York: Abingdon, 1925); Brightman, *A Philosophy of Ideals* (New York: Henry Holt, 1928).

52 Edgar S. Brightman to Georgia Harkness, October 4, 1922, Edgar S. Brightman Collection, Department of Special Collections, Boston University; Albert C. Knudson, *Present Tendencies in Religious Thought* (New York: Abingdon, 1924); Knudson, *Philosophy of Personalism*.

53 Knudson, *Present Tendencies in Religious Thought*, 190–250; Knudson, "Bowne as Teacher and Author," 5–14.

54 Ernst Troeltsch, *Psychologie und Erkenntnistheorie in der Religionswissenschaft* (Tübingen: Mohr, 1905), 38–47; Albert C. Knudson, "Religious Apriorism," in *Studies in Philosophy and Theology*, ed. E. C. Wilm (New York: Abingdon, 1922), 93–127; Knudson, *Present Tendencies in Religious Thought*, 225–46.

55 Troeltsch, *Psychologie und Erkenntnistheorie in der Religionswissenschaft*, 42–45, "belongs," 44; Knudson, *Present Tendencies in Religious Thought*, 240–44; Knudson, *Philosophy of Personalism*, 250–54.

56 Knudson, *Philosophy of Personalism*, "a crude," 14.

57 McTaggart, *Studies in the Hegelian Dialectic*; Edward Caird, *Evolution of Religion*; John Caird, *Fundamental Ideas of Christianity*; William Stern, *Psychologie der Veräderungauffassung* (Breslau: Preuss & Jünger, 1906); Charles Renouvier, *Manuel républicaine de l'homme et du citoyen* (Paris: A. Colin, 1904); Royce, *Religious Aspect of Philosophy*; W. E. Hocking, *The Meaning of God in Human Experience* (New Haven: Yale University Press, 1912); Mary Whiton Calkins, *The Persistent Problems of Philosophy* (New York: Macmillan, 1925).

58 George Croft Cell to Albert C. Knudson, July 5, 1905, Albert C. Knudson Papers; Knudson, *Philosophy of Personalism*, 17–87.

59 Knudson, *Philosophy of Personalism*, 62–67.

60 Knudson, *Philosophy of Personalism*, 72–75.

61 Leibniz, *Discourse on Metaphysics*; Knudson, *Philosophy of Personalism*, 158–62, 216–18, 185–88.

62 Knudson, *Philosophy of Personalism*, "the polemic," 336.

63 Knudson, *Philosophy of Personalism*, "the picturing" and "its value," 375; S. Paul Schilling, "Albert Cornelius Knudson: Person and Theologian," in *The Boston Personalist Tradition in Philosophy, Social Ethics, and Theology*, ed. Paul Deats and Carol Robb (Macon, Ga: Mercer University Press, 1986), "amazing," 83; Albert Cornelius Knudson, *Basic Issues in Christian Thought* (New York: Abingdon, 1950), "sophisticated," 113; Douglas Clyde Macintosh, *The Reasonableness of Christianity* (New York: Scribner's, 1926), 163–65; Douglas Clyde Macintosh, *The Problem of Knowledge* (New York: Macmillan, 1915), 334; Macintosh, *Theology as an Empirical Science* (New York: Macmillan, 1919).

64 Knudson, *Philosophy of Personalism*, "only as being," 384.

65 James T. Carlyon, "Bowne in the Classroom," *Personalist* 28 (1947): "of course I cannot," 271; William James, *Pragmatism and The Meaning of Truth* (Cambridge, Mass.: Harvard University Press, 1978 [1907]), 18; Ralph Barton Perry, *The Present Conflict of Ideals* (New York: Longmans, Green, 1918), 202, 218; Knudson, *Philosophy of Personalism*, 418–25.

66 Earl B. Marlatt to Albert C. Knudson, February 5, 1926, quote Albert C. Knudson Papers; Leslie, "Albert Cornelius Knudson, the Man," 13; Leslie, "Albert Cornelius Knudson: An Intimate View," 360; Schilling, "Albert Cornelius Knudson, Person and Theologian," 82.

67 Brightman, *Religious Values*, "seemingly" and "deepest," 134; Brightman, *Introduction to Philosophy*, 332–33.

68 Newhall, "Edgar Sheffield Brightman," 14–15; Brightman, "Religion as Truth," 1:75. Brightman was especially influenced by Edmund Noble, *Purposive Evolution: The Link between Science and Religion* (New York: Henry Holt, 1926).

69 Brightman, "Religion as Truth," 1:56–57; Brightman, *Problem of God*.

70 William James, *The Varieties of Religious Experience* (1902; reprint, New York: Modern Library, 1999), 570–72, "the real," 571; H. G. Wells, *God the Invisible King* (New York: Cassell, 1917), "my friend," 172; F. W. J. Schelling, *Philosophical Investigations into the Essence of Human Freedom*, trans. Jeff Love and Johannes Schmidt (Albany: State University of New York, 2006 [1st German ed., 1809]), 27–68.

71 Francis J. McConnell, *Is God Limited?* (New York: Abingdon, 1924), "no solution," 63; McConnell, *The Christlike God: A Survey of the Divine Attributes from the Christian Point of View* (New York: Abingdon, 1927), 85–89; Brightman, *Problem of God*, 10.

72 Brightman, *Problem of God*, "required," 138.

73 Ralph Tyler Flewelling, "Notes and Discussions: The Problem of God," *Personalist* 11 (1930): 275–79, "we cannot," 276; Brightman, *Personality and Religion*, finite-infinite God, 71–100; Andrew Banning, "Professor Brightman's Theory of a Limited God," *Harvard Theological Review* 27 (July 1934): 145–68; Ted B. Clark, "The Doctrine of a Finite God," *Review and Expositor* 52 (1955): 21–43; Joseph J. Labaj, *An Exposition of the Problem of Evil and Its Solution in the Writings of Edgar Sheffield Brightman* (Rome: Pontificia Universitas Gregoriana, 1964).

74 Brightman, *Philosophy of Religion*, 240–304, 305–41, "whatever," 337; "an advance," 341; Edgar S. Brightman, *The Finding of God* (New York: Abingdon, 1931), 166–93.

75 Brightman, *Finding of God*, "any consciousness," 94; Brightman, "Religion as Truth," 1:63; Edgar S. Brightman, *The Spiritual Life* (New York: Abingdon, 1942), 23–25.

76 Edgar S. Brightman, "Personality as a Metaphysical Principle," in *Personalism in Theology*, 41–45.

77 Brightman, "Personality as a Metaphysical Principle," 45–46.

78 Brightman, "Personality as a Metaphysical Principle," 53–56; Edgar S. Brightman, "What Is Personality?" *Personalist* 20 (1939): 129–38.

79 Knudson, *Philosophy of Personalism*, 87; Knudson, *Doctrine of God*, 311; Brightman, "Personality as a Metaphysical Principle," 56–57; Edgar S. Brightman, *Is God a Person?* (New York: Association Press, 1932), 4–15, "the purpose," 14; Georgia Harkness, *The Recovery of Ideals* (New York: Scribner's, 1937). On Brightman and Harkness concerning idealism, see Dorrien, *Making of American Liberal Theology: Idealism, Realism, and Modernity*, 398–404.

80 Knudson, *Doctrine of God*, 15–16; Albert C. Knudson, "The Theology of Crisis," in *Report of the Biennial Meeting of the Conference of Theological Seminaries in the United States and Canada Bulletin* 6 (1928): 52–77.

81 Knudson, *Doctrine of God*, 67–85, 125–45, 223–25, 352–60; Rudolf Otto, *The Idea of the Holy*, trans. John W. Harvey, 2nd ed. (London: Oxford University Press, 1950 [1st German ed., 1917; 1st English ed., 1923]), 116–20, 140–46.

82 Knudson, *Doctrine of God*, 174–87; Albert C. Knudson, "Methodism," in *An Encyclopedia of Religion*, ed. Vergilius Ferm (New York: Philosophical Library, 1945), 488; Knudson, *The Validity of Religious Experience* (New York: Abingdon, 1937), "the strongest," 21; Albert C. Outler, *The Wesleyan Theological Heritage: Essays of Albert C. Outler*, ed. Thomas C. Oden and Leicester R. Longden (Grand Rapids: Zondervan, 1991), 21–37, 39–54, 97–110, 111–24; Richard Watson, *Theological Institutes* (New York: Emory and Waugh, 1831); William Burt Pope, *Compendium of Christian Theology*, 3 vols. (New York: Phillips & Hunt, 1880); Miner Raymond, *Systematic Theology*, 3 vols. (New York: Nelson & Phillips, 1877); Miley, *Systematic Theology*.

83 Knudson, *Doctrine of God*, 180–92.

84 Knudson, *Doctrine of God*, 203–41, 285–324.

85 Knudson, *Doctrine of God*, 418–28; McConnell, *Christlike God*, 70; Knudson, *Christian Thought*, 85–86, 122–41.

86 Knudson, *Doctrine of Redemption*, 388–432, "it was a," 412; Knudson, "The Social Gospel and Theology," *Personalist* 5 (1924): 102–14, "the conversion," 109; Olin Curtis, *The Christian Faith Personally Given in a System of Doctrine* (Grand Rapids: Kregel, 1956 [1905]), 373.

87 Charles Hartshorne, "The Unity of Being" (Ph.D. diss., Harvard University, 1923); Hartshorne, "Some Causes of My Intellectual Growth," in *The Philosophy of Charles Hartshorne*, ed. Lewis Edwin Hahn (LaSalle, Ill.: Open Court, 1991), 20–23; Hartshorne, *The Darkness and the Light: A Philosopher Reflects upon His Fortunate Career and Those Who Made It Possible* (Albany: State University of New York Press, 1990), 45–54, 109–96; Hartshorne, "How I Got That Way," in *Existence and Actuality: Conversations with Charles Hartshorne*, ed. John B. Cobb Jr. and Franklin I. Gamwell (Chicago: University of Chicago Press, 1984), ix–xvii.

88 Charles Hartshorne to Edgar S. Brightman, October 18, 1934, "literal participation"; Brightman to Hartshorne, December 10, 1934, Edgar S. Brightman Papers. For published collections of this correspondence, see Robert A. Gillies, ed., "The Brightman-Hartshorne Correspondence, 1934–1944," *Process Studies* 17 (1988): 9–18; and Randall E. Auxier and Mark Y. A. Davies, eds., *Hartshorne and Brightman on God, Process, and Persons: The Correspondence, 1922–1945* (Nashville: Vanderbilt University Press, 2001).

89 Edgar S. Brightman to Charles Hartshorne, December 10, 1934; Hartshorne to Brightman, February 10, 1935; Brightman to Hartshorne, January 30, 1938; Hartshorne to Brightman, December 22, 1938; Hartshorne to Brightman, May 8, 1939; Brightman to Hartshorne, May 12, 1939, Edgar S. Brightman Papers; Hartshorne, *Man's Vision of God* (Chicago: Willett, Clark, 1941); Brightman, review of *Man's Vision of God*, by Charles Hartshorne, *Journal*

of Religion 22 (1942): 96–99; Hartshorne to Brightman, January 22, 1942; Brightman to Hartshorne, September 25, 1942, Edgar S. Brightman Papers.

90 Edgar S. Brightman to Charles Hartshorne, October 31, 1942; Hartshorne to Brightman, November 9, 1942; Brightman to Hartshorne, January 31, 1943; Hartshorne to Brightman, January 13, 1944, Edgar S. Brightman Papers.

91 Edgar S. Brightman, "South of the Rio Grande," *Religion in Life* 15 (1946): 191–201, "it takes," 191; Brightman, "Personalism in Latin America," *Personalist* 24 (1943): 147–62; Brightman, *The Future of Christianity* (New York: Abingdon, 1937), 80; Brightman, "The Church, the Truth, and Society," in *Theology and Modern Life: Essays in Honor of Harris Franklin Rall*, ed. Paul A. Schilpp (Chicago: Willett, Clark, 1940), 253–62, "a God who" and "a more generous," 262; Brightman, *Finding of God*, "modernists," 40.

92 Brightman, *Moral Laws* (New York: Abingdon, 1933); Brightman, *Nature and Values* (New York: Abingdon, 1945); Brightman, *Persons and Values* (Boston: Boston University Press, 1952).

93 Brightman, "Bowne," 258–60, 264–65; Brightman, "A Temporalist View of God," *Journal of Religion* 12 (1932): 545–55; Brightman, *Person and Reality*, quotes 323.

94 Brightman, *Philosophy of Religion*, 347–49; Brightman, *Person and Reality*, 46–48, "messages" and "wherever," 46.

95 Brightman, *Person and Reality*, 46–54, quotes 51.

96 Brightman, *Person and Reality*, "in real," 324; Martin Heidegger, *Kant und das Problem der Metaphysik* (Bonn: Cohn, 1929), 183.

97 Brightman, *Person and Reality*, "is fantastic" and "horrible," 324; "we must," 325; Bradley, *Appearance and Reality*, 210.

98 Brightman, *Person and Reality*, "if there," 327; F. S. C. Northrop, *The Logic of the Sciences and the Humanities* (New York: Meridian Books, 1947).

99 Bradley, *Appearance and Reality*, 218; J. M. E. McTaggart, "The Unreality of Time," *Mind* 17 (1908): "of something," 474; Brightman, *Person and Reality*, "lost," 327; Bowne, *Theism*, 224, 222; Bowne, *Metaphysics*, "has no," 186; "a fact of," 182; Borden Parker Bowne, *Philosophy of Theism* (New York: Harper & Brothers, 1887), 191, "hence the divine," 153.

100 Brightman, *Person and Reality*, "the temporal," 328.

101 Albert C. Knudson, *The Philosophy of War and Peace* (New York: Abingdon, 1947), "benevolent" and "energetic," 82; "national" and "rising," 87; "many" and "civilizing," 90; Knudson, *The Principles of Christian Ethics* (New York: Abingdon, 1943), 262–80.

102 Knudson, *Philosophy of Personalism*, 83; Edgar S. Brightman, "Authority and Personality," *Journal of Bible and Religion* 12 (1944): "a repudiation," 6; Burrow, *Personalism*, 107–8.

103 Walter G. Muelder, "Report from the Dean: The School of Theology," *Bostonia* 20 (1947): 13; Muelder, "Christian Social Ethics Looks Forward," *Nexus* 21 (1964): 3–4; Bogumil Gacka, *Interview with Emeritus Dean Walter Muelder*

(Stockbridge, Mass.: Marian Press, 1996), 2–3; Muelder, "Communitarian Christian Ethics: A Personal Statement and a Response," in *Toward a Discipline of Social Ethics: Essays in Honor of Walter George Muelder*, ed. Paul Deats Jr. (Boston: Boston University Press, 1972), 296.

104 Walter G. Muelder, "Individual Totalities in Ernst Troeltsch's Philosophy of History" (Ph.D. diss., Boston University, 1933); Muelder, *Moral Law in Christian Social Ethics* (Richmond: John Knox, 1966), 61–119; Muelder, *The Ethical Edge of Christian Theology: Forty Years of Communitarian Personalism* (Lewiston, N.Y.: Edwin Mellen Press, 1983), 6, 22; Muelder, *Foundations of the Responsible Society* (New York: Abingdon, 1959); Muelder, "Communitarian Dimensions of the Moral Laws," in *Boston Personalist Tradition*, 237–39; Gacka, *Interview with Emeritus Dean Walter Muelder*, 15; Troeltsch, *Der Historismus und seine Probleme*; Troeltsch, *Gesammelte Schriften*, 3:118–21.

105 Walter G. Muelder, "Personality and Christian Ethics," in *Personalism in Theology*, 187; Muelder, "Individual Totalities in Ernst Troeltsch's Philosophy of History"; Muelder, "Communitarian Dimensions of the Moral Laws," 240–41; Muelder, "Religion and Postwar Reconstruction," *World Affairs Interpreter* (Autumn 1942): 275–85.

106 Troeltsch, *Gesammelte Schriften*, 3:118–21; Muelder, "Communitarian Dimensions of the Moral Laws," 240–42; Muelder, *Moral Law*, 32–34; Walter G. Muelder, "Norms and Valuations in Social Science," in *Liberal Learning and Religion*, ed. Amos N. Wilder (New York: Harper & Brothers, 1951); Muelder, "Theology and Social Science," in *Christian Social Ethics in a Changing World*, ed. John C. Bennett (New York: Association Press, 1966); Muelder, "Religion and Postwar Reconstruction," 275, 280; John E. Boodin, *The Social Mind* (New York: Macmillan, 1939).

107 Royce, *Religious Aspect of Philosophy*, "the sense of," 175; Royce, *The Problem of Christianity*, 2 vols. (New York: Macmillan, 1913), "the Beloved" and "the Realm," 1:172.

108 Muelder, "Personality and Christian Ethics," 200–203; Muelder, "Communitarian Dimensions of the Moral Laws," 240–42; Muelder, "An Autobiographical Introduction: Forty Years of Communitarian Personalism," "a *socius*," 7; Muelder, *Moral Law*, 23–47.

109 Walter G. Muelder, "A Philosophy for Post-War Pacifism," *Fellowship* (December 1944): 200.

110 Muelder, "Philosophy for Post-War Pacifism," 200–201.

111 Muelder, "Philosophy for Post-War Pacifism," 201; see Walter G. Muelder, "Pacifism and Politics: A Reply to Felix Greene," *Fellowship* (June 1947): 93–94; Michael Dwayne Blackwell, *Pacifism in the Social Ethics of Walter George Muelder* (Lewiston, N.Y.: Edwin Mellen Press, 1995), 253–82.

112 Stanley High, "Methodism's Pink Fringe," *Reader's Digest* (February 1950): 134–38, quotes 135; C. Eric Lincoln and Paul Deats Jr., "Walter G. Muelder: An Appreciation of His Life, Thought, and Ministry," in *Toward a Discipline of Social Ethics*, 3; Muelder, "Autobiographical Introduction," 34. The School of

Theology's pacifist contingent during Muelder's era included Schilling, church historian Richard B. Cameron, psychologist of religion Paul E. Johnson, registrar Wayne Jones, and librarian Jannette E. Newhall.

113 Walter G. Muelder, "Minorities Can Be Integrated," *Intercollegian* (February 1953): 16–17; Muelder, "Communitarian Dimensions of the Moral Laws," in *Boston Personalist Tradition*, 249–50; Gunnar Myrdal, *An American Dilemma*, 2 vols. (New York: Harper & Brothers, 1944).

114 Robert M. MacIver, *The More Perfect Union* (New York: Macmillan, 1948), 9–10; MacIver, *The Web of Government* (New York: Macmillan, 1947); Muelder, "Communitarian Dimensions of the Moral Laws," 249–50.

115 Walter G. Muelder, *Religion and Economic Responsibility* (New York: Scribner's, 1953), 156–58; see Muelder, "New Theology and Old Social Gospel," *New Christian Advocate* (October 1958): 26–28.

116 Muelder, *Religion and Economic Responsibility*, quote xi; Amsterdam Assembly, World Council of Churches, "The Church and the Disorder of Society" (Amsterdam: World Council of Churches, 1948).

117 Amsterdam Assembly, World Council of Churches, "Church and the Disorder of Society," 192; Muelder, *Religion and Economic Responsibility*, 6–38, 92–96, 97–116, quote 36.

118 Walter G. Muelder, "The Togetherness of Men and Women" (1958), in *Ethical Edge*, 321–36, quote 321.

119 Muelder, "Togetherness of Men and Women," 328–29.

120 Muelder, "Togetherness of Men and Women," 331–35, quotes 330, 333.

Chapter 7

1 Bernard Eugene Meland, "A Long Look at the Divinity School and Its Present Crisis," *Criterion* 1 (1962): 21–30, quote 30; Dorrien, *Making of American Liberal Theology: Idealism, Realism, and Modernity*, 151–285.

2 Foster, *Finality of the Christian Religion*; Foster, *The Function of Religion in Man's Struggle for Existence* (Chicago: University of Chicago Press, 1909); Shailer Mathews, *The Messianic Hope in the New Testament* (Chicago: University of Chicago Press, 1905); Mathews, *The Church and the Changing Order* (New York: Macmillan, 1909); Mathews, *The Social Gospel* (New York: Macmillan, 1910); Mathews, *The Faith of Modernism* (New York: Macmillan, 1924)

3 William James, "Does 'Consciousness' Exist?" *Journal of Philosophy, Psychology, and Scientific Methods* 1 (1904), in *The Writings of William James*, ed. John J. McDermott (Chicago: University of Chicago Press, 1977), 169–83, "are clinging," 169; James, *Pragmatism and The Meaning of Truth*; James, *Essays in Radical Empiricism* (New York: Longmans, Green, 1912); James, *The Will to Believe and Other Essays in Popular Philosophy* (Cambridge, Mass.: Harvard University Press, 1982 [1897]); James, *Some Problems of Philosophy: A Beginning of an Introduction to Philosophy* (New York: Longmans, Green, 1911); John Dewey, *The Quest for Certainty* (New York: Minton, Balch, 1929).

4 James, *Pragmatism and The Meaning of Truth*, 172–73; James, *Essays in Radical Empiricism*, 36–61.

5 Gerald Birney Smith, "The Task and Method of Systematic Theology," *American Journal of Theology* 14 (1910): 215–33; Shailer Mathews, "Theology and the Social Mind," *Biblical World* 46 (1915): 204–48; Mathews, "The Kingdom of God," *Biblical World* 35 (1910): 420–27; Mathews, "The Historical Study of Religion," in *A Guide to the Study of the Christian Religion*, ed. Gerald Birney Smith (Chicago: University of Chicago Press, 1916), 19–80; Shirley Jackson Case, "The Study of Early Christianity," in Smith, *Guide to the Study of the Christian Religion*, 239–326; Gerald Birney Smith, "Systematic Theology and Christian Ethics," in Smith, *Guide to the Study of the Christian Religion*, 483–579.

6 Douglas Clyde Macintosh, "The Reaction against Metaphysics in Theology" (Ph.D. diss., University of Chicago, 1911), 1–86; Macintosh, "Personal Idealism, Pragmatism, and the New Realism," *American Journal of Theology* 14 (1910): 650–56; Macintosh, "Hocking's Philosophy of Religion: An Empirical Development of Absolutism," *Philosophical Review* 23 (1914): 27–47; Macintosh, "Toward a New Untraditional Orthodoxy," in Ferm, *Contemporary American Theology*, 282–303.

7 Macintosh, *Problem of Knowledge*; Macintosh, *Theology as an Empirical Science*; Macintosh, *Reasonableness of Christianity*; Henry Nelson Wieman, Douglas Clyde Macintosh, and Max Carl Otto, *Is There a God? A Conversation* (Chicago: Willett, Clark, 1952), 131–41, "we have," 140.

8 Douglas Clyde Macintosh, "Experimental Realism in Religion," in *Religious Realism*, ed. Douglas Clyde Macintosh (New York: Macmillan, 1931), 307–409; Macintosh, *The Problem of Religious Knowledge* (New York: Harper & Brothers, 1940).

9 Macintosh, "Experimental Realism in Religion," 377–79; Macintosh, *Reasonableness of Christianity*, 46–50.

10 Edward Scribner Ames, *Religion* (New York: Henry Holt, 1929), 154–55; Shailer Mathews, *The Growth of the Idea of God* (New York: Macmillan, 1931), "an experienced," 219; "for God is," 226.

11 Gerald Birney Smith, "An Overlooked Factor in the Adjustment between Religion and Science," *Journal of Religion* 7 (1927): 337–59; Smith, "Traditional Religion in a Scientific World," *Journal of Religion* 8 (1928): 487–90; Smith, *Current Christian Thinking* (Chicago: University of Chicago Press, 1928), 169–70; Smith, "Theological Thinking in America," in *Religious Thought in the Last Quarter-Century*, ed. Gerald Birney Smith (Chicago: University of Chicago Press, 1927), 95–115.

12 Bernard E. Meland, *The Realities of Faith: The Revolution in Cultural Forms* (New York: Oxford University Press, 1962), 109–11, "it is," 109; Meland, "Present Crisis," 24–25; Charles Harvey Arnold, *Near the Edge of Battle: A Short History of the Divinity School and the "Chicago School of Theology," 1866–1966* (Chicago: Divinity School Association, 1966), 65.

13 Henry Nelson Wieman, "The Confessions of a Religious Seeker," *American Journal of Theology and Philosophy* 12 (1991), 67–119; Wieman, "Theocentric Religion," in Ferm, *Contemporary American Theology*, 1:339–52; Wieman, "Intellectual Autobiography of Henry Nelson Wieman," in *The Empirical Theology of Henry Nelson Wieman*, ed. Robert W. Bretall (New York: Macmillan, 1963), 3–18; Wieman, "Experience, Mind, and Concept," *Journal of Philosophy* 21 (1924): 561–72; Meland, *Realities of Faith*, "it was as if," 111; Alfred North Whitehead, *Inquiry into the Principles of Natural Knowledge* (Cambridge: Cambridge University Press, 1919); Whitehead, *Concept of Nature*; Whitehead, *The Principle of Relativity* (Cambridge: Cambridge University Press, 1922).

14 Meland, "Present Crisis," "strangely," 25; Wieman, "Confessions of a Religious Seeker," "I felt," 104.

15 Henry Nelson Wieman, *Religious Experience and Scientific Method* (New York: Macmillan, 1926), 5–16, "Something" and "the mere," 5.

16 Wieman, *Religious Experience and Scientific Method*, 21–47.

17 Wieman, *Religious Experience and Scientific Method*, 5–59, "a dry," 48; "these are," 50; Henry Nelson Wieman, "Two Views of Whitehead," review of *Religion in the Making*, by Alfred North Whitehead, *The New Republic* 11 (1927): 361–62; Wieman, "Religion Redefined," review of *Religion in the Making*, by Whitehead, *Journal of Religion* 7 (1927): 487–90.

18 Wieman, "Confessions of a Religious Seeker," "a vastly" and "to call it," 78; Henry Nelson Wieman, *The Wrestle of Religion with Truth* (New York: Macmillan, 1928), 1–7, 28–31, "and God is," 3; Alfred North Whitehead, *Religion in the Making* (New York: Macmillan, 1927), "what the individual" and "from God," 16–17; Wieman, "Two Views of Whitehead," 362.

19 Wieman, *Wrestle of Religion with Truth*, 179–90; Whitehead, *Religion in the Making*, 88–105, 149–60.

20 Henri Bergson, *Creative Evolution*, trans. Arthur Mitchell (New York: Henry Holt, 1911); Bergson, *The Creative Mind: An Introduction to Metaphysics*, trans. Mabelle L. Andison (New York: Philosophical Library, 1946); Alexander, *Space, Time, and Deity*; Morgan, *Emergent Evolution*; Morgan, *Life, Mind, and Spirit*; Whitehead, *Science and the Modern World*; Whitehead, *Symbolism, Its Meaning and Effect* (New York: Macmillan, 1927); Lewis S. Ford, *The Emergence of Whitehead's Metaphysics, 1925–1929* (Albany: State University of New York Press, 1986); Martin Heidegger, *Being and Time*, trans. John Macquarrie and Edward Robinson (New York: Harper & Row, 1962); Heidegger, *The Basic Problems of Phenomenology*, trans. Albert Hofstadter (Bloomington: Indiana University Press, 1988); L. Susan Stebbing, review of *Process and Reality*, by Alfred North Whitehead, *Mind* 39 (1930): 466–75; Dickinson S. Miller, "Two Views of Whitehead," review of *Religion in the Making*, by Whitehead, *New Republic* 11 (1927): 362–63; Wieman, *Wrestle of Religion with Truth*, 185; Wieman, "Two Views of Whitehead," 361–62; Gene Reeves and Delwin Brown, "The Development of Process Theology," in *Process Philosophy and Christian*

Thought, ed. Delwin Brown, Ralph E. James Jr., and Gene Reeves (Indianapolis: Bobbs-Merrill, 1971), 22–23.

21 Alfred North Whitehead, *Process and Reality: An Essay in Cosmology* (New York: Macmillan, 1929), 27–54. Since this is the edition of Whitehead's book that was available to Wieman and the early process school, it is the one I will cite. This edition contained numerous typographical and editing errors, as did an English edition published by Cambridge. A corrected edition, edited by David Ray Griffin and Donald W. Sherburne, was published in 1978 by Free Press.

22 Whitehead, *Process and Reality*, 27–54, quotes 43–44; Alfred North Whitehead, *Adventures of Ideas* (New York: Macmillan, 1933; repr., New York: Free Press, 1967), 175–90; William A. Christian, *An Interpretation of Whitehead's Metaphysics* (New Haven: Yale University Press, 1959), 11–13.

23 Whitehead, *Process and Reality*, quotes 521, 522. The quotes do not change in the Griffin and Sherburne corrected edition, 343–46.

24 Whitehead, *Process and Reality*, quotes 523, 524, 526.

25 Henry Nelson Wieman, "A Philosophy of Religion," review of *Process and Reality*, by Alfred North Whitehead, *Journal of Religion* 10 (1930): 137–39; Wieman, "Theocentric Religion," 1:345–46; Lionel Thornton, *The Incarnate Lord* (London: Longman, Green, 1928).

26 Wieman, "Theocentric Religion," 1:345–46.

27 Henry Nelson Wieman and Bernard Eugene Meland, *American Philosophies of Religion* (Chicago: Willett, Clark, 1936), 233–38; Whitehead, *Process and Reality*, 517–18. The Griffin/Sherburne edition eliminates the comma after "and that these elements," 341.

28 Wieman and Meland, *American Philosophies of Religion*, 239–40.

29 Henry Nelson Wieman and Walter Marshall Horton, *The Growth of Religion* (Chicago: Willett, Clark, 1938); Wieman, *The Source of Human Good* (Carbondale: Southern Illinois University Press, 1946); Wieman and Regina Westcott-Wieman, *Normative Psychology of Religion* (New York: Thomas Y. Crowell, 1935).

30 Bernard Eugene Meland, "The Root and Form of Wieman's Thought," in *Empirical Theology of Henry Nelson Wieman*, 44–68; Daniel Day Williams, "Wieman as a Christian Theologian," in *Empirical Theology of Henry Nelson Wieman*, 73–96.

31 Markus Barth to Bernard M. Loomer, August 31, 1965, Bernard M. Loomer Papers, box 5, Regenstein Library, University of Chicago; Nancy Frankenberry, "Bernard Loomer: Introduction," in *The Chicago School of Theology: Pioneers in Religious Inquiry*, 2 vols., ed. W. Creighton Peden and Jerome A. Stone (Lewiston, N.Y.: Edwin Mellen Press, 1996), 2:285; John F. Hayward, "For Bernie: In Memory of Bernard Loomer," *Criterion* (Winter 1986): 9–11; Bernard MacDougall Loomer, "The Theological Significance of the Method of Empirical Analysis in the Philosophy of A. N. Whitehead" (Ph.D. diss., University of Chicago, 1942).

32 Charles Hartshorne to Granville Henry, October 20, 1969, Charles Hartshorne Papers, Center for Process Studies, Claremont School of Theology; Hartshorne, *The Philosophy and Psychology of Sensation* (Chicago: University of Chicago Press, 1934), 13–14, 207–8, 269–70; Hartshorne, *Darkness and the Light*, 109–96; Hartshorne, "Philosophy After Fifty Years," in *Mid-Twentieth Century American Philosophy: Personal Statements*, ed. Peter A. Bertocci (New York: Humanities Press, 1974), 140–46; Hartshorne, "How I Got That Way," ix–xvii.

33 Charles Hartshorne, *Beyond Humanism: Essays in the New Philosophy of Nature* (Chicago: Willett, Clark, 1937), 178–86, "the doctrine," 185; Charles Sanders Peirce, *Values in a Universe of Chance*, ed. Philip P. Wiener (Garden City, N.Y.: Doubleday, 1958).

34 Reviews of Charles Hartshorne, *Man's Vision of God and the Logic of Theism*, by John C. Bennett, *Christendom* 7 (1942): 102–4; Reinhold Niebuhr, *Christianity and Society* 7 (1942): 43–44; Douglas Clyde Macintosh, *Review of Religion* 6 (1942): 443–48; Hartshorne, *Man's Vision of God and the Logic of Theism* (New York: Harper & Brothers, 1941).

35 Charles Hartshorne, *Whitehead's Philosophy: Selected Essays, 1935–1970* (Lincoln: University of Nebraska Press, 1972), 1–7, "a warm," 1; "my primary," 3; Hartshorne, "Is Whitehead's God the God of Religion?" *Ethics* 53 (1943): 219–27; Ivor Leclerc, *Whitehead's Philosophy: An Expository Introduction* (London: Allen & Unwin, 1959), 3; Hartshorne, "A Reply to My Critics," in *Philosophy of Charles Hartshorne*, 640; John B. Cobb Jr., "Hartshorne's Importance for Theology," in *Philosophy of Charles Hartshorne*, 170; see Christian, *Whitehead's Metaphysics;* Victor Lowe, *Understanding Whitehead* (Baltimore: Johns Hopkins University Press, 1962); Auxier and Davies, *Hartshorne and Brightman*.

36 Charles Hartshorne, "Whitehead and Ordinary Language," *Southern Journal of Philosophy* 8 (1970): 437–45, in *Whitehead's Philosophy*, 171–82; Hartshorne, "Whitehead in Historical Context," in Hartshorne and Creighton Peden, *Whitehead's View of Reality* (New York: Pilgrim Press, 1981), 8–9, quote 9; Hartshorne, "Reply to My Critics," 645–47; Hartshorne, "Whitehead's Idea of God," in *The Philosophy of Alfred North Whitehead*, ed. Paul Arthur Schilpp (Evanston, Ill.: Northwestern University Press, 1941), 557–58.

37 Lewis S. Ford, "Hartshorne's Interpretation of Whitehead," in *Philosophy of Charles Hartshorne*, 313–37, "a genuine," 315; Ford, ed., *Two Process Philosophers: Hartshorne's Encounter with Whitehead*, AAR Studies in Religion (Tallahassee, Fla.: American Academy of Religion, 1973); Whitehead, *Process and Reality*, 220, 336; A. H. Johnson, *Whitehead's Theory of Reality* (Boston: Beacon Press, 1952); Johnson, *Whitehead's Philosophy of Civilization* (Boston: Beacon Press, 1958); Victor Lowe, Charles Hartshorne, and A. H. Johnson, *Whitehead and the Modern World: Science, Metaphysics, and Civilization; Three Essays on the Thought of Alfred North Whitehead* (Boston: Beacon Press, 1950).

38 Hartshorne, "Whitehead in Historical Context," 21–24; Charles Hartshorne, postscript to Santiago Sia, *God in Process Thought: A Study in Charles Hartshorne's*

Concept of God (Dordrecht, the Netherlands: Martinus Nijhoff, 1985), 119; Hartshorne, "Whitehead's Idea of God," 513–59; Edgar A. Towne, *Two Types of New Theism: Knowledge of God in the Thought of Paul Tillich and Charles Hartshorne* (New York: Peter Lang, 1997), 156–60; Ralph E. James, *The Concrete God: A New Beginning for Theology; The Thought of Charles Hartshorne* (Indianapolis: Bobbs-Merrill, 1967), 108–11; Ford, "Hartshorne's Interpretation of Whitehead," 315–16; Christian, *Whitehead's Metaphysics*, 396–99

39 Charles Hartshorne, *The Divine Relativity: A Social Conception of God* (New Haven: Yale University Press, 1948), "just as," 39; Hartshorne, "Theological Values in Current Metaphysics," *Journal of Religion* 26 (1946): 157–67.

40 Hartshorne, *Divine Relativity*, 25–34; Hartshorne, postscript to *God in Process Thought*, "a rare," 118; Charles Hartshorne, *Creative Synthesis and Philosophic Method* (London: SCM Press, 1970), 19–42; Nancy Frankenberry, "Hartshorne's Method in Metaphysics," in *Philosophy of Charles Hartshorne*, 291–312.

41 Morris R. Cohen, *Preface to Logic* (New York: Henry Holt, 1944), 74–75; Hartshorne, *Divine Relativity*, x–xi, 60–115; Charles Hartshorne, "Introduction: The Standpoint of Panentheism," in *Philosophers Speak of God*, ed. Charles Hartshorne and William L. Reese (Chicago: University of Chicago Press, 1953; repr., Amherst, N.Y.: Humanity Books, 2000), 2–5.

42 Hartshorne, "Introduction: The Standpoint of Panentheism," "we should," 8–15.

43 Hartshorne and Reese, *Philosophers Speak of God*, 15–25, 58–75, 211–24, 395–410, 365–94, 76–164, 165–210.

44 Charles Hartshorne, *Reality as Social Process: Studies in Metaphysics and Religion* (New York: Free Press, 1953); Hartshorne, *The Logic of Perfection* (LaSalle, Ill.: Open Court, 1962); Hartshorne, *Anselm's Discovery: A Re-Examination of the Ontological Proof for God's Existence* (LaSalle, Ill.: Open Court, 1965).

45 Daniel Day Williams, *The Spirit and the Forms of Love* (New York: Harper & Row, 1968); Williams, *The Andover Liberals: A Study in American Theology* (New York: King's Crown Press, 1941); Williams, "The Perplexity and the Opportunity of the Liberal Theology in America," *Journal of Religion* 25 (1945): 168–78; Williams, "Tradition and Experience in American Theology," in *The Shaping of American Religion*, ed. James Ward Smith and A. Leland Jamison (Princeton: Princeton University Press, 1961), 443–95; Williams, *God's Grace and Man's Hope* (New York: Harper & Brothers, 1949); Bernard M. Loomer, "Christian Faith and Process Philosophy," *Journal of Religion* 29 (1949): 171–203; Loomer, "Neo-Naturalism and Neo-Orthodoxy," *Journal of Religion* 28 (1948): 79–91; Williams, "Truth in the Theological Perspective," *Journal of Religion* 28 (1948): 242–49; Williams, "Some Queries to Professor Meland on His Paper, 'How Is Culture a Source of Theology?'" *Criterion* 3 (1964): 28–33; Bernard E. Meland, "How Is Culture a Source of Theology?" *Criterion* 3 (1964): 10–21; Meland, "The Root and Form of Wieman's Thought," 44–68; Williams, "Wieman as a Christian Theologian," 73–96.

46 Meland, "Present Crisis," 21–30; Clark M. Williamson, "Bernard Meland: What Kind of Theologian?" *Journal of Religion* 60 (1980): 369–90, Sittler quote 369.

47 Bernard Eugene Meland, "The Confessions of a Frustrated Theologian" (1944), unpublished autobiographical essay, Bernard Eugene Meland Papers, Regenstein Library, University of Chicago, 1–6, "my father really stepped," 3; "we were people," 5.

48 Meland, "Confessions of a Frustrated Theologian," "quiet love" and "it was," 6; Bernard Eugene Meland, "Fifty Years of Religious Inquiry" (1979), unpublished autobiographical essay, Bernard Eugene Meland Papers, Regenstein Library, University of Chicago, 1–2; Meland, "Interpreting the Christian Faith within a Philosophical Framework," *Journal of Religion* 33 (1953): 87–102, "despite," 89; Meland, *America's Spiritual Culture* (New York: Harper & Brothers, 1948), 51; Tyron Inbody, *The Constructive Theology of Bernard Meland: Postliberal Empirical Realism* (Atlanta: Scholars Press, 1995), 5–6.

49 Meland, "Confessions of a Frustrated Theologian," 7–10, quotes 8, 9; Meland, "Fifty Years of Religious Inquiry," 3–4.

50 Meland, "Fifty Years of Religious Inquiry," 4–7, Mathews quote 6; Meland, "Confessions of a Frustrated Theologian," 10–12, "effervescence" quote 10; Bernard E. Meland, "Towers of the Mind" (1946), unpublished autobiographical essay, Bernard Eugene Meland Papers, Regenstein Library, University of Chicago, 2–3.

51 Meland, "Towers of the Mind," quote 10; Meland, "Fifty Years of Religious Inquiry," 9–10.

52 Meland, "Confessions of a Frustrated Theologian," 13–18, "here was," 13; Meland, "Towers of the Mind," 55–56, "fixed and complacent," 56; Meland, "Fifty Years of Religious Inquiry," 11–12; Bernard Eugene Meland, "Some Autobiographical Reflections: Bearing on Works Preceding *Faith and Culture*" (1969), unpublished paper, Bernard Eugene Meland Papers, Regenstein Library, University of Chicago, 6.

53 Meland, "Some Autobiographical Reflections," 6; Bernard Eugene Meland, "The Range of Our Dedications," *Divinity School News* 14 (1947): 1–4; Inbody, *Constructive Theology of Bernard Meland*, 15–16.

54 Meland, "Confessions of a Frustrated Theologian," quotes 20–21; Bernard Eugene Meland, "A Critical Analysis of the Appeal to Christ in Present-Day Religious Interpretations" (Ph.D. diss., University of Chicago, 1929).

55 Bernard Eugene Meland, *Modern Man's Worship: A Search for Reality in Religion* (New York: Harper & Brothers, 1934), 36–37, 139–40; Meland, "The Religion of Henry Nelson Wieman," *Christian Register* (October 1933): 677–79; Meland, "Is God Many or One?" *Christian Century* 50 (1933): 725–26; Meland, "Mystical Naturalism and Religious Humanism," *New Humanist* 8 (1935): 72–74; Meland, "Rudolf Otto and the New Church Worship in Germany," *Homiletic Review* 103 (1932): 261–66; Meland, "Friedrich Heiler and the High Church

Movement in Germany," *Journal of Religion* 12 (1933): 139–49; Paul Tillich, "Logos und Mythos der Technik," *Logos* 16 (1927): 356–65; Tillich, "Mythos und Mythologie," in vol. 4 of *Die Religion in Geschichte und Gegenwart*, 2nd ed. (Tübingen: Mohr, 1930), 664–69; Reinhold Niebuhr, *An Interpretation of Christian Ethics* (New York: Scribner's, 1935), 2–7; Niebuhr, "The Truth in Myths," in *The Nature of Religious Experience: Essays in Honor of Douglas Clyde Macintosh*, ed. J. S. Bixler et al. (New York: Harper & Brothers, 1937), 121–33.

56 Meland, *Modern Man's Worship*, 179–80, 185–86, quote 179; Bernard Eugene Meland, "Toward a Valid View of God," *Harvard Theological Review* 24 (1931): 202–3; Meland, "Towers of the Mind," 18–21.

57 Bernard Eugene Meland, "The Faith of a Mystical Naturalist," *Review of Religion* 1 (1937): 270–78, quotes 270–71; Meland, "Towers of the Mind," 19–21; Wieman and Meland, *American Philosophies of Religion*.

58 Wieman and Meland, *American Philosophies of Religion*, 272–305; Meland, "Faith of a Mystical Naturalist," 270–78.

59 Wieman and Meland, *American Philosophies of Religion*, 300–305; Meland, "Towers of the Mind," quote 23.

60 Meland, "Towers of the Mind," 24–27, 33–45; Inbody, *Constructive Theology of Bernard Meland*, 25.

61 Bernard Eugene Meland, "In Praise and Life" (1937–1939), unfinished manuscript, Bernard Eugene Meland Papers, Regenstein Library, University of Chicago; Meland, "Towers of the Mind," 24–32.

62 Meland, "Towers of the Mind," "it was as if," 32; Bernard Eugene Meland, "First Principles as Guides to University Education," *School and Society* 44 (1936): 648–50; Meland, *Higher Education and the Human Spirit* (Chicago: University of Chicago Press, 1953), 10–18, 48–51; Meland, "The New Language in Religion," *Religion in the Making* 2 (1942): 275–89; reprinted in Bernard E. Meland, *Essays in Constructive Theology: A Process Perspective*, ed. Perry LeFevre (Chicago: Exploration Press, 1988), 141–55.

63 Meland, "New Language in Religion," quotes 144, 150; Bernard Eugene Meland, "God, the Unlimited Companion," review of *Man's Vision of God and the Logic of Theism*, by Charles Hartshorne, *Christian Century* 59 (1942): 1289–90; Meland, "At Home in the Universe," in *Contemporary Religious Thought: An Anthology*, ed. Thomas S. Kepler (Nashville: Abingdon Press, 1941), 284–89; Meland, "Growth Toward Order," *Personalist* 21 (1940): 257–66; James, "Does Consciousness Exist?" 169–83.

64 Bernard Eugene Meland, "Theological Perspective," *Religion in Life* 13 (1943/44): 100–106, quotes 100, 102.

65 Meland, "Theological Perspective," quotes 102, 103, 104.

66 Bernard Eugene Meland, "Some Unresolved Issues in Theology," *Journal of Religion* 24 (1944): 233–39, quote 236; Meland, "Some Autobiographical Reflections," 9.

67 Meland, "Some Unresolved Issues in Theology," 234–37; Meland, "Towers of the Mind," 54–74; Meland, "Some Autobiographical Reflections," 7–9; Bernard Eugene Meland, "Toward a Common Christian Faith," *Christendom* 2 (1937): 388–99.

68 Bernard E. Meland, *Seeds of Redemption* (New York: Macmillan, 1947), quotes 5; Meland, *The Church and Adult Education* (New York: American Association for Adult Education, 1939); Meland, "The Tragic Sense of Life," *Religion in Life* 10 (1941): 212–22; Meland, "The Spiritual Outreach of the Liberal Arts College," *Religious Education* 35 (1940): 219–23; Meland, "Some Philosophic Aspects of Poetic Perception," *Personalist* 21 (1941): 384–92; Meland, "For Self-Realization: Religious Education," *Adult Education Bulletin* 6 (1942): 178–79; Meland, "Two Paths to the Good Life," *Personalist* 23 (1942): 53–61; Meland, *Write Your Own Ten Commandments* (Chicago: Willett, Clark, 1938).

69 Mathews, *Faith of Modernism*, 5–6; Meland, *Seeds of Redemption*, 8–9, 39–44.

70 Meland, *Seeds of Redemption*, 127–38; Meland, *America's Spiritual Culture*, 3–21, 29–36, 91–93, "singing," 91.

71 Bernard Eugene Meland, *The Reawakening of Christian Faith* (New York: Macmillan, 1949), 4–12, 34–54, 71–74, 91.

72 Meland, *Reawakening of Christian Faith*, 46–47, 50–61.

73 Meland, "Confessions of a Frustrated Theologian," "what we need" and "while I have," 11; Meland, "Interpreting the Christian Faith," "there is," 89; Bernard Eugene Meland, "New Dimensions of Liberal Faith," *Christian Century* 74 (1957): 961–63; Meland, "The Persisting Liberal Witness," *Christian Century* 79 (1962): 1157–59; Meland, "Modern Protestantism: Aimless or Resurgent?" *Christian Century* 80 (1963): 1494–97; Meland, "A Time of Reckoning—An Editorial," *Journal of Religion* 24 (1949): 1–4; Meland, "This Upsurge of Faith," *Christian Century* 72 (1955): 562–63; Meland, "Reflections on the Early Chicago School of Modernism," *American Journal of Theology and Philosophy* 5 (1984): 9–12. Meland taught a series of courses on "The History of Liberal Theology."

74 Meland, "Fifty Years of Religious Inquiry," "the cultic," 27; Meland, "Interpreting the Christian Faith," "matrix," 91, "in any," 94; Bernard Eugene Meland, "Myth as a Mode of Awareness and Intelligibility," *American Journal of Theology and Philosophy* 8 (1987): 109–19.

75 Meland, "Interpreting the Christian Faith," 93–94; Meland, "Some Autobiographical Reflections," 15–18.

76 Bernard Eugene Meland, *Faith and Culture* (Carbondale: Southern Illinois University Press, 1953), quote 32.

77 Meland, *Faith and Culture*, quotes 54, 184.

78 Meland, *Faith and Culture*, quotes 201, 212, 216.

79 Meland, "New Dimensions of Liberal Faith," "to repossess," 963; Meland, *Realities of Faith*, i–iii, 165–66, 287–306, 309–20.

80 Bernard Eugene Meland, *Fallible Forms and Symbols: Discourses on Method in a Theology of Culture* (Philadelphia: Fortress, 1976), vii, 42–46; Meland, "Some Autobiographical Reflections," 21–22; Meland, review of *The Impact of American Religious Liberalism*, by Kenneth Cauthen, *Church History* 32 (1963): 492–93; Meland, "Can Empirical Theology Learn Something from Phenomenology?" in *The Future of Empirical Theology*, ed. Bernard Eugene Meland (Chicago: University of Chicago Press, 1969), 283–305; Meland, "The Structure of Christian Faith," *Religion in Life* 37 (1968/69): 551–62; Meland, "The New Realism in Religious Inquiry," *Encounter* 31 (1970): 311–24; Meland, "Language and Reality in the Christian Faith," *Encounter* 34 (1973): 173–90; Meland, "The Mystery of Existing and Not Existing," *Union Seminary Quarterly Review* 30 (1975): 165–75.

81 Meland, *Fallible Forms and Symbols*, 48–49.

82 Meland, "Can Empirical Theology Learn Something from Phenomenology?" quotes 291; Meland, *Higher Education and the Human Spirit*, 61; Inbody, *Constructive Theology of Bernard Meland*, 124–25; Meland, "Fifty Years of Religious Inquiry," 30.

83 Bernard Eugene Meland, "Analogy and Myth in Postliberal Theology," *Perkins School of Theology Journal* 15 (1962): 19–27; reprinted in Meland, *Essays in Constructive Theology*, 157–65, "a degree," 162; Schubert M. Ogden, *Christ without Myth: A Study Based on the Theology of Rudolf Bultmann* (Dallas: Southern Methodist University Press, 1979 [1961]); John B. Cobb Jr., *A Christian Natural Theology: Based on the Thought of Alfred North Whitehead*, 2nd ed. (Louisville: Westminster John Knox, 2007 [1965]).

84 Meland, "Analogy and Myth," quotes 162–63.

85 Meland, "Analogy and Myth," "a rebel," 163; Meland, *Fallible Forms and Symbols*, 99–100, 132–42.

86 Meland, "The Empirical Tradition in Theology at Chicago," in *The Future of Empirical Theology*, 57–62, quotes 62; Langdon Gilkey, *Maker of Heaven and Earth: A Study of the Christian Doctrine of Creation* (Garden City, N.Y.: Doubleday, 1959); Gilkey, *Naming the Whirlwind: The Renewal of God-Language* (Indianapolis: Bobbs-Merrill, 1969); Joseph Haroutunian, *Wisdom and Folly in Religion* (New York: Scribner's, 1940); Haroutunian, *God with Us* (Philadelphia: Westminster, 1965); Joseph Sittler, *Doctrine of the Word in the Structure of Lutheran Theology* (Philadelphia: Muhlenberg Press, 1948); Sittler, *The Care of the Earth* (Philadelphia: Fortress, 1964); Brian Gerrish, *Grace and Reason: A Study in Luther's Theology* (New York: Oxford University Press, 1962).

87 Cobb Jr., *Christian Natural Theology*, "basic," xii; Dorrien, *Making of American Liberal Theology: Crisis, Irony, and Postmodernity*, 190–268.

88 Edgar Towne, "God and the Chicago School in the Theology of Bernard Meland," *American Journal of Theology and Philosophy* 10 (1989): 3–19; Jerome A. Stone, *The Minimalist Vision of Transcendence: A Naturalist Philosophy of Religion* (Albany: State University of New York Press, 1992), 58–61; Nancy

Frankenberry, *Religion and Radical Empiricism* (Albany: State University of New York Press, 1987), 134–36; William Dean, "Empiricism and God," in *Empirical Theology: A Handbook*, ed. Randolph Crump Miller (Birmingham, Ala.: Religious Education Press, 1992), 123–25; Bernard Loomer, "Meland on God," *American Journal of Theology and Philosophy* 5 (1984): 18–143; Tyron Inbody, "The Contribution of Bernard Meland to the Development of a Naturalistic Historicist Concept of God," *American Journal of Theology and Philosophy* 20 (1999), 259–79; Inbody, *Constructive Theology of Bernard Meland*, 175–204; Delores Joan Rogers, *The American Empirical Movement in Theology* (New York: Peter Lang, 1990).

89 Meland, *Faith and Culture*, "a temporal," 212; Meland, *Fallible Forms and Symbols*, 151; Bernard Eugene Meland, "Prolegomena to Inquiry into the Reality of God," *American Journal of Theology and Philosophy* 1 (1980): 71–82; Meland, "'Ultimate Mystery' and Structured Thought," *American Journal of Theology and Philosophy* 10 (1989): 153–57, 155; Inbody, "Contribution of Bernard Meland," 261–62.

90 Inbody, *Constructive Theology of Bernard Meland*, 175; Meland, *Fallible Forms and Symbols*, "a collective," 176.

91 Meland, "Empirical Tradition in Theology at Chicago," 36; Bernard M. Loomer, "The Size of God," *American Journal of Theology and Philosophy* 8 (1987): 43–51; John B. Cobb Jr., "Response to Loomer," *American Journal of Theology and Philosophy* 8 (1987): 52–55; Marvin C. Shaw, "The Romantic Love of Evil: Loomer's Proposal of a Reorientation in Religious Naturalism," *American Journal of Theology and Philosophy* 10 (1989): 33–42; William Dean, *American Religious Empiricism* (Albany: State University of New York Press, 1986), 32–33; Nancy Frankenberry, "Taking Measure of 'The Size of God,'" *American Journal of Theology and Philosophy* 8 (1987), 77–84.

92 Meland, *Seeds of Redemption*, "we do not understand," 63; "living is suffering," "there is no," and "the complex interweaving," 106; Meland, "Tragic Sense of Life," 212–22; Frankenberry, *Religion and Radical Empiricism*, 136; Inbody, "Contribution of Bernard Meland," 266–67.

93 Meland, *Reawakening of Christian Faith*, 56; Tyron Inbody, "Bernard Meland: 'A Rebel among Process Theologians,'" *American Journal of Theology and Philosophy* 5 (1984): 43–71; Bernard Eugene Meland, "Narrow Is the Way Beyond Absurdity and Anxiety," *Criterion* 5 (1966): 3–9, "the mind's," 8; John B. Cobb Jr., *Transforming Christianity and the World: A Way Beyond Absolutism and Relativism*, ed. Paul F. Knitter (Maryknoll, N.Y.: Orbis Books, 1999).

94 Williamson, "Bernard E. Meland: What Kind of Theologian?" 369; Larry E. Axel, *The Writings of Larry E. Axel (1946–1991): Studies in Liberal Religious Thought*, ed. Michael Shermis (Lewiston, N.Y.: Edwin Mellen Press, 1992), 151–60, 175–91; John B. Spencer, "Meland as a Resource for Political Ethics," in *Process Philosophy and Social Thought*, ed. John B. Cobb Jr. and W. Widick Schroeder (Chicago: Center for the Scientific Study of Religion, 1981),

153–70; Marjorie Suchocki, "Anxiety and Trust in Feminist Experience," *Journal of Religion* 60 (1980): 459–471; Creighton Peden, *The Chicago School: Voices in Liberal Religious Thought* (Bristol, Ind.: Wyndham Hall Press, 1987), 104–31.

Chapter 8

1 Paul Tillich, "Autobiographical Reflections of Paul Tillich," in *The Theology of Paul Tillich*, ed. Charles Kegley and Robert Bretall (New York: Macmillan, 1952), 7; Tillich, *The Interpretation of History*, trans. N. A. Rasetzki and Elsa Talmey (New York: Scribner's, 1936), 3–7; Wilhelm Pauck and Marion Pauck, *Paul Tillich: His Life and Thought* (New York: Harper & Row, 1989), 1–14, 30; Wilhelm Pauck, *From Luther to Tillich: The Reformers and Their Heirs* (New York: Harper & Row, 1984), 158–61. Near the end of his life Tillich published a revised edition of part 1 of *Interpretation of History*, under the title *On the Boundary: An Autobiographical Sketch* (New York: Scribner's, 1964).

2 Tillich, *Interpretation of History*, 6–8; Pauck and Pauck, *Paul Tillich*, 19–28; Paul Tillich, foreword to Martin Kähler, *The So-Called Historical Jesus and the Historic Biblical Christ* (1896), trans. Carl E. Braaten (Philadelphia: Fortress, 1988), vii–viii; Schelling, *System of Transcendental Idealism*; Schelling, *Philosophy of Nature*; Schelling, *Essence of Human Freedom*; Wilhelm Pauck, *From Luther to Tillich*, 168–73. On Kähler, see Dorrien, *Word as True Myth*, 109–16.

3 Paul Tillich, *Die religionsgeschichtliche Konstruktion in Schellings positiver Philosophie, ihre Voraussetzungen und Prinzipien* (Breslau: Fleischmann, 1910); Tillich, *Mystik und Schuldbewusstein in Schellings philosophischer Entwicklung* (Gütersloh: Bertelsmann, 1912).

4 Paul Tillich, *Der Begriff des Uebernatürlichen, sein dialektischer Charakter und das Prinzip der Identät, dargestellt an der supranaturalistischen Theologie vor Schleiermacher* (Königsberg: Madrasch, 1915); Tillich, "Autobiographical Reflections," "my enthusiasm," 7; Tillich, *The New Being* (New York: Scribner's, 1955), 52; Jerome Stone, "Tillich and Schelling's Later Philosophy," in *Kairos and Logos*, ed. John Carey (Cambridge, Mass.: North American Paul Tillich Society, 1978), 11–44; Horst Fuhrmanns, *Schellings Philosophie der Weltalter. Schelling Philosophie in den Jahren 1806–1821* (Düsseldorf: L. Schwann, 1954), 75–82. This discussion of Tillich adapts material from Dorrien, *Making of American Liberal Theology: Idealism, Realism, and Modernity*, 483–516.

5 "To Be or Not to Be," *Time* 73 (1959): "many of them," 47; Ronald Stone, *Politics and Faith: Reinhold Niebuhr and Paul Tillich at Union Theological Seminary in New York* (Macon, Ga.: Mercer University Press, 2012), 9–11.

6 Tillich, "Autobiographical Reflections," 12; Pauck and Pauck, *Paul Tillich*, 46–54; Tillich, *My Search for Absolutes* (New York: Simon and Schuster, 1967), 39; Tillich, *On the Boundary*, 52.

7 Paul Tillich to Emanuel Hirsch, February 20, 1918, in *E. Hirsch and P. Tillich-Briefwechsel 1917–18*, ed. Hans-Walter Schuette (Berlin: *Die Spur*, 1973),

"gloomy," 21; Tillich, *Interpretation of History,* "the experience," 35; D. Mackenzie Brown, *ed.*, *Ultimate Concern: Tillich in Dialogue* (New York: Harper & Row, 1965), "personal," 153; Paul Tillich, "Über die Idee einer Theologie der Kultur," in *Religionsphilosophie der Kultur; zwei Entwürfe von Gustav Radbruch und Paul Tillich* (Berlin: Reuther & Reichard, 1920), 27–52; Tillich, "Christentum und Sozialismus," *Das neue Deutschland* 8 (1919): 106–10.

8 Paul Tillich, "Christentum und Sozialismus," 106–10; Tillich and Richard Wegener, *Der Sozialismus als Kirchenfrage: Leitsätze von Paul Tillich und Richard Wegener* (Berlin: Gracht, 1919), in Tillich, *Gesammelte Werke,* 14 vols. (Stuttgart: Evangelisches Verlagswerk, 1962–1975); Günther Dehn, *Die Alte Zeit, Die Vorigen Jahre: Lebenserinnerungen* (Munich: Chr. Kaiser, 1962), 212–13, 223; "Brief von Prof. Dr. Eduard Heimann an den Verfasser über die einzelnen Mitglieder des Kairos-Kreises," appendix 1 in Eberhard Amelung, *Die gestalt der Liebe* (Gütersloh: Gerd Mohn, 1972), 215; Eduard Heimann, *Kapitalismus und Sozialismus* (Potsdam: Alfred Protte, 1931); Heimann, *Die soziale Theorie des Kapitalismus* (Tübingen: J.C.B. Mohr, 1929); Adolf Löwe, *Economics and Sociology: A Plea for Cooperation in the Social Sciences* (New York: Routledge, 1935); Joan Campbell, *Joy in Work, German Work: The National Debate, 1800–1945* (Princeton: Princeton University Press, 2014), 306.

9 Paul Tillich, "Kairos," *Die Tat* 14 (1922): 330–50; Tillich, "Masse und Religion," *Blätter für religiösen Sozialismus* 2 (1921): 1–7, 9–12; Tillich, "Die Theologie als Wissenschaft," *Vossische Zeitung* 512 (1921): 2–3; Tillich, "Religiöse Krisis," *Vivos voco* 11 (1922): 616–21; Tillich, *Das System der Wissenschaften nach Gegenständen und Methoden* (Göttingen: Vandenhoeck & Ruprecht, 1923), discussion of the Unconditioned, 129–30; Tillich, "Zur Klärung der religiösen Grundhaltung," *Blätter für religiösen Sozialismus* 3 (1922): 46–48; Tillich, *Interpretation of History,* 123–75; Tillich, "Basic Principles of Religious Socialism" (1923), in *Political Expectation,* ed. James Luther Adams, trans. James Luther Adams and Victor Nuovo (New York: Harper & Row, 1971), 58–88.

10 Tillich, "Basic Principles of Religious Socialism," "it has," 60.

11 Tillich, "Basic Principles of Religious Socialism," "the more," 74.

12 Tillich, "Basic Principles of Religious Socialism," "as a universal," 82.

13 Paul Tillich, "Die religiöse und philosophische Weiterbildung des Sozialismus," *Blätter für religiösen Sozialismus* 5 (1924): 18; Pauck and Pauck, *Paul Tillich,* "I have," 83; Hannah Tillich, *From Time to Time* (New York: Stein and Day, 1973).

14 Paul Tillich, *Die religiöse Lage der Gegenwart* (Berlin: Ullstein, 1926); English ed., *The Religious Situation,* trans. H. Richard Niebuhr (New York: Henry Holt, 1932).

15 Tillich, *Religiöse Verwirklichung* (Berlin: Furche Verlag, 1929); reprint, Tillich, *The Protestant Era,* ed. and trans. James Luther Adams (London: Nisbet, 1951), 74–92, "revelation," 91; Tillich, "Kritisches und positives Paradox: eine Aufeinandersetzung

mit Karl Barth und Friedrich Gogarten," *Theologische Blätter* 2 (1923): 263–69; Karl Barth, "The Paradoxical Nature of the 'Positive Paradox': Answers and Questions to Paul Tillich," in *Beginnings of Dialectic Theology*, "frosty," 147.

16 Heppenheim Conference contributors, *Sozialismus aus dem Glauben* (Zürich: Rotaphel-Verlag, 1929), 11–20, 102–6, 228–45; August Rathmann, "Tillich als religiöser Sozialist," in Tillich, *Gesammelte Werke*, 13:566–67; John R. Stumme, introduction to Paul Tillich, *The Socialist Decision*, trans. Franklin Sherman (German ed., Potsdam: Alfred Protte, 1933; New York: Harper & Row, 1977), xvii–xviii.

17 Martin Jay, *The Dialectical Imagination: A History of the Frankfurt School and the Institute of Social Research, 1923–1950* (Boston: Little, Brown, 1973), 5–12; Karl Korsch, *Three Essays on Marxism* (New York: Monthly Review, 1971), 11–15; Paul Breines, introduction to *Three Essays on Marxism*, 3–8; Max Horkheimer and Theodor W. Adorno, *Dialectic of Enlightenment*, trans. John Cumming (New York: Continuum, 1988), 3–42; Paul Tillich, "Sozialismus: II. Religiöser Sozialismus," in *Die Religion in Geschichte und Gegenwart*, reprinted in *Political Expectation*, 40–57; Tillich, "Sozialismus," *Neue Blätter für den Sozialismus* 1 (1930): 1–12; Tillich, "The Class Struggle and Religious Socialism" (1929), trans. James Luther Adams, in *Paul Tillich on Creativity*, ed. Jacquelyn Ann Kegley (Lanham, Md.: University Press of America, 1989), 104–5; Tillich, "The Protestant Principle and the Proletarian Situation," 1931 pamphlet, in *Protestant Era*, 242–47.

18 Pauck and Pauck, *Paul Tillich*, 125–27; Hannah Tillich, *From Time to Time*, 147; Stumme, introduction to *Socialist Decision*, xxiii.

19 Tillich, *Socialist Decision*, "it holds," xxxiv.

20 Tillich, *Socialist Decision*, 27–44, 66–93, 127–50.

21 Karl Marx, *Economic and Philosophic Manuscripts of 1844*, trans Martin Milligan (Amherst, N.Y.: Prometheus Books, 1988).

22 Tillich, *Socialist Decision*, "the spirit of" and "there is," 116.

23 Tillich, *Socialist Decision*, "in the last," "on national," and "concrete," 87.

24 Tillich, *Socialist Decision*, "demonic," 173.

25 Tillich, *On the Boundary*, 46; Hannah Tillich, *From Time to Time*, 147–56.

26 "Men of Learning, Jews and Non-Jews, Fired by Nazis," *Manchester Guardian Weekly* (1933); reprinted by Jewish Telegraphic Agency, June 11, 1933, www.jta .org/1933/06/11; Paul Tillich, "The Ninth Anniversary of German Book Burning" (May 18, 1942), in *Against the Third Reich: Paul Tillich's Wartime Addresses to Nazi Germany*, trans. Matthew Lon Weaver, ed. Ronald H. Stone and Matthew Lon Weaver (Louisville: Westminster John Knox, 1998), 32–35; Pauck and Pauck, Paul Tillich, 129–31.

27 Pauck and Pauck, *Paul Tillich*, 126–38; Hannah Tillich, *From Time to Time*, 151–56; Henry Sloane Coffin, *A Half Century of Union Theological Seminary, 1896–1945* (New York: Scribner's, 1954), 134–35, "my," 135.

28 Paul Tillich, *Systematic Theology,* 3 vols. (Chicago: University of Chicago, 1951, 1957, 1963), "he is," 1:10.

29 Tillich, *Systematic Theology,* 1:12.

30 Tillich, *Systematic Theology,* 1:14–15, quotes 14.

31 Tillich, *Systematic Theology,* 1:16–18, quote 16; 2:97–180.

32 Tillich, *Systematic Theology,* 1:40–45.

33 Tillich, *Systematic Theology,* quote 1:46; see 2:118–36.

34 Paul Tillich, "Das religiöse symbol," *Blätter für deutsche Philosophie* 1 (1928); revised version, Tillich, "The Religious Symbol," *Journal of Liberal Religion* 2 (1940): 13–33; further revised version, Tillich, "The Religious Symbol," in *Symbolism in Religion and Literature,* ed. Rollo May (New York: G. Braziller, 1960), 75–98; Paul Tillich, *Theology of Culture,* ed. Robert C. Kimball (New York: Oxford University Press, 1959), 36–38.

35 Tillich, "Religious Symbol," in *Symbolism in Religion and Literature,* 87–89, quote 89.

36 Paul Tillich, *Dynamics of Faith* (New York: Harper & Brothers, 1957), 48–54, quote 50; Tillich, *Systematic Theology,* 2:152; Tillich, *Biblical Religion and the Search for Ultimate Reality* (Chicago: University of Chicago Press, 1955), 78–85.

37 Paul Tillich, "The Meaning and Justification of Religious Symbols," in *Religious Experience and Truth,* ed. Sidney Hook (New York: New York University Press, 1961), 4, 10; Tillich, "Religious Symbol," in *Symbolism in Religion and Literature,* quote 91; Tillich, *Theology of Culture,* 53–67; Tillich, *Dynamics of Faith,* 53–54; Tillich, *Systematic Theology,* 2:152.

38 Paul Tillich, *The Courage to Be* (New Haven: Yale University Press, 1952); Tillich, "Marx and the Prophetic Tradition," *Radical Religion* 1 (1935): 21–29; Tillich, "The Church and Communism," *Religion in Life* 6 (1937): 347–57; Tillich, "Marxism and Christian Socialism," *Christianity and Society* 7 (1942): 13–18; Tillich, "How Much Truth Is There in Karl Marx?" *Christian Century* 65 (1948): 906–8; Tillich, "Existentialism and Religious Socialism," *Christianity and Society* 15 (1949): 8–11; Tillich symposium with Max Horkheimer, Adolf Löwe, and Friedrich Pollock, "Theorie und Praxis" (1945), in Brian Donnelly, *The Socialist Émigré: Marxism and the Later Tillich* (Macon, Ga.: Mercer University Press, 2003), "I once," 20.

39 Paul Tillich, "Beyond Religious Socialism," *Christian Century* 66 (1949): 732–33; Tillich, "Autobiographical Reflections," "if the prophetic," "prophetic, humanistic," and "calculating," 13; "I lost," 19.

40 Pauck and Pauck, *Paul Tillich,* 177–95; James Luther Adams, "Introduction: The Storms of Our Times and *Starry Night,*" in Towne, *Thought of Paul Tillich,* 17–18. This reflection registers the author's conversations with Wilhelm Pauck and James Luther Adams.

41 Robert Fitch, "The Social Philosophy of Paul Tillich," *Religion and Life* 27 (1958): 247–56; Alistair MacLeod, *Paul Tillich: An Essay on the Role of Ontology*

in His Philosophical Theology (London: Allen & Unwin, 1973), 19; Clark Kucheman, "Justice and the Economic Order: A Critical and Constructive Study of the Economic Thought of Paul J. Tillich" (Ph.D. diss., University of Chicago, 1965); Stumme, *Socialism in Theological Perspective*, discussion of Amelung, 14; Dennis P. McCann, "Tillich's Religious Socialism: 'Creative Synthesis' or Personal Statement?" in Towne, *Thought of Paul Tillich*, 81–101; Terence M. O'Keefe, "Paul Tillich's Marxism," *Social Research* 48 (1981): 472–99; Walter A. Weisskopf, "Tillich and the Crisis of the West," in Towne, *Thought of Paul Tillich*, 63–78; Ronald Stone, "Paul Tillich: On the Boundary Between Protestantism and Marxism," *Laval Théologique et Philosophie* 45 (1989), 393–401; Guy Hammond, "Tillich and the Frankfurt Debates about Patriarchy and the Family," in *Theonomy and Autonomy: Studies in Paul Tillich's Engagement with Modern Culture*, ed. John J. Carey (Macon, Ga.: Mercer University Press, 1982), 89–110; James Champion, "Tillich and the Frankfurt School: Parallels and Differences in Prophetic Criticism," *Soundings* 69 (1986): 529; Donnelly, *Socialist Émigré*.

42 Paul Tillich, *Love, Power, and Justice: Ontological Analyses and Ethical Applications* (London: Oxford University Press, 1954).

43 Paul Tillich, "Reply to Interpretation and Criticism," in *Theology of Paul Tillich*, 345–46.

44 Tillich, "Reply to Interpretation and Criticism," 346.

45 Paul Tillich, *Christianity and the Encounter of World Religions* (New York: Columbia University Press, 1963; repr., Minneapolis: Fortress, 1994), 39–47; Tillich, "On the Boundary Line," *Christian Century* 77 (1960), 1435–36.

46 Tillich, *Christianity and the Encounter of World Religions*, 25–26; Troeltsch, *Religion in History*.

47 Tillich, *Theology of Culture*, 3–9; Tillich, *Christianity and the Encounter of World Religions*, quote 61–62.

48 Paul Tillich, "The Significance of the History of Religions for the Systematic Theologian," in *The Future of Religions*, ed. Jerald C. Brauer (New York: Harper & Row, 1966), quote 87; see Tillich, *Protestant Era*, 238–40; Tillich, *Christianity and the Encounter of World Religions*, 20.

49 Tillich, "Significance of the History of Religions," 80–94, quotes 88, 94.

50 Ved Mehta, *The New Theologian* (New York: Harper & Row, 1965), quote 51; Pauck and Pauck, *Paul Tillich*, 275.

51 Paul Tillich, *A History of Christian Thought*, ed. Carl E. Braaten (New York: Simon and Schuster, 1968), 411–17.

52 David Held, *Introduction to Critical Theory: Horkheimer to Habermas* (Berkeley: University of California Press, 1980); David Ingram, *Critical Theory and Philosophy* (New York: Paragon House, 1990); Zoltan Tar, *The Frankfurt School: The Critical Theories of Max Horkheimer and Theodor W. Adorno* (New York: Schocken Books, 1977); Raymond Geuss, *The Idea of Critical Theory* (Cambridge: Cambridge University Press, 1981).

53 Tillich, "Class Struggle and Religious Socialism," "primarily," "to a powerful," and "as a genuine," 104.

54 James Luther Adams, "Reminiscences of Paul Tillich" (1987), in *An Examined Faith: Social Context and Religious Commitment*, ed. George W. Beach (Boston: Beacon Press, 1991), 125–33, "you can't," 127; Tillich, *Systematic Theology*, 3:297–93; Tillich, "Class Struggle and Religious Socialism," "religious socialism," 105; see James Luther Adams, "Theology and Modern Culture: Paul Tillich," in *On Being Human Religiously*, ed. Max L. Stackhouse (Boston: Beacon Press, 1976), 225–54; Adams, *Paul Tillich's Philosophy of Culture, Science, and Religion* (New York: Harper & Row, 1965), 203–4.

55 Tillich, "Protestant Principle," 239.

56 Tillich, "Protestant Principle," 242, 247.

57 Tillich, *Systematic Theology*, 1:79–81, 235–89.

58 Tillich, *Love, Power, and Justice*, 11–24.

59 Tillich, *Love, Power, and Justice*, "is reason," 33.

60 Dorrien, *New Abolition*; Dorrien, *Breaking White Supremacy*; Dorrien, *Social Ethics in the Making*.

Chapter 9

1 W. E. B. Du Bois, *Darkwater: Voices from within the Veil* (New York: Harcourt, Brace, 1920; repr., New York: Dover, 1999), quotes 4, 5; Du Bois to Mary Burghardt Du Bois, July 21, 1883, in *The Correspondence of W. E. B. Du Bois*, 2 vols., ed. Herbert Aptheker (Amherst: University of Massachusetts Press, 1973), 1:3–4; Dorrien, *New Abolition*, 158–95.

2 Du Bois, *Darkwater*, 6; W. E. B. Du Bois, *Dusk of Dawn: An Essay toward an Autobiography of a Race Concept* (New York: Harcourt Brace and World, 1940), 12, 108–9; Du Bois, *The Autobiography of W. E. B. Du Bois* (New York: International Publishers, 1968), 62, 72; "W. E. B. Du Bois Interview with William T. Ingersoll," May 1960, Columbia University Oral History Project, Butler Library, Columbia University; David Levering Lewis, *W. E. B. Du Bois: Biography of a Race, 1868–1919* (New York: Henry Holt, 1993), 27.

3 Du Bois, *Darkwater*, 6.

4 W. E. B. Du Bois, *The Souls of Black Folk* (Chicago: A. C. McClurg, 1903; repr., New York: Dover, 1994), "then it dawned," 2; Du Bois, *Autobiography of W. E. B. Du Bois*, "began to feel," 83; Du Bois, *Dusk of Dawn*, 13.

5 Du Bois, *Darkwater*, "now it was," 7; Du Bois, *Dusk of Dawn*, 18–23; Du Bois, *Autobiography of W. E. B. Du Bois*, "half-guilty," 102; W. E. B. Du Bois to the Reverend Scudder, February 3, 1886, in *Correspondence of W. E. B. Du Bois*, 1:5.

6 W. E. B. Du Bois, "The Religion of the American Negro," *New World* 9 (1900): "a sort of," 614–15; Du Bois, *Dusk of Dawn*, 32–33; Du Bois, *Autobiography of W. E. B. Du Bois*, 109, 126; W. E. B. Du Bois to the Harvard College Admissions Office, October 29, 1887, in *Correspondence of W. E. B. Du Bois*,

1:6; George Frederick Wright, *The Logic of Christian Evidences* (Andover, Mass.: Warren F. Draper, 1880).

7 Du Bois, *Darkwater,* "I dreamed," 9; Du Bois, *Autobiography of W. E. B. Du Bois,* 157; Lewis, *W. E. B. Du Bois,* "these are," 135; "I rejoice," 134; W. E. B. Du Bois to Hon. Rutherford B. Hayes, April 3, 1892, in *Correspondence of W. E. B. Du Bois,* 1:16–17; Du Bois to President D. C. Gilman, October 28, 1892, in *Correspondence of W. E. B. Du Bois,* 1:20–21; Du Bois, *Dusk of Dawn,* 42–48.

8 Du Bois, *Darkwater,* "suddenly," 9; W. E. B. Du Bois to Trustees of the John F. Slater Fund, March 10, 1893, in *Correspondence of W. E. B. Du Bois,* 1:23–25; D. C. Gilman to Du Bois, April 13, 1894, in *Correspondence of W. E. B. Du Bois,* 1:29; Du Bois, *Dusk of Dawn,* 42–48.

9 W. E. B. Du Bois, "Strivings of the Negro People," *Atlantic Monthly* 80 (1897): 194–98, amplified version reprinted as chapter 1, "Of Our Spiritual Strivings," in *Souls of Black Folk,* 1–7, quotes 1, 2; for a similar passage, see Du Bois, *The Philadelphia Negro: A Social Study* (Philadelphia: University of Pennsylvania Press, 1899; repr., New York: Oxford University Press, 2007), 397. For works that attribute a strong Hegelian influence on Du Bois, see Joel Williamson, *The Crucible of Race: Black-White Relations in the American South Since Emancipation* (New York: Oxford University Press, 1984), 402–13; Paul Gilroy, *The Black Atlantic: Modernity and Double Consciousness* (Cambridge, Mass.: Harvard University Press, 1993), 134–35; Robert Gooding-Williams, "Philosophy of History and Social Critique in *The Souls of Black Folk,*" *Social Science Information* 26 (1987): 106–8; and Jacqueline Stevens, "Beyond Tocqueville, Please!" *American Political Science Review* 89 (1995): 987–90. For works contending that Du Bois was influenced by Emerson or Herder, see Arnold Rampersad, *The Art and Imagination of W. E. B. Du Bois* (Cambridge, Mass.: Harvard University Press, 1976), 74–75; Cornel West, *The American Evasion of Philosophy: A Genealogy of Pragmatism* (Madison: University of Wisconsin Press, 1989), 142–43.

10 Ralph Waldo Emerson, "The Transcendentalist," in *Nature, Addresses, and Lectures,* ed. Robert E. Spiller and Alfred R. Ferguson (Cambridge, Mass.: Harvard University Press, 1979), 201–16; Du Bois, "Strivings of the Negro People," 2, 3.

11 Du Bois, "Strivings of the Negro People," 2, 7.

12 W. E. B. Du Bois, "The Conservation of Races," Address to the American Negro Academy, March 5, 1897, originally published by the American Negro Academy in vol. 2 of *Occasional Papers* (Washington, D.C., 1897); reprinted in Du Bois, *Pamphlets and Leaflets,* ed. Herbert Aptheker (White Plains, N.Y.: Kraus-Thomson, 1986), and Du Bois, *W. E. B. Du Bois: A Reader,* ed. David Levering Lewis (New York: Henry Holt, 1995), 20–27, quotes 21. Citations refer to the Holt edition.

13 Du Bois, "Conservation of Races," 21–22.

14 Du Bois, "Conservation of Races," 24, 25, 26.

15 Du Bois, "Conservation of Races," 26, 27.

16 Herbert Spencer, *First Principles* (New York: D. Appleton, 1864); Spencer, *The Principles of Sociology*, 3 vols. (New York: D. Appleton, 1876–1897); Richard Hofstadter, *Social Darwinism in American Thought* (Boston: Beacon Press, 1955), 31–50; George W. Stocking Jr., *Race, Culture, and Evolution: Essays in the History of Anthropology* (Chicago: University of Chicago, 1968), 234–69; Stephen Jay Gould, *Ontogeny and Phylogeny* (Cambridge, Mass.: Harvard University Press, 1977); Charles Darwin, *The Descent of Man* (New York: J. Murray, 1874), 166–68.

17 Ernst Haeckel, *The History of Creation*, 2 vols. (1876; 6th ed., New York: D. Appleton, 1914), quote 2:249; Robert J. Richards, *The Tragic Sense of Life: Ernst Haeckel and the Struggle Over Evolutionary Thought* (Chicago: University of Chicago Press, 2008), 255–61.

18 Du Bois, *Dusk of Dawn*, "actual," 51; Du Bois, "Conservation of Races," in *Pamphlets and Leaflets*, "same," 10.

19 Albion W. Small, *An Introduction to the Study of Society* (New York: American Book, 1894); Thomas F. Gossett, *Race: The History of an Idea in America* (New York: Schocken Books, 1965), 54–83; George M. Frederickson, *Racism: A Short History* (Princeton: Princeton University Press, 1998), 51–75; M. K. Richardson and G. Keuck, "Haeckel's ABC of Evolution and Development," *Biological Reviews* 77 (2002): 495–528. Small founded the *American Journal of Sociology* in 1895.

20 Williamson, *Crucible of Race*, 397–405, quote 405.

21 Henry Louis Gates Jr., introduction to the Bantam reprint edition of W. E. B. Du Bois, *The Souls of Black Folk* (New York: Bantam, 1989 [1903]), xvii–xviii; Gates, *The Signifying Monkey: A Theory of African-American Literary Criticism* (New York: Oxford University Press, 1988), 207; Lawrie Balfour, *Democracy's Reconstruction: Thinking Politically with W. E. B. Du Bois* (Oxford: Oxford University Press, 2011), 73–74; Robert Gooding-Williams, *In the Shadow of Du Bois: Afro-American Political Thought in America* (Cambridge, Mass.: Harvard University Press, 2009), 66–129; Gooding-Williams, "Philosophy of History," 106–8; Cornel West, *Prophesy Deliverance! An Afro-American Revolutionary Christianity* (Philadelphia: Westminster, 1982), 30–31; Lawrence D. Bobo, "Reclaiming a Du Boisian Perspective on Racial Attitudes," *ANNALS of the American Academy of Political and Social Science* 568 (2000): 186–202; Adolph L. Reed Jr., *W. E. B. Du Bois and American Political Thought: Fabianism and the Color Line* (New York: Oxford University Press, 1997), 107–25; Ernest Allen Jr., "Du Boisian Double Consciousness: The Unsustainable Argument," *Massachusetts Review* 43 (2002): "double," 217; Gilroy, *Black Atlantic*, 111–45; Paul Gilroy, *Against Race: Imagining Political Culture Beyond the Color Line* (Cambridge, Mass.: Harvard University Press, 2000), 51–52; Terence L. Johnson, *Tragic Soul-Life: W. E. B. Du Bois and the Moral Crisis Facing American Democracy;* (New York: Oxford University Press,

2012); Eboni Marshall Turman, *Toward a Womanist Ethic of Incarnation* (New York: Palgrave Macmillan, 2013).

22 John A. Hobson, *The Problem of the Unemployed: An Inquiry and an Economic Policy* (London: Methuen, 1896); Hobson, *The War in South Africa: Its Causes and Effects* (1900); Hobson, *Imperialism* (London: Allen & Unwin, 1948 [1902]); W.E.B. Du Bois, "African Roots of the War," *Atlantic Monthly* 115 (May 1915), 707–14.

23 Du Bois, "African Roots of the War," quote 712–13.

24 W. E. B. Du Bois, "The Future of Wilberforce University," *Journal of Negro Education* 9 (1940): quotes 564–65.

25 Du Bois, *Souls of Black Folk*, 1–7; Du Bois, *Darkwater*, "Credo," 1–2; "The Second Coming," 60–62; "Jesus Christ in Texas," 70–77; "Hymn to the Peoples," 161–62; Du Bois, "Untitled," in *Creative Writings by W. E. B. Du Bois*, ed. Herbert Aptheker (Millwood, N.Y.: Kraus-Thomson, 1985), "the tattered," 41.

26 Martin Luther King Jr., *Stride Toward Freedom: The Montgomery Story* (New York: Harper & Brothers, 1958), 20; Marshall Frady, *Martin Luther King Jr.: A Life* (New York: Penguin, 2002), 11–13; Lewis V. Baldwin, *There Is a Balm in Gilead: The Cultural Roots of Martin Luther King Jr.* (Minneapolis: Fortress, 1991), 16–17; Taylor Branch, *Parting the Waters: America in the King Years, 1954–63* (New York: Simon and Schuster, 1988), 40–41.

27 L. D. Reddick, *Crusader without Violence* (New York: Harper & Row, 1959), 43–51; Martin Luther King Sr., with Clayton Riley, *Daddy King: An Autobiography* (New York: William Morrow, 1980), 26, 88; Branch, *Parting the Waters*, 46–47. Reddick was close to the King family and is an invaluable source on the tangled name story, and Daddy King's memoir sought to straighten out longstanding confusions about it.

28 Martin Luther King Jr. to Alberta Williams King, October 1948, in *The Papers of Martin Luther King, Jr.*, vol. 1, *Called to Serve, January 1929–June 1951*, ed. Clayborne Carson, Ralph E. Luker, and Penny A. Russell (Berkeley: University of California Press, 1992), 161; King, "The Christian Pertinence of Eschatological Hope," November 29, 1949–February 15, 1950, in *Papers of Martin Luther King, Jr.*, 1:268–73, "will be a society," 1:272–73; King, "The Humanity and Divinity of Jesus," November 29, 1949–February 15, 1950, in *Papers of Martin Luther King, Jr.*, 1:257–62; King, "Six Talks in Outline," September 13–November 23, 1949, in *Papers of Martin Luther King, Jr.*, 1:242–51; King, "A View of the Cross Possessing Biblical and Spiritual Justification," November 29, 1949–February 15, 1950, in *Papers of Martin Luther King, Jr.*, 1:263–67; King, "Preaching Ministry," September 14–November 24, 1948, in *Papers of Martin Luther King, Jr.*, vol. 4, *Advocate of the Social Gospel*, ed. Clayborne Carson et al. (Berkeley: University of California Press, 2007), 69–72, "I am a," 72.

29 King, *Stride Toward Freedom*, "his message," 84; Martin Luther King Jr., "Pilgrimage to Nonviolence," *Christian Century* 77 (1960): 439–41; Coretta Scott

King, *My Life with Martin Luther King Jr.* (New York: Holt, Rinehart & Winston, 1969), 71; David J. Garrow, *Bearing the Cross: Martin Luther King Jr. and the Southern Christian Leadership Conference* (New York: Quill, 1986), 41; Charles E. Cobb Jr., *This Nonviolent Stuff'll Get You Killed* (New York: Basic Books, 2014).

30 Martin Luther King Jr. Papers Project, "The Student Papers of Martin Luther King, Jr.: A Summary Statement on Research," *Journal of American History* 78 (1991): 23–31; David Thelen, "Becoming Martin Luther King, Jr.: An Introduction," *Journal of American History* 78 (1991): 11–22; David J. Garrow, "King's Plagiarism: Imitation, Insecurity, and Transformation," *Journal of American History* 78 (1991): 86–92; Keith D. Miller, "Martin Luther King, Jr., and the Black Folk Pulpit," *Journal of American History* 78 (1991): 120–23, "his professors'," 121; David Levering Lewis, "Failing to Know Martin Luther King, Jr.," *Journal of American History* 78 (1991): 81–85, "who" and "a picture," 84, 85; Clayborne Carson, with Peter Holloran, Ralph E. Luker, and Penny Russell, "Martin Luther King, Jr., as Scholar: A Reexamination of His Theological Writings," *Journal of American History* 78 (1991): 93–105; John Higham, "Habits of the Cloth and Standards of the Academy," *Journal of American History* 78 (1991): 106–10; Keith D. Miller, "Composing Martin Luther King, Jr.," *PMLA* 105 (1990): 70–82; Miller, *Voice of Deliverance: The Language of Martin Luther King, Jr., and Its Sources* (New York: Free Press, 1992; repr., Athens, Ga.: University of Georgia Press, 1998), 53–66; Miller, "Martin Luther King, Jr. Borrows a Revolution: Argument, Audience and Implications of a Secondhand Universe," *College English* 48 (1986): 249–65; Theodore Pappas, "A Doctor in Spite of Himself: The Strange Career of Martin Luther King, Jr.'s Dissertation," *Chronicles* 15 (1991): 25–29; Richard Lischer, *The Preacher King: Martin Luther King Jr. and the Word That Moved America* (New York: Oxford University Press, 1995), 45; David Levering Lewis, *King: A Biography* (1st ed., 1970; 3rd ed., Urbana: University of Illinois Press, 2003); Lewis V. Baldwin, "Martin Luther King, Jr., the Black Church, and the Black Messianic Vision," *Journal of the Interdenominational Theological Center* 12 (1984/85): 93–108; Baldwin, "Family and Church: The Roots of Martin Luther King, Jr.," *National Baptist Union-Review* 91 (1987): 1, 3; Baldwin, "Understanding Martin Luther King, Jr., within the Context of Southern Black Religious History," *Journal of Religious Studies* 13 (1987): 1–26; Baldwin, *Balm in Gilead*, 3.

31 Miller, "Composing Martin Luther King," 70–82; see Miller, *Voice of Deliverance*, 45–92; Miller, "Martin Luther King, Jr. Borrows a Revolution," 249–65; David J. Garrow, "The Intellectual Development of Martin Luther King, Jr.," reprinted in *Martin Luther King, Jr.: Civil Rights Leader, Theologian, Orator*, 3 vols., ed. David J. Garrow (New York: Carlson Publishing, 1989), 2:443.

32 J. Pius Barbour to Martin Luther King Jr., July 21, 1955, in *Papers of Martin Luther King, Jr.*, 2:564–66; Lischer, *Preacher King*, 68–69; Lewis, *King*, 33; Garrow, *Bearing the Cross*, 41.

33 Martin Luther King Jr., "A Conception and Impression of Religion Drawn from Dr. Brightman's Book Entitled *A Philosophy of Religion*," in *Papers of Martin Luther King, Jr.*, 1:407–16, quote 415–16.

34 "Conversation between Cornish Rogers and David Thelen," Rogers quote 45; Baldwin, *There Is a Balm*, Lenud quote 40; Walter G. Muelder, "Philosophical and Theological Influences in the Thought and Action of Martin Luther King, Jr.," *Debate and Understanding* 1 (1977): 183.

35 Martin Luther King Jr., "Final Examination Answers, Personalism," January 1952, in *Papers of Martin Luther King, Jr.*, 2:110–12; Dorrien, *Making of American Liberal Theology: Crisis, Irony and Postmodernity*, 17–28.

36 Martin Luther King Jr., "An Exposition of the First Triad of Categories of the Hegelian Logic—Being, Non-Being, Becoming," February 4–May 22, 1953, in *Papers of Martin Luther King, Jr.*, 2:196–201; King, *Stride Toward Freedom*, 100–101; Martin Luther King Jr., interview with Tom Johnson, *Montgomery Adviser* (January 19, 1956); cited in John J. Ansbro, *Martin Luther King, Jr.: Nonviolent Strategies and Tactics for Social Change* (Lanham, Md.: Madison Books, 2000), 122; Miller, "Composing Martin Luther King," 76–77.

37 Martin Luther King Jr., "Reinhold Niebuhr's Ethical Dualism," May 9, 1952, in *Papers of Martin Luther King, Jr.*, 2:142–51, quotes 150; see Walter G. Muelder, "Reinhold Niebuhr's Conception of Man," *Personalist* 26 (1945): 284–92; King, *Stride Toward Freedom*, 100; King, "The Theology of Reinhold Niebuhr," April 1953–June 1954, in *Papers of Martin Luther King, Jr.*, 2:269–79.

38 Martin Luther King Jr., "A Comparison and Evaluation of the Theology of Luther with That of Calvin," May 15, 1953, in *Papers of Martin Luther King, Jr.*, 2:174–91, quotes 189–90; Knudson, *Doctrine of Redemption*, 222–333; Bowne, *Studies in Christianity*, 85–193; Anders Nygren, *Agape and Eros*, trans. Philip Watson (Philadelphia: Westminster, 1953).

39 Martin Luther King Jr., "Qualifying Examination Answers, Systematic Theology," December 17, 1953, in *Papers of Martin Luther King, Jr.*, 2:228–33, 228, 232.

40 Martin Luther King Jr., "Contemporary Continental Theology," September 13, 1951–January 15, 1952, in *Papers of Martin Luther King, Jr.* 2:113–38; Walter Marshall Horton, "Tillich's Role in Contemporary Theology," in *Theology of Paul Tillich*, 36–37; Jack Stewart Boozer, "The Place of Reason in Paul Tillich's Concept of God" (Ph.D. diss., Boston University, 1952); Raphael Demos, review of vol. 1 of *Systematic Theology*, by Paul Tillich, *Journal of Philosophy* 49 (1952): 692–708; George F. Thomas, "The Method and Structure of Tillich's Theology," in *Theology of Paul Tillich*, 86–105; David E. Roberts, "Tillich's Doctrine of Man," in *Theology of Paul Tillich*, 109–30; *Papers of Martin Luther King, Jr.*, 2:339–40; L. Harold DeWolf, "First Reader's Report," February 26, 1955, *in Papers of Martin Luther King, Jr.*, 2:333–34; S. Paul Schilling, "Second Reader's Report," February 26, 1955, in *Papers of Martin Luther King, Jr.*, 2:334–35. The committee's members were DeWolf, Schilling, Peter Bertocci,

John H. Lavely, Richard M. Millard, Jannette E. Newhall, and at least formally Muelder.

41 Martin Luther King Jr., "A Comparison of the Conceptions of God in the Thinking of Paul Tillich and Henry Nelson Wieman," in *Papers of Martin Luther King, Jr.*, 2:339–44; Tillich, vol. 1 of *Systematic Theology*; Wieman, *Religious Experience and Scientific Method*, quote 9; James Cone, *Martin & Malcolm & America* (Maryknoll, N.Y.: Orbis Books, 1991), "as if," 31.

42 King, "Comparison of the Conceptions," quotes 512–13.

43 King, "Comparison of the Conceptions," "neither swallows," 533; Miller, *Voice of Deliverance*, "today almost," 62; David L. Chappell, *A Stone of Hope: Prophetic Religion and the Death of Jim Crow* (Chapel Hill: University of North Carolina Press, 2004), "from thousands," 53.

44 Chappell, *Stone of Hope*, 53–54; David Garrow, *Protest at Selma: Martin Luther King Jr. and the Voting Rights Act of 1965* (New Haven: Yale University Press, 1978), 221; see Garrow, "Intellectual Development of Martin Luther King," 2:451; Miller, *Voice of Deliverance*, 7, 17, 61; Chappell recognizes that Niebuhr was much closer to Rauschenbusch's version of the social gospel than Niebuhr's polemical rhetoric about it suggested, which helps Chappell get the main thing right: "The prophetic core of the Social Gospel at its best may explain the attraction it held for Martin Luther King Jr." (quote 310).

45 King, *Stride Toward Freedom*, quote 100.

46 Bayard Rustin, "New South . . . Old Politics" (1956), in *Time on Two Crosses: The Collected Writings of Bayard Rustin*, ed. Devon W. Carbado and Donald Weise (San Francisco: Cleis, 2003), 95–101; Adam Fairclough, *To Redeem the Soul of America: The Southern Christian Leadership Conference and Martin Luther King Jr.* (Athens: University of Georgia Press, 2001), 37–55.

47 Martin Luther King Jr., interview with Alex Haley, *Playboy* (January 1965), in *A Testament of Hope: The Essential Writings and Speeches of Martin Luther King Jr.*, ed. James M. Washington (New York: HarperCollins, 1991), 340–77, quote 345.

48 King, *Testament of Hope*, quote 346.

49 King, *Testament of Hope*, quotes 348, 349, 353.

50 King, *Testament of Hope*, quotes 353, 354, 355.

51 Martin Luther King Jr., "Nonviolence: The Only Road to Freedom," *Ebony* 21 (1966): 27–30; King, "Dr. King's Speech—Frogmore—November 14, 1966," King Papers, box 11, The King Center, Atlanta, quotes 6, 7.

52 King, "Dr. King's Speech," 7.

53 Martin Luther King Jr., "A Time to Break Silence," speech at Riverside Church, April 4, 1967, in *Testament of Hope*, quotes 240, 241.

54 "Dr. King's Disservice to His Cause," *Life* (April 21, 1967): 4; Carl Rowan, "Martin Luther King's Tragic Decision," *Reader's Digest* (September 1967): 37–42; Rowan, *Breaking Barriers: A Memoir* (Boston: Little, Brown, 1991), 246–48; "Dr. King's Error," *New York Times* (April 7, 1967); "A Tragedy," *Washington Post* (April 6, 1967); "NAACP Decries Stand," *New York Times* (April 11,

1967); editorial, *Pittsburgh Courier* (April 16, 1967); Max Lerner, "The Color of War," *New York Post* (April 7, 1967); Martin Luther King Jr., "To Charter Our Course for the Future," speech to Southern Christian Leadership Conference, May 22, 1967, Penn Community Center, Frogmore, SC, "my name," King Papers, box 12, The King Center, Atlanta.

55 Martin Luther King Jr., *Where Do We Go from Here: Chaos or Community?* (New York: Harper & Row, 1967; repr., Boston: Beacon Press, 2010), quotes 5, 10, 12.

56 King, *Where Do We Go from Here*, quotes 45–46, 47.

57 King, *Where Do We Go from Here*, quote 66.

58 Andrew Kopkind, "Soul Power," *New York Review of Books* (August 24, 1967): 3–6; David J. Garrow, "Where Martin Luther King Jr. Was Going: *Where Do We Go* and the Traumas of the Post-Selma Moment," *Georgia Historical Quarterly* 75 (1991): 719–21; Taylor Branch, *At Canaan's Edge: America in the King Years, 1965–68* (New York: Simon and Schuster, 2006), 637–38; Renata Adler, "Letter from the Palmer House," *New Yorker* (September 23, 1967): 71.

59 Martin Luther King Jr., *Conscience for Change* (Boston: Beacon Press, 1968; repr., *The Trumpet of Conscience* [Boston: Beacon Press, 2010]), quote 79.

60 Martin Luther King Jr., *Address to the Southern Christian Leadership Conference*, Penn Community Center, Frogmore, SC, May 22, 1967, in *The Radical King*, ed. Cornel West (Boston: Beacon Press, 2015), 126.

61 Cone, *Black Theology and Black Power*; Cone, *Black Theology of Liberation*; J. Deotis Roberts, *Liberation and Reconciliation: A Black Theology* (Philadelphia: Westminster, 1971); Gustavo Gutiérrez, *A Theology of Liberation: History, Politics, and Salvation*, trans. Caridad Inda and John Eagleson (Maryknoll, N.Y.: Orbis Books, 1973); Juan Luis Segundo, *The Liberation of Theology* (Maryknoll, N.Y.: Orbis Books, 1976); José Míguez Bonino, *Doing Theology in a Revolutionary Situation* (Philadelphia: Fortress, 1975).

62 Rosemary Radford Ruether, *Disputed Questions: On Being a Christian* (Nashville: Abingdon, 1982), 17–29, "sense of," 21; Ruether, *Women and Redemption: A Theological History* (Minneapolis: Fortress, 1998), "ghettoized," 221; Ruether, "Beginnings: An Intellectual Autobiography," in *Journeys: The Impact of Personal Experience on Religious Thought*, ed. Gregory Baum (New York: Paulist Press, 1975), 34–56; Dorrien, *Making of American Liberal Theology: Crisis, Irony, and Postmodernity*, 179–89.

63 Ruether, *Disputed Questions*, quote 29; Ruether, "Beginnings," 36–38; Rosemary Radford Ruether, "Robert Palmer: First the God, Then the Dance," *Christian Century* 107 (1990): 125–26.

64 Ruether, *Disputed Questions*, quote 76; Ruether, *Women and Redemption*, 222; Ruether, "Beginnings," 43–46; Rosemary Radford Ruether, *Gregory of Nazianzus: Rhetor and Philosopher* (London: Oxford University Press, 1969).

65 Ruether, *Disputed Questions*, "one lived," 82.

66 Rosemary Radford Ruether, *The Church against Itself: An Inquiry into the Conditions of Historical Existence for the Eschatological Community* (New York: Herder and Herder, 1967), quote 235; Ruether, "A Question of Dignity, a Question of Freedom," in *What Modern Catholics Think about Birth Control*, ed. William Birmingham (New York: New American Library, 1964), 233–40.

67 Rosalind Hinton, "A Legacy of Inclusion: An Interview with Rosemary Radford Ruether," *Cross Currents* 52 (2002): 28–37, "every time," 30; see Ruether, *Church against Itself*; Ruether, "Question of Dignity," 233–40; Rosemary Radford Ruether, *The Radical Kingdom: The Western Experience of Messianic Hope* (New York: Paulist Press, 1970); Ruether and Eugene Bianchi, *From Machismo to Mutuality: Essays on Sexism* (New York: Paulist Press, 1975); Ruether, ed., *Religion and Sexism: Images of Women in the Jewish and Christian Religious Traditions* (New York: Simon and Schuster, 1973).

68 *Womanspirit Rising: A Feminist Reader in Religion*, ed. Carol Christ and Judith Plaskow (New York: HarperCollins, 1979), quote 21; Rosemary Radford Ruether, "Motherearth and the Megamachine: A Theology of Liberation in a Feminine, Somatic and Ecological Perspective," *Christianity & Crisis* 31 (1972): 267–73, reprinted in *Womanspirit Rising*, 43–52, and Ruether, *Liberation Theology: Human Hope Confronts Christian History and American Power* (New York: Paulist Press, 1972), 115–26.

69 Ruether, "Motherearth and the Megamachine," 118–21, quote 119–20.

70 Ruether, "Motherearth and the Megamachine," quotes 121, 122.

71 Ruether, "Motherearth and the Megamachine," quotes 124.

72 Ruether, *Disputed Questions*, "never to" 53; Ruether, "Beginnings," "these scholars," 52.

73 Ruether, *Disputed Questions*, 53–54; Rosemary Radford Ruether, *New Woman, New Earth: Sexist Ideologies and Human Liberation* (New York: Seabury Press, 1975), 89–133; Ruether, *Faith and Fratricide: The Theological Roots of Anti-Semitism* (New York: Seabury Press, 1974).

74 Rosemary Radford Ruether, *Sexism and God-Talk: Toward a Feminist Theology*, 2nd ed. (Boston: Beacon Press, 1993 [1983]), 12–46, quotes 18, 24.

75 Ruether, *Sexism and God-Talk*, 22–33, quote 32.

76 Ruether, *Sexism and God-Talk*, quotes 229–30; on Daly's gynocentric dualism, see Rosemary Radford Ruether, *Gaia & God: An Ecofeminist Theology of Earth Healing* (San Francisco: HarperCollins, 1992), 147–48; see Dorrien, *Soul in Society*, 262–71.

77 Ruether, *Sexism and God-Talk*, quotes 231.

78 Rosemary Radford Ruether, *Women-Church: Theology and Practice of Feminist Liturgical Communities* (San Francisco: Harper & Row, 1985), 52; Zillah R. Eisenstein, *The Radical Future of Liberal Feminism* (New York: Longman, 1981); Ruether, *Sexism and God-Talk*, 216–22.

79 Ruether, *Sexism and God-Talk*, 223–34; Ruether, *New Woman, New Earth*, 162–214.

80 Ruether, *Sexism and God-Talk*, 23–31, 116–38, quotes 24, 137, 138; Rosemary Radford Ruether, *To Change the World: Christology and Cultural Criticism* (New York: Crossroad, 1981), 45–56; Ruether, "Feminist Theology and Spirituality," in *Christian Feminism: Visions of a New Humanity*, ed. Judith L. Weidman (New York: Harper & Row, 1984), 15–16.

81 Ruether, *Gaia & God*, 246; Dorrien, *Soul in Society*, 314–16.

82 Ruether, *Gaia & God*, 247–49.

83 Ruether, *Gaia & God*, 252–53.

84 Hinton, "Legacy of Inclusion," "legitimize," 30; Russell, Ross, Ellis, Gebara, and Hinton made their remarks at a conference honoring Ruether at Garrett-Evangelical Theological Seminary on April 3–4, 2002; Letty M. Russell, "Wise Woman Bearing Gifts," *Cross Currents* 53 (2003): 116–20, quotes 116, 118; Susan A. Ross, "Teaching Feminist Theology to College Students: The Influence of Rosemary Radford Ruether," *Cross Currents* 53 (2003): 111–15, quotes 115; Marc H. Ellis, "At the End of an Era: A Meditation on Ecumenism, Exile, and Gratitude," *Cross Currents* 53 (2003): 104–10; Ivone Gebara, "Ecofeminism: A Latin American Perspective," *Cross Currents* 53 (2003): 93–103, quote 103; Rosalind Hinton, "Contextualizing Rosemary," *Cross Currents* 53 (2003): 86–92; Hinton, "Legacy of Inclusion," 31; Rosemary Radford Ruether and Marc H. Ellis, eds., *Beyond Occupation: American Jewish, Christian, and Palestinian Voices for Peace* (Boston: Beacon Press, 1990); Ruether, "The Women of Palestine: Steadfastness and Self-Help in the Occupied Territories," *Christianity & Crisis* 47 (1987): 434–38.

85 Mary McClintock Fulkerson, "Contesting the Gendered Subject: A Feminist Account of the *Imago Dei*," in *Horizons in Feminist Theology: Identity, Tradition, and Norms*, ed. Rebecca S. Chopp and Sheila Greeve Davaney (Minneapolis: Fortress, 1997), 107–9, "a kind of," 109; Fulkerson, *Changing the Subject: Women's Discourses and Feminist Theology* (Minneapolis: Fortress, 1994), 53–58, "in a realm," 55; Ellen T. Armour, "Questioning 'Woman' in Feminist/Womanist Theology: Irigaray, Ruether, and Daly," in *Transfigurations: Theology and the French Feminists*, ed. C. W. Maggie Kim, Susan M. St. Ville, and Susan M. Simonaitis (Minneapolis: Fortress, 1993), 150–56; Delores S. Williams, "The Color of Feminism," *Christianity & Crisis* 45 (1985), 164–65, quote 164; Rosemary Radford Ruether, "Feminist Theology in the Academy," *Christianity & Crisis* 45 (1985), 57–62; Williams, "The Color of Feminism: or, Speaking the Black Woman's Tongue," *Journal of Religious Thought* 43 (1986), 42–58; Daphne Hampson, *Theology and Feminism* (Oxford: Basil Blackwell, 1990), 27–29, quote 29; Sheila Greeve Davaney, "Continuing the Story, but Departing the Text: A Historicist Interpretation of Feminist Norms in Theology," in Chopp and Davaney, *Horizons in Feminist Theology*, 201; Kwok Pui-lan, *Postcolonial Imagination & Feminist Theology* (Louisville: Westminster John Knox, 2005), 147.

86 Elisabeth Schüssler Fiorenza, *In Memory of Her: A Feminist Theological Reconstruction of Christian Origins* (New York: Crossroad, 1983), 17–18, "can be," 19; see Fiorenza, *Discipleship of Equals: A Critical Feminist Ekklesia-logy of Liberation* (New York: Crossroad, 1993), 53–79; Fiorenza, *Bread Not Stone: The Challenge of Feminist Biblical Interpretation* (Boston: Beacon Press, 1984).

87 Hinton, "Legacy of Inclusion," 32.

88 Hinton, "Legacy of Inclusion," 32–33.

89 Hinton, "Legacy of Inclusion," "I don't think," 32; Ruther to author, "it's telling," February 18, 2005, Pilgrim Place, Claremont, California.

Chapter 10

1 Pope Pius X, *Lamentabili Sane*, July 3, 1907; Pius X, *Pascendi Dominici Gregis*, September 8, 1907, in *The Papal Encyclicals*, ed. Anne Freemantle (New York: New American Library, 1963), 202–7, 197–201; Yves Congar, *Vraie et fausse réforme dans l'Eglise* (Paris: Editions du Cerf, 1950); Henri de Lubac, *Le Mystere du surnaturel* (Paris: Aubier, 1965); Lubac, *Mémoire sur l'occasion de mes écrits* (Namur: Culture et Verité, 1989); Pierre Teilhard de Chardin, *The Phenomenon of Man* (New York: Harper & Row, 1959); John Courtney Murray, *We Hold These Truths: Catholic Reflections on the American Proposition* (New York: Sheed and Ward, 1960); Joseph Maréchal, *Le point de départ de la métaphysique*, 2nd ed., 5 vols. (Paris: Descleé de Brouwer, 1944–1949); Joseph Donceel, ed. and trans., *A Maréchal Reader* (New York: Herder and Herder, 1970); Karl Rahner, *Geist in Welt: Zur Metaphysik der endlichen Erkenntnis bei Thomas von Aquin*, 2nd ed., rev. Johannes B. Metz (München: Kösel-Verlag, 1957 [1940]); English edition, *Spirit in the World*, trans. William Dych (New York: Herder and Herder, 1957).

2 David Tracy, "Lonergan's Interpretation of St. Thomas Aquinas: The Intellectualist Nature of Speculative Theology" (Ph.D. diss., Gregorian University, Rome, 1969); Todd Breyfogle and Thomas Levergood, "Conversation with David Tracy," *Cross Currents* 44 (1994): Tracy quote 311; author's interview with Langdon B. Gilkey, July 21, 2002.

3 Martin Heidegger, *Kant and the Problem of Metaphysics*, 5th ed., trans. Richard Taft (Bloomington: Indiana University Press, 1997 [1st German ed., 1929]), 3–41, 137–50; Rahner, *Spirit in the World*, 57–77, 117–79; Bernard J. F. Lonergan, SJ, *Insight: A Study of Human Understanding* (New York: Philosophical Library, 1957), 7–12, 70–86, 687–706; Lonergan, *Method in Theology* (New York: Herder and Herder, 1972), "a normative," 4; David Tracy, *The Achievement of Bernard Lonergan* (New York: Herder and Herder, 1970).

4 Tracy, *Achievement of Bernard Lonergan*, "in its," 238; Lonergan, *Method in Theology*, "theologians of different" and "quite conservative," 333, 332.

5 David Tracy, "Lonergan's Foundational Theology: An Interpretation and a Critique," in *Foundations of Theology: Papers from the International Lonergan*

Congress 1970, ed. Phillip McShane, SJ (Notre Dame: University of Notre Dame Press, 1971), 197–222, quote 214.

6 David Tracy, *Blessed Rage for Order: The New Pluralism in Theology* (New York: Seabury Press, 1975), 6–7; Van A. Harvey, *The Historian and the Believer: The Morality of Historical Knowledge and Christian Belief* (New York: Macmillan, 1966).

7 Tracy, *Blessed Rage for Order*, 10–12, Tracy's paraphrase of Lonergan, 12; Lonergan, *Method in Theology*, 53–55.

8 Tracy, *Blessed Rage for Order*, 22–32.

9 Tracy, *Blessed Rage for Order*, quotes 32, 33.

10 Tracy, *Blessed Rage for Order*, 43–71; Paul Ricoeur, *Interpretation Theory: Discourse and the Surplus of Meaning* (Fort Worth: Texas Christian University Press, 1976); Ricoeur, *The Conflict of Interpretations: Essays in Hermeneutics*, ed. Don Ihde (Evanston, Ill.: Northwestern University Press, 1974).

11 Tracy, *Blessed Rage for Order*, 91–118; Emile Durkheim, *The Elementary Forms of Religious Life* (New York: Macmillan, 1915); Peter Berger, *The Sacred Canopy: Elements of a Sociological Theory of Religion* (Garden City, N.Y.: Doubleday, 1967); Clifford Geertz, "Religion as a Social System," in *The Religious Situation: 1968*, ed. Donald Cutler (Boston: Beacon Press, 1968), 639–88; Lonergan, *Insight*, 279–81, 319–431; Lonergan, *Method in Theology*, 3–27; Stephen Toulmin, *The Uses of Argument* (New York: Cambridge University Press, 1958); Schubert M. Ogden, *The Reality of God* (New York: Harper & Row, 1966), 27–34.

12 Tracy, *Blessed Rage for Order*, 160–61; Thomas Aquinas, *Summa Theologica*, 5 vols. (New York: Benziger Brothers, 1948), 5:1a., q.20.

13 Tracy, *Blessed Rage for Order*, 172–203, quote 177.

14 Dulles, review of *Blessed Rage for Order*, by David Tracy, 304–10; John B. Cobb Jr., review of *Blessed Rage for Order*, by David Tracy, *Christian Century* 93 (1976): 369–71; Edward Farley, review of *Blessed Rage for Order*, by David Tracy, *Christian Century* 93 (1976); Gordon D. Kaufman, review of *Blessed Rage for Order*, by Tracy, and *Ecclesial Man*, by Edward Farley, *Religious Studies Review* 2 (1976): 7–13; Harvey Cox, "How Pluralistic Is Tracy's Revisionism?" *Review of Books and Religion* 5 (1976): 1.

15 Dulles, review of *Blessed Rage for Order*, by David Tracy, 304–10, quote 310; Cobb Jr., review of *Blessed Rage for Order*, by Tracy, 369–71; Farley, review of *Blessed Rage for Order*, by Tracy, quote 371–72; Kaufman, review of *Blessed Rage for Order*, by Tracy, and *Ecclesial Man*, by Farley, 7–13; Cox, "How Pluralistic Is Tracy's Revisionism?" 1.

16 Van A. Harvey, "The Pathos of Liberal Theology," *Journal of Religion* 56 (1976): 382–91, quote 385; Gerald O'Collins, SJ, review of *Blessed Rage for Order*, by David Tracy, *Gregorianum* 57 (1976): 778–81.

17 David Tracy, "Theology as Public Discourse," *Christian Century* 92 (1975): 280–83, quotes 283.

18 David Tracy, "Presidential Address: The Catholic Analogical Imagination," *Proceedings of the Catholic Theological Society of America* 32 (1977): 234–44; David

Tracy and John B. Cobb Jr., *Talking About God: Doing Theology in the Context of Modern Pluralism,* 1977 Walter and Mary Tuohy Lectures (New York: Seabury Press, 1983), 17–28; Helen James John, *The Thomist Spectrum* (New York: Fordham University Press, 1966); William Hill, *Knowing the Unknown God* (New York: Philosophical Library, 1971); Bernard Montagnes, *La Doctrine de l'analogie de l'être d'aprés St. Thomas d'Aquinas* (Louvain: Nauevelauts, 1963); Ralph McInerny, *The Logic of Analogy* (The Hague: Martinus Nijhoff, 1961); Eric Mascall, *Existence and Analogy* (London: Longmans, Green, 1949); Cornelio Fabro, *Participation et causalité selon S. Thomas d'Aquin* (Louvain: Publications universitaires de Louvain, 1961); Louis-Bertrand Geiger, *La participation dans la philosophie de S. Thomas d'Aquin* (Paris: J. Vrin, 1953); Victor Preller, *Divine Science and the Science of God: A Reformulation of Thomas Aquinas* (Princeton: Princeton University Press, 1967); David Burrell, CSC, *Analogy and Philosophical Language* (New Haven: Yale University Press, 1975); Burrell, *Aquinas: God and Action* (Notre Dame: University of Notre Dame Press, 1979).

19 Tracy and Cobb, *Talking About God,* 24–28.

20 David Tracy, *The Analogical Imagination: Christian Theology and the Culture of Pluralism* (New York: Crossroad, 1981), 3–46, 110–15, 154–78; T. S. Eliot, "What Is a Classic?" in *Selected Prose of T. S. Eliot,* ed. Frank Kermode (New York: Harcourt Brace Jovanovich, 1975), 115–32; Frank Kermode, *The Classic* (New York: Viking, 1975); Hans-Georg Gadamer, *Truth and Method* (New York: Sheed and Ward, 1975), 73–91; Karl Rahner, *Foundations of Christian Faith: An Introduction to the Idea of Christianity,* trans. William V. Dych (New York: Seabury Press, 1978), 153–62.

21 Tracy, *Analogical Imagination,* quotes 424, 362; C. H. Dodd, *The Apostolic Preaching and Its Development* (London: Hodder & Stoughton, 1936); Rudolf Bultmann, *The History of the Synoptic Tradition,* trans. John Marsh (New York: Harper & Row, 1963); Norman Perrin, *What Is Redaction Criticism?* (Philadelphia: Fortress, 1969); Ernst Fuchs, *Zum hermeneutischen Problem in der Theologie; Die existentiale Interpretation* (Tübingen: Mohr, 1959); Gerhard Ebeling, *Word and Faith,* trans. James W. Leitch (Philadelphia: Fortress, 1963); Robert Funk, *Language, Hermeneutic, and Word of God* (New York: Harper & Row, 1966).

22 Shea, "Review Symposium," 313–19, quotes 319, 318, 313; see Werner Jeanrond, "Theology in the Context of Pluralism and Postmodernity: David Tracy's Theological Method," in *Postmodernism, Literature and Theology,* ed. David Jasper (London: Macmillan, 1993), 145–61; Richard Lints, "The Postpositivist Choice, Tracy or Lindbeck?" *Journal of the American Academy of Religion* 61 (1993): 655–77; Kristin E. Heyer, "How Does Theology Go Public? Rethinking the Debate between David Tracy and George Lindbeck," *Political Theology* 5 (July 2004): 307–27; O'Brien, "Review Symposium," 326–28, quotes 328; Bernard Cooke, "Review Symposium: Four Perspectives," *Horizons* 8 (1981): 324–26; Ted Peters, review of *Analogical Imagination,* by David Tracy, *Christian*

Century 98 (1981): 1101–3, quote 1102; John B. Cobb Jr., review of *Analogical Imagination*, by Tracy, *Religious Studies Review* 7 (1981): 281–84, quote 283; T. Howland Sanks, SJ, "David Tracy's Theological Project: An Overview and Some Implications," *Theological Studies* 54 (1993): 698–727, quote 716; Gregory Baum, review of *Analogical Imagination*, by Tracy, *Religious Studies Review* 7 (1981): 284–90, quote 284.

23 Burrell, "Review Symposium," 319–23, quotes 323, 320; see David Burrell, CSC, review of *Analogical Imagination*, by David Tracy, *Commonweal* (May 22, 1981): 310–11.

24 David Tracy, "Author's Response," *Horizons* 8 (1981): 329–39; Breyfogle and Levergood, "Conversation with David Tracy," 305.

25 David Tracy, "God, Dialogue and Solidarity: A Theologian's Refrain," *Christian Century* 107 (1990); reprinted in *How My Mind Has Changed*, ed. James M. Wall and David Heim (Grand Rapids: Eerdmans, 1991), 88–99, "I may" and "the most," 91; Breyfogle and Levergood, "Conversation with David Tracy," "it's a very," 302.

26 David Tracy, *Plurality and Ambiguity: Hermeneutics, Religion, Hope* (San Francisco: Harper & Row, 1987).

27 Stephen Happel and David Tracy, *A Catholic Vision* (Philadelphia: Fortress, 1984); Tracy, "God, Dialogue and Solidarity," "there is a dark," 93.

28 Tracy, *Plurality and Ambiguity*, quotes x, 85, 93; Richard Rorty, *Philosophy and the Mirror of Nature* (Princeton: Princeton University Press, 1979), 266–67.

29 David Tracy, *On Naming the Present: God, Hermeneutics, and Church* (Maryknoll, N.Y.: Orbis Books, 1994), 138; Tracy, *Plurality and Ambiguity*, quotes 93–94; Thomas Merton, *The Asian Journal of Thomas Merton* (New York: New Directions, 1968); John B. Cobb Jr., *Beyond Dialogue: Toward a Mutual Transformation of Christianity and Buddhism* (Philadelphia: Fortress, 1982); William Johnston, *The Still Point: Reflections on Zen and Christian Mysticism* (New York: Fordham University Press, 1971).

30 Tracy, *Plurality and Ambiguity*, 111–12.

31 David Tracy, *Dialogue with the Other: The Inter-Religious Dialogue* (Grand Rapids: Eerdmans, 1990), 30–47, quotes 30; William James, *The Varieties of Religious Experience* (New York: Modern Library, 1999 [1902]), 37; James, *A Pluralistic Universe* (Cambridge, Mass.: Harvard University Press, 1979 [1908]); James, *Will to Believe and Other Essays*; Gadamer, *Truth and Method*, 91–119, 235–354; Martin Heidegger, *Holzwege* (Frankfurt: Klostermann, 1950); Heidegger, *Poetry, Language, Thought*, trans. Albert Hofstadter (New York: Harper & Row, 1971); Heidegger, *Basic Writings*, ed. David Farrell Krell (New York: Harper & Row, 1977), 143–87, 319–39.

32 Tracy, *Dialogue with the Other*, quotes 74, 75; Frederich Franck, ed., *The Buddha Eye: An Anthology of the Kyoto School* (New York: Crossroad, 1982); Masao Abe, *Zen and Western Thought*, ed. William La Fleur (Honolulu: University of

Hawaii Press, 1985); Kitaro Nishida, *Intelligibility and the Philosophy of Nothingness* (New York: Greenwood Press, 1973).

33 *Meister Eckhart: The Essential Sermons, Commentaries, Treatises and Defense*, trans. and ed. Edmund Colledge, OSA, and Bernard McGinn (New York: Paulist Press, 1981); Bernard McGinn, "The God Beyond God: Theology and Mysticism in the Theology of Meister Eckhart," *Journal of Religion* 61 (1981): 1–19; Tracy, *Dialogue with the Other*, 79–89.

34 Tracy, *Dialogue with the Other*, 92; *John Ruusbroec: The Spiritual Espousals and Other Works*, ed. James A. Wiseman, OSB (New York: Paulist Press, 1985).

35 Tracy, *Dialogue with the Other*, quote 82. Tracy's interpretation of Ruysbroeck was influenced by Louis Dupré, *The Common Life* (New York: Crossroad, 1984).

36 Tracy, *Dialogue with the Other*, 97; Tracy, "God, Dialogue and Solidarity," "there are now," 98. A revised version of the latter essay is also reprinted in *Dialogue with the Other*, 1–7.

37 Tracy, *On Naming the Present*, 3–22, quotes 5, 18, 22. "Nihilism with a happy ending" was coined by literary critic Alan Bloom.

38 Breyfogle and Levergood, "Conversation with David Tracy," 294–97; David Tracy, "The Hidden God: The Divine Other of Liberation," *Cross Currents* 46 (1996): 5–16; Tracy, "The Post-Modern Re-Naming of God as Incomprehensible and Hidden," *Cross Currents* 50 (2000): 240–47; Lois Malcolm, "An Interview with David Tracy," *Christian Century* 119 (2002): 24–30; Scott Holland, "This Side of God: A Conversation with David Tracy," *Cross Currents* 52 (2002): 54–59.

39 Tracy, "Hidden God," 5–16; Tracy, "Post-Modern Re-Naming of God," 240–47; David Tracy, *This Side of God* (Chicago: University of Chicago Press, forthcoming).

40 Breyfogle and Levergood, "Conversation with David Tracy," 294–97; Holland, "This Side of God," 54–59; Tracy, "Post-Modern Re-Naming of God," 240–47.

41 Breyfogle and Levergood, "Conversation with David Tracy," quotes 300; see Hans Urs von Balthasar, *The Glory of the Lord: A Theological Aesthetics*, 7 vols., ed. Joseph Fessio, SJ, and John Riches (Edinburgh: T&T Clark, 1982); Austin Farrer, *The Glass of Vision* (London: Dacre Press, 1948); Farrer, *A Rebirth of Images* (London: Dacre Press, 1949); Balthasar, *Theo-Drama: Theological Dramatic Theory*, 4 vols., trans. Graham Harrison (San Francisco: Ignatius Press, 1988–1994); Balthasar, *The Glory of the Lord: A Theological Aesthetics*, 7 vols., trans. Erasmo Leiva-Merikakis et al., ed. John Riches et al. (San Francisco: Ignatius Press, 1982–1989); Rowan Williams, *A Ray of Darkness* (Boston: Cowley, 1995).

42 Tracy, "Hidden God," 7–8; see David Tracy, "Form & Fragment: The Recovery of the Hidden and Incomprehensible God," 1999 Palmer Lecture, Center of Theological Inquiry, Princeton Theological Seminary, Princeton, N.J., in *The Concept of God in Global Dialogue*, ed. Werner G. Jeanrond and Aasuly Lande (Maryknoll, N.Y.: Orbis Books, 2005), 98–114.

43 Tracy, "Hidden God," quotes 8–10; B. A. Gerrish, *The Old Protestantism and the New: Essays on the Reformation Heritage* (Chicago: University of Chicago Press, 1982), 131–49; Gerrish, *Grace and Reason*; John Dillenberger, *God Hidden and Revealed: The Interpretation of Luther's Deus Absconditus and Its Significance for Religious Thought* (Philadelphia: Muhlenberg Press, 1953); Hellmut Bandt, vol. 8 of *Luthers Lehre vom verborgenen Gott: Eine Untersuchung zu dem offenbarungsgeschichtlichen Ansatz seiner Theologie*, Theologische Arbeiten (Berlin: Evangelische Verlaganstalt, 1958).

44 Tracy, "Hidden God," 10–12.

45 Tracy, "Hidden God," 12; Breyfogle and Levergood, "Conversation with David Tracy," 307; Malcolm, "Interview with David Tracy," 28–29.

46 Tracy, "Hidden God," quote 13.

47 Tracy, "Post-Modern Re-Naming of God," 240–47, quote 243; Taylor, *Altarity*; John D. Caputo, ed., *The Religious* (Oxford: Blackwell, 2002); Philippa Berry and Andrew Wernick, eds., *Shadow of Spirit: Postmodernism and Religion* (New York: Routledge, 1992).

48 Breyfogle and Levergood, "Conversation with David Tracy," 302.

49 Malcolm, "Interview with David Tracy," 28–29; Holland, "This Side of God," 59.

50 Peter C. Hodgson, *Winds of the Spirit: A Constructive Christian Theology* (Louisville: Westminster John Knox, 1994), 332–33; Hodgson, "A Theologian of Mediation: Personal Recollections from Half a Century," *Spire* 24 (2003): 14–18.

51 Peter C. Hodgson, *The Formation of Historical Theology: A Study of Ferdinand Christian Baur* (New York: Harper & Row, 1966), 275–84; Hodgson to author, November 23, 2004, "I now see"; Hodgson, *Summer Sermons, Winter Thoughts* (Eugene, Ore.: Cascade Books, 2018), 83; Edward Farley, *The Transcendence of God: A Study in Contemporary Philosophical Theology* (Philadelphia: Westminster, 1960); Farley, "Reflecting on Some Reflections: A Third-Order Essay," *Religious Studies Review* 24 (1998): 152.

52 Heidegger, *Holzwege*, "that event," 61; Hodgson, "Theologian of Mediation," 15; see Heidegger, *Poetry, Language, Thought*; Gerhard Ebeling, *The Nature of Faith*, trans. Ronald Gregor Smith (Philadelphia: Muhlenberg Press, 1961), 44–71; Ebeling, *Word and Faith*, 201–46; James M. Robinson, "The German Discussion of the Later Heidegger," in *The Later Heidegger and Theology: New Frontiers in Theology*, ed. Robinson and John B. Cobb Jr. (New York: Harper & Row, 1963), 3–76.

53 Peter C. Hodgson, *Jesus—Word and Presence: An Essay in Christology* (Philadelphia: Fortress, 1971), "word," 276; "absolute," 290.

54 Peter C. Hodgson, *Children of Freedom: Black Liberation in Christian Perspective* (Philadelphia: Fortress, 1974), quotes 20, 30; Hodgson, *New Birth of Freedom: A Theology of Bondage and Liberation* (Philadelphia: Fortress, 1976), xiii–xiv.

55 Hodgson, *New Birth of Freedom*, 265–355; Paul Ricoeur, *Freedom and Nature: The Voluntary and the Involuntary*, trans. Erazim V. Kohák (Evanston, Ill.: Northwestern University Press, 1966), 128.

56 Letty M. Russell, review of *New Birth of Freedom*, by Peter C. Hodgson, *Theology Today* 33 (1977): 428–30; Frederick Herzog, "Birth Pangs: Liberation Theology in North America," *Christian Century* 93 (1976): 1120–25; Herzog, review of *New Birth of Freedom*, by Hodgson, *Christian Century* 94 (1977): "theological," 543.

57 Hodgson, *Winds of the Spirit*, "I felt" and "a bridge," 335.

58 Edward Farley, *Requiem for a Lost Piety: The Contemporary Search for the Christian Life* (Philadelphia: Westminster, 1966); Farley, "Reflecting on Some Reflections," 152; Farley, *Ecclesial Man: A Social Phenomenology of Faith and Reality* (Philadelphia: Fortress, 1975).

59 Farley, *Ecclesial Man*, 14–15.

60 Farley, *Ecclesial Man*, 24–50, 44–45; Edmund Husserl, *Ideas: General Introduction to Pure Phenomenology* (London: Allen & Unwin, 1931); Husserl, *Logical Investigations*, 2 vols., trans. J. N. Findlay (London: Routledge and Kegan Paul, 1970); Husserl, *Formal and Transcendental Logic*, trans. D. Cairns (The Hague: Martinus Nijhoff, 1969); Gilkey, *Naming the Whirlwind*, 242, 244; Lonergan, *Insight*, 415.

61 Farley, *Ecclesial Man*, quote 56.

62 Farley, *Ecclesial Man*, 9, 85–98, 106–85.

63 Farley, *Ecclesial Man*, 215–27, quote 128; Emil Brunner, *The Misunderstanding of the Church* (Philadelphia: Westminster, 1953), 6, 10–12.

64 Farley, "Reflecting on Some Reflections," quote 153; Hodgson, *Summer Sermons*, "because of," 87.

65 Peter C. Hodgson and Robert H. King, eds., *Christian Theology: An Introduction to Its Traditions and Tasks*, 2nd ed. (Philadelphia: Fortress, 1985 [1982]); see Rebecca S. Chopp and Mark Lewis Taylor, eds., *Reconstructing Christian Theology* (Minneapolis: Fortress, 1994).

66 Edward Farley and Peter C. Hodgson, "Scripture and Tradition," in Hodgson and King, *Christian Theology*, 61–65.

67 Farley and Hodgson, "Scripture and Tradition," 64–81; David H. Kelsey, *The Uses of Scripture in Recent Theology* (Philadelphia: Fortress, 1975); James Barr, *The Bible in the Modern World* (London: SCM Press, 1973); Barr, *Old and New in Interpretation* (London: SCM Press, 1966).

68 Edward Farley, *Ecclesial Reflection: An Anatomy of Theological Method* (Philadelphia: Fortress, 1982), quotes 166, 168.

69 Farley, *Ecclesial Reflection*, quotes 171, 183.

70 Farley, *Ecclesial Reflection*, 185–87, 193–299, 308–25; Edward Farley, *Theologia: The Fragmentation and Unity of Theological Education* (Philadelphia: Fortress, 1983); Farley, *The Fragility of Knowledge: Theological Education in the Church and the University* (Philadelphia: Fortress, 1988); Farley, *Good and Evil:*

Interpreting a Human Condition (Minneapolis: Fortress, 1990), 1–26; Farley, *Divine Empathy: A Theology of God* (Minneapolis: Fortress, 1996), 3–22, 111–32; Karl Jaspers, *Philosophical Faith and Revelation*, trans. E. B. Ashton (New York: Harper & Row, 1962).

71 Farley, *Divine Empathy*, 132–33.

72 Farley, *Divine Empathy*, 134–50, 252–85, 300–315, "the cipher," 141; Edward Farley, *Deep Symbols: Their Postmodern Effacement and Reclamation* (Valley Forge, Pa.: Trinity Press International, 1996), 42–73; Paul Lakeland, review of *Divine Empathy*, by Farley, *Theological Studies* 58 (1997): 558–60; Kathryn Tanner, review of *Divine Empathy*, by Farley, *Modern Theology* 14 (1998): 555–60; Martin R. Tripole, SJ, review of *Good and Evil*, by Farley, *Theological Studies* 52 (1991): 568–69; William C. Placher, review of *Good and Evil*, by Farley, *Christian Century* 108 (1991): 728–29; Wendy Farley, "Divine Empathy and Deep Symbols," *Religious Studies Review* 24 (1998): 147–52.

73 Peter Hodgson, ed. and trans., *Ferdinand Christian Baur on the Writing of Church History* (Oxford: Oxford University Press, 1968); Strauss, *Life of Jesus*; editor's preface to Hegel, *Lectures on the Philosophy of Religion*, quote 1:xi.

74 G. W. F. Hegel, *The Christian Religion: Lectures on the Philosophy of Religion*, part 3, *The Revelatory, Consummate, Absolute Religion*, ed. and trans. Peter Hodgson (Missoula, Mont.: Scholars Press, 1979); Hegel, *Lectures on the Philosophy of Religion*.

75 Editor's preface to Hegel, *Lectures on the Philosophy of Religion*, 1:xi; Hodgson, *Winds of the Spirit*, quotes 335; Peter C. Hodgson, *Hegel and Christian Theology: A Reading of the Lectures on the Philosophy of Religion* (Oxford: Oxford University Press, 2007), v–vi.

76 Peter C. Hodgson, *Revisioning the Church: Ecclesial Freedom in the New Paradigm* (Philadelphia: Fortress, 1988), quotes 51, 11, 17.

77 Hodgson, *Revisioning the Church*, quotes 55, 104; Gutiérrez, *Theology of Liberation*; Leonardo Boff, *Ecclesiogenesis: The Base Communities Reinvent the Church* (Maryknoll, N.Y.: Orbis Books, 1986); Fiorenza, *In Memory of Her*; Ruether, *Women-Church*.

78 Peter C. Hodgson, *God in History: Shapes of Freedom* (Nashville: Abingdon, 1989), quotes 7.

79 Hodgson, *God in History*, 39–44, quote 43.

80 Hodgson, *God in History*, quote 45.

81 Hegel, *Lectures on the Philosophy of World History*, trans. Nisbet, 54; Hodgson, *God in History*, quotes 45, 47; see Toews, *Hegelianism*; William J. Brazill, *The Young Hegelians* (New Haven: Yale University Press, 1970).

82 Hodgson, *God in History*, 44–49, quotes 46; Barth, *Doctrine of God*, section 28.

83 Hegel, *Lectures on the Philosophy of Religion*, 3:194, 370; Hodgson, *God in History*, 98–103, quotes 101–2; Ricoeur, *Conflict of Interpretations*, 440–97.

84 Hodgson, *God in History*, 108–12, quote 112; Hegel, *Encyclopedia of the Philosophical Sciences*, 381.

85 Hodgson, *God in History*, 198–205, quote 205.

86 Hodgson, *God in History*, 205–8; Hegel, *Phenomenology of Spirit*, 264–65, 410–16.

87 Hodgson, *God in History*, 234–46, quotes 240, 246.

88 Peter C. Hodgson, *Liberal Theology: A Radical Vision* (Minneapolis: Fortress, 2007), "in my view," 73; William Jones, *Is God a White Racist? A Preamble to Black Theology* (Garden City, N.Y.: Doubleday, 1973).

89 Hodgson, *Liberal Theology*, "demonstrates" and "African American," 74.

90 Hodgson, *Liberal Theology*, "into" and "suppressed," 75.

91 Hodgson, *Winds of the Spirit*, quotes 3, 5; Peter C. Hodgson, *Christian Faith: A Brief Introduction* (Louisville: Westminster John Knox, 2001).

92 Hodgson, *Winds of the Spirit*, 37–41, 53–66, 77–83, 93–96, 101–14, quotes 41, 111.

93 Peter C. Hodgson, *Summer Sermons, Winter Thoughts* (Eugene, Ore.: Cascade Books, 2018), "theology has" and "visions," 94; Hodgson, *Winds of the Spirit*, "my old," 337.

94 Catherine Keller, *Apocalypse Now and Then: A Feminist Guide to the End of the World* (Boston: Beacon Press, 1996), "perpetual," 140; Keller, *From a Broken Web: Separation, Sexism, and Self* (Boston: Beacon Press, 1986), "the most," 2; Dorrien, *Making of American Liberal Theology: Crisis, Irony, and Postmodernity*, 501–12.

95 Keller, *From a Broken Web*, quote 3.

96 Keller, *From a Broken Web*, 93–154; Nancy Chodorow, *The Reproduction of Mothering: Psychoanalysis and the Sociology of Gender* (Berkeley: University of California Press, 1978); Dorothy Dinnerstein, *The Mermaid and the Minotaur: Sexual Arrangements and Human Malaise* (New York: Harper Colophon, 1977).

97 Keller, *From a Broken Web*, quotes 162, 167.

98 Keller, *From a Broken Web*, quote 183.

99 Keller, *From a Broken Web*, quotes 184, 188, 189, 201, 229.

100 Catherine Keller to author, "I was," conversation on May 8, 2019; Keller, *From a Broken Web*, 201–52, quotes 211, 251.

101 Keller, *Apocalypse Now and Then*, quotes xi, 12–13; see Catherine Keller, "Why Apocalypse, Now?" *Theology Today* 49 (1992): 183–95.

102 Keller, *Apocalypse Now and Then*, quote 20; Julia Kristeva, *Powers of Horror: An Essay on Abjection* (New York: Columbia University Press, 1982), 11.

103 Keller, *Apocalypse Now and Then*, 128–30, "eco-social," 130; Julia Kristeva, "Women's Time," *Signs: Journal of Women in Culture and Society* 7 (1981): 13–35.

104 Keller, *Apocalypse Now and Then*, quotes 247, 248, 258; Mary Daly, *Gyn/Ecology* (Boston: Beacon Press, 1978), "waged" 105.

105 Keller, *Apocalypse Now and Then*, quotes 262, 285, 276; see Catherine Keller, "Power Lines," *Theology Today* 52 (1995): 188–203.

106 Keller, *Apocalypse Now and Then*, quotes 298, 301, 291, 307.

107 Peter C. Hodgson, review of *Apocalypse Now and Then*, by Catherine Keller, *Journal of the American Academy of Religion* 66 (1998): 441–44, quote 443; Miroslav Volf, review of *Apocalypse Now and Then*, by Keller, *Modern Theology* 14 (1998): 563–65, quotes 564, 565.

108 Mary Grey, review of *Apocalypse Now and Then*, by Catherine Keller, *Ecotheology* 5–6 (1998/99): 239–42, quote 239; Elizabeth A. Say, review of *Apocalypse Now and Then*, by Keller, *Cross Currents* 48 (1998): 257–59, quote 259; Tina Pippin, review of *Apocalypse Now and Then*, by Keller, *Critical Review of Books in Religion* 10 (1997): 296–98.

109 Catherine Keller, "The Last Laugh: A Counter-Apocalyptic Meditation on Moltmann's *The Coming of God*," *Theology Today* 54 (1997): 381–91.

110 Catherine Keller, "Seeking and Sucking: On Relation and Essence in Feminist Theology," in Chopp and Davaney, *Horizons in Feminist Theology*, 54–78, quotes 68, 71; Elisabeth Schüssler Fiorenza, *Jesus: Miriam's Child, Sophia's Prophet: Critical Issues in Feminist Christology* (New York: Continuum, 1994), quote 54.

111 Keller, "Seeking and Sucking," quotes 75, 78.

112 Catherine Keller, "Introduction: The Process of Difference, the Difference of Process," in *Process and Difference: Between Cosmological and Poststructuralist Postmodernisms*, ed. Catherine Keller and Anne Daniell (Albany: State University of New York Press, 2002), 1–29, quotes 2, 7.

113 Keller, "Introduction," 10–11; Whitehead, *Process and Reality*, "in watertight," 10.

114 Keller, "Introduction," 12.

115 Catherine Keller, "Process and Chaosmos: The Whiteheadian Fold in the Discourse of Difference," in Keller and Daniell, *Process and Difference*, 55–72, quotes 57, 68, 69; Gilles Deleuze, *The Fold: Leibniz and the Baroque*, trans. Tom Conley (Minneapolis: University of Minnesota Press, 1993), "sort of," 76; Deleuze, *Difference and Repetition*.

116 Catherine Keller, *Face of the Deep: A Theology of Becoming* (New York: Routledge, 2003).

117 Keller, *Face of the Deep*, quotes xv, xvii.

118 Keller, *Face of the Deep*, quotes 9.

119 Keller, *Face of the Deep*, quotes 10, 12; Jacques Derrida, *Of Grammatology*, trans. Gayatri Chakravorti Spivak (Baltimore: Johns Hopkins University Press, 1976); Jürgen Moltmann, *God in Creation: A New Theology of Creation and the Spirit of God*, trans. Margaret Kohl (New York: Harper & Row, 1985), 79–87.

120 Keller, *Face of the Deep*, quotes 35; Karl Barth, *Church Dogmatics*, vol. 3, bk. 1, *The Doctrine of Creation*, trans G. W. Bromiley and R. J. Ehrlich (Edinburgh: T&T Clark, 1960), 105; see Alexander Heidel, *The Babylonian Genesis: A Complete Translation of All the Published Cuneiform Tablets of the Various Babylonian Creation Stories* (Chicago: University of Chicago Press, 1951), 1:28–43, 19; William P. Brown, *Structure, Role, and Ideology in the Hebrew*

and Greek Texts of Genesis 1:1–2, 3, Society of Biblical Literature Dissertation Series 132 (Atlanta: Scholar's Press, 1993); Richard S. Hess and David Toshio Tsumera, eds., *"I Studied Inscriptions from Before the Flood": Ancient Near Eastern, Literary, and Linguistic Approaches to Genesis 1–11* (Winona Lake, Ind.: Eisenbrauns, 1994).

121 Keller, *Face of the Deep*, quotes 172, 219; Joseph Bracken, SJ, *The Divine Matrix: Creativity as Link between East and West* (Maryknoll, N.Y.: Orbis Books, 1995), 59.

122 Keller, *Face of the Deep*, 4, 240, quotes 219, 222; see John B. Cobb Jr. and David R. Griffin, *Process Theology: An Introductory Exposition* (Philadelphia: Westminster John Knox, 1976), 65–68.

123 Laurel C. Schneider, review of *Face of the Deep*, by Catherine Keller, *Journal of Religion* 84 (2004): 639–40; Jonathan Baxter, review of *Face of the Deep*, by Keller, *Reviews in Religion and Theology* 10 (2003): 418–21, quotes 421; B. Jill Carroll, review of *Face of the Deep*, by Keller, *Theology Today* 61 (2004): 389–90, quotes 390; Douglas Sturm, review of *Face of the Deep*, by Keller, *Soundings* 87 (2004): 236–41, quote 241.

124 Keller, *Face of the Deep*, 229.

125 Keller, *Face of the Deep*, quotes 230, 238; Catherine Keller, *God and Power: Counter-Apocalyptic Journeys* (Minneapolis: Fortress, 2005); Keller, *On the Mystery: Discerning God in Process* (Minneapolis: Fortress, 2008).

126 Catherine Keller, *Cloud of the Impossible: Negative Theology and Planetary Entanglement* (New York: Columbia University Press, 2015), "cloudy," 8; Jacques Derrida, "Sauf le nom (Post Scriptum)," in *On the Name*, trans. David Wood, John P. Leavey Jr., and Ian McLeod (Stanford: Stanford University Press, 1995), "is to be," 75; "more than," 43; Derrida, "A Certain Impossible Possibility of Saying the Event," in *The Late Derrida*, ed. W. J. Mitchell and Arnold Davidson (Chicago: University of Chicago Press, 2007), 227–40.

127 H. G. Senger, "Nikolaus von Kues," in *Nimm und lies. Christliche Denken von Origenes bis Erasmus von Rotterdam* (Stuttgart: W. Kohlhammer, 1991), 333–59; C. L. Moran, "A Road Not Taken: Nicholas of Cusa and Today's Intellectual World," *Proceedings of the American Catholic Philosophical Association* 57 (1983): 68–77; Karsten Harries, *Infinity and Perspective* (Cambridge: MIT Press, 2001), 42–64; Nicholas of Cusa, *Da Docta Ignorantia*, in *Nicholas of Cusa: Selected Spiritual Writings*, trans. H. Lawrence Bond (New York: Paulist Press, 1997), 85–206.

128 Keller, *Cloud of the Impossible*, "cloud-writing" is the title and theme of chapter 2, 50–86; Gregory of Nyssa, *The Life of Moses* (New York: Paulist Press, 1978); Denys Turner, *The Darkness of God: Negativity in Christian Mysticism* (Cambridge: Cambridge University Press, 1995), 17–22; Eugene Thacker, *After Life* (Chicago: University of Chicago Press, 2010), 34–35.

129 Nicholas of Cusa, *Da Docta Ignorantia*, "there are," 159; Nicholas of Cusa, *De Visione Dei*, in *Nicholas of Cusa*, 233–91; Nicholas of Cusa, *On Not Other*

(*De Li Non Aliud*), *Complete Philosophical and Theological Treatises of Nicholas of Cusa*, trans. Jasper Hopkins (Minneapolis: Arthur J. Banning, 2001); Jasper Hopkins, *Nicholas of Cusa on God as Not Other: A Translation and an Appraisal of De Li Non Aliud* (Minneapolis: University of Minnesota, 1979); Peter J. Casarella, "Nicholas of Cusa and the Power of the Possible," *American Catholic Philosophical Quarterly* 64 (1990): 7–34; Keller, *Cloud of the Impossible*, 110–17; Johannes Hoff, *The Analogical Turn: Rethinking Modernity with Nicholas of Cusa* (Grand Rapids, Eerdmans, 2013).

130 Nicholas, *De Visione Dei*, "we see," 257; Nicholas, *On Not Other*, 2:1112; Keller, *Cloud of the Impossible*, "experimental," 103; "an illicit," 110.

131 Keller, *Cloud of the Impossible*, "if we" and "once we," 111; Nicholas of Cusa, "On the Summit of Contemplation," in Hopkins, *Nicholas of Cusa on God as Not Other*, "that than," 294.

132 Keller, *Cloud of the Impossible*, "one can say," 107; Whitehead, *Process and Reality*, "a tenderness," 346; Nicholas of Cusa, *De Visione Dei*, "sweetness," 247; "a most astonishing" and "the natural," 246.

133 Whitehead, *Process and Reality*, 21; Keller, *Cloud of the Impossible*, 109; Roland Faber, "De-Ontologizing God: Levinas, Deleuze, and Whitehead," in Keller and Daniell, *Process and Difference*, 209–34.

134 Keller, *Cloud of the Impossible*, 306–7.

Chapter 11

1 Dorrien, *Kantian Reason and Hegelian Spirit*, 489–99; Joseph Donceel, "On Transcendental Thomism," *Continuum* 7 (1969): 164–68; Rahner, *Geist in Welt*.

2 Lotze, *Grundzüge der Religionsphilosophie*; Lotze, *Metaphysik*; Lotze, *Logik*; Rudolf Eucken, *Knowledge and Life*, trans. W. Tudor Jones (New York: G. P. Putnam's Sons, 1914); Eucken, *Collected Essays*, ed. and trans. Meyrick Booth (London: T. Fisher Unwin, 1914); Seth, *Hegelianism and Personality*; Seth, *Scottish Philosophy*; Rashdall, *Philosophy and Religion*; Howison, *Limits of Evolution*; Bowne, *Metaphysics*; Bowne, *Theory of Thought and Knowledge*; Knudson, *Philosophy of Personalism*.

3 Karl Rosenkranz, *Geschichte der kantischen Philosophie* (Leipzig: Voss, 1840); Marheineke, *Die Grundlinien der christlichen Dogmatik*; Rosenkranz, *Encyklopädie der theologischen Wissenschaften*; Karl Ludwig Michelet, *Vorlesungen über die Persöhnlichkeit Gottes und Unsterblichkeit der Seele oder die ewige Persöhnlichkeit des Geistes* (Berlin: F. Dümmler, 1841); Edward Caird, *The Critical Philosophy of Immanuel Kant* (Glasgow: James Maclehose, 1889); Caird, *Evolution of Religion*; C. C. J. Webb, *God and Personality* (London: Allen & Unwin, 1919); Josiah Royce, *The World and the Individual* (New York: Macmillan, 1900); Hocking, *Meaning of God*; Brightman, *Person and Reality*; Cohen, *Kants Theorie der Erfahrung*, 589–92; Ernst Cassirer, *Substanzbegriff und Funktionsbegriff*:

Untersuchungen über die Grundfragen der Erkenntniskritik (Berlin: Cassirer, 1910); Cassirer, "Paul Natorp," *Kant-Studien* 30 (1925): 273–98.

4 Immanuel Kant, *Critique of Judgment*, trans. James Creed Meredith (Oxford: Clarendon, 1973), "the parts," 21.

5 Friedrich Schlegel, *Athenaeumsfragment* ("Athenaeum Fragments"), in *Philosophical Fragments*, 116; Beiser, *German Idealism*, 435–61.

6 Heidegger, *Kant and the Problem of Metaphysics*, "in the radicalism," "pure reason," and "awoke," 118; Mark C. Taylor, "Infinite Restlessness," in *Hegel and the Infinite: Religion, Politics, and Dialectic*, ed. Slavoj Žižek, Clayton Crockett, and Creston Davis (New York: Columbia University Press, 2011), "such an," 107.

7 Fichte, *Science of Knowledge*; Schelling, *Vom Ich als Princip der Philosophie*, 1:151; Schelling, *Philosophy of Nature*; Fuhrmanns, *F. W. J. Schelling*, 2:51–52; Schelling, *System der gesammten Philosophie*, 6:148; Schelling, *System of Transcendental Idealism*; Friedrich W. J. Schelling, *The Unconditional in Human Knowledge: Four Early Essays (1794–1796)*, trans. Fritz Marti (Lewisburg, Pa.: Bucknell University Press, 1980), 90–95.

8 G. W. F. Hegel, "The Spirit of Christianity and Its Fate" (1899), in *Early Theological Writings*, trans. T. M. Knox (Chicago: University of Chicago Press, 1948), quote 296; Dorrien, *Kantian Reason and Hegelian Spirit*, 162–68.

9 Martin Heidegger, *Hegel's Concept of Experience*, trans. Kenley Dove (New York: Harper & Row, 1970), "the presentation" and "the presentation," 48.

10 Martin Heidegger, *Schelling's Treatise on the Essence of Freedom*, trans. Joan Stambaugh (Athens: Ohio University Press, 1985), "not in the mere," 161; Taylor, "Infinite Restlessness," 104; Nancy, *Hegel*, "inaugural," 3; "not in the solace," 4.

11 Nancy, *Hegel*, "every instance," 5; "an upsurge" and "the full," 9.

12 Nancy, *Hegel*, 9–12, 55–65, "being unto," 55.

13 Nancy, *Hegel*, "sentimental," 60; "it is recognition," 59; "infinite," 62.

14 Otto Pfleiderer, *Philosophy and Development of Religion*, 2 vols. (Edinburgh: W. Blackwood and Sons, 1894); Troeltsch, *Absoluteness of Christianity*.

15 Albrecht Ritschl, *Die christliche Lehre von der Rechtfertigung und Versöhnung*, 3 vols. (Bonn: Adolph Marcus, 1870–1874); Ritschl, *Christian Doctrine*; Herrmann, "Der evangelische Glaube und die Theologie Albr. Ritschls," 1–25; Harnack, *What Is Christianity?*

16 Herrmann, *Die Metaphysik in der Theologie*; Herrmann, *Die Religion im Verhältnis zum Welterkennen und zur Sittlichkeit*; Herrmann, "Albrecht Ritschl," 405–6; Herrmann, "Kants Bedeutung für das Christentum," 104–22; Herrmann, "Die Auffassung der Religion in Cohens and Natorps Ethik," in *Gesammelte Schriften*, 377–405; Troeltsch, *Die Absolutheit der Christentums und die Religionsgeschichte*; Troeltsch, "Historical and Dogmatic Method in Theology" and "Dogmatics of the History-of-Religions School," in *Religion in History*, 11–32, 87–108; Troeltsch, *Christian Faith*, 16–17, 91–92; Ecke, *Die theologische Schule Albrecht Ritschls und die Evangelische Kirche der Gegenwart*; Rathje, *Die Welt des freien Protestantismus*, 102–3.

17 Tillich, *Love, Power, and Justice*, "God as," 12.

18 O'Regan, *Heterodox Hegel*.

19 Žižek, *Sublime Object of Ideology*, xxix–xxx.

20 Hegel, *Philosophy of Right*, paragraphs 257–71, quotes 258, 155–56.

21 Hegel, *Philosophy of Right*, quote 358, 222.

22 Hegel, *Philosophy of Right*, 355–60, 220–23; Hegel, *Lectures on the Philosophy of World History*, trans. Nisbet, "America" and "the country," 170; "the dregs," 166.

23 Enrique Dussel, *Politica de la liberación: Historia mundial y critica* (Madrid: Trotta, 2007), "just a few," 380.

24 Enrique Dussel, "Eurocentrism and Modernity," in *The Postmodernism Debate in Latin America*, ed. John Beverly, José Oviedo, and Michael Aronna (Durham, N.C.: Duke University Press, 1995), "but modernity" and "the moment," 66.

25 Dussel, *Philosophy of Liberation*, "reprehensible," 61; "only the praxis," 15; Dussel, "World System and 'Transmodernity,'" *Nepantla* 3 (2002): 221–44; Dussel, *Etica de la liberación en la edad de la globalización y de la exclusión* (Mexico City: Universidad Autónoma Metropolitana, 1998).

26 Dussel, *Philosophy of Liberation*, "puts the system," 63–64; "reprehensible," 61; "only the praxis," 15; Dussel, "World System and 'Transmodernity,'" *Nepantla* 3 (2002): 221–44; Dussel, *Etica de la liberación en la edad de la globalización y de la exclusión* (Mexico City: Universidad Autónoma Metropolitana, 1998).

27 Walter D. Mignolo, *The Darker Side of Western Modernity: Global Futures, Decolonial Options* (Durham, N.C.: Duke University Press, 2011), "with Europe," 151; "as the justification," 152; Diana Hugh quote 152.

28 Bruno Bosteels, "Hegel in America," in Žižek, Crockett, and Davis, *Hegel and the Infinite*, "the question," 74; Susan Buck-Morss, "Hegel and Haiti," *Critical Inquiry* 16 (2000): "the project," 865.

29 Gayatri Chakravorty Spivak, *A Critique of Postcolonial Reason: Toward a History of the Vanishing Present* (Cambridge, Mass.: Harvard University Press, 1999), "because it attempts," "it is, strictly," and "and these will," 49; Spivak, "A Literary Representation of the Subaltern: A Woman's Text from the Third World," in *In Other Worlds: Essays in Cultural Politics* (New York: Routledge, 1988), 241–68.

30 Gayatri Chakravorty Spivak, "Subaltern Studies: Deconstructing Historiography," in *Selected Subaltern Studies*, ed. Ranajit Guha and Gatatri Chakravorty Spivak (Oxford: Oxford University Press, 1988), "the historian," 16; Bosteels, "Hegel in America," 74.

31 Bosteels, "Hegel in America," "or even" and "into the," 75; Malabou, *Future of Hegel*, 39–56, 115–30; Catherine Malabou, "Is Confession the Accomplishment of Recognition? Rousseau and the Unthought of Religion in the *Phenomenology of Spirit*," in Žižek, Crockett, and Davis, *Hegel and the Infinite*, 19–30.

32 Theodor Adorno, *Hegel: Three Studies*, trans. Shierry Weber Nicholsen (Cambridge: MIT Press, 1994), 13–32; Adorno, *Negative Dialectics*, trans. E. B.

Ashton (New York: Seabury Press, 1973), 300–350; Horkheimer and Adorno, *Dialectic of Enlightenment.*

33 Jürgen Habermas, "The Dialectics of Rationalization: An Interview with Jürgen Habermas," *Telos* 49 (1981): 6–7; Habermas, "Psychic Thermidor and the Rebirth of Rebellious Subjectivity," in *Habermas and Modernity*, ed. Richard J. Bernstein (Cambridge: MIT Press, 1985), 67–77; Habermas, "The German Idealism of the Jewish Philosophers," in *Philosophical-Political Profiles* (Cambridge: MIT Press, 1983), 41; Habermas, *Knowledge and Human Interests*, trans. Jeremy J. Shapiro (Boston: Beacon Press, 1971), 91–186; Habermas, *Theory and Practice*, trans. John Viertel (Boston: Beacon Press, 1973); Martin Heidegger, *An Introduction to Metaphysics*, trans. Ralph Manheim (New Haven: Yale University Press, 1959), "inner truth," 199.

34 Jürgen Habermas, *Legitimation Crisis*, trans. Thomas McCarthy (Boston: Beacon Press, 1975); Habermas, *Communication and the Evolution of Society*, trans. Thomas McCarthy (Boston: Beacon Press, 1979), 1–68.

35 Habermas, *Communication*, "the goal," 3.

36 Jürgen Habermas, *The Theory of Communicative Action*, 2 vols., trans. Thomas McCarthy (Boston: Beacon Press, 1984, 1987), 1:8–42, 143–272; Habermas, *Between Facts and Norms: Contributions to a Discourse Theory of Law and Democracy*, trans. William Rehg (Cambridge: MIT Press, 1996).

37 Habermas, *Theory of Communicative Action*, 2:113–98, 301–403.

38 Jürgen Habermas, *The Philosophical Discourse of Modernity: Twelve Lectures*, trans. Frederick G. Lawrence (Cambridge: MIT Press, 1987), 131–210.

39 Habermas, *Philosophical Discourse of Modernity*, "network," 162; "the familiar," 161.

40 Habermas, *Philosophical Discourse of Modernity*, 211–65; Thomas McCarthy, introduction to *Philosophical Discourse of Modernity*, xiv.

41 Habermas, *Philosophical Discourse of Modernity*, 266–93, "irritating," 273; "Foucault's dramatic," 275–76.

42 Habermas, *Philosophical Discourse of Modernity*, "a different" 40.

43 Jürgen Habermas, *The Inclusion of the Other: Studies in Political Theory* (Cambridge: MIT Press, 1998); Axel Honneth, *The Struggle for Recognition: The Moral Grammar of Social Conflicts*, trans. Joel Anderson (Cambridge: MIT Press, 1996); Nancy Fraser and Axel Honneth, *Redistribution or Recognition? A Political-Philosophical Exchange*, trans. Joel Golb, James Ingram, and Christiane Wilke (London: Verso, 2003); Fraser, *Scales of Justice: Reimagining Political Space in a Globalizing World* (New York: Columbia University Press, 2010); Rudolf Siebert, *From Critical Theory of Society to Theology of Communicative Praxis* (Lewiston, N.Y.: Edwin Mellen Press, 1987); Seyla Benhabib, *Critique, Norm, and Utopia: A Study of the Foundations of Critical Theory* (New York: Columbia University Press, 1986); Kenneth Baynes, *The Normative Grounds of Social Criticism* (Albany: State University of New York Press, 1992); David Ingram, *Habermas and the Dialectic of Reason* (New Haven: Yale University Press, 1987);

Hille Haker, *Recognition and Responsibility: Critical Theory and Christian Ethics*, forthcoming; Christopher Latiolais, "Reconstructing and Deconstructing the Ideals of Reason: Habermas and the Constructive Role of Narrative," *Journal of the Interdisciplinary Crossroad* 1 (2004).

44 See Dorrien, *Social Ethics in the Making*, 637–40.

45 Sharon D. Welch, *Communities of Resistance and Solidarity: A Feminist Theology of Liberation* (Maryknoll, N.Y.: Orbis Books 1985), 32–54.

46 Welch, *Communities of Resistance and Solidarity*, quotes 72.

47 Welch, *Communities of Resistance and Solidarity*, quotes 79, 80.

48 Sharon D. Welch, *A Feminist Ethic of Risk*, rev. ed. (Minneapolis: Fortress, 2000), 14–37; Emilie M. Townes, *Breaking the Fine Rain of Death: African American Health Issues and a Womanist Ethic of Care* (New York: Continuum, 1998), "socially shared," 26; Townes, *In a Blaze of Glory: Womanist Spirituality as Social Witness* (Nashville: Abingdon, 1995), "a respect-filled," 138.

49 Welch, *Feminist Ethic of Risk*, 123–58, quote 135.

50 Welch, *Feminist Ethic of Risk*, quotes 168.

51 Sharon D. Welch, "Sporting Power: American Feminism, French Feminisms, and an Ethic of Conflict," in Kim, Ville, and Simonaitis, *Transfigurations*, 171–98; Sheila G. Davaney, "The Limits of the Appeal to Women's Experience," in *Shaping New Vision: Gender and Values in American Culture*, ed. Clarissa W. Atkinson, Constance H. Buchanan, and Margaret R. Miles (Ann Arbor: University of Michigan Research Press, 1987), 32–48; Jacquelyn Grant, *White Women's Christ and Black Women's Jesus: Feminist Christology and Womanist Response* (Atlanta: Scholars Press, 1989), 195–209.

52 Sharon D. Welch, *After the Protests Are Heard* (New York: New York University Press, 2019).

53 Tillich, *Love, Power, and Justice*, "but whenever," 67.

54 Tillich, *Love, Power, and Justice*, "is not dead," 108.

55 Tillich, *On the Boundary*, "whenever," 83.

56 Tillich, *On the Boundary*, quote 83.

57 Tillich, *On the Boundary*, 86; Tillich, *Protestantisches Prinzip und proletarische Situation* (Bonn: Friedrich Cohen, 1931); Tillich, *Protestant Era*, 237–59.

58 Schelling, *Grounding of Positive Philosophy*, 108, 129–30, 150.

59 Schelling, *Grounding of Positive Philosophy*, "externalize," 153.

60 William Desmond, *Hegel's God: A Counterfeit Double?* (Aldershot: Ashgate, 2003), 9–67, 88–120; Desmond, "Between Finitude and Infinity: On Hegel's Sublationary Infinitism," in Žižek, Crockett, and Davis, *Hegel and the Infinite*, "the humanists," 127.

61 Desmond, *Hegel's God*, 91–113; Desmond, "Between Finitude and Infinity," 120–25, "the more," 126; Hegel, *Lectures on the Philosophy of Religion*, "to exist," 3:292.

62 Desmond, "Between Finitude and Infinity," "is no," 127.

63 Hodgson, *Hegel and Christian Theology*, quote 267.

64 Hegel, *Lectures on the Philosophy of Religion*, 2:567–76, quotes 574, 575; Hodgson, *Hegel and Christian Theology*, 269.

65 Stephen Crites, *Dialectic and Gospel in the Development of Hegel's Thinking* (University Park: Pennsylvania State University Press, 1998), 517–26; Shanks, *Hegel and Religious Faith*, quote 7; Hodgson, *Hegel and Christian Theology*, 270; Lauer, *Hegel's Concept of God*, 162–202.

66 G. R. G. Mure, *A Study of Hegel's Logic* (Oxford: Oxford University Press, 1950), 320–31; Williams, *Recognition*, 267–72.

67 Karl Popper, *The Open Society and Its Enemies*, 2 vols. (London: Routledge, 1945).

68 Hegel, *Phenomenology of Spirit*, #758, "this God," 459; Martin Luther, "Heidelberg Disputation" (1518), in *Luther's Works*, vol. 31, *Career of the Reformer I*, ed. Harold Grimm (Philadelphia: Muhlenberg Press, 1957), "because men," 54.

69 G. W. F. Hegel, *Lectures on Natural Right, 1817–1818*, trans. M. Stewart and Peter C. Hodgson (Berkeley: University of California Press, 1995), quotes #164.

70 Williams, *Tragedy, Recognition, and the Death of God*, 364–66; Eberhard Jüngel, "'Die Weltgeschichte st das Weltgericht' aus theologischer Perspektive," in *Die Weltgeschichte—das Weltgericht?* ed. R. Bubner and W. Mesch (Stuttgart: Klett-Cotta, 2001), 23.

71 Hegel, *Philosophy of Right*, 10; Hegel, "Spirit of Christianity," "it is," 247.

72 Hegel, *Philosophy of Right*, "is the rose," 12; Hegel, *Lectures on the Philosophy of World History*, ed. and trans. Hodgson and Brown, "shallow" and "as merely," 489–90; Jüngel, "Die Weltgeschichte st das Weltgericht," 25; Wolfhart Pannenberg, *Systematische Theologie*, 3 vols. (Göttingen: Vandenhoeck & Ruprecht, 1993), 3:682–83; Williams, *Tragedy, Recognition, and the Death of God*, 370; Hegel, *Lectures on the Philosophy of Religion*, 1:378–79.

73 Hegel, *Phenomenology of Spirit*, "it wins," #32, 19; Hegel, *Lectures on the Philosophy of Religion*, 3:125–32, "monstrous," "all that," and "the death," 3:125.

74 James Cone, *The Cross and the Lynching Tree* (Maryknoll, N.Y.: Orbis Books, 2011), quotes 37.

75 Dorrien, *New Abolition*; Dorrien, *Breaking White Supremacy*; Cone, *Cross and the Lynching Tree*, quote 22.

76 Whitehead, *Religion in the Making*, "the common," 95; Whitehead, *Process and Reality*, corrected edition, "the ultimate," 340; Thandeka, "I've Known Rivers: Black Theology's Response to Process Theology," *Process Studies* 18 (1989): 282–93, "process" and "the manners," 285.

77 Monica A. Coleman, *Making a Way Out of No Way: A Womanist Theology* (Minneapolis: Fortress, 2008), "one of," "accept," and "God resists," 82; see Henry James Young, "Process Theology and Black Liberation: Testing the Whiteheadian Metaphysical Foundations," *Process Studies* 18 (1989): 259–67; Young, *Hope in Process: A Theology of Social Pluralism* (Minneapolis: Fortress, 1990); Theodore Walker Jr., *Mothership Connections: A Black Atlantic Synthesis*

of Neoclassical Metaphysics and Black Theology, SUNY Series in Constructive Postmodern Thought (Albany: State University of New York Press, 2004).

78 Ford, "Hartshorne's Interpretation of Whitehead," 313–37; Ford, *Two Process Philosophers*; Whitehead, *Process and Reality*, 220, 336; Johnson, *Whitehead's Theory of Reality*; Hartshorne, "Whitehead and Ordinary Language," 437–45; Hartshorne and Peden, *Whitehead's View of Reality*, 8–9; Hartshorne, "Whitehead's Idea of God," 557–58; Hartshorne, postscript to *God in Process Thought*, 119.

79 Hartshorne, *Divine Relativity*; Hartshorne, "Theological Values in Current Metaphysics," 157–67.

80 David Ray Griffin, "Hartshorne's Differences from Whitehead," in Ford, *Two Process Philosophers*, 35–57; James, *Concrete God*, 108–11; Charles Hartshorne, "Interrogation of Charles Hartshorne," in *Philosophical Interrogations*, ed. Sydney Rome and Beatrice Rome (New York: Holt, Rinehart & Winston, 1964), 321–54, "a new Consequent," 323.

81 Towne, *Two Types of New Theism*, 156–60; Christian, *Whitehead's Metaphysics*, 396–99; Lewis S. Ford, *Transforming Process Theism* (Albany: State University of New York Press, 2000); John B. Cobb Jr., "A Challenge to American Theology and Philosophy," *American Journal of Theology and Philosophy* 15 (1994): 123–36.

82 Gottfried Thomasius, *Beiträge zur kirchlichen Christologie* (1845), in *God and Incarnation: A Library of Protestant Thought*, ed. Claude Welch (New York: Oxford University Press, 1965), 48–94; W. F. Gess, *Die Lehre von der Person Christi* (Basel: Bahnmaiers Buchhandlung, 1856); Isaak August Dorner, *History of the Development of the Doctrine of the Person of Christ*, 5 vols., trans. William Lindsay Alexander (Edinburgh: T&T Clark, 1878); Dorner, *Divine Immutability: A Critical Reconsideration*, trans. Robert R. Williams and Claude Welch (Minneapolis: Fortress, 1994).

83 Karl Barth, *Church Dogmatics*, vol. 2, bk. 2, *The Doctrine of God*, trans. G. W. Bromiley et al. (Edinburgh: T&T Clark, 1957), 145–94; Hans Urs von Balthasar, *Mysterium Paschale*, trans. Aidan Nichols (Grand Rapids: Eerdmans, 1993), 11–147; Karl Rahner, *Schriften Zur Theologie* (Zurich: Benziger, 1962), 4:103–33; Eberhard Jüngel, *Gott als Geheimnis der Welt* (Tübingen: Mohr, 1977); Moltmann, *Crucified God*; Robert Jenson, *Systematic Theology*, 2 vols. (Oxford: Oxford University Press, 1997), 1:179–93; Wolfhart Pannenberg, *Systematic Theology*, 3 vols., trans. Geoffrey W. Bromiley (Grand Rapids: Eerdmans, 1994), 2:397–453.

84 Dorrien, *Democratic Socialist Vision*, 18–47.

85 William Temple, *Mens Creatrix: An Essay* (London: Macmillan, 1917); Temple, *Christus Veritas: An Essay* (London: Macmillan, 1924).

86 William Temple, *Nature, Man, and God* (London: Macmillan, 1934), quote ix–x.

87 Temple, *Nature, Man, and God*, quote 66.

88 Temple, *Nature, Man, and God*, 57–81.

89 Temple, *Nature, Man, and God*, quotes 128.

90 Temple, *Nature, Man, and God*, quote 133.

91 Temple, *Nature, Man, and God*, 257–59; Whitehead, *Process and Reality*, "the great," 497.

92 Temple, *Nature, Man, and God*, quote 269; see Jack F. Padgett, *The Christian Philosophy of William Temple* (The Hague: Martinus Nijhoff, 1974), 67–79.

93 Temple, *Nature, Man, and God*, quotes 295.

94 Temple, *Nature, Man, and God*, quote 306–7.

95 Temple, *Nature, Man, and God*, quotes 315, 317.

96 Karl R. Popper and John C. Eccles, *The Self and Its Brain: An Argument for Interactionism* (Heidelberg: Springer-Verlag, 1977); Geoffrey Madell, *Mind and Materialism* (Edinburgh: Edinburgh University Press, 1988); W. D. Hart, *The Engines of the Soul* (Cambridge: Cambridge University Press, 1988); Daniel E. Dennett, *Consciousness Explained* (Boston: Little, Brown, 1991); Paul M. Churchland, *Matter and Consciousness: A Contemporary Introduction to the Philosophy of Mind* (Cambridge: MIT Press, 1988); Colin McGinn, *The Problem of Consciousness: Essays Towards a Resolution* (Oxford: Basil Blackwell, 1991); Thomas Nagel, *Mortal Questions* (London: Cambridge University Press, 1979); John Searle, *The Rediscovery of the Mind* (Cambridge: MIT Press, 1992); Searle, "Minds and Brains without Programs," in *Mindwaves: Thoughts on Intelligence, Identity, and Consciousness*, ed. Colin Blakemore and Susan Greenfield (Oxford: Basil Blackwell, 1987), 209–33.

97 David Ray Griffin, *Unsnarling the World-Knot: Consciousness, Freedom, and the Mind-Body Problem* (Berkeley: University of California Press, 1998), 46–76; Griffin, *Religion and Scientific Naturalism: Overcoming the Conflicts* (Albany: State University of New York Press, 2000), 137–78; Marjorie H. Suchocki, *The End of Evil: Process Eschatology in Historical Context* (Albany: State University of New York Press, 1988); David Ray Griffin, review of *End of Evil*, by Suchocki, *Process Studies* 18 (1989): 57–62; Suchocki, "Evil, Eschatology, and God: Response to David Griffin," *Process Studies* 18 (1989): 63–69; Griffin to author, March 12, 2003.

Index

Abernathy, Ralph, 366
absolute dependence, Schleiermacher's
     concept of, 151–52
absolute idealism: in British philosophy,
     208–9; Coleridge and, 95; Hegel and,
     113–14, 118–19, 484–86; Kant and,
     47, 73–74; Knudson and, 232–37;
     Muelder and, 260; post-Kantians and,
     116–17; Schelling and, 118–19
Absolute Knowing, Hegel's Spirit and,
     121–23
*The Absoluteness of Christianity and the
     History of Religions*, 219–20
abstract thought, Hegel's discussion of,
     134
The Achievement of Bernard Lonergan
     (Tracy), 390
Adams, James Luther, 328, 334
Adorno, Theodor, 323, 468
African Americans: citizenship and,
     350–51; Du Bois' double conscious-
     ness and, 344–48; feminist theology
     and, 383–86; social Darwinism and,
     349–52
After the Protests Are Heard (Welch), 478

Aids to Reflection (Coleridge), 96–97
Akhilananda (Swami), 242
Alcott, Amos Bronson, 99
Alexander, Samuel, 230, 273
Allen, Ernest, Jr., 351
Allison, Henry, 46
Altizer, Thomas J.J., xi, 391
American Academy of Religion, 400
An American Dilemma (Myrdal), 263
American Journal of Sociology, 349
American Missionary Association
     (AMA), 341–42
American Negro Academy, 346–49
American Philosophies of Religion (Wie-
     man & Meland), 293–94
American philosophy: absolute idealism
     in, 212–18; personal idealism in,
     205–7; post-Kantianism and, 456–62;
     Tillich and, 323–25, 329, 337
American transcendentalism, 98–99
Ameriks, Karl, 46
Ames, Edward Scribner, 268, 272,
     291–94
The Analogical Imagination (Tracy), 394–
     95, 397–99

Anglicanism: Coleridge and, 92–93,
    97–99; personal idealism and, 206;
    rationalism, 9–10, 12–13
Anselm, 38, 152–53
anti-Semitism: Hegel and, 141; in Kant's
    work, 66–67; Ruether on, 377, 383;
    Tillich and, 323–24
antiwar movement: King and, 370–71;
    Ruether and, 376
*Aphorisms on Ignorance and Absolute
    Knowing* (Göschel), 162
Apocalypse Now and Then (Keller), 428
apocalypticism, Keller and, 428–29
apophasis, Hegel on, 486–91
appearance, Kant's discussion of, 48–49
Aquinas, Thomas, 255; *see also* Thomism
Aristotle: Hegel and, 2, 113, 115, 122,
    127; Kant's discussion of, 41–45;
    Tillich and, 336
Armour, Ellen T., 384
Athanasius, 248
atheism: Kant's discussion of, 56–60;
    master-slave dialectic and, 129; Tillich
    on, 332–33
Atlantic Monthly, 344–46
atonement theology, 213–14
aufgehoben, Hegel's concept of, 137–38
Augustine, Tillich and, 336
Augustinian/Anselmian tradition of
    God's existence, 38
authority: Christian theology and role of,
    3; liberal theology and, 10
The Autobiography of W. E. B. Du Bois,
    340

Bagnall, Robert, 354
Baker, Ella, 366–67
Balfour, Lawrie, 351
Balthasar, Hans Urs von, 404, 495
Barbour, J. Pius, 355, 358–59, 363
Barth, Karl: Brunner and, 303; on God,
    495; Hegel and, 1–2, 27, 165–
    66, 196–200; Hodgson and, 421;
    Kierkegaard and, 195–96; King and,
    362; Meland on, 298, 301; neo-
    orthodoxy of, 265; on philosophy,

196; Ritschlians and, 26–27; theology
    of, 192–99; Tillich and, 311, 317–18,
    329; Tracy on, 391
Bataille, Georges, 114, 472
Bauer, Bruno, 114, 161, 199; Marx and,
    166–67, 169
Bauer, Edgar, 169
Baum, Gregory, 391
Baur, Ferdinand Christian: Harnack
    and, 19–20; Hegel and, 115, 145–46;
    historicism and, 14–15; historicism of,
    218, 220–21; Hodgson and, 408–9;
    Schleiermacher and, 106
Baxter, Jonathan, 437
Baynes, Kenneth, 473
The Beauties of Archbishop Leighton
    (Coleridge), 95–96
beauty, Kant on, 35–37
Beauvoir, Simone de, 128, 429
Beebe, James A., 236
Being and Time (Heidegger), 317
Beiser, Frederick, 46, 114–15
Benary, Agathon, 160, 162
Benary, Ferdinand, 162
Benhabib, Seyla, 473
Bennett, John C., 294
Bennett, Jonathan, 45
Bergson, Henri, 295–96
Berkeley, George: Kant and, 39, 44–45,
    50–51, 61; on senses and thought, 67;
    subjective idealism of, 207–8, 445–46
Berlinische Monatsschrift, 63
Bernard of Clairvaux, 401
Bertocci, Peter, 361
Bevel, James, 366, 373
Beyond God the Father (Daly), 429
Beyond Humanism (Hartshorne), 282–83
"Beyond Religious Socialism" (Tillich),
    328
biblical criticism, 217–18; Knudson and,
    226
biblical inerrancy, Bowne's criticism of,
    213–14
Biographia Literaria (Coleridge), 94–96
Bird, Graham, 46
Birmingham church bombings, 356, 368

Bismarck, Otto von, 26
black nationalism, Du Bois and, 350
Black Power movement, King and, 369–70
black social gospel; *see* social gospel movement: Du Bois and, 354–55; evolution of, 11–13; King and, 355–74; neo-Hegelianism and, 490–92
Blätter für Religiösen Sozialismus (Leaves for Religious Socialism) (journal), 313, 316
Blessed Rage for Order (Tracy), 390–91, 394–96, 398–99
Bliss, W. D. P., 5, 12
Bobo, Lawrence, 351
Boehme, Jacob, 94–95, 331, 336, 439
Bonino, José Míguez, 374
Boodin, John E., 259, 294
Bookbinder, Hilarious, 180
Boozer, Jack, 362
Borowski, Ludwig Ernst, 30
Bosanquet, Bernard, 208
Bosteels, Bruno, 115, 466–67
Boston personalism, 206
Boston University: Bowne at, 207–8, 217; Brightman at, 228–29, 257; King at, 358–60; Knudson at, 226–27, 249; liberal theology and, 269–70; Muelder at, 258; theology at, 269–70
Boumann, Ludwig, 163
Bousset, Wilhelm, 218
Bowne, Borden Parker, 12; Brightman and, 228–31, 237, 256; death of, 227–28; Knudson and, 226–28, 231–37, 248–49; Muelder and, 259, 260–61; personal idealism of, 205–18, 231–37, 256–57, 294, 360–61
Bowne, Joseph, 207
Bowne, Margaret, 207
Braaten, Carl, 414
Bracken, Joseph, 436
Bradley, F. H., 208, 269
Branch, Taylor, 364
Brandom, Robert, 115
Braniss, Christlieb J., 106
Brauer, Jerald C., 304

Brecht, Bertholt, 323
Bretschneider, Karl Gottlieb, 106–7
Briggs, Sheila, 414
Brightman, Edgar S., 205–6; Barbour and, 359; Bowne and, 228–31, 237, 252–53; ethics and value theory and, 252–53; on evil, 238; Hartshorne and, 250–51, 287–88; Kant and, 256–57; King and, 357, 359–61; Knudson and, 227–30, 233–37, 247, 252–53; McConnell and, 240–41; Mueder and, 258–66; personalism and, 237–57, 294; personalist theology and, 237–57; social gospel and, 249–50; tragedies in life of, 238–39
British culture, Kant's discussion of, 66
British philosophy: absolute idealism and, 208–9; theology and, 205–6
British theology: Harnack and, 19–20; liberal theology, 9–12; philosophy and, 205–6; Schleiermacher and, 85–86
Broad Church tradition, 9, 12–13, 97, 99
Broca, Paul, 349
Brock, Rita Nakashima, 431
Brown, Robert F., 418
Brown, William Adams, 294, 357–58
Brunner, Emil, 303, 311
Bruno, Giordano, 94–95
Buber, Martin, 128, 195
Buckham, John Wright, 228
Buck-Morss, Susan, 466
Budde, J. F., 33
Buddhism, 330; Tracy on, 400–403
Bultmann, Rudolf, 311, 317, 391
Burbidge, John W., 115
Burrell, David, 396–98, 414
Bushnell, Horace, 215, 357
Butler, Joseph, 10
Butler, Judith, 115

Cady Stanton, Elizabeth, 215
Caird, Edward, 209, 226, 233, 497
Caird, John, 209, 233
Calhoun, Robert L., 294, 408
Calkins, Mary W., 233

Calvinism, 9; Tracy on, 404; Troeltsch
    and, 223
Cannon, Katie, 477
Capital (Marx), 172–78
capitalism: Du Bois' criticism of, 352;
    liberal theology and, 4; Marx's critique
    of, 171–78; Tillich's critique of, 316
Carlyle, Thomas, 98
Carové, Friedrich W., 160, 162
Carroll, B. Jill, 437
Cartesian ego, Hegel's discussion of, 127
Case, Shirley Jackson, 268
Cassirer, Ernst, 46, 323, 447
Catholicism: Bowne and, 217–18; Hegel
    and, 115, 159–60; Ruether and,
    375–77; theology in, 387–88; Tillich's
    criticism of, 320; Tracy's theology and,
    387–408; Troeltsch on, 219–23
causality, Kant's discussion of, 42–43
Champion, James, 329
Channing, William Ellery, 99, 215
Chappell, David L., 364
Chardin, Pierre Teilhard de, 388
Chicago school, 232; Brightman's
    critique of, 242; decline of, 303–4;
    liberal theology and, 267–70; Macin-
    tosh and, 235, 270–72; Meland and,
    289–90, 291–307, 297–98; nature
    and God in, 247; Smith and, 272–73;
    Whitehead and, 251, 273–74
*Children of Freedom: Black Liberation in
    Christian Perspective* (Hodgson), 409
Chopp, Rebecca S., 414
Christ, Carol, 377
"Christabel" (Coleridge), 91
Christian, William, 283, 494
Christian Century magazine, 328
Christianity: Barth on, 197–99; Bowne's
    discussion of, 213–18; Coleridge
    on, 91–99; Harnack's definition of,
    17–18; Hegel's discussion of, 115–16,
    125, 149–64, 197–99; "Judaizing"
    and "Hellenizing" factions in, 14–15,
    17–19; Kant on, 57–58, 66–69;
    Kierkegaard on, 187, 189–92; left-
    Hegelianism and, 114; master-slave

dialectic in, 129–33; Neoplatonism
    and, 255–56; personal idealism,
    211–13; post-Kantian religion and,
    74; Ruether's theology and, 375–86;
    Schleiermacher and, 76–77, 100–111;
    theology of religion and, 99–111,
    219–25; Tillich's discussion of, 324–
    37; Tracy on Buddhism and, 400–402;
    Troeltsch on, 219–25
Christianity and the Social Crisis (Raus-
    chenbusch), 357
A Christian Natural Theology (Cobb),
    304–5
Christian socialism, 264, 359
*The Christian Doctrine of Justification and
    Reconciliation* (Ritschl), 16
The Christian Faith (Schleiermacher),
    100–107, 110
Christian Theology in Outline (Brown),
    357
Christliche Dogmatik (Barth), 195–96
Christlichprotestantische Dogmatik (Herr-
    mann), 24
The Christlike God (McConnell), 239–40
Christmas Eve (Schleiermacher), 100
Christ the Representative (Sölle), 164
Church Dogmatics (Barth), 196
Churchmen's Union for the Advance-
    ment of Liberal Religious Thought,
    12–13
The Church Against Itself (Ruether),
    376–77
civil rights: Hodgson and, 409; King
    and, 355–57, 365–74; Muelder and,
    263; Ruether and, 376–77, 385–86
Civil Rights Act of 1964, 368
civil society, Marx's discussion of, 168
Clarke, Samuel, 10
Clarke, William Newton, 296–97,
    357–58
class struggle, 316; feminist liberation
    and, 380–81
"The Class Struggle and Religious Social-
    ism" (Tillich), 334
Climacus, Johannes (pseud.): *see* Kierke-
    gaard, Søren

Cloud of Unknowing, 439

Cobb, John B., Jr.: Hartshorne and, 288; Hodgson and, 400, 414, 420, 423; Keller and, 425, 433; Meland and, 295; Tracy and, 395, 397–98; Whitehead and, 267, 302–5, 494

Coe, George Albert, 218, 228

Coffin, Henry Sloane, 323

Cohen, Hermann, 46, 447

Cohen, Morris R., 286

Coleman, Monica, 1, 492–93; religious philosophy of, 92–99

Coleridge, Samuel Taylor, 74; American Transcendentalists and, 98–99; Fichte and, 116; poetry of, 91; religious issues in work of, 94–99; transcendental reason and, 90–99

Collins, Arthur, 46

commodities, Marx's discussion of, 174–78

Communication and the Evolution of Society (Habermas), 469

The Communion of the Christian with God (Herrmann), 21–24

communism: Du Bois and, 354–55; King and, 327–28; Marx and Engels embrace of, 170–71

The Communist Manifesto (Marx and Engels), 171

Communities of Solidarity and Resistance (Welch), 474–75

The Concept of Irony (Kierkegaard), 180

Concluding Unscientific Postscript (Kierkegaard), 181, 184–85, 190–92

Cone, James, xii, 363, 374, 423–24, 490

Congar, Yves, 388

Congregationalism, 9

Conradi, Kasimir, 160, 162

Constantius, Constantin, 180

A Contribution to the Critique of Political Economy (Marx), 171–74

Copeland, M. Shawn, 414

cosmopolitanism, Kant's discussion of, 69–70

Cotton, Dorothy, 367

The Courage to Be (Tillich), 327–28

Cousin, Victor, 99

Cox, Harvey, 395

"Credo" (Du Bois), 354

Creuzer, Georg Friedrich, 139

crisis theology: Barth's concept of, 27, 195; Tillich and, 313–23

Crites, Stephen, 485

Critique of Judgment (Kant), 71, 118, 447, 449–50

Critique of Practical Reason (Kant), 53–54; self-determination in, 69–70

Critique of Pure Reason (Kant), 34; critical interpretations of, 45–48, 50–51, 61–67; deceptive representations and, 48–49; metaphysics and, 54; modern philosophy and influence of, 52; reason discussed in, 39–45, 69–72

Crockett, Clayton, 115

Croft Cell, George, 233

The Cross and the Lynching Tree (Cone), 490

Crozer Seminary, 357

Crusius, Christian August, 33

culture: Du Bois' double consciousness and, 344–46; Kant on, 37; Keller on sexism in, 424–25; liberalism and, 4; Meland on decline of, 300–301; Ruether on sexism and, 377–78; Schleiermacher on religion and, 83; separation of religion from, 5–6; Tillich on religion and, 313

Culture Protestant nationalism, 3–4

Cummings, Edward, 343

Curtis, Olin A., 226, 248

Daly, Mary: Keller and, 428–30; Kristeva on, 429; Ruether and, 374–75, 377, 379–81, 385; Welch and, 475–76

Darkwater (Du Bois), 340, 354

Darwinian evolution: Bowne's discussion of, 207, 215–16; racism and, 348; Ritschl and, 15–16

Dasein (determinate being), Hegel's concept of, 137

Das System der Wissenschaften (Tillich), 314

Daub, Karl, 109, 139, 143, 160–61

Davaney, Sheila Greeve, 384

Dean, William, 307

Debs, Eugene, 353

deceptive representations, Kant's discussion of, 48–49

deconstructionism: Hegel and, 115; Tracy and, 401

De Docta Ignorantia (On Learned Ignorance) (Nicholas of Cusa), 439–40

Dehn, Günther, 313, 319, 323

deists: Enlightenment movement, 9; in Germany, 10

"Dejection: An Ode" (Coleridge), 91

Delbrück, Johann F. F., 106

Deleuze, Gilles, 433–34; on Hegel, 113; Hegel and, 202–3; Tracy and, 401, 403

de Man, Hendrik, 318–19

democracy: Du Bois' discussion of, 352–54; imperialism and, 352–53

The Democratic Socialist Vision (Dorrien), 496

Demos, Raphael, 362

De Nys, Martin J., 115

Der Historismus und seine Probleme (Troeltsch), 224–25

Der Historismus und seine Überwindung (Troeltsch), 224–25

Derrida, Jacques: on difference, 8; Habermas and, 471–72; Hegel and, 113, 115, 202–3, 468; Keller and, 435, 438; Tracy and, 401, 403–4

Descartes, René: Hegel on, 153–54; Kant and, 29, 32, 38–39, 45, 47–48; Knudson and, 234–35; Solomon's discussion of, 124; Temple and, 496–97

de Silentio, Johannes, 180

Desmond, William, 115, 483–84

Deutsche Jahrbücher, 166–67

DeVreis, Dawn, 414

Dewart, Leslie, 391

de Wette, Wilhelm Martin L., 108–9, 141, 145, 162

Dewey, John, 268–70, 468; Meland and, 299; Wieman on, 273, 294

DeWolf, L. Harold, 249, 251, 257, 358, 360–62

Dial (journal), 99

Dialectical Society, 360, 363

Dialectic of Enlightenment (Adorno & Horkheimer), 468

dialectics: Hegel's discussion of, 134–38; Marx and, 172–78, 329–30; Tillich's discussion of, 330

Die bestimmte Religion, Hegel's concept of, 148–49

Die Metaphysik in der Theologie (Herrmann), 20–21

Die offenbare Religion, Hegel's concept of, 152

Die Religion im Verhältnis zum Welterkennen und zur Sittlichkeit (Herrmann), 21

Die vollendete Religion, Hegel's concept of, 152

Diez, Carl Immanuel, 117

The Difference between Fichte's and Schelling's System of Philosophy (Hegel), 118

Diggs, James R. L., 354

Dionysius, 439

dipolar theism, 282, 285–89

Dissenters movement, 90

divine polarity, Hartshorne's concept of, 283–89

divine self-manifestation, Tillich's discussion of, 330–31

The Divine Relativity (Hartshorne), 285, 493

The Doctrine of God (Knudson), 245–46

The Doctrine of Redemption (Knudson), 245–46

Dohna, Count Wilhelm, 76–77

Donnelly, Brian, 329

Dorner, Isaak August, 495

double consciousness: black scholarly criticism of, 350–52; Du Bois' concept of, 339–40, 344–45

dualism, Kant's discussion of, 47–48, 50, 62, 70, 73

Du Bois, Alexander, 340

Du Bois, Alfred, 340

Du Bois, James, 340

Du Bois, Mary Silvina Burghardt, 340–41

Du Bois, W. E. B., 178; black scholarly criticism of, 350–52; black social gospel and, 354–55; on capitalism and democracy, 352–54; double consciousness theory of, 339–40, 344–45; early life and career of, 340–44; Hegel and, 339–40; liberalism and, 5; liberation theology and, 339; process tradition and, 1; on racism, 345–48

Dulles, Avery, 395

Dusk of Dawn (Du Bois), 340

Dussel, Enrique, 464–66

Eastern religions: Brightman's study of, 242, 251–52; Hegel's discussion of, 148–49; Tillich's discussion of, 330; Tracy on, 399–400, 407–8

Ebeling, Gerhard, 409

Ebenezer Baptist Church, 356

Eberhard, J. A., 60–61, 76, 87

ecclesia, Farley's concept of, 413

Ecclesial Man: A Social Phenomenology of Faith and Reality (Farley), 411–12, 414

Ecclesial Reflection: An Anatomy of Theological Method (Farley), 414–15

Eckhart, Meister, 146–47, 401–2, 405

eco-feminism, Ruether and, 382–83

The Economic and Philosophical Manuscripts of 1844 (Marx), 320

economic theory: liberalism and, 4; Marx's impact on, 173–78; Tillich's discussion of, 320

ecumenical movement: Muelder and, 265–66; Tracy and, 389

"The Education of the Human Race" (Lessing), 59

ego-theism, Emerson's theory of, 98

Eichhorn, Johann, 6, 91

Einstein, Albert, 323

Eiselen, Johann F. G., 160

Eisenstein, Zillah, 381

Either/Or (Kierkegaard), 180, 184

Eleastics, 201

elitism, in liberal theology, 12

Ellis, Marc H., 383

Ely, Richard, 12

Emerson, Ralph Waldo, 97–98, 345–46

Encyclopedia of the Philosophical Sciences (Hegel), 110, 134, 137–39, 143

Engel, J., 60

Engels, Friedrich, 167–71, 177–78

Engels/Kautsky economic materialism, 320

Enlightenment: evolution of liberal theology and, 9–13; Hegel and, 463–64; Kant's interpretation of, 29–31, 33–34, 52–53, 63, 458; popular philosophers' criticism of, 62; Prussian liberal philosophy and, 60–67; religion and, 6; Tillich's discussion of, 331

Epistle to the Romans (Barth), 192–93

Erasmus, 405

Erdmann, Johann Eduard, 161

Eremita, Victor, 180

Essays and Reviews, 12–13

The Essence of Christianity (Feuerbach), 161

essentialism, Ruether linked to, 380–86

ethics, Brightman on, 252–53

Eucken, Rudolf, 205

Eurocentrism: Hegel and, 464–78; liberal theology and, 7–9; Troeltsch's embrace of, 225

Evangelical Church of the Prussian Union, 143

Evangelical Social Congress, 18

Evans, James H., Jr., 414

evil: Brightman's discussion of, 238; Hegel on, 486–88; Kant's discussion of, 58

evolution, Brightman's examination of, 238–39

existence, Kant on, 38–39

existentialism, Tillich's work in, 327–29

Fabro, Carnelio, 396

Face of the Deep (Keller), 434–35, 437–38

Fackenheim, Emil, 115

faith: *Glaubenslehre* (Schleiermacher's doctrine of faith), 101–11, 152; Kant on knowledge and, 54–60; Tracy on, 394

Fallible Forms and Symbols (Meland), 302–3

Fanon, Frantz, 128

Farley, Edward, 387, 395, 408–9, 411–17; process tradition and, 1

Farrer, Austin, 404

Faustus Socinus, 331

Fear and Trembling (Kierkegaard), 180

Feder, Johann G. H., 50, 60–61

Federal Council of Churches, 228, 262

Federation of Theological Schools, 282

feeling: Hegel on, 110–11, 146, 162; Schleiermacher on, 81–82, 102–3, 107–11, 162

Fellowship of Reconciliation (FOR), 357, 359

feminist liberation theology: Keller and, 387–88, 425–42; Ruether and, 374–86; Welch and, 474–77

Feuerbach, Ludwig: Hegel and, 114, 161, 164, 166–67, 486; Marx and, 168–69

Fichte, J. G.: American transcendentalists and, 98–99; Brightman's critique of, 242–43; Coleridge and, 92–94; Findlay's discussion of, 123; on freedom, 447; Hegel and, 115–16, 118, 155–56, 486–87; Kant and, 47, 70, 73, 116, 451–52; Schelling and, 117–18; Tillich and, 310

fideism, 7, 100; Herrmann and, 21; Levinas and, 201–2

Filson, Floyd V., 265

The Finality of the Christian Religion (Foster), 269

Findlay, J. N., 123

First International, 171

Fisk, Clinton B., 342

Fisk University, 342–43

Fitch, Robert, 329

Flewelling, Ralph T., 218, 241

Ford, Lewis, 302, 305, 494

Förster, Friedrich C., 160–63

Forstman, Jack, 414

Foster, George Burman, 268–70, 272

Foucault, Michel, 403, 472–73; Welch and, 475–76

Foundations of the Metaphysics of Morals (Kant), 54, 57

Francis, Convers, 99

Franco-Prussian Yearbook (*Deutsch-Französische Jahrbücher*), 167

Frankfurt Institute for Social Research, 318

Frankfurt school: Habermas and, 468–70; Tillich and, 332–33

Franklin, Benjamin, 4

Fraser, Nancy, 473–74

Frederick Wilhelm III (King), 89

Freedmen's Bureau, 341–42

freedom: Hegel's discussion of, 127–33; Hodgson's discussion of, 410–11, 422–23; Kant's discussion of, 71–72, 448–49

Frei, Hans, 408

French culture: Kant's discussion of, 66; Schleiermacher's discussion of, 85–86

French Revolution, Kant's discussion of, 68

Fricker, Edith, 90

Fricker, George, 92

Fricker, Sarah, 90, 92

Friedrich Wilhelm I (King), 31–32

Friedrich Wilhelm II (King) (Frederick the Great), 31–33, 60, 62–63, 68–69, 167

Friend (newspaper), 92

Fries, J. F., 140–42, 162

From a Broken Web (Keller), 425

Fuchs, Ernst, 409

Fulkerson, Mary McClintock, 384

Fuller, Margaret, 99

fundamental theology, 394

Furness, William Henry, 99

The Future of Christianity (Brightman), 251–52

Gabler, Georg Andreas, 160, 162

Gadamer, Hans-Georg, 392, 395, 399

Gaia & God (Ruether), 382

Gandhi, Mahatma, King and, 357–59, 368, 371–72

Gans, Eduard, 150, 160, 162–63

Gardner, Sebastian, 46

Garrett Evangelical Theological Seminary, 377
Garrigou-Lagrange, Reginald, 396
Garrow, David, 358
Garve, Christian, 50, 60–61
Gass, Joachim Christian, 110
Gates, Henry Louis, 350–51
Gebara, Ivone, 383
Geiger, Louis-Bertrand, 396
gender equity: feminist theology and, 381–86; Muelder on, 265–66
Gerhart, Mary, 414
German philosophy: Kant and, 68; theology and, 205–6
The German Ideology (Marx), 169
Germany: Coleridge and Wordsworth in, 91–92; Du Bois' travels in, 343–44; Hegel's nationalism and, 463–64; in Kant's life, 30; liberal theology in, 9–13; Troeltsch and, 222
Gerrish, Brian, 304, 405
Gess, W. F., 495
Gestalt, Hegel's concept of, Christianity and, 115–16
Gieseler, J. K. L., 109
Gilkey, Langdon, 304, 389, 391, 412, 414
Gilroy, Paul, 351
Gilson, Etienne, 396
Gladden, Washington, 12
Glaubenslehre (Schleiermacher's doctrine of faith), 101–11, 152
Gnosticism: Ruether on, 380; Schleiermacher linked to, 106
Godhead beyond God, Eckhart's concept of, 402
God in History: Shapes of Freedom (Hodgson), 419–23
Goethe, Johann W., Schleiermacher and, 75, 77, 84–85
Gontard, Susette, 118
Gooding-Williams, Robert, 351
Gordon, George A., 228
Göschel, Karl Friedrich, 160–62
Gospels, Tracy's discussion of, 406
Gottschick, Johannes, 14
Gottschow, Hannah, 316–17

Grant, Jacquelyn, 477
Great Britain: democracy and imperialism in, 352–53; Harnack and, 19–20; liberal theology in, 9–12; Schleiermacher's discussion of, 85–86
Greek religion and philosophy, Hegel's discussion of, 131, 149
Green, Joseph, 37
Green, Ronald, 538n56
Green, T. H., 208
Greenfield, 307
Gregory of Nazanianzus, 376
Gregory of Nyssa, 439
Grey, Mary, 431
Griesbach, Johann Jakob, 6
Griffin, David Ray, 267, 305, 432–33, 494, 500–501
Grundrisse der Kritik der Politischen Oekonomie, 174–75
Grunow, Eleonore, 79, 86–87
Gunkel, Hermann, 218, 435
Gunner, Byron, 354
Gutiérrez, Gustavo, 374, 391, 405
Gyn/Ecology (Daly), 429

Habermas, Jürgen, 115, 130, 463, 468–74; feminist scholarship and, 476–77
Haeckel, Ernst, 349
Haker, Hille, 115, 473
Haldane, Richard B., 208
Haley, Alex, 368–69
Hamann, Johann G., 61–64, 68
Hamilton, William, 391
Hammond, Guy, 329
Hampson, Daphne, 384
Hardenberg, Friedrich von (Novalis), 116, 118
Häring, Theodore, 14
Harkness, George, 230–31
Harnack, Adolf von, 3, 14; Barth and, 192; Brightman and, 228; Kant and, 67; Knudson and, 227; liberal theology and, 17–20, 332; Troeltsche on, 220–21
Haroutunian, Joseph, 304
Harrison, Beverly, 377
Hart, Albert Bushnell, 343

Hartman, Klaus, 129–30
Hartshorne, Charles, 249–51; dipolar theism and, 282–89; Meland and, 299–300, 303; Whitehead and, 267–68, 492–94
Hartt, Julian, 414
Harvard Divinity School, absence of feminist theology at, 375, 379
Harvey, Van, 391, 395
Haufniensis, Vivilius, 180
Haydon, A. Eustace, 294
Headlam, Stewart, 5
Hedge, Frederick Henry, 98–99
Hefner, Philip, 307
Hegel, Georg Wilhelm Friedrich: on absolute idealism, 113–14, 118–20; Barth and, 27, 165–66, 196–200; Baur and, 14–15; Bowne and, 208; Brightman and, 252; Coleridge and, 93; critiques of, 1–2; death of, 162–63; Du Bois and, 339–40, 344–45, 350; Dussel on, 464–66; early life and career, 117–18; Farley and, 417; on freedom and spirit, 127–33; Habermas and, 473–74; heterodox influences on, 460–61; Hodgson and, 417–25; Hölderlin and, 117; Kant and, 46–47, 67, 70–71, 73, 113, 117, 119–23, 142–43, 153–54; Keller and, 441–42; kenosis theology and, 495; Kierkegaard and, 165–66, 179–92; King and, 339–40, 361; Knudson's study of, 226, 236; Levinas on, 1–2, 113, 165–66, 199–202; liberal theology and, 11–12; on logic, 114–15, 133–64, 186–87; on love, 451–53; Marx and, 1–2, 140–41, 161–62, 165–68, 172, 333; Meland and, 296; Mignolo on, 466; modern philosophy and, 6–7; Nancy's interpretation of, 453–55; neo-Hegelian theology and, 481–91; postcolonial criticism of, 462–78; Prussian reform movement and, 140–41; religious philosophy and, 1–2, 142–64, 444–56; Schelling and, 115–19, 139; Schleiermacher and, 105–6, 110–11, 142–46, 150–52;

social idealism and legacy of, 478–81; Spinoza and, 113, 115, 147–48; Tholuck and, 20; Tillich and, 115, 309, 334–37, 444, 480–81; Troeltsch and, 221; on United States, 7–8
Hegel, Ludwig, 139
Hegel, Marie, 139
Hegel: A Re-Examination (Findlay), 123
"Hegel's Concept of Geist" (Solomon), 123
Hegel's God (Desmond), 483–84
Heidegger, Martin: Brightman on, 254; Habermas and, 468, 471–72; Hegel and, 115, 453–54; Hodgson in, 409; on Kant, 389; Kant and, 451; phenomenology and, 249, 387; Tillich and, 317; Tracy and, 401; on Western metaphysics and God, 2; Whitehead and, 277–78
Heiler, Frederick, 291
Heimann, Eduard, 313, 318
Heine, Heinrich, 31
Heller, Hermann, 323
Henning, Leopold, 161–63
Henrich, Dieter, xiii, 70–72, 115
Heraclitus, 336
Herder, Johann Gottfried, 62–64, 91–92
hermeneutics, revisionist theology and, 392, 395
Herrmann, Johann Wilhelm, 3; Barth and, 192; Brightman and, 228–29; de-Judaized Christianity and, 14, 67; Harnack and, 17, 25–26; liberal theology and, 20–26; personal idealism and, 232; post-Kantianism and, 459; Troeltsch and, 24–25
Herron, George, 5, 12
Herz, Henriette, 77, 79, 88
Herz, Marcus, 77
Herzog, Frederick, 411
heterodoxy, Hegel and, 460–61
Heyward, Carter, 431
hiddenness, Luther's concepts of, 405–6
High, Stanley, 262, 299
Hinrichs, H. W. F., 143, 146, 161–62
Hinton, Rosalind, 383
Hirsch, Emanuel, 313

historical criticism, 6

historicism: Chicago School and, 268; Hegel on theology and, 145–46, 158–64; Kierkegaard on, 191–92; Knudson and, 247; Ritschl and, 13–16; of Troeltsch, 26–28, 218–25

History and Class Consciousness (Lukács), 468

Hobson, John, 5, 352

Hocking, William Ernest, 28, 209, 212, 229, 233; absolute idealism and, 260, 294; Brightman and, 249; Wieman and, 273

Hodgson, Peter C., 115, 387; freedom and presence, 408–14, 417–25; Hegel and, 419–23, 484–85; Keller and, 430–31; process tradition and, 1; Scripture principle and, 415

Hoffmann, A. F., 33

Hofgeismar Circle, 318

Hölderlin, Friedrich, 47, 116–18, 155–56, 452

Holland, Scott, 5

Holy Roman Empire, 30

The Holy Family (Marx), 169–70

Honneth, Axel, 115, 473–74

Horkheimer, Max, 114, 318, 323

Horstmann, Rolf-Peter, 115

Horton, Myles, 337

Horton, Walter Marshall, 294

Hosmer, Frank, 341–42

Hotho, Heinrich G., 161–63

Hough, Williston S., 226

Houlgate, Stephen, 115

Howard University, Ruether and, 376–77

Howison, George Holmes, 208, 209, 212, 233

Hugh, Diana, 466

Hülsen, August Ludwig, 116

human agency, Marx and Engels on, 170–71

Humboldt, Wilhelm von, 89

Hume, David: Coleridge on, 94; Kant and, 29, 34–35, 39, 42, 45, 51–52

Husserl, Edmund, 82, 249, 387, 412–14

Hutchinson, Sara, 92

Huxley, Thomas H., 347, 349

"Hymn to the Peoples" (Du Bois), 354

Hyppolite, Jean, 114, 128

I and Thou (Buber), 195

idealism: *see* variations on, e.g., romantic idealism: Kant's philosophy and, 44–49, 61, 67–68; realism *vs.*, 443–44

The Ideal of the Holy (Otto), 246

idolatry, Tillich's discussion of, 330

"I Have a Dream" (King), 355–56, 365–66

imagination, Coleridge's discussion of, 93–94

Immortality in Post-Kantian Idealism (Brightman), 230

imperialism, capitalism and, 352–53

Imperialism (Hobson), 352

Inbody, Tyron, 307

The Incarnate Lord (Thornton), 279

The Inclusion of the Other (Die Einbeziehung des anderen) (Habermas), 474

Independent Social Democratic Party (USPD), 313, 315–16

individual: absolute idealism and, 208–9; in liberal theology, 4

Ingram, David, 474

Insight: A Study of Human Understanding (Lonergan), 389

intellectual intuition, Kant's discussion of, 50

internal relations theory, 230

interreligious discourse, Tracy and, 399–401

intersubjectivity: Hegel's dialectics and, 113–64; Kant's philosophy and, 46–48

In the Spirit of Hegel (Solomon), 123–24

An Introduction to Philosophy (Brightman), 238

Introduction to Philosophy (Brightman), 230

Irigaray, Luce, 429

Is God a White Racist? (Jones), 423–24

Is God Limited? (McConnell), 239

"I've Been to the Mountaintop" (King), 365

Jachmann, Reinhold Bernhard, 30
Jacobi, Friedrich Heinrich, 61–63, 100,
117, 146, 162, 201–2
Jaeschke, Walter, 418
Jahrbücher für wissenschaftliche Kritik
(Yearbooks for Scientific Criticism)
(journal), 161
James, William, 239; Du Bois and,
343–45; Hartshorne and, 287–88;
interreligious discourse and, 400–401;
Keller and, 427; Knudson and, 236;
Meland and, 290–93, 295–96, 299,
302–3; personal idealism and, 206,
212; pragmatism of, 268–70, 273;
Wieman on, 273
Jaruzelski, Wojciech, 461
Jaspers, Karl, 416
Jefferson, Thomas, 4
Jesus: Herrmann's discussion of, 21–23;
Knudson on, 247; Schleiermacher's
discussion of, 104–11
Jesus—Word and Presence (Hodgson), 409
John of the Cross, 401
Johnson, A. H., 284
Johnson, Elizabeth, 430
Johnson, Mathilde, 227
Johnson, Mordecai, 337, 355, 357–59,
363, 491
Johnson, Terence L., 351
Jones, Rufus, 249, 294
Jones, William, 423–24
Judaism: Christianity and, 14–15, 17–
19; Hegel's discussion of, 149–51;
Kant's anti-Semitic discussion of, 66–
67; Ruether and, 377; Schleiermacher
on Christianity and, 104–5
Jüngel, Eberhard, 115, 488

Kaftan, Julius, 14, 227
Kähler, Martin, 20, 27, 309–11
Kairos Circle, 313
kairos socialism, Tillich's development of,
313–15, 329
Kaiser Wilhelm Gesellschaft, 18
Kandinsky, Wassily, 323
Kant, Immanuel: American transcen-
dentalists and, 98–99; Bowne and,

208–18, 234–37; Brightman and,
256–57; Coleridge's study of, 91–
99; dialectic of, 134; early life and
education, 31–33; on Enlightenment,
29–31, 33–34, 52–53, 63; Findlay's
discussion of, 123; Hegel and, 46–47,
67, 70–71, 73, 113, 117, 119–23,
142–43, 153–54; Hegelian Geist and,
124–26; Herrmann and, 25; interpretive traditions of, 45–48; Kierkegaard
on, 183, 190–92, 539n56; Knudson
and, 234–37; on law and nationhood,
69; legacy of, 29–31, 67–68; liberal
theology and, 4, 6–8, 10–11; on
morality, 52–60; Newtonian physics
and, 33–34; post-Kantian reaction to,
60–67; racism and white superiority
in, 36–37, 64–65; religion and, 1–2,
53–60, 73–74, 147; religious idealism
and, 446–50; Ritschl on, 13–14, 16;
Schelling and, 118–19; Schleiermacher
and, 76; on self-determination, 69–70;
sufficient reason principle and, 34–35;
Thomism and, 388; Tillich and, 310
Kant and the Problem of Metaphysics
(Heidegger), 451
Kantian Reason and Hegelian Spirit
(Dorrien), 120
Kapp, Christian, 161
Kattenbusch, Ferdinand, 14
Kaufman, Gordon, 395, 414
Keats, John, 95
Keller, Catherine: feminist theology and,
387–88, 425–42; Hodgson and, 414;
liberal theology and, 267; process
tradition and, 1; Whitehead and, 305,
425–42
Kelsey, David, 414
Kelsey, George, 363
kenosis theology, 62, 495
Kierkegaard, Søren: Barth and, 192–95;
critique of Hegel by, 1–2; Hegel and,
113, 165–66, 179–92, 478, 483;
Herrmann and, 23–24; on Kant, 183,
190–92, 539n56; Marx and, 178;
Meland on, 298, 301; Tillich and,
309, 317

King, Coretta Scott, 367
King, Henry Churchill, 228
King, Martin Luther, Jr., xi; anti-war movement and, 370–71; Black Power movement and, 369–70; black social gospel and, 355–74, 491; at Boston University, 359–61; early life and career, 356–57; liberation theology and, 339; personal idealism and, 206, 364–74; plagiarism charges against, 358, 362–63; Poor People's Campaign and, 372–74; process tradition and, 1; scholarship of, 358–59; sermons of, 365–66; social gospel and, 337
King, Martin Luther, Sr., 356–57
King, Robert H., 414
Klee, Paul, 323
knowledge, Kant's discussion of, 40–45, 54–55
Knowledge and Human Interests (Habermas), 468–69
Knudson, Albert C., 205–6, 215; Bowne and, 226–28, 231–37, 248–49; Brightman and, 229–30, 236–37, 241–44, 247; McConnell and, 239–41, 248; Methodism and, 205–6, 215, 231, 246–47; Mueller and, 260; personalist theology and, 225–26, 231–37, 245–46, 257; on personality, 244
Köhler, Wolfgang, 323
Kojève, Alexander, 114, 129–30, 455
Kreines, James, 115
Kristeva, Julia, 428–29
Kroner, Richard, 115, 317
"Kubla Khan" (Coleridge), 91
Kucheman, Clark, 329
Küng, Hans, 388

labor, Marx and Engels on division of, 170–71, 175–78
Lacan, Jacques, 114, 455
Ladd, G. T., 212
Lagarde, Paul de, 15; Troeltsch and, 218–19
Lamarckian theory, racism and, 347–49
Lamentabili Sane, 388

Lange, Friedrich Albert, 447
Lange, J., 33
Latin American liberation theology, 374
Latin American philosophy, 251–52
Latiolais, Christopher, 474
Lauer, Quentin, 115
Lawson, James, 368, 409
League of Communists, 171
Lectures on the Natural Right, 1817–1818 (Hegel), 487–88
left-Hegelians, 114–15, 161–64; Marx and, 166–67; master-slave dialectic and, 129
Legitimation Crisis (Habermas), 469
Leibniz, G. W., 29, 32, 34, 38–39; Bowne and, 233–34; Hegel on, 153; on idealism, 44–45; Troeltsch and, 224; Whitehead and, 278
Leighton, Robert, 95–96
Lenud, Philip, 360
Leo, Heinrich, 161
Lessing, G. E, 59, 117, 184
Levinas, Emmanuel: on difference, 8; Hegel and, 1–2, 113, 165–66, 199–202, 486–87; on Kierkegaard, 195; on Western metaphysics and God, 2
Levison, Stanley, 366–67, 370
Lewis, C. I., 249
Lewis, Daniel Levering, 358
Lewis, Thomas A., 115
liberalism: Bowne's discussion of, 213–14; feminist theology and, 381–86; religion and, 4–5; socialism and, 5–6, 321–23
liberal theology: Barth and, 197–99; Bowne's discussion of, 214–18; evolution of, 9–13; Harnack and, 17–20; Herrmann and, 20–26; Kantian morality and, 73–74; Kierkegaard on, 191–92; King and, 357–58; Macintosh's discussion of, 271–72; Meland on, 300–301; principles of, 2–4; Ritschlian school and, 12–17; Schleiermacher and, 108–11; social gospel and, 12; Tillich and, 331; Tracy on, 391; Whitehead's influence on, 267–81

liberation theology: feminist theology, 374–86; Hodgson's discussion of, 410–12, 419–20, 423–24; King and, 374; oppression and, 339; religious philosophy and, 1–2; Tracy's omission of, 394–95
Liberation Theology (Ruether), 374
The Life of Jesus Critically Examined (Strauss), 161
Linnaeus, Carl, 64
Lippmann, Walter, 294
Lischer, Richard, 358
Locke, John, 4, 29, 94, 97, 445–46
logic, Hegel's philosophy of, 114–15, 133–64, 186–87
The Logic of Christian Evidence (Wright), 343
Logos theology, 220; Tillich's discussion of, 330–31, 336
Lonergan, Bernard, 389–93, 405, 412, 460
Loofs, Friedrich, 14
Loomer, Bernard, 251, 281–82, 288, 299, 303–4
Lorde, Audre, 339, 477
Lososophia (Coleridge), 93
Lotze, Rudolf Hermann, 13, 16–17; personal idealism and, 205–8; Troeltsch and, 218–19
Love, Power, and Justice (Tillich), 329
Löwe, Adolf, 313, 318, 323
Lowe, Victor, 283
Lowe, Walter, 414
Lowery, Joseph, 366
Lubac, Henri de, 388
Lucinde (Schlegel), 78
Lücke, Gottfried Christian, 109
Lukács, Georg, 468
Luther, Martin: Barth and, 193; Herrmann on, 23; Ritschl on, 15; Tracy on, 404–6
Lutheran theology: Hegel and, 157, 159; Ritschl on, 15
Lyman, Eugene, 294
Lyrical Ballads (Coleridge and Wordsworth), 91

Macintosh, Douglas Clyde, 232, 235; Chicago school and, 270–72, 281, 286; Lyman and, 294
MacIver, Robert M., 263
MacLeod, Alistair, 329
Magna Carta Libertatum of 1215, 4
Maimonides, 255
Malabou, Catherine, 115, 467–68
Mann, Thomas, 323
Man's Vision of God and the Logic of Theism (Hartshorne), 283
Marburg school, 46, 447
Marcel, Gabriel, 195
March on Washington, 355, 368
Marcuse, Herbert, 114, 128, 468
Maréchal, Joseph, 388–89, 460
Marheineke, Philipp, 110, 113, 160–63, 417
Marlatt, Earl B., 237
Marsh, Daniel L., 236–37, 262
Marsh, James, 97
Marson, Charles, 5
Marx, Heinrich, 166
Marx, Karl, xi; banishment of, 169; early life and career of, 166–67; Hegel and, 1–2, 140–41, 161–62, 165–68, 172, 320, 333, 463; left-Hegelianism and, 114; master-slave dialect and, 128, 131; political economics and, 166–78; social idealism and legacy of, 478–81; Tillich and, 309, 320, 480–81
Marxism: Hegel's influence on, 128–33; political economics and, 166–78; Tillich and, 315–16, 318–20, 328–30, 333–37, 480–81
Mascall, Eric, 396
master-slave dialect: Hegel's development of, 127–33; left-Hegelianism and, 114
Mathews, Shailer, 268–70, 272–74, 281, 286; Meland and, 290–94
Maurice, Frederick Denison, 11, 97
Mays, Benjamin E., 337, 355, 357, 363
McCann, Dennis, 329
McCarthy, Thomas, 472
McConnell, Francis, 228, 239–41, 248
McDowell, John, 115

McFague, Sallie, 414

McTaggart, J. M. E., 209, 232, 256, 455; rational idealism and, 269

Mead, George Herbert, 468

mechanical causation, Bowne and, 211

mechanistic theory: Lotze's discussion of, 207–8; Whitehead and, 277–78

Mediating theology, 14

mediation: Hegel's discussion of, 122–23, 137; Kierkegaard on, 188–92; Tillich on, 315

Medicus, Fitz, 310

Meiklehohn, Alexander, 228

Meland, Bernard E., 267, 274, 281–82, 289–307; early life and career, 289–90; Tracy on, 392; Whitehead and, 294–95, 299–300, 302–3; Wieman and, 291–95, 299

Mendelssohn, Moses, 78

Mennicke, Karl, 313, 318, 323

Mercadante, Linda, 414

Merleau-Ponty, Maurice, 114, 165

Merton, Thomas, 400

metaphysics: Hartshorne and, 288–89; Hegel and, 115, 129–30; Kant and, 32–34, 38, 53–60, 71; Meland and, 296; revisionist theology and, 392; Whitehead on, 277–78

Metaphysics (Bowne), 256

Method in Theology (Lonergan), 389–90

Methodism: Knudson and, 205–6, 215, 231, 246–47; Muelder's activism and, 261–62

"Methodism's Pink Fringe" (High), 262

Michaelis, Johann David, 6

Michelet, Karl Ludwig, 161–63

Mignolo, Walter, 466

Miley, John, 246

Miller, George Frazier, 354, 364

Miller, Keith, 358

Milton, John, 4, 91

Mitchell, Hinkley, 217, 226–27

modern philosophy: Hegel's influence on, 165, 465; Kierkegaard and, 188–92; post-Kantianism and, 458–62

modern theology: Catholicism and, 388; Chicago School and, 268–70; Hegel's influence on, 165; ideology of, 6; Ritschlian school and, 13; Tracy's discussion of, 391–408

Moltmann, Jürgen, 391, 431, 435

Montgomery bus boycott, 359

Moore, Douglas, 360

Moore, G. E., 113

morality: Kant on, 39–40, 52–60, 73–74; of knowledge, Tracy's concept of, 390–91; Tracy on religion and, 393

Moral Laws (Brightman), 252

moral optimism, Macintosh's discussion of, 271–72

Moravian Brethren, 74–75

Morehouse College, 356–57

Morgan, C. Lloyd, 230, 273

Muelder, Epke Hermann, 258

Muelder, Walter: King and, 358, 361–62; personalist theology and, 206, 249, 251, 257; social gospel and, 337; third-generation personalism and, 258–66

Müller, Friedrich, 349

Müller, Julius, 14, 20

Mure, G. R. G., 486

Murray, John Courtney, 388

Murray, Pauli, 337

Muste, A. J., 357–58

Myrdal, Gunnar, 263–64

mysticism, in Tracy's theology, 399–408

myth, Tillich's theory of, 326–27

Nancy, Jean-Luc, 115, 453–55, 467–68

Napoleon: Hegel's view of, 119–20; Prussia and, 87–88

Nash, Diane, 367

National Association for the Advancement of Colored People (NAACP), 352, 366

nationalist ideology, African American embrace of, 351–52

Natorp, Paul, 228, 447

naturalism: English Romanticism and, 91–92; meaning and, 67–68

natural religions, Hegel's discussion of, 131

Nature, Man and God (Temple), 496

Nature and Values (Brightman), 252

Nazism, Tillich and, 319–23

Neander, August, 110

neo-Calvinist theology, 196–97

A Neo-Hegelian Theology (Shanks), 164

neo-Hegelian theology: legacy of, 481–91; Marxism and, 128; postcolonialism and, 462–78

neo-Lamarckian theory, racism and, 349–51

neo-orthodoxy: American institutions of, 408–9; Herrmann and, 26; Meland on, 298, 300; Muelder's criticism of, 265; Tracy on, 391

Neoplatonism: Brightman on, 255; Tracy and, 401, 403–4, 407

neo-supernaturalism, 293–94

Neue Blätter für den Sozialismus (journal), 318–19

New Birth of Freedom (Hodgson), 409–10

Newtonian physics, 33–34

New Woman, New Earth (Ruether), 374

Nicholas of Cusa, 94–95, 331, 438–41

Niebuhr, H. Richard, 323, 408

Niebuhr, Reinhold, 271, 294, 478, 524n75; Cone and, 490; Kant and, 448–49; King and, 358–59, 361–62, 364–65; liberal theology, 408; Meland and, 300; Tillich and, 303, 336–37

Nietzsche, Friedrich, 312; master-slave morality of, 128; Tillich and, 317; on Western theism, 2

"The Nightingale" (Coleridge), 91

Nitzsch, Karl Immanuel, 14, 107–9

nonviolence, King on, 368–71

Northrop, F. S. C., 255–56, 294

Notabene, Nicolaus, 180

noumena, Kant's concept of, 49–50, 58–59, 70–72, 96

Novalis: *see* Hardenberg, Friedrich von (Novalis)

Nygren, Anders, 361–62

Obama, Barack, 477–78

Observations on the Feeling of the Beautiful and Sublime (Kant), 35–37

Ogden, Schubert, 423; Chicago school and, 267; Hartshorne and, 288, 494; Tracy and, 393–94, 414; Whitehead and, 302–3

O'Keefe, Terence, 329

Old Left, civil rights movement and, 367

Olsen, Regine, 180

The One Possible Basis for a Demonstration of the Existence of God, 38–39

On Religion: Speeches to Its Cultured Despisers (Schleiermacher), 79–86, 105–6

On the Bondage of the Will (Luther), 405

"On the Idea of a Theology of Culture" (Tillich), 313

On the Not Other (Nicholas of Cusa), 440

ontology of being, 130

O'Regan, Cyril, 460–61

original sin, Kant on, 57–59

otherness, Levinas on, 199

Otherwise than Being (Levinas), 201–2

Otto, Max C., 294

Otto, Rudolf, 245–46, 291–92, 317

Outler, Albert C., 246

An Outline of Christian Theology (Clarke), 296–97, 357

pacificism, Muelder's belief in, 261–62

Palmer, George Herbert, 212, 343

Palmer, Robert, 375

panentheism, Keller and, 436–37

panlogical system, Hegel's concept of, 113–15

Pannenberg, Wolfhart, 489

Panofsky, Erwin, 323

pantheism: Hartshorne and, 250–51, 287–89; Hegel and, 147–48, 161–62; Schleiermacher and, 80–85, 107–11

Pantisocracy, 90

Parker, Theodore, 99

Parmenides: Hegel and, 8, 130, 201; Levinas and, 199–201

Pascendi Dominici Gregis, 388

patchwork theory, Kant and, 46–47

Paton, H. J., 43

patriarchy, feminist theology and, 377, 379–81, 384

Patripassianism, 240

Pauck, Wilhelm, 327–28

Pauline theology: Ritschl on, 15; Troeltsch and, 220

Paulus, Heinrich, 145

Peabody, Elizabeth Palmer, 99

Peabody, Francis Greenwood, 343

Peace of Westphalia, 30

Peirce, Charles Sanders, 249, 283, 468

"Perpetual Peace: A Philosophical Sketch" (Kant), 69

Perry, Ralph Barton, 236, 249, 273

personal idealism: American philosophy and, 225–37; Bowne and, 205–18; Brightman and, 229–37, 244; Knudson and, 231–37; philosophy and, 1–2, 204–5; post-Kantianism and, 456–62

Personalist, 241

personalist theology: Brightman and, 237–57; King and, 355–56, 362–74; Knudson and, 228–37; Mueller on, 266; third-generation personalism and, 258–66

personality: Brightman's concept of, 237–57; Mueller's concept of, 259–66

personal redemption, Ritschlian school, 16–17

Person and Reality (Brightman), 252

Persons and Values (Brightman), 252

Peters, Ted, 397

Pfleiderer, Otto, 205

phenomena, Kant's concept of, 49–50, 58–59, 70–72, 96

phenomenology: Hartshorne's rejection of, 249; Hegel and, 114–15, 129–30

The Phenomenology of Spirit (Hegel): critical analysis of, 123–25; dialectic in, 134, 139; Judaism in, 149–50; Kierkegaard's discussion of, 186–87; master-slave dialect in, 127–33; publication of, 119–23; religion in, 149

philosophes, 60

Philosophical Fragments (Kierkegaard), 181–85

The Philosophical Discourse of Modernity (Habermas), 471

Philosophische Bibliothek, 61

Philosophisches Magazin, 61

philosophy: psychology and, 243–44; radical empiricism and, 269; theology and, 100–111, 205–6; Tillich on, 333–37

A Philosophy of Ideals (Brightman), 230

A Philosophy of Religion (Brightman), 253, 357, 359

Philosophy of Right (Hegel), 137–38, 140–42, 462–64; Marx's criticism of, 168

Philosophy of Theism (Bowne), 256

The Philosophy of Personalism (Knudson), 230–32, 237

physics, philosophy and, 255–56

Pickle, Joe, 307

Pietism: Herrmann's discussion of, 23; Kant and, 31–33, 60–61; Schleiermacher and, 74–75, 101–2, 158–59; Tholuck and, 158–59

Pinkard, Terry, 115, 130, 139

Pippin, Robert, 115, 124–25, 130

Pippin, Tina, 431

Plaskow, Judith, 377

Plato: dialectic of, 134; geometry and, 255; Hartshorne and, 284; Hegel and, 113, 121; Kant and, 44–45, 70; Kierkegaard on, 180; Levinas, 201; Ruether's critique of, 378; Schleiermacher's and Schlegel's translation of, 86, 88

Plotinus, 287–88

Plurality and Ambiguity (Tracy), 399–400

Poelchau, Harold, 319

Polanyi, Karl, xi

political philosophy: democracy and imperialism in, 352–53; liberalism and, 4; Ruether and, 376; Troeltsch on, 222

Poor People's Campaign, 372–74

Pope, William Burt, 246

Popper, Karl, 487

Popularphilosophie movement, 60–67

postcolonialism, Hegel in context of, 463–78

post-Hegelianism, legacy of, 8

post-Kantianism: Bowne and, 210–18; Chicago School and, 272; Hegel and, 119, 153–64, 482–83; Kierkegaard and, 187–92; liberal theology and, 73–74; participants in, 116; race and racism and, 447–48; religious idealism and, 446–50, 456–62; Schelling and, 119; theology of religious feeling and, 100–111; Whitehead and, 500–503

postmodernism: feminist theology and, 431; Habermas' critique of, 471–73; Hegel and, 202–3; Kierkegaard and, 195; religious philosophy and, 387; Tracy's theology and, 388–89, 399–408

poststructuralism: Keller and, 430–31; Ruether and, 383–84

Powell, Adam Clayton, Sr., 12, 491

practical reason, Kant on religion and, 10–11

practical theology, Tracy and, 398

pragmatism: Chicago School and, 268–70, 273; Peirce and, 283

Prefaces (Notabene), 180

Present Tendencies in Religious Thought (Knudson), 230–31

Prichard, H. A., 45

Pringle-Pattison, Andrew Seth, 205, 209, 233

The Problem of Christianity (Royce), 260

The Problem of God (Brightman), 239–41

Process and Reality (Whitehead), 277–80, 282, 284, 492

Process Studies (journal), 302

process theology, 27; Keller and, 433–34; Meland and, 302; religious philosophy and, 1–2; Tracy and, 393–94; Whitehead and, 267–81, 492–95

production, Marx's discussion of, 177–78

Progressive Era, liberal theology and, 11, 27

Prolegomena to Any Future Metaphysic (Kant), 51–52

prophetic tradition, Tracy's discourse on, 404

Protestant theology: Ritschl on, 15; Ruether and, 375; Tillich on, 314, 334–37; Tracy and, 395; Troeltsch and, 222–23

The Protestant Era (Tillich), 324, 334, 408

Proudhon, Pierre-Joseph, 168–69

Prussian nationalism: German liberal theology in, 13; Harnack and, 17–18; Hegel's criticism of, 140; Kant's critique of, 60; Marx and, 167; Schleiermacher's loyalty to, 87–90

Prussian Union Church, Ritschl and, 15–16

psychology: Keller on, 425; philosophy and, 243–44

Pui-lan, Kwok, 384

pure being, Hegel's concept of, 135–36

pure thought, Hegel on, 138–39

Puritanism, 4; Congregationalism and, 9; Du Bois and, 342

race and racism: black social gospel and, 355; Du Bois' double consciousness theory and, 341–47; Du Bois' table of races and, 347–48; feminist theology's failures concerning, 384–86; Hodgson on, 410; imperialism and, 352; Kant and, 447–48; in Kant's work, 36–37, 64–65; King's fury concerning, 366–74; Knudson and, 249; liberal theology and, 7; Muelder's activism on, 261–63; neo-Lamarckian theory and, 349–51; science and, 64–65; social Darwinism and, 348–52

Rade, Martin, 14

Radford, Rebecca Cresap Ord, 375

radical liberals, 5–6; Du Bois and, 353

The Radical Future of Liberal Feminism (Eisenstein), 381

The Radical Kingdom (Ruether), 374

Rahner, Karl, 388–89, 391, 393, 396, 405, 460

Ramsey, Ian, 395

Ransom, Reverdy, 5, 12, 354, 491

Rashdall, Hastings, 205

rationalism: Brightman on, 241–42, 254–57; Schleiermacher and, 81–82; Tillich on, 315

Ratzel, Friedrich, 347

Rauschenbusch, Walter, xi, 12, 261, 264, 357–59

Raymond, Miner, 246

Readers Digest, 262

reason: Hegel on cunning of, 2; Hegel's discussion of, 127; Kant discussion of, 35–40, 53–60, 69–72, 96

The Reawakening of Faith (Meland), 299

Recognition: Fichte and Hegel on the Other (Williams), 486

redemption: liberal theology and, 11; Schleiermacher's discussion of, 104–11

Reed, Adolph, 351

Reformed confessions, 195

Reid, Thomas, 61

Reimarus, Hermann Samuel, 10

Reinhardt, Max, 323

Reinhold, Karl Leonhard, 61

Reischle, Max, 14

relativism, Knudson's criticism of, 232

religion: Bowne's discussion of, 213–18; Chicago School concept of, 269–70; in Hegelian scholarship, 115, 125; Hegel's discussion of, 125, 130–33, 142–64; Kant on, 1–2, 53–60, 73–74, 147; Kierkegaard on, 179–92; liberal ideology and, 4–5; Marx's criticism of, 169–71; Meland on, 294–95; theology of, 218–25, 333–37; Tillich's theology of, 218–25, 330–37; Wieman on, 274–76

Religion and Sexism (Ruether), 374–86

Religion in the Making (Whitehead), 273, 492

Religionsgeschichtliche Schule, 20, 25, 218

Religion within the Boundaries of Mere Reason (Kant), 54, 57–58, 60, 68

Religious Aspect of Philosophy (Royce), 290

The Religious Aspect of Philosophy (Royce), 260

religious feeling, theology of, 99–111

religious idealism: evolution of, 443–56; Hegel and, 456–62; post-Kantianism and, 456–62

religious philosophy, theology as, 1–9

The Religious Situation (Tillich), 317, 323

religious socialism, Tillich and, 313–23, 328–29, 334–37

Religious Values (Brightman), 230, 238

Renaissance humanism, liberal theology and, 4

Renouvier, Charles, 232

Repetition (Constantius), 180, 184

"Restoration" of 1915, 109

revelation, Herrmann's concept of, 23

revisionist theology: Farley and, 408; Hodgson and, 408; Tracy and, 388–408

Rheinische Zeitung, 167

Ricardo, David, 173, 176–78

Rickert, Heinrich, 221

Ricoeur, Paul, 389, 392, 395, 421

right-Hegelians, 113–14, 161–64; master-slave dialectic and, 129

"The Rime of the Ancient Mariner" (Coleridge), 91

Ripley, George, 99

Ripley, Sophia, 99

Rist, Johannes, 156, 489–90

Ritschl, Albrecht, 3; Barth's discussion of, 27; Herrmann and, 21–22; historicism of, 13–16; Knudson and, 231–32; on liberal theology, 14–17; liberal theology and, 11–14; post-Kantianism and, 458–59; Troeltsch on, 222

Ritschlian school: Brightman's critique of, 229; Herrmann and, 20–24; liberal theology and, 12–28; Macintosh and, 270–72; Meland on, 300; personal redemption and social religion in, 16–17; post-Kantianism and, 458–60; Tillich and, 26, 309; Troeltsch and, 26, 218–19

Ritschlian school theology, 3–4

Roberts, J. Deotis, 374

Rogers, Cornish, 360

Romanticism: Coleridge and, 90–91,

95–99; Hegel and, 117, 145–46; Kant and, 30–31, 73–74, 450–51; Schleiermacher and, 75–77, 84–85

Rorty, Richard, 399

Rosen, Stanley, 113

Rosenkranz, Johann Karl Friedrich, 161

Ross, Susan A., 383

Rötscher, Heinrich T., 161

Rousseau, Jean-Jacques, 29, 35, 39; Hegel and, 467–68

Royce, Josiah, 209, 212; absolute idealism and, 260–61, 294; Du Bois and, 343; Meland and, 290; personal idealism and, 226, 233, 249; rational idealism and, 269

Ruether, Herman, 376

Ruether, Rosemary Radford: feminist liberation theology and, 374–86; liberation theology and, 339–40; process tradition and, 1

Ruge, Arnold, 114, 162, 168

Rupp, George, xiii, 115

Russell, Bertrand, 113, 277

Russell, Letty, 377, 383, 411

Russian-Prussian Seven Year War, 35

Rust, Isaak, 106, 161–62

Rustin, Bayard, 359, 366–68, 370

Ruysbroeck, Jan, 401–2

Sabellianism, 248

Saivings, Valerie, 304

Sanks, T. Howland, 398

Sartre, Jean-Paul, 114, 128

Sawicki, Marianne, 414

Say, Elizabeth A., 431

Schaller, Julius, 161

Schelling, Friedrich, 14; absolute idealism and, 47, 73–74, 95, 100, 116–17; American transcendentalists and, 98–99; Brightman and, 239; Brightman's critique of, 243; Coleridge and, 92–95; Fichte and, 117–18; Hegel and, 115–19, 139–40, 155–56, 481–83; on Hegel's panlogical system, 113; Kant and, 46–47, 70; Meland and, 296; post-Kantianism and, 116; Tillich and, 309–11, 313, 326, 334–36, 480–81

Schiller, J. C. Friedrich, 118

Schilling, S. Paul, 249

Schlegel, August, 118–19

Schlegel, Caroline, 118–19

Schlegel, Dorothea, 118

Schlegel, Friedrich, 47; Hegel and, 118; post-Kantianism and, 116; Schleiermacher and, 73, 77–79, 85–86

Schleiermacher, Charlotte, 78

Schleiermacher, Friedrich: Barth's discussion of, 27; early life and education, 74–76; on feeling and rationalism, 82–83; Hegel and, 105–6, 110–11, 142–46, 150–52; Herrmann and, 23–24; Herz and, 77; Kant and, 25, 67, 76–77, 79–82; King and, 357; Knudson and, 225–26, 231–32, 248–49; legacy of, 387; liberal theology and, 9–11; Meland on, 300; personalist theology and, 247–48; post-Kantianism and, 458–59; Prussian patriotism of, 86–90, 140–41; relationships of, 77–78, 86–87; on religion, 1–2, 6–8, 73–74, 79–85, 87–88; Romanticism and, 78–79; Schlegel and, 73, 77–78, 85–86; on theology, 89–90, 99–111; Tholuck and, 20; Tillich and, 309–10, 335; on Trinity, 158–59; University of Berlin and, 88–89; women and, 77–79, 86–87

Schleiermacher, Gottlieb, 74–76

Schlitt, Dale M., 115

Schmid, Heinrich J. T., 106

Schmidt, Karl Ludwig, 323

Schmoller, Gustav von, 343–44

Schopenhauer, Arthur, 210–11, 283; Brightman and, 252; Tillich and, 336

Schubert, Paul, 408

Schultz, Johann, 61

Schulze, Johannes, 163

Schüssler Fiorenza, Elisabeth, 384–85, 414, 431–32

Schwarz, Friedrich H. C., 139

science: Brightman's examination of, 238–39; Chicago school and role of, 270, 272–75; Hartshorne and, 282–89; Hegel and, 139; Kant on knowledge and, 32–34; Macintosh's discussion of, 271–72; Schleiermacher on religion and, 83; Tracy on religion and, 392–93

Science of Logic (Hegel), 110; dialectic in, 135–39; publication of, 133–34

Scottish Enlightenment, 33, 61

Scripps College, 375

scriptural authority, liberal theology and, 10–11

Scripture principle, 414–15

Scudder, Vida, 12

"The Second Coming" (Du Bois), 354

Seeds of Redemption (Meland), 298

Segundo, Juan Luis, 374

self-consciousness: Hegel's discussion of, 126–27; Schleiermacher's doctrine of faith and, 102–3, 107–11; sociality and, 127–33

self-determination: Hegel's discussion of, 121–23; Kantian idealism and, 69–72

Sellars, Roy W., 294

Semler, Johann S., 6, 75

sensation as mental act, in Scottish philosophy, 61

sensibility, Kant's discussion of, 41–45

sexism: in Kant, 37; Keller on, 425; Ruether on tribal culture and, 377–78

Sexism and God-Talk (Ruether), 379–80, 382

The Shaking of the Foundations (Tillich), 324

Shanks, Andrew, 115, 164, 485

Sheldon, Henry C., 226, 228

Shelley, Mary Wollstonecraft, 95

Shelley, Percy Bysshe, 95

Sherburne, Donald, 494

shining present, Brightman's discussion of, 253–54

Shuttlesworth, Fred, 366

Siebert, Rudolf, 474

sin, Bowne's discussion of, 215–16

Sinzheimer, 323

Sittler, Joseph, 304

skepticism, Kant's rejection of, 43, 46–48, 56–61

Small, Albion, 349

Smiley, Glenn, 359, 366

Smith, Adam, 173, 176–78

Smith, Gerald Birney, 268–69, 272–73, 290–92, 294

Smith, Norman Kemp, 46

Smith, Steven G., 201

social Darwinism, racism and, 348–52

Social Democratic Party (SPD), 313, 315–16, 319–23

social ethics: feminist scholarship on, 474–75; Troeltsch on, 222–25

social gospel movement: *see* black social gospel: American philosophy and, 337; Bowne and, 216, 218, 228; Brightman and, 229–37; Chicago school and, 272; evolution of, 11–13; King and, 357–58; Knudson and, 226, 249; Meland and, 297–99; Muelder and, 263–66

socialism: Du Bois and, 353; Hegel's master-slave dialect and, 128; King and, 367–74; Muelder and, 261; Tillich and religious socialism, 313–23, 328

The Socialist Decision (Tillich), 319–23

social justice: King and, 374; Ruether and, 383–86; social gospel movement and, 12

social philosophy, Hegel and, 114–15, 129–30

social salvation, social gospel movement and, 12

social science, racism and, 349–52

social structure: revisionist theology and, 392–93; social gospel movement and, 12

social subjectivity, Hegel's discussion of, 2, 113–14

The Social Teaching of the Christian Churches (Troeltsch), 222

Socrates, 179; dialectic of, 134; Kierkegaard on, 180–82

Sölle, Dorothee, 164

Solomon, Robert C., 115, 123–24

The Souls of Black Folk (Du Bois), 344, 354

Southern black church, civil rights movement and, 367–69

Southern Christian Leadership Conference (SCLC), 366–72

Southey, Robert, 90

space and time: Brightman on, 255; Kant's idealism of, 44–49, 61

speculative philosophy, Hegel's discussion and, 134, 141

Spencer, Herbert, 207, 211, 216, 218, 348–52

Spencer, John, 307

Spinoza, Baruch: Hegel and, 2, 113, 115, 147–48, 152–53; Schleiermacher and, 81; substance doctrine of, 116

Spirit (*Geist*): Absolute Knowing and, 121–23; freedom and, 127–33; Gestalt and, 115–16; Hegelian dialectics of, 113–64; Hegel's concept of, 2, 122–23; logic of, 131–33; philosophical interpretations of, 123–25; religion and, 125, 145–64; Tillich's discussion of, 320

Spirit in the World (Rahner), 388

The Spirit and the Forms of Love (Williams), 288–89

Spivak, Gayatri Chakravorty, 467

Sprachpragmatik und Philosophie (Habermas), 469

Stages on Life's Way (Kierkegaard), 180, 184

Steffens, Heinrich, 109

stereotypes, Kant's reliance on, 36–37

Stern, Robert, 115

Stern, William, 232

Stewart, J. Michael, 418

Stone, Ronald, 329

Strauss, David Friedrich, 15, 114–15, 161, 455

Strawson, P. F., 45

"Strivings of the Negro People" (Du Bois), 344–45

Strong, Augustus, 12

Stroup, George W., 414

structured relations theory, 306–7

Stubenrauch, Samuel, 75–76

Student Nonviolent Coordinating Committee, 366–67

A Study of Hegel's Logic (Mure), 486

Sturm, Douglas, 307, 437

subjective idealism: of Berkeley, 207; Kant and, 45–48; Kierkegaard and, 188; legacy of, 445–46

subjectivity: Hegel's discussion of, 124–25; Keller on, 425–26; Kierkegaard on, 188–92

sublation, Hegel's concept of, 137–38

substance, Spinoza's doctrine of, 116

Suchocki, Marjorie, 305, 414, 494

surplus value, Marx's discussion of, 176

symbolism: Farley on, 416–17; Tillich on myth and, 326–27

systematic theology, Tracy and, 394–96

Systematic Theology (Tillich), 324, 334, 362

Talented Tenth discourse, black criticism of, 351

Tanner, Kathryn, 414

Taussig, Frank W., 343

Taylor, Charles, 115, 130, 453

Taylor, Mark C., 115, 451, 453

Temple, William, 205, 209, 495–503

Teresa of Avila, 401

TeSelle, Eugene, 414

Testem benevolentiae, 388

Thandeka, 492

Theism (Bowne), 256

theodicy: Brightman's examination of, 238–39; Whitehead and, 492–95

Theologische Studien und Kritiken, 107

theology: Brightman's work in, 230–37; Catholicism and, 387–88; Hegel's discussion of, 144–64; Kantian morality and, 73–74; logic and, 133–34; philosophy and, 100–111, 205–6; of religion, 218–25, 330–37; religious philosophy as, 1–9; Tillich on, 324–26, 330–37

A Theology for the Social Gospel (Rauschenbusch), 357

theonomy, Tillich's concept of, 314–23

Theory of Communicative Action (Habermas), 470

Theory of Thought and Knowledge (Bowne), 209–10

"The Three Dimensions of a Complete Life" (sermon), 365–66

thing-in-itself: Hegel's discussion of, 125–26, 481–82; Kant's concept of, 45–46, 49–50, 73–74, 457–58

third-generation personalism, 258–66

Thirty Years' War, 30

This Side of God (Tracy), 403, 407

Thistlethwaite, Susan Brooks, 414

Tholuck, Friedrich August Gottreu, 14, 20, 23, 158–59, 162

Thomas, George, 360

Thomas, Norman, 353

Thomasius, Gottfried, 495

Thomism, 388; post-Kantianism and, 460; Tracy and, 389, 391, 393, 396

Thoreau, Henry David, 99

Thornton, Lionel, 279–80

Thurman, Howard, 337, 355, 491

Thus Spoke Zarathustra (Nietzsche), 312

Tillich, Johannes, 309–10; on religious socialism, 313–23

Tillich, Mathilde, 310

Tillich, Paul: American career of, 323–37; Barth and, 192, 195; early life and career, 309–10; Hegel and, 115, 309, 334–37, 444, 480–81; King and, 363–64; legacy of, 387, 478–81; Meland and, 300; neo-supernaturalism and, 294; Niebuhr and, 303; politics and, 312–13; post-Kantianism and, 309, 444; process tradition and, 1; religious socialism and, 313–23; Ritschlian school and, 26; Tracy and, 397; wartime experiences of, 311–12, 335

Totality and Infinity (Levinas), 199

Toulmin, Stephen, 393

Tourgée, Albion, 5

Towne, Edgar A., 307, 494

Townes, Emilie, 476

Tracy, David, 414; Catholic theology and, 387–408; Keller and, 438; mysticism of, 399–408; process tradition and, 1, 393–94

Transcendental Club, 99

Transcendental Deduction, Kant's concept of, 43–44, 46

transcendental idealism, Kant and, 45–49

transcendental object, Kant's doctrine of, 49

transcendental reason, Coleridge and, 90–99

Traub, Friedrich, 14

Treitschke, Heinrich von, 343–44

Trendelenburg, Adolf, 186

tribal culture, Ruether on sexism and, 377–78

Trinity: Bowne's discussion of, 217–18; Coleridge's discussion of, 91–99; Hegel's discussion of, 154–59, 197–99, 483–85; Knudson on, 247–48

Troeltsch, Ernst, 3, 14; Bowne and, 218; Chicago school and, 272; Herrmann and, 24–25; historicism of, 26–28; Knudson and, 231–32; liberal theology and, 20; Muelder and, 258–61; personal idealism and, 205–6; post-Kantianism and, 459; theology of religion and, 218–25, 331

Tübingen school, 106, 117, 218

Turman, Eboni Marshall, 351

Twesten, August, 109

Tzschirner, Heinrich Gottlieb, 106

Über die Religion: Reden an die Gebildeten unter ihren Verächtern (On Religion: Speeches to Its Cultured Despisers, 1799) (Schleiermacher), 9–10

Ullmann, Carl, 109

Ulrichi, Hermann, 207

Umbreit, F. W. C, 109

understanding: Coleridge on, 94, 96; Hegel's discussion of, 120, 127; Kant's categories of, 42–48, 127

Union Theological Seminary, 232, 269–70; Tillich at, 323–25, 329

Unitarianism, 98–99; liberal theology and, 4

United States: democracy and imperialism in, 352–53; Hegel's view of, 7–8, 464; liberal theology in, 9–12; personal idealism in, 205–7; Troeltsch's view of, 225

"The Unity of Being" (Hartshorne), 249
University of Berlin, founding of, 89
University of Chicago Divinity School, 274, 283; Meland and, 290–91, 297, 301–2, 304–7; Tillich at, 329

Vaihinger, Hans, 46
The Validity of Religious Experience (Knudson), 245
value theory: Brightman and, 252–53; Chicago school and, 270–72
Van Dusen, Henry P., 294
The Varieties of Religious Experience (James), 239, 293, 400–401
Vatican I Council, 396
Vatican II reforms, 388–89
Vatke, Wilhelm, 162
Veit, Dorothea Mendelssohn, 78
Verdinglichung ("reification"), Marx's concept of, 174–78
The Vicarious Sacrifice (Bushnell), 357
Vietnam war: King's opposition to, 370–71; Ruether's opposition to, 376
Vio, Thomas de (Cardinal Cajetan), 396
Vischer, Friedrich Theodor, 161
The Vision of God (Nicholas of Cusa), 439–40
Vivian, C. T., 366
Volf, Miroslav, 431
von Westphalen, Jenny, 167
von Willich, Ehrenfried, 87–88
von Willich, Henriette von Kathen, 87–88
Voting Rights Act of 1965, 369

Wagner, Adolf, 343–44
Walker, Ralph, 46
Walker, Wyatt, 366
Walter, Bruno, 323
Ward, Harry, 12
Ward, James, 205, 209
Washington, Booker T., 346, 350
Wasianski, Ehregott A. Christian, 30
Watchman journal, 90–91
Watson, Richard, 246

Webb, C. C. J., 209
Weber, Alfred, 323
Weber, Max, 222, 470
Wegener, Richard, 310–11
Weimar Republic, Tillich and, 315
Weiss, Bernhard, 227
Weisskopf, Walter, 329
Weitling, Wilhelm, 168
Welch, Sharon, 1, 414, 474–77
Wells, H. G., 239
Wells, Ida B., 5
Werder, Karl Friedrich, 161, 162
Wesley, John, 214–15, 246, 248–49
West, Cornel, 351
Western metaphysics, Hegel on, 2
Westphal, Kenneth, 115
Westphal, Merold, 115
Wever, Margarethe, 311
"What Real Progress Has Metaphysics Made in Germany since the Time of Leibniz and Wolff?" (Kant), 71
Where Do We Go from Here: Chaos or Community? (King), 371–72
Whitehead, Alfred North: Brightman and, 253; Chicago school and, 251, 273–74, 282; early life and career, 277–78; feminist theology and, 388; Hartshorne and, 249–51, 282–89; Hodgson and, 420, 422–23; internal relations theory and, 230; Keller and, 425–27, 432–34, 436, 441–42; legacy of, 305–7; liberal theology and legacy of, 267–81; Meland and, 294–95, 299–300, 302–3; process tradition and, 1, 28, 492–95; Ruether and, 382–83; Schleiermacher and, 82–83; Temple and, 496–503; Tracy and, 393; Wieman on, 276–81, 294
white superiority: in Kant, 36–37, 64–65; Ruether's feminist theology linked to, 380–86; Welch's discussion of, 477–78
Wieman, Henry Nelson, 28; Chicago school and, 251, 273–76; Hartshorne, 286–89; King and, 359–60, 363–64;

Meland and, 291–95, 299, 302–3; Whitehead and, 277–81
Wilberforce University, 354
Wilhelm Meister's Apprenticeship (Goethe), 77
will: Du Bois on power of, 343; Luther on, 405; Tillich on concept of, 336
Williams, Alberta, 356
Williams, Alfred Daniel, 356
Williams, Daniel Day, 27–28, 267, 281–82, 288–89, 408
Williams, Delores, 384
Williams, Hosea, 366
Williams, Robert R., 115, 201–2, 414, 417
Williams, Rowan, 115, 404
Williamson, Joel, 350
Wilmore, Gayraud, 409
Wilson, John Cook, 207
Windelband, Wilhelm, 221
Winds of the Spirit (Hodgson), 424
Wissenschaftslehre (The Science of Knowledge) (Fichte), 116, 451–52
Wobbermin, Georg, 14
Wolf, Friedrich August, 87
Wolfers, Arnold, 313
Wolff, Christian, 31–34
Wolff, Robert Paul, 45
Wöllner, Johann, 60, 68–69
women: civil rights movement sexism and, 366–67; Kant on, 35; Mueller on rights for, 265–66
Wordsworth, Dorothy, 91
Wordsworth, William: Coleridge and, 90–94, 99; Emerson and, 98
Workshop on Constructive Theology, 414
World Council of Churches (WCC), 264–66
World Society of Revolutionary Communists, 171
Wrede, William, 218
Wright, George Frederick, 343
Wright, Marian, 372
Wright, Richard R., Jr., 12, 354

Xenophanes, 336

Yeomans, Christopher, 115
Young, Andrew, 366

Žižek, Slavoj, 115, 455, 461, 467–68